the
bread
bible

ALSO BY ROSE LEVY BERANBAUM

The Cake Bible
Rose's Christmas Cookies
The Pie and Pastry Bible

Rose Levy Beranbaum

the bread bible

photographs by gentl & hyers / edge
illustrations by alan witschonke

foreword by michael batterberry

W. W. Norton & Company
New York   London

Manufacturing by The Maple-Vail Book Manufacturing Group
Book design by Jean Orlebeke
Production manager: Andrew Marasia

Library of Congress Cataloging-in-Publication Data

Beranbaum, Rose Levy.
The bread bible / by Rose Levy Beranbaum ; photographs by Gentl & Hyers/Edge ; illustrations by Alan Witschonke ; foreword by Michael Batterberry.
    p. cm.
Includes bibliographical references and index.
    ISBN 0-393-05794-1
    1. Bread. I. Title.

TX769.B365 2003
641.8'15—dc21

2003044550

W. W. Norton & Company, Inc., 500 Fifth Avenue, New York, N.Y. 10110
www.wwnorton.com

W. W. Norton & Company Ltd., Castle House, 75/76 Wells Street, London W1T 3QT

1 2 3 4 5 6 7 8 9 0

To my paratrooper father, Robert Maxwell Levy, who gave me his wings, the courage to fly, and the freedom to dream.

For the generous bread bakers who shared their recipes with me and bread bakers everywhere.

To the memory of Lionel Poilâne, one of the greatest bread bakers of all time.

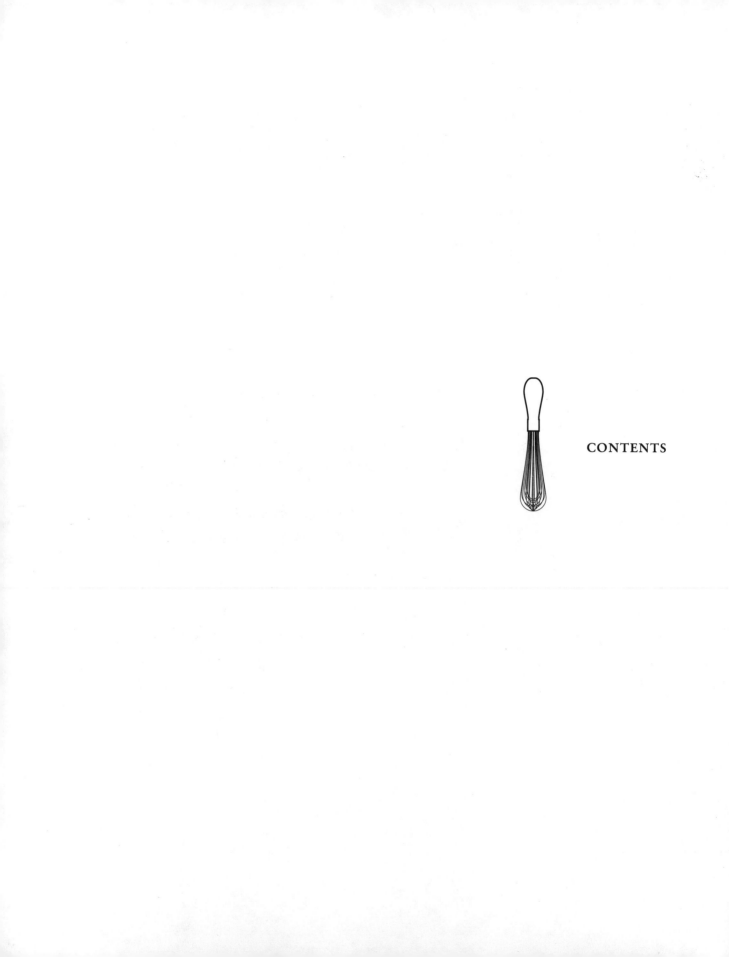

CONTENTS

Foreword

by Michael Batterberry
Founding Editor of *Food Arts* and *Food & Wine* magazines

IF CIVILIZATION, AS IS GENERALLY ACCEPTED, WAS BORN OF THE FIRST settled riverbank farms, bread made from harvested grains may well have been its first, and most profound, culinary expression. Millennia ago, bread became synonymous with the absolutely essential. In ancient Egypt, the word for bread meant "life," the force of which still shows remarkable staying power, according to the scholarly English food writer Jane Grigson, who, roaming widely in the groves of academe, observed that her scattered archaeologist friends all gave place of honor at their tables to small Near Eastern flatbreads, edible talismans keeping them in day-to-day physical touch with earliest recorded times. Over the centuries, bread's kinship with the sacred continued to grow: the sacramental bread and wine of the Christian communion service; the Passover matzoh, unleavened flatbread to ceremoniously commemorate the Jewish Exodus; the Puritans' "white bread of God," symbolizing the purity of their Lord. Parenthetically, in feudal connotation, the titles "Lord" and "Lady" signified the provider and the doler-out of bread, respectively.

Seen from these perspectives, the title of Rose Levy Beranbaum's invaluable new book, *The Bread Bible,* seems hardly a stretch. If civilization were to fall, this volume could be used as an appropriate tool to help jump-start it.

When Rose decides to delve into a subject, as devoted readers will readily swear on stacks of her earlier *The Cake Bible,* she immerses herself like an oceanographer descending in a bathysphere to probe the darkest deeps. Personal experience confirms this. After mutually agreeing that Rose would write for *Food Arts* magazine a comprehensive study, of interest to professional chefs, on the topic of sugars, more numerous, she said, than we imagined, she resurfaced many months later with a text so exhaustively researched, so scrupulously tested, that it went on to win two coveted food journalism awards, one American, the other global, the following year.

As an elementary human need, bread runs a close third to air and water. Back in the 1970s in New York, a French diplomat once described to me over dinner his experiences in a German POW camp during World War II. The shortage of food was acute, and to keep up morale, he and his captive fellow officers, Frenchmen to the genetically coded core, entertained each other with the minute details of sumptuous prewar cuisine they had partaken of back home. As time wore on, engulfing hunger led them to reminisce about simpler and simpler fare, homey family dishes, beloved childhood treats, until, at the famished last, to stave off despair, the only thing they cared to deliberate narrowed to the subtle nuances of bread and the arguable superiority of its variable scent, crust, crumb, flavor, even its sound.

Had she been alive then, Rose, with her limitless supply of bread tales, could have nightly played Scheherazade to the imprisoned French. "Bakers say that the bread's song," she writes, "is the sound of the crust crackling as it cools," an unbottled genie remark that swiftly conjures up for me an encounter with chef Alain Sailhac, Dean of the French Culinary Institute. Outside a bread baking kitchen classroom, he snatched a warm baguette from a rolling rack, grinned with delight upon pressuring it gently close to his ear, as if testing the merits of an elephantine cigar, and then thrust it at me, urging, "Listen, listen!"

Bread, that miraculous metamorphosis of flour, water, and yeast, becomes a living thing shortly after the introduction of the yeast, the metabolic action of which is fermentation. Rising bread dough is a warm and companionable being, if you listen to Rose, who, after a couple of decades of pulling loaves from the oven, can still pose the question, "Could it be that I'm only completely happy now when a bread is *happening* [the italics are mine] somewhere nearby?"

The goal of bread baking, she states succinctly, "is to get good volume and a beautiful crust." A born teacher with a dual scientific and artistic bent, she is determined to lead you to this victorious and glorious end. To spare readers taking any avoidable chances, Rose has carved in hearthstone what she declines as "The Ten Essential Steps of Making Bread," a canon that entails, aside from mixing, shaping, and baking, the procedures of pre-fermenting, dividing and preshaping, slashing, glazing, cooling, slicing, and storing.

And that's just for openers. A quotation that I apparently utter with the repetitiveness of a mantra is Escoffier's declaration that "the art of cookery is the constant expression of the present." Trust Rose to understand this fully, as she uninterruptedly demonstrates with constant pitch-perfect responses to the craving for technical know-how of today's younger generations. Throughout *The Bread Bible,* she follows up recipe procedures with expository passages beneath the heading "Understanding." A fragmentary example: "allowing the batter to rest enables the flour to absorb the liquid evenly," as in the case of her Yorkshire Popovers, which she confesses to have been perfecting for fifteen years. Further amplification comes in the form of bulleted "Pointers for Success," i.e., helpful hints typified by this one for producing flawless Soft Golden Potato Bread: "If not using the dry milk, you can replace the water with 1/2 cup plus 1 tablespoon of milk, preferably nonfat, scalded (brought to just under the boiling point) and cooled to lukewarm."

Elsewhere she drops random tips with the profligacy of Johnny Appleseed. If, for example, you don't possess a piping bag for loose muffin dough, simply scrape it into a gallon-size heavy-duty Ziploc bag, zip, and snip off the tip of a lower corner. An avid runner in private life, she'll even happily put you through the paces of home-curing olives for olive bread, should you care to go those extra ten miles.

Yet another boon is that the author is never shy about recommending specific brand names, often with sourcing information, that have passed her rigorous testing muster, be it an electric mixer, household flour mill, baking pan, frozen Maine blueberry, or freshest-tasting extract.

The planet-circling sources of some of her recipes provide further evidence of her attunement with Escoffier's dictum. Present-day bread bakers, even if bonded for life to soulfully comforting treasures hoarded in their grandmothers' recipe files, simultaneously exhibit an insatiably far-ranging appetite, as well as a sophisticated connoisseurship, for the best the world has to offer. An inveterate traveler who makes each trip a Mount McKinley tasting expedition (we've seen her in softly smiling, gently spoken, all-devouring action), Rose has compiled in this landmark volume recipes of her own invention, along with others gathered from a pantheon of some of the world's most talented, dedicated, and skillful bakers of everything from traditional hearth breads to newly created bread based desserts.

The years this oeuvre has taken, the author concludes, she now looks back on as a humbling as well as an elevating experience, "opening the way for a lifetime of continued discovery," a path that readers, taking her hand, can follow, too, to the end of their bread-enlightened days.

Introduction

THIS IS MY BREAD BIOGRAPHY. IT IS A PERSONAL HISTORY OF BREAD FROM MY first memory of its appearance into my existence—the bagel my mother gave me as a teething ring—to my most recent achievement—a bread risen entirely from my own sourdough starter. Some of the recipes along this journey were created from my imagination. Others were inspired by breads tasted on my travels abroad. Still others are treasures shared by other bakers that I have made my own, as all bakers are wont to do. The experience of putting together this book and researching all the aspects of bread making has been one of the steepest and most gratifying learning curves of my life. And it has been a humbling experience as well, opening the way for a lifetime of continued discovery.

Occasionally people suggest that making bread, particularly kneading it, must be a great way to get out aggression. The irony is that when I start making bread, I am immediately blissed out and any possible aggression immediately evaporates. I don't need to pound the bread with my fists to arrive at this blessed state. In fact, when I don't have a bread going, I feel that something is missing. Could it be that I'm only completely happy now when a bread is happening somewhere nearby?

There is a satisfaction derived from the act of baking bread that I get from no other kitchen activity. Perhaps the most engaging aspect is that yeast is a dormant live organism one is bringing to life and feeding so that it will grow and expand, providing texture and flavor in the bread. It always seems utterly amazing that flour, water, yeast, and salt, judiciously proportioned, transform into the most perfect loaf of bread.

Coincidentally, my serious interest in wine began about eight years ago, the same time I started working seriously on this bread book. It was at the Huia vineyard in South New Zealand, when the vintner was explaining to me why he had to cool down the fermenting wine to prevent undesirable flavors, that it hit me how incredibly similar the process of making bread is to that of making wine. Both rely on yeast fermentation, time, and temperature control to produce fantastic flavors in the end product. The wild yeast for wine is present on the grapes' skin; for bread it is present on the wheat. But both usually rely on the addition of a commercial yeast starter or culture.

The sugar in the grape feeds the yeast that produces alcohol and carbon dioxide, the two end products of fermentation, just as the sugar in the flour feeds the yeast to the same end. And just as a specific variety of grape or blend of grapes produces a specific variety of wine, different varieties of flour produce different types of bread. Surely it is more than coincidence that the ancient tradition of Hebrew grace before the meal begins with the prayer of thanks for the wine and immediately follows with the prayer of thanks for the bread—the only two parts of the meal thus honored. Though I don't speak conversational Hebrew, these Hebrew prayers are ingrained in my soul. And I think of bread and wine as the foundation of my culinary existence.

My first experience of eating home-baked bread was not until I was seventeen and a freshman at the University of Vermont. A local resident paid my boyfriend with a loaf of her bread for mowing the lawn. It vaguely captured my attention—he was so pleased about it. He made fried egg sandwiches for us for a hunting trip—something I would normally have rejected on concept (both the fried egg and the hunting)—but I was in love, it was so cold, and I was so hungry . . . and it was an epiphany. My first school vacation back in New York I borrowed "The Joy of Cooking" from Rosalind Streeter, a neighbor and friend of my mother's, and made my first bread. It is a tribute to the perfect instructions that so was the bread.

But the seed of desire to bake bread actually had already been planted deeply within me by my craftsman father, whose dream it was to make a real hearth beehive oven. I remember the first time he mentioned it, and my reaction: Why? Now, all these years later, I share the dream. One of my favorite childhood stories was my father's about his canoeing trip up the Hudson River. (I was a city kid, but with the benefit of a genuine backwoods—by choice—father.) A short while before the trip he had begun a sourdough starter, from a book called *Camping and Woodcraft* by Horace Kephart. My father's plan was to make sourdough muffins in a reflector baker, which got its heat from the sun. During portage, when he had to carry the canoe across land, he tightened the caps on the jars to keep the liquid starter from spilling if they tilted. Apparently he had created a very active starter, because during one of the portages he heard an explosion, muffled by the bedding that was wrapped around the jars. It didn't take long for him to realize that it was the starter. His bedding all needed to be washed, and this incident spelled the end of his short-lived sourdough experiments. But he was captivated by the possibilities of the fermentation, so he passed the scepter to me. It was fortunate that the starter exploded, because he remembers that it was so alive it had streaks of color. When this happens it means that undesirable bacteria have taken over and the starter needs to be discarded. Had he used it for baking, he would at the very least have been taken ill. Perhaps I would never even have been born to write this book!

I never had the experience of home-baked bread as a child, but the three first smells I remember loving were honeysuckle, fresh-ground coffee, and, most of all, the smell of baking bread from the Silvercup Factory when we crossed the Queensboro Bridge every weekend. For me it was the one good thing about returning to the city from Far Rockaway, where I was born.

When my father visited his mother in the Bronx, he would always stop by his favorite bakery and bring home a fragrant fresh loaf of Jewish rye and another of cornbread. But I also enjoyed shopping with my maternal grandmother and watching the Pechter's rye bread shuddering its way through the then-new electric slicing machine. I even loved the little piece of printed paper that stuck to the loaf and always made sure to save one of the tiny crusty end pieces, which my grandmother called the *crychick*, for my little brother. I wasn't sure if it was a Russian or Jewish word, but I found the sound adorable and perfectly descriptive.

Bread in one form or another is part of everyone's childhood memories. Bread has been a part of our civilization for a long time. Yeast-leavened wheat bread and the milling of wheat flour are thought to have originated about five thousand years ago in Egypt. Bread is now basic to all cultures. The time-honored quote of Brillat Savarin, "Show me what they eat and I'll tell you who they are," works wonderfully when applied to bread. For example, is it light and delicate, soft and fluffy, dense and hardy, complex and chewy? Is the bread cut into neat slices or torn into crusty pieces? Is it enjoyed for its own value or simply used as a vehicle to hold a filling? Bread is considered so vital to life by the Swiss that during World War II they created a bread they referred to as hundred-year-old bread, a bread that could last for years buried underground, in case a soldier became lost and needed it for survival. The armed forces were given maps to enable them to find the hidden bread. Self-contained bakery trucks were created to produce the bread. I learned of this from my friend Albert Uster, who purchased one of these loaves from the Swiss government a few years ago for his business in Gaithersburg, Maryland.

While it's true that bread ties us to our past, it does much more than that. It also connects us to our present reality. In this day and age, when many children think milk comes from the supermarket and don't even know what a potato looks like, baking bread puts them in touch with the most fundamental source of their need for nourishment. Beyond that, making bread yourself nourishes both body and soul.

It's surprising how many people prefer bread even to cake! (Although in my house, they still expect cake as well and probably always will.) For years now, I've served my breads as the appetizer or first course of a dinner. And the bread has never been the vehicle for another substance; it serves as the main event, enhanced only by a gilding of butter, or a little dunking of olive oil with a second quick dip in roasted spices for accent.

Another of bread's many charms is that it requires no decoration or extraneous elements. The form and color it takes are its own beauty. I'm not a big fan of what I think of as "tortured bread." It's fun to see elaborately sculpted breads in the window of a bakery or to use one as a bread basket, but for eating, the texture is best when it has been less handled and manipulated.

Every bread baker I know would love to have everyone baking bread. It stems from the desire to share the pleasure. Here's my advice: Start a tradition. Find a favorite bread recipe and try different proportions of flours or vary the additions of seeds. Retype the recipe the way you prefer to mix the dough, leaving out variations or other unnecessary notes once you know the recipe and technique. Share the bread with friends or family, and soon people will associate you with this particularly delicious and personal offering—and it will be *your* bread. I am simply serving as the starter (or pre-ferment) for your bread-baking adventures. I encourage you with all my hearth to take it from there and make it your own! It will change your life.

I was moved by a quote from Carmen Jackson Crofton I once read in a 1999 issue of the *Washington Post* food section referring to her mother's holiday rolls: "I'm not sure my mother really understands just what her cooking means to me. It represents everything warm and good and cozy."

One of the things that has made me the most joyful and grateful in the process of creating this book is discovering that I had entered an incredibly warm, welcoming, and supportive bread community. Never have I met people more willing to share, to teach, to join hands, and, yes, to cast bread on the water. (Perhaps this is an overused expression, but surely it couldn't be more appropriate than in this context!) There is hardly a bread baker I do not adore on first meeting. I am greatly indebted to the many wonderful bakers who welcomed me into their world, eager to share their own points of view and knowledge from years of experience in large-scale production, but equally eager to embrace new ideas. One of the very first was Amy Quazza, chef bread instructor at the French Culinary Institute, who for years invited me to take her class. Fortunately I did before finishing this book, because it opened my eyes to the differences between home and commercial baking, and in one mere week turned me into an expert bread shaper.

Prior to this book I thought of myself as a "pastry person." But when I was doing a "stage" in the bread-baking kitchen of Restaurant Daniel, one of the pastry cooks suggested that "the difference between a pastry chef and bread baker is that bread baking requires absolute devotion and passion." I knew I had crossed the divide. I realized that upon considering all the joyous moments of my existence on this earth, I am most content when making bread. But I was still undecided whether I should continue with this book. I told Daniel's chef boulanger Mark Fiorentino that I was considering giving it up because, unlike cake and pastry, which I had managed to control to my satisfaction, my bread never turned out exactly the same way two times in a row. This masterful but modest craftsman looked at me from his towering height, smiled, and said, "Neither does mine; I don't know what I'm doing half the time." With this kind encouragement I was up and running again. Yes, bread is big parts alchemy, instinct, and artistry. And although I've come to the level of repeatability where my breads at least weigh the same amount every time, I've also come to the realization that it's actually quite delightful that, despite the most precise and detailed directions, no two breads are ever exactly the same. Your bread won't be exactly like mine, but it will be wonderful. In this world of ever-increasing homogenization, bread remains one absolutely great way to express individuality.

When I started this book, I realize now that I actually knew little about bread-baking theory. I had studied it, superficially, in college and had been baking bread for years, but without really understanding the process. However, this served partly as an advantage, because I was free to create without assumptions as to what would and would not work. I soon discovered that there were many diametrically opposed theories about all aspects of bread making, and that I could establish my own as well from personal experience and assessment.

The truth is I had never thought I could make bread at home as good as bakery bread. But to my delight, I proved myself 100 percent wrong. I now feel that the best bread is one you make according to your own taste, with your own hands, that comes out of your own oven.

In a way I'm sorry the mystery is gone, but in another sense it will always be there, continuing to evolve, and the wonder will certainly always remain. There are so many variables in bread baking. Bread is like life—you can never control it completely. Come to think of it, bread IS life.

Rose Levy Beranbaum
New York City

Credits and Acknowledgments

As I get older, I am ever more appreciative of the steadily enlarging network of friends and colleagues who participate in my life and work. Thankfully, the central core has remained a constant: My husband of 28 years, Elliott R. Beranbaum, who never once complained about my turning our apartment into a bakery production site, and my soul mates and loyal friends Jeanne Bauer and David Shamah, who have participated so generously in the creation of this book.

The greatest energy, passion, and commitment equal to my own, making this book all it could be, came wholeheartedly and unconditionally from my beloved and gifted editor and friend, Maria D. Guarnaschelli. This is our seventh book together, our third "bible," and the magic is better than ever.

I also want to acknowledge the significant contributions of my friends and business managers Monica Netupsky and Norman Perry; my dearest friend Elizabeth Karmel, who gave them to me; Erik Johnson of Norton for his wonderful judgment and calm organizational skills; Judith Sutton, copy editor beyond my dreams; Alexandra Nickerson for an excellent index; and the entire production and sales department of W. W. Norton: Andrew Marasia; Nancy Palmquist; Susan M. Sanfrey; Debra Morton Hoyt; William Rusin and his team throughout the country; Drake McFeely, president; Jeannie Luciano, publishing director; Starling Lawrence, editor in chief. Never have I felt more welcomed, supported, and at home at a publishing house.

Thank you Alan Witschonke for your extraordinary line drawings; Gentl & Hyers for your amazing photographs; Michael Pederson and Amy Quazza for putting your hearts and skills into styling the bread for photography and rising to the occasion on the coldest week of the winter of 2003; Alex Gant for your hospitality as studio manager, not to mention drop-dead cappuccino; Helen Raffels for your continued friendship and artistry.

Thank you Pat Adrian, for keeping my books in the forefront in "The Good Cook"; Diane Gregory for your unfailing support and spiritual genius; Yoko Nakajima for recipe testing; Kenny Sossa and Eddy Perez, for your ever present willingness to taste and critique.

Special thanks to the many bread bakers who welcomed me so enthusiastically into the fold: Vicky J. Caparulo, Maggie Glezer, Lauren Groveman, David Norman, Mark Farantino, friends at the King Arthur Flour Company (Brinna Sands, Shannon Zappala, Joe Caron, Tod Bramble, Jeffrey Hamelman, Robin Sargeant, Sue Gray, Sue Baker, Sue Miller), Dan Lieder, Cat (Catherine) Liviakis, Amy Quazza, Didier Rosato, Peter Reinhart, Amy Scherber, Vinnie Scotto, Kathleen Weber, Hans Welker, chef Director Bread Program at the French Culinary Institute, and friends at Tom Cat Bakery (Noel Comess, James Rath, Matthew Reich).

Deep gratitude to the technical expertise and generosity of Tim Huff of General Mills, Bill Weekley of SAF Yeast, and science/food writer Bob Wolke, for reviewing the extensive technical sections of this book; also to the flour millers Paul Drumm of Kenyon Grist Mill in Rhode Island and Joe Lindley of Lindley Mills in North Carolina for sharing their unique expertise, my friend Jens Schmidt for his profound knowledge of wine production and fermentation, and Ruth Dundas Schmidt for her brilliantly detailed bread machine reports.

Also deep gratitude to Daniel Boulud for my invaluable *stage* in the bread baking kitchen of his Restaurant Daniel.

Heartfelt thanks to my friends at *Food Arts* magazine: Michael Batterberry, publisher, for his beyond-words foreword for this book; Jim Poris, senior editor, for his generous supply of flour research information; Gary Tucker, senior editor, for his loyal support and true friendship, taking me out for regular culinary airings. And to my friend Barbara Kuck, of The Culinary

Archives and Museum at Johnson and Wales, for providing a home both for my archives and my PBS baking series *Baking Magic with Rose*; and to my friend Madeleine Schamah, for her generous heart and for keeping me and the entire production crew so well-fed; as well as Susan and Bob Jassie of Alyson's Orchard in Walpole, New Hampshire, for providing us with a wonderful location.

Undying gratitude to my dear friends and producers Margie Poore, Alec Fatalovich, and most of all their daughter Jennifer Fatalovich, for believing in me and providing the "show" to my "tell." Also great appreciation to my friend Brian Maynard of KitchenAid for continuing to improve an already magnificent mixer.

Special thanks to my dear friends and colleagues Reiko Akehi, Neil Bernstein, Diane Boate, Lois Dash, Angelica Pulvirenti, and Suvir Saran for their contributions; Dorothy Cann Hamilton of the French Culinary Institute; Syndi Seid of Advanced Etiquette; and Charlie Trotter, for celebrating my books with fantastic parties; John Guarnaschelli for his concern and wisdom; Jerry Ruotolo both for his beautiful author's photo and for introducing me to his son Rob Ruotolo, now my computer guru, who has kept my computers impressively fit and able to complete this book.

Also special thanks to Kenny Amador, my tech-support knight of the Wolf Range, hearth of my bread baking existence.

the
bread
bible

1.

The Ten Essential Steps of Making Bread

1. FERMENTING AND PRE-FERMENTING

Fermentation

Fermentation is what happens when yeast comes in contact with the flour and water. Fermentation is what makes wine out of fruit sugars and beer out of grains. In all cases, it occurs when yeast consumes the sugars from starches producing, among other things, bubbles of carbon dioxide gas. In the case of bread baking, it is carbon dioxide bubbles that do the leavening and give it its great texture.

Yeast is a living, single-cell plant. It eats sugars and produces carbon dioxide and ethyl alcohol as it grows and multiplies. Only certain strains are used in bread baking. Flour is a carbohydrate. Like all carbohydrates, the starch molecules are made up of hundreds of sugar molecules. When the yeast, water, and flour are combined, enzymes in the flour break down the carbohydrates into sugar. The yeast, a microscopic single-cell organism, eats this sugar, grows and multiplies, and gives off carbon dioxide and alcohol. As it is produced, the carbon dioxide is held in by a network of gluten strands, or protein, formed by kneading together the flour and water, and it leavens or causes the bread to rise. The alcohol produced by the yeast gives the bread flavor. Both the carbon dioxide and the alcohol evaporate into the air during baking.

Flavor also comes from the action of the bacteria present in the environment, which compete with the yeast for the sugar in the flour. These beneficial bacteria produce flavorful acids such as acetic and lactic acid.

Temperature control is a very important factor in fermentation. Bakers use varying temperatures to get the results they want. Artisan bakers, for example, almost always prefer a cool slow rise, or fermentation, of the dough.

Yeast is active at temperatures between 33° and 130°F. At warmer temperatures, the yeast is more active and grows and multiplies more quickly. The fermentation process itself produces heat. When fermentation takes places at too high a temperature, however (over 90°F), unpleasant off flavors are produced in the bread.

When chilled, the yeast goes into dormancy, slowing its activity and producing more alcohol. This decreased activity gives the bacteria a chance to feed on the sugar, develop more, and produce more acetic acid. Temperatures of 40° to 55°F are ideal for the formation of acetic acid; 55° to 90°F results in the formation of the blander lactic acid. Acetic acid imparts a far more sour quality to bread than lactic acid. As an added benefit, acetic acid also strengthens the dough's structure, although too much of this acidity would ultimately weaken it. Some bakers prefer the milder flavor provided by lactic acid.

Length of fermentation is another important factor that determines both the flavor and the color of the bread. If the dough ferments for too long, the yeast and bacteria will consume all of the sugar in the flour, and the bread will have a pale crust and bland flavor. Some residual sugar in the dough is necessary both for flavor and to brown the crust.

Pre-fermentation

My friend Rob Ruotolo, who is also my computer guru and has therefore tasted a good many of the breads in this book, made a revealing comment. He said that all of my breads have one thing in common that he values greatly. "Not only are they delicious while I eat them, the flavor lingers in my mouth for a long while afterwards." There is a reason for this, and it is the pre-ferment, or dough starter. The most flavorful breads, then, usually involve making a pre-ferment, or dough starter. This starts the fermenting process before the final mixing of the dough. To make a pre-ferment, you simply take part of the flour, water, and yeast for the dough and mix it before the rest of the dough. This pre-ferment sits at room temperature, or in the refrigerator, to ferment and develop flavor until you use it to make the rest of the dough. The longer fermentation it offers develops extra gluten strength for the dough, adds depth and complexity of flavor, with a long finish, and increases the shelf life of the bread. It also makes it possible to use less yeast, which allows the taste of the wheat to emerge. In fact, the longer the pre-ferment, the less the yeast you need.

Too high a proportion of pre-ferment would make the bread too sour and weaken the gluten network or structure. Most bread recipes, however, will be markedly improved by using a pre-ferment. Simply put, by making a pre-ferment, you will bring out the full flavor potential of the flour. But some breads, such as the Prosciutto Ring bread (page 370), have so much flavor from these powerful ingredients that a starter is probably not worth the extra time and effort. For breads like this, the *"straight,"* or *"direct," method* of mixing dough is ideal: all the flour, water, and yeast are mixed together at the beginning.

Note that most pre-ferments, with the exception of sourdough or levain, use commercial yeast, as opposed to wild yeast.

There are several different types of pre-ferments. They vary mainly by the amount of water they contain. Don't be put off by strange-sounding names, like *barm, biga, chef, desem, levain, madre bianca, mother, pâte fermentée, poolish, sponge, starter,* or *sourdough starter.* At first these terms put me off, and I was resolved to avoid them in this book, thinking that the all-encompassing term *starter* was all I really needed, but gradually these special words became familiar friends. This common language serves not only to distinguish the type of starter but also to connect us to a history and family of bread bakers around the world. So I will define each of the terms here, and as they appear in almost every recipe, they will become familiar to you too.

PÂTE FERMENTÉE (OLD DOUGH) AND "ALTUS BRAT" (OLD BREAD)

The easiest way to deepen the flavor of your bread is simply to save a small piece of dough from one batch to add at the end of mixing the next one (during the last couple of minutes, since the structure is already developed). The "old dough" can stay at room temperature for up to 6 hours or be refrigerated for up to 48 hours. If you don't make bread that often, wrap the dough airtight and freeze it for up to 3 months.

The old-time practice, originating in Germany, of adding *altus brat,* or old bread, is another way of increasing depth of flavor with minimal work. It entails adding a small quantity of stale bread that has been soaked in water, squeezed dry, and allowed to ferment overnight at room temperature (see the variation in the recipe for Authentic Pumpernickel Bread, page 329).

Old dough or old bread is usually added at 25 percent the weight of the total flour in the bread, but the percentage can be much higher.

THE SPONGE METHOD

Another easy way to deepen the flavor of your bread is to make a sponge from some of the flour, water, and yeast in the recipe. Some books describe a sponge as having a stiff consistency. I prefer a more liquid one because it makes it possible to whisk bubbles into the sponge. These bubbles set up many little air pockets. During fermentation, the yeast produces carbon dioxide (gas), which enters the air pockets and enlarges them. Thus, whisking the sponge helps to produce a bread that has a more even and airy crumb. I learned this valuable technique from Gale Sher's book *From a Baker's Kitchen* when I first began baking bread many years ago.

I usually make a sponge with equal volumes of flour and water (for example, 3 cups/16.5 ounces/468 grams flour to 3 cups/25 ounces/709 grams water). This is about one and a half times the weight of the flour in water

(151 percent hydration—the percentage of dough by weight that is water). And it was a little less than half the yeast called for in the recipe.

Though not as complex as a biga or levain (see below), a sponge still results in far more flavor than combining all the ingredients at once. Because my sponge uses all of the water in the recipe, and is therefore more liquid, it enables the yeast to grow faster and can be used after only 1 hour, or, ideally, 4 hours at room temperature. Alternatively, it can refrigerated for up to 24 hours, resulting in greater acidity and more depth of flavor. I like to make a "flour blanket" with the remaining flour and yeast to sprinkle on top of the sponge. It provides a protective cover, insulating the sponge and preventing it from drying out. I love to watch as cracks gradually develop in the flour blanket, indicating that the yeast is growing and swelling. When the sponge bub-

PROCESS: Sponge dough starter breaking through the flour blanket, indicating that the yeast is growing and swelling

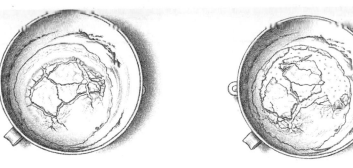

bles up through the flour blanket, I often push a little of the flour over it, but this is not strictly necessary, as I also cover the bowl as an added safeguard.

A sponge can be made with anywhere from 30 to 50 percent of the total flour used in the bread. The less flour, the more liquid the consistency and the faster the growth of the yeast; however, there must be adequate flour for the yeast to ferment.

HOW TO IMPART DEPTH OF FLAVOR TO YOUR FAVORITE BREAD RECIPES

To convert almost any bread recipe to the sponge method, simply divide the total amount of flour by 2.5 and combine it with all of the water and about half (or a little less, if a more convenient measure) of the yeast. Mix the remaining flour with the remaining dry ingredients except for the salt, which will usually be added after the first stage of mixing the dough, and sprinkle it lightly over the sponge to form a blanket. Allow it to stand for 1 to 4 hours at room temperature—or, preferably, for 1 hour at room temperature and up to 24 hours refrigerated. After about 3 hours in the refrigerator, the yeast will become dormant and most, but not all, activity will stop, enabling the ever-present bacteria to grow and develop wonderfully flavorful esters (formed from the organic acids and alcohol produced in the cold environment). The yeast will remain alive under these conditions for as long as 24 hours.

POOLISH

A poolish (thought to have been named for Polish bakers in France) is made the same day or the day before the bread and is always fermented at room temperature, to ensure the formation of milder flavors. It is usually made with equal parts flour and water by weight. It uses between one-third and one-half of the total water in the recipe, which is **22 to 33 percent of the total amount of flour**. The amount of yeast that is added to a poolish decreases proportionately with the length of fermentation. If too much yeast is added before a long overnight pre-ferment, the yeast will exhaust all the sugar in the flour.

　　The recommended amount of yeast based on the weight of flour in the poolish: At a temperature of 72° to 80°F for a 3-hour fermentation, 0.5 percent instant yeast is recommended; for 6 hours, 0.23 percent instant yeast; for 8 hours, 0.17 percent instant yeast; and for 12 hours, 0.03 to 0.05 percent instant yeast. In order to ensure a lower acidity, the ideal time to add the poolish to the dough is when it has matured. At this point it will have domed slightly and will be just beginning to deflate. A long poolish produces more interesting aromas and requires less yeast. It also gives a longer window of maturity (up to 2 1/2 hours).

BIGA

A biga, an Italian pre-ferment, is close to the consistency of bread dough (from 50 to 78.7 percent water [hydration]). It is usually mixed at least 6 to 24 hours ahead and used within 3 days. Because of its stiff consistency, it is the strongest (in terms of gluten) of the pre-ferments and is particularly useful in breads with a high water content, such as ciabatta, to strengthen the network of gluten. If a biga overmatures and deflates, the bread will have smaller holes. If the biga is refrigerated for much past 3 days, it will become too acidic, weakening the gluten and adding a very sour flavor. It can, however, be frozen for up to 3 months; it will lose some yeast activity but will still contribute complexity to the flavor of the bread. What I most love about a biga is the flexibility of time it gives you. It takes only a few minutes to mix, and then, any time within the next 3 days, all you add is the rest of the flour, a little yeast, and the salt, and you're well on your way to fantastic bread! My biga is fairly soft, so it integrates easily into the rest of the dough. If your biga is stiffer, cut it into a few pieces before adding it.

To make a biga: Use at least one-third the volume of water used in the recipe (e.g., the recipe calls for 1 cup water, use 1/3 cup for the biga) and double its volume in flour (in this case, 2/3 cup). **This will be about 30 percent of the total amount of flour,** but it's fine to use up to 55 percent of the total amount of flour, which will add more strength to the dough (also of course adjusting the volume of water to fall within the 55 to 78.7 percent of the flour ratio). For 1/2 to 2/3 cup flour, use 1/16 teaspoon of the yeast in the recipe in the biga. If you are using a total of 1 cup to 1 1/3 cups flour in the biga, double the yeast used in the biga (1/8 teaspoon).

If time does not allow for a minimum of 8 hours fermentation for the biga, double the yeast given in the recipe for the biga (be sure to subtract the appropriate amount from the dough) and allow it to stand for at least 2 hours, or until at least doubled in volume. Stir it down, and use it or store in the refrigerator or freezer.

SOURDOUGH STARTERS

Sourdough, levain, and *barm* are synonymous terms that refer to dough starters created from wild yeast (*Saccharomyces exiguus*). The main factor that distinguishes sourdough starters from others is that they can be kept alive for long periods of time—even centuries. Recipes often call for organic grapes to make a wild yeast starter because of the wild yeast present on their skins, but, in fact, flour, preferably organic, and water are really all you need. (If you want to purchase sourdough cultures, see page 572. To learn more about sourdough, and for a recipe for making your own starter, see page 425.)

A healthy sourdough starter can be the sole leavening in a bread dough, but many bakers boost their starter with a little commercial cake yeast (up to 0.2 percent of the weight of the flour, or, if using instant yeast, 0.6 percent of the weight of the flour) for added rising security, without affecting other qualities such as flavor, color of the crust, and shelf life. Professional bakers refer to a sourdough starter as a *chef* or *seed culture* in the first stages of its development. When it is fully developed and mature, at which point it is strong enough to raise a bread dough, it is referred to as a *sourdough culture*. The chef is usually started with whole wheat or rye flour, but once it is established, full of live and vigorous yeast cells, it is maintained or refreshed with all white flour. (In Germany, sourdough starter is made entirely with rye flour.) While a sourdough starter is the most complex of the pre-ferments, it is not necessarily the most sour. If it is used and refreshed with flour and water daily, at room temperature, it develops more of the milder lactic acid than the more sour acetic acid. The degree of sourness is also strongly influenced by both the strain of the wild yeast and the type of bacteria present in it.

A sourdough starter is usually made up of equal weights of flour and water, but it can range from 50 percent water for a stiff starter to 125 percent water for a liquid starter. In short, to make a sourdough starter requires only flour and water, then several refreshment feedings of the same, and patience, to grow the wild yeast on the flour and to attract bacteria from the environment.

If you have a liquid sourdough starter, you can turn it into a stiff sourdough starter simply by stirring in bread flour until it is firm enough to knead for a few minutes on a counter to a biscuit-dough consistency. The stiffer starter ferments more slowly and does not require as cold a temperature to slow down fermentation. This means it can be refreshed less often. And, because a warmer temperature results in a more mellow flavor, a stiff starter is ultimately less sour than a liquid one.

Although a sourdough starter will stay alive for at least a week without having to be refreshed with flour and water, it will become progressively more acidic, and thus produce a very sour bread. This makes it impractical for the home baker who does not bake bread every day.

San Francisco Sourdough is a wild yeast starter that contains a unique strain of bacteria (*Lactobacillus sanfrancisco*). This bacteria is responsible for the bread's sour flavor and thick crust.

The Lalvain du Jour starters from France (see Sources page 572) require only 12 hours to develop, compared to a traditional homemade wild yeast levain, which takes weeks and requires frequent refreshing with flour and water. Breads made from the Lalvain starters use the same basic technique as a sourdough bread, with the addition of commercial yeast. The Lalvain represents 0.3 percent of the flour (or water) used in the sourdough starter. Instant yeast that is added just before mixing the dough represents 0.4 percent of the total amount of flour in the recipe. Lalvain starters are combined with equal weights of water and flour. For the Lalvain starter, **39 percent of the total** flour and 42.3 percent of the total water in the recipe are used (see the recipe for Low-Risk Sourdough on page 473). The recommended amount of Lalvain in a sourdough starter is 0.4 percent of the flour used for a 12- to 20-hour room-temperature fermentation. This might seem high but actually is not, as the product is only partially yeast—the rest is bacteria.

You can also use a Lalvain starter to add a subtle very mildly sour and absolutely delicious flavor to a sponge in the following way: For every cup of flour used in the sponge, use 1/8 teaspoon Lalvain Pain de Campagne starter in place of the yeast. Then for the flour mixture (the rest of the dough), use 1/4 teaspoon instant yeast per cup of flour in the mixture. Allow the sponge to sit at room temperature for 8 to 12 hours, then mix the dough as usual. The first rise should be 2 hours at 75° F. If you want to speed it up slightly, though, it's fine to increase the 1/4 teaspoon of instant yeast to 3/8 teaspoon per cup of flour.

TO CONVERT A RECIPE USING A BIGA (A STARTER MADE WITH COMMERCIAL YEAST) TO A SOURDOUGH STARTER USING LALVAIN DU JOUR STARTER

Increase the water in the starter to equal the weight of the flour in the starter, and subtract that amount from the water used for rest of the dough. When replacing the yeast, keep in mind that 4.2 ounces/120 grams (3/4 cup plus 1 1/2 tablespoons) unbleached all-purpose flour requires 1/8 teaspoon (0.4 grams) Lalvain. For example, for a biga starter using 1/4 cup/59 grams water and 1/2 cup plus 1 1/2 teaspoons/75 grams flour, increase the water to 1/4 cup plus 1 tablespoon/75 grams. Replace the 1/16 teaspoon/0.2 grams of instant yeast with 1.6 times the amount Lalvain: a slightly rounded 1/16 teaspoon/0.3 grams. Then use 1 tablespoon less water in the dough.

When to Add a Starter to the Dough

Some bakers add stiff starters such as biga or pâte fermentée (old dough), to the dough after it has been mixed. They reason that the biga or old dough has already had 3 to 5 minutes of mixing, and it might be overmixed if added at the beginning. I haven't found this to be true with the small amounts of dough I make using home equipment, however, so I add the starter right at the beginning of the dough-mixing process.

Temperature of the Pre-ferment (Starter)

When you refrigerate a pre-ferment, it takes several hours for it to get below 50°F. It will never become as cold as the refrigerator, because the continued fermentation, even at a very slow rate, produces a small amount of heat.

When you mix dough by hand, it is best to have the pre-ferment at room temperature, as it will incorporate more easily, and not much heat is built up in the hand-kneading process. When you use a mechanical mixing device such as a stand mixer, however, the temperature of the dough increases by between just under 1°F to as much as 3°F for every minute of mixing. Thus, the pre-ferment can be used at a lower temperature to compensate for the friction built up by the mixer (when overheated, gluten breaks down and off flavors develop).

Since the temperature of the pre-ferment directly affects the temperature of the finished dough, if it is cold, it will take longer for the first rise, and if it is too cold, it may not absorb the liquid (hydrate) fully (see mixing/kneading, page 45). If I have refrigerated the pre-ferment, I usually take it out about 30 minutes ahead of mixing the dough if using a stand mixer, and about 45 minutes ahead if using a bread machine. If using a food processor, I use it cold from the refrigerator, because so much heat builds up during processing.

If you haven't refrigerated the pre-ferment, however, it works well to refrigerate it for 15 to 30 minutes before mixing the dough.

UNDERSTANDING HOW TO CREATE YOUR OWN BREAD RECIPES OR TO ADJUST BREAD RECIPES TO SUIT YOUR TASTE

I strongly recommend you weigh the ingredients on a scale when you make the bread recipes in this book. If you do, both the weight and size of the baked loaf will come out precisely as given (or with very minor variations). If you choose to use cup measures, the amounts will be less precise and you may need to adjust the amount of flour or water by feel as indicated in each recipe. With either method, once you know the percentages of the ingredients needed to make bread (see below), you will be able to develop your own recipes if you so desire. Weighing, however, is a lot easier and more precise than measuring with cups.

Commercial bakers use what is called the "baker's percentage" for ease in calculating the weight of ingredients in their bread recipes (also known as formulas). The flour represents 100 percent and every other ingredient is calculated as a percentage of the flour's weight. This system is easy to use, but it does not take into account the amount of starch, water, or fat in other ingredients added to the basic flour/water/yeast/salt formula, such as milk, butter, cheese, bananas, or potatoes. The baker's percentage also divides the percentages between the pre-ferment (dough starter) and the rest of the dough, making it difficult to evaluate at a glance the overall water content (known as hydration), starch content, and fat content.

To address this problem, I have included what I call "The Dough Percentage" in each recipe. These percentages of ingredients enable you to see at a glance the total water content, salt, yeast, and fat content. These percentages not only give you a better understanding of the entire makeup of the bread, they also enable you to make adjustments to suit your own taste. For example, if you find a particular recipe either a little too salty or not quite salty enough, drop or raise the percentage of salt slightly—and once you have found the level you prefer, you can use the same ratio for other similar breads. (It's like having your own custom-made template.) Keep in mind, however, that other ingredients in the recipe may call for variations in the basic percentages. The Olive Bread (page 383), for example, with its salty olives, has only 1.3 percent added salt compared to the usual range of 1.5 to 2.5 percent.

If a bread you make seems a bit dry, you can simply adjust the water. Of course some breads, such as bagels, are intended to be drier, and some, such as ciabatta or focaccia, are by nature very wet in order to achieve the characteristic large holes.

A RANGE OF INGREDIENT PERCENTAGES FOR HEARTH BREADS BY WEIGHT

Flour: 100%
Water: 54.6 to 83.9%
Instant yeast: 0.25 to 1.03%
Salt: 1.5 to 2.6%

Using different types of flour will also make significant changes in both the flavor and the texture of the bread. When adding whole wheat flour, I use 7.2 percent of the white flour, which adds a pleasantly wheaty flavor without either bitterness or making the crumb more compact. Even the addition of

1 percent whole wheat can make a huge flavor difference, as in the baguette. (My preferred ratio of rye flour is 16.9 percent for rye bread and 30.1 percent for pumpernickel.)

If you change the balance of different types of flours, the water amount will also need to be changed slightly; i.e., if you use more whole wheat or rye flour, you will need to add a little more water—or, better still, start with a little less flour. If you are using a large amount of freshly ground whole wheat flour rather than an older white wheat, start with a little less water in the recipe.

AN EXAMPLE OF A BASIC HEARTH BREAD

BY WEIGHT
Water is 66.6% of the weight of the flour

OR

Flour is 150% (1 1/2 times) the weight of the water
Instant yeast is 0.5% of the weight of the flour
Salt is 2.1% of the weight of the flour and 425% (4 1/4 times the weight of the yeast)

BY VOLUME
(flour is measured by dipping a cup used for measuring solids into the flour bin and sweeping off the excess with a metal spatula or knife)

Water is 43% of the volume of the flour

OR

Flour is 233% of volume of the water
Instant yeast is 0.5% of the volume of the flour
Salt is double the volume of the instant yeast (1% of the volume of the flour)

AN EXAMPLE USING 1 CUP OF BREAD FLOUR (WEIGHING 5.5 OUNCES/156 GRAMS) AND 66.6% AVERAGE AMOUNT OF WATER (HYDRATION)

1 cup bread flour (5.5 ounces/156 grams)

7 tablespoons (3.6 ounces/104 grams) water

1/4 teaspoon (0.78 gram) instant yeast

1/2 teaspoon (3.3 grams) salt

FOR THE SAME AMOUNT OF WATER (HYDRATION) USING UNBLEACHED ALL-PURPOSE FLOUR

(Since all-purpose flour weighs less than bread flour for the same volume, the water must be decreased)

1 cup all-purpose flour (5 ounces/142 grams)

6.5 tablespoons (3.3 ounces/95 grams) water

(The salt and yeast will still fall within the acceptable range of 1.5 to 2.6% for the salt and 0.25 to 1.03% for the yeast, or can be decreased very slightly.)

Added Ingredients

The maximum amount of seeds and grains that can be supported by a given amount of dough and still result in a good crumb (rather than becoming coarse and crumbly) is 60 percent (based again on the weight of the flour). My usual preference is 33.3 percent, as in the Tyrolean Ten-Grain Torpedo (page 394). The weight of dried fruits and nuts added, however, can be as much as 100 percent (based on the weight of the flour); the Cranberry Walnut Bread (page 408) uses 95 percent. Here again, you can tailor these percentages to your personal preference if you understand the makeup of these ingredients and their effect on the dough.

Essentially there are two basic types of ingredients that are added to bread. One type is integrated into the structure of the dough during mixing and, once mixed, can no longer be identified readily—such as butter, oil, eggs, and potatoes. The other type stays separate from the dough's structure, though it is supported by the network of gluten, and maintains its distinguishing features—such as seeds, whole grains, or nuts.

When adding an ingredient of the first type, it is necessary to understand what it is composed of (fiber or starch, water, and/or fat) and its effect on the dough in order to keep the ingredients in balance. The chart on pages 569–70, from the USDA handbook *Composition of Foods*, lists these components for common ingredients added to bread, and an explanation of each ingredient's function in the dough is given below.

When adding ingredients of the second type, there are several considerations involved. Too much of this type of ingredient will weigh down the dough and make it too dense. If using close to the maximum amount permissable, you will need to increase the yeast by about 1 1/2 times. The sharp edges of some nuts and grains will cut some of the gluten strands that support the rise of the dough, so it will be necessary to use a higher-protein flour, such as bread flour, and/or add vital wheat gluten.

The characteristics of the added ingredient are another important consideration. Nuts, for example, benefit both in flavor and in texture if toasted lightly before they are added to a dough. (Toasting also serves to keep walnuts from turning blue in the dough!) Grains, on the other hand, require softening by soaking for several hours before adding them to the dough.

(*Note:* The above information is based on both my personal experience and extensive research from invaluable periodicals, textbooks, and cookbooks, as referenced in the Bibliography, page 607.)

2. MIXING AND KNEADING

Whether you mix the dough by hand or machine, making dough always begins with mixing together the flour, water, yeast, dough starter (pre-ferment), if using one, and salt. Since the salt can kill the yeast if it comes in direct contact with it, it is best to add it after you mix the yeast into the flour.

Once you have moistened the flour, the next step is to knead the dough to begin to develop the gluten a little. Then allow the dough to rest for 20 minutes to give it a chance to absorb the water more evenly. This rest is referred to as the *autolyse* and is used widely by artisan bakers. The concept came from the renowned French bread-baking professor Raymond Calvel, author of *The Taste of Bread, How to Maintain It and How to Recapture It (Le Gout du Pain, Comment le Préserver, Comment le Retrouver)* (see Bibliography, page 607). The autolyse is a simple but very effective method of making dough less sticky and more extensible (easier to stretch). A less sticky dough is easier to handle and requires less added flour to keep it from sticking to your fingers and the counter while you knead it. After the rest (autolyse), the dough is kneaded to realign the strands of gluten and strengthen them to form the network structure of the dough. Doughs made with the autolyse method are higher in moisture, with more open crumb in the baked bread.

Hand Versus Machine Kneading

I used to be a total devotee of hand kneading; I once wrote, "Not for me a bread machine that would rob me of the pleasure of touching the dough." What changed my mind? Brinna Sands of King Arthur Flour, another person who felt the same way about hand kneading until she discovered how ideal bread machines or electric mixers are for kneading very sticky doughs, the only kind of dough that will give you the desirable open-holed texture characteristic of certain artisan-type breads. I still get to touch the dough to my heart's content at many stages of production. But during the initial mixing process I prefer to use a machine, not only because it totally sidesteps the temptation to add excess flour, but also because making bread as often as I have in the past several years was beginning to result in the inevitable repetitive stress injuries, particularly to my wrists.

I now have a large variety of mixing devices of varying sizes and types, including a Breadman Ultimate bread machine, 6-quart and 5-quart KitchenAid stand mixers, a 5 1/2-quart Kenwood stand mixer, a KitchenAid food processor, a Cuisinart food processor, a 6 1/2-quart Bosch Universal spiral-type mixer (the bowl doesn't move but the motion of the blades is similar to a spiral mixer), an 8-quart Electrolux Magic Mill ("The Assistant") spiral mixer, and a 20-quart Hobart mixer. I love them all and I use them all, depending on the amount and type of dough I'm mixing. (Some are very similar to others with only minor variations, but I wanted to try out as many mixing devices as possible before making any recommendations.)

Essentially it comes down to this: when I'm making doughs that are 1 1/2 pounds or under, I use the bread machine—but only for mixing and kneading (I don't use its rising or baking cycles). For doughs from 1 pound up to about 3 pounds (with about 6 cups of flour), I use a 5-quart stand mixer. For doughs up to 6 pounds (12 cups) of flour, I use a 6-quart stand mixer. I also use the food processor to mix and knead some doughs, as long as they are not very soft. For some doughs over 3 pounds and up to 12 pounds, I use the spiral-type mixers (they also work well for the 1-pound doughs). And for a larger quantity of dough, I use the big Hobart.

Here are the virtues and drawbacks I've found of mixing and kneading by hand and in these machines.

By Hand

PROS

> Teaches how to feel the way gluten develops in the dough

> Avoids overmixing the dough

> Avoids overheating the dough

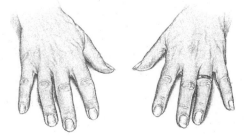

CONS

> Easy to add too much flour

> Difficult to achieve adequate development of high-gluten-flour doughs

> Possible stress injury to wrists and arms from kneading

Basic Technique for the Hand Method (Kneading by Hand)

Reserve about one-eighth of the total amount of flour, to be added only as needed.

Whisk the instant yeast and flour together before whisking in the salt. The salt should then be added to the flour and yeast to ensure that it is mixed in evenly.

EQUIPMENT:
Dough mixing bowl and
wooden spoon

If the sponge or biga has been refrigerated, take it out about 1 hour before mixing.

Mix the dough with a wooden spoon or your hand until the flour is moistened. Knead the dough, still in the bowl, until it holds together, then empty it out onto a counter dusted with some of

TECHNIQUE: **KNEADING BY HAND**

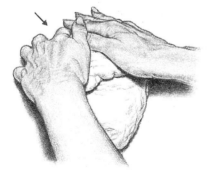

Folding the top of the dough down
toward you

Firmly pushing the dough down and away
from you with the heels of your hands

the reserved flour. Knead the dough for 5 minutes, adding as little of the reserved flour as possible. It will be very sticky.

Invert the bowl over the dough and allow it to rest for 20 minutes. Then continue kneading for another 5 to 10 minutes or until it is very smooth and elastic.

The Bread Machine

PROS

> Doesn't "walk" on the counter, as some mixers can

> Nonstick container and dough blade make it easy to remove all the dough and to clean as well

> A perfect contained environment in which to proof the dough (I sometimes even put the loaf pan in it, with a small container of water under it, for the final shaped rise)

EQUIPMENT:
Breadman "Ultimate" bread machine

> Mixes small amounts of dough well

> Incorporates a minimum amount of air during mixing (the flour doesn't get "bleached" from oxygenation)

> Mixing is with minimal friction, raising the temperature of the dough less than 1°F per minute of mixing (it is best to start the mixing at about 67°F, because after resting and kneading, the dough will be about 74°F).

CONS

> It can handle only a small amount of dough

> Most models do not have a programmable dough feature and so automatically heat the dough during mixing, causing it to rise faster during the first proofing

Basic Technique for the Bread Machine Method

If using a chilled sponge or biga, remove it to room temperature **45 minutes before mixing.**

Add the liquid ingredients first, then add the dry ingredients. Scrape the corners if flour or dough collects in them. Program the machine for a manual cycle. Do a 3-minute mix and immediately hit the pause button so that the dough can rest for 20 minutes for the autolyse. Since "pause" on most machines is only 10 minutes, set a timer for 9 minutes so you can press the pause button a second time before it starts kneading the dough.

Add the salt when the kneading cycle begins. Knead for about 10 minutes.

If your bread machine heats the dough so the finished dough is above 80°F, cool it by scraping it onto a lightly floured counter and flattening it as much as possible. Cover it with plastic wrap that has been lightly greased with cooking spray or oil and allow it to rest for 15 minutes. Then knead it lightly and set it in the dough-rising container bowl to proof as usual.

Instructions for bread machines always say not to soak the bowl and blade; I'm sure this is because soaking and then scrubbing risks damage to the nonstick coating. But with this type of coating, all you have to do is allow it to air-dry and the bits of dried dough will slide right out.

(*Note:* If making more than 1 pound of dough, I usually hold a piece of plastic wrap over the work bowl during the first 2 minutes of mixing to keep the flour from jumping out.)

The Stand Mixer

PROS

>   The average 5-quart mixer can handle as much as 6 cups of flour (3 pounds of medium-stiff dough) without straining the motor, but it also works well with smaller amounts (particularly with the paddle attachment). If a dough is very stiff, such as a bagel dough, I only mix up to 1 1/2 pounds of dough at a time. The KitchenAid Professional 6-quart mixer can handle as much as 12 cups of flour (6 pounds of medium-stiff dough).

> The KitchenAid 5-quart and the Hobart Commercial mixer both have an ice water jacket attachment ideal for keeping the dough at the optimal temperature.

> It works well with very sticky doughs, such as focaccia.

> The KitchenAid and Kenwood have adjustments for lowering and raising the bowl to ensure that the dough hook or paddle reaches very close to the bottom.

CONS

> Most stand mixers will "walk" on the counter with stiff doughs; mix these at a lower speed and *never* walk away from the mixer when it's on.

> The temperature of the dough will rise from 2° to 3°F per minute of mixing, depending on the stiffness of the dough. It is best to start mixing most doughs at 55° to 60°F, because after the 20-minute rest (autolyse) and kneading, the dough will reach 75° to 78°F.

EQUIPMENT:
KitchenAid® mixer with water jacket attachment

Basic Technique for the Stand Mixer

Unless the dough is a very liquid one (such as the focaccia dough, page 205), I usually prefer to use the dough hook rather than the paddle attachment. However, with very small amounts of dough in a large mixer, the paddle attachment often works better, because it reaches closer to the bottom of the bowl.

If using a sponge or biga that has been refrigerated, remove it to room temperature 30 minutes before mixing. If not using a sponge (where the water has already been whisked in by hand), I add the water with the mixer on low speed.

Start on the lowest speed possible until the flour is moistened. Then drape the top of the bowl with a towel or plastic wrap and allow it to sit for 20 minutes.

Knead most dough on #4 if using a KitchenAid, #3 if using a Kenwood; for very stiff doughs, use #2 on a KitchenAid, #1 on a Kenwood. Once you raise the speed, keep the mixer at that speed, or the dough can "unmix" and become sticky. This can be reversed once or twice, but after that the dough will not return to its original state.

Most doughs require 7 to 10 minutes of kneading.

The Food Processor

PROS

> Speed, speed, speed (dough mixes in under 1 1/2 minutes)!

CONS

> Dough overheats unless the liquid is cold when added (but ice-cold liquid will kill the yeast)

> Too soft a dough will lift up the blade and/or be hard to remove from the work bowl

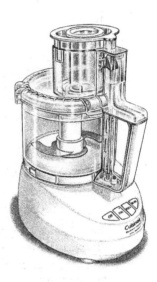

EQUIPMENT:
Cuisinart food processor

Basic Technique for the Food Processor Method

Refer to the instruction booklet for your model to determine the maximum amount of flour to use and which blades are appropriate for which amount of flour. If you have the Cuisinart "PowerPrep Plus" model, use the dough button, which slows down the blades if the dough starts to strain the motor, when mixing the dough.

Note that although tearing destroys gluten formation, cutting, as with the food processor's metal blade, does no harm because the gluten strands will reconnect after processing.

Start by adding the dry ingredients, and the chilled sponge or biga if using, to the work bowl. Then, with the motor on, gradually add the chilled liquid ingredients. Process the mixture for about 1 1/2 minutes to knead it. Remove the dough from the work bowl and knead it for about 10 seconds to equalize the temperature, as the dough nearest the blade tends to be warmer.

The Spiral Mixer (such as the Bosch Universal and Electrolux Magic Mill)
PROS

> Easily handles large amounts of dough; also works with smaller amounts

> Heats the dough less than a stand mixer

> Oxygenates the dough less than a stand mixer

> The Magic Mill does not "walk" on the counter

CONS

> Doesn't work as well as a stand mixer for small amounts of very sticky dough, such as brioche

Basic Technique (and Special Tips) for Spiral Mixers

With doughs over 3 pounds (about 6 cups of flour) hold out about one-third of the flour. Start mixing on the lowest possible speed, gradually adding the reserved flour until the dough is moistened. Allow the dough to rest for 20 minutes before kneading.

THE BOSCH UNIVERSAL

If doing an overnight-refrigerated sponge, remove it to room temperature 30 minutes before mixing. If using a chilled biga, remove it to room temperature 15 minutes before mixing.

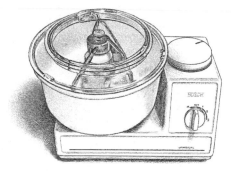

EQUIPMENT:
The Bosch Universal

When mixing less than 1 1/2 pounds of dough (about 3 cups of flour), use the smaller blade. Drape a towel or plastic wrap over the bowl during the 20-minute rest.

Knead on medium-low speed, (#2) for 7 to 10 minutes.

THE ELECTROLUX MAGIC MILL

The heavy stainless steel bowl holds the temperature, so, if using an overnight-refrigerated sponge, take it out of the refrigerator 1 hour ahead of mixing. If using a chilled biga, take it out 30 minutes ahead.

EQUIPMENT:
Electrolux Magic Mill "Assistant" Mixer

When mixing less than 4 pounds of dough (about 8 cups/2 1/2 pounds flour), use the dough hook. If mixing less than 3 pounds of dough (about 6 cups/almost 2 pounds flour), adjust the hook so that it stays 3/4 inch away from the sides of the bowl. Use the scraper with the dough hook only when the dough is very sticky.

For larger amounts, use the roller and scraper. For 8 pounds of dough (16 cups/5 pounds flour), set the roller 1 1/2 inches away from the sides of the bowl. For over 8 pounds of dough (5 pounds flour), set the roller 2 inches away from the sides of the bowl.

Drape a towel or plastic wrap over the top of the bowl during the 20-minute rest.

Knead on medium-low (the second mark on the wheel) for 7 to 10 minutes.

THE 20-QUART HOBART

PROS

> Handles large amounts of dough

> Uses a 10-quart or 20-quart bowl without needing an adapter

> Ice water jacket attachment is ideal for keeping the dough at the optimal temperature

CONS

> Oxygenates the dough

> "Walks" on the bench or floor

Basic Technique for the 20-Quart Hobart

Use the "stir" setting to keep the flour from jumping out of the bowl. Then switch to speed 1 to mix; add the liquid while mixing. Use speed 2 to knead the dough for 7 to 10 minutes.

The Basic Mixing Method—in Full Detail

My mixing method, evolved over the years, is an amalgamation of Gail Sher's technique of beating air into the sponge, Paula Wolfert's technique gleaned from a French pastry chef of blanketing the sponge with flour, and Brinna Sands of King Arthur and Shirley Corriher's urging to make a very wet dough. Shirley also came up with the revolutionary suggestion of adding ice water to bread dough before mixing it. Since I had found it convenient to chill the sponge overnight, it occurred to me that if I left it close to refrigerator temperature, that would be similar to adding ice water to a room-temperature dough. The results were excellent.

With the advent of the improved instant yeast that does not require proofing in warm water before adding it to the dough, I then decided to add about half of the yeast to the sponge and half to the flour mixture (flour blanket). This was before I learned that the instant yeast should not be added to a cold dough or to one below 70°F because at lower temperatures, some of the yeast will die. (In theory, instant yeast can be added directly to flour, but the dough must be at 70° to 95°F, or else warm water should be used to dissolve [rehydrate] it.) But the method had always worked so well for me I've continued to use it. On mixing, as the dough heats up, and during subsequent rising, most of the yeast from the flour blanket will be activated. Some of it may die, but a certain proportion of dead yeast can be desirable for both flavor and relaxation of the dough. Since my doughs were rising in the amount of time I considered to be optimal for flavor development, and since the final results of texture and flavor were what I wanted them to be, I have retained this method.

The first quantity of yeast sits first in the sponge for at least 1 hour at room temperature, at which point the fermentation will elevate the temperature of the sponge to about 87°F. After the first hour in the refrigerator, it will be about 71°F. After 2 1/2 hours (total of 4 1/2 hours) it will still be at 67°F, which means that the sponge method will result in full activation of the yeast.

AUTOLYSE

This technique of mixing the flour and water before adding salt was developed by the renowned French bread-baking professor Raymond Calvel and it has been embraced widely by the artisan bread-baking community. Briefly mixing only the flour and water, both at room temperature, and letting the mixture sit for 20 minutes (or longer) allows the flour to absorb the water evenly and requires less mixing time to arrive at the ideal structural strength of the gluten, therefore resulting in less oxygenation (incorporation of air) of the dough. When a dough is oxygenated, the baked crumb will be less golden, and more white, and the flavor is diminished. With a traditional autolyse, the salt and yeast are added after the rest period. The salt is added later because it draws water away from the flour and slows absorption of water (hydration). If the autolyse, or rest, is more than 30 minutes, the yeast is added later so that it doesn't start to ferment before mixing. If sugar is added to a dough, it is also always added after the autolyse for the same reason the salt is. If a small amount of fat is added to a dough, it can be put in right after the autolyse, but a larger amount, as in a brioche, will be added after the dough has been fully kneaded to maximize gluten development.

I have modified the autolyse method slightly for the home baker, adding the yeast in the beginning to ensure even mixing and to avoid its direct contact with the salt, which would kill the yeast. (With the hand method, I whisk the salt with the flour in the beginning to ensure even incorporation and minimize yeast contact.) Also, when mixing by machine, since part of the flour is already moistened (hydrated) in the pre-ferment (starter), I am less concerned with moistening the remaining flour quickly. Though cold temperatures do slow down the speed of water absorption, I opt to chill the dough to avoid excess buildup of heat during mixing. In commercial bakeries, a "friction factor" is used to determine the temperature of the water needed to arrive at the correct dough temperature. If you have a KitchenAid or Hobart mixer with an ice water jacket attachment, you can have all the ingredients at room temperature before mixing. Conversely, if your sponge is at room temperature, you can refrigerate it in the bowl for about 30 minutes before mixing.

Raising the temperature of the dough above 90°F results in undesirable flavors; below 70°F, and the flour will not absorb water (hydrate) evenly, and that will affect the consistency of the crumb. However, this is a big temperature window and the home baker really needn't be too concerned as long as he or she stays within this range. Controlling the precise finished temperature is critical in commercial baking because it affects the entire production schedule. A dough with too low a finished temperature will take longer to rise, and a dough with too high a finished temperature will take less time to rise, both of which affect loading the loaves into the oven, cooling time, and delivery.

The optimal finished temperature is considered to be 72° to 78°F for doughs made with wheat flour. If rye flour is 20 percent or more of the total weight of the flour, the finished temperature of the dough should be 82°F. This higher temperature strengthens the network of gluten in the wheat flour, ensuring that it is strong enough to support the rye flour.

HOW TO DETERMINE WHEN DOUGH IS ADEQUATELY KNEADED

Dough is kneaded after the initial mixing both to realign the strands of gluten that have begun to develop and to strengthen them, to form the network structure of the dough. Kneading, whether by hand or machine, is a way of mixing the dough by stretching it, which is what makes the gluten network stronger. Dough that has been kneaded properly is shiny and elastic. If you pull off a little

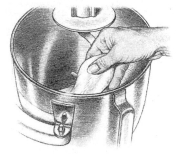

TECHNIQUE: Pulling the dough to test extensibility (stretchiness)

piece of it, you will feel its considerable extensibility—i.e., it is stretchy. A firm dough such as pumpernickel will spring back quickly when pressed with a fingertip. Softer doughs, such as the Ricotta Loaf (page 285), will be springy but will not fill the impression as quickly.

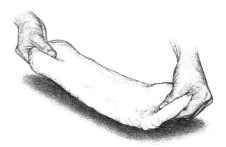

TECHNIQUE: Stretching dough into a rectangle

The "windowpane test" used by some bakers entails pulling off a small piece of dough and stretching it: it should not tear, and if held up to the light, it should be translucent. I do not use the windowpane test to determine dough strength because some doughs, such as those containing a lot of seeds, will always tear when stretched. Others, such as Pugliese (page 360), become extensible at a later stage during rising, which stretches and strengthens the dough, and during pulling, "turning" or folding it over on itself.

ORDER OF ADDING INGREDIENTS WHEN MAKING DOUGH

In commercial baking, it is generally considered more desirable to start with a drier dough and add water as you work to complete the kneading process. This is because flour doesn't absorb water (hydrate) quickly or evenly if added after the initial dough is mixed. But professional bakers are experienced at knowing how much water to add. For home bakers, I feel it is far easier to start with a moister dough and add flour only if necessary. If, by chance, the dough needs more water after mixing, it is best to use a spritzer. Make sure the water in the spritzer is fresh (it should not have been standing for more than 2 days).

3. RAISING (PROOFING) AND TURNING THE DOUGH

After a dough is mixed, it is always allowed to rise and double at least once after shaping and usually two or sometimes even three times before the final shaped rise, in order to develop more structure and flavor. Each time the dough rises and expands, it in effect exercises the strands of gluten, making them stronger.

There are two basic methods for **raising**. The one I use most often is simply to allow the dough to rise until doubled, or until a fingertip pressed into the top of the dough makes an impression that does not fill back up. Each time a risen dough is pushed down and deflated, it will still retain some air, because the gluten becomes stronger and more elastic during the rise. Each subsequent time the dough is capable of rising more than what would originally have been double. This means that with each subsequent rising, the dough needs

TECHNIQUE: Testing dough with fingertip to see whether it has risen

more space to double in size than it did for the first rise. This is why I specify a container that is larger than double the initial size of the dough in the recipes.

The second method, used by most professional artisan bakers, is to "turn" the dough after every 30 to 60 minutes, until it has doubled. "**Turning**" the dough by gently deflating it, stretching it, and folding, or "rounding," it also develops the gluten and retains the gases that form. Another essential reason for "turning" the dough is to redistribute the yeast and gas bubbles and to dispel some of the carbon dioxide and alcohol. If the yeasts were not moved, they would eventually consume all the immediately available sugar and suffocate in their carbon dioxide and alcohol waste products.

The more times the dough is allowed to rise, the finer and more even the crumb will be. Some doughs that are very soft and extensible, such as brioche, can as much as triple in one rise without deflating, but others, such as breadstick dough, will overstretch the gluten and tear it if allowed to overrise. It is truly amazing to witness the power of the yeast the first time this happens: the overrisen dough can blow the cover right off a container.

STEP-BY-STEP ILLUSTRATIONS FOR TURNING DOUGH:
THE BUSINESS-LETTER FOLD

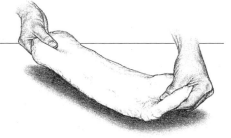

1> Stretching dough into a rectangle

2> Folding the bottom third of the dough rectangle over the center

3> Folding the top edge of the dough down to the bottom edge

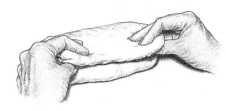

4> Dough turned oo the closed edge is on the left

5> Folding the bottom third of the dough rectangle over the center a second time

6> Folding the top edge of the dough down to the bottom edge a second time

1> Stretching out the left side of the dough

2> Folding the left side of the dough over
toward the center

3> Folding the stretched top of the
dough down toward the center

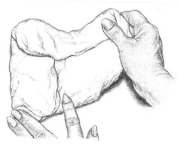

4> Stretching out the right side of
the dough

5> Folding the right side of the dough over
toward the center

Containers

If you have a very active dough and can't be around to control it by deflating it at necessary intervals, there *is* something you can do. Use a covered plastic container that is only a little larger than double the volume of the dough, and set a heavy weight on top of it. My favorite containers are clear acrylic with lids, purchased from food service suppliers. They have volume markings on the side, which make it easy to see when the dough has doubled. Alternatively, you can mark the height the dough should rise to with a piece of tape.

EQUIPMENT AND PROCESS:

Clear acrylic dough-rising container

Pushing down the dough into the dough-rising container

Dough rising until doubled in the dough-rising container

Temperature

Room temperature of 75° to 80°F is considered the ideal temperature in which to raise the dough. If the doughs are at around 75°F after mixing, they will take 1 to 1 1/2 hours for the first rise. Some doughs that have a lower than usual amount of yeast, such as the baguette, can take up to 3 hours. A slow rise promotes more flavor development and larger holes in the crumb.

If the room is cold or if you need to speed the rise, rather than increase the yeast, which would result in a more yeasty flavor (which might mask some of the desirable wheaty flavor), you can increase the temperature of the rising environment easily with a homemade or purchased acrylic proof box. I always use one to raise dough because it makes it unnecessary to cover the dough with greased plastic wrap. If you want to raise the temperature in the box, set 1 cup of hot (or close to boiling) water in it, as far from the dough as possible. If there is

EQUIPMENT AND PROCESS:
Bread rising in acrylic proof box

room, use two, one in each corner. Replace the water with new hot water every 30 minutes. You can also set the container holding the bread on top of a heating pad set to low or medium to keep the water hot. (Set at medium, my heating pad is 82° to 86°F.) If the room temperature is acceptable, fill the cup with room-temperature water to provide a moist environment and to prevent drying out of the upper crust.

An oven *without* a pilot light but with the oven light turned on will be an ideal 75° to 80°F. An oven with a pilot light is too hot.

It is helpful to know when estimating rising time according to room temperature that the rate of fermentation, or rising, is about double for every 15°F increase in temperature.

Overnight (Unshaped) Refrigerator Rise

Refrigerator temperatures vary depending both on how they are set and how often the door is opened. In my refrigerator, which runs between 34° and 37°F, 1 1/2 to 2 pounds of dough, starting at about 71°F, will be about 65°F after 3 hours of chilling and most activity will have quieted down. After a thorough chilling of 8 hours, the dough temperature goes down to about 47°F. (It will not get quite as low as the refrigerator temperature because there is still some yeast activity, although minimal.)

Since the dough is still fairly warm during the first 3 hours in the refrigerator (and if it is a larger quantity it will take even more than 3 hours to chill enough to go into dormancy), it is helpful to place the dough in a large oiled bag and flatten it before refrigerating, so it will cool more quickly. Deflate the dough every hour for the first 3 hours if it is continuing to rise and get puffy.

4. DIVIDING AND PRESHAPING THE DOUGH

Most of my recipes make only one loaf of bread. One of the advantages to this is that you can shape the dough immediately after deflating it. For those recipes that require dividing, it is necessary to preshape the dough and allow it to relax afterward, or the dough will be too stretchy to shape well.

When dividing dough, it is important to cut it with a bench scraper, a sharp chef's knife, or scissors. Pulling or tearing it will weaken the gluten. You can divide the dough by eye into equal pieces or "scale" it by weight, which is, of course, more exact. It is usually necessary to "patch" the pieces of dough in order to get equal loaves. I use scissors to cut off the excess dough and then just set it onto smaller pieces. During shaping, it will became fully integrated and reconnected into the dough's structure.

If the dough is very wet, a quick, sure touch helps to keep it from sticking to your fingers. Use the bench scraper as an extension of your hand to lift and move the dough.

After dividing the dough, set each piece on the lightly floured counter and gently preshape it into a round by pulling up the edges to the top. Without flipping it over, use a bench scraper to move it to a separate lightly floured part of the counter. Cover it with oiled plastic wrap and allow it to sit for about 20 minutes or until relaxed and extensible (when you pull it gently, it stretches without tearing).

5. SHAPING THE DOUGH

For many people, shaping the dough is the scariest part of bread baking, but the truth is, you don't have to worry: there's no such thing as an imperfect bread. Artisan hearth breads should look a little rough, free-form, and distinctive. And the more you shape bread, the more proficient you become. I look forward to this stage of the baking process, especially after having spent a week at the French Culinary Institute baking program with chef Amy Quazza, hand-shaping breads until I could do it in my sleep. If you want to get really good fast, offer your services at your local bakery. Meantime, here are a few basic principles of loaf shaping, along with fantastically beautiful and useful step-by-step drawings by Alan Witschonke.

GENERAL TIPS ON SHAPING

> If dough is shaped when cold, the components will not be evenly distributed, so the resulting crumb may have bubbles and the texture be uneven. If the dough has been refrigerated, remove it to room temperature 30 minutes to 1 hour before shaping. (Brioche however, is such a soft, moist dough, it is best rolled when cold, as it will require less flour to keep it from sticking.)

> Always place the dough smooth (skin) side down on a very lightly floured counter or a sheet of Roul'pat (see Equipment, page 586) to begin shaping. Too much flour causes the dough to slip. You want the dough to grab slightly onto the counter as you push against it to tighten the outer "skin," which will help to support and maintain the shape of the loaf.

> Tighter shaping will prolong proofing but results in better shape and texture. A taut outer skin holds the shape of the bread. Use an unfloured or barely floured work surface so that the dough can grab onto it and tug slightly during shaping.

> If a recipe calls for shaping a bread into a round (boule) and you prefer the long torpedo (*batard*) shape, it's fine to choose that instead—and vice versa.

> If a shaped dough has been refrigerated, it will take about 1 hour to come to room temperature.

> After dough is shaped, it can be frozen for up to 2 weeks, though I think there is more disturbance of fermentation and more loss of flavor at this point than if frozen after baking. If you plan to freeze a dough, it is best to use 10 to 25 percent more yeast to compensate for freezing damage; use the larger amount if planning to freeze the dough for the full 2 weeks.

Shaping a Round (Boule)

Begin by gently pressing down the dough into a round patty, dimpling the dough with your fingertips to deflate any large bubbles. Draw up the edges to the center. Pinch them together and turn the dough over so that the pinched

STEP-BY-STEP ILLUSTRATIONS FOR SHAPING A ROUND LOAF (BOULE):

1> Flattening the dough

2> Drawing up the edges into the center

3> Pinching the edges of the dough together at the top

4> Drawing the dough down with cupped hands to tighten the skin

5> Rotating the dough back and forth, using a circular motion

part is at the bottom. With cupped hands, stretch the dough down on all sides to form a taut skin, and pinch it again at the bottom.

Transfer the round ball of dough to an unfloured part of the counter and, with your hands on either side of the dough, push it to and fro while rotating it clockwise. You will feel the dough tighten and take on a rounder shape, with taut skin.

Shaping Round Rolls

For very small rolls, it works best simply to roll the dough between the lightly floured palms of your hands. For larger rolls, place the dough on a barely floured counter, cup your hand over it, and, with gentle pressure, roll the dough clockwise until you feel it take shape. It will round, and, as the gluten strengthens, seem to rise up into your hand (a lovely feeling!).

Shaping a Loaf

Begin by gently pressing the dough (or lightly rolling it with a rolling pin) into a wide rectangle; the exact size is not important at this point. (A long side of the dough should be facing toward you.) Dimple the dough with your fingertips to deflate any large bubbles. Fold over the right side of the dough to a little past the center. Fold over the left side of the dough to overlap it slightly. Press the center overlap section with the side of your hand to seal the dough. (If you have a lot of experience shaping, you may prefer at this point to rotate the dough 90 degrees—a quarter turn.) Starting at the top edge of the dough, roll it over three or four times, until it reaches the bottom edge of the dough: With each roll, press with your thumbs to seal it and at the same time push it away from you slightly to tighten the outer skin. As you roll and press, the dough will become wider. If it is not as long as the pan, place both hands close together on top of the dough and, rolling back and forth, gradually work your way toward

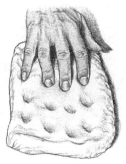

TECHNIQUE:
Dimpling the dough

STEP-BY-STEP ILLUSTRATIONS FOR
SHAPING A RECTANGULAR LOAF:

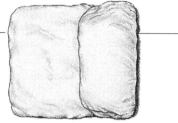

1> Folding the right side of the dough
over to a little past the center

2> Folding the left side of the dough
over to overlap the right edge
slightly

3> Rolling down the top edge of the dough

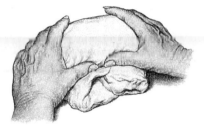

4> Pushing the dough away from
you to tighten and seal the roll

5> Rolling the dough down again
and pushing the roll down and
away from you with your thumbs

6> Rolling the dough down to the bottom
edge and sealing it with your thumbs

7> Rolling the dough back and forth to elongate it into a rectangular loaf slightly
longer than the pan

continued >

8> Tucking the ends of the loaf under

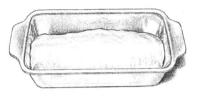

9> Shaped loaf in the pan

the ends, gently stretching the dough. For the most even shape, it is important to keep a tight skin on the surface of the dough and not to tear it. If you want the edges of the loaf to be smooth, tuck the sides under.

Shaping a Torpedo (Batard)

The most attractive shape for an elongated loaf is fuller in the middle and slightly pointed at the ends, like an elongated football. Begin by gently pressing the dough into a rectangle 1 or 2 inches narrower than you want the finished loaf to be, as it will widen during shaping. Have a long side facing toward you. Dimple the dough with your fingertips to deflate any large bubbles. Starting at the long top edge, bring each corner of the dough to meet at the center, forming a triangle at the top. Fold the tip of the triangle down to the center (this creates a fuller center section). Seal the seam with your thumbs, pushing the dough slightly away from you at the same time to increase the surface tension. Roll the dough down three-quarters of the way, again sealing it with your thumbs and pushing it back. Fold the dough down one more time so it reaches the bottom edge and seal it with your thumbs, pressing down and moving along the entire length of the dough. Roll the dough toward you so that the seam is centered at the bottom.

STEP-BY-STEP ILLUSTRATIONS FOR SHAPING A TORPEDO
(BATARD):

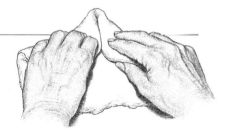

1> Bringing the upper corners of the dough
down to meet at the center

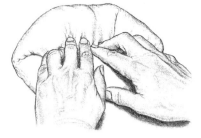

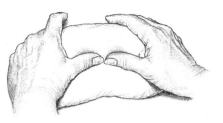

2> Folding the peak down to meet
the edges at the center

3> Sealing the dough with your
thumbs and pushing it away
from you to increase surface
tension

4> Rolling the dough
down three-quarters of
the way, then sealing it
and pushing it away
with your thumbs

5> Folding the dough
down to the bottom
edge and sealing it
with your thumbs

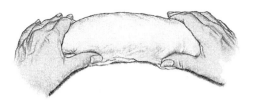

6> Pressing along the entire
length of the seam with your
thumbs

7> Dough rolled forward so seam is centered underneath

For torpedo-shaped rolls, start by rolling the pieces of dough into balls. Then taper them by placing both hands on top and rolling back and forth to elongate them, applying more pressure to the ends to taper them evenly.

Shaping a Baguette

Starting with the stubby preshaped dough rectangle, with a long side facing you, gently pat and stretch the dough into an 8-by-5-inch rectangle. Fold the bottom up over a little past the center and the top down to the center. With the side of your hand, seal the dough in the center, creating a trough. Then

STEP-BY-STEP ILLUSTRATIONS FOR
SHAPING A BAGUETTE:

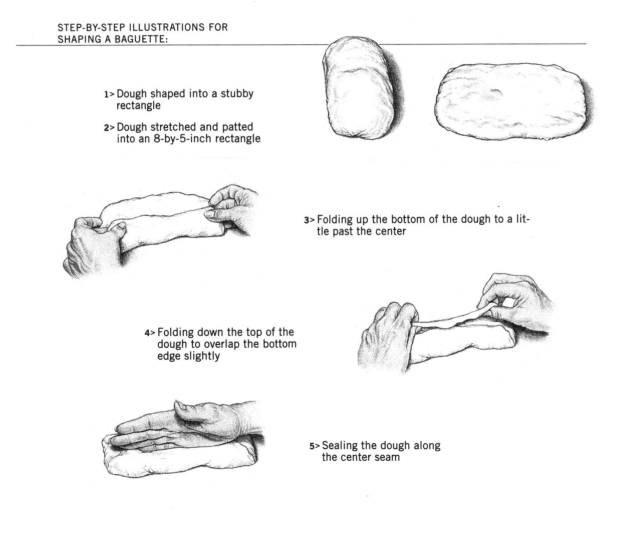

1> Dough shaped into a stubby rectangle

2> Dough stretched and patted into an 8-by-5-inch rectangle

3> Folding up the bottom of the dough to a little past the center

4> Folding down the top of the dough to overlap the bottom edge slightly

5> Sealing the dough along the center seam

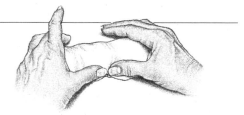

6> Option #1: Rolling down the top of the
dough to meet the bottom edge and sealing it with your thumbs

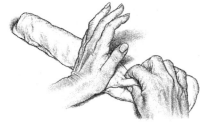

Option #2: Rolling down the top of the
dough and sealing it with your palms as
you go

7> Pinching any open-
ings in the seam to
seal it

8> Rolling the dough
back and forth to
elongate it

9> Stretching the dough to a
length of 14 inches

10> Placing the dough in the pan

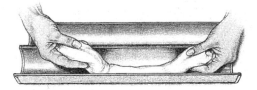

bring the top edge down to the bottom and seal, using the heel of your hand or your thumbs, pressing only on the seam to maintain as much air as possible in the rest of the dough. (If the seam doesn't seal, pinch it together between your thumbs and index fingers first.) Try to keep the length at about 8 inches. Roll the dough slightly toward you so that the seam is centered underneath.

Allow the dough to rest, covered (or place it in a couche; see page 78), for 30 to 45 minutes, until it is very light and soft enough to stretch. Then gently stretch each piece to 14 inches.

Shaping a Braided Loaf

A braided dough must be firm enough to hold the shape of the braid. For perfectly symmetrical strands, each piece of dough can be shaped as you do for the baguette. But a more casual approach works well too. The important part is achieving a final shape similar to the torpedo, fuller

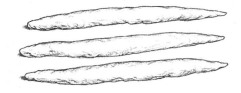

Three tapered ropes of dough

in the center and tapered at the ends. Cut the dough into 3 or 4 equal pieces. Cover them with plastic wrap or a damp towel, and allow them to rest for 10 minutes.

For a rougher shape, start by rolling each piece of dough on the counter into as long a rope as possible. Work with one piece at a time, keeping the rest covered. Lift each piece of dough from one end with one hand while using the other hand to pull and stretch it gently downward to form a 15- to 16-inch-long rope, (if making a 4-strand braid, roll 14 to 15 inches long), flouring your hands lightly if the dough is sticky.

A *three-strand braid* is most symmetrical when you start at the middle and then continuing braiding out to each end. It will be about 15 inches long.

If making a *four-strand braid*, taper the top of each dough rope to about 5 inches in so that it is narrower than the rest of the rope, as otherwise this part of the dough tends to bunch up and be too fat. Pinch the 4 ropes together

1> Braid started in the center, the outside strand
crossed over the center strand, alternating
from side to side

2> Pinching the end of the braid tightly

3> Finishing the braid by crossing
the outside strand under the
center strand, alternating from
side to side

4> The finished braid: ends
pinched, tucked under, and
pushed toward the center

at their tops and braid, pulling and stretching the dough slightly as you go.
Keep pinching the ends together, as they tend to pull apart as you braid.
Stretch the dough more as you come to the end of
the braid so that it comes to more of a point, then
pinch the strands together at the end. Moisten
both pinched ends with a little water to help them
hold together during rising, and tuck them under a
little, pushing the ends of the loaf together a little
so that it is fatter in the center.

Most amazing of all is the *single-strand braid*. At
first it may seem impossible to master, but once you
try it you will see that it it's quicker than any other

VARIATION:
A 3-braided challah coiled into a
round, with the end tucked under

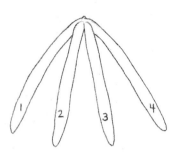

1> Four ropes pinched together at the top

2> Starting braid by slipping 1 under both 2 and 3

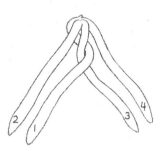

3> Crossing 1 over 3

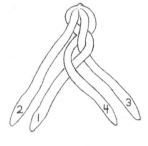

4> Slipping 4 under both 3 and 1 and then crossing it over 1

5> Slipping 2 under both 1 and 4 and then crossing it over 4

6> Slipping 3 under both 4 and 2 and then crossing it over 2

method. Start with a 20-inch-long rope made with one-third of the dough (at least 7 ounces/200 grams). In order for the loaf to be symmetrical, have the bottom hand of the strand thicker than the rest, because it has to form a loop and then be stretched which will thin it. The other end of the strand is then thrust deeply into the top loop so that it holds in place. If the dough seems dry, brush the end with water to make sure that it sticks and doesn't pull loose from the knot.

Finished 4-braided loaf with ends pinched together and tucked under

The easiest option of all is to make a **simulated** braided loaf using a molded loaf pan produced by Nordicware (see Sources, page 598). You simply shape the dough into a loaf and press it into the pan. It takes on the impressions of the pan, so it imitates an elaborately shaped bread.

STEP-BY-STEP ILLUSTRATIONS FOR
SHAPING A SINGLE-STRAND BRAID:

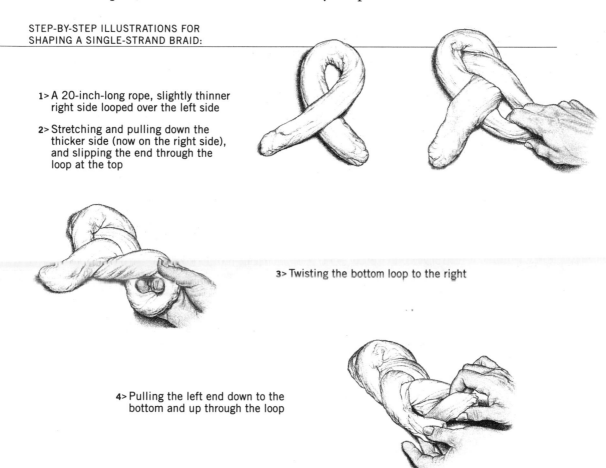

1> A 20-inch-long rope, slightly thinner right side looped over the left side

2> Stretching and pulling down the thicker side (now on the right side), and slipping the end through the loop at the top

3> Twisting the bottom loop to the right

4> Pulling the left end down to the bottom and up through the loop

5> Using both hands to slip the end through the loop so it shows on top

Dough-Shaping Equipment

LOAF PANS

Breads that are baked in pans have the support of the sides of the pan to maintain their shape. In order to get the most attractive shape, the amount of dough has to match the volume of the pan. Too little dough, and the bread will not have an attractive crest. Too much dough, and it will mushroom over the edges and be misshapen and top-heavy.

EQUIPMENT:

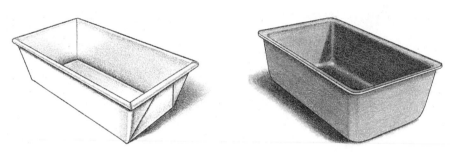

Chicago Metallics loaf pan,
example of a standard loaf pan

T-Fal loaf pan

Bread pans vary widely as to volume. Even when the dimensions are the same, the degree of slope from the top rim to the bottom of the pan will affect the amount of dough the pan can hold. When you are using a pan for the first time, I recommend greasing the pan lightly and pressing the unshaped dough into it to see how it will fit. It should be no higher than 1/2 inch from the top of the pan. If there is too little dough for the pan, use a smaller pan. If there is too much dough, remove some and bake it as a roll, or save it to add to your next batch of dough (see Pâte Fermentée [Scrap Dough], page 337).

All doughs baked in loaf pans should rise until the center is about 1 inch above the sides of the pan. New pans need to be well greased the first time.

Then, if they are wiped clean instead of washed, they will generally not require more than the lightest film if any at all. Even nonstick pans should be greased lightly. I use cooking spray and wipe out any excess with a piece of plastic wrap.

TECHNIQUE:
Measuring the height of risen dough

BANNETONS OR DOUGH-RISING BASKETS

Bread that is baked free-form, either directly on an oven stone or on a baking sheet, is either made stiff enough with a high proportion of flour to hold its shape or is shaped and risen in a floured banneton to give extra support. Bannetons can be beautiful willow baskets from France, unlined or lined with coarse woven cloth, or they can be plastic baskets or even colanders lined with clean kitchen towels. It is

EQUIPMENT: **DOUGH-RISING BANNETONS**

Cloth-lined banneton

Willow banneton

Spiral willow banneton

Cloth-lined oblong banneton

Colander with a kitchen towel, an improvised banneton

important to have a porous container so that the dough can breathe. Otherwise, the moisture of the dough may cause it to stick to the cloth and the dough will collapse and deflate when unmolded. It is fine, however, to place it in a plastic proof box, even one with hot water.

Unlined willow bannetons need to be dusted with flour from a sifter to keep the dough from sticking. Cloth-lined bannetons require a heavier coating of flour, rubbed into the cloth. Rice flour, which is silky-fine, is ideal. Some of the flour will be absorbed into the surface (skin) of the dough and help give it support. Often on unmolding, the dough will deflate somewhat, but if it has been prepared correctly it will rise back up to an amazing extent when set in a hot steamy oven.

If you are using a colander and floured towel, and the risen bread is more than 1 inch below the top, you should support the bread when inverting it so that it doesn't fall and deflate. Cut a cardboard circle small enough to fit into the colander and touch the bread. Place a piece of parchment on top of the bread and then invert it onto the cardboard. Then slide the bread with the parchment beneath it off the cardboard and onto the stone or baking sheet.

COUCHES

The French word *couche* means bed, and that is the name given to the cloth that is folded to make a bed for long loaves, such as baguettes, to rest during rising. It is made of the same special coarse woven cloth used to line bannetons, and it needs to be dusted with flour in the same way. A slim narrow board or baker's peel is used to roll the dough off the cloth onto the baking stone.

Overnight Shaped Refrigerator Rise

Placing the shaped dough in a loaf pan or free-form on a baking sheet and allowing it to sit overnight in the refrigerator results in extra depth of flavor and a lovely blistering of the crust. I usually allow the shaped dough a beginning rise of 30 minutes at room temperature before refrigerating it. Because the dough continues to rise during the first 3 hours of refrigeration, it is often fully proofed by the next day, so all that is needed is for it to warm at room temperature for an hour while the oven is preheating. If the dough hasn't risen enough, I allow it to sit at room temperature until it is fully proofed. A cup of hot water in the plastic proof box (see page 588) also helps to speed the process if necessary.

The Final (Shaped) Proof or Rise

For the most attractive design in the top crust, the final shaped dough should be underproofed slightly so that it will open up widely at the slash (see below). It is at this stage when the impression left if a finger is gently pressed into the dough fills back up very slowly. Soft rich doughs such as brioche, however, should be allowed a full proof so that they do not pull in at the sides when baked. A braided challah also needs a full proof so that it doesn't rise much after going into the oven and reveal a pale portion of the dough that the glaze did not reach.

6.   SLASHING (SCORING) AND STENCILING

Making cuts or slashes in the dough to release the steam that builds up during baking is not strictly necessary. It is done to determine exactly how and where the dough will split and to ensure that it splits in a clean line, not in a ragged, uncontrolled tear. If the slash is not deep or long enough, the crust will continue to open and split raggedly at both ends of the slash.

Breads baked in loaf pans will open on their own in an attractive way just under the crest of the loaf if not slashed, so slashing a long line down the center is optional, as a design feature. Round loaves that have been raised in bannetons are sometimes also left to open freely to enhance the artisanal look with unpredictably irregular cracks. They are proofed right side (smooth side) up in the banneton, and when unmolded and baked they open at the weakest point.

The key to effective slashing is a razor-sharp blade. Slashing may strike fear into the heart of a new bread baker because it seems impossible at first to duplicate the swift, decisive motion of a professional baker. If the motion is too slow, the cutting device may drag the dough into an unattractive line. There are two ways I know of around this problem. One is simply to use the

STEP-BY-STEP ILLUSTRATIONS FOR MAKING DECORATIVE
SLASHES AND SCORING THE DOUGH:

1> Making a tic-tac-toe slash

2> Making a single cross slash

3> Finished single cross slash

4> Making a starfish slash

5> Finished starfish slash

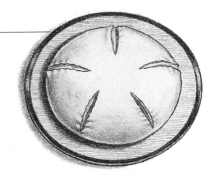

6> The lantern slash

7> Making a double slash

8> Finished double slash

9> Making a spiral slash

10> A spiral-slashed torpedo
(batard)

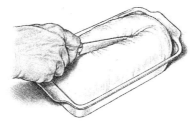

11> Holding the knife at an
angle to make an ear
(grigne)

12> Slashing a long line down
the center

tip of a sharp knife or the tip of a single-edged razor blade to mark the dough, and then to go over it until the cut is deep enough. The other is to use small sharp shears to cut through the dough. This works especially well with a fragile airy dough with a dry crust—the sort that usually is shaped in a banneton. I find a single-edged razor blade makes the best cut. It often helps to allow the bread to sit uncovered for 5 minutes to form a slight skin before slashing.

The two important considerations in slashing are the depth and the angle of the cut. If the cut is too deep, the crust will stand up away from the dough. If it is too shallow, the center of the dough will rise up and completely fill in the opening, so it will resemble a scar more than a design. Usually a depth of 1/4 to 1/2 inch works well. If the dough has risen to the point where it has doubled and the impression left by your finger remains rather than slowly filling in, it is best to go with a 1/4-inch-deep slash, because the dough will not rise as much from the heat of the oven. If you like the look of a wide-open cut, you will need to underproof the dough slightly, as mentioned above, just to the point that the impression doesn't spring back but fills in slowly. Then a 1/2-inch-deep slash works well, because the dough will continue to rise more and fill in more of the cut.

Usually the blade of the cutting device is held at a right angle (straight up) to the dough when slashing. But in order to get what is called an "ear," grigne (grin in French), bloom, or ridged cut, it is necessary to hold the blade at an angle so that it cuts down into the dough on an angle.

It's fine to be creative about your slashes. It's a great way to personalize your loaf.

Stenciling is another interesting method of giving a unique design to the bread. It's easy to do. Just before the loaf goes into the oven, set a stencil (purchased or homemade, perhaps your initial) over the dough and sift some flour on top of it. Carefully lift the stencil away. During baking, the flour from the exposed area of the stencil will not brown as much as the rest of the crust, making a beautiful contrast and design.

7.   GLAZING

The purpose of a glaze is to give the crust a shiny appearance and, sometimes, depending on the glaze, a deeper color. A glaze can also serve as "glue" to attach a scattering of seeds such as poppy, caraway, or sesame.

If a bread is glazed, it should not be sprayed with water before baking or steamed during the beginning of baking, because the water (which would otherwise produce a shine) will dull the glaze.

Some breads look best without any glaze. Rustic breads that are proofed in flour-dusted bannetons are not glazed or misted with water because the flour on the surface of the dough gives an attractive artisanal appearance to the crust.

For extra shine, a glaze can be applied both before baking and again when the bread is taken out of the oven. A glaze can also be applied before rising and again before baking; this helps to keep the crust from drying. After the dough has risen, use a light hand when brushing on the glaze so as not to deflate it.

If slashing the dough, do it after applying the glaze so that there is a more dramatic contrast between the slashed interior crumb and the crust.

Egg yolk glazes result in the deepest coloring of the crust, and you may need to tent the loaf loosely with foil after the first 20 minutes or so of baking to prevent overbrowning.

TYPES OF GLAZES

>   **A crisp crust:** Water (brushed or spritzed)

>   **A powdery, rustic chewy crust:** Flour (dusted)

>   **A soft velvety crust:** Melted butter, preferably clarified (1/2 tablespoon per average loaf)

>   **A crisp light brown crust:** 1 egg white (2 tablespoons) and 1/2 teaspoon water, lightly beaten and strained (the ideal sticky glaze for attaching seeds)

>   **A medium shiny golden crust:** 2 tablespoons egg (lightly beaten to measure) and 1 teaspoon water, lightly beaten

>   **A shiny deep golden brown crust:** 1 egg yolk (1 tablespoon) and 1 teaspoon heavy cream, lightly beaten

>   **A shiny medium golden brown crust:** 1 egg yolk (1 tablespoon) and 1 teaspoon milk, lightly beaten

>   **A very shiny hard crust:** 1 1/2 teaspoons cornstarch and 6 tablespoons water: whisk the cornstarch with 2 tablespoons of the water. Bring the remaining 1/4 cup water to a boil and whisk the cornstarch mixture into it; simmer for about 30 seconds, or until thickened and translucent. Cool to room temperature, then brush on the bread before baking and again as soon as it comes out of the oven.

8.   BAKING

Helen Charley's *Food Science* was the first food textbook I was assigned when I was a student at the University of Vermont many years ago. I was impressed even then by this simple but profoundly explicit definition of what happens during the baking phase of bread preparation: "The pressure of the expanding gas coupled with the ability of the gluten to stretch and confine the steam is responsible for the marked expansion of the gluten as it bakes. Once the gluten is inflated, pressure from the expanding steam maintains its volume until heat has had time to set the protein."

The goal in baking is to get good volume and a beautiful crust. Volume is determined by *oven spring*, which takes place during the first third of the baking cycle, when the rate of fermentation rapidly increases, until the heat kills the yeast. But the most significant part of the rise is produced by the gradual expansion of the gas and the moisture in the dough that turns to steam.

As the temperature rises, the outer surface of the dough dries and the crust starts to form. The goal is to delay the formation of this crust until the gases have accomplished their work so the dough can expand to its full capacity. One way this is achieved is by *steaming* the oven. The steam condenses on the dough, keeping it moist and able to expand while also helping the enzymes in the dough to break down the carbohydrates into sugars that will enable the crust to brown. The steam also serves to gelatinize the surface starches, which gives the crust a glossy sheen. So, to sum it up: *Steam produces increased volume, optimal browning, and shine.*

The two essential factors for hearth breads with crisp crust are intense initial heat and initial moisture. But in order to maintain the crisp crust, especially in very moist breads such as the ciabatta, the moisture has to be vented toward the end of baking. This can be accomplished by leaving the oven door partially ajar during the last 5 or 10 minutes of baking, and if your oven has a convection option, by turning it on at that point. You don't want to use convection in the beginning of baking, however, because it will blow out the moisture. In fact, in some electric ovens, you can see the moisture coming out of the vent. If possible, cover the vent for the first 10 minutes of baking.

Soft breads and those that contain higher amounts of honey, sugar, fat, and/or egg require lower temperatures to prevent burning, but they also benefit from steaming. Lower temperatures of 350° to 375°F result in a thicker crust, which is actually a good thing because it provides extra stability for these soft breads that could cave in at the sides (referred to as *shelling*).

The major problem with any oven is that the moment the door is opened, the temperature drops at least 25 degrees and often as much as 50 degrees. For this reason, I usually set the oven at 25 to 50 degrees above the desired temperature and lower it as soon as the bread is in the oven and the door closed. The unavoidable loss of heat is why it is preferable to create steam just when putting the bread into the oven rather than spritzing every few minutes and losing heat every time the door is open. (Besides, the amount of water added by spritzing is surprisingly little.)

Baking stones or unglazed quarry tiles help significantly to recover the lost heat more quickly, as they retain heat. They also serve to provide more even baking, to give the bread its initial heat boost, and to pull the moisture out of the bottom crust. The stone or tiles should be preheated with the oven for at least 45 minutes, or, preferably, 1 hour.

The oven should never be opened during the first 15 minutes of baking. But after that point, it's usually fine to open it quickly and turn the bread halfway around to promote more even browning. If the bread is on a pan or parchment, this is also a good time to remove it and set it directly onto the stone. The bread can be turned halfway through the baking time instead but I can never resist opening the oven door to see what it looks like at the first safe opportunity.

Placing the Bread in the Oven

I don't bake directly on the oven stone (except for matzoh) until the crust is set and won't stick to the stone, because I intensely dislike the smell of burning cornmeal or flour, which would be necessary to keep it from sticking. If this does not bother you, it's fine to use a baker's peel, lightly sprinkled with coarse cornmeal or flour, preferably semolina, to transfer the shaped dough to the stone. Use a sharp thrust to slide it from the peel.

My usual method is to shape a free-form loaf and set it on a Silpain- or Silpat-lined pan, preferably a perforated one, and then set the pan on the stone. When I use parchment, I use a peel to slide it onto the stone. The bread can be left on the parchment for the entire baking period, but I prefer to remove it after the first 15 minutes of baking so that the bottom crust does not steam and gets as crisp as possible.

Methods of Steaming

To create the most steam as quickly as possible requires a metal pan that retains heat, ideally a cast-iron skillet (reserved for this purpose or it will rust), but an aluminum sheet pan will also do. Set the pan on the floor of the oven before preheating it (or the shelf just above if there is a heating element on the floor).

Use a spritzer or brush to moisten the surface of the dough just before it goes into the oven. *Note: Do not steam the oven or mist the bread if the bread has been glazed or dusted with flour.*

TECHNIQUE:
Spraying the dough with water before baking

ICE CUBE METHOD

This is my preferred method because it is the safest. It produces a lot of steam, though not as much or as quickly as using boiling water. Most of the steam produced, however, will be trapped inside the oven, in contrast to the boiling water method (see below), unless you work very quickly.

Just before setting the bread in the oven, take out of the freezer about 1/2 cup of ice cubes (5 to 6 cubes, about 1/4 cup of water when melted). The moment the bread is in the oven, pull the waiting pan forward (using a thick pot holder) and toss the cubes into the pan. Immediately close the door. The pan will slide in on its own and almost all the steam will remain in the oven.

TECHNIQUE:
Adding ice cubes to pre-heated pan for creating steam

BOILING WATER METHOD

This produces good steam but so quickly that you have to work fast to keep it in the oven. Wear a protective oven mitt, and avert your face: steam burns are painful.

Just before the bread is ready to go into the oven, pour 1 cup of boiling water into a 2-cup or larger measuring cup with a spout. Set the bread in the oven, pull the waiting pan slightly forward, and quickly pour in the boiling water. Immediately shut the door. (If your oven door has a glass window, protect it by laying a towel over it when pouring the boiling water, or you risk cracking the glass.)

How to Tell When the Bread Is Done

There's nothing like an instant-read thermometer to know for sure. I've thumped the bottom of many a loaf and not always been entirely certain of what I'm hearing or if the hollow sound is quite "hollow" enough.

Bread loses on the average 7 to 8 percent of its raw dough weight in baking. As the temperature rises, the moisture in the dough turns to steam and evaporates. For crusty breads, you want as much evaporation as possible without drying out the bread (which is difficult to do in any case without over-browning the crust). I bake most of my breads to between 200° and 211°F; I take brioche and other egg-rich breads out at 180° to 190°F. I bring soft white sandwich loaves to the higher temperature in order to strengthen their side crust; In fact, I sometimes unmold them and return them to the oven with the door partially ajar for 5 minutes to brown and set the crust.

If the bread tests done and the crust is still pale, turn up the oven as far as it will go and bake the bread, watching it carefully, until browned. It usually takes only about 3 minutes.

A dark brown crust offers more depth of flavor in the crumb beneath as well as the crust itself. But too dark a crust, veering toward burned, is bitter and unpleasant to my taste. If this should happen, it helps to use a grater to remove any burned areas. Try to do it as soon as possible before the burned aroma permeates the bread.

WHERE TO INSERT THE THERMOMETER

It hurts to make a hole in a beautiful crust, especially a smooth one, so try to insert the thermometer in an inconspicuous area: for example, an existing air bubble hole. With a bread that has been baked in a loaf pan, you can insert the thermometer just under the crown. To get an accurate reading, be sure to insert the thermometer into the center of the loaf, which is the last part to finish baking.

TECHNQIUE:
Inserting a thermometer into the center of the bread to test for doneness

High-Altitude Bread Baking

Yeast breads seem to fare better at high altitudes than do chemically leavened baked goods, such as cakes. A few minor alterations, however, will be helpful. Because of the lower air pressure, yeast breads will rise more quickly; cutting back a little on the yeast and allowing the dough to rise at cooler temperatures will help to slow it down. Bill Weekley of the Le Saffre Yeast Corporation, who owned a bakery at a 5,000-foot elevation, reports that reducing the yeast by about 10 percent and using stronger (higher-protein) flour helps to maintain volume. Interestingly, rather than increasing the water to compensate for the drier atmosphere, it is necessary to decrease it slightly, he says, because the lower atmospheric pressure causes too soft a dough to rise too much and collapse.

9.   COOLING

Bakers say that the sound of the crust crackling as it cools is the bread's song. It is indeed lovely and gratifying, because when you hear it, you know you've done a good job. After a while, you will find yourself listening for it.

It is important to cool breads with a crisp crust on a rack so that there is enough air circulation to allow the moisture to escape. Breads with a soft crust that are very fragile, such as the egg-rich panettone, need a cushioning support while cooling. I cover a soft pillow with a plastic bag and set the bread on it, turning it occasionally to help it to cool evenly.

Cooling is part of the baking process. If cut while still hot, most bread will be unpleasantly pasty and even gummy. It is almost always better to allow the bread to cool completely and then reheat it briefly if you want to serve it warm. One exception is sticky buns, which are perfect in both texture and flavor practically from the moment they come out of the oven.

10. SLICING AND STORING

For slicing firm, crisp-crusted breads, a long knife with deep serrations is ideal. Some breads, however, such as a rustic prosciutto bread or a baguette, have a much more appealing texture when broken or torn rather than when clean cut. Breads that are very soft, such as brioche or soft white sandwich bread, are best cut with either an electric knife or the Furi knife with rounded serrations (see page 593).

If an uncut loaf of bread is left at room temperature until the next day, the crust will soften unless it is stored uncovered or placed in a brown paper bag. If storing it for more than 10 hours, I prefer to sacrifice the crust and keep the interior crumb as fresh as possible by putting it in a plastic zip-seal bag or vacuum-sealing it in a container (see page 596). The next day, it can be placed in a 350° to 400°F oven, depending on the original baking temperature of the bread, for about 10 minutes, which will recrisp the crust and freshen the crumb. I love the efficiency of my Cuisinart convection toaster oven, which is large enough for a 9-inch round loaf but small enough to preheat in minutes.

If you are planning to store the bread for any length of time, it is better to freeze it than refrigerate it, as in the refrigerator, it gets stale faster.

If you are planning to freeze a loaf, it is best to underbake it by about 5 minutes so that the internal temperature is 180° to 190°F. After it has cooled completely, it should be wrapped airtight. (I use the original brand Saran wrap—not the new type—which is airtight, and then place it in a freezer-weight bag, expressing as much air as possible from the bag.) Defrost the loaf at room temperature for several hours, then finish the baking for 10 or 15 minutes at the same temperature at which it was originally baked.

Once a bread has been cut, it is important to keep the cut edge from exposure to air to prevent the entire loaf from drying out. The easiest way is to stand it on this cut end. Often my husband comes home to several mountain peaks of bread on our marble counter, resembling a Japanese Zen rock garden.

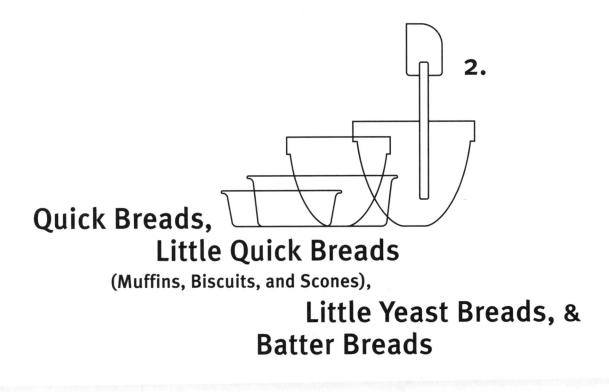

Quick Breads,
Little Quick Breads
(Muffins, Biscuits, and Scones),
Little Yeast Breads, &
Batter Breads

2.

PEOPLE OFTEN ASK ME ABOUT THE DIFFERENCES AMONG THE VARIOUS categories of baked goods. The confusion is understandable, because there are many "crossovers" and the boundaries are sometimes fuzzy. Brioche, for example, can be considered a cake, a pastry, or a bread, depending on how it is used (what it is filled or topped with) and when it is eaten.

All baked goods have three ingredients in common: flour, liquid, and salt. I define where they fall on the baking spectrum, from quick bread (essentially a cake), to yeast bread, by the proportion of liquid each contains in relation to the flour. Batter breads have the most liquid of all, quick breads less, and yeast hearth breads still less, with pastry the least of all.

Fat is another significant ingredient in baked goods. The degree of its presence or its absence helps to sharpen the definition of categories. Almost all cakes and pastries have fat, which is what makes them tender; only some breads have fat, and it's generally a far smaller amount, making them much more chewy.

Quick Breads (The Dough Percentage: 88.3 to 196.7% water, 34.7 to 101.6% fat)

These are the easy ones, so quickly done and forgiving you have to question if they are really in fact "bread." If yeast is included in your definition of bread then they are not. Generally, however, these are referred to as "breads" because they are baked in a loaf shape and are less delicate and sweet than cakes or pastries. Quick breads are usually leavened with baking powder or baking soda and are often served sliced, in a bread basket, or sometimes as dessert. The Southwestern Corn Spoon Bread, which is baked in a round dish and usually served as a side dish, is an exception, but belongs in this category because it is leavened with baking powder and shares the same range of flour, liquid, and fat.

Little Quick Breads

Muffins (The Dough Percentage: 95 to 132% water, 42.4 to 59.2% fat)
These are essentially small cakes made with less leavening than most cakes and all-purpose flour, rather than cake flour, for a firmer crumb, sometimes containing slightly less sugar. The corn fingers are muffins baked in a different shape.

Muffins freeze well for up to 3 months. Frozen muffins can be reheated in a preheated 400°F oven for 15 to 20 minutes, or until a metal cake tester inserted briefly into the center feels warm. Room-temperature muffins can be reheated in a 400°F oven for 4 minutes.

Biscuits and Scones (The Dough Percentage: 36 to 108.1% water, 20.4 to 69.4% fat)
Biscuits and scones, which are shaped and baked free-form, not in a tin or pan, are closer to bread on the baking spectrum. In fact, I think of them as the missing link between bread and pastry because they are more crumbly and delicate than bread but more substantial than pastry. That is because most biscuits and scones have more liquid than a basic pie dough, for example, and, although sometimes less, often around the same amount of fat. The "extra" liquid develops more protein, making them chewier (unless compensated for by more fat) and heavier than a piecrust or pastry.

Little Yeast Breads (The Dough Percentage: 51 to 68.6% water, 0 to 16.3% fat)

These are actually small classic yeast breads, but the doughs are shaped and baked in unusual ways that give them unique crumb and crust characteristics.

English muffins, for example, are made with what is essentially the same dough as a soft white bread (just a little less water and butter, and a little more yeast and salt), but they are baked on a griddle instead of in an oven, which makes the difference. Pretzel dough (for soft pretzels) has 51 percent water while bagel dough, which is very similar, has 63.8 percent water. Pretzels are dipped in lye and salted to produce their distinctive shiny crust; bagels are boiled in malted water before baking, which gives them a dense crumb and a thick chewy crust that is also shiny but less so than pretzels. Bialy dough is almost the same as bagel dough, with a slightly higher amount of water; it also contains high-gluten flour, for maximum chew. Since bialys are not boiled before baking, they are lighter and less chewy than bagels, with a dull, almost papery thin crust.

Batter Breads (The Dough Percentage: 113 to 229% water, 45 to 50.6% fat)

Crumpets fall somewhere between a batter and a bread, containing double the water of a basic bread and three times the yeast. Popovers and Dutch babies contain no yeast and are leavened entirely by egg and steam. They have almost double the liquid of crumpets, so they are technically more like cream puffs than like bread. However, I have included them in this chapter because popovers make such a terrific substitute for dinner rolls, and Dutch babies, which are really giant popovers, make the most impressive edible containers for butter-sautéed fruit and fresh berries.

Carrot Bread > page 103
Carrot Bread sandwiches with
cream cheese (foreground)

Cinnamon Crumb Surprise > page 97

Flaky Scone > page 139

Crumpets > page 175

Crumpets with clotted
cream and honey

Butter Popovers > page 178

Perfect Pizza with Steamed Clams and Ricotta
> page 192

Squares of Rosemary
Focaccia Sheet > page 205

Cinnamon Crumb Surprise

Topped with fragrant cinnamon crumbs, this golden loaf has a hidden treat in the middle: a tart layer of buttery apple slices, nestled inside a layer of cinnamon crumbs. This is a real favorite in our house, perfect with coffee or tea; I also enjoy it with a glass of cold milk.

TIME SCHEDULE

Oven Temperature: 350°F
Baking Time: 50 to 60 minutes

Makes: an 8-by-4-by-3-inch-high loaf

Crumb Topping and Filling

INGREDIENTS	MEASURE	WEIGHT	
	volume	ounces	grams
light brown sugar	1/4 cup firmly packed	1.25 ounces	36 grams
granulated sugar	1 1/2 tablespoons	0.7 ounce	19.2 grams
walnuts	3/4 cup	3 ounces	85 grams
cinnamon	1 teaspoon	--	--
unsifted cake flour	1/4 cup plus 2 tablespoons	1.75 ounces	50 grams
unsalted butter, melted	3 tablespoons	1.5 ounces	43 grams
pure vanilla extract	1/4 teaspoon	--	--

EQUIPMENT

a heavy-duty stand mixer with paddle attachment OR
a hand-held mixer;

a 9-by-5-inch loaf pan, bottom greased and lined with parchment, then sprayed with Baker's Joy or greased and floured (if using a non-stick pan and Baker's Joy, there is no need to line the pan)

1 > **Preheat the oven.** Preheat the oven to 350°F 30 minutes before baking. Have an oven shelf at the middle level.

2 > **Make the crumb mixture.** In a food processor fitted with the metal blade, pulse the sugars, nuts, and cinnamon until the nuts are coarsely chopped. Reserve 1/2 cup for the filling. Add the flour, butter, and vanilla to the remainder and pulse briefly just until the butter is absorbed. Empty it into a bowl and refrigerate for about 20 minutes to firm up, then use your fingertips to form a coarse, crumbly mixture for the topping.

Apple Filling and Butter

INGREDIENTS	MEASURE	WEIGHT	
room temperature	volume	ounces	grams
1 small tart apple (5.5 ounces/155 grams)	1 heaping cup slices	4.5 ounces	130 grams
lemon juice	2 teaspoons	--	8 grams
1 large egg	3 tablespoons	1.75 ounces	50 grams
2 large egg yolks	2 tablespoons	about 1 ounce	32 grams
sour cream	1/2 cup	4.2 ounces	120 grams
pure vanilla extract	1 teaspoon	--	4 grams
sifted cake flour	1 1/2 cups	5.3 ounces	150 grams
sugar	3/4 cup	5.3 ounces	150 grams
baking powder	1/4 teaspoon	--	1.2 grams
baking soda	3/8 teaspoon	--	1.8 grams
salt	1/8 plus 1/16 teaspoon (scant 1/4 teaspoon)	--	1.2 grams
unsalted butter, softened	9 tablespoons	4.5 ounces	128 grams

3 > **Prepare the filling and mix the batter.** Just before mixing the batter, peel and core the apple. Cut into 1/4-inch-thick slices, and toss with the lemon juice.

In a medium bowl, lightly combine the egg, the yolks, about one fourth of the sour cream, and the vanilla.

In a mixer bowl, or other large bowl, combine the cake flour, sugar, baking powder, baking soda, and salt. Mix on low speed (#2 if using a KitchenAid, with the paddle attachment) for 30 seconds to blend. Add the butter and the remaining sour cream and mix until the dry ingredients are moistened. Increase the speed to medium if using a stand mixer (#4 KitchenAid), or high speed if using a hand-held mixer, and beat for 1 minute to aerate and develop the structure. Scrape down the sides of the bowl. Gradually add the egg mixture in two batches, beating for 20 seconds after each addition to incorporate the ingredients and strengthen the structure. Scrape down the sides.

4 > Fill the pan. Scrape about two-thirds of the batter into the prepared pan. Smooth the surface. Sprinkle with the reserved 1/2 cup crumb mixture and top with the apple slices, arranging them in two rows of overlapping slices. Drop the reserved batter in large blobs over the fruit and spread it evenly, preferably with a small offset spatula. (The batter will be 3/4 inch from the top of the pan.) Sprinkle with the crumb topping.

5 > Bake the bread. Bake for 50 to 60 minutes or until a wooden toothpick inserted in the center comes out clean and the bread springs back when pressed lightly in the center (an instant-read thermometer inserted into the center will read about 200°F). Tent loosely with buttered foil after 45 minutes to prevent overbrowning.

6 > Cool the bread. Remove the bread from the oven and set it on a wire rack to cool for 10 minutes. Place a folded kitchen towel on top of a flat plate and cover it with plastic wrap. Oil the plastic wrap. Loosen the sides of the bread with a small metal spatula, and invert it onto the plate. Grease a wire rack and reinvert the bread onto it, so that it is right side up. Cool completely, about 1 1/2 hours, before wrapping airtight.

POINTERS FOR SUCCESS

> It is not necessary to sift the flour if you are weighing it. However, if you measure it, sift it into the cup and then level it off, without shaking or tapping the cup at all.

> It's fine to use all-purpose flour, which will result in a slightly firmer texture, but it is imperative that it be *bleached* all-purpose; otherwise, the butter is likely to drop to the bottom, making an unpleasant tasting and rubbery layer.

> It is essential that the oven be hot enough to set the structure quickly to support the crumb topping and keep it from sinking.

THE DOUGH PERCENTAGE

Flour:	100%
Water:	88.3% (includes the water in the butter and egg whites)
Salt:	0.8%
Fat:	38.5% (includes the fat in the egg yolks and sour cream)

Cranberry-Banana-Walnut Quick Bread

My friend Jeanne Bauer has been talking about her Aunt Ceil's cranberry-banana-nut bread for years, and when I started this book, I finally paid serious attention. Now I know why. This recipe has everything going for it. Cranberry tempers the sweetness of banana, while banana rounds out the acidity and bite of the cranberry. In fact, I found the cranberry so delicious I doubled the original amount, which also decreased the sweetness. Cutting the cranberries in half is well worth the effort, as it both helps them to keep their shape by preventing them from bursting and also helps them absorb the sugar.

Moist and crunchy, this bread is also delicious toasted. It stays fresh for at least 4 days, and the flavor and texture actually improve on standing for at least 12 hours. It is perfect plain or spread lightly with whipped cream cheese.

TIME SCHEDULE

Oven Temperature: 350°F
Baking Time: 55 to 65 minutes

Makes: an 8 1/2-by-4 1/2-by-3 1/2-inch-high loaf/37.5 ounces/1062 grams

INGREDIENTS	MEASURE	WEIGHT	
room temperature	volume	ounces	grams
walnuts	1 cup	4 ounces	114 grams
bleached all-purpose flour (use only Gold Medal or Pillsbury)	2 cups minus 1 tablespoon	9.5 ounces	273 grams
baking soda	1 teaspoon	--	5 grams
salt	1 teaspoon	--	6.6 grams
unsalted butter, softened	8 tablespoons	4 ounces	113 grams
sugar, preferably turbinado	1 cup	7 ounces	200 grams
2 large eggs, lightly beaten	6 tablespoons (3 fluid ounces)	3.5 ounces	100 grams

INGREDIENTS	MEASURE	WEIGHT	
room temperature	volume	ounces	grams
1 very ripe large banana	**3/4 cup**	**about 5.5 ounces**	**152 to 162 grams**
sour cream	**1 1/2 tablespoons**	**0.7 ounce**	**23 grams**
pure vanilla extract	**1 teaspoon**	--	--
cranberries, fresh or frozen, cut in half	**2 cups**	**7 ounces**	**200 grams**

EQUIPMENT

a heavy-duty stand mixer with paddle attachment OR
a hand-held mixer;

a 9-by-5-inch loaf pan, greased with cooking spray or oil

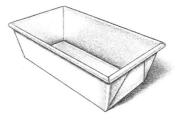

1 > **Preheat the oven.** Preheat the oven to 325°F 20 minutes before baking. Have an oven shelf at the middle level.

2 > **Toast the nuts.** Toast the walnuts on a baking sheet until just beginning to color, about 7 minutes. Empty them onto a paper towel and rub them lightly to remove any loose skin. Allow the nuts to cool. Then break or coarsely chop them.

3 > **Mix the batter.** In a medium bowl, whisk together the flour, baking soda, and salt. In a mixer bowl or other large bowl, cream the butter and sugar on medium speed if using a stand mixer (#4 KitchenAid, with the paddle attachment), or high speed if using a hand-held beater until light, about 3 minutes.

Add the eggs, banana, sour cream, and vanilla all at once and continue beating for about 1 minute or until thoroughly blended. Add the flour mixture and beat on low speed (#2 KitchenAid) for 20 seconds or until moistened. Add the cranberries and walnuts and continue beating for another 20 seconds or until well incorporated. (The batter will weigh about 2 pounds, 9 ounces/1 kg, 158 grams.)

4 > **Fill the pan and bake the bread.** Scrape the batter into the prepared pan. (It will be about 3/4 inch from the top.) Bake for 55 to 65 minutes or until the bread is golden and springs back when pressed lightly in the middle. Tent loosely with foil after the first 30 minutes to prevent overbrowning. The bread will develop an attractive split after the first 20 minutes or so of baking.

5 > Cool the bread. Set the pan on a wire rack to cool for 10 minutes. Loosen the sides of the bread, unmold it, and cool completely, top side up.

POINTERS FOR SUCCESS

> Toasting the walnuts only lightly brings out their flavor without making them bitter and keeps them from turning blue in the batter. As much of the walnut skin as possible is discarded, also to avoid any bitterness.

UNDERSTANDING

I use the traditional creaming method for this recipe because the method of mixing all the dry ingredients together and then adding fat and liquid to them would make this quick bread too tender.

THE DOUGH PERCENTAGE

Flour:	100%
Water:	123.5% (includes the water in the butter, egg whites, sour cream, cranberries, and banana)
Salt:	2.1%
Fat:	34.7% (includes the fat in the egg yolks and sour cream)

Carrot Bread

Carrot cake is an American favorite, appearing in many guises, from muffins to layers in a wedding cake. My quick bread version has an exceptionally high proportion of carrots and a low proportion of sugar and oil. The only spice used is cinnamon, so the flavor of the carrots really stands out.

You can spread the slices with softened sweet butter or whipped cream cheese, but the bread is also wonderful on its own.

The zucchini variation below has a similar moist texture but an entirely different flavor because the zucchini stays in the background, allowing the cinnamon and toasted walnuts to be the stars.

As with all vegetable-and-oil-based breads, the moisture will be distributed most evenly if the bread is allowed to stand for a day. The advantage is that such breads will keep perfectly at room temperature for as long as 3 days.

TIME SCHEDULE

Oven Temperature: 350°F
Baking: 1 hour
Standing Time: overnight

Makes: an 8 1/2-by-4 1/2-by-3 1/4-inch-high loaf/35 ounces/994 grams

INGREDIENTS	MEASURE	WEIGHT	
room temperature	volume	ounces	grams
unbleached all-purpose flour (use only Gold Medal, King Arthur, or Pillsbury)	1 1/2 cups plus 1 1/2 tablespoons	8 ounces	227 grams
baking powder	1/2 tablespoon	--	7.3 grams
baking soda	1/2 teaspoon	--	2.5 grams
salt	1/2 teaspoon	--	3.3 grams
cinnamon	2 teaspoons	--	4.5 grams
3 large eggs	scant 5 fluid ounces	5.25 ounces	150 grams (weighed without shells)
safflower oil	1/2 liquid cup	3.75 ounces	107 grams
sugar, preferably turbinado	1 cup	7 ounces	200 grams
finely grated carrots	3 1/2 cups	12 ounces	340 grams
raisins	1 cup	5 ounces	144 grams

EQUIPMENT

a heavy-duty stand mixer with paddle attachment OR
a hand-held mixer;

a 9-by-5-inch loaf pan, sprayed with nonstick vegetable oil or
greased

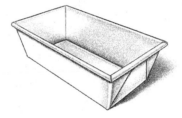

1 > **Preheat the oven.** Preheat the oven to 350°F 20 minutes before baking. Have an oven shelf on the rung below the middle level.

2 > **Mix the batter.** In a medium bowl, whisk together the flour, baking powder, baking soda, salt, and cinnamon.

In a large bowl or a mixer bowl, using a wooden spoon or a hand-held or stand mixer on low speed (#2 if using a KitchenAid, with the paddle attachment), mix together the eggs, oil, and sugar for 1 minute or until blended. Add the flour mixture and continue stirring or beating on low speed just until incorporated, about 20 seconds. Add the carrots and continue stirring or beating for another 12 seconds. Stir in the raisins with a large rubber spatula or the wooden spoon.

3 > **Fill the pan and bake the bread.** Scrape the batter into the bread pan. (It will be about 1/2 inch from the top.) Bake for about 1 hour or until the top is golden and a cake tester inserted in the center comes out clean.

4 > Cool the bread. Set the pan on a wire rack to cool for 10 minutes. Then run a small spatula between the sides of the pan and the bread and unmold it onto an oiled wire rack. Turn it right (top) side up and allow it to cool completely.

5 > Let the bread stand. Wrap the loaf well in plastic wrap and allow it to sit overnight to distribute the moisture. (If you just can't wait to taste it, don't worry: the bread won't fall apart as long as it is allowed to cool completely before cutting.)

VARIATION

Zucchini Bread (a 35 3/4-ounce/1015-gram loaf)   The zucchini does not contribute significant flavor to this quick bread the way the carrots do. Most of this bread's flavor comes from the cinnamon, turbinado sugar, and toasted walnuts. What the zucchini does add are moistness and structure. Because this bread is so spicy and flavorful, it would be fine to replace the whole eggs with 4 1/2 large egg whites (4.5 fluid ounces/9 tablespoons), making it entirely cholesterol-free.

Substitute 3 cups (12 ounces/340 grams) grated zucchini for the carrots and 1 cup (4 ounces/113 grams) coarsely broken or chopped walnuts, lightly toasted, for the raisins. Add 2 tablespoons more flour to compensate for the extra moisture of the zucchini.

UNDERSTANDING

Carrots are 88.2 percent water and zucchini is 94 percent, which is why the variation requires a little extra flour.

The baking soda serves to give an attractive deep brown color to both loaves.

There is no need to soak the raisins, as they absorb moisture from the carrots and plump up on their own. If you prefer to omit the raisins, add 1/3 cup more flour. (In addition to the extra flour, you can also add up to 1 cup [4 ounces/113 grams] coarsely broken or chopped walnuts, lightly toasted, to the carrot bread.)

THE DOUGH PERCENTAGE

Flour:	**100%** (includes the fiber in the carrots)
Water:	**145%** (includes the water in the carrots and egg whites)
Salt:	**1.3%**
Oil:	**47.4%** (includes the fat in the egg yolks)

Chocolate Chocolate Chip Bread

This quick bread is dark, dense, chocolaty, and tender. I developed this recipe for my book *The Cake Bible* and it is as popular in 2003 as it was at its debut in 1988! The only change I've made is the addition of chocolate mini chips or chopped chocolate for extra intensity.

The optional Kahlúa glaze results in excellent flavor synergy, provides extra moistness, and elevates this dessert "bread" to holiday or special-occasion fare.

TIME SCHEDULE

Oven Temperature: 350°F
Baking Time: 50 to 60 minutes

Makes: an 8-by-4-by-3-inch-high loaf

INGREDIENTS	MEASURE	WEIGHT	
	volume	ounces	grams
unsweetened cocoa (Dutch-processed)	3 tablespoons plus 1/2 tablespoon	0.75 ounce	21 grams
boiling water	3 tablespoons	1.5 ounces	44 grams
pure vanilla extract	1/2 tablespoon	--	6 grams
3 large eggs	scant 5 fluid ounces	5.25 ounces	150 grams (weighed without shells)
sifted cake flour	1 1/4 cups	4.5 ounces	125 grams
sugar, preferably turbinado	3/4 cup plus 2 tablespoons	6 ounces	175 grams
baking powder	3/4 teaspoon	--	3.6 grams
salt	1/4 teaspoon	--	1.7 grams
unsalted butter, softened	13 tablespoons	6.5 ounces	184 grams
Optional: chocolate mini chips or bittersweet chocolate (chopped medium-fine)	3 tablespoons	1 ounce	28 grams

a heavy-duty stand mixer with paddle attachment OR
a hand-held mixer;

an 8-by-4-inch (4-cup) loaf pan, OR, if using the chocolate chips, an
8 1/2-by-4 1/2-inch (5-cup) loaf pan, bottom greased and lined
with parchment, then sprayed with Baker's Joy OR greased and
floured (if using a nonstick pan and Baker's Joy, there is no need to
line the pan)

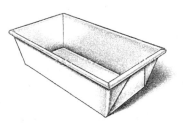

1 > Preheat the oven. Preheat the oven to 350°F 30 minutes before baking. Have an
oven shelf at the middle level.

2 > Make the soft cocoa paste. In a medium bowl, whisk together the cocoa and
boiling water until smooth. Allow it to cool to room temperature, then gently whisk
in the vanilla and eggs. It will be fluid.

3 > Mix the batter. In a mixer bowl or other large bowl, combine the cake flour,
sugar, baking powder, and salt. Mix on low speed (#2 if using a KitchenAid, with
the paddle attachment) for 30 seconds to blend. Add half the chocolate paste and the
butter and mix until the dry ingredients are moistened. Increase the speed to medium
if using a stand mixer (#4 KitchenAid), or high if using a hand-held mixer, and beat
for 1 minute to aerate and develop the structure. Scrape down the sides of the bowl.
Gradually add the remaining chocolate paste in two batches, beating for 20 seconds
after each addition to incorporate the ingredients and strengthen the structure.
Scrape down the bowl. With a rubber spatula, fold in the optional chocolate mini
chips or bittersweet chocolate.

4 > Fill the pan. Scrape the batter into the prepared pan and smooth the surface
with a spatula. (The batter will be almost 1/2 inch from the top of the 4-cup pan.)

5 > Bake the bread. Bake for 50 to 60 minutes or until a wooden toothpick inserted
in the center comes out clean. An instant-read thermometer inserted into the center
will read about 200°F. Tent loosely with buttered foil after 25 minutes to prevent
overbrowning. (The bread shouldn't start to shrink from the sides of the pan until
after removal from the oven.)

6 > Cool the bread. Set the bread on a wire rack to cool for 10 minutes. Loosen the sides of the bread with a small metal spatula and invert it onto an oiled wire rack. Reinvert so that it is top side up and cool completely.

VARIATION

For an extra-moist cake and a subtle background coffee accent, brush the bread with coffee syrup.

To make the syrup: In a small pan, stir together 1/4 cup water and 2 tablespoons sugar. Bring to a full rolling boil, stirring to dissolve the sugar. Cover and remove from the heat. When the syrup is cool, add 1 tablespoon Kahlúa. As soon as the bread is removed from the oven, brush half the syrup onto the top. Let the bread cool for 10 minutes, then invert it onto a lightly oiled rack and brush the bottom and sides with the remaining syrup. Reinvert it to finish cooling top side up.

POINTERS FOR SUCCESS

> It is not necessary to sift the flour if you are weighing it. However, if you measure it, be sure to sift it into the cup and then level it off, without shaking or tapping the cup at all.

> To get an attractive split down the middle of the crust, wait until the natural split is about to develop, about 20 minutes into the baking, and, with a lightly oiled sharp knife, make a shallow slash 6 inches long down the middle of the bread. This must be done quickly so that the oven door does not remain open very long, or the bread could fall. When the top crust splits, it will open along this slash.

> Be sure to use a wooden toothpick to test when the bread is done, as it will spring back if lightly pressed when still underdone.

> There is no need to poke holes in the bread for the Kahlúa syrup to be absorbed; it enters quite readily, and the holes would mar the surface.

THE DOUGH PERCENTAGE

Flour:	**100%** (includes the starch in the cocoa)
Water:	**151.4%** (includes the water in the butter and egg whites)
Salt:	**1.2%**
Fat:	**38.5%** (includes the fat in the egg yolks and cocoa)

Southwestern Corn Spoon Bread

My friend and longtime collaborator David Shamah is a font of ingenious ideas. This recipe was inspired by one of his suggestions, and it is the best spoon bread I've ever had. It forms a crisp and golden cheesy crust on top, and inside it is light yet moist and full flavored. It's terrific as an accompaniment to barbecued chicken, pork chops, sausages, or ham—I actually love this spoon bread so much I think of these other dishes more as an accompaniment to it!

TIME SCHEDULE

Oven Temperature: 375°F
Baking Time: 30 to 35 minutes

Serves: 4

Filling

INGREDIENTS	MEASURE	WEIGHT	
room temperature	volume	ounces	grams
unsalted butter	**4 tablespoons**	**2 ounces**	**57 grams**
1 small onion, chopped	2/3 cup	3 ounces	86 grams
chipotle chile in adobo (see step 2), or 1/2 jalapeño pepper, seeded and finely chopped	about 1 tablespoon	--	12.5 grams 11 grams
1 large garlic clove, minced	2 teaspoons	0.25 ounce	7 grams
1/2 roasted red bell pepper, peeled, seeded, and chopped	1/2 cup	3 ounces	85 grams
2 small ears corn-husked and cooked, kernels	1 cup (or 11 ounce can niblets, drained)	5 ounces	142 grams
cilantro, chopped	1/4 cup	--	20 grams

EQUIPMENT

a 4- to 6-cup ceramic casserole or soufflé dish, buttered or greased with cooking spray or oil

1 > **Preheat the oven.** Preheat the oven to 375°F 20 minutes before baking.

2 > **Sauté the filling.** Place a medium (10-inch) skillet over medium-low heat and add the butter. When it is melted, add the onion and jalapeño (if not using the chipotle). Sauté, stirring occasionally, until the onion is softened and golden. Add the garlic and sauté, stirring constantly, for 30 seconds. Remove the pan from the heat and stir in the red pepper, corn, and cilantro. If using the chipotle, remove most of the seeds and chop it fine. Combine it with enough of the adobo sauce to make 1 tablespoon and stir into the filling. Cool completely.

Batter

INGREDIENTS	MEASURE	WEIGHT	
room temperature	volume	ounces	grams
bleached all-purpose flour (such as Gold Medal or Pillsbury)	1/2 cup plus 1/2 tablespoon	2.5 ounces	75 grams
yellow cornmeal, preferably stone-ground (such as Kenyon's)	1/2 cup	2.25 ounces	64 grams
sugar	3 tablespoons	1.3 ounces	38 grams
baking powder	1 1/4 teaspoons	--	6 grams
salt	3/4 plus 1/8 teaspoon	--	5.8 grams
black pepper	1/8 teaspoon	--	--
heavy cream	1/3 liquid cup	2.75 ounces	80 grams
milk	1/3 liquid cup	2.75 ounces	80 grams
1 large egg, divided:			
yolk	1 tablespoon plus 1/2 teaspoon	0.65 ounce	18.6 grams
white	2 tablespoons	1 ounce	30 grams
cream of tartar	1/8 teaspoon		
sharp cheddar cheese, shredded	1 heaping cup, divided	2.5 ounces	70 grams
Optional: red pepper flakes, if not using the chipotle	1/8 teaspoon	--	--

3 > **Mix the batter.** In a medium bowl, stir together the flour, cornmeal, sugar, baking powder, salt, and black pepper.

In a glass measuring cup or small bowl, lightly whisk together the cream, milk, and egg yolk.

In a medium bowl, whisk the egg white until foamy. Add the cream of tartar and whisk until stiff peaks form when the beater is lifted slowly.

Stir the egg/milk mixture and corn mixture into the flour mixture just until it is evenly moistened. Fold in all but 1/2 cup (1 ounce/28 grams) of the cheese, then fold in the egg white just until incorporated.

4 > Bake the spoon bread. Pour the batter into the prepared casserole. Sprinkle with the remaining cheese and the optional red pepper flakes. Bake for 30 to 35 minutes or until the top is puffed and golden brown and springs back when lightly pressed in the center with your finger (an instant-read thermometer inserted in the center will read about 160°F). Serve at once.

STORE   Any leftovers can be refrigerated for up to 5 days.

POINTERS FOR SUCCESS

>   To roast a red pepper, line a gas burner with foil to catch any dripping juices. Hold the pepper over the heat with tongs, turning it occasionally so that the skin blisters and chars all over. (Or, if you have electric range, roast it under the boiler.) Place it in a plastic bag for a few minutes to steam, to help separate the skin from the pepper. Then remove and discard as much of the skin as possible.

>   To cook the fresh corn, boil the ears in unsalted water for 5 to 7 minutes or until just tender when pierced with a cake tester or skewer. Canned niblets are the best alternative to fresh corn. An 11-ounce can of niblets, drained, equals 9.6 ounces/272 grams; half is 4.8 ounces/113 grams. If niblets are unavailable, use frozen corn, thawed.

>   The spoon bread reheats well, particularly in a microwave.

>   The recipe can be doubled easily.

THE DOUGH PERCENTAGE

Flour:	100%
Water:	114.9% (includes the water in the vegetables and egg white)
Salt:	4.2%
Fat:	54.7% (includes the fat in the cream, milk, egg yolk, and cheese)

Quintessential Corn Muffins

The secret to this muffin's pure corny flavor, golden yellow color, craggy crown, and tender open crumb is using the best, freshest stone-ground cornmeal (see page 556) and the addition of sour cream. Blueberries provide an appealing sweetness, but I love the taste of corn by itself so much I usually make them without blueberries.

TIME SCHEDULE

Oven Temperature: 400°F
Baking Time: 15 to 18 minutes

Makes: 6 Muffins

INGREDIENTS	MEASURE	WEIGHT	
	volume	ounces	grams
cornmeal, preferably stone-ground (such as Kenyon's)	1/2 cup	2.25 ounces	64 grams
bleached all-purpose flour (use only Gold Medal or Pillsbury)	1/2 cup plus 1/2 tablespoon	2.6 ounces	75 grams
sugar	2 tablespoons plus 2 teaspoons	about 1 ounce	33 grams
baking powder	1 teaspoon	--	4.6 grams
baking soda	1/4 teaspoon	--	1.2 grams
salt	1/2 teaspoon	--	3.3 grams
1 large egg	2 tablespoons plus 1/2 teaspoon	1.75 ounces	50 grams (weighed out of the shell)
sour cream	2/3 cup	5.7 ounces	161 grams
unsalted butter, melted and cooled	2 tablespoons	1 ounce	28 grams
Optional: small blueberries, fresh or frozen	2/3 cup	2.75 ounces	80 grams
Optional: cornmeal for dusting	scant 1/2 teaspoon	--	--

six 6-ounce soufflé ramekins or custard cups, OR
a 6-cup muffin pan, all lined with foil or paper liners,
preferably lightly sprayed with Baker's Joy or cooking spray

1 > Preheat the oven. Preheat the oven to 400°F 20 minutes before baking. Have an oven shelf at the middle level.

2 > Mix the batter. In a medium bowl, whisk together the cornmeal, flour, sugar, baking powder, baking soda, and salt.

In a glass measuring cup or small bowl, lightly whisk together the egg and sour cream.

Stir the egg mixture into the flour mixture just until it is moistened. There should still be some lumps. Fold in the melted butter just until incorporated. Fold in the optional blueberries. You should still see little lumps.

3 > Fill the muffin containers. Spoon the batter into the ramekins, custard cups, or muffin cups, filling them almost to the top (2.25 ounces/67 grams in each; 2.75 ounces/80 grams if using the blueberries). Use a small metal spatula or the back of a teaspoon to smooth the tops if necessary. If using a muffin pan, fill any empty cups half-full with water. For a crunchy top, place the 1/2 teaspoon cornmeal in a small strainer, hold it over the muffins, and stir the cornmeal with a spoon, so that it sprinkles evenly over the tops.

4 > Bake the muffins. Bake for 15 to 18 minutes or until the tops are golden brown and a wooden toothpick inserted into the middle comes out clean.

5 > Cool the muffins. Unmold the muffins and cool them top side up on a wire rack. Serve room temperature.

NOTE The muffins can be reheated in a 400°F oven for about 4 minutes.

VARIATION

Blue Cornmeal Muffins Blue cornmeal has a similar flavor to yellow but offers an intriguing blue/gray color, particularly attractive with the addition of the blueberries. It is usually ground finer than yellow and absorbs slightly more liquid; increase the sour cream to 3/4 cup (6.5 ounces/182 grams). Place a scant 2.5 ounces/70 grams batter (3 ounces/85 grams if using the blueberries) in each muffin cup.

POINTERS FOR SUCCESS

> A #30 ice cream scoop (2-tablespoon capacity) works well for transferring the batter to the muffin containers.

> The muffins can be frozen, well wrapped, for up to 3 months. Reheat in a pre-heated 400°F oven for 15 to 20 minutes or until a metal cake tester inserted briefly into the center feels warm.

UNDERSTANDING

When mixing the batter, it is important to work quickly, as the water will begin to activate the baking soda. Lumps in the batter are desirable (the flour will still get hydrated completely during baking) because if you mix the batter until it is smooth, the tops of the muffins will be rounded instead of craggy and the muffins will not be as tender since more gluten will be formed. Mixing by hand helps to avoid overmixing.

Filling any empty muffin cups with water prevents the heat from being drawn to them and adds moisture.

THE DOUGH PERCENTAGE

Flour:	100%
Water:	104.7% (includes the water in the sour cream, butter, and egg white)
Salt:	2.4%
Fat:	42.4% (includes the fat in the sour cream and egg yolk)

Corn Fingers

These corn fingers, baked in a mold so they resemble little individual ears of corn, are tender, fine-grained, and slightly sweet, with little nubbins of corn in each bite and the glad surprise of occasional hot pepper flakes. They seem to dissolve in the mouth yet have a full corn flavor.

TIME SCHEDULE

Oven temperature: 425°F
Baking Time: 15 minutes

Makes: 12 to 13 corn fingers

INGREDIENTS	MEASURE	WEIGHT	
room temperature	volume	ounces	grams
bleached all-purpose flour (use only Gold Medal or Pillsbury)	1/2 cup plus 1/2 tablespoon	2.5 ounces	75 grams
yellow cornmeal, preferably stone ground (such as Kenyon's)	1/2 cup	2.25 ounces	64 grams
sugar	2 tablespoons plus 2 teaspoons	1 ounce	33 grams
baking powder	1 1/4 teaspoons	--	6 grams
salt	1/2 teaspoon	--	3.3 grams
hot pepper flakes	1/2 to 1 teaspoon (to taste)	--	--
2 small ears corn, husked and cooked, kernels cut off the cobs	1 cup	5 ounces	142 grams
unsalted butter, melted	4 tablespoons	2 ounces	57 grams
heavy cream	1/3 liquid cup	2.7 ounces	77 grams
whole milk	1/3 liquid cup	2.8 ounces	80 grams
1 large egg, divided:			
yolk	1 tablespoon plus 1/2 teaspoon	0.65 ounce	18.6 grams
white	2 tablespoons	1 ounce	30 grams

2 cast-iron corn-finger molds, lightly greased with cooking spray or oil (or make in 2 batches if you only have one mold)

1 > Preheat the oven. Preheat the oven to 425°F 20 minutes before baking. Have an oven shelf at the middle level. Just before mixing the batter, preheat the molds.

2 > Mix the batter. In a medium bowl, stir together the flour, cornmeal, sugar, baking powder, salt, and hot pepper flakes. Add the corn and stir until coated.

In a glass measuring cup or small bowl, lightly whisk together the melted butter, cream, milk, and egg yolk.

In a medium bowl, beat the egg white until soft peaks form when the beater is lifted slowly.

Stir the butter, milk and egg mixture into the flour mixture just until moistened. There should still be lumps. Fold in the egg white just until incorporated. You should still see little lumps.

3 > Fill the molds. Spoon or pipe (use a pastry bag with a plain 1/2-inch-wide tip) the batter into the molds, filling them almost to the top. Use a small metal spatula or the back of a teaspoon to smooth the batter if necessary. Fill any empty depressions half-full with water.

4 > Bake the corn fingers. Bake for 15 minutes or until the tops are golden brown.

5 > Unmold the corn fingers and cool. To unmold, loosen the sides of each corn finger with a small metal spatula, place a wire rack over the mold, and invert them onto the rack. Repeat with the second mold. These corn fingers are wonderfully tender, so they require care while still warm to avoid breaking them. Serve warm or at room temperature.

POINTERS FOR SUCCESS

> To cook the corn, boil the ears in unsalted water for 5 to 7 minutes or until just tender when pierced with a cake tester or skewer.

> Piping the batter is neater and faster than using a spoon. A coated fabric pastry bag works better for this soft batter because it is stiffer than a plastic bag, making it

easier to handle the batter. (The baked corn fingers will look the same no matter which method you choose.)

> Corn fingers freeze well for several weeks. Wrap each one airtight in plastic wrap and place in heavy-duty freezer bags. Reheat in a preheated 400°F oven for about 7 minutes.

UNDERSTANDING

Fresh corn needs to be cooked in order to remove some of its liquid, or the batter will be too liquid.

Blue cornmeal can be substituted for the yellow cornmeal, but a few teaspoons of liquid should be added to compensate for the higher absorption capability of blue cornmeal.

Filling any empty depressions with water prevents the heat from being drawn to them and adds moisture.

THE DOUGH PERCENTAGE

Flour:	100%
Water:	107.9% (includes the water in the cream, milk, butter, and egg white)
Salt:	2.4%
Fat:	59.4% (includes the fat in the cream, milk, and egg yolk)

Blueberry Muffins

Blueberry muffins are my favorite, so over the years I've been tweaking my recipe toward perfection. This latest version has a little less sugar than the last and though it's still delicious made with buttermilk, I find that sour cream gives it the most mellow and rich flavor. I also love the soft crumb contrasting with the crisp sugary top.

In August, when the tiny blueberries from Maine are available, I make a double batch of these muffins and freeze them for weekend breakfast treats. One of my best finds this year is a mail-order source for frozen Maine blueberries (see Sources, page 572).

TIME SCHEDULE

Oven Temperature: 375°F
Baking Time: 25 to 35 minutes

Makes: 6 muffins

INGREDIENTS	MEASURE	WEIGHT	
room temperature	volume	ounces	grams
unsalted butter	**4 tablespoons**	**2 ounces**	**56 grams**
sugar	**1/2 cup**	**3.5 ounces**	**100 grams**
grated lemon zest	**2 teaspoons**	--	**4 grams**
1 large egg	--	**1.75 ounces**	**50 grams**
pure vanilla extract	**1/2 teaspoon**	--	--
bleached **all-purpose flour (use only Gold Medal or Pillsbury)**	**about 1 cup**	**4.75 ounces**	**135 grams**
baking soda	**3/8 teaspoon**	--	**1.9 grams**
salt	**1/4 plus 1/16 teaspoon**	--	**2 grams**
sour cream	**1/3 cup**	**about 2.75 ounces**	**80 grams**
small blueberries, rinsed and dried	**3/4 cup (rounded)**	**3.5 ounces**	**100 grams**

Topping

sugar	3/4 teaspoon	--	3 grams
nutmeg, preferably freshly grated	dusting	--	--

EQUIPMENT

six 6-ounce soufflé ramekins or custard cups OR
a 6-cup muffin pan, all lined with foil or paper liners,
preferably lightly sprayed with Baker's Joy or cooking spray

1 > Preheat the oven. Preheat the oven to 375°F 20 minutes before baking. Have an oven shelf at the middle level.

2 > Mix the batter. In a large bowl, with a wooden spoon, cream the butter, sugar and lemon zest until light and fluffy. Beat in the egg and vanilla.

    In a small bowl, whisk together the flour, baking soda, and salt. Spoon half of the flour mixture and half the sour cream onto the butter/sugar mixture and, using a rubber spatula, fold in until most of the flour disappears. Repeat with the remaining flour and sour cream, folding in just until the flour disappears. Fold in the blueberries.

3 > Fill the muffin containers. Spoon the batter into the ramekins, custard cups, or muffin cups, filling them almost to the top. Fill any empty muffin cups half-full with water. Dust the tops with the sugar and nutmeg.

4 > Bake the muffins. Bake for 25 to 35 minutes or until the muffins spring back when pressed lightly in the center with a fingertip and a wooden toothpick inserted in the center comes out clean.

5 > Cool the muffins. Unmold the muffins and turn right side up on a wire rack to cool. Serve warm or at room temperature.

NOTE The muffins can be reheated in a 400°F oven for about 4 minutes.

POINTERS FOR SUCCESS

> I like the rich flavor of sour cream and the slightly more open texture it gives the muffins, but if you prefer to use buttermilk, it can easily be substituted. For the best flavor when using buttermilk, substitute 1 teaspoon baking powder for the baking soda.

> A #30 ice cream scoop (2-tablespoon capacity) works well for transferring the batter to the muffin containers.

> The muffins can be frozen, well wrapped, for up to 3 months. Reheat in a preheated 400°F oven for 15 to 20 minutes or until a metal cake tester inserted briefly into the center feels warm.

UNDERSTANDING

Filling any empty muffin cups with water prevents the heat from being drawn to them and adds moisture.

THE DOUGH PERCENTAGE

Flour:	100%
Water:	95% (includes the water in the sour cream, butter, and egg white)
Salt:	1.5%
Fat:	49.1% (includes the fat in the sour cream and egg yolk)

Big Banana Muffins

This recipe is adapted from my banana cake, one of the most popular recipes in my book *The Cake Bible*. The texture and flavor of the toasted walnuts, or poppy seeds or chocolate, are a great new addition. I bake them in a Texas muffin pan, which has cups that have an 8-ounce capacity, compared to the usual 6 ounces. Texas, the largest state in America, is big on big, which is how this muffin pan got its name! It seemed particularly appropriate for these muffins because they are big on flavor as well as size. This batter can also be baked in a loaf pan, and can feature chocolate chips. See the variations at the end of the recipe.

TIME SCHEDULE

Oven Temperature: 350°F
Baking Time: 25 to 30 minutes

Makes: 5 muffins

INGREDIENTS	MEASURE	WEIGHT	
room temperature	volume	ounces	grams
1 very ripe banana, peeled and lightly mashed	**1/2 cup**	**4 ounces**	**113.5 grams**
sour cream	**1/4 cup**	**about 2 ounces**	**60 grams**
1 large egg	**3 tablespoons**	**1.75 ounces**	**50 grams** (weighed without shell)
grated lemon zest	**1 teaspoon**	**--**	**2 grams**
pure vanilla extract	**3/4 teaspoon**	**--**	**--**
bleached **cake flour or** _bleached_ all purpose flour	**1 cup scant** 3/4 cup	**3.5 ounces**	**100 grams**
sugar, preferably turbinado	**6 tablespoons**	**2.6 ounces**	**75 grams**
baking powder	**1/2 teaspoon**	**--**	**2.4 grams**
baking soda	**1/2 teaspoon**	**--**	**2.5 grams**
salt	**1/4 teaspoon**	**--**	**1.7 grams**
unsalted butter, softened	**5 tablespoons**	**2.5 ounces**	**71 grams**
walnuts, toasted and chopped medium-fine	**1/2 cup**	**1.75 ounces**	**50 grams**

EQUIPMENT

a heavy-duty stand mixer with paddle attachment OR a hand-held mixer;

a Texas muffin pan lined with foil or paper liners, preferably lightly sprayed with Baker's Joy or cooking spray

1 > **Preheat the oven.** Preheat the oven to 350°F 20 minutes before baking. Have an oven shelf at the middle level.

2 > **Mix the batter.** In a food processor fitted with the metal blade, process the banana and sour cream until smooth. Add the egg, lemon zest, and vanilla and process until blended.

In a mixer bowl or other large bowl, combine the flour, sugar, baking powder, baking soda, and salt and beat on low speed (#2 if using a KitchenAid, with the paddle attachment) for about 1 minute, until well mixed. Add the butter and half the banana mixture and beat until the dry ingredients are moistened. Raise the speed to medium (#4 KitchenAid) or high if using a hand-held electric mixer and beat for 1 1/2 minutes. Scrape down the sides of the bowl. Add the remaining banana mixture in two parts, beating for about 20 seconds after each addition or until well mixed. On low speed, beat in the walnuts.

3 > Fill the muffin containers. Spoon or pipe the batter into the muffin containers, filling them three-quarters full. Pour a little water into the unfilled muffin cup to prevent uneven baking.

4 > Bake the muffins. Bake for 25 to 30 minutes or until the muffins spring back when pressed lightly in the center.

5 > Cool the muffins. Remove the muffins from the oven and unmold them at once onto a wire rack. Turn top side up and cool until just warm or room temperature.

STORE   Stored airtight at room temperature, these have just as lovely a texture and flavor the next day. The muffins can be reheated for about 4 minutes in a 400°F oven.

VARIATION

Banana Loaf   This recipe can also be baked in an 8-by-4-inch bread pan for 40 to 50 minutes or until a wooden skewer inserted in the center comes out clean.

POINTERS FOR SUCCESS

>   Use *bleached* all-purpose flour for a firmer more bread-like texture. Use cake flour for a softer, lighter crumb.

>   For finely grated zest, use a citrus zester (a small implement with tiny scraping holes), a vegetable peeler, or fine grater to remove the yellow portion only of the peel. The white pith beneath is bitter. If using a zester or peeler, finish by chopping the zest with a sharp knife.

>   For the best flavor and sweetness, use a banana that is very ripe, with black spots all over the skin.

>   It is not necessary to sift the flour if you are weighing it. However, if you measure it, be sure to sift it into the cup and then level it off, without shaking or tapping the cup at all.

>　　A #30 ice cream scoop (2-tablespoon capacity) works well for transferring the batter to the muffin containers. But I find it easiest to use a heavy-duty gallon zip-seal bag as a disposable piping bag. Scrape the batter into the bag, zip it closed, and cut off the tip.

>　　The muffins can be frozen for up to 3 months. Frozen muffins can be reheated in a preheated 400°F oven for 15 to 20 minutes or until a metal cake tester inserted briefly into the center feels warm.

>　　These are also delicious made with 2 tablespoons poppy seeds instead of the walnuts.

>　　For a chocolate chip version, fold 1/4 cup / 1.5 ounces / 42 grams of mini chocolate chips (or chocolate chopped medium fine) into the finished batter.

>　　For a chocolate swirl version, stir 1 ounce / 28 grams melted cooled bittersweet chocolate into 1/2 cup of the batter. Add it to the top of the batter in the loaf pan or muffin cups and swirl it in.

NOTE　For calculation purposes if making these muffins in larger quantities, it is useful to know that the banana peel represents about 25 percent of the weight of the banana.

THE DOUGH PERCENTAGE

Flour:	100% (includes the starch in the banana)
Water:	132% (includes the water in the sour cream, butter, egg white, and banana)
Salt:	1.4%
Fat:	59.2% (includes the fat in the sour cream and egg yolk)

Biscuits

Biscuits are a truly American tradition, emanating from the South, where no meal is considered complete with them. In this chapter I have included the three basic types of biscuits:

> baking powder–butter biscuits

> baking powder–shortening biscuits

> baking powder with yeast biscuits

I have also incorporated two less familiar but very appealing additions to the basic biscuit: hard-cooked egg yolks, because they contribute a velvety texture, and sweet potato, for its beautiful color and moisture-holding ability.

POINTERS FOR SUCCESS FOR MAKING BISCUITS

> To hard-cook eggs to produce moist but firm yolks that are all yellow (no green on the outside): Place the room temperature eggs in a small nonreactive saucepan with a tight-fitting cover and add enough cold water to cover them. Bring the water to a boil, cover tightly, and remove the pan from the heat. Allow it to sit for 10 minutes. Drain and set the eggs in a bowl of ice water to cool completely before peeling.

> If you measure the flour instead of weighing it, you may need to adjust the texture of the dough by adding either a little more flour or a little more liquid.

> Be sure to knead the dough to develop the gluten-forming protein, or it will not have enough structure to rise during baking.

> When shaping biscuits, flour your hands and the counter. Most of this flour does not get absorbed by the dough. Because a thin dusting of it will stay on the sur-

face of the dough, do not use self-rising flour for this purpose. The baking powder in it would never be activated and would impart a bitter taste to the crust of the biscuits.

> Unbaked biscuits can be frozen for up to 3 months. Bake without defrosting, adding 10 to 15 minutes to the baking time.

> To reheat leftover or frozen baked biscuits, spritz or sprinkle them all over with water and heat in a preheated 300°F oven for 15 minutes. A cake tester briefly inserted into the center will feel warm; the outside will be crispy and the inside will be soft.

Butter Biscuits

These are the biscuits I want when I make strawberry shortcake. The butter and hard-boiled egg yolk give them the most extraordinary golden color, velvety texture, and pleasing flavor.

TIME SCHEDULE

Oven Temperature: 375°F
Baking Time: 15 to 20 minutes

Makes: nine 2 1/2-by-1 1/2-inch-high biscuits

INGREDIENTS	MEASURE	WEIGHT	
	volume	ounces	grams
unsalted butter, cold	**6 tablespoons**	**3 ounces**	**85 grams**
White Lily self-rising flour or	**2 cups**	**10 ounces**	**290 grams**
bleached all-purpose flour	1 1/4 cups	6.5 ounces	182 grams
plus cake flour	2/3 cup	2.3 ounces	86 grams
plus baking powder	1 tablespoon	0.5 ounce	14.7 grams
plus salt	1 teaspoon	--	6.6 grams
sugar	**3 tablespoons**	**1.3 ounces**	**37.5 grams**
2 large eggs, hard-cooked (see page 125), yolks only	--	**1.3 ounces**	**37 grams**
heavy cream or		**6 ounces**	**174 grams**
buttermilk	**3/4 liquid cup**	6.3 ounces	182 grams
(or a combination of the two)		(6.3 ounces)	(178 grams)
Optional topping:			
melted butter, cooled	1 tablespoon	0.5 ounce	14 grams
sugar for sprinkling	about 1 teaspoon	--	--

EQUIPMENT

a baking sheet, a cushioned baking sheet, OR 2 baking sheets placed one on top of the other, lined with a nonstick liner such as Silpat or parchment;

a baking stone OR baking sheet;

a 2 1/2-inch scalloped cookie or biscuit cutter

1 > **Chill the butter.** Cut the butter into small bits. Refrigerate for at least 30 minutes, or freeze for 10 minutes.

2 > **Preheat the oven.** Preheat the oven to 400°F 20 minutes before baking. Have an oven rack at the middle level and place a baking stone or baking sheet on it before preheating.

3 > **Mix the dough.** In a large bowl, whisk together the flour (and the baking powder and salt if not using self-rising flour) and sugar. Add the butter and, with your fingertips, press it into the flour to make small pieces that resemble coarse meal. (Or use an electric mixer, with the paddle attachment if a stand mixer, on low speed.)

Press the egg yolks through a fine strainer into the flour mixture, and whisk to distribute them evenly. Stir in the cream (and/or buttermilk) just until the flour is moistened and the dough starts to come together so you can form it into a ball with your hands. Empty it onto a lightly floured counter and knead it a few times until it develops a little elasticity and feels smooth. Dust the dough lightly with flour if it feels a little sticky, and pat or roll it 3/4 inch thick (the shape doesn't matter).

4 > **Shape the dough.** Have a small dish of flour for dipping the cutter. Dip the cutter into flour before each cut and cut cleanly through the dough, lifting out the cutter without twisting it so that the edges are straight, for the maximum rise, kneading the dough scraps briefly so they won't get tough, pat or roll out, and cut out more biscuits.

For biscuits with soft sides, place the biscuits almost touching (about 1/4 inch apart) on the baking sheet. For crisp sides, place them 1 inch apart. Brush off any excess flour. For a crisp top, brush with the melted butter and sprinkle lightly with the sugar.

5 > **Bake the biscuits.** Place the biscuits in the oven on the hot baking stone or hot baking sheet, raise the temperature to 400°F and bake for 5 minutes. Lower the tem-

perature to 375°F and continue baking for 10 to 15 minutes or until golden (an instant-read thermometer inserted in the center of a biscuit will read about 200°F).

Split the biscuits in half, preferably using a three-tined fork to keep them from compressing and to create a rustic rough split.

VARIATION

Ginger Biscuits: These are great for peach shortcake.   Add 2 tablespoons finely chopped crystallized ginger (1 ounce/28 grams) to the flour mixture and add 1 tablespoon (1/3 ounce/17 grams) grated fresh ginger when adding the liquid.

UNDERSTANDING

White Lily flour (see Sources, page 572) really produces the softest, lightest biscuits, but any bleached all-purpose flour in combination with cake flour will also be fine for these.

THE DOUGH PERCENTAGE

Flour:	100%
Water:	41.7% to 66.4% (includes the water in the butter and cream and/or buttermilk)
Salt:	2.4%
Fat:	20.4 to 69.4% (includes the fat in the egg yolks and cream and/or buttermilk)

Touch-of-Grace Biscuits

Shirley Corriher is the Queen of Southern biscuits. This recipe for her biscuits has appeared in articles and cookbooks, including her own *CookWise*. There are several secrets to these fluffy biscuits: the traditional Southern soft (low-protein) White Lily flour, Crisco, and a lot of liquid (more than double the usual amount!). Another secret is the Southern tradition of the "rising oven." This means that when the biscuits are placed in the oven, the temperature is turned up so that a burst of heat rises up, giving extra lift to the biscuits. I have adopted this great tradition for all my biscuits!

Heavy cream will make a more tender biscuit, while buttermilk will make a slightly lighter biscuit with a subtle tang. Compared to the Butter Biscuits (page 127), these have less fat but more sugar and liquid, making them feathery. Because they are made with shortening, they have less flavor than biscuits made entirely with butter, but the trade-off is that they are whiter, lighter, and fluffier. Of course they can be spread with butter after baking if you can't just eat biscuits without the butter flavor. They are also tasty Southern-style, sandwiched with ham and pepper jelly. And they make an excellent accompaniment to any dinner.

TIME SCHEDULE

Oven Temperature: 475°F, then 500°F, then 475°F
Baking Time: 15 to 20 minutes

Makes: nine 2 1/2-by-2-inch-high biscuits

INGREDIENTS	MEASURE	WEIGHT	
	volume	ounces	grams
White Lily self-rising flour or	**1 1/2 cups**	**7.5 ounces**	**217 grams**
bleached all-purpose flour	1 cup	5 ounces	142 grams
plus cake flour	about 1/2 cup	1.75 ounces	60 grams
plus baking powder	2 teaspoons	0.3 ounce	9.8 grams
plus salt	3/4 teaspoon	--	5 grams
sugar	**3 tablespoons**	**1.3 ounces**	**37.5 grams**
salt	**1/4 teaspoon**	--	**1.6 grams**
vegetable shortening, cold	**3 tablespoons**	**1.25 ounces**	**36 grams**
heavy cream or		**10.2 ounces**	**290 grams**
buttermilk	**1 1/4 cups**	10.6 ounces	302 grams
(or a combination of the two)		(10.4 ounces)	(296 grams)
bleached all-purpose flour **(NOT self-rising)**	**1 cup**	**5 ounces**	**142 grams**
Optional topping melted butter, cooled	1 tablespoon	0.5 ounce	14 grams

EQUIPMENT

an 8-inch cake pan (OR 6-inch cake pan for half the recipe), lightly greased;

a baking stone OR baking sheet;

optional: a #30 ice cream scoop (2-tablespoon capacity)

1 > **Preheat the oven.** Preheat the oven to 475°F 30 minutes before baking. Have an oven shelf at the middle level and place a baking stone or baking sheet on it before preheating.

2 > **Mix the dough.** In a medium bowl (about 1 1/2 quarts), whisk together the flour (and the baking powder if not using self-rising flour), sugar, and salt (1 teaspoon in all if not using self-rising flour). Add the shortening in teaspoon-sized pieces and, with your finger-tips, press the shortening into the flour until pea-sized or smaller. (Or use an electric mixer on low speed.)

Stir in the cream (and/or buttermilk). The biscuit dough will be very soft, like mashed potatoes. Allow it to sit for 2 to 3 minutes: it will stiffen slightly.

3 > Shape the dough. Spread the all-purpose flour in a pie plate or cake pan. To shape the biscuits using the ice cream scoop or a large spoon, scoop up a biscuit-sized lump of the dough (a heaping scoopful) and drop it onto the flour. Sprinkle the top lightly with some of the flour. Pick up the biscuit with your hand and shape it into a round, gently shaking off any excess flour: it works well to hold the biscuit in your left hand, with fingers partially closed so that thumb and index finger form the letter C. With your right hand, tamp down the top of the dough so that the biscuit is 1 inch high and 2 inches wide.

Put each biscuit in the cake pan as soon as it is shaped, placing them snugly-up against each other so that the soft dough will rise up instead of spreading sideways during baking. If desired, dip the brush in the melted butter (avoid the milk solids that will have sunk to the bottom) and brush the top of the biscuits.

4 > Bake the biscuits. Place the biscuits in the oven on the hot baking stone or baking sheet. Raise the heat to 500°F and bake for 5 minutes. Lower the heat to 475°F and continue baking for 10 to 15 minutes, until biscuits have doubled in size and are lightly browned (an instant-read thermometer inserted into the center will read about 160°F).

Allow the biscuits to cool in the pan for 1 to 2 minutes, then empty them onto a plate. Pull the biscuits apart and split them in half, preferably using a three-tined fork to keep them from compressing and to create a rustic rough split rather than a clean cut.

UNDERSTANDING

These biscuits must be arranged tightly together in a pan for support because their high moisture content would otherwise cause them to lose their shape during baking before they set.

The oven temperature can be higher than for biscuits made with butter because vegetable shortening doesn't brown as quickly as butter.

THE DOUGH PERCENTAGE

Flour:	100%
Water:	81 to 108.1% (includes the water in the cream and/or buttermilk)
Salt:	3.2%
Shortening:	20.4 to 69.4%

Angel Light Biscuits

To create biscuits as light as an angel's wings, I added yeast, in addition to baking powder, to my Butter Biscuit recipe. The yeast makes it possible to prepare this dough up to three days ahead of baking the biscuits, which means you can have hot biscuits on the table in no time.

TIME SCHEDULE

Minimum Rising Time: 5 1/2 hours
Oven Temperature: 375°F, then 400°F, then 375°F
Baking Time: 15 to 20 minutes

Makes: nine 2 1/2-by-2-inch-high biscuits

INGREDIENTS	MEASURE	WEIGHT	
	volume	ounces	grams
unsalted butter, cold	**6 tablespoons**	**3 ounces**	**85 grams**
White Lily self-rising flour or	**2 cups**	**10 ounces**	**290 grams**
bleached all purpose flour	1 1/4 cups	6.5 ounces	182 grams
plus cake flour	2/3 cup	2.3 ounces	86 grams
plus baking powder	1 tablespoon	0.5 ounce	14.7 grams
plus salt	1 teaspoon	--	6.6 grams
sugar	**3 tablespoons**	**1.3 ounces**	**37.5 grams**
instant yeast (see page 561 for brands)	**2 teaspoons**	--	**6.4 grams**
2 large eggs, hard-cooked **(see page 125), yolks only**	--	**1.3 ounces**	**37 grams**
heavy cream or		**about 7 ounces**	**203 grams**
buttermilk	**3/4 liquid cup plus**	about 7.5 ounces	212 grams
(or a combination of the two)	**2 tablespoons**	(7 ounces)	(213 grams)
Optional topping:			
melted butter, cooled	1 tablespoon	0.5 ounce	14 grams
sugar for sprinkling	about 1 teaspoon	--	--

a baking sheet, a cushioned baking sheet, OR 2 baking sheets placed one on top of the other, lined with a nonstick liner such as Silpat or parchment;

a baking stone OR baking sheet;

a 2 1/2-inch scalloped cookie or biscuit cutter

1 > **Chill the butter.** Cut the butter into small bits. Refrigerate for at least 30 minutes, or freeze for 10 minutes.

2 > **Mix the dough.** In a large bowl, whisk together the flour (and baking powder and salt if not using self-rising flour), sugar, and yeast. Add the butter and, with your fingertips, press it into the flour to make small pieces that resemble coarse meal. (Or use an electric mixer on low speed.)

Press the egg yolks through a fine strainer into the flour mixture, and whisk to distribute them evenly. Stir in the cream and (and/or buttermilk) just until the flour is moistened and the dough starts to come together so you can form it into a ball with your hands. The dough will be very soft and sticky.

3 > **Let the dough rise.** Cover the dough tightly with plastic wrap and allow it to rise for about 1 1/2 hours (ideally at 75° to 80°F) or until it becomes puffy but hasn't quite doubled.

Pat the dough down gently and refrigerate it, tightly covered, for 4 hours, or for up to 3 days.

4 > **Shape the dough and let it rise.** Have a small dish of flour ready for dipping the cutter. Scrape the dough onto a lightly floured counter and knead it a few times until it develops a little elasticity and feels smooth. Dust the dough lightly with flour if necessary, and pat or roll it 3/4 inch thick (the shape doesn't matter).

Dip the cutter into flour before each cut and cut cleanly through the dough, lifting out the cutter without twisting it so that the edges are straight, for the maximum rise. Knead the dough scraps briefly, pat or roll out, and cut out more biscuits.

For biscuits with soft sides, place the biscuits almost touching (about 1/4 inch apart) on the baking sheet. For crisp sides, place the biscuits 1 inch apart.

Cover the biscuits with plastic wrap and allow them to rise for about 1 hour (ideally at 80° to 85°F) or until 1 inch high.

5 > Preheat the oven. Preheat the oven to 375°F 30 minutes before baking. Have an oven shelf at the middle level and place a baking stone or baking sheet on it before preheating.

6 > Bake the biscuits. Gently brush any excess flour from the biscuits. For a crisp top, brush with the melted butter and sprinkle lightly with the sugar. Place the biscuits in the oven on the hot baking stone or baking sheet, raise the temperature to 400°F and bake for 5 minutes. Lower the temperature to 375°F and continue baking for 10 to 15 minutes or until lightly browned. (An instant-read thermometer inserted into the center of a biscuit will read about 200°F).

Split the biscuits in half, preferably using a three-tined fork to keep them from compressing and to create a rustic split.

UNDERSTANDING

White Lily flour (see Sources page 572) really produces the softest, lightest biscuits, but any brand of bleached all-purpose flour in combination with cake flour will be fine for these.

THE DOUGH PERCENTAGE

Water:	47.4 to 75.8% (includes the water in the butter)
Yeast:	2.37%
Salt:	2.4%
Fat:	31 to 56.7%% (includes the fat in the egg yolks)

Sweet Potato Biscuits

You will never find a better use for leftover sweet potatoes or yams! They contribute a very subtle flavor and sweetness, which I balance by using less sugar than usual, but what I value most is the moistness and deep dark gold color they add. These biscuits are especially delicious sandwiched with ham and honey mustard.

TIME SCHEDULE

Minimum Rising Time: 5 1/2 hours
Oven Temperature: 375°F, then 400°F, then 375°F
Baking Time: 15 to 20 minutes

Makes: nine 2 1/2-by-2-inch-high biscuits

INGREDIENTS	MEASURE	WEIGHT	
	volume	ounces	grams
unsalted butter, cold	**6 tablespoons**	**3 ounces**	**85 grams**
White Lily self-rising flour or	**2 cups**	**10 ounces**	**290 grams**
bleached all-purpose flour	1 1/4 cups	6.5 ounces	182 grams
plus cake flour	2/3 cup	2.3 ounces	86 grams
plus baking powder	1 tablespoon	0.5 ounce	14.7 grams
plus salt	1 teaspoon	--	6.6 grams
sugar	**2 tablespoons**	**about 0.75 ounce**	**25 grams**
instant yeast (see page 561 for brands)	**2 teaspoons**	**--**	**6.4 grams**
2 large eggs, hard-cooked (see page 125), (yolks only)	**--**	**1.3 ounces**	**37 grams**
heavy cream or		**5.4 ounces**	**153 grams**
buttermilk	**2/3 cup**	5.6 ounces	160 grams
(or a combination of the two)		(5.5 ounces)	(156 grams)
baked sweet potato or yam, sieved at room temperature	**1/4 cup plus 2 tablespoons**	**3.3 ounces**	**95 grams**
Optional topping			
melted butter, cooled	1 tablespoon	0.5 ounce	14 grams
sugar for sprinkling	about 1 teaspoon	--	--

EQUIPMENT

a cookie sheet, a cushioned cookie sheet, OR 2 baking sheets placed one on top of the other, lined with a nonstick liner such as Silpat or parchment;

a baking stone OR baking sheet;

a 2 1/2-inch scalloped cookie or biscuit cutter

1 > **Chill the butter.** Cut the butter into small bits. Refrigerate for at least 30 minutes, or freeze for 10 minutes.

2 > **Mix the dough.** In a large bowl, whisk together the flour (and baking powder and salt if not using self-rising flour), sugar, and yeast. Add the butter and, with your fingertips, press it into the flour to make small pieces that resemble coarse meal. (Or use an electric mixer on low speed.)

Press the egg yolks through a fine strainer into the flour mixture and whisk to distribute them evenly.

Whisk the cream (and/or buttermilk) into the sweet potato or yam. With a rubber spatula or wooden spoon, stir into the flour mixture just until the flour is moistened and the dough starts to come together so you can form a ball with your hands. The dough will be very soft and sticky.

3 > **Let the dough rise.** Cover the dough tightly with plastic wrap and allow it to rise for about 1 1/2 hours (ideally at 75°F to 80°F) or until it becomes puffy but hasn't quite doubled. Pat the dough down gently and refrigerate it, tightly covered, for 4 hours, or up to 3 days.

4 > **Shape the dough and let it rise.** Have a small dish of flour ready for dipping the cutter. Using an oiled spatula or dough scraper, scrape the dough onto a lightly floured counter and knead it a few times until it develops a little elasticity and feels smooth. Dust the dough lightly with flour if it feels sticky, and pat or roll it 3/4 inch thick (the shape doesn't matter).

Dip the cutter into flour before each cut and cut cleanly through the dough, lifting out the cutter without twisting it so that the edges will be straight, for the maximum rise. Knead the dough scraps briefly, pat or roll out, and cut out more biscuits.

For biscuits with soft sides, place the biscuits almost touching (about 1/4 inch apart) on the baking sheet. For crisp sides, place them 1 inch apart.

Cover the biscuits with plastic wrap and allow them to rise for about 1 hour (ideally at 80°F to 85°F) or until they are 1 inch high.

5 > Preheat the oven. Preheat the oven to 375°F 30 minutes before baking. Have an oven shelf at the middle level and place a baking stone or baking sheet on it before preheating.

6 > Bake the biscuits. Gently brush any excess flour from the biscuits. For a crisp top, brush with the melted butter and sprinkle lightly with the sugar. Place the biscuits in the oven on the hot baking stone or baking sheet, raise the temperature to 400°F, and bake for 5 minutes. Lower the temperature to 375°F and continue baking for 10 to 15 minutes or until lightly browned (an instant-read thermometer inserted into the center of a biscuit will read about 200°F).

Split the biscuits in half, preferably using a three-tined fork to keep them from compressing and to create a rustic split.

UNDERSTANDING

White Lily flour (see Sources, page 572) really produces the softest, lightest biscuits but any brand of bleached all-purpose flour in combination with cake flour will be fine for these.

Using both baking powder and yeast ensures a light and tender texture despite the extra moisture. Less flour and less liquid is used than for the "plain" angel butter biscuits to balance the additional liquid from the sweet potato.

The hard-cooked egg yolks add a little extra tenderness because of the fat they contain, but their main contribution is a velvety softness on the tongue.

THE DOUGH PERCENTAGE

Flour:	100%
Water:	**54.3 to 74%** (includes the water in the heavy cream and/or buttermilk and the sweet potato)
Yeast:	**2.71%**
Salt:	**2.2%**
Fat:	**28.1 to 45.8%** (includes the fat in the egg yolks and cream and/or buttermilk)

Flaky Scones

It is only in the past ten years that the scone (pronounced "skawn," as in gone) has appeared on the breakfast scene, threatening to upstage even the bagel. Catherine G. Brown, in her book *Scottish Cooker* (Mercat Press, Edinburgh, 1999), writes that these small "tea cakes" go back at least to the eighteenth century, when the poet Robert Burns "rightly described them as 'souple [soft] scones, the wale [choicest] of food.'" The Chambers Scots Dictionary suggests that the word *scone* is from the Gaelic *sgonn*, meaning a shapeless mass. Any way you slice it, one can't ask for a more perfect breakfast, tea, or coffee break bread.

These flaky scones are ample and comforting—crisp on the outside, soft, moist, and layered inside with a pure butter flavor and just the right touch of chewy-sweetness from the currants. I've tried and rejected many other recipes. These, from master baker Patty Jackson of Tuscan Square, in New York City, are the best. They are prepared by layering butter pieces into the dough much in the style of puff pastry, giving the scones a slightly flaky texture. But since they contain only about one-third butter to flour (puff pastry uses equal parts) and are made with heavy cream instead of water, they offer a far more substantial, soul-satisfying texture.

If you want each scone to be a perfect even triangle, there will be some waste. Personally, I prefer to use every scrap of the delicious dough and embrace the rustic misshapen ones along with the classic three-sided variety.

TIME SCHEDULE

Oven Temperature: 400°F
Baking Time: 15 to 20 minutes

Makes: twelve or sixteen 4-in by-1 1/2-inch-high scones

INGREDIENTS	MEASURE	WEIGHT	
	volume	ounces	grams
unsalted butter, cold	1 cup	8 ounces	227 grams
unbleached all-purpose flour, preferably Hecker's	4 1/4 cups	21.25 ounces	608 grams
sugar	1/2 cup	3.5 ounces	100 grams
baking powder	2 teaspoons	--	9.6 grams
baking soda	1/2 teaspoon	--	2.5 grams
salt	1/4 teaspoon	--	1.7 grams
heavy cream	2 liquid cups	16.3 ounces	464 grams
currants	1 cup	4.5 ounces	131 grams

EQUIPMENT

2 half sheet pans lined with nonstick liners such as Silpat or parchment;

a baking stone OR baking sheet

1 > Chill the butter. Cut the butter into 1-inch cubes. Refrigerate for at least 30 minutes, or freeze for 10 minutes.

2 > Mix the dough. In a large bowl, whisk together the flour, sugar, baking powder, baking soda, and salt. Add the butter and with your fingertips, press the cubes into large flakes. (Or use an electric mixer, mixing until the butter is the size of small walnuts.)

Stir in the cream just until the flour is moistened and the dough starts to come together in large clumps. Stir in the currants. Knead the dough in the bowl just until it holds together, and turn it out onto a lightly floured board.

3 > Preheat the oven. Preheat the oven to 400°F 30 minutes before baking. Have an oven rack at the middle level and set a baking stone or baking sheet on it before preheating.

4 > Shape the dough. Lightly flour the top of the dough (or use a floured pastry sleeve), and roll it out into a long rectangle 1 inch thick and about 8 inches by 12 inches; use a bench scraper to keep the edges even by smacking it up against the sides of the dough. Fold the dough in thirds, lightly flour the board again, and rotate the dough so that the closed side faces to the left. Roll it out again and repeat the "turn" 3 more times, refrigerating the dough, covered with plastic wrap, for about 15 minutes as necessary only if it begins to soften and stick.

Roll out the dough once more. Trim the edges so that it will rise evenly. (To use the scraps, press them together and roll out, giving them 2 turns, then roll the dough into a 1-inch-thick square and cut it into 2 triangles.)

Cut the dough in half lengthwise so you have 2 pieces, each about 4 inches by 12 inches. Cut each piece of dough into triangles with about a 3-inch-wide base and place them about 1 inch apart on the prepared baking sheets. (The dough will rise but not expand sideways.) If the dough is soft, cover it well with plastic wrap and freeze for 15 minutes or refrigerate for 1 hour before baking.

5 > **Bake the scones.** Bake the scones one sheet at a time: cover the second sheet with plastic wrap and refrigerate while you bake the first one, then bake the second pan directly from the refrigerator. Place the pan on the hot baking stone or hot baking sheet and bake the scones for 15 to 20 minutes or until the edges begin to brown and the tops are golden brown and firm enough so that they barely give when pressed lightly with a finger (an instant-read thermometer inserted into the center of a scone will read about 200°F). Check the scones after 10 minutes of baking, and if they are not browning evenly, rotate the baking sheet from front to back. Do not overbake, as they continue baking slightly on removal from the oven and are best when slightly moist and soft inside.

6 > **Cool the scones.** Place two linen or cotton towels on two large racks and, using a pancake turner, lift the scones from the baking sheets and set them on top. Fold the towels over loosely and allow the scones to cool until warm or at room temperature. (Since linen or cotton "breathes," the scones will have enough protection to keep from becoming dry and hard on the surface but will not become soggy.)

VARIATIONS

Dried Cranberry Scones   Substitute dried cranberries for the currants for more tang.

Lemon Poppy Seed Scones   Omit the currants and add 3 tablespoons (1 ounce/28 grams) poppy seeds and 2 tablespoons (0.5 ounce/12 grams) finely grated lemon zest to the flour mixture.

POINTERS FOR SUCCESS

>   To reheat frozen scones, bake them in a preheated 300°F oven for 20 minutes. The outside will be crisp and a cake tester inserted briefly in the center will feel warm.

UNDERSTANDING

Hecker's flour has a protein content that is higher than Gold Medal unbleached all-purpose (averaging 10.5 percent) but lower than King Arthur all-purpose (11.7 percent). Any of the three flours will produce excellent scones, but Hecker's is my preference because it results in the best compromise between tenderness and flakiness.

THE DOUGH PERCENTAGE

Flour:	100%
Water:	49% (includes the water in the butter and cream)
Salt:	0.3%
Fat:	57.7% (includes the fat in the cream)

Rich and Creamy Ginger Scones

These scones are lighter and more delicate than the Flaky Scones (page 139). They contain a little more butter and a little less cream. The cream is whipped for added lightness, and the tops are dusted with sugar for sparkle and crunch.

I like to use both candied ginger and ground ginger because the ground ginger distributes evenly through the dough and the candied ginger gives little unexpected hits of flavor. Use the best crystallized ginger you can find. I love the Australian variety, but when I go to Paris I always bring back some of Fouquet's incomparable ginger. He imports fresh ginger from Thailand and candies it himself.

Since these scones are so fabulously rich, I prefer to make them smaller than the usual, but if you prefer big ones, simply cut 6 wedges instead of 8. This is a delightful recipe not only because it is so delicious, but because it is so quick and easy to mix. If you freeze the butter cubes and flour mixture the night before, these scones can be on your breakfast table the next morning in forty-five minutes, ready to eat!

TIME SCHEDULE

Oven Temperature: 400°F
Baking Time: 15 to 20 minutes

Makes: twelve or sixteen 3 1/2-by-1 1/4-inch-high scones

INGREDIENTS	MEASURE	WEIGHT	
	volume	ounces	grams
unsalted butter, cold	12 tablespoons	6 ounces	170 grams
heavy cream	3/4 liquid cup	6 ounces	174 grams
unbleached all-purpose flour, preferably King Arthur or Hecker's	2 cups	10 ounces	284 grams
sugar, preferably turbinado	1/3 cup	2.3 ounces	66 grams
baking powder	1 tablespoon	0.5 ounce	14.7 grams
ground ginger	1 teaspoon	--	--
salt	1/8 teaspoon	--	--
grated lemon zest	1 teaspoon	--	2 grams
crystallized ginger, cut into 1/8- to 1/4-inch pieces, or mini-diced crystallized ginger	2/3 cup	4 ounces	113 grams

Topping

heavy cream	2 teaspoons		
sugar, preferably turbinado	1 tablespoon	--	12 grams

EQUIPMENT

two 12-inch pizza pans OR a large cookie sheet, sprayed with Baker's Joy or greased and floured;

a baking stone OR baking sheet

1 > **Chill the butter and whip the cream.** If using the food processor, cut the butter into 3/4-inch cubes and freeze for at least 15 minutes. They should be very solid. If mixing the dough by hand, cut the butter into 3/4-inch cubes and refrigerate for at least 30 minutes or until very firm.

Whip the cream just until soft peaks form when the beater is lifted. Cover and place in the refrigerator.

2 > **Preheat the oven.** Preheat the oven to 400°F 30 minutes before baking. Have an oven rack at the middle level and set a baking stone or baking sheet on it before preheating.

3 > Mix the dough.

Food Processor Method

In a food processor with the metal blade, combine the flour, sugar, baking powder, ground ginger, salt, and lemon zest. Add the butter and process for 10 to 15 seconds or until the mixture resembles fine meal.

Empty the mixture into a large bowl and stir in the crystallized ginger. Make a well in the center. Add the whipped cream to the well and, with a rubber spatula or a dough scraper, stir the flour mixture into the cream until all of it is moistened. Knead the dough in the bowl just until it holds together, then turn it out onto a lightly floured counter. Knead it about 8 times, until it can be shaped into a smooth ball. (The dough will weigh about 28.5 oz/810 grams.)

Hand Method

In a large bowl, whisk together the flour, sugar, baking powder, ground ginger, salt, and lemon zest. Add the butter and rub it between your fingers until the mixture resembles fine meal. Stir in the crystallized ginger.

Make a well in the center of the mixture. Add the whipped cream to the well and, with a rubber spatula or a dough scraper, stir the flour mixture into the cream until all of it is moistened. Knead the dough in the bowl just until it holds together, then turn it out onto a lightly floured counter. Knead it about 8 times, until it can be shaped into a smooth ball. (The dough will weigh about 28.5 ounces/810 grams.)

Both Methods

4 > Shape and chill the dough. Cut the dough in half. Shape each half into a smooth ball, press it into a 3/4-inch-thick disk about 6 inches in diameter, and wrap well with plastic wrap. Freeze for 15 minutes, or refrigerate for 1 hour.

5 > Cut the dough. With a long sharp knife, cut each disk into 6 or 8 wedges. Brush the tops with the heavy cream and sprinkle evenly with the sugar. Lift the wedges onto the prepared baking sheets, leaving at least 1 1/2 inches between them.

6 > Bake the scones. Place the pan on the hot baking stone or hot baking sheet and bake the scones for 15 to 20 minutes or until the edges begin to brown and the tops are golden brown and firm enough so that they barely give when pressed lightly with a finger (an instant-read thermometer inserted into the center of a scone will read about 200°F). Check the scones after 10 minutes of baking, and if they are not browning evenly, rotate the baking sheet from front to back. Do not overbake as they continue baking slightly on removal from the oven and are best when slightly moist and soft inside.

7 > **Cool the scones.** With a pancake turner, transfer the scones to a wire rack to cool completely.

VARIATION

Stollen Christmas Scones I love the flavor of stollen but not the texture, which is invariably dry. With stollen scones, however, you have the best of both worlds. Chef Dietmar Eilbacher, of the Culinary Institute of America at Greystone, in California, served them at a Spice Conference to universally rave reviews.

Reduce the ground ginger to 3/4 teaspoon and add 1/2 teaspoon each ground allspice, cinnamon, coriander, and anise, and a pinch of cloves and mace. In addition to the lemon zest, add 2 teaspoons grated orange zest.

Replace the crystallized ginger with 3 tablespoons (1.75 ounces/50 grams) candied orange peel and add 1/3 cup (1.75 ounces/50 grams) raisins and 3/4 cup (2.5 ounces/70 grams) chopped almonds at the same time. Bake the scones one sheet at a time: cover the second sheet with plastic wrap and refrigerate while you bake the first one, then bake the second pan directly from the refrigerator.

Add 2 teaspoons vanilla extract to the heavy cream at the end of whipping.

Bake at the same temperature.

POINTERS FOR SUCCESS

> If you are in a hurry, these scones will still be delicious without whipping the cream. The idea came from cookbook writer Cindy Mushet, and it makes the scones slightly airy in texture.

> If it's warm in your kitchen, place the flour, sugar, baking powder, salt, and ginger in a container or zip-seal plastic bag and freeze for at least 15 minutes before mixing the dough.

> The unbaked scones can be individually wrapped in plastic wrap and frozen for up to 3 months. To bake, place one or more still-frozen scones on a prepared baking sheet, brush with cream, sprinkle with sugar, and bake frozen. Add 5 to 7 minutes to the baking time. They have a more even shape when baked frozen.

> The scones can be frozen for up to 3 months. Reheat in a preheated 300°F oven for about 20 minutes. The outside will be crunchy and a cake tester briefly inserted in the center and removed will feel warm.

The scones tend to stick to parchment. Using Baker's Joy or greasing and flouring the pans works best.

THE DOUGH PERCENTAGE

Flour:	100%
Water:	43.9% (includes the water in the butter and cream)
Salt:	0.3%
Fat:	70.5% (includes the fat in the cream)

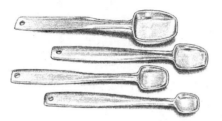

Royal Irish Soda Bread

This started off as authentic Irish soda bread, which in Ireland is usually made with at least part whole wheat flour, buttermilk, salt, and baking soda. By test four, all the good things—like butter, sugar, and raisins soaked in Irish whiskey—had crept in and before I knew it I had the makings of a scone-like bread, but a less rich one, as it has only half the butter. The butter and sugar add tenderness, moisture, and flavor and soaking the raisins in the Irish whiskey, an inspiration from my editor, Maria, works wonderfully to protect them from overbrowning on the surface and to give them a mellow flavor. I use only baking soda as the leavening, which is activated and released fully by the acidity in the buttermilk. There is no added baking powder, which is responsible for the odd metallic aftertaste so often associated with this bread.

The bread takes just minutes to mix and is baked immediately after mixing. It is especially delicious spread with plenty of creamy Irish whiskey butter (see below). Shaping the dough into rolls makes it ideal for a bread basket, as the crust prevents the crumb from getting dry on standing the way slices of the bread would. See the variation.

If you like an earthy wheaty flavor, use the optional whole wheat flour. The bread will still have a surprisingly light texture.

TIME SCHEDULE

Oven Temperature: 375°F
Baking Time: 35 minutes

Makes: a 7-by-3-inch-high round loaf/24 ounces/680 grams

INGREDIENTS	MEASURE	WEIGHT	
	volume	ounces	grams
raisins	1 scant cup	4.5 ounces	129 grams
Irish whiskey or hot water	1/2 liquid cup	3 ounces	85 grams
unsalted butter, cold	4 tablespoons	2 ounces	56 grams
unbleached all-purpose flour (or 1 cup all-purpose and 1 cup whole wheat flour)	2 cups	10.5 ounces	300 grams
sugar	3 tablespoons	1.3 ounces	37.5 grams
baking soda	1 teaspoon	--	5 grams
salt	3/4 teaspoon	--	5 grams
buttermilk	3/4 liquid cup plus 1 tablespoon	7 ounces	200 grams

EQUIPMENT

a baking sheet, lined with a nonstick liner such as Silpat or parchment, OR greased with cooking oil or spray

1 > **Soak the raisins.** In a small bowl, combine the raisins and whiskey. Cover with plastic wrap and allow to sit, stirring once, until the raisins are softened, about 30 minutes (or let stand for as long as overnight).

Drain, and reserve the whiskey to use in the Irish whiskey butter. You should have about 3 tablespoons.

2 > **Preheat the oven.** Preheat the oven to 375°F 20 minutes before baking. Have an oven shelf just below the center of the oven.

3 > **Mix and knead the dough.** Cut the butter into about 8 slices so that it begins to soften a little and will be easier to mix into the flour.

In a large bowl, stir together the flour, sugar, baking soda, and salt. With your fingertips, rub in the butter until the mixture resembles coarse crumbs. Stir in the raisins. With a wooden spoon or rubber spatula, stir in the buttermilk just until the dry ingredients are moistened and the dough comes together.

Empty the dough onto the counter and knead it lightly about 8 times, until smooth but still a little sticky. If it sticks to the counter, use a bench scraper to gather it together—try to avoid adding extra flour. Flour your hands if absolutely necessary. (The dough will weigh about 22.5 ounces/640 grams.)

4 > Shape the dough. Roll the dough into a 6-inch round (it will be 1 3/4 inches high). If it sticks, flour it lightly. Place it on the prepared baking sheet and, with a single-edged razor blade or sharp knife, make a 1/2-inch-deep slash from one side of the dough to the other, then make a second slash across it to form a cross.

5 > Bake the bread. Bake the bread for 30 minutes or until it is golden brown and a wooden skewer comes out clean (an instant-read thermometer inserted into the center will read about 190°F).

6 > Cool the bread. If you have a linen, cotton, or loose-weave towel, place it on a wire rack and place the bread on top. Fold the towel over loosely and allow the bread to cool until just warm (about 40 minutes) or at room temperature. (The towel keeps the top crust soft, but since it "breathes," the bread will not become soggy.) Or simply cool the bread on a rack.

VARIATION

Royal Irish Soda Rolls (makes fifteen 2 1/2-inch-by-1 1/2-inch-high rolls; 1.5 ounces/44 grams each) After kneading the dough, roll it into a long rope and divide it into 8 equal pieces (about 1.75 ounces/50 grams each). Roll each piece of dough between the palms of your hands, or with one cupped hand on the counter, into a ball about 1 1/2 inches across. Set the balls about 2 inches apart on the prepared baking sheet, in 3 rows of 5 balls each. With a single-edged razor blade or sharp knife, cut a 1/4-inch-deep cross in each one. Bake for 15 to 20 minutes or just until beginning to brown (an instant-read thermometer inserted into the center of a roll will read about 190°F).

If you have a linen, cotton, or loose-weave towel, place it on a wire rack and set the rolls on top. Fold the towel over loosely and allow them to cool until just warm (15 to 20 minutes) or at room temperature. Or simply cool the rolls on a rack.

Irish Whiskey Butter

3 tablespoons reserved Irish whiskey from the raisins
1 tablespoon sugar
9 tablespoons (4 1/2 ounces/128 grams) unsalted butter, softened

In a small microwaveable bowl, stir together the whiskey and sugar. Cover with plastic wrap and microwave until hot about 20 seconds. (Alternatively, use a small saucepan and stir constantly.) Stir to dissolve the sugar. Cover and allow to cool completely.

In a small bowl, with a small whisk or spoon, gradually stir the Irish whiskey mixture into the butter until incorporated. It will be a caramel brown color. Store at cool room temperature for up to 2 days, or refrigerate for up to 2 weeks.

POINTERS FOR SUCCESS

> This bread freezes beautifully for up to 1 month. To reheat it, bake it uncovered in a preheated 300°F oven for 20 to 30 minutes, or until a cake tester inserted in the center briefly feels warm.

UNDERSTANDING

This recipe calls for double the baking soda of most standard Irish soda bread recipes. It results in a smoother top crust, higher rise, and a more golden color, as opposed to the usual reddish-brown color.

THE DOUGH PERCENTAGE

Flour:	100%
Water:	63%
Salt:	1.7%
Fat:	16.3% (includes the fat in the buttermilk)

Levy's Bagels

My first bread memory and my first teething ring are one and the same. It was my mother, a dentist, who considered the bagel an ideal natural teething ring because of its firm yet forgiving texture. But it was my father who brought us freshly baked bagels on a string every Friday afternoon after he made his weekly delivery of bagel peels. In the 1940s, after the war, and the early 1950s, when times were hard, my father, a skilled cabinet maker, turned to bagel peel production and eventually laid claim to the exclusive bagel peel business in the greater New York area, including the five boroughs and all of New Jersey. That did not make us rich, but we had all the bagels we could eat.

A peel is a flat wooden pallet with a long pole as handle, designed for transferring bread to and from an oven. The peels used for bagels are only slightly wider than the bagels themselves. In traditional bagel production, after being boiled in salted water, the bagels are placed on a wooden board and set in the oven, which may be as deep as twenty feet. Once the tops of the bagels are firm, a piece of string is run under the bagels to release them and they are inverted onto the hot oven shelf. The peel is used to move them about so that they bake evenly and to remove them from the oven.

Nowadays, bagels are loved around the world, but today's bagels are not the bagels of my childhood. Those were dense and chewy, plain golden brown—no poppy seed, onion, or "everything," and certainly no boutique blueberry bagels with the texture of cake. (The first time I heard about those I felt as if the world as I knew it was coming to an end.) My bagels were served cut crosswise in half, so that to my childish imagination they delightfully resembled telephones, and each cut half was spread with a big lump of sweet butter. As I bit off each piece, my attentive grandmother would apply a new lump of butter. When I got older, I ate bagels the way the grownups did, cutting them in half horizontally, digging out the softer centers, and toasting them before filling the cavities thus created with butter.

I hadn't had a bagel that pleased me as much in years, as the texture of bagels has become ever more compromised in the direction of an airy bread. I was afraid to make them myself because that wasn't the tradition. So when I started working on this recipe, I made sure my father was there to set the standard. He did more than that. He drew from his memory of sixty years ago a technique he had observed of shaping the bagels by rolling them first into a rope, which strengthens the dough and makes the baked bagels extra chewy. When I asked him whether they approached the bagels of his memory, to my delight, he said, "They're better!" I suspect that's because they are less dense in texture and the flavor more complex due to a simple sponge starter and an overnight rise.

This dough can be made by hand, but it requires sufficient kneading to develop the gluten and as it is a stiff dough, it requires strong hands. I prefer using a stand mixer. Since a 5-quart KitchenAid stand mixer can handle only a half recipe of the dough, I am providing directions for a half batch of 5, as well as providing directions for a full batch of 10 for those who have a larger stand mixer.

TIME SCHEDULE

Dough Starter (Sponge): minimum 1 hour, maximum 24 hours
Minimum Rising Time: 1 hour
Oven Temperature: 500°F, then 450°F
Baking Time: 35 minutes

Makes: ten (five if making the smaller batch) 4-by-1 1/2-inch-high bagels/about 4.5 ounces/127 grams each

Dough Starter (Sponge)—Full Recipe

INGREDIENTS	MEASURE	WEIGHT	
	volume	ounces	grams
instant yeast (see page 561 for brands)	1 teaspoon	--	3.2 grams
water, at room temperature (70° to 90°F)	2 1/4 liquid cups	18.7 ounces	531 grams
King Arthur high-gluten flour, preferably, or bread flour	3 cups	16.5 ounces	468 grams

Dough Starter (Sponge) — Half Recipe

INGREDIENTS	MEASURE	WEIGHT	
	volume	ounces	grams
instant yeast (see page 561 for brands)	1/2 teaspoon	--	1.6 grams
water, at room temperature (70° to 90°F)	1 liquid cup plus 2 tablespoons	9.3 ounces	265.5 grams
King Arthur high-gluten flour, preferably, or bread flour	1 1/2 cups	8.25 ounces	234 grams

EQUIPMENT

a heavy-duty stand mixer with dough hook attachment;

a baking stone (dusted with cornmeal if baking the bagels directly on it);

1 or 2 half sheet pans (not black) lined with parchment and oiled or greased with cooking spray or oil (oil is not necessary if coating the bottom of the bagels with seeds), or a peel dusted with cornmeal;

parchment OR 2 clean kitchen towels, one dusted with flour;

a slotted skimmer

1 > **Make the sponge.** In a mixing bowl or the bowl of a stand mixer, place the yeast, water, and flour. Whisk about 2 minutes, until very smooth; scrape down the sides. The sponge will be very thick. Cover the bowl with plastic wrap.

Flour Mixture — Full Recipe

INGREDIENTS	MEASURE	WEIGHT	
	volume	ounces	grams
Optional: unsalted butter	3 tablespoons	1.5 ounces	42 grams
King Arthur high-gluten flour, preferably, or bread flour	2 1/3 cups	12.75 ounces	364 grams
instant yeast	1 teaspoon	--	3.2 grams
malt powder or barley malt syrup	1 tablespoon 1 tablespoon	0.3 ounce 0.7 ounce	9.3 grams 21 grams
sugar	1 tablespoon	about 0.5 ounce	12.5 grams
salt	1 tablespoon	0.75 ounce	21 grams
black pepper	1 teaspoon	--	--

The Flour Mixture — Half Recipe

INGREDIENTS	MEASURE	WEIGHT	
	volume	ounces	grams
Optional: unsalted butter	1 1/2 tablespoons	1.25 ounces	21 grams
King Arthur high-gluten flour, preferably, or bread flour	**1 cup plus about 3 tablespoons**	**6.4 ounces**	**182 grams**
instant yeast (see page 561 for brands)	**1/2 teaspoon**	--	**1.6 grams**
malt powder or barley malt syrup	**1/2 tablespoon** 1/2 tablespoon	-- --	**4.7 grams** 10.5 grams
sugar	**1/2 tablespoon**	about 0.25 ounce	**6.2 grams**
salt	**1/2 tablespoon**	0.3 ounce	**10.5 grams**
black pepper	**1/2 teaspoon**	--	--

2 > Combine and add the ingredients for the flour mixture. In a medium bowl, whisk together 2 cups (11 ounces/312 grams) of the flour if making the full recipe, or 1 cup (5.5 ounces/156 grams) if making the half recipe, the yeast, malt, sugar, salt, and pepper. Sprinkle the mixture lightly over the sponge; do not stir. Cover with plastic wrap and let stand for 1 to 4 hours at room temperature, or, for the best flavor development, 1 hour at room temperature and then refrigerated overnight, or up to 24 hours. (During this time, the sponge will bubble through the flour mixture in places; this is fine.)

3 > Mix the Dough

Hand Method

If the sponge/flour mixture has been refrigerated, let it stand at room temperature for 30 minutes. If using the butter, allow it to soften at room temperature for about 15 minutes.

Add the butter, if using, to the sponge/flour mixture. With a wooden spoon or your hand, stir the flour mixture into the sponge until it becomes too stiff to mix. Knead the dough in the bowl until it comes together, then scrape it onto a lightly floured counter. Knead the dough for 5 minutes just to begin to develop the gluten structure; use a bench scraper to scrape the dough and gather it together as you knead it. At this point it will be sticky. Cover it with the inverted bowl and allow it to rest for 20 minutes. (This rest will make the dough less sticky.)

Knead the dough for another 10 to 15 minutes or until it is very smooth and elastic. It should be barely tacky (slightly sticky) to the touch. If desired, add the remaining flour until it is no longer tacky. More flour will make a heavier, chewier bagel, which some prefer. (The dough will weigh about 3 pounds/1 kg/440 grams).

Mixer Method
Add the butter if using it and all but 2 tablespoons of the remaining flour and mix with the dough hook, starting on low speed (#2 if using a KitchenAid), mix until all the flour is moistened, about 1 minute. Raise the speed to medium (#4 KitchenAid) and knead for 10 minutes if using high-gluten flour, 5 to 7 minutes if using bread flour, adding the remaining 2 tablespoons flour toward the end if the dough doesn't pull away from the bowl. It should be very elastic and smooth and should jump back when pressed with a fingertip. Empty it onto the counter and knead in a little more flour if it is tacky (slightly sticky) to the touch. More flour will make a heavier, chewier bagel, which some prefer. (The dough will weigh about 3 pounds/1 kg 440 grams if making the full recipe, 1 1/2 pounds/720 grams if making the half recipe.)

Both Methods
4 > **Let the dough rise.** Place the dough in a 4-quart (or 2-quart for half the recipe) dough-rising container or bowl, lightly greased with cooking spray or oil. Press the dough down and lightly spray or oil the top. Cover the container with a lid or plastic wrap. With a piece of tape, mark the side of the container at approximately where double the height of the dough would be. Allow the dough to rise, ideally at 75° to 80°F, for 1 to 2 hours or until doubled.

Deflate the dough by firmly pushing it down. Give it an envelope turn and set it back in the container. Oil the top of the dough, cover it, and refrigerate it for at least 4 hours, or overnight for the most flavor. (If you want to make the bagels later, at this point the dough can be wrapped and refrigerated for up to 2 days. Let the dough stand at room temperature for 30 minutes before shaping.)

5 > **Shape the dough and let it rise.** Set a sheet of the parchment or lightly floured towel on a countertop near the stovetop. (Alternatively, line the baking sheet(s) with parchment or floured towels and place the shaped bagels on them so that you can move them easily when you are ready to boil them.)

Transfer the dough to an unfloured counter. Cut it in half and place one piece, covered, in the refrigerator. Cut the dough into 5 equal pieces (5 ounces/144 grams each). Allow the dough to rest for about 10 minutes.

Use either of the following methods to shape the dough, working with one piece at a time and keeping the remaining pieces covered. Place each bagel as you shape it on the parchment or floured towel, and cover gently with oiled plastic wrap or a second towel.

Shaping Method #1
Begin by drawing up the sides of the piece of dough and pinching them together to form a round ball. Turn the ball over so the pinched seam is on the bottom. Stick

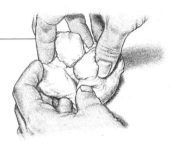

1> Drawing up the sides of the dough

2> Pinching the dough together at the top

3> Making a hole with your index
   finger in the center of the dough

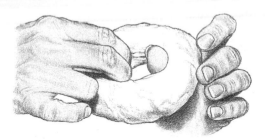

4> Hooking the dough around your
   thumb and pulling the dough with the
   fingers of your other hand

5> Stretching the dough make a 2 1/2-inch
   hole

continued >

CHAPTER 2 / *Quick Breads, Little Quick Breads, Little Yeast Breads, and Batter Breads*   **157**

your index finger all the way through the center of the ball, to make a hole. Hook the bagel over your thumb and insert the index finger of your other hand into the hole, stretching and rotating it to make a hole about 2 1/2 inches in diameter. (The bagel will resemble a ring at this point but when boiled, it will puff up and the hole will close in to bagel size, about 1 inch.)

Shaping Method #2
To develop slightly more chewiness, roll each piece of dough on an unfloured counter into a 12-inch-long rope. Make a ring, overlapping the ends by 2 inches and joining them by pressing down and rolling on the overlap until it is the same thickness as the rest of the dough ring. There will be a 1-inch hole in the center. This technique results in rounder, slightly higher bagels with smaller holes.

SHAPING METHOD #2

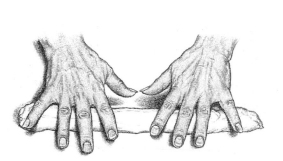 

1> Rolling the dough into a 12-inch long rope

2> Making a ring by twisting one end of the dough over to overlap the other end by 2 inches

3> Pressing down and rolling the dough

Both Methods
Allow the bagels to rise for about 15 minutes or until they puff slightly.

6 > **Preheat the oven.** Preheat the oven to 500°F 30 minutes before baking. Have an oven shelf at the lowest level and place a baking stone or baking sheet on it before preheating.

Water Bath and Toppings

INGREDIENTS	MEASURE	WEIGHT	
	volume	ounces	grams
molasses or	2 tablespoons	1.5 ounces	42 grams
sugar	1/4 cup	1.75 ounces	50 grams
baking soda	1 teaspoon	--	--

Glaze and Toppings

INGREDIENTS	MEASURE	WEIGHT	
	volume	ounces	grams
2 large egg whites	1/4 liquid cup	about 2 ounces	60 grams
cold water	1 teaspoon	--	--
poppy, sesame, or caraway seeds; kosher or sea salt; minced onions sautéed in vegetable oil; and/or dried garlic chips or dehydrated onions softened in hot water	(3 to 4 tablespoons seeds)	--	--

7 > **Boil the bagels.** If you are using seeds for topping the bagels, instead of setting the boiled bagel onto the parchment or towel, scatter half the seeds evenly over a jelly-roll or cake pan and set the boiled bagel on top of the seeds, rather than on the parchment or towel, then transfer to the peel or baking sheet as directed below. There is no need to grease the baking sheets in this case.

Bring a large pot (about 9 inches by 4 inches high) of water to a boil. Stir in the molasses or sugar and baking soda until dissolved. With a skimmer, transfer the bagels, one at a time, to the boiling water, without crowding them; cook them in batches of 2 to 3 at a time so that they can swim around without touching one another. If they are slightly underrisen, they may sink at first but will then rise to the surface. Boil for 30 seconds to 2 minutes on each side, gently flipping them over with the skimmer; the longer time will make a thicker crust. Remove the boiled bagels, shaking off excess water over the pot and set onto parchment or the unfloured towel to drain, then move them, using a pancake turner, to the prepared baking sheet(s) or peel, after just 30 seconds to 1 minute, so that they don't stick. (If necessary, boil and bake the bagels in two batches; in that case, set the pot aside until ready to

TECHNIQUE:
Removing bagels from boiling water with a slotted skimmer

boil the next batch, and bring the mixture back to a boil before sliding the bagels into the boiling water.) The bagels will look wrinkled at this stage. Don't worry—their appearance vastly improves on baking.

8 > Glaze the bagels. Whisk together the egg whites and cold water to break up the whites. Pass through a sieve into a bowl, and brush each bagel with the glaze. Do not let the glaze drip onto the baking sheet or peel, or it will glue them down. Brush with a second coat of glaze and, if desired, sprinkle any topping of your choice evenly over the bagels. (If you are using seeds, lift each bagel with a thin pancake turner or your hand, and, holding it over the pan with the seeds, sprinkle some more seeds on top. This way, you don't have any seeds that would burn on the baking sheet.)

TECHNIQUE: Brushing bagels with egg-white glaze, then sprinkling them with poppy seeds

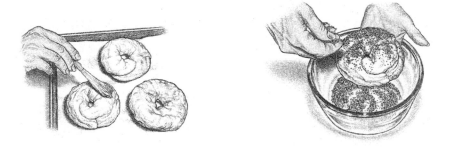

9 > Bake the bagels. If using baking sheets, place one sheet directly on the hot oven stone or hot baking sheet. If using a peel, slide the bagels onto the hot stone. Bake for 5 minutes. Lower the temperature to 450°F and bake for 20 minutes. Turn off the oven, without opening it and let the bagels remain for 5 minutes. Then open the oven door and leave the bagels in the oven for 5 more minutes.

10 > Cool the bagels. Transfer the bagels to a wire rack and cool completely. (If baking a second batch, bring the oven temperature back to 500°F. If using a baking stone, to prepare it for the next batch, use an oven-sweep or brush (see page 594) to sweep any cornmeal from the stone onto a baking sheet, and discard it.)

STORE The bagels keep well for 1 day at room temperature in a paper bag. For longer storage, wrap each in plastic wrap, place in plastic freezer bags, and freeze for up to 1 month. Thaw, still wrapped, at room temperature.

> High-gluten flour guarantees a bagel with maximum chewiness. Alternatively, use King Arthur bread flour, which has a higher gluten-forming protein content than other bread flours available to the consumer. You could also add up to 1/4 cup/1.3 ounces/38 grams of vital wheat gluten to a lower-protein unbleached flour.

> Butter, though not traditional, will produce a softer and lighter crumb. My preference is bagels made without it.

> The barley malt contributes flavor and the slightest hint of sweetness.

> Don't flour the counter when shaping the bagels using the rolling method, or the dough will not be sticky enough to seal the ends.

UNDERSTANDING

Baking soda helps to create a golden color in the crust. Molasses contributes extra shine.

THE DOUGH PERCENTAGE

Flour:	100%
Water:	63.8%
Yeast:	0.8%
Salt:	2.4%
Butterfat:	(if using the optional butter): 3.5%

Bialys

There are some who divide the world between bagel lovers and bialy lovers. The dough for both is actually very similar, but the difference in shaping and baking techniques sets them apart. A bagel is brown, chubby, and almost cakey, with a soft and chewy crust. It can be left plain or sprinkled with a variety of toppings. A bialy is flat, with a springy/soft crumb and a crisp papery thin shell of a flour-dusty white crust. It always has a filling in the center, from a "schmear" of caramelized onions to a more substantial chopped onion and poppy seed combination. If you find the idea of oil-poached garlic appealing, see the recipe for the for Focaccia with Pockets of Garlic (page 207).

Kossar's, on the lower east side of New York, is close to Greenwich Village, where I live, and even closer to where my great-grandparents lived years before I was born. Kossar's is considered by New Yorkers to be the last word in bialys, so I was delighted when Whitey, one of the top bakers, who has worked there for twenty five years, offered to give me a lesson in making and shaping bialy dough. He also gave me the secret to keeping the dough from puffing too much in the center. I made bialys at home the very next day and was thrilled with their success.

Don't worry if the dough puffs a little more than it should—it will make it easier to cut in half. Delicious when freshly baked or lightly toasted after cooling, this simple and amazing bread, spread with butter, is as soul-satisfying as bread ever gets.

TIME SCHEDULE

Starter: straight dough method
Minimum Rising Time: about 3 1/2 hours
Oven Temperature: 475°F
Baking: 6 to 8 minutes

Makes: six 4-by-1 1/4-inch-high bialys about 2.75 ounces/82 grams each or six flat 5-by-1-inch-high bialys coated with poppy seeds 2.5 ounces/72.5 grams each

INGREDIENTS	MEASURE	WEIGHT	
	volume	ounces	grams
King Arthur high-gluten bread flour, preferably, or bread flour	2 cups	10.5 ounces	300 grams
instant yeast (see page 561 for brands)	1/2 teaspoon	--	1.6 grams
salt	1 teaspoon	--	6.6 grams
water, at room temperature (70° to 90°F)	3/4 liquid cup plus 2 tablespoons (7 fluid ounces)	7.25 ounces	206 grams

EQUIPMENT

a heavy-duty stand mixer with dough hook attachment;

a half sheet pan lined with a nonstick liner such as Silpain or parchment;

a baking stone OR baking sheet

1 ▸ **Mix the dough.** In the bowl, whisk together the flour and the yeast, then whisk in the salt (this keeps the yeast from coming in direct contact with the salt which would kill it). With the dough hook, on low speed (#2 if using a KitchenAid), gradually add the water, mixing for about 1 minute or until the flour mixture is moistened. Raise the speed to medium (#4 KitchenAid) and continue mixing for 7 minutes. The dough should clean the bowl but be soft and elastic. Add a little extra flour or water if necessary. (The dough will weigh about 17.75 ounces/506 grams.)

2 > **Let the dough rise.** Place the dough in a 1 1/2-quart or larger dough-rising container or bowl, lightly greased with cooking spray or oil. Press down the dough and lightly spray or oil the top. Cover the container with a lid or plastic wrap. With a piece of tape, mark the side of the container at approximately where double the height of the dough would be. Allow the dough to rise, ideally at 75° to 80°F, for 1 1/2 to 2 hours or until it has doubled.

3 > **Shape the dough and let it rise.** Deflate the dough by firmly pushing it down, and transfer it to a floured counter. Cut the dough into 6 equal pieces (about 3 ounces/84

grams each). Work with one piece at a time, keeping the remaining dough covered. Maintaining as much air as possible in the dough, round each piece by pulling the dough together to form a pouch, stretching to make a smooth skin, and pinching it together where the edges meet. Set it on a floured baking sheet or tray, pinched side down. (The rounds will be 2 1/2 inches by 1 1/2 inches high.) Flour the tops and cover with plastic wrap.

Allow the bialys to rise for about 2 hours at 75° to 80°F or until almost doubled; when pressed lightly in the center, they should keep the impression. If the dough is underrisen, it will puff up in the center instead of maintaining the characteristic hollow crater. The trick for underrisen dough is to make a small hole in the center before adding the filling. Since the dough bakes so quickly, it's easy to test bake one to see if the dough is ready. If you want to be on the safe side, make the hole anyway.

Onion–Poppy Seed Filling

Makes: 2 tablespoons, about 1.25 ounces/38 grams

INGREDIENTS	MEASURE	WEIGHT	
	volume	ounces	grams
vegetable oil	2 1/4 teaspoons	--	--
onion, chopped	6 tablespoons	1.5 ounces	43 grams
poppy seeds	3/4 teaspoon	--	--
sea salt	1/4 teaspoon	--	--
black pepper	to taste	--	--

4 > **Make the onion–poppy seed filling.** In a small sauté pan, heat the oil. Add the onion and sauté over medium heat, stirring often, for about 5 minutes or until translucent. Remove from the heat and add the poppy seeds, salt, and pepper to taste. Cool.

5 > **Preheat the oven.** Preheat the oven to 475°F 30 minutes before baking. Have an oven shelf at the lowest level and place a baking stone or baking sheet on it, and a sheet pan on the floor of the oven, before preheating.

6 > **Make the craters for the filling.** Holding each piece of dough with both hands, with your thumbs in the middle and almost touching, pinch the center of the dough tightly between your thumbs and first two fingers and stretch the dough to 4 1/2 to 5 inches in diameter, forming a crater in the center. Place it on the lined baking sheet and spoon 1 teaspoon of onion–poppy seed filling into the center.

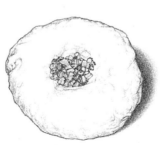

Pinching the center of the dough
and stretching it to make a crater

Onion–poppy seed mixture
placed in center of bialy

7 > **Bake the bialys.** Place the baking sheet with the bialys directly on the hot oven stone or hot baking sheet, or, if using parchment, use a peel or a cookie sheet to slide the parchment with the bialys onto the stone or sheet. Toss 1/2 of ice cubes into the sheet pan on the oven flour, and immediately shut the door. Bake for 6 to 10 minutes or until pale golden and mottled with brown spots (an instant-read thermometer inserted into the center will read about 211°F.).

8 > **Cool the bialys.** Remove the baking sheet or parchment from the oven and, with a pancake turner, transfer the bialys to wire racks to cool until just warm.

STORE   The bialys keep well for 1 day at room temperature in a paper bag. For longer storage, wrap each in airtight plastic wrap and place in freezer bags in the freezer for up to 1 month. Thaw, still wrapped, at room temperature.

VARIATION

To make crisper flat bialys (a favorite in New York), brush the tops with a mixture of 1 large egg white beaten with 1/2 teaspoon water and sprinkle with poppy seeds (use 3 times the weight of the egg white in poppy seeds). Cover with plastic wrap and press down on the bialys with a sheet pan or cookie sheet to make 5 1/2- to 6-inch rounds. Remove the plastic wrap and use the wide end of a chopstick to make about 12 holes in each bialy. Bake as above, but add a few minutes so that the bialys turn golden brown.

POINTERS FOR SUCCESS

>   High-gluten flour ensures maximum chewiness because it has more gluten-forming proteins, which give a stronger structure to the bread. Alternatively, use King

Arthur bread flour, which has a higher gluten-forming protein content than other bread flours. You could also add up to 1/4 cup/1.3 ounces/38 grams of vital wheat gluten to the flour.

>   A stand mixer is far superior to hand mixing for developing the gluten.

>   If you prefer the traditional "schmear" of browned onion paste to the onion and poppy seed filling, simply puree a medium onion in a food processor, spread it on a nonstick baking sheet, and bake for about 1 hour in a 350°F oven, stirring a few times, until lightly browned. Use only about 1/4 teaspoon on the center of each bialy.

THE DOUGH PERCENTAGE

Flour:	100%
Water:	68.6%
Yeast:	0.53%
Salt:	2.2%

English Muffins

This incredibly smooth and supple dough is almost identical to the one for Basic Soft White Sandwich Loaf (page 244), with slightly less butter and slightly more yeast but it is cooked on a griddle rather than baked in an oven. It has that elusive English muffin flavor but is so much more delicious than store-bought muffins in large part because of the sponge pre-ferment technique. An electric griddle is ideal because it holds its temperature so evenly without adjustment. Of course, it's also great for the Crumpets (page 175) and your favorite pancakes.

TIME SCHEDULE

Dough Starter (Sponge): minimum 4 hours, maximum 24 hours
Rising Time: about 3 hours
Griddle Temperature: 275°F (low heat for frying pan)
Cooking Time: 50 minutes

Makes: ten 3-by-just-under-1-inch-high muffins

Dough Starter (Sponge)

INGREDIENTS	MEASURE	WEIGHT	
	volume	ounces	grams
unbleached all-purpose flour (use only Gold Medal, King Arthur, or Pillsbury)	1 cup plus 1 1/2 tablespoons	5.5 ounces	156 grams
water at room temperature (70° to 90°F)	3/4 liquid cup	6.2 ounces	177 grams
honey	1 tablespoon	0.75 ounce	20 grams
instant yeast (see page 561 for brands)	1/2 teaspoon	--	1.6 grams

EQUIPMENT

a heavy-duty stand mixer with dough hook attachment;

a cast-iron griddle OR large heavy skillet;

a 3 1/2-inch biscuit cutter (OR a clean tuna can with top and bottom removed, thoroughly washed to remove any odors)

1 > **Make the sponge.** In the bowl of a stand mixer or another large bowl, place the flour, water, honey, and instant yeast. Whisk until very smooth, incorporating air, about 2 minutes. The sponge will be the consistency of a thick batter.

Flour Mixture

INGREDIENTS	MEASURE	WEIGHT	
	volume	ounces	grams
unbleached all-purpose flour (use only Gold Medal, King Arthur, or Pillsbury)	1 cup plus 1 1/2 tablespoons	5.5 ounces	156 grams
dry milk, preferably nonfat (or replace the water with the scalded milk that has been cooled to lukewarm)	2 tablespoons	1.5 ounces	40 grams
instant yeast	1/2 teaspoon	--	1.6 grams
unsalted butter, softened	3 tablespoons	1.5 ounces	42 grams
salt	1 1/4 teaspoons	--	8.3 grams
cornmeal	about 1/3 cup	about 1.5 ounces	about 42 grams
melted butter, preferably clarified	1 teaspoon	0.3 ounce	9 grams

2 > **Combine the ingredients for the flour mixture.** In a medium bowl, whisk together the flour (reserve 1/4 cup if mixing by hand), dry milk, and yeast. Sprinkle this on top of the sponge; do not stir. Cover tightly with plastic wrap. Allow to ferment for 1 to 4 hours at room temperature, or, for the best flavor development, 1 hour at room temperature and 8 or up to 24 hours in the refrigerator; if mixing by hand, remove

the sponge from the refrigerator about 1 hour before mixing the dough. During this time, the sponge will bubble through the flour blanket in places; this is fine.)

3 > Mix the dough.

Mixer Method

Add the butter and mix with the dough hook on low speed (#2 if using a KitchenAid) until the flour is moistened enough to form a rough dough. Scrape down any bits of dough. Drape plastic wrap over the top of the bowl and allow the dough to rest for 15 to 20 minutes.

Sprinkle on the salt and knead the dough on medium speed (#4 KitchenAid) for 10 minutes. It will be smooth and shiny but tacky enough to stick slightly to your fingers. Add a little flour or water if necessary. (The dough will weigh about 19.75 ounces/568 grams.)

Hand Method

Add the butter and salt and, with a wooden spoon or your hand, stir until all the flour is moistened. Knead the dough in the bowl until it comes together, then scrape it onto a lightly floured counter. Knead the dough for 5 minutes, just to begin to develop the gluten structure, adding as little of the reserved 1/4 cup of flour as possible; use a bench scraper to scrape the dough and gather it together as you knead it. At this point, it will be very sticky. Cover it with the inverted bowl and allow it to rest for 20 minutes. (This rest will make the dough less sticky and easier to work with.)

Knead the dough for another 5 minutes or until it is very smooth and elastic. It should still be tacky enough to stick slightly to your fingers. If the dough is very sticky, add some or all of the remaining reserved flour, or a little extra. (The dough will weigh about 19.75 ounces/568 grams.)

Both Methods

4 > Let the dough rise. Using an oiled spatula or bench scraper, scrape the dough into a 2-quart dough-rising container or bowl, lightly greased with cooking spray or oil. Press down the dough and lightly spray or oil the top. Cover the container with a lid or plastic wrap. With a piece of tape, mark the side of the container at approximately where double the height of the dough would be. Allow the dough to rise, ideally at 75° to 80°F, for about 1 1/2 hours or until doubled.

With oiled fingers, gently deflate the dough by pressing it down, and knead it lightly in the container. Oil the top of the dough, cover it, and refrigerate it for at least 1 hour, or up to 24 hours, to chill and firm the dough.

5 > Shape the dough and let it rise. Sprinkle a half sheet pan or the counter evenly with about two-thirds of the cornmeal. On a lightly floured counter, roll out the dough to a rectangle 8 inches wide by 12 inches long and about 1/4 inch thick. Spray the biscuit cutter with Baker's Joy or flour it, and cut out 6 rounds. They will shrink back to 3 inches once cut, and their height will be closer to 1/2 inch. Set the pieces of dough on top of the cornmeal, leaving about 2 inches between them, and dust the tops lightly. Cover them with a large container, or cover loosely with oiled plastic wrap, and allow them to rise for about 45 minutes or until about 3/4 inch high.

Meanwhile, knead the dough scraps together and press them into a disk. Set it on a flat plate, cover it with plastic wrap, and refrigerate it for at least 1 hour, or up 8 hours to relax the gluten. Then roll the dough on a floured counter to a little larger than 7 inches square by about 1/4 inch thick and cut out 4 more rounds of dough. Allow them to rise, and proceed as for the first batch.

6 > Preheat the griddle or frying pan. If using an electric griddle, preheat it to 275°F. If using a skillet, heat it over low heat until a drop of water sizzles on contact.

7 > Cook the muffins. Brush the griddle or pan lightly with the melted butter using a pancake turner, add the muffins (in batches if necessary) and cook for 10 minutes or until browned underneath. Turn and continue cooking until the bottom is browned (an instant-read thermometer inserted into the center should read about 190°F).

8 > Cool the muffins. Transfer the muffins to a wire rack to cool completely.

STORE The muffins can be stored in a paper bag overnight, frozen, well wrapped (split before freezing), for up to 3 months.

SERVE Split the muffins, using a fork or two forks back to back to create a rough surface full of "nooks and crannies." Toast them, preferably using the top brown element in a toaster oven or a broiler until lightly browned. Heaven.

THE DOUGH PERCENTAGE

Flour:	100%
Water:	60% (includes the water in the honey and butter)
Yeast:	1%
Salt:	2.8%
Fat:	10.9%

Pretzel Bread

This bread was created by Mark Fiorentino, chef boulanger, and Daniel Boulud for the dinner menu of Daniel's bistro DB in New York City. It is a wondrously chewy, flavorful bread shaped like a tiny football, with the shiny salt-sprinkled crust of a classic pretzel. This incredibly popular little bread has been a secret recipe up until now, but Daniel generously offered it to me to share with everyone. Wouldn't this be delicious fun for a Super Bowl party!

TIME SCHEDULE

Dough Starter: straight dough method
Rising Time: 1 1/2 hours
Oven Temperature: 400°F
Baking Time: 15 to 20 minutes

Makes: twelve 1 1/2-by-4-by-1-inch-high little breads about 1 ounce/28 grams each

INGREDIENTS	MEASURE	WEIGHT	
	volume	ounces	grams
bread flour, preferably King Arthur special	1 1/2 cups minus 1 tablespoon	about 8 ounces	225 grams
whole wheat flour	3 tablespoons	scant 1 ounce	25 grams
instant yeast (see page 561 for brands)	3/4 teaspoon	--	2.4 grams
Optional: malt powder	1/2 teaspoon	--	1.5 grams
salt	1 1/8 teaspoon	--	7.4 grams
water, at room temperature (70° to 90°F)	1/2 liquid cup plus 2 teaspoons	4.5 ounces	127 grams
Optional: unsalted butter	1 tablespoon	0.5 ounce	14 grams

EQUIPMENT

a heavy-duty stand mixer with dough hook attachment;

half sheet pans, lined with foil and greased with cooking spray or oil;

a baking stone OR baking sheet

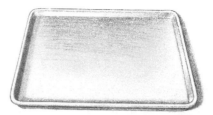

1 > Mix the dough. In the mixer bowl, whisk together the flours, yeast, and optional malt powder. Then whisk in the salt (this keeps the yeast from coming in direct contact with the salt, which would kill it). With the dough hook, on low speed (#2 if using a KitchenAid) add the water, mixing until all the flour is moistened. Add the butter, if desired. Raise the speed to medium (#4 KitchenAid) and knead for 7 minutes. If the dough does not form a smooth ball after 5 minutes, add a little more water by the 1/2 teaspoon. The dough should be very stiff and only somewhat elastic. (The dough will weigh 14 ounces/400 grams.)

2 > Shape the dough. Empty the dough onto a counter. Cut the dough into 12 pieces and shape them into flattened balls 3 1/2 inch wide by 2 1/2 inches high. Let them sit covered for 1 hour. They will not increase in size, but will relax to 4 inches wide by 2 inches high.

Cut each piece of dough into 4 pieces and then cut each piece into 3 (about 1.3 ounces/33 grams each). Roll each one into a ball. Shape into a tapered 4-inch-long football, 1 inch wide in the middle, by placing both hands on top and rolling back and forth to elongate it, applying more pressure to the ends to taper them. Set the footballs on a baking sheet about 2 inches apart.

3 > Let the dough rise. Cover the footballs with oiled plastic wrap and let sit for 30 minutes, just so that they rise very slightly.

Refrigerate, uncovered, for 1 hour so the dough is firm enough to dip in the lye solution without losing its shape (no need to refrigerate if you are brushing the pretzels with egg white and not using the lye solution).

4 > Preheat the oven. Preheat the oven to 400°F 30 minutes before baking. Have an oven shelf at the lowest level and place a baking stone or baking sheet on it, and a cast-iron skillet or sheet pan on the floor of the oven, before preheating.

5 > Make the lye solution. Be very careful when working with lye, as it is extremely caustic and will burn if it comes in direct contact with your skin. In a small stainless steel, glass, or other nonreactive container, mix the lye with the boiling water (cover your nose with a handkerchief until the lye is dissolved to avoid irritation). Allow the mixture to cool.

Lye 4% Solution

INGREDIENTS	MEASURE	WEIGHT	
	volume	ounces	grams
lye	1 teaspoon gently rounded	0.3 ounce	9.5 grams
water	1 liquid cup	8.3 ounces	236 grams
salt, preferably sel gris	1/2 teaspoon	--	3.3 grams

6 > **Slash and glaze the dough.** With a sharp knife or single-edged razor blade, make 2 long shallow slightly diagonal slashes in each bread. **Avoid touching the lye solution with your bare fingers.** Use tongs or rubber gloves to dip each piece of dough in the lye solution, then set it on the prepared pan. (Each batch uses 2 tablespoons of lye solution. Sprinkle the top of the dough with the salt, and bake immediately.

7 > **Bake the breads.** Quickly but gently set the baking sheet on the hot baking stone or hot baking sheet. Toss 1/2 cup of ice cubes into the pan beneath, and immediately shut the door. Bake for 15 to 20 minutes or until deep golden brown (an instant-read thermometer inserted in the center will read about 200°F).

8 > **Cool the pretzels.** Remove the pan from the oven and using tongs, lift the breads onto racks to cool until just warm.

POINTERS FOR SUCCESS

> Only a lye solution will give you the typical pretzel crust, but these little breads are so delicious they are worth making even without the lye glaze. Red Devil lye is available in hardware or plumbing supply stores.

> Alternatively, an egg white glaze will still provide an attractive shiny glaze: Whisk together 1 egg white with 1/2 teaspoon cold water to break up the white. Put it through a sieve into a bowl, and brush each bread with the glaze. Do not let the glaze drip onto the baking sheet or peel, or it will glue them down. Brush with a second coat of the glaze and sprinkle with the salt.

UNDERSTANDING

The optional malt adds its own flavor.

The optional butter adds flavor, softens the crumb slightly, and keeps the bread soft the following day.

Slightly underproofing the dough will cause it to burst open more along the slashes.

THE DOUGH PERCENTAGE

Flour:	100% (bread: **89.3%**, whole wheat: **10.7%**)
Water:	**51%**
Yeast:	**0.96%**
Salt:	**4.3%**

Crumpets

These spongy fried little disks with holes lacing through the top have an interesting floury quality you either love or hate. Toasting crisps the crust and completes the cooking.

The secret to the airiest possible crumpet is the second rising after the addition of the baking soda. Toasted and buttered, they are traditional for breakfast or tea.

TIME SCHEDULE

Rising Time: 1 1/2 hours
Griddle Temperature: 275°F (low heat for frying pan)
Frying Time: about 10 minutes

Makes: six 4-by-3/8-inch-high crumpets

INGREDIENTS	MEASURE	WEIGHT	
	volume	ounces	grams
unbleached all-purpose flour (use only Gold Medal, King Arthur, or Pillsbury)	1 cup plus 1 1/2 tablespoons	5.5 ounces	156 grams
dry milk, preferably nonfat (or replace the water with scalded milk that has been cooled to lukewarm)	2 tablespoons	0.7 ounce	20 grams
instant yeast (see page 561 for brands)	1 teaspoon	--	3.2 grams
sugar	1/2 teaspoon	--	--
salt	1/2 teaspoon	--	3.5 grams
water, at room temperature or warm	3/4 liquid cup plus 2 tablespoons, divided	7 ounces	198 grams
baking soda	1/4 teaspoon	--	--
melted butter, preferably clarified	1 teaspoon	--	4 grams

A heavy-duty stand mixer with paddle attachment OR
a hand-held mixer;

a griddle OR cast-iron skillet OR other heavy pan;

six 4 inch-by-1/2-inch-high rings OR large tuna cans
with top and bottom removed, thoroughly washed to
remove any odors

1 > **Mix the batter.** In a large mixer bowl or other large bowl, with the paddle attachment on low speed (#2 if using a KitchenAid, with the paddle attachment), beat together the flour, dry milk, yeast, sugar, and salt. Add the 3/4 cup water and, gradually raising the speed to medium (#5 KitchenAid), beat for about 5 minutes, until completely smooth.

2 > **Let the batter rise.** Using an oiled rubber spatula, scrape the batter into a dough-rising container or bowl with at least 1-quart capacity. With a piece of tape, mark the side at where double the height of the dough would be. Cover and allow it to rise until doubled, about 1 hour.

3 > **Add the baking soda and the remaining water and let the dough rise again.** In a small bowl, mix together the baking soda and the remaining 2 tablespoons water. Stir into the batter (this will deflate it again) and allow it to rise until almost doubled, about 30 minutes. The batter will be filled with bubbles.

4 > **Preheat the griddle or frying pan.** If using an electric griddle, preheat it to 275°F. If using a skillet, heat it over low heat until a drop of water sizzles when added.

5 > **Fry the crumpets.** Brush the griddle or pan and the inside of the crumpet rings lightly with the melted butter. Set the rings in the pan (cook the crumpets in 2 batches if necessary). Use a ladle or large spoon to pour the batter into the rings filling them about two-thirds full. The batter will rise to the top during cooking. Cook the crumpets for 10 minutes or until they are nicely browned underneath and have lost their shine and appear dull on top (to check, using tongs, lift off a ring and slide a spatula underneath). Turn the crumpets and continue cooking until the bottoms are browned.

6 > Cool the crumpets. Remove the crumpets to a wire rack to cool completely.

STORE   The crumpets can be stored overnight in a paper bag or frozen, well wrapped, for up to 3 months: thaw before toasting.

SERVE   Toast the crumpets until they are warmed through and the outsides are crisp.

UNDERSTANDING

Crumpets fall somewhere between a batter and a bread, containing double the water of a basic bread and three times the yeast plus baking soda.

THE DOUGH PERCENTAGE

Flour:	100%
Water:	113%
Yeast:	2%
Salt:	2.1%

Butter Popovers

Popovers are often made simply with flour, eggs, and milk, without butter, but butter not only adds its unmistakably good flavor, it also improves the texture. These popovers, crisp on the outside and almost cake-like spongy on the inside, are incredibly tender and delicious, and they also have something very special to recommend them: unlike regular popover batter, which must be mixed at least two hours before baking, these can go straight into the oven *immediately after mixing*! They are good as a dinner roll or a brunch treat with butter and preserves. They can even be baked several hours ahead and recrisped just before serving.

TIME SCHEDULE

Oven Temperature: 425°F
Baking Time: 1 hour

Makes: 6 large (about 4 inches high) popovers or 12 small ones (muffin size)

INGREDIENTS	MEASURE	WEIGHT	
	volume	ounces	grams
Wondra flour	1 cup plus 3 tablespoons (measured by shaking from container into cup)	about 5 ounces	145 grams
salt	1/2 teaspoon	--	--
sugar	1/2 teaspoon	--	--
whole milk	1 liquid cup	8.5 ounces	242 grams
2 large eggs	3 fluid ounces	3.5 ounces	100 grams (weighed without shells)
unsalted butter, melted and cooled but still liquid	4 tablespoons, divided	2 ounces	56 grams

EQUIPMENT

a 6-cup popover pan OR 12-cup mini popover pan (if
using black metal, lower the initial 425°F to 400°F) OR
a 12-cup standard muffin pan

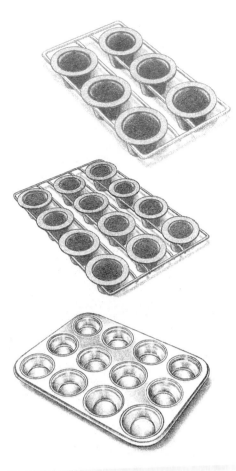

1 > **Preheat the oven.** Preheat the oven to 425°F 30
minutes before baking. Set a rack on the second rung
from the bottom.

2 > **Mix the batter.** In a large bowl, whisk together the
flour, salt, and sugar. Using a whisk, slowly stir in the
milk. Continuing with the whisk or using a hand-held
electric or rotary beater, add the eggs one at a time,
beating for about 1 minute after each addition,
then beating until the batter is smooth. Beat in 2
tablespoons of the melted butter. (Small lumps of
butter will remain visible.) Transfer the batter to a
pitcher. If not using immediately, cover and refrigerate for up to 24 hours; beat lightly before pouring
the batter into the pans.

3 > **Prepare the pan.** Use a small pastry feather or
brush to coat the entire interior of the pan with the remaining melted butter. Place
1 teaspoon of butter in each of the 6 popover cups. Or, if using the muffin pan, use
1/2 teaspoon in each cup.

Three to 5 minutes before baking, place the popover or muffin pan in the oven to
heat until the butter is very hot and beginning to brown (don't allow it to burn). Place
a large sheet of aluminum foil on the rack under the tin to catch any bubbling fat.

4 > **Fill the pan and bake the popovers.** Remove the pan from the oven and pour the
batter on the hot butter, filling the cups half-full. Bake for 15 minutes. Lower the
heat to 350°F and continue baking for 40 to 45 minutes for the large popovers, 20 to
25 minutes for the muffin-sized ones. They will pop well above the sides of the
popover or muffin cups, rising to about three times their original height.

5 > **Ten minutes before the end of the baking time, release the steam.** Open the oven
door and quickly make a small slit in the side of each raised popover to release the
steam and allow the centers to dry out more.

6 > Cool the popovers slightly. With pot holders, gently lift out the popovers one at a time, holding each one from the top, and set them on a wire rack to cool slightly. If you are not ready to serve them, they can be cooled to room temperature, then reheated later on a baking sheet in a 350°F oven, for 5 minutes. The crisp outer shell will keep them from collapsing.

VARIATION

Yorkshire Popovers   Substitute an equal amount of rendered beef fat for the butter.

POINTERS FOR SUCCESS

>   In place of Wondra flour, you can use 1 cup/5 ounces/145 grams (measured by dip-and-sweep) *bleached* all-purpose flour (use only Gold Medal or Pillsbury). In that case, mix 2 tablespoons of the melted butter with the flour mixture before adding the milk, refrigerate the batter for at least 2 hours, or up to 24 hours before baking.

>   If you would like to make only half a batch, fill any empty popover or muffin cups with water. This creates steam, which will help the popovers rise. If you leave the cups empty, the heat is drawn more to them than to the filled cups, slowing the baking and decreasing the rise.

UNDERSTANDING

Wondra flour is a granular form of flour developed in the 1960s by General Mills. It is equal in protein content to bleached all-purpose flour but dissolves instantly in liquid because it has been subjected to a process called agglomeration (also used to make instant coffee powder and powdered milk). It is produced essentially by misting flour with water and then spray-drying it with compressed air, which separates the flour into particles of even size and shape that will not clump together when mixed with liquid. That even absorption of liquid is what makes it possible to bake these popovers immediately after mixing the batter.

There is no chemical leavening in this batter. Leavening is provided by the egg and also by steam from the milk as it heats in the oven.

THE DOUGH PERCENTAGE

Flour:	100%
Water:	188% (includes the water in the milk, butter, and egg whites)
Salt:	2.3%
Fat:	45% (includes the fat in the milk and egg yolks)

Dutch Baby

A Dutch baby is actually a giant crater-shaped popover, perfect for accommodating a filling of sautéed caramelized apples, peaches, or fresh berries and a billow of crème fraîche or whipped cream.

As is so often the case, it is the simplest things that require the most work to perfect. My goal was for a Dutch baby that had crisp, puffy sides but a tender, almost custardy bottom (as opposed to an eggy/rubbery one). The final result of many tests is this crunchiest, puffiest, and most tender version. The secrets are coating the flour with the butter before adding the milk, and adding 2 extra egg whites and enough sugar to tenderize and flavor the batter.

TIME SCHEDULE

Advance Preparation: minimum 1 hour, maximum 24 hours
Oven Temperature: 425°F
Baking Time: 1 hour

Serves: 4 to 6

Batter

INGREDIENTS	MEASURE	WEIGHT	
	volume	ounces	grams
bleached all-purpose flour (use only Gold Medal or Pillsbury)	1 cup	5 ounces	142 grams
sugar	3 tablespoons	1.3 ounces	37 grams
salt	1/4 teaspoon	--	1.7 grams
unsalted butter, melted	4 tablespoons, divided	2 ounces	56 grams
milk	1 liquid cup	8.5 ounces	242 grams
2 large eggs plus 2 large egg whites	5 fluid ounces	5.6 ounces (weighed without shells)	160 grams
pure vanilla extract	1 teaspoon	--	--

an 11-inch steel Dutch baby pan OR cast-iron skillet (if using the skillet, lower the initial 425°F to 400°F)

1 > Mix the batter.

Food Processor Method

In a food processor with a metal blade, process the flour, sugar, and salt, for a few seconds to mix. Add 2 tablespoons of the melted butter and process until it is the size of tiny peas, about 20 seconds. Scrape the sides of the container. With the motor on, add the milk, eggs and egg whites, and vanilla and process for about 20 seconds or until the batter is smooth.

Hand Method

In a medium bowl, stir together the flour, sugar, and salt. Add 2 tablespoons of the melted butter and use a fork to mash and mix it in until it is the size of tiny peas. With a rotary beater or whisk, slowly beat in the eggs and then egg whites one at a time, beating for about 1 minute after each addition. Then beat until the batter is fairly smooth (small lumps of butter will remain visible). Beat in the vanilla extract.

Both Methods

2 > Let the batter rest. Allow the batter to sit at room temperature for 1 hour before baking, or cover and refrigerate it for up to 24 hours. Allow it to come to room temperature and beat it lightly before baking.

3 > Preheat the oven. Preheat the oven to 425°F 30 minutes before baking. Have a rack in the bottom third of the oven.

4 > Prepare the pan. Remelt the remaining 2 tablespoons butter in the pan. Use a small pastry feather or brush to coat the entire interior with the butter.

Three minutes before baking, place the pan in the oven and heat it until the butter is hot and bubbling.

5 > Fill the pan and bake the Dutch baby. Remove the pan from the oven and pour the batter on top of the hot butter. Bake for 15 minutes. Lower the heat to 350°F and continue baking for 30 minutes or until puffed around the edges above the sides of the pan and golden brown. *About 15 minutes before the end of the baking time, open the oven door and quickly make 3 small slits in the center of the Dutch baby to release the steam and allow the center to dry more.*

Apple Filling

INGREDIENTS	MEASURE	WEIGHT	
	volume	ounces	grams
unsalted butter, softened	4 1/2 tablespoons	2.2 ounces	63 grams
2 pounds Granny Smith or other tart apples (about 6 medium) peeled, cored, and sliced 1/4 inch thick	6 cups sliced	25 ounces	717 grams
freshly squeezed lemon juice	2 teaspoons	--	10 grams
light brown sugar	3 tablespoons	1.5 ounces	40 grams
granulated sugar	3 tablespoons	1.3 ounces	38 grams
ground cinnamon	3/4 teaspoon	--	--
nutmeg, preferably freshly grated	1/4 teaspoon	--	--
salt	1/4 plus 1/16 teaspoon	--	--
Optional garnish: crème fraîche or whipped cream	1 cup	about 8 ounces	232 grams

6 > While the Dutch baby is baking, prepare the apples. In a large nonreactive frying pan, melt the butter over the medium heat until bubbling. Add the apple slices and sprinkle them with the lemon juice, brown sugar, granulated sugar, cinnamon, nutmeg, and salt. Sauté the apples, stirring occasionally, for 12 to 15 minutes. After about the first 5 minutes of cooking, the apples will begin to exude liquid. Raise the heat slightly until it evaporates, then lower the heat to medium and continue cooking until the slices are glazed and tender when pierced with a cake tester or sharp knife. Turn off the heat and cover to keep warm.

7 > Fill the Dutch baby and serve. Slide the Dutch baby onto a serving plate (slip a spatula between the sides of the pan and the pastry if necessary to dislodge it) and fill it with the apples. If desired, spoon some crème fraîche or whipped cream on top, and pass the rest.

REHEAT Place the Dutch baby on a baking sheet and heat it in a preheated 350°F oven for about 10 minutes. The texture of the dough will not be as moist and tender as when freshly baked.

For a *Baby Dutch Baby,* to serve 2, simply divide the recipe in half and use an 8-inch ovenproof skillet (preferably cast-iron). Decrease the baking time at 350°F to 15 minutes and make the slits 10 minutes before the end of the baking time.

POINTERS FOR SUCCESS

> To core and slice the apples, cut them in half and use a melon baller to scoop out the cores. Slice each half into quarters, and then each piece into 3 slices, or 4 if the apples are very large.

> If you prefer a more chewy, slightly less puffy version, simply leave out the extra egg whites.

UNDERSTANDING

Letting the batter rest allows the flour to absorb the liquid evenly. Coating some of the flour with the melted butter keeps the proteins in the flour from absorbing as much of the milk and forming gluten. A certain amount of gluten development is necessary in order to support the puff. I tried using one-quarter cake flour instead of coating the flour with butter, and the batter would not puff at all! Replacing the milk with buttermilk decreased the puffing by three-quarters due to the effect of the buttermilk's acidity on the gluten. Adding powdered buttermilk to the milk for flavor, however, has no effect on the puffing.

Adding extra whole eggs to the basic recipe would toughen the dough, making it rubbery, but the extra egg whites make it airier, crisper, and more tender.

This batter is actually quite similar to cream puff pastry dough, with half the butter, 1 less egg, and 1 less egg white. Cream puff dough is cooked slightly before baking, making it stiff enough to pipe. The extra butter in cream puff dough keeps it from becoming rubbery because of the extra egg, and the resulting puff is crisper on the outside than the Dutch baby, but the insides of the two are actually quite similar.

The leavening in this batter is provided entirely by the egg.

THE DOUGH PERCENTAGE

Flour:	100%
Water:	229% (includes the water in the milk, butter, and egg whites)
Salt:	1.2%
Fat:	46% (includes the fat in the milk and egg yolks)

Flatbreads

3.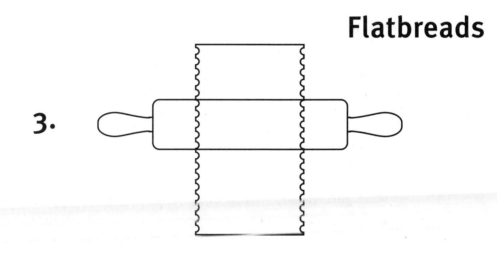

THIS IS EVERYONE'S FAVORITE CATEGORY, FROM PIZZA, THE ULTIMATE healthful fast food and a meal in itself, to pitas that inflate like little balloons to make fantastic sandwiches to herbed matzoh, which bubbles but doesn't rise because it contains no leavening and is fabulous as an appetizer.

Pizza is so important to me I made a pilgrimage to New Haven to sample the renowned Frank Pepe's version and gratefully received some helpful tips from his daughter, who, as luck would have it, was our waitress. I also had a precious private lesson from Vinny Scotto, who made thousands of pizzas when working at Al Forno in Providence, Rhode Island, where the American thin-crust pizza craze began, and continues to make them in his own restaurant, Gonzo, in New York's Greenwich Village. All of this was synthesized into my final favorite version offered here, along with favorite suggested toppings. One of them, the steamed clams, came from dinners enjoyed at a New Jersey restaurant on the Delaware River, near our country home, that specialized in steamers and pizza. We would always order steamers as an appetizer and I would save a few of my plump butter-dipped steamers to set on top of our main-course pizza. Nowadays anything goes atop a pizza, and I'm all for it, as long as it isn't too thick a layer, because my number one criterion for pizza is that it have a crisp crust.

In the north of Italy, pizza is called *focaccia*. By either name it can be crisp or soft and chewy, round, oblong, or rectangular, thick or thin, and lightly adorned with herbs or laden with multiple toppings. But when I think of pizza, I think of a thin round of dough topped with cheese and other savory ingredients, whereas when I think of focaccia, at least as I know it in America, I imagine rectangular doughs of varying thicknesses but always somewhat thicker than pizza, with dimples containing tiny pools of olive oil and a scattering of herbs and, perhaps, garlic. The focaccia recipes in this chapter include a range of different types of dough and radically different mixing techniques, which are responsible for their differing textures, from cake-like to chewy. All have a much higher proportion of water than most recipes which is responsible for their light texture. The Grilled Focaccia (page 216) has the lowest amount of water (69.9 percent) and is mixed the least, resulting in a crisp crust and soft, cake-like interior. The Focaccia Layered with Fresh Herbs (page 209) contains 78.7 percent water and is vigorously hand-kneaded, resulting in an exceptionally light and airy crumb, with a layer of fresh herbs just under the crisp top crust. The Rosemary Focaccia Sheet (page 205) contains an amazing 113.5 percent water and is beaten in a stand mixer for twenty minutes. This creates a light but extraordinarily chewy dough.

Pita, the flatbread of the Middle East, which puffs up during baking to form a pocket in the middle, is, interestingly enough, almost identical to my basic pizza dough or grilled focaccia dough (65 percent water), but it is made with a higher-protein flour and is kneaded to develop gluten, which enables the dough to support its rise.

Much as I adore pizza, focaccia, and pita, the flavorful flatbreads of India could have held me willing captive during my stay in Delhi many years ago. As most Indian homes do not possess a tandoor oven, tandoori breads (and tandoori chicken) were considered restaurant fare. But every night at the home of my friends the Puris, a never-ending procession of chapati arrived during the meal. I have included my favorite Indian flatbread rarely found in this country: a fried paratha, which is like a more refined, slightly flaky chapati, stuffed with spicy ground meat.

UNDERSTANDING

The proportions of the basic essential ingredients in flatbreads fall into the range of 53 to 113.5 percent water, 0 to 1.6 percent instant yeast, and 1.3 to 2.9 percent salt. These percentages are based on the Baker's Percentage, in which every ingredient is based on the flour which is given the value of 100 percent. Some of these breads also contain from 1.4 to 12.7 percent butterfat or oil.

Perfect Pizza Dough

I have given a great deal of thought to pizza dough because, like the rest of the world, I adore pizza. When thin-crusted grilled pizza arrived on the scene, I was convinced that it was the answer, but as it became trendy, and the crust became so thin it became brittle and so grilled it became charred, I realized that what I like most in a pizza crust is something between a thin, crisp crust and the more bready old style. After years of handing over my crust edges to my husband, I realized that I had achieved my goal of crisp, light, and chewy crust when I found myself with an empty plate and no crust edges to offer!

The secret of this special crust is a wet dough that has very little gluten, which keeps it tender. The secret to a well-shaped but crisp crust without the grittiness of cornmeal was given to me by the contractor for my country kitchen, Andy Badding, who became a good friend. While going to college in his hometown of Buffalo, he worked at a pizza parlor where he learned the secret of starting the pizza on a pan, then, once set, sliding it directly onto the baking stone. This means that no cornmeal is necessary for the bottom of the dough and the crust is perfectly crunchy.

After trying many flours, I have found that *unbleached* all-purpose flour produces the most tender crust, but my number one preference is actually for the Italian-style low-protein flour (see page 551) that makes the dough easier to stretch and gives it slight extra chew without making it tough.

Another important thing I discovered is that unless you have a pizza oven that gets as hot as 600°F, it is better not to add the topping until the last five minutes of baking, so the cheese doesn't become tough and the other toppings overcooked. Also, though I love the flavor of fresh mozzarella available in Italian cheese shops, it does not develop the stringiness I enjoy in a pizza topping, so I use a commercial brand. Keep in mind that tempting as it is to load the dough with delicious things, too much topping added to a pizza while it is baking makes for a soggy crust.

Pizza makes a casual, friendly, easy-going meal. I include the classic Margherita topping in the recipe, with my other top favorites as variations, but they are only rough guides. Pizza can be anything you want it to be: feel free to experiment. Here's one case where exact quanties can be thrown to the winds. (Bet you never thought to hear me say this!)

One of my favorite pizzas is Arugula Pizza Bianca (page 193), consisting simply of mozzarella, Parmigiano-Reggiano, and ricotta, with arugula and a drizzle of olive oil tossed on after baking. It's kind of like a salad atop a pizza.

The Alsatian onion pizza came into being when I made my Alsatian Onion Tart for *The Pie and Pastry Bible*. That filling was so marvelous that I tried it out on some pizza dough. I ended up preferring it to the tart crust!

This recipe makes a 10-inch pizza, which I find perfect for two. It can be divided in half to make two 7-inch pizzas (same 10-minute baking time) or increased to make several 7- or 10-inch pizzas. Pizza larger than 10 inches makes for unwieldy slices.

TIME SCHEDULE

Minimum Rising Time: 2 hours
Oven Temperature: 475°F
Baking Time: 10 to 15 minutes

Makes: 7 ounces/200 grams dough/one 10-inch pizza (or two 7-inch pizzas)
Serves: 2

INGREDIENTS	MEASURE	WEIGHT	
	volume	ounces	grams
flour, preferably King Arthur Italian-style or *unbleached* all-purpose flour (use only Gold Medal, King Arthur, or Pillsbury)	3/4 cup plus 1 tablespoon	4 ounces	113 grams
instant yeast (see page 561 for brands)	1/2 teaspoon	--	1.6 grams
sugar	1/2 teaspoon	--	2 grams
salt	1/2 teaspoon	--	3.3 grams
water, at room temperature (70° to 90°F)	1/3 liquid cup	2.75 ounces	79 grams
olive oil	4 teaspoons	0.6 ounce	18 grams

2 smaller pizza pans, about 9 1/2 inches, OR
1 large pizza pan, about 12 1/2 inches, preferably black steel;

a baking stone

1 > **One hour before shaping, or for best flavor development, 8 to 24 hours ahead, mix the dough.** In a small bowl, whisk together the flour, instant yeast, and sugar. Whisk in the salt (this keeps the yeast from coming into direct contact with the salt, which would kill it). Make a well in the center and pour in the water. Using a rubber spatula or wooden spoon, gradually stir the flour into the water until all the flour is moistened and a dough just begins to form, about 20 seconds. It should come away from the bowl but still stick to it a little, and be a little rough looking, not silky smooth. Do not overmix, as this will cause the dough to become stickier.

2 > **Let the dough rise.** Pour the oil into a 2-cup measuring cup (to give the dough room to double in size) or a small bowl. With oiled fingers or an oiled spatula, place the dough in the oiled cup and turn it over to coat on all sides with the oil. Cover it tightly. If you want to use it soon, allow it to sit at room temperature for 1 hour or until doubled. For the best flavor development, make the dough at least 6 hours or up to 24 hours ahead, and allow it to sit at room temperature for only 30 minutes or until slightly puffy. Then set the dough, still in the measuring cup, in the refrigerator. Remove it 1 hour before you want to put it in the oven.

3 > **Prepare the Margherita topping (see Step 7) or one of the tomato toppings from page 193.**

4 > **Preheat the oven.** Preheat the oven to 475°F 1 hour before baking. Have an oven shelf at the lowest level and place a baking stone on it before preheating.

5 > **Shape the pizza and let it rise.** With oiled fingers, lift the dough out of the measuring cup or bowl. Holding the dough in one hand, pour a little of the oil left in the cup or bowl onto the pizza pan(s), and spread it all over the pan(s) with your fingers. (If making 2 pizzas, divide the dough in half.) Set the dough on the pan(s) and press

it down with your fingers to deflate it gently. Shape it into a smooth round by tucking under the edges. If there are any holes, knead it very lightly until smooth. Allow the dough to sit for 15 minutes, covered, to relax it.

Using your fingertips, press the dough from the center to the outer edge to stretch it into a 10-inch circle (7 inches for the 2 pizzas), leaving the outer 1/2 inch thicker than the rest to form a lip. If the dough resists stretching (as will happen if you have activated the gluten by overkneading it), cover it with plastic wrap and let it rest for a few minutes longer before proceeding. Brush the surface of the dough with any remaining olive oil. Cover it with plastic wrap and allow it to sit for 30 to 45 minutes, until it becomes light and slightly puffy with air.

6 > **Bake the pizza.** Set the pizza pan directly on the hot stone and bake for 5 minutes.

7 > **Add the toppings.**

Pizza Margherita

6 tablespoons Tomato Sauce (page 193)
3/4 to 1 cup (3 to 4 ounces/85 to 113 grams) coarsely grated mozzarella
Optional: 1/4 cup ricotta (2 ounces/60 grams)

Remove the pan from the oven and spread the tomato sauce on the dough, leaving a narrow boarder. Strew the mozzarella over the sauce. If desired, drop little blobs of the ricotta on top. Return the pan to the stone for 5 minutes or until the cheese is melted and the crust golden; or, for an extra crisp and browned bottom crust, using a pancake turner or baker's peel, slide the pizza from the pan directly onto the stone. After 2 minutes, slip a small metal spatula under one edge, and if the bottom is golden, raise the pizza to a higher shelf.

8 > **Serve the pizza.** Transfer the pizza to a cutting board and cut with a pizza wheel, sharp knife, or scissors.

VARIATION

Margherita with Steamed Clams   After fully baking the pizza, arrange 12 steamed clams, preferably steamers or littlenecks, on top of the melted cheese. It's especially delicious if you dip them in melted butter first. If using canned clams, drain them well and simmer them in a little olive oil with a smashed garlic clove and light sprinkling of parlsey.

Cinnamon Raisin Loaf > page 260

Basic Soft White Sandwich Loaf > page 244

Basic Soft White Sandwich Loaf
with peanut butter and jelly

Stages of Poolish (sponge starter)
for baguette > page 337:
(*top*): fully risen; (*bottom*): just beginning
to recede, ready to use

Left page, top: Stages of liquid sourdough starter > page 433 (*from left to right*): 1) just fed; 2) risen; 3) liquidy-stretchy risen levain
bottom: Stages of stiff sourdough starter (*from left to right*): 1) just fed; 2) risen; 3) stretchy-ropey risen levain

Basic Sourdough loaves with cheeses, fruits, and nuts > page 444

Golden Semolina Torpedo with ricotta
and honey > page 365

TOMATO TOPPINGS

Pizza Tomato Sauce (makes 3/4 cup, enough for two 10-inch pizzas)

1 cup (8 ounces/230 grams), peeled, seeded, and chopped ripe tomatoes, (include any juices) or canned
  crushed tomatoes, with their juices
1 tablespoon olive oil
1 large garlic clove, chopped
1/4 teaspoon hot pepper flakes
2 teaspoons chopped fresh oregano or 1/2 teaspoon dried
1/4 teaspoon sugar
1/4 teaspoon salt
Freshly ground black pepper to taste

In a small saucepan, combine all of the ingredients and simmer, stirring frequently, until reduced to about 3/4 cup, 10 to 12 minutes. Taste for seasoning, and cool.

I prefer to leave this chunky, but to make a smooth sauce, simply process it for a few seconds in a food processor.

Oven-Dried Cherry or Grape Tomatoes

With a small sharp paring knife or serrated knife, slice tomatoes horizontally in half and place them cut side up on a jelly-roll pan or cookie sheet. (You will need about 22 tomatoes [3.5 ounces/100 grams] for a 10-inch pizza, to replace the tomato sauce.) Sprinkle lightly with salt, a little sugar, and a little olive oil. Bake in a 250°F oven until the tomatoes start to shrivel but are still juicy, about 2 hours. Simply scatter the tomatoes on top of the mozzarella cheese before the last 5 minutes of baking.

FAVORITE PIZZA VARIATIONS

Arugula Pizza Bianca

1/4 cup (2 ounces/57 grams) ricotta
1 1/2 tablespoons grated Parmigiano-Reggiano
3/4 to 1 cup (3 to 4 ounces/85 to 113 grams) coarsely shredded whole-milk mozzarella, preferably
  Polly-O or The Mozzarella Company (see Sources, page 572)
2 cups loosely packed (1 1/2 ounces/42 grams) trimmed arugula
Salt and freshly ground black pepper to taste
Extra virgin olive oil

After the first 5 minutes of baking, remove the pizza pan from the oven and spread the ricotta over the dough, leaving a narrow border. Sprinkle the Parmesan on top and then the shredded mozzarella. Return the pan to the stone for 5 minutes or until the cheese is melted and the crust golden; or, for an extra crisp and browned bottom crust, using a pancake turner or baker's peel, slide the pizza from the pan directly onto the stone. After 2 minutes, slip a small metal spatula under one edge, and if the bottom is golden, raise the pizza to a higher shelf.

Remove the pizza from the oven and top with arugula, salt, pepper, and a sprinkling of extra virgin olive oil.

Mushroom Pizza Bianca (White Pizza)

2 scant tablespoons olive oil
8 ounces (227 grams) button mushrooms, sliced (2 1/2 cups)
Rounded 1/4 teaspoon salt
1 large garlic clove, smashed
3/4 to 1 cup (3 to 4 ounces/85 to 113 grams) coarsely shredded whole-milk mozzarella, preferably
 Polly-O or The Mozzarella Company (see Sources, page 572)
1/4 teaspoon dried oregano
Hot pepper flakes to taste

In a large sauté pan, heat the olive oil over low heat. Add the mushrooms in a single layer, sprinkle with the salt, and add the garlic. Cook for about 20 minutes, stirring often, until the liquid has evaporated and the mushrooms are just beginning to brown. Allow them to cool, and discard any large pieces of garlic.

After the first 5 minutes of baking, remove the pizza pan from the oven and sprinkle the mozzarella all over the dough. Top with the mushrooms, leaving a narrow border and spreading them evenly. Sprinkle with the oregano and hot pepper flakes. Return the pan to the stone for 5 minutes or until the cheese is melted and the crust golden; or, for an extra crisp and browned bottom crust, using a pancake turner or baker's peel, slide the pizza from the pan directly onto the stone. After 2 minutes, slip a small metal spatula under one edge, and if the bottom is golden, raise the pizza to a higher shelf.

Red and Gold Bell Pepper, Onion, and Gorgonzola Dolce

1 1/2 tablespoons olive oil
1 medium onion, halved lengthwise and thinly sliced
1 red bell pepper, cored, seeded, and cut lengthwise into strips
1 orange bell pepper, cored, seeded, and cut lengthwise into strips
Salt and freshly ground black pepper
3/4 cup (3 ounces) crumbled sweet Gorgonzola (dolce) or Taleggio
A few leaves of fresh basil, sliced into thin strips (chiffonade)
Optional: 6 anchovy fillets

In a large (12-inch) sauté pan, heat the olive oil over medium heat. Add the onion and bell pepper and cook, stirring often, until the peppers are tender when pierced with a fork, about 15 minutes. Transfer to a plate. Add salt and pepper to taste and let cool, then separate the peppers from the onion.

After the first 5 minutes of baking, remove the pizza pan from the oven and spread the onion evenly over the surface, leaving a narrow border. Arrange the peppers in a spiral on top of the onions. Strew little bits of the Gorgonzola or Taleggio on top and sprinkle with the basil. Return the pan to the stone for 5 minutes or until the cheese is melted and the crust golden; or, for an extra crisp and browned bottom crust, using a pancake turner or baker's peel, slide the pizza from the pan directly onto the stone. After 2 minutes, slip a small metal spatula under one edge, and if the bottom is golden, raise the pizza to a higher shelf. Garnish, if desired, with the anchovy fillets.

Alsatian Onion Pizza

1 tablespoon olive oil
1 tablespoon unsalted butter
3 medium yellow onions, halved, very thinly sliced (use the 1-millimeter slicing disk of a food processor)
   (3 1/2 cups/1 pound/454 grams)
1/8 teaspoon sugar
1/4 teaspoon salt
1/8 teaspoon freshly ground black pepper
1 medium garlic clove, minced
1/2 teaspoon fresh thyme leaves
2 tablespoons (0.25 ounce/7 grams) loosely packed grated Swiss Gruyére
4 black oil-cured olives, halved and pitted

In a large heavy skillet, heat the oil and butter over low heat until bubbling. Add the onions and sprinkle with the sugar, salt, and pepper. Cover tightly and cook, without stirring, for about 45 minutes over the lowest possible heat. The onions will be soft and will have released a little liquid.

Raise the heat to medium and cook uncovered, stirring often, until all liquid has evaporated and the onions are deep gold in color. Reduce the heat to low, add the garlic and thyme, and cook for 3 minutes, stirring often. Remove from the heat. (You will have 3/4 cup/6 ounces/172 grams of onion mixture.)

After the first 5 minutes of baking, remove the pizza pan from the oven and spread the onion mixture evenly over the dough, leaving a narrow border. Sprinkle evenly with the Gruyère and arrange the olives decoratively on top. Return the pan to the stone for 5 minutes or until the cheese is melted and the crust golden; or, for an extra crisp and browned bottom crust, using a pancake turner or baker's peel, slide the pizza from the pan directly onto the stone. After 2 minutes, slip a small metal spatula under one edge, and if the bottom is golden, raise the pizza to a higher shelf.

POINTERS FOR SUCCESS

> The pizza dough can be frozen after the first 5 minutes of baking for up to 3 months. When ready to use, simply add the toppings and bake for 5 minutes or until the cheese has melted.

> A proof box or plastic box (see page 588) is great for covering the shaped pizza dough to keep it from drying. Plastic wrap works well but requires a little care when lifting it off the dough.

> DeMarle (see page 586) makes a special Silpain pizza mold ideal for individual 7-inch pizzas. The mold holds 6 pizzas: you can make 6 pizzas if you multiply the recipe by 3, or cut the molds into individual sizes. After shaping the dough, set the mold(s) on a layer of paper towels to absorb any excess oil, so that it won't ooze onto the baking stone. The baked pizzas release easily from the mold after baking; just flex it slightly, and the pizzas pop right out.

> Ovens vary for both top and bottom browning, so adjust accordingly. If your oven reaches 500°F and you use a preheated baking stone, the initial baking of the dough, without the topping, may take only 2 minutes. If the bottom crust is fully browned before the topping and top crust are baked, simply transfer it from the stone onto a higher shelf. If the bottom isn't browning enough, slip the pizza from the pan directly onto the hot stone. Once you gain a sense of the heat of your oven, you can use the same technique for every pizza.

VARIATION

Grilled Pizza   An outdoor gas or charcoal grill is the ideal way to make pizza during hot weather to avoid heating up the kitchen. A black steel pizza pan (see page 590) ensures that the heat is perfectly even and browns the bottom crust impeccably.

Preheat a covered gas grill to 500°F according to manufacturer's directions. Or, if using a charcoal grill, build the coals on one side of the grill and light the fire 40 minutes ahead. With any grill, leave all the vents open.

If using a gas grill, turn one side of it to low. Place the pizza, still on the pan, on the hotter side of the grill and grill, covered, for 2 minutes. Slide a pancake turner underneath the dough to loosen it and slip it directly onto the cooler side of grill (use tongs if you have them) for just a few seconds—you'll smell it browning. Lift an edge with the pancake turner to check, and as soon as deep brown grill marks appear, return the pizza to the pan and transfer it to a heatproof surface (cover the grill to keep in the heat). Add the toppings and return the pizza, on the pan, to the cooler side of the grill. Cover the grill and cook for 7 to 8 minutes longer or until the cheese is melted and the crust begins to brown around the edges.

THE DOUGH PERCENTAGE

Flour:	100%
Water:	69.9%
Yeast:	1.4%
Salt:	2.9%
Oil:	11.9%

Potato Flatbread Pizza

This potato flatbread is actually a pizza dough made softer, moister, and lighter with the addition of mashed potatoes, egg, and butter. The resulting dough is as soft as a down pillow, the crust crisp on the outside with just enough chew on the inside. It has become a permanent appetizer on the Grouse Mountain menu, with daily varying herbed and spicy toppings, cut into squares and presented in an overlapping circle.

The mushroom/onion topping given here is the one I enjoyed when first introduced to this flatbread. You could also use any of the toppings on pages 192–95. The instructions here are for one large 10-inch pizza (or six large pizzas for a crowd), but the basic recipe can also be divided in half to make 2 smaller pizzas; see the variation on page 199.

Special thanks to Rick Kangas, chef at the Grouse Mountain Grill in Beaver Creek, Colorado, for offering this recipe.

TIME SCHEDULE

Minimum Rising Time: about 2 hours
Oven Temperature: 475°F
Baking Time: 5 minutes

Makes: 7 ounces/200 grams dough, One 10-inch flatbread
Serves: 2 as an appetizer, 1 as a main dish

INGREDIENTS	MEASURE	WEIGHT	
	volume	ounces	grams
unbleached all-purpose flour (use only Gold Medal, King Arthur, or Pillsbury)	3/4 cup	3.5 ounces	100 grams
instant yeast (see page 561 for brands)	1/4 teaspoon	--	0.8 gram
sugar	2 teaspoons	--	8 grams
salt	3/8 teaspoon	--	2.5 grams
mashed potato	2 tablespoons plus 2 teaspoons	1.3 ounces	38 grams
unsalted butter, softened	1/2 tablespoon	0.25 ounce	7 grams
water, preferably potato water, at room temperature (70° to 90°F)	3 tablespoons	1.5 ounces	44 grams
lightly beaten egg	1 1/2 teaspoons	0.3 ounce	8 grams
olive or vegetable oil	1 teaspoon	--	4.5 grams

EQUIPMENT

a pizza pan, about 12 1/2 inches, preferably black steel;

a baking stone

1 > **Mix the dough.** In a small bowl, whisk together the flour, yeast, and sugar. Then whisk in the salt (this keeps the yeast from coming in direct contact with the salt, which would kill it). Add the mashed potato and butter and, with a wooden spoon or rubber scraper, mix just until incorporated in clumpy bits. Add the water and egg and stir in until blended. Using an oiled spatula or dough scraper, scrape the dough onto a counter and knead it lightly for about 15 seconds, just to form a smooth dough with a little elasticity.

2 > **Let the dough rise.** Pour the oil (1 teaspoon for the smaller batch, 2 tablespoons for the larger batch into a container (2 cups for the smaller one, 3 quarts for the larger one) and place the dough in it. Turn it over to coat on both sides with the oil. Cover tightly and allow it to sit at room temperature for 30 minutes or until slightly puffy.

Set the dough, still in the container, in the refrigerator for up to 24 hours; remove 1 hour before you are ready to put it in the oven. Or, instead, just let it sit at room temperature for another 30 minutes to 1 hour, until doubled.

3 > Prepare the mushroom/onion topping below (or any of the toppings on pages 192–95).

4 > Preheat the oven. Preheat the oven to 475°F 1 hour before baking. Have an oven shelf at the lowest level and place a baking stone on it before preheating.

5 > Shape the dough and let it rise. With oiled fingers, lift the dough out of the container. Pour a little of the oil from the container onto the pizza pan(s), and spread it with your fingers. Press down on the dough with your fingers to deflate it gently and shape it into a smooth round by tucking under the edges. (If making the larger batch, cut the dough into 6 equal pieces and shape each into a ball.) Set the dough on the pizza pan(s) and allow it to sit for 15 minutes, covered, to relax.

Using your fingertips, press each ball of dough out into a 10-inch circle, leaving the outer 1/2 inch thicker than the rest to form a lip. If the dough resists stretching, cover it and let it rest for a few minutes longer before proceeding. Sprinkle the surface of the dough with any remaining olive oil. Cover with plastic wrap and allow to sit for 30 to 45 minutes, until the dough becomes light and slightly puffy with air.

6 > Bake the flatbread(s). Set the pan(s) with the flatbread directly on the hot stone in batches, as necessary, and bake for 5 minutes. Remove the pan(s) from the oven and spread with the mascarpone cheese. Strew with the topping of your choice (reserve the Parmesan cheese). Slip a pancake turner or baker's peel between the dough and the pan and slide the flatbread directly onto the stone. Bake for 5 minutes or until the crust is golden. After 2 minutes, slip a small metal spatula under one edge, and if the bottom is golden, raise the flatbread to a higher shelf.

7 > Serve the flatbread(s). Transfer the flatbread to a cutting board. Dust with the Parmesan cheese and cut with a pizza wheel, sharp knife, or scissors into about 9 squares. Arrange them slightly overlapping, on a serving plate.

VARIATION

For 2 individual 7-inch flatbreads, divide the smaller amount of dough in half and halve the topping. The baking time will remain the same.

Mushroom and Onion Topping

FOR ONE 10-INCH FLATBREAD	FOR SIX 10-INCH FLATBREADS
BACON BITS	
1 strip bacon (about 1 ounce/28 grams)	6 strips (about 6 ounces/170 grams)
SPINACH AND ONION	
1 teaspoon extra virgin olive oil	2 tablespoons
2 cups (2 ounces/56 grams) loosely packed small spinach leaves	4 cups (8 ounces/226 grams)
1/3 cup (1 ounce/28 grams) thinly sliced red onion	2 cups (6 ounces/170 grams)
Pinch of salt	1/4 teaspoon
Grinding of black pepper	to taste
SPICY MUSHROOMS	
1 teaspoon extra virgin olive oil	2 tablespoons
2/3 cup (2 ounces/56 grams) sliced cremini mushrooms	4 cups (8 ounces/226 grams)
1 small clove garlic, smashed	3 large garlic cloves, smashed
Pinch of salt	1/4 teaspoon
Grinding of black pepper	to taste
Pinch of chopped fresh thyme	about 1/4 teaspoon
Pinch of chopped fresh rosemary	about 1/4 teaspoon
Pinch of red pepper flakes	about 1/4 teaspoon
CHEESE GLAZE AND SPRINKLE	
2 tablespoons (1 ounce/28 grams) mascarpone cheese	3/4 cup (6 ounces/170 grams)
1 tablespoon (1/4 ounce/7 grams) grated Parmigiano-Reggiano	6 tablespoons (1.5 ounces/42 grams)

1 > **Make the bacon bits.** Cut the bacon into 1/2-inch pieces. Fry it until crisp. Drain on a paper towel.

2 > **Sauté the spinach and onion.** In a medium sauté pan, heat the olive oil over low heat. Add the spinach and onions and sprinkle with the salt and pepper. Sauté for about 3 minutes or until the spinach is wilted and the onions softened. Set aside.

3 > **Make the spicy mushrooms.** In a medium (large for the larger recipe) sauté pan, heat the olive oil over low heat. Add the sliced mushrooms and the garlic. Sprinkle with the salt, pepper, thyme, rosemary, and red pepper flakes Cook for about 10 minutes, stirring often, until the liquid has evaporated and the mushrooms are just beginning to brown. Allow them to cool, and discard any large pieces of garlic.

Dinner Rolls This flatbread dough also makes excellent dinner rolls. It's simply a matter of different shaping.

Preheat the oven to 350°F 30 minutes before baking. Have an oven shelf at the lowest level and place an oven stone or baking sheet on it before preheating.

Shape the dough into balls, using about 1/4 cup (2 ounces/56 grams) dough for each, and set them about 3 inches apart on a baking sheet lined with a Silpain or parchment. Cover with a large plastic box, or cover with plastic wrap greased with cooking spray or oil. Let them rise until doubled, 30 to 60 minutes.

Gently set the baking pan directly on the stone or baking sheet and bake the rolls until golden brown, 15 to 20 minutes (an instant-read thermometer inserted in the center will register about 212°F). Brush them with melted butter and cool slightly on racks. Serve warm.

To make the flatbread ahead

Bake the flatbread for a total of 7 minutes on the pizza pan. Transfer it to a rack to cool. When ready to serve, spread it with the mascarpone cheese and strew on the toppings (or use the topping of your choice). With a pancake turner or baker's peel, set it directly on the preheated oven stone or baking sheet and bake it in a preheated 475°F oven for about 3 minutes or until the crust is golden. Dust it with the Parmesan cheese and cut it into portions.

POINTERS FOR SUCCESS

> For 1 cup of mashed potatoes, you will need approximately 3 medium potatoes (10 ounces/281 grams). Boil in water to cover for about 25 minutes or until tender. Cool slightly, and press through a potato ricer or peel and mash them with a fork.

> The flatbread can also be cooked on a grill (see Grilled Pizza page 196) but care must be taken, as the potato in the dough makes it brown more quickly.

UNDERSTANDING

If you save the water from the boiled potatoes, it makes an excellent replacement for plain water in the dough because it benefits yeast production while providing more potato flavor. The water is not salted because salt slows down the yeast activity or, in large amounts, can kill the yeast. Extra salt is added to the dough to balance the addition of the potato.

THE DOUGH PERCENTAGE

Flour:	**100%** (includes the starch from the potato)
Water:	**74%** (includes the water in the potato, egg white, and butter)
Yeast:	**0.74%**
Salt:	**2.3%**
Fat:	**4.2%**

Recipe for Six Potato Flatbreads for a Crowd

Makes: 2 pounds, 10.3 ounces/1210 grams dough
Serves: 12

INGREDIENTS	MEASURE	WEIGHT	
	volume	ounces	grams
unbleached all-purpose flour (use only Gold Medal, King Arthur, or Pillsbury)	4 1/4 cups	21 ounces	600 grams
instant yeast (see page 561 for brands)	1/2 tablespoon	--	4.8 grams
sugar	1/4 cup	1.75 ounces	50 grams
salt	2 1/4 teaspoons	0.5 ounce	15 grams
mashed potatoes	1 cup	about 8 ounces	232 grams
unsalted butter, softened	3 tablespoons plus 1 teaspoon	1.6 ounce	47 grams
water, at room temperature (70° to 90°F)	1 liquid cup plus 2 tablespoons (9 fluid ounces)	9.3 ounces	265 grams
1 large egg, lightly beaten	3 tablespoons	2 ounces (weighed without the shell)	56 grams
olive or vegetable oil	2 tablespoons	0.5 ounce	27 grams

EQUIPMENT

6 pizza pans, about 12 1/2 inches, preferably black steel;

a baking stone;

a stand mixer with dough hook

1 > **Mix the dough.** In the mixer bowl, whisk together the flour, yeast, and sugar. Then whisk in the salt (this keeps the yeast from coming in direct contact with the salt, which would kill it).

Add the mashed potatoes and butter and, with the dough hook on low speed (#2 if using a KitchenAid), mix just until incorporated in clumpy bits. With the mixer still on low, add the water and egg and mix just until blended. Scrape the dough onto a counter and knead it lightly for about 30 seconds, just to form a smooth dough with a little elasticity.

Proceed as directed in the recipe on page 197, starting with step 2.

Rosemary Focaccia Sheet

This intriguing dough presents an apparent contradiction: it is incredibly light yet moist and satisfyingly chewy. Consider the percentage of water in this dough! In relation to the flour, it has 113.5 percent water, making it the highest percentage of any dough in this book. Who would have thought it even possible to make a dough this wet and still produce bread? And that is the secret of its incredible texture. The exceptionally high amount of water keeps the gluten in the flour from breaking down during the very long beating process. This enables the dough to develop into long stretchy strands that hold the air and give a chewy texture. It will remain a soupy batter until toward the very end of the twenty-minute beating, when it suddenly metamorphoses into a shiny, smooth, incredibly elastic dough.

I adapted this recipe from my favorite neighborhood bakery, the Sullivan Street Bakery in New York City. I love the dough so much I prefer it as the main feature, simply sprinkled with a little fruity olive oil and rosemary, sparkling with fleur de sel or sea salt. I also love it with the simple addition of oil-poached garlic cloves (see the variation below).

TIME SCHEDULE

Rising Time: about 5 hours
Oven Temperature: 475°F
Baking Time: 13 minutes

Makes: a 16-by-11-by-1-inch-high focaccia

INGREDIENTS	MEASURE	WEIGHT	
	volume	ounces	grams
unbleached all-purpose flour (use only Gold Medal, King Arthur, or Pillsbury)	2 3/4 cups	13.6 ounces	390 grams
instant yeast (see page 561 for brands)	3/8 teaspoon	--	1.2 grams
water, at room temperature (70° to 90°F.)	2 liquid cups minus 2 tablespoons	15.5 ounces	442 grams
sugar	3/4 teaspoon	--	3 grams
salt	3/4 teaspoon	--	5.2 grams
extra virgin olive oil	2 tablespoons plus 2 teaspoons, divided	1.25 ounces	36 grams
fresh rosemary needles or dried rosemary	2 teaspoons 1/2 teaspoon	--	--
fleur de sel or sea salt	1/4 teaspoon	--	--

EQUIPMENT

a heavy-duty stand mixer with paddle attachment;

a half sheet pan (12 inches by 17 inches);

a baking stone OR baking sheet

1 > Mix the dough. In the mixer bowl, with the paddle attachment on low speed (#2 if using a KitchenAid), combine the flour and yeast. With the mixer running, gradually add the water, mixing just until the dough comes together, about 3 minutes. It will be very soupy. Increase the speed to medium (#4 KitchenAid) and beat until the dough is transformed into a smooth, shiny ball, about 20 minutes.

Add the sugar and salt and beat until they are well incorporated, about 3 minutes.

2 > Let the dough rise. Using an oiled spatula or dough scraper, scrape the dough into a 1 1/2-quart dough-rising container or bowl, lightly greased with cooking spray or oil. The dough will look like melted mozzarella. Lightly spray or oil the top of the dough. Cover the container with a lid or plastic wrap. With a piece of tape, mark the side of the container at approximately where double the height of the dough would be. Allow the dough to rise (ideally at 75° to 80°F) for about 4 hours or until it has at least doubled.

3 > **Shape the dough and let it rise.** Coat the sheet pan with a heaping tablespoon of the olive oil. Pour the dough onto it—it will be thin enough to pour but very stretchy. Coat your hands with a little of the remaining olive oil and spread the dough as thin as possible without tearing it. Let it relax for 10 minutes, then spread it to almost fill the entire sheet, trying to maintain the bubbles in the dough. (If the dough is still very elastic and resists stretching, allow it to rest for another 10 minutes.)

Cover the pan with a large plastic box or greased plastic wrap and allow to rise until one and a half times its original volume, about 1 hour.

4 > **Preheat the oven.** Preheat the oven to 475°F 1 hour before baking. Have an oven shelf at the lowest level and place a baking stone or baking sheet on it before preheating.

5 > **Sprinkle on the toppings and bake the focaccia.** Uncover the dough and drizzle the remaining olive oil evenly over it. Sprinkle evenly with the rosemary and salt. Place the pan directly on the hot stone or hot baking sheet and bake for 12 to 13 minutes or until the top is golden. Remove from the oven and drizzle on a little extra virgin olive oil, if desired. Serve immediately.

VARIATION

Focaccia with Pockets of Garlic   If you love garlic, meltingly soft pockets of poached garlic added to the dough make a welcome addition to the crisp, light bread. Be sure to prepare the garlic ahead so that you can use the garlic-infused oil for the focaccia.

This method of "roasting" garlic also makes it milder than the usual oven roasting, as long as you do not allow it to brown. In early summer, when garlic scapes, the newly forming garlic cloves are available at the farmer's market. I like to use these tiny tips of pinky-size garlic pearls, which are exceptionally sweet and mild.

1 large head of garlic (about 2 1/2 inches wide)
About 1 cup extra virgin olive oil

1 > **Peel the garlic cloves: you should have about 2/3 cup.** Place them in a small saucepan and cover them with the olive oil, adding more if the oil does not cover the garlic completely.

2 > **Cover the pan and leave it partially uncovered if the oil starts to bubble.** Bring the oil just to a boil over low heat. Turn down the heat as low as possible (use a heat dif-

fuser if necessary) and poach the garlic at a bare simmer (if the oil starts to bubble too much, partially uncover the pan) for 20 to 30 minutes, until a cake tester or metal skewer inserted in it goes in fairly easily but not so soft that it turns to mush. Smaller cloves may take only 15 minutes, so remove them as they are softened. (You can also poach garlic by placing the partially covered [ovenproof] pan in a preheated 250°F oven for the same amount of time.)

3 > **Lift the garlic from the oil with a slotted spoon, and let the oil cool.** Use the garlic-infused oil in place of the olive oil to prepare the focaccia, if desired, and refrigerate the remainder for other uses.

4 > **Slice any large garlic cloves lengthwise in half or in thirds.** After pouring the dough onto the sheet pan, make about 32 evenly spaced depressions in the dough with your fingertip (8 rows of 4 across), and gently press a garlic clove into each one. As the dough rises, it will partially enclose the garlic and protect it from becoming any darker than golden during baking.

UNDERSTANDING

The sugar and salt are added at the end of beating to give the gluten a chance to develop fully so that the baked focaccia will be nice and chewy.

THE DOUGH PERCENTAGE

Flour:	100%
Water:	113.5%
Yeast:	0.3%
Salt:	1.3%
Oil:	12.7%

Focaccia Layered with Fresh Herbs

This amazingly light bread has a thin crisp top crust hiding a fine layer of bright green herbs beneath it. Its delicately flavored moist, tender crumb is filled with large holes; its top is golden and sparkling with crystals of salt. The secrets to this special flavor and texture are durum flour (a golden flour with sweet wheaty flavor), a very moist dough, and a long slow rise. This bread teaches two very interesting and useful techniques: working with a very sticky dough by hand with a unique kneading method that can be used for any similar dough, and laminating herbs into a crust the way you would butter into puff pastry. It is a craftsperson's bread and thoroughly enjoyable to make. It is equally enjoyable to eat, both on its own, or split and used as a sandwich bread.

Master this recipe, and you will be able to make most any sticky dough from ciabatta to pugliese by hand. Special thanks to Maggie Glezer, creator of the recipe.

TIME SCHEDULE

Rising Time: about 5 1/2 hours
Oven Temperature: 450°F
Baking Time: 15 minutes

Makes: a 14-by-7-by-1 3/4-inch-high focaccia about 17 ounces/486 grams
Serves: 4 to 6

INGREDIENTS	MEASURE	WEIGHT	
	volume	ounces	grams
unbleached all-purpose flour (use only Gold Medal, King Arthur, or Pillsbury)	1 cup plus 1 tablespoon	5.3 ounces	150 grams
durum flour (see page 546)	1 cup	5.3 ounces	150 grams
instant yeast (see page 561 for brands)	1/4 teaspoon	--	0.8 gram
water, at room temperature (70° to 90°F)	1 liquid cup	8.2 ounces	236 grams
extra virgin olive oil	1 tablespoon	1 scant ounce	13.5 grams
salt	1 teaspoon	--	6.6 grams
fresh herb leaves of your choice (one type, or a mixture)	1 cup, very loosely packed	about 0.5 ounce	about 13 grams

Topping

extra virgin olive oil	1 tablespoon	--	13.5 grams
coarse salt	1/4 teaspoon	--	1.7 grams

EQUIPMENT

a large sheet of parchment, floured;

a baking stone OR baking sheet

1 > At least 7 hours and up to 15 hours before eating, make the dough. In a medium bowl, whisk together the all-purpose flour, durum flour, and yeast. Add the water and oil and, with your fingers or an oiled rubber spatula, mix just until uniformly combined. The dough will be very sticky. Cover the bowl tightly with plastic wrap and allow it to rest for 20 minutes. (This rest will make the dough less sticky and easier to work with.)

2 > Knead the dough. Sprinkle the 1 teaspoon salt onto the dough and mix it in with your fingers. Scrape the dough onto an unfloured counter and knead it for 10 minutes in the following manner: Squeeze the dough very firmly between the thumbs and index fingers of both hands, moving down the length of the dough and squeezing hard enough so that your thumbs and fingers go right through the dough until they touch each other. When you have reached the end of the dough, flip it over with your fingers and repeat the squeezing process. Even though the dough will not hold together in one piece because it is so sticky, do not add any flour. It will gradually become smoother, but it will still be sticky enough to cling to your hands. Use a bench scraper when necessary to bring the dough together. (It will become firmer and less sticky with each subsequent deflating, folding, and resting period.)

3 > Let the dough rest. Scrape the dough into an unoiled bowl and cover it tightly with a lid or plastic wrap. (Depending on how much dough still clings to your fingers, the dough will weigh 17.6 to 18 ounces/500 to 510 grams.) Allow it to sit for 30 minutes to begin rising just a little.

4 > Turn the dough and let it rise. With an oiled dough scraper, transfer the dough to a lightly floured counter, and lightly flour the top of the dough. Gently flatten it without deflating it completely. Fold in all four sides to make a tight package. Return it to the bowl, cover it, and allow it to sit for another 30 minutes.

5 > Turn the dough and let it rise again. Repeat the flouring, deflating, and folding process. Return the dough to the bowl and allow it to sit for 2 to 3 hours, until doubled. It will be full of large bubbles and should spring back when you press it.

6 > Shape the dough. Transfer the dough to a floured counter and flour it well. With your hands, without popping the bubbles, tuck in the sides to make a smooth package. Flour the dough, cover it with plastic wrap, and let it rest for 10 to 15 minutes.

With floured hands, gently stretch and press the dough into a 10-by-6-inch rectangle a scant 1 inch thick. Transfer the dough to the floured parchment and flour the top of the dough. With a slender rolling pin, roll out one-quarter (1 1/2 inches) of a long side into a thin 4 1/2-inch-wide flap that will be large enough to cover the thicker unrolled portion of the dough when folded over. Press with the rolling pin where the thin sheet joins the dough to make a sharp demarcation. If necessary, use more flour to keep the dough from sticking. Brush off any flour from the thick part of the dough, and brush it lightly with water.

7 > Add the herbs. Dip the herb leaves in water, shake off excess droplets, and arrange them close together but not overlapping on the thick portion of the dough. Fold the thin portion of the dough over the herbs to cover them completely. Pat gently to push out any air bubbles and tuck the edges under all around. Dust the top of the dough lightly with flour and, starting from a short end, roll over it lightly and evenly until the herbs come into sharp relief but do not break through the dough, and any trapped air is expelled. Roll both lengthwise and crosswise to keep the dough as even a rectangle as possible. It should be about 6 inches wide by 14 inches long and 1/2 inch high.

STEP-BY-STEP ILLUSTRATIONS FOR LAYERING
FOCACCIA DOUGH WITH FRESH HERBS:

1> Squeezing the dough with the thumbs
and index fingers of both hands

2> Squeezing the entire length of the dough

3> Flipping the dough over
with your fingers

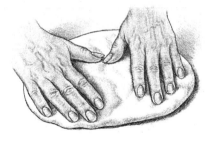

4> Stretching and flattening the
dough into a rectangle

5> Folding in all four sides
to make a tight package

6> Tucking the sides under to
make a smooth package

7> Stretching and pressing the dough into a rectangle

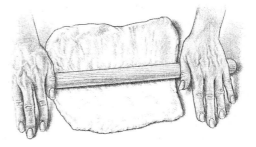

8> Rolling out one quarter of one long side into a thin flap

9> Herbs spread across the dough

10> Folding the dough flap over the herbs

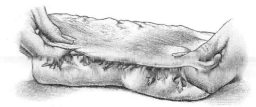

11> Rolling until the herbs come into sharp relief

12> Pressing deep dimples into the dough

8 > Let the shaped dough rise. Cover the dough with a large plastic box, or dust it lightly with flour and cover it with plastic wrap. Allow it to rise for about 2 hours or until puffy and 1 inch high; when pressed lightly, the indentation should slowly fill in.

9 > Preheat the oven. Preheat the oven to 450°F 1 hour before baking. Have an oven shelf in the upper third of the oven and place a baking stone or baking sheet on it, and a sheet pan on the floor of the oven, before preheating.

10 > Oil and dimple the dough, and sprinkle it with salt. With a clean dry brush, brush any flour from the surface of the dough. Gently brush on the 1 tablespoon olive oil (you can use your fingers to spread the oil, but press very gently so as not to deflate the dough). With your fingers, press dimples all over the dough, about 1 inch apart, going down to the bottom of the dough without breaking through. Sprinkle with the coarse salt.

11 > Bake the focaccia. Use a baker's peel or cookie sheet (no sides) to slip the bread, still on the parchment, onto the hot baking stone or hot baking sheet. Toss 1/2 cup of ice cubes into the pan beneath and immediately shut the oven door. Bake for 10 minutes. Remove the bread from the parchment, turn it around, and set it directly on the stone or baking sheet. Bake for another 5 minutes or until golden (an instant-read thermometer inserted into the center will read about 210°F).

12 > Cool the focaccia. With a sturdy pancake turner, lift the focaccia from the baking sheet or stone and transfer the focaccia to a wire rack to cool briefly, until warm.

POINTERS FOR SUCCESS

>   Choose your favorite herbs or a mixture of three, such as flat-leaf parsley, minced chives, and sage, or parsley, rosemary, and thyme.

>   Use only the leaves, and discard any tough or woody stems.

>   If desired, you can sprinkle on about 1/4 cup crumbled fresh goat cheese or grated Parmigiano-Reggiano along with the herbs. The top flap of dough will keep the cheese from drying out.

UNDERSTANDING

Durum flour, which is milled from a very hard wheat flour called durum wheat (see page 546), is sometimes marketed as "extra-fancy pasta flour" or "farina-grade pasta flour." It is used for pasta because it gives it a desirably firm al dente texture. Avoid semolina, which is also from durum wheat but is a much coarser grind.

Durum flour offers more delicious flavor and more attractive golden color than white wheat flour. It is combined with unbleached all-purpose flour for this recipe because the white wheat flour forms stronger gluten, which lightens the dough, and is more absorbent, resulting in a softer, moister dough as well.

THE DOUGH PERCENTAGE

Flour:	100%
Water:	78.7%
Yeast:	0.27%
Salt:	2.3%
Oil:	9%

Grilled Focaccia

Focaccia and pizza dough are really the same balance of flour, water, salt, and yeast, but focaccia is generally shaped thicker than pizza and boasts many small depressions in the top crust that contain little puddles of olive oil. Because the dough is thicker, baked focaccia has a soft layer inside a crunchy top and bottom crust. The dough can even be shaped thick enough to split open and use as a sandwich bread.

Cooking focaccia on the grill gives it that wonderful smoky flavor. The goal is to give it attractive browned grill marks without charring the bottom crust. The trick is to cook the dough on a baking sheet for the first 2 minutes, just to set it, so that it can then be slipped onto the grill for a few seconds, just until it begins to brown. Not only does this give the focaccia a fantastic flavor, it is a great way to avoid heating up your kitchen in hot weather.

TIME SCHEDULE

Minimum Rising Time: about 2 hours
Gas Grill Temperature: 500°F
Grilling Time: 10 minutes

Makes: a 9-by-6-by-1/2-inch-high focaccia

INGREDIENTS	MEASURE	WEIGHT	
	volume	ounces	grams
flour, preferably King Arthur Italian style, or *unbleached* all-purpose flour (use only Gold Medal, King Arthur, or Pillsbury)	3/4 cup plus 1 tablespoon	4 ounces	113 grams
instant yeast (see page 561 for brands)	1/2 teaspoon	--	1.6 grams
sugar	1/2 teaspoon	--	2 grams
salt	1/2 teaspoon	--	3.3 grams
water at room temperature or warm	1/3 liquid cup	2.75 ounces	79 grams
olive oil	4 teaspoons	0.6 ounce	18 grams
fresh rosemary needles	1 scant tablespoon	--	--
fleur de sel or coarse sea salt	to taste	--	--
black pepper	to taste	--	--
garlic, coarsely chopped	to taste	--	--
Optional: extra virgin olive oil for sprinkling	to taste	--	--

EQUIPMENT

a grill;

a baking sheet;

a long pancake turner and/or tongs

1 > Mix the dough. In a small bowl, whisk together the flour, yeast, and sugar. Then whisk in the salt (this keeps the yeast from coming into direct contact with the salt, which would kill it). Make a well in the center and pour in the water. Using a rubber spatula or wooden spoon, gradually stir the flour into the water until all the flour is moistened and a dough just begins to form, about 20 seconds. It should come away from the bowl but still stick to it a little, and be a little rough looking, not silky smooth. Do not overmix, as this will cause the dough to become stickier.

2 > Let the dough rise. Pour the oil into a 2-cup measuring cup (to give the dough room to double) or a small bowl. With oiled fingers or an oiled spatula, place the dough in the cup or bowl and turn it over to coat on all sides with the oil. Cover it tightly and allow it to sit at room temperature for 30 minutes or until slightly puffy.

Set the dough, still in the cup or bowl, in the refrigerator for up to 24 hours; remove 1 hour before you are ready to put it in the oven. Or, instead, simply let it sit at room temperature for another 30 minutes to 1 hour, until doubled.

3 > **Shape the focaccia and let it rise.** With oiled fingers, lift the dough out of the cup or bowl. Holding the dough in one hand, pour a little of the oil left in the cup or bowl onto the baking sheet and spread it all over the pan with your fingers. Set the dough on top and press it down with your fingers to deflate it gently. Shape it into a smooth round by tucking under the edges. If there are any holes, knead very lightly until smooth. Let the dough rest for 15 minutes, covered, to relax it.

Using your fingertips, press the dough from the center to the outer edge to stretch it into a rectangle about 9 inches by 6 inches and 1/4 inch high. If the dough resists, cover it with plastic wrap and continue pressing on it with your fingers. Brush the top of the dough with any oil remaining in the measuring cup or bowl and cover it with plastic wrap. Let the dough rise for 20 to 30 minutes more or until light and spongy looking.

4 > **Preheat a covered gas grill to 500°F according to manufacturer's directions.** Or, if using a charcoal grill, build the coals on one side of the grill and light the fire 40 minutes ahead.

5 > **Sprinkle on the toppings and grill the focaccia.** Using your fingertips, press deep dimples at 1-inch intervals all over the dough. Sprinkle it with the rosemary, salt and pepper.

If using a gas grill, turn one side of it to low. Place the focaccia, still on the baking sheet, on the hotter side of the gas or charcoal grill and grill, covered, for 2 minutes. Slide a pancake turner underneath the dough to loosen it and slip it directly onto the cooler side of grill (use tongs if you have them) for just a few seconds—you'll smell it browning. Lift an edge with the pancake turner to check, and as soon as deep brown grill marks appear, return the focaccia to the baking sheet and slide it over to the cooler side of the grill. Sprinkle on the garlic, cover the grill, and cook 7 to 8 minutes longer or until the top begins to brown around the edges.

6 > **Serve the focaccia.** Slip the pancake turner under the focaccia and transfer it to a cutting board. Sprinkle it with extra olive oil if desired, cut it into strips with a serrated knife, and serve immediately.

To bake focaccia: Preheat the oven to 475°F 30 minutes before baking. Have an oven shelf at the lowest level and place baking stone or heavy baking sheet on it before preheating.

Place the baking sheet with the focaccia on the hot stone or hot baking sheet and bake for 5 minutes. Add the garlic, if desired, slide a pancake turner underneath the dough to loosen it, and slip it directly onto the stone. Continue baking for another 5 minutes or until the top begins to brown around the edges.

POINTERS FOR SUCCESS

> If you are planning to use the focaccia as a sandwich bread, double the recipe. Press it into a rectangle the same size but 1/2 inch high; it will bake to 1 inch high. (Add a few minutes to the grilling or baking time.)

UNDERSTANDING

Less salt is used in this dough than for most other doughs so that extra salt can be sprinkled on top. It adds not only an attractive décor but also a pleasant taste sensation.

THE DOUGH PERCENTAGE

Flour:	100%
Water:	69.9%
Yeast	1.4%
Salt:	1.4%
Oil:	11.9%

Sicilian Vegetable Pizza Roll

My friend Angelica Pulvirenti grew up in a tiny village of Ispica, near the ancient town of Ragusa, my favorite city in Sicily. Most people in those days did not have their own ovens, so, as the only daughter, it was her proud responsibility to take the family bread to the communal oven in town for baking. She still remembers how the bread was placed in her mother's bed under the wool covers to rise, as it was the warmest spot in the house.

This indescribably good filled bread roll is a recipe Angelica has been making every Christmas for as long as she can remember. Of course, she makes it the way people who have been cooking and baking all their lives do, without a recipe and without weighing or measuring anything—purely by heart. It was fun watching her trying to slow down to contemplate, measure, and re-create it for this book.

Jerusalem artichokes add an earthy flavor to the garlicky broccoli filling, faintly reminiscent of globe artichokes. Also called sunchokes, they are available during the cool months of the year starting around October, but this bread will still be delicious without them.

This dough is really a pizza dough, but it is developed more to make it strong enough to hold the filling. It is rolled out into a large rectangle, topped with the filling, and then rolled up like a jelly roll to create a beautiful spiral of vegetables in the dough.

TIME SCHEDULE

Rising Time: 20 minutes
Oven Temperature: 475°F, then 400°F
Baking Time: 30 minutes

Makes: an 18-by-4 1/2-by-2-inch-high loaf
Serves: 12 to 16

Filling

INGREDIENTS	MEASURE	WEIGHT	
	volume	ounces	grams
olive oil	1/3 liquid cup	2.5 ounces	72 grams
broccoli florets, cut into small pieces (about 3/4 inch)	8 cups (2 bunches)	14.5 ounces	412 grams
3 to 4 Jerusalem artichokes, peeled, and thinly sliced	1 rounded cup slices	about 4 ounces	118 grams
5 large garlic cloves, thinly sliced and julienned	1/2 cup julienned	about 1.5 ounces	42 grams
salt	1 teaspoon	0.2 ounce	6.6 grams
black pepper	to taste	--	--

EQUIPMENT

heavy-duty aluminum foil;

a half sheet pan;

a baking stone OR baking sheet

1 > **Make the filling.** In a large skillet, heat the olive oil over medium heat (Angelica calls it "happy heat"). Add the broccoli and sauté, stirring constantly, for 3 minutes or just until it starts to change color. Add the Jerusalem artichokes and garlic and sprinkle with salt. Cover and cook, stirring often, for about 3 minutes or until tender-crisp. (The broccoli will continue cooking slightly during baking.) Sprinkle on the pepper and cool completely.

Dough

Makes: 27.7 ounces/792 grams

INGREDIENTS	MEASURE	WEIGHT	
	volume	ounces	grams
unbleached all-purpose flour (use only Gold Medal, King Arthur, or Pillsbury)	3 1/4 cups	about 16.5 ounces	468 grams
instant yeast (see page 561 for brands)	2 teaspoons	--	6.4 grams
sugar	2 teaspoons	--	8.3 grams
salt	1 1/2 teaspoons	--	10 grams
water, at room temperature (70° to 90°F)	1 1/3 liquid cups	11 ounces	312 grams
whole wheat flour (or *unbleached* all-purpose flour) for rolling the dough	1/4 cup	1.25 ounces	35 grams
olive oil	3 tablespoons, divided	about 1.5 ounces	40 grams

2 > **Mix the dough.** In a medium bowl, whisk together the flour, yeast, and sugar. Then whisk in the salt (this keeps the yeast from coming in direct contact with the salt, which would kill it). Make a well in the center of the flour, add the water, and, with a rubber spatula or wooden spoon, stir it in until blended.

Sprinkle the counter with some of the whole wheat (or all-purpose) flour. Using an oiled spatula or dough scraper, scrape the dough out onto the counter and knead it for 10 minutes or until smooth and resilient. It will be very sticky during the first 5 minutes of kneading. (If it is still sticky after 5 minutes, cover it with the inverted bowl and let it rest for 20 minutes.) Add more flour if necessary only after the first 5 minutes. (The dough can also be made in a stand mixer with a dough hook; mix on medium speed [#4 if using a KitchenAid] for 7 minutes.)

3 > **Let the dough rest.** Clean the counter and sprinkle it with more whole wheat (or all-purpose) flour. Set the dough on top and allow it to sit, covered with plastic wrap, for 20 to 30 minutes to relax before rolling.

4 > **Preheat the oven.** Preheat the oven to 475°F 1 hour before baking. Have an oven shelf at the lowest level and place a baking stone or baking sheet on it before pre-heating.

5 > **Shape the dough.** Using 1 tablespoon of the olive oil, brush a 4-inch band of oil down the center of a 20-inch-long piece of heavy-duty foil.

Roll the dough into an 18-by-16-inch rectangle. Strew the filling evenly over the dough. Roll up the dough from a longer side, using a long plastic ruler to help support the dough as you roll it (slip the edge of the ruler slightly under the dough and use it to lift up and roll the dough). Pinch the edge of the dough firmly to make a tight seam. Turn the dough so that the seam is underneath. Pinch the ends of the dough firmly together and tuck them under.

Roll the loaf onto the foil so that the seam remains underneath, and lift it onto the pan, leaving it on the foil. Brush the top with 1 tablespoon of the olive oil and make 3 small slashes in the top of the dough.

6 > **Bake the bread.** Set the baking sheet on the hot stone or hot baking sheet and bake for 10 minutes. Lower the heat to 400°F and bake for 10 minutes. Rotate the pan and continue baking for 10 minutes or until the loaf is golden all over.

7 > **Brush the loaf with oil and cool it slightly.** Remove the baking sheet from the oven and set it on a wire rack. Brush the top of the loaf with the remaining 1 tablespoon olive oil. Allow it to cool for about 10 minutes.

8 > **Serve the bread.** Transfer it to a carving board and use a serrated knife to cut it into 1/2- to 3/4-inch slices.

POINTERS FOR SUCCESS

>   This bread freezes well, and slices of it reheat to fabulous full flavor in just 10 minutes in a preheated 350°F oven. I like to spread the slices first with duxelles (page 390) to keep the filling moist, while crisping the crust. This intense mushroom filling is a fantastic flavor synergy with the Jerusalem artichokes. Slices are also delicious reheated and then drizzled with a little truffle or extra virgin olive oil.

THE DOUGH PERCENTAGE

Flour:	100%
Water:	62%
Yeast:	1.27%
Salt:	2%
Oil:	8%

Pita Bread

Once you have tasted homemade pita bread, you will be hooked for life. Not only is it more delicious, with a softer and moister texture than the commercial variety, it happens to be easy to prepare—and the dough can be made and refrigerated as much as four days ahead of baking. It's also great fun to watch the pitas puff up like little balloons while baking.

This Middle-Eastern "pocket bread" is ideal to use for hummus and other dips, and for all manner of sandwiches. I like to make small 4-inch pitas and cut them into wedges, but for stuffing, the larger size is best. Simply cut off a small piece from the top and with a knife, gently separate the inside to form a pocket.

TIME SCHEDULE

Minimum Rising Time: 1 hour
Oven Temperature: 475°F
Baking Time: 3 minutes per bread

Makes: twelve 4-inch pitas or eight 6-inch pitas

INGREDIENTS	MEASURE	WEIGHT	
	volume	ounces	grams
unbleached all-purpose flour (use only Gold Medal, King Arthur, or Pillsbury)	3 cups plus a scant 1/4 cup	16 ounces	454 grams
salt	2 teaspoons	0.5 ounce	13.2 grams
instant yeast (see page 561 for brands)	2 teaspoons	--	6.4 grams
olive oil	2 tablespoons	1 ounce	27 grams
water, at room temperature (70° to 90°F)	1 1/4 liquid cups	10.4 ounces	295 grams

EQUImpMENT

a baking stone OR cast-iron skillet OR a baking sheet

1 > About 1 1/2 hours before shaping, or for best
flavor development, 8 hours to 3 days ahead, mix
the dough.

Mixer Method

In the bowl of a stand mixer, combine all the ingredients. With the paddle attachment, mix on low speed (#2 if using a KitchenAid) just until all the flour is moistened, about 20 seconds. Change to the dough hook, raise the speed to medium (#4
KitchenAid), and knead for 10 minutes. The dough should clean the bowl and be
very soft and smooth and just a little sticky to the touch. Add a little flour or water if
necessary. (The dough will weigh about 27.75 ounces/793 grams.)

Hand Method

In a large bowl, combine all the ingredients except for a scant 1/4 cup of the flour.
With a wooden spoon or your hand, mix until all the flour is moistened. Knead the
dough in the bowl until it comes together.

   Sprinkle a little of the reserved flour onto the counter and scrape the dough
onto it. Knead the dough for 5 minutes, adding as little of the reserved flour as possible. Use a bench scraper to scrape the dough and gather it together as you knead it.
At this point it will be very sticky. Cover it with the inverted bowl and allow it to rest
for 5 to 20 minutes. (This rest will make the dough less sticky and easier to work
with.)

   Knead the dough for another 5 to 10 minutes or until it is soft and smooth and
just a little sticky to the touch. Add with a little flour or water if necessary. (The
dough will weigh about 27.75 ounces/793 grams.)

Both Methods

2 > Let the dough rise. Using an oiled spatula or dough scraper, scrape the dough
into a 2-quart or larger dough-rising container or bowl, lightly greased with cooking
spray or oil. Press the dough down and lightly spray or oil the top of it. Cover the
container with a lid or plastic wrap. With a piece of tape, mark the side of the container at approximately where double the height of the dough would be. Refrigerate
the dough overnight (or up to 3 days), checking every hour for the first 4 hours and
pressing it down if it starts to rise.

3 > Preheat the oven. Preheat the oven to 475°F 1 hour before baking. Have an oven shelf at the lowest level and place a baking stone, cast-iron skillet, or baking sheet on it before preheating.

4 > Shape the dough. Cut the dough into 8 or 12 pieces. Work with one piece at a time, keeping the rest covered with a damp cloth. On a lightly floured counter, with lightly floured hands, shape each piece into a ball and then flatten it into a disk. Cover the dough with oiled plastic and allow it to rest for 20 minutes at room temperature.

Roll each disk into a circle a little under 1/4 inch thick. Allow them to rest, uncovered, for 10 minutes before baking.

5 > Bake the pita. Quickly place 1 piece of dough directly on the stone or in the skillet or on the baking sheet, and bake for 3 minutes. The pita should be completely puffed but not beginning to brown. The dough will not puff well if it is not moist enough. See how the pita puffs, then, if necessary, spray and knead each remaining piece with water until the dough is soft and moist; allow to rest again and reroll as before. (However, those that do not puff well are still delicious to eat.) Proceed with the remaining dough, baking 3 or 4 pieces or a time if using a stone or baking sheet. Using a pancake turner, transfer the pita breads to a clean towel, to stay soft and warm. Allow the oven to reheat for 5 minutes between batches. The pitas can be reheated for about 30 seconds in a hot oven before serving.

To cook the pitas on the stovetop

Preheat a griddle or cast-iron skillet over medium-high heat. Lightly grease the surface and cook the pitas one at a time. Cook for about 20 seconds, then turn the dough and continue cooking for 1 minute or until big bubbles appear. Turn the dough again and cook until the dough balloons. If the dough begins to brown, lower the heat. The entire cooking process for each pita should be about 3 minutes.

VARIATION

For a whole wheat version, use half whole wheat, and half white flour. If using regular whole wheat flour, for best results, grind it very fine or process it in a food processor for 5 minutes to break the bran into smaller particles. Finely ground 100% whole wheat flour (atta), available in Middle-Eastern food markets, is the finest grind available. Or, for a milder but wheatier flavor and golden color, try 100% white whole wheat flour (see Sources, page 572). You will need to add 1/4 cup more water, for a total of 1 1/2 cups (12.4 ounces/354 grams).

This dough is actually the same as my pizza dough, but it is made with a higher-protein flour and is kneaded to develop enough gluten to support the rise during baking, when the pitas inflate like little balloons to form the inner pocket.

THE DOUGH PERCENTAGE

Flour:	100%
Water:	65%
Yeast:	1.4%
Salt:	2.9%
Oil:	6.2%

Mediterranean Matzoh

I grew up with store-bought matzoh, munching it with great pleasure every Passover, thickly spread with sweet butter, sprinkled lightly with salt, or sometimes drizzled with schmaltz (chicken fat). It's hard to compete with tradition and happy childhood memories, but when I was visiting Tom Cat, the huge bread bakery in Queens, New York, that supplies so many of New York's best restaurants with rustic breads, head baker James Rath introduced me to a matzoh of a different stripe, created by co-owner Noel Comess. Paper-thin, crackling crisp, with a hint of rosemary and a suspicion of olive oil—I knew I had met a matzoh too good to save only for the Passover table (where it represents the unleavened bread made by the Jews during their long exodus from Egypt, when time did not allow for yeast-raised bread). In fact, two friends, Anna and Morry Schwartz, were visiting from Australia, and the four of us went through two huge Tom Cat matzohs as appetizers with Champagne. This matzoh needs nothing more than one bite for you to want to make it in your kitchen.

Don't expect these matzohs to look like the evenly ridged squares that come out of a box. They are far more interesting, in a free-form sort of way. They resemble crackers with many beautiful bubbles of varying sizes.

TIME SCHEDULE

Minimum Resting Time: 40 minutes
Oven Temperature: 450°F
Baking Time: 5 to 6 minutes per matzoh

Makes: six 11-inch rounds about 3 ounces/83 grams each

INGREDIENTS	MEASURE	WEIGHT	
	volume	ounces	grams
unbleached all-purpose flour (use only Gold Medal, King Arthur, or Pillsbury)	2 3/4 cups	13.7 ounces	390 grams
finely ground whole wheat flour	1/4 cup	1.25 ounces	35 grams
salt	1 1/8 teaspoons	0.25 ounce	7.5 grams
water, at room temperature (70° to 90°F)	1 liquid cup	8.2 ounces	236 grams
olive oil	1/4 liquid cup (plus a little extra for oiling the dough)	about 2 ounces	about 54 grams
fresh rosemary, finely chopped	1/2 tablespoon	--	2 grams

EQUIPMENT

a baking stone and peel OR 2 large baking sheets, lightly dusted with flour or cornmeal

1 > Mix the dough.

Mixer Method

In the bowl of a stand mixer, whisk together the flours and salt. Make a well in the center and pour in all but 1 tablespoon of the water, the olive oil, and rosemary. With the paddle attachment, mix on medium speed (#4 if using a KitchenAid) until the dough cleans the sides of the bowl. If the dough does not come together after 1 minute, add the remaining water 1/2 teaspoon at a time. Don't worry if it seems sticky; adding more flour if necessary will not destroy the texture. Transfer the dough to a counter, and knead it lightly 1 to 2 minutes, until smooth and satiny. (It will be a round ball that flattens after relaxing.)

Hand Method

Place the flours on a counter or in a bowl, and sprinkle with the salt. Make a well in the center and add the olive oil. Add all but 1 tablespoon of the water in three or four additions, using your fingers and a bench scraper or spatula to work the flour into the liquid until you can form a ball. If necessary, add the final tablespoon of water. Knead the dough until it is very smooth and elastic and feels like satin, about 5 minutes, adding extra flour only if it is still very sticky after kneading for a few minutes.

Both Methods

2 > **Oil the dough and let it rest.** Pour about 1 teaspoon olive oil onto a small plate and turn the dough in it so that it is coated all over. Leave the dough on the plate, cover it with plastic wrap, and allow it to sit at room temperature for at least 30 minutes, or refrigerate it overnight.

3 > **Preheat the oven.** Preheat the oven to 450°F 1 hour before baking. Have an oven shelf at the middle level and place a baking stone on it before preheating.

4 > **Shape and bake the dough.** Cut the dough into 6 equal parts and shape them into balls. Flatten them into disks, cover, and allow them to sit for about 10 minutes.

Work with one piece of dough at a time, keeping the rest covered. Place a dough disk on a floured counter and flour the top of it Roll it into a rough circle 12 to 13 inches in diameter. As you roll, lift the dough and slide it on the counter at regular intervals, flouring as necessary to prevent sticking.

Slide the dough onto the prepared peel or a baking sheet. If using a peel, slide the dough onto the hot stone by jiggling the peel as you gradually pull it forward. If using a baking sheet, set the baking sheet directly on the stone.

Bake for 1 minute, then, with a fork or the tip of a knife, poke any big bubbles that may have formed. Continue baking for 2 minutes more. Hold a clean pot holder in one hand, and use a large pancake turner to lift the matzoh and flip it over onto the pot holder. Slide the matzoh back onto the stone or baking sheet and bake for another 2 to 3 minutes or until the raised bubbles are lightly browned.

5 > **Cool the matzoh.** With a pancake turner, remove the matzoh from the oven and set it on a wire rack to cool completely while you shape and bake the remaining dough. If the matzoh isn't crisp after cooling, you can return it briefly to the oven. If desired, gently brush off any flour on the surface with a pastry feather or soft brush.

POINTERS FOR SUCCESS

> While each matzoh is baking, there is just enough time to roll the next one. If the dough is hard to roll, cover it and let it rest for a minute or so.

UNDERSTANDING

Amazingly, when analyzing the proportion of ingredients, I discovered that, to the gram, the formula for this recipe is identical to my strudel recipe, containing the same amount of flour, oil, water, and salt! Strudel, however, is stretched to a transparent thinness, brushed with clarified butter, and wrapped around moist fillings, producing a crisp, flaky, and tender dough, unlike matzoh, which is baked flat, unfilled, and unbuttered, resulting in a brittle crisp bread. The olive oil in the matzoh, though not traditional, provides extra crispness and flavor.

THE DOUGH PERCENTAGE

Flour:	100% (all-purpose: 91%, whole wheat: 9%)
Water:	55.5%
Yeast:	0%
Salt:	1.8%
Oil:	1.4%

Kheema Paratha

The flatbreads of India are many and varied, but of all the flatbreads that do not require a special tandoor oven, the paratha, which is cooked on a griddle, is my favorite. The dough for this bread contains less water than pita and, instead of yeast, relies on a special technique of rolling, folding, and layering with melted butter to make it puff into a tender, almost flaky bread. Parathas are sautéed in a little butter on a disk-like iron pan called a tawa, available in Middle-Eastern and Indian markets, but they can also be made in a cast-iron skillet. Sautéing rather than baking in an oven is what gives the paratha its crisp exterior.

Paratha is usually served plain to accompany dinner. Torn pieces are used as an edible "fork" to lift the food. Paratha is sometimes filled with a mixture of spicy onion and potato or cauliflower, but it was only when I visited India that I enjoyed kheema paratha, filled with spiced ground meat. On my return, I found the perfect recipe for the kheema filling in Madhur Jaffrey's *An Invitation to Indian Cooking*. The optional Middle-Eastern cilantro-based sauce is a terrific accompaniment.

TIME SCHEDULE

Minimum Resting Time: 30 minutes
Sautéing Time: about 2 1/2 minutes per bread

Makes: 4 parathas (with enough filling for 8; extra filling can be frozen for as long as 3 months, or used to fill tacos and tortillas)

Dough

Makes: about 17 ounces/482 grams

INGREDIENTS	MEASURE	WEIGHT	
	volume	ounces	grams
whole wheat chapati flour (atta) or half whole wheat and half *unbleached* all-purpose flour (such as Gold Medal or Pillsbury)	2 cups, lightly spooned	10.2 ounces	290 grams
salt	1 teaspoon	0.2 ounce	6.6 grams
Optional: dry milk, preferably nonfat (or replace half the water with scalded milk that has been cooled to lukewarm)	1 1/2 tablespoons	about 0.5 ounce	11.7 grams
water, at room temperature (70° to 90°F)	3/4 liquid cup	6.2 ounces	177 grams

EQUIPMENT

a 9-inch tawa OR cast-iron skillet

1 > **Make the dough.**

Food Processor Method

In a food processor fitted with the metal blade, combine the flour(s), salt, and the optional dry milk. With the motor running, gradually pour in the water. Remove the cover and pinch the dough. If it holds together and feels moist, continue processing for 45 seconds: the dough should form a ball. If necessary, pulse in a little more water. The dough should be very smooth and soft and only very slightly tacky (sticky).

Hand Method

In a medium bowl, whisk together the flour(s), salt, and the optional dry milk. Make a well in the center. Pour about 1/2 cup of the water into the well, stirring it into the flour with your hand or a rubber spatula. Gradually add only enough of the remaining water as necessary to pick up all the dry flour particles and form a soft dough.

Transfer the dough to an unfloured countertop and knead it for 10 to 15 minutes; it works best if you use your knuckles, as the dough tends to stick to your palms. As the dough starts drying slightly, dip your knuckles into a little warm water and continue kneading. The dough should be very smooth and soft and only very slightly tacky (sticky).

Both Methods

2 > **Let the dough rest.** Place the dough in a lightly oiled bowl and spray the top lightly with nonstick vegetable spray. Cover tightly with plastic wrap and place it in a warm spot for a minimum of 30 minutes or up to 3 hours.

Kheema (Ground Meat Filling)

Makes: 2 cups

INGREDIENTS	MEASURE	WEIGHT	
	volume	ounces	grams
vegetable oil	2 tablespoons	1 ounce	28 grams
1 bay leaf	--	--	--
1 small cinnamon stick	--	--	--
3 whole cloves	--	--	--
1 medium onion, finely chopped	1 cup	5 ounces	142 grams
a 1/2-inch piece of ginger, peeled and minced	4 teaspoons	--	--
3 medium garlic cloves, minced	--	--	--
coriander seeds	1/2 tablespoon	--	--
cumin seeds	1/2 tablespoon	--	--
ground turmeric	1/2 teaspoon	--	--
plain yogurt	1 tablespoon	--	--
tomato sauce	1 tablespoon	--	--
ground beef, preferably chuck	--	1 pound	454 grams
ground mace	1/8 teaspoon	--	--
nutmeg, preferably freshly grated	1/8 teaspoon	--	--
salt	3/4 teaspoon	--	5 grams
cayenne pepper	1/4 to 1/2 teaspoon	--	--
water	1/4 liquid cup	--	--
clarified butter (or ghee)	1/4 liquid cup	1.75 ounces	48 grams
Optional: Yemenite Green Sauce (page 237)	1 cup	8.3 ounces	237 grams

3 > **Make the kheema while the dough is resting (or up to 3 days ahead).** In a heavy medium (10-inch) skillet, heat the oil over medium heat until hot. Add the bay leaf, cinnamon stick, and cloves and fry for a few minutes, until the bay leaf begins to

darken slightly. Lower the heat, add the onion, ginger, and garlic, and sauté, stirring, for 10 minutes or until the onion darkens to medium brown.

Meanwhile, in a small sauté pan, dry-roast the coriander and cumin seeds over medium heat, stirring often, for about 2 minutes or until they smell fragrant. Allow them to cool, then grind them in a spice mill or coffee grinder.

Add the coriander, cumin, and turmeric to the onion mixture and sauté for about 2 minutes, stirring constantly. Add the yogurt and cook, stirring constantly, for 1 minute. Add the tomato sauce and cook, stirring constantly, for about 3 minutes.

Add the meat and raise the heat to medium. Sauté, breaking up lumps with a slotted spoon or spatula, for 5 to 7 minutes or until the meat is browned.

Stir in the mace, nutmeg, salt, cayenne pepper, and water. Lower the heat to the lowest possible setting or (use a heat diffuser if you have one), cover, and simmer, stirring about every 10 minutes to prevent scorching, for 45 minutes. If all the water evaporates before this time, add a few tablespoons more, but the mixture should be dry at the end of cooking. Taste and add a little more salt, if desired.

Let the filling cool, then remove and discard the bay leaf, cinnamon, and cloves.

4 > Shape the dough. On a floured surface, roll the dough into a long rope. Divide it into 8 even pieces. Work with one piece of dough at a time, keeping the rest of the dough covered with plastic wrap to prevent it from drying out. Shape each piece into a ball, dust it lightly with flour, and set on a baking sheet or counter.

Working with one piece of dough at a time again, keeping the rest covered, flatten a ball of dough with floured fingers and roll it into a 5-inch circle, flouring the surface and the dough lightly as necessary to keep it from sticking. Brush off any excess flour and brush the surface of the dough with clarified butter. Fold the dough in half, dust off the flour, and brush again with clarified butter. Fold it over one more time and set it aside.

5 > Shape the parathas. When all the dough has been shaped, roll out each triangular piece into a rough 7-inch round. It helps to use your fingers to stretch the dough gently. The rolled dough rounds can be stacked if separated by wax paper or plastic wrap.

Work with 2 pieces of dough at a time. Sprinkle 1/4 cup of the kheema filling evenly over one dough round and top with a second round. Fold the edges over about 1/4 inch and press to seal in the filling.

Turn the paratha seam side down on a lightly floured counter and roll very gently, so that the meat filling does not come through the dough, to a 7- to 8-inch round; roll firmly over the thicker edges.

6 > Fry the parathas. Heat the tawa or sauté pan over medium heat until a drop of

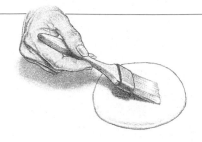

1> Brushing excess flour off the dough

2> Brushing the dough with clarified butter

3> Brushing the folded dough with
   clarified butter

4> Paratha folded over a second time

5> Rolling folded dough into a rough
   circle

water will sizzle on it. Lower the heat to medium-low and brush the pan with some of the remaining clarified butter. Place a paratha in the pan and fry until the bottom has brown spots and is golden and crisp, about 1 1/2 minutes. Brush the surface with a little more of the butter and, using a pancake turner, flip it over and fry the second side until golden, about 1 minute. The dough will puff up but then deflate once it is removed from the heat.

7 > **Serve the parathas.** With a pizza wheel or sharp knife cut the paratha into 4 wedges. Keep them warm in a low oven, loosely covered with foil, while you cook the

remaining breads. (The parathas can also be reheated in this way for about 10 minutes, or eaten at room temperature.) Serve with the green sauce if you like.

Yemenite Green Sauce (Schug)

My friend Meera Freeman gave me the recipe for this spicy sauce.

Makes: 1 cup (8.3 ounces/237 grams)

INGREDIENTS	MEASURE	WEIGHT	
	volume	ounces	grams
cardamom seed (from 6 pods)	1/4 teaspoon	--	--
1 small clove	--	--	--
cumin seeds, lightly toasted	1/2 teaspoon	--	--
salt	1/2 teaspoon	--	--
black pepper	1/4 teaspoon	--	--
2 garlic cloves	--	--	--
3 small hot green chiles, seeds and ribs removed	1/4 cup	about 1 ounce	31 grams
3 mild green chiles, seeds and ribs removed	1/4 cup	about 1 ounce	31 grams
1 large bunch cilantro, leaves and fine stems only	2 cups	about 1.5 ounces	42 grams
olive oil	1/4 liquid cup	2 ounces	56 grams

Grind the spices, salt, and pepper together in a mortar or a small spice or coffee grinder. Combine with the remaining ingredients in a food processor fitted with the metal blade and process until the consistency of a sauce, stopping to scrape down the sides two or three times.

POINTERS FOR SUCCESS

> The whole wheat flour must be fresh (see page 553), or it will not form as strong a dough and the meat filling will break through it.

> Use the higher amount of cayenne pepper if you want a little fire in the filling. The smaller amount is barely perceptible.

UNDERSTANDING

Using 100% finely ground whole wheat flour (atta), available in Indian or Middle-Eastern food markets, you can make the most delicate and deliciously wheaty dough.

1> Stretching the dough into a round

2> Kheema filling scattered over the top

3> Placing a second round of dough over the filling

4> Pressing the edges to seal in the filling

5> Folding the edges over and pressing down to seal

6> Rolling the turned-over dough into an 8-inch round

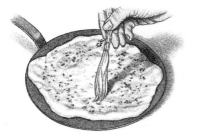

7> Brushing the paratha while it is frying on the tawa

8> Flipping the paratha over with a pancake turner

If using ordinary whole wheat flour, it is necessary to use one third to one-half unbleached all-purpose flour to provide the necessary elasticity. If using regular whole wheat flour, process it in a food processor for several minutes to reduce the size of the bran and germ, then sift it to remove any coarse particles. The resulting dough will be more chewy than the 100% whole wheat dough. Using half milk and half water instead of all water results in a more supple dough. I like to use lard in place of the clarified butter because its flavor is so compatible with the filling.

THE DOUGH PERCENTAGE

Flour:	100%
Water:	61%
Yeast:	0%
Salt:	2.3%

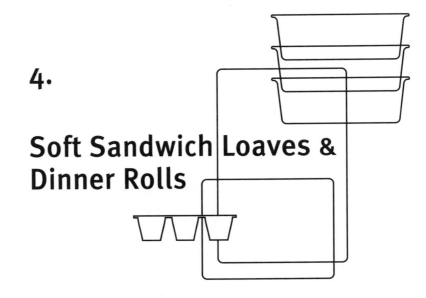

4.

Soft Sandwich Loaves & Dinner Rolls

DESPITE THE GROWING APPEAL OF FULL-FLAVORED, CRUSTY, AND CHEWY artisan breads, there will always be a place in our hearts for soft white sandwich bread. Just as when the French think of bread, a baguette surely pops into mind, when we think of bread, it is a soft white loaf. There's nothing to be ashamed of: the manufacture and standardization of the commercial loaf of sliced white bread at an affordable price is one of the miracles of American technology, and we love our soft, squishy white commercial sandwich bread. It sets the standard for the all-American peanut butter and jelly sandwich, or for warm cinnamon-raisin spiral toast with butter. It was my goal in developing a base recipe for this type of bread to achieve the ultimate in softness and lightness but with the integrity of a full homemade flavor, in contrast to the relatively bland commercial variety that serves as a mere vehicle for a filling. As for the texture, though many enjoy this type of bread freshly baked, at its absolute squishiest, I enjoy it still more lightly toasted, which emphasizes its airiness rather then its softness.

Although I find the basic soft sandwich recipe I developed to be nearly perfect just the way it is, I came up with several other fun and delicious versions by adding banana, potato, sweet potato or yam, Cheddar cheese, ricotta, and cottage cheese. These additions change the flavor, color, and texture, usually in subtle but sometimes more apparent, and always interesting ways.

All of these soft bread doughs are also wonderful for making classic dinner rolls. Make them for dinner parties, special occasions, and holidays. Of course they will also make the best hot dog and hamburger buns.

In addition to the basic soft white bread, I have included two soft sandwich loaves made partly with whole-grain wheat, Cracked Wheat Loaf and Flaxseed Loaf. They are not as soft as the sandwich loaves made with white flour, but you will enjoy the extra texture and wheatiness provided by these flavorful grains.

POINTERS FOR SUCCESS FOR MAKING SOFT BREADS

> It is fine to use bread flour instead of unbleached all-purpose flour for these breads, but the flours suggested will result in the softest texture.

> Adding 1 to 3 percent whole wheat flour will contribute significant wheaty flavor without affecting the texture of the bread.

> Soft breads need to be baked long enough so that the crust is strong enough to support the high rise and not cave in at the sides after baking.

> These loaves must not be cut when still hot, or they will collapse.

> Cut these soft breads with an electric knife or a serrated knife.

UNDERSTANDING

The secrets to the soft texture of these breads are unbleached all-purpose white flour, a high percentage of liquid, and a high proportion of butter. The airiness of texture is due to the high percentage of liquid and the milk, which strengthen the gluten (protein) structure of the bread. I think of this type of bread as an eggless brioche. Because it has no egg, it stays soft even on the second day after baking. And it freezes perfectly for up to 3 months. A higher amount of pre-ferment (sponge dough starter) gives a fuller flavor to this 100 percent white wheat flour bread, so almost 50 percent of the total amount of flour is used in the sponge compared to the usual 30 percent.

The proportion of basic essential ingredients in soft white sandwich breads falls into the range of 63.9 to 74.4 percent water, 0.74 to 1.64 percent instant yeast, 1.9 to 2.3 percent salt, and 4.4 to 17.9 percent butterfat. These percentages are based on the Baker's Percentage, in which every ingredient is based on the flour, which is given the value of 100 percent. The water and fat percentages include what is contained in any of the added ingredients.

Basic Soft White Sandwich Loaf

This is my best white bread for sandwiches, dinner rolls, cinnamon swirl or herb swirl breads, and toast. I developed it to match my childhood memory of my favorite bread, Silvercup, a soft, light, and airy bread like today's Wonder Bread, which made the best toast. This homemade version has the same texture but has a more yeasty and fuller flavor. In fact, this bread is like a brioche, with less butter and no egg. It has an even yet open crumb but is softer and lighter in texture. Part of the secret of its light texture is that, like brioche, it is made from an exceptionally moist dough. Lightly toasted and topped with soft scrambled eggs, it is nothing short of ambrosial. Michael Batterberry, publisher of *Food Arts* magazine, tasted this bread and said, "Mmmm. . . . This is what Wonder Bread, in its soul, really always wanted to be!"

TIME SCHEDULE

Dough Starter (Sponge): minimum 1 hour, maximum 24 hours
Minimum Rising Time: about 3 1/2 hours
Oven Temperature: 350°F
Baking Time: 50 minutes

Makes: two 8-by-4-by-4 1/2-inch-high loaves 1 1/4 pounds/581 grams

Dough Starter (Sponge)

INGREDIENTS	MEASURE	WEIGHT	
	volume	ounces	grams
unbleached all-purpose flour (use only Gold Medal, King Arthur, or Pillsbury)	2 1/4 cups plus 2 1/2 tablespoons	12 ounces	341 grams
water, at room temperature (70° to 90°F)	scant 1 3/4 liquid cups	14.3 ounces	405 grams
honey	2 tablespoons plus 1 teaspoon	1.5 ounces	45 grams
instant yeast (see page 561 for brands)	3/4 teaspoon	--	2.4 grams

two 8 1/2-in-4 1/2-inch loaf pans, lightly greased with cooking spray or oil;

a baking stone OR baking sheet

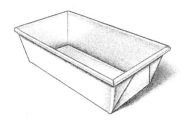

1 > Make the sponge. In a mixer bowl or other large bowl, combine the flour, water, honey, and instant yeast. Whisk until very smooth, to incorporate air, about 2 minutes. The sponge will be the consistency of a thick batter, Scrape down the sides of the bowl, and cover with plastic wrap.

Flour Mixture and Dough

INGREDIENTS	MEASURE	WEIGHT	
	volume	ounces	grams
unbleached all-purpose flour (use only Gold Medal, King Arthur, or Pillsbury)	2 cups plus 3 tablespoons	about 11 ounces	311 grams
dry milk, preferably nonfat	1/4 cup	1.5 ounces	40 grams
instant yeast	3/4 teaspoon	--	2.4 grams
unsalted butter, softened	9 tablespoons	4.5 ounces	128 grams
salt	2 1/4 teaspoons	--	15 grams
Optional: melted butter	1 tablespoon	0.5 ounce	14 grams

2 > Make the flour mixture and add to the sponge. In a medium bowl, whisk together the flour (reserve 1/4 cup if mixing by hand), dry milk, and instant yeast. Sprinkle this on top of the sponge and cover tightly with plastic wrap. Allow it to ferment for 1 to 4 hours at room temperature. (During this time, the sponge will bubble through the flour blanket in places: this is fine.)

3 > Mix the dough.

Mixer Method

Add the butter to the bowl and mix with the dough hook on low speed (#2 if using a KitchenAid) for 1 minute or until the flour is moistened enough to form a rough dough. Scrape down any bits of dough. Cover the bowl with plastic wrap and allow the dough to rest for 20 minutes.

Sprinkle on the salt and knead the dough on medium speed (#4 KitchenAid) for 7 to 10 minutes. It will not come away from the bowl until the last minute or so of kneading; it will be smooth and shiny and stick to your fingers. With an oiled spatula, scrape down any dough clinging to the sides of the bowl. If the dough is not stiff, knead in a little flour. If it is not at all sticky, spray it with a little water and knead it in. (The dough will weigh about 44.25 ounces/1258 grams.)

Hand Method

Add the salt and butter to the bowl and, with a wooden spoon or your hand, stir until all the flour is moistened. Knead the dough in the bowl until it comes together, then scrape it onto a lightly floured counter. Knead the dough for 5 minutes, enough to develop the gluten structure a little, adding as little of the reserved flour as possible to keep the dough from sticking. Use a bench scraper to scrape the dough and gather it together as you knead it. At this point, it will be very sticky. Cover it with the inverted bowl and allow it to rest for 20 minutes. (This resting time will make the dough less sticky and easier to work with.)

Knead the dough for another 5 minutes or until it is very smooth and elastic. It should still be tacky (sticky) enough to cling slightly to your fingers a little. If the dough is still very sticky, however, add some of the remaining reserved flour, or a little extra. (The dough will weigh about 44.25 ounces/1258 grams.)

Both Methods

4 > Let the dough rise. Using an oiled spatula or dough scraper, scrape the dough into a 4-quart dough-rising container or bowl, lightly oiled with cooking spray or oil. Push down the dough and lightly spray or oil the surface. Cover the container with a lid or plastic wrap. With a piece of tape, mark the side of the container at approximately where double the height of the dough would be. Allow the dough to rise (ideally at 75° to 80°F) until doubled, 1 1/2 to 2 hours.

Using an oiled spatula or dough scraper, scrape the dough onto a floured counter and press down on it gently to form a rectangle. It will be full of air and resilient. Try to maintain as many of the air bubbles as possible. Pull out and fold the dough over from all four sides into a tight package, or give it 2 business letter turns and set it back in the container. Again oil the surface, cover, and mark where double the height would now be. (It will fill the container fuller than before because it is puffier with air.) Allow the dough to rise for 1 to 2 hours or until it reaches the mark.

5 > Shape the dough and let it rise. Turn the dough out onto a lightly floured counter and cut it in half. Shape each piece into a loaf: begin by gently pressing the dough (or lightly rolling it with a rolling pin) into a wide rectangle; the exact size is not important at this point. (A long side of the dough should be facing toward you.) Dimple the dough with your fingertips to deflate any large bubbles. Fold over the right side of the dough to a little past the center. Fold over the left side of the dough to overlap it slightly. Press the center overlap section with the side of your hand to seal the dough. (If you have a lot of experience shaping, you may prefer at this point to rotate the dough 90 degrees—a quarter turn.) Starting at the top edge of the dough, roll it over three or four times, until it reaches the bottom edge of the dough: with each roll, press with your thumbs to seal it and at the same time push it away from you slightly to tighten the outer skin. As you roll and press, the dough will become wider. If it is not as long as the pan, place both hands close together on top of the dough and, rolling back and forth, gradually work your way toward the ends, gently stretching the dough. For the most even shape, it is important to keep a tight skin on the surface of the dough and not to tear it. If you want the edges of the loaf to be smooth, tuck the sides under.

Place the loaves in the prepared loaf pans; the dough will be about 1/2 inch from the top of the pans. Cover them with a large container, or cover them loosely with oiled plastic wrap, and allow to rise until the center is about 1 inch above the sides of the pan, 1 1/2 to 2 hours. When the dough is pressed with a fingertip, the depression will very slowly fill in.

6 > **Preheat the oven.** Preheat the oven to 350°F 45 minutes before baking. Have an oven shelf at the lowest level and place a baking stone or baking sheet on it, and a cast-iron skillet or sheet pan on the floor of the oven, before preheating.

7 > **Bake the bread.** Quickly but gently set the pans on the hot baking stone or hot baking sheet. Toss 1/2 cup of ice cubes into the pan beneath and immediately shut the door. Bake for 50 minutes or until medium golden brown and a skewer inserted in the middle comes out clean (an instant-read thermometer inserted into the center will read about 210°F). Halfway through baking, turn the pans around for even baking.

8 > **Glaze and cool the bread.** Remove the bread from the oven and set it on a wire rack. Brush the top of the bread with the optional melted butter. Unmold and cool top side up on a wire rack until barely warm, about 1 hour.

ULTIMATE FULL FLAVOR VARIATION

For the best flavor development, in Step 2, allow the sponge to ferment for 1 hour at room temperature and then refrigerate it for 8 to 24 hours. If using the hand mixing method, remove it from the refrigerator about 1 hour before mixing the dough.

>   If not using the dry milk, you can replace 1 cup of the water with 1 cup milk, preferably nonfat, scalded (brought to the boiling point) and cooled to lukewarm.

UNDERSTANDING

A greater amount of sponge dough starter (pre-ferment) offers a fuller flavor in this "plain" bread, so almost 50 percent of total amount of flour is used in the sponge, compared to the usual 30 percent of hearth breads.

If using liquid milk, it is scalded to deactivate the enzyme in it that could make the dough sticky.

Baking the bread at too high a temperature, would result in too thin a crust, which would cause keyholing, or caving in at the sides of the loaf. Therefore, this bread is baked at 350°F. It is also important for the bread to be thoroughly baked so that the crust is firm enough to prevent it from compressing. The loaves should not be cut until completely cool for the same reason.

THE DOUGH PERCENTAGE

Flour:	100%
Water:	66.3% (includes the water in the butter and honey)
Yeast:	0.74%
Salt:	2.3%
Butterfat:	15.9%

Butter-Dipped Dinner Rolls

When I was growing up, it was unthinkable to have dinner without bread on the table. Sliced rye was the usual fare for weekday suppers, but at my refined great-aunt Polly's, where dining was an occasion, it was always dinner rolls. To my mind, they represented the elegance of a bygone era. I still remember how she firmly taught me to break off a piece politely rather than to bite into it as my natural impulse dictated! When I grew up and started eating out at fine restaurants, I discovered that dinner rolls are a part of formal dining and was grateful for the lesson in manners.

TIME SCHEDULE

Dough Starter (Sponge): minimum 1 hour, maximum 24 hours
Minimum Rising Time: about 3 1/2 hours
Oven Temperature: 400°F
Baking Time: 15 to 20 minutes

Makes: 12 rolls

Dough Starter (Sponge)

INGREDIENTS	MEASURE	WEIGHT	
	volume	ounces	grams
unbleached all-purpose flour (use only Gold Medal, King Arthur, or Pillsbury)	1 cup plus 3 tablespoons	6 ounces	170 grams
water, at room temperature (70° to 90°F)	3/4 liquid cup plus 2 tablespoons	7 ounces	202 grams
honey	1 tablespoon plus 1/2 teaspoon	0.7 ounce	22 grams
instant yeast (see page 561 for brands)	1/4 teaspoon	--	0.8 gram

a baking stone OR baking sheet;

an 8-inch square pan OR 9-inch round pan (baked in
the square pan, each roll resembles a perfectly shaped
little loaf, 2 inches by 2 1/2 inches by 2 1/2 inches high
[1.6 ounces/46.7 grams])

1 > **Make the sponge.** In a mixer bowl or other large bowl, combine the flour, water,
honey, and instant yeast. Whisk until very smooth, to incorporate air, about 2 minutes. The sponge will be the consistency of a thick batter. Scrape down the sides of
the bowl and cover with plastic wrap.

Flour Mixture and Dough

INGREDIENTS	MEASURE	WEIGHT	
	volume	ounces	grams
unbleached all-purpose flour (use only Gold Medal, King Arthur, or Pillsbury)	1 cup plus 1 1/2 tablespoons	5.5 ounces	156 grams
dry milk, preferably nonfat	2 tablespoons	0.7 ounce	20 grams
instant yeast	1/2 teaspoon	--	1.6 grams
unsalted butter, softened	4 1/2 tablespoons	2.2 ounces	64 grams
salt	1 1/8 teaspoons	--	7.5 grams
unsalted butter, melted and cooled	4 tablespoons	2 ounces	56 grams

2 > **Combine the ingredients for the flour mixture and add to the sponge.** In a
medium bowl, whisk together the flour (reserve 1/4 cup if mixing by hand), dry milk,
and instant yeast. Sprinkle this on top of the sponge and cover tightly with plastic
wrap. Allow it to ferment for 1 to 4 hours at room temperature. (During this time the
sponge will bubble through the flour blanket in places: this is fine.)

3 > **Mix the dough.**

Mixer Method
Add the butter to the bowl and mix with the dough hook on low speed (#2 if using a
KitchenAid) for 1 minute or until the flour is moistened enough to form a rough
dough. Scrape down any bits of dough. Cover the top of the bowl with plastic wrap
and allow the dough to rest for 20 minutes.

Sprinkle on the salt and knead the dough on medium speed (#4 KitchenAid) for 7 to 10 minutes. It will not come away from the bowl until toward the last minute or so of kneading; it will be smooth and shiny and stick to your fingers. With an oiled spatula, scrape down any dough clinging to the sides of the bowl. If the dough is not stiff, knead in a little flour. If it is not at all sticky, spray it with a little water and knead it in. (It will weigh about 22 ounces/629 grams.)

Hand Method

Add the salt and butter to the bowl and, with a wooden spoon or your hand, stir until all the flour is moistened. Knead the dough in the bowl until it comes together, then scrape it onto a lightly floured counter. Knead the dough for 5 minutes, enough to develop the gluten structure a little, adding as little of the reserved flour as possible to keep the dough from sticking. Use a bench scraper to scrape the dough and gather it together as you knead it. At this point, it will be very sticky. Cover it with the inverted bowl and allow it to rest for 20 minutes. (This resting time will make the dough less sticky and easier to work with.)

Knead the dough for another 5 minutes or until it is very smooth and elastic. It should still be tacky (sticky) enough to cling slightly to your fingers. If the dough is still very sticky, however, add some of the remaining reserved flour, or a little extra. (The dough will weigh about 22 ounces/629 grams.)

Both Methods

4 > **Let the dough rise.** Using an oiled spatula or dough scraper, scrape the dough into a 2-quart dough-rising container or bowl, lightly oiled with cooking spray or oil. Push down the dough and lightly spray or oil the surface. Cover the container with a lid or plastic wrap. With a piece of tape, mark the side of the container at approximately where double the height of the dough would be. Allow the dough to rise (ideally at 75° to 80°F) until doubled, 1 1/2 to 2 hours.

Using an oiled spatula or dough scraper, scrape the dough onto a floured counter and press it gently into a rectangle. It will be full of air and resilient. Try to maintain as many of the air bubbles as possible. Pull out and fold the dough over from all four sides into a tight package, or give it 2 business letter turns and set it back in the container. Again oil the surface, cover, and mark where double the height would now be. (It will fill the container fuller than before because it is puffier with air.) Allow the dough to rise for 1 to 2 hours or until it reaches the mark.

5 > **Shape the rolls, glaze them, and let them rise.** You need to cut each half of the dough into 12 even pieces: the easiest way to do this is first to roll the dough gently into a long log and cut it into 4 equal pieces, then cut each piece into 3 equal pieces (each one should weigh 1 3/4 ounces/50 grams). Work with one piece at a time, keeping the remaining dough covered.

If the dough is sticky, flour your hand—but not the counter, so that the dough has a little resistance to help shape it. Roll each piece of dough, cupping your hand over it, to make a smooth ball. Seal the small indentation that forms in the bottom by pinching it tightly. This will help to make a tight skin on the outside of the roll, which will give it an even shape during baking.

Pour the butter into a small bowl. Dip each dough ball into the melted butter and coat all sides, using a pastry feather or brush as necessary, then place it pinched side down in the pan, making 3 rows of 4 rolls each. (The rows of 4 will be touching each other but the rows of 3 will have spaces around them. Because of the spaces, the dough will elongate into loaf shapes.) Repeat with the second batch.

Cover the pans with a large container, or cover loosely with oiled plastic wrap, and allow the rolls to rise for about 1 1/2 hours, until doubled; the center of the tops will almost reach the top of the pan. When the dough is pressed with a fingertip, the indentation will remain.

6 > Preheat the oven. Preheat the oven to 400°F 1 hour before baking. Have an oven shelf at the lowest level and place an oven stone or baking sheet on it, and a sheet pan or cast, iron skillet on the floor of the oven, before preheating.

7 > Bake the rolls. Quickly but gently set the pans on the hot baking stone or hot baking sheet, and toss 1/2 cup of ice cubes into the pan beneath. Immediately shut the door, and bake for 20 minutes or until medium golden brown (an instant-read thermometer inserted into the center will read about 212°F). If planning to reheat the rolls to serve later, bake them only for 15 minutes or until pale golden (about 180°F).

8 > Cool the rolls. Remove the rolls from the oven. Unmold and cool them top side up on wire racks until just warm, about 20 minutes, then pull apart.

NOTE To reheat the rolls, set them on a baking sheet and heat for about 5 minutes in a preheated 375°F oven.

A SELECTION OF SHAPES FOR DINNER ROLLS

Little Round Rolls (Makes 18)

EQUIPMENT

a large baking sheet, greased or lined with a Silpain or parchment

Cut the dough into 18 pieces: each should be about 2 tablespoons in volume and weigh about a little over 1 ounce/33 grams; this will result in 1 1/2-inch balls of dough (about the size of golf balls). Work with one piece at a time, keeping the remaining dough covered. Roll each piece into a ball between the palms of your hands, dip it in the butter, and place the rolls about 1 1/2 inches apart on the prepared baking sheet, staggering the rows.

Cover the pan with a large plastic container or cover loosely with oiled plastic wrap. Allow the rolls to rise for about 1 1/2 hours, until doubled. When the dough is pressed with a fingertip, the indentation will remain.

Proceed with Step 6, but bake for about 5 minutes less, as these rolls are a little smaller.

Parker House Rolls (Makes 18)

EQUIPMENT

a large baking sheet, greased or lined with a Silpain or parchment

Cut the dough into 18 pieces: each should be about 2 tablespoons in volume and weigh about a little over 1 ounce/33 grams; this will result in 1 1/2-inch balls of dough (about the size of golf balls). Work with one piece at a time, keeping the remaining dough covered.

Roll each piece into a ball between the palms of your hands, then flatten to a 1/4-inch-thick disk, 2 1/2 inches in diameter. Brush with melted butter and fold in half, pressing lightly on the fold. Set the rolls 1 inch apart on the prepared baking sheet and brush them with melted butter again.

Cover the pan with a large container, or cover loosely with oiled plastic wrap. Allow the rolls to rise for about 1 1/2 hours, until doubled. When the dough is pressed with a fingertip, the indentation will remain.

Folding the dough round in half for Parker House Rolls

Proceed with Step 6, but bake for about 5 minutes less, as these rolls are a little smaller.

Cloverleaf Rolls (Makes 18)

EQUIPMENT

muffin tins or 6-ounce custard cups, greased

Cut the dough into 18 pieces: each should be about 2 tablespoons in volume and weigh about a little over 1 ounce/33 grams; this will result in 1 1/2-inch balls of dough (about the size of golf balls). Work with one piece at a time, keeping the remaining dough covered.

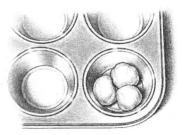

Cloverleaf Rolls

Roll each piece into a ball between the palms of your hands, then cut into 3 equal pieces. Shape these into balls by rolling them between the palms of your hands, and place a set of 3 balls in each greased muffin cup or custard cup. Brush them with the melted butter.

Cover the pans or cups with a large container, or cover loosely with oiled plastic wrap. Let the dough rise until almost doubled, 30 to 45 minutes. The rolls should be 2 inches wide by 1 inch high. Brush with any remaining melted butter.

Proceed with Step 6, but bake for about 5 minutes less, as these rolls are a little smaller.

ULTIMATE FULL FLAVOR VARIATION

For the best flavor development, in Step 2, allow the sponge to ferment for 1 hour at room temperature and then refrigerate it for 8 to 24 hours. If using the hand mixing method, remove it from the refrigerator about 1 hour before mixing the dough.

VARIATIONS

Rosy Red Bread   The water leftover from boiling beets is a wonderful natural food color. Used in place of water in the dough, it adds a very subtle indefinable flavor and an absolutely gorgeous color. (The natural acidity of bread dough sets the color.) For a paler pink color, cut the beet liquid by half with water. What little girl could resist her own little pink loaf! When lightly toasted and spread with a little butter and garnet-colored raspberry jam, the interplay of colors adds unexpected pleasure to every bite.

Lagniappe: Little Oyster Loaves   My absolute favorite use for these Butter-Dipped Mini Loaves is adapted from an idea in M. F. K. Fisher's book *The Art of Eating*. It makes a quick and easy lunch or brunch dish. Simply cut off the top of a roll (reserve this "lid") and hollow out the center. Brush the inside of the lid and the inside of the loaf with melted butter and toast in a preheated 400°F oven for 3 minutes or just until lightly crisp, not golden. Meanwhile, dust 3 medium oysters with cornmeal and sauté them quickly in butter. The object is to crisp the outsides and heat the insides without really cooking them much. Stuff them into the loaf and drizzle with more butter, and a little heavy cream, if desired. Top with the lid and serve. Prepare for bliss!

POINTERS FOR SUCCESS

>   If not using the dry milk, you can replace 1 cup of the water with 1 cup milk, preferably nonfat, scalded (brought to the boiling point) and cooled to lukewarm. (It is scalded to deactivate the protease enzyme in it, which would slow down yeast production and can cause breakdown of the protein in the flour, resulting in a sticky and weakened dough.)

> I learned the technique of dipping shaped balls of dough (before they rise) in clarified or strained butter at George Lang's restaurant, Gundel, in Budapest, Hungary. This process infuses the entire crust with a delicious buttery flavor.

THE DOUGH PERCENTAGE

Flour:	100%
Water:	66.3% (includes the water in the butter and honey)
Yeast:	0.74%
Salt:	2.3%
Butterfat:	15.9%

Pullman Loaf Sandwich Bread (Pain de Mie)

The *Pain de mie* is the basic white sandwich bread of France. This bread has a minimum of crust, the result of baking the loaf in a special straight-sided covered pan. The cover prevents a full rise, producing the tight fine crumb and minimum of crust.

This soft, fine-grained loaf is very similar to the Basic Soft White Sandwich Bread recipe, but it is one of the quickest and easiest yeast breads to make. It is made without a dough starter and uses a larger than usual amount of yeast so that it only takes an hour to rise. It is a bread with which to start your yeast bread baking adventures.

TIME SCHEDULE

Starter: straight dough method
Rising Time: 1 to 1 1/2 hours
Oven Temperature: 425°F
Baking Time: 1 hour

Makes: a 15-by-4-by-3 1/4-inch-high loaf 35.7 ounces/1015 grams

INGREDIENTS	MEASURE	WEIGHT	
	volume	ounces	grams
unbleached all-purpose flour (use only Gold Medal, King Arthur, or Pillsbury)	4 cups	20.5 ounces	585 grams
dry whole milk	1/4 cup	1.5 ounces	40 grams
instant yeast (see page 561 for brands)	1 tablespoon	--	9.6 grams
unsalted butter, softened	6 tablespoons	3 ounces	85 grams
water at room temperature (70° to 90°F)	1 1/2 liquid cups	12.5 ounces	354 grams
honey	2 tablespoons	1.5 ounces	40 grams
salt	2 teaspoons	--	13.2 grams

a Pullman loaf pan (16 inches by 4 inches by 4
inches), lightly greased with cooking spray or oil

1 > Mix the dough.

Mixer Method

In a large mixer bowl, whisk together the flour, dry milk, and yeast. Add the butter
and mix with the dough hook on low speed (#2 if using a KitchenAid), then add the
water, honey, and salt. When all the flour is moistened, raise the speed to medium
(#4 KitchenAid) and beat for 7 minutes. The dough will be smooth, shiny, and
slightly sticky to the touch. If the dough is not stiff, knead in a little flour. If it is not
at all sticky, spray it with a little water and knead it in. (It will weigh about 38.5
ounces/1102 grams.)

Hand Method

In a large bowl, whisk together all but 1/4 cup of the flour, the dry milk, and yeast.
Add the butter and, with a wooden spoon or your hand, stir in the water, honey, and
salt until the flour is moistened. Knead the dough in the bowl until it comes together,
then scrape it onto a lightly floured counter. Knead for 5 minutes, enough to develop
the gluten structure a little, adding as little of the reserved flour as possible to keep
the dough from sticking. Use a bench scraper to scrape the dough and gather it
together as you knead it. At this point, it will be very sticky. Cover it with the
inverted bowl and allow it to rest for 20 minutes. (This resting time will make the
dough less sticky and easier to work with.)

Knead the dough for another 5 minutes or until it is very smooth and elastic. It
should still be tacky (sticky) enough to cling slightly to your fingers. If the dough is
still very sticky, however, add some of the remaining reserved flour, or a little extra.
(It will weigh about 38.5 ounces/1102 grams.)

Both Methods

2 > Shape the dough and let it rise. On a lightly floured counter, shape the dough
into a football. Flour the top and cover it with plastic wrap. Allow it to relax for
10 to 15 minutes. Remove the plastic wrap and gently deflate the dough, using your
fingertips to spread it into a rectangle about 10 inches by 8 inches. Flour the counter
as necessary to keep it from sticking.

Give the dough one business-letter turn, then press or roll it out again to about 12 inches by 5 inches and shape it into a 16-inch-long loaf (see page 69). Set it in the prepared pan. Grease the top of the pan and slide it into place, leaving it a few inches ajar so that you can gauge the progress of the rising dough (be sure to insert the lid starting with the curved end farthest from you down, so that when you slide the lid open, it does not scrape across the bread!). Cover the exposed area with plastic wrap if not using a proof box. Cover the pan with a large container or set it in a warm area, and allow it to rise until it is about 1/2 inch below the top of the lid, 1 to 1 1/2 hours. When the dough is pressed with a fingertip, the depression will very slowly fill in.

3 > **Preheat the oven.** Preheat the oven to 425°F 30 minutes before baking. Have an oven shelf at the lowest level. (Do NOT use an oven stone.)

4 > **Bake the bread.** Gently place the pan in the oven and bake for 30 minutes. Quickly slide off the lid, turn the pan around, for even baking, and continue baking for about 30 minutes until deeply brown. If the bread starts getting too dark after 20 minutes, tent it loosely with foil.

5 > **Cool the bread.** Remove the bread from the oven and unmold it onto a large wire rack. Cool it top side up until barely warm, about 1 hour.

POINTERS FOR SUCCESS

> Instead of purchasing this special pan, however, you can make a "covered" pan by using a heavy baking sheet topped with a metal weight, though, of course, if the pan is tapered, the loaf will not make perfectly square *slices* like traditional pain de mie.

> If not using the dry milk, you can replace 1 cup of the water with 1 cup milk, scalded (brought just under the boil) and cooled to lukewarm.

UNDERSTANDING

This bread is not given a resting time (autolyse) before adding the salt, because the object is to create a slightly weak dough. A more developed strong dough would have larger holes and tend to keyhole (cave in) at the sides as well as the top.

It is essential to bake this bread for the full baking time, as a dark firm crust will keep it from caving in or collapsing: even so, the center still tends to dip about 1/2 inch. However, if one-third of the recipe is baked in a 5 1/3- to 6-cup pan, it will dip only about 1/8 inch. Baking time is 40 to 50 minutes—no need to tent with foil.

THE DOUGH PERCENTAGE

Flour:	100%
Water:	**63.9%** (includes the water in the butter and honey)
Yeast:	**1.64%**
Salt:	**2.3%**
Butterfat:	**11.8%**

Cinnamon Raisin Loaf

Soft white raisin bread spiraled with cinnamon sugar is one of America's most popular breads. I love the sweetness and moistness the raisins contribute to the crumb but have to accept the fact that not everyone is a raisin lover. So if you must, omit the raisins—you will still have a terrific bread.

Of course, if you are a raisin lover, you can instead occasionally omit the cinnamon spiral for a more versatile raisin bread that makes fantastic sandwiches, from ham to grilled cheese. And, to have it both ways, you can easily convert the raisin bread into cinnamon toast by brushing it with melted butter and sprinkling it with a mixture of 1/2 teaspoon or more of cinnamon to 1 tablespoon of sugar.

Gaps in the spiral are common in a spiraled bread. To minimize the gaps, for this bread, I add the raisins to the dough rather than to the cinnamon sugar.

TIME SCHEDULE

Dough Starter (Sponge): minimum 1 hour, maximum 24 hours
Minimum Rising Time: about 3 1/2 hours
Oven Temperature: 350°F
Baking Time: 50 minutes

Makes: two 8-by-4-by-4 1/2-inch-high loaves, about 1 1/2 pounds/700 grams with raisins; 1 1/4 pounds/581 grams without

Dough Starter (Sponge)

INGREDIENTS	MEASURE	WEIGHT	
	volume	ounces	grams
unbleached all-purpose flour (use only Gold Medal, King Arthur, or Pillsbury)	2 1/4 cups plus 2 1/2 tablespoons	12 ounces	341 grams
water, at room temperature (70° to 90°F)	scant 1 3/4 liquid cups	14.3 ounces	405 grams
honey	2 tablespoons plus 1 teaspoon	1.5 ounces	45 grams
instant yeast (see page 561 for brands)	3/4 teaspoon	--	2.4 grams

EQUIPMENT

two 8 1/2-by-4 1/2-inch loaf pans, lightly greased with cooking spray or oil;

a baking stone OR baking sheet

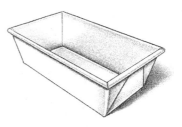

1 > **Make the sponge.** In a mixer bowl or other large bowl, combine the flour, water, honey, and instant yeast. Whisk until very smooth to incorporate air, about 2 minutes. The sponge will be the consistency of a thick batter. Scrape down the sides of the bowl and cover it with plastic wrap.

Flour Mixture and Dough

INGREDIENTS	MEASURE	WEIGHT	
	volume	ounces	grams
unbleached all-purpose flour (use only Gold Medal, King Arthur, or Pillsbury)	2 cups plus 3 tablespoons	about 11 ounces	311 grams
dry milk, preferably nonfat	1/4 cup	1.5 ounces	40 grams
instant yeast	3/4 teaspoon	--	2.4 grams
unsalted butter, softened	9 tablespoons	4.5 ounces	128 grams
salt	2 1/4 teaspoons	--	15 grams
Optional: melted butter	1 tablespoon	0.5 ounce	14 grams

2 > **Combine the ingredients for the flour mixture and add to the sponge.** In a medium bowl, whisk together the flour (reserve 1/4 cup if mixing by hand), dry milk,

and instant yeast. Sprinkle this on top of the sponge and cover tightly with plastic wrap. Allow it to ferment for 1 to 4 hours at room temperature. (During this time the sponge will bubble through the flour blanket in places: this is fine.)

Raisins

INGREDIENTS	MEASURE	WEIGHT	
	volume	ounces	grams
raisins	1 cup	5 ounces	144 grams

3 > Mix the dough.

Mixer Method

Add the butter to the bowl and mix on low speed with the dough hook (#2 if using a KitchenAid) for 1 minute or until the flour is moistened enough to form a rough dough. Scrape down any bits of dough. Cover the top of the bowl with plastic and allow the dough to rest for 20 minutes.

Sprinkle on the salt and knead the dough on medium speed (#4 KitchenAid) for 7 to 10 minutes. It will not come away from the bowl until toward the last minute or so of kneading; it will be smooth and shiny and stick to your fingers. With an oiled spatula, scrape down any dough clinging to the sides of the bowl. If the dough is not stiff, knead in a little flour. If it is not at all sticky, spray it with a little water and knead it in. (It will weigh about 44.25 ounces/1258 grams.) Cover the bowl with plastic wrap and allow the dough to relax for 10 minutes.

Add the raisins and mix on low speed (#2 KitchenAid) for about 2 minutes to incorporate them evenly. But don't worry too much about how well they distribute, because deflating and folding the dough after the first rise will distribute them more evenly.

Hand Method

Add the salt and butter to the bowl and, with a wooden spoon or your hand, stir until all the flour is moistened. Knead the dough in the bowl until it comes together, then scrape it onto a lightly floured counter. Knead the dough for 5 minutes, enough to develop the gluten structure a little, adding as little of the reserved flour as possible to keep it from sticking. Use a bench scraper to scrape the dough and gather it together as you knead it. At this point, it will be very sticky. Cover it with the inverted bowl and allow it to rest for 20 minutes. (This resting time will make the dough less sticky and easier to work with.)

Knead the dough for another 5 minutes or until it is very smooth and elastic. It should still be tacky (sticky) enough to cling slightly to your fingers. If the dough is still very sticky, however, add some of the remaining reserved flour, or a little extra. (The dough will weigh about 44.25 ounces/1258 grams.) Cover the bowl with plastic wrap and allow the dough to relax for 10 minutes.

Add the raisins and, with an oiled wooden spoon or your hand, mix in the raisins to incorporate them evenly. But don't worry too much about how well they distribute, because deflating and folding the dough after the first rise will distribute them more evenly.

Both Methods

5 > **Let the dough rise.** Using an oiled spatula or dough scraper, scrape the dough into a 4-quart dough-rising container or bowl, lightly oiled with cooking spray or oil. Push down the dough and lightly spray or oil the surface. Cover the container with a lid or plastic wrap. With a piece of tape, mark the side of the container at approximately where double the height of the dough would be. Allow the dough to rise (ideally at 75° to 80°F) until doubled, 1 1/2 to 2 hours.

Using an oiled spatula or dough scraper, scrape the dough into a floured counter and press down on it gently to form a rectangle. It will be full of air and resilient. Try to maintain as many of the air bubbles as possible. Give the dough 1 business letter turn and set it back in the container. Oil the surface again, cover, and refrigerate for 1 hour to firm the dough for rolling.

Cinnamon Sugar Spiral Filling (optional)

INGREDIENTS	MEASURE	WEIGHT	
	volume	ounces	grams
sugar	1/4 cup plus 2 tablespoons	2.6 ounces	75 grams
cinnamon	4 teaspoons	0.3 ounce	9 grams
lightly beaten egg	2 tablespoons	about 1 ounce	32 grams

6 > **Make the optional cinnamon sugar spiral filling.** In a small bowl, whisk together the sugar and cinnamon.

7 > **Shape the dough and let it rise.** Turn the dough out onto a lightly floured counter and cut it in half. Keep one piece of dough covered while you work with the other piece.

To make raisin bread without the cinnamon spiral: **Shape each piece into a loaf and place the dough in the prepared loaf pans; it will be about 1/2 inch from the top of the pans.**

To make a spiral bread: **You may want to refrigerate half the dough so that you don't have to rush the shaping of the first piece.**

On a lightly floured counter, roll out one piece of dough to a rectangle 7 1/2 inches wide by 14 inches long and about 1/4 inch thick. Using your fingertips, gently press (dimple) the dough all over to deflate air bubbles that result in gaps in the spiral. Brush the dough with the lightly beaten egg (about 1 tablespoon per loaf) leaving a 3/4-inch margin all around.

Sprinkle half the cinnamon sugar evenly over the dough, leaving a 3/4-inch margin on all sides. Starting from the short end closest to you, roll the dough up tightly, as you would a jelly roll; brush the top of the dough with egg and squeeze the dough gently all along the length of the roll with each roll so that it will adhere well to the filling. If necessary, use your hands to push in the ends of the roll so that it does not get larger than 7 1/2 inches long. When you come to the end, make a seam by tightly pinching the edge of the dough to seal in the filling. Push in any inner coils of dough on the sides that may have worked their way out and pinch the ends of the dough tightly together to seal. Tuck them under so that the loaf will fit into the pan.

Place the roll seam side down in a prepared pan; it will be about 1/2 inch from the top of the pan. Repeat for the second loaf.

Cover the pans with a large container, or cover loosely with oiled plastic wrap. Allow to rise about 1 to 2 hours or until the center is 1 1/2 inches above the sides of the pan. When the dough is pressed lightly with your fingertip, the indentation will remain.

8 > Preheat the oven. Preheat the oven to 350°F 45 minutes before baking. Have an oven shelf at the lowest level and place a baking stone or baking sheet on it before preheating.

9 > Bake the bread. Quickly but gently set the pans on the hot baking stone or hot baking sheet, and immediately shut the door. Bake for 50 minutes or until the bread is medium golden brown and a skewer inserted in the middle comes out clean (an instant-read thermometer inserted into the center will read about 211°F). Halfway through baking, turn the pans around for even baking.

10 > Glaze and cool the bread. Remove the pans from the oven and set them on a wire rack. Brush the tops of the breads with melted butter. Unmold and cool top side up on a wire rack until barely warm, about 1 hour.

VARIATION

Herb Spiral Loaves   In place of the cinnamon sugar, use 2/3 cup (1 ounce/28 grams) minced parsley, 2/3 cup (1.25 ounces/32 grams) minced scallions (white and green parts) or chives, and 2 pinches of salt.

ULTIMATE FULL FLAVOR VARIATION

For the best flavor development of the dough, in Step 2, allow the sponge to ferment for 1 hour at room temperature and then refrigerate it for 8 to 24 hours. (If using the hand mixing method, remove it from the refrigerator about 1 hour before mixing the dough.)

POINTERS FOR SUCCESS

> If not using the dry milk, you can replace 1 cup of the water with 1 cup milk, preferably nonfat, scalded (brought to just under the boiling point) and cooled to luke-warm. (The milk is scalded to deactivate the protease enzyme in it, which would slow down yeast production and can cause breakdown of the protein in the flour, resulting in a sticky and weakened dough.)

> I find that a whole egg wash works best to prevent gaps in a spiraled dough.

> When chilling the dough before shaping, you can refrigerate it for as long as 24 hours.

UNDERSTANDING

Using unsoaked raisins keeps the crumb from darkening. The raisins soften from the liquid in this moist dough.

"Shelling," the separation of the top layer, resulting in a large gap, is a potential problem with spiraled bread. It can be caused by underproofing (not allowing the shaped dough to rise fully, resulting in an increased oven spring that could cause this separation). Allowing the shaped dough to rise longer before baking will help to prevent it from having gaps because there will be less sudden oven spring.

THE DOUGH PERCENTAGE

Flour:	100%
Water:	66.3% (includes the water in the butter and honey)
Yeast:	0.74%
Salt:	2.3%
Butterfat:	15.9%

Potato Sandwich Loaf

The addition of potato to the basic soft white bread recipe produces a slightly heavier and denser bread. The potato contributes moisture and an earthy undertone, and toasting concentrates this appealing flavor. This bread is a wonderful accompaniment to all manner of fillings from pot roast to gravlax, and it also makes lovely cucumber and dill tea sandwiches.

TIME SCHEDULE

Dough Starter (Sponge): minimum 1 hour, maximum 24 hours
Minimum Rising Time: about 3 1/2 hours
Oven Temperature: 475°F, then 375°F
Baking Time: 25 to 30 minutes

Makes: an 8-by-4-by-4 1/2- to 5-inch-high loaf 18.7 ounces/531 grams

Dough Starter (Sponge)

INGREDIENTS	MEASURE	WEIGHT	
	volume	ounces	grams
1 medium potato, washed but not peeled		6 ounces	170 grams
unbleached all-purpose flour (use only Gold Medal, King Arthur, or Pillsbury)	3/4 cup plus 1 tablespoon	4 ounces	117 grams
Water, from boiling the potato, at room temperature (70° to 90°F)	1/2 liquid cup *minus* 1 tablespoon	3.5 ounces	100 grams
honey	1 tablespoon	0.75 ounce	20 grams
instant yeast (see page 561 for brands)	1/4 teaspoon	--	0.8 gram

EQUIPMENT

an 8 1/2-by-4 1/2-inch loaf pan, lightly greased with cooking spray or oil;

a baking stone OR baking sheet

1 > Boil the potato and make the sponge. Boil the potato in unsalted water for 20 to 30 minutes or until tender. Drain, reserving the potato water, and let cool slightly. Measure out 1/2 cup minus 1 tablespoon of potato water and let it cool to lukewarm. Peel the potato and put it through it a ricer or strainer, or mash it gently to make a smooth puree; measure or weigh out 1/2 cup (4.5 ounces/128 grams).

In a mixer bowl or other large bowl, combine the flour, potato water, honey, and yeast. Whisk until very smooth, to incorporate air, about 2 minutes. The sponge will be the consistency of a thick batter. Scrape down the sides of the bowl and cover it with plastic wrap.

Flour Mixture and Dough

INGREDIENTS	MEASURE	WEIGHT	
	volume	ounces	grams
unbleached all-purpose flour (use only Gold Medal, King Arthur, or Pillsbury)	1 1/4 cups	6.3 ounces	180 grams
dry milk, preferably nonfat	2 tablespoons	0.5 ounce	16 grams
instant yeast	3/4 teaspoon	--	2.4 grams
unsalted butter, softened	4 teaspoons	0.6 ounce	18.5 grams
riced or mashed potato (from above)	1/2 cup	4.5 ounces	126 grams
salt	1 teaspoon	--	6.6 grams
Optional: melted butter	1/2 tablespoon	0.25 ounce	7 grams

2 > Combine the ingredients for the flour mixture and add to the sponge. In a medium bowl, whisk together flour (reserve 2 tablespoons if mixing by hand), the dry milk, and yeast. Sprinkle this on top of the sponge and cover tightly with plastic wrap. Allow it to ferment for 1 to 4 hours at room temperature. (During this time the sponge will bubble through the flour blanket in places: this is fine.)

3 > Mix the dough.

Mixer Method

Add the butter and mashed potato to the bowl and mix with the dough hook on low speed (#2 if using a KitchenAid) for 1 minute or until the flour is moistened enough to form a rough dough. Scrape down any bits of dough. Cover the bowl with plastic wrap and allow the dough to rest for 20 minutes.

Sprinkle on the salt and knead the dough on medium speed (#4 KitchenAid) for 7 to 10 minutes. It will be smooth, shiny, and tacky (sticky) enough to stick to your fingers. With an oiled spatula, scrape down any dough clinging to the sides of the bowl. If the dough is not stiff, knead in a little flour. If it is not at all sticky, spray with and knead it in a little water. (The dough will weigh about 20.5 ounces/583 grams.)

Hand Method

Add the salt, butter, and mashed potato to the bowl and, with a wooden spoon or your hand, stir until all the flour is moistened. Knead the dough in the bowl until it comes together, then scrape it onto a lightly floured counter. Knead the dough for 5 minutes, just to begin to develop the gluten structure, adding as little of the reserved flour as possible. Use a bench scraper to scrape the dough and gather it together as you knead it. At this point, it will be very sticky. Cover it with the inverted bowl and allow it to rest for 20 minutes. (This resting time will make the dough less sticky and easier to work with.)

Knead the dough for another 5 minutes or until it is very smooth and elastic. It should still be tacky (sticky) enough to cling slightly to your fingers a little. If the dough is still very sticky, however, add some of the remaining reserved flour, or a little extra. (The dough will weigh about 20.5 ounces/583 grams.)

Both Methods

4 > **Let the dough rise.** Using an oiled spatula or dough scraper, scrape the dough into a 2-quart dough-rising container or bowl, lightly greased with cooking spray or oil. Push down the dough and lightly spray or oil the top. Cover the container with a lid or plastic. With a piece of tape, mark the side of the container at approximately where double the height of the dough would be. Allow the dough to rise (ideally at 75° to 80°F) until it has doubled, 1 to 2 hours.

Using an oiled spatula or dough scraper, scrape the dough onto a floured counter and gently press it down to form a rectangle. It will be full of air and resilient. Try to maintain as many of the air bubbles as possible. Pull out and fold the dough over from all 4 sides into a tight package, or give it 2 business letter turns, and set it back in the container. Again oil the surface, cover, and mark where double the height would now be. (It will fill the container fuller than before because it is puffier with air.) Allow it to rise for 1 1/2 to 2 hours or until doubled. When the dough is pressed with a fingertip, the depression will very slowly fill in.

5 > **Shape the dough and let it rise.** Turn the dough onto a lightly floured counter and shape it into a loaf (see page 67 for illustrated directions). Place in the prepared loaf pan; it should be no higher than 1/2 inch from the top of the pan. Cover with a large container, or cover loosely with oiled plastic wrap, and allow to rise until the center is about 1 1/2 inches above the sides of the pan, 1 1/2 to 2 hours.

6 > **Preheat the oven.** Preheat the oven to 475°F 1 hour before baking. Have an oven shelf at the lowest level and place a baking stone or baking sheet on it, and a cast-iron skillet or sheet pan on the floor of the oven, before preheating.

7 > Bake the bread. Quickly but gently set the pan on the hot baking stone or hot baking sheet. Toss 1/2 cup of ice cubes into the pan beneath and immediately shut the door. Bake for 5 minutes. Lower the heat to 375°F and continue baking for 20 to 25 minutes or until the bread is medium golden brown and a skewer inserted in the middle comes out clean (an instant-read thermometer inserted into the center will read about 190°F). Halfway through baking, turn the pans around for even baking.

8 > Glaze and cool the bread. Remove the bread from the oven and set it on a wire rack. Brush the top of the bread with the melted butter, if using. Unmold and cool it top side up on a wire rack until barely, warm, about 1 hour.

ULTIMATE FULL FLAVOR VARIATION

For the best flavor development, in Step 3, allow the sponge to ferment for 1 hour at room temperature and then refrigerate it for 8 to 24 hours. If using the hand mixing method, remove it from the refrigerator about 1 hour before mixing the dough.

VARIATION

Purple Potato Bread Using mashed purple potatoes produces amazing results. The baked bread has a lovely mauve crumb, whose color disappears entirely on freezing. On toasting, however, the color magically reappears. This would obviously make a great hit with children.

POINTERS FOR SUCCESS

> You can replace the potato water and the dry milk with scalded milk that has been cooled to lukewarm.

> To replace the mashed potato with potato flour, add 2 tablespoons plus 1 teaspoon (1 scant ounce/25.5 grams) potato flour to the flour mixture and, just before mixing the dough, add 1/2 cup minus a scant 1 tablespoon (3.7 ounces/105 grams) water. Although this is an exact equivalent and will result in essentially the same texture and flavor in the bread, the dough usually rises a little more using potato flour because it is incorporated more evenly into the dough.

UNDERSTANDING

The amount of potato used in this bread is only about half of that used in the Potato Buttermilk Bread (page 319), so the potato flavor is very subtle (it's more apparent if using the potato boiling water).

Less butter is used here than in the Basic Soft White Sandwich Loaf (page 244) because the potato enriches it with moisture and flavor.

The oven starts at a high temperature because this produces the highest possible rise for this bread. This bread can bake at a higher temperature than the Soft White Sandwich Loaf because the potato gives it more structure, so it does not require as thick a crust.

THE DOUGH PERCENTAGE

Flour:	**100%** (includes the starch in the potato)
Water:	**63.2%** (includes the water in the butter, honey, and potato)
Yeast:	**1%**
Salt:	**2.2%**
Butterfat:	**4.6%**

Banana Feather Loaf

No, this is not a cake-like banana bread. This is a real bread, very similar to the Potato Sandwich Loaf (page 266), with the same base. It is equally moist, without being at all chewy, and it is much lighter and softer. In fact, this is the lightest of all my breads. It becomes firmer on the second day but retains its moistness and lightness. I love it with lemon curd and also with peanut butter. The flavor of banana is subtle and becomes more assertive when toasted.

TIME SCHEDULE

Dough Starter (Sponge): minimum 1 hour, maximum 24 hours
Minimum Rising Time: about 3 1/2 hours
Oven Temperature: 425°F, then 375°F
Baking Time: 25 to 30 minutes

Makes: an 8-by-4-by-4 1/2-inch-high loaf 18 ounces/528 grams

Dough Starter (Sponge)

INGREDIENTS	MEASURE	WEIGHT	
	volume	ounces	grams
unbleached all-purpose flour (use only Gold Medal, King Arthur, or Pillsbury)	1/2 cup plus 1 tablespoon	about 2.75 ounces	80 grams
water, at room temperature (70° to 90°F)	scant 1/2 liquid cup (3 1/2 fluid ounces)	3.6 ounces	103 grams
honey	1 tablespoon	0.75 ounce	20 grams
instant yeast (see page 561 for brands)	1/4 teaspoon	--	0.8 gram

EQUIPMENT

an 8 1/2-by-4 1/2-inch loaf pan, lightly greased with cooking spray or oil;

a baking stone OR baking sheet

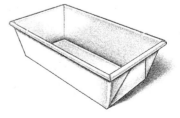

1 > Make the sponge. In a mixer bowl or other large bowl, combine the flour, water, honey, and yeast. Whisk until very smooth, to incorporate air, about 2 minutes. The sponge will be the consistency of a thick batter. Scrape down the sides of the bowl and cover it with plastic wrap.

Flour Mixture and Dough

INGREDIENTS	MEASURE	WEIGHT	
	volume	ounces	grams
unbleached all-purpose flour (use only Gold Medal, King Arthur, or Pillsbury)	about 1 1/2 cups	7.25 ounces	207 grams
instant yeast	3/4 teaspoon	--	2.4 grams
dry milk, preferably nonfat	2 tablespoons	0.7 ounce	20 grams
unsalted butter, softened	4 teaspoons	0.6 ounce	18.5 grams
1 very ripe medium banana, lightly mashed	1/2 cup	4 ounces	113 grams
salt	1 teaspoon	--	6.6 grams
Optional: melted butter	1/2 tablespoon	0.25 ounce	7 grams

2 > Combine the ingredients for the flour mixture and add to the sponge. In a medium bowl, whisk together the flour (reserve 1/4 cup if mixing by hand), yeast, and dry milk. Sprinkle this on top of the sponge and cover tightly with plastic wrap. Allow it to ferment for 1 to 4 hours at room temperature. (During this time the sponge will bubble through the flour blanket in places: this is fine.)

3 > Mix the dough.

Mixer Method
Add the butter and mashed banana to the bowl and mix with the dough hook on low speed (#2 if using a KitchenAid) for 1 minute or until the flour is moistened enough to form a rough dough. Scrape down any bits of dough. Cover the bowl with plastic wrap and allow the dough to rest for 20 minutes.

Sprinkle on the salt and knead the dough on medium speed (#4 KitchenAid) for 7 to 10 minutes. It will be smooth and shiny and tacky enough to stick to your fingers. With an oiled spatula or dough scraper, scrape down any dough clinging to the sides of the bowl. If the dough is not stiff, knead in a little flour. If it is not at all sticky, spray with a little water and knead it in. (The dough will weigh about 19.5 ounces/559 grams.)

Hand Method

Add the butter, mashed banana, and salt to the bowl and, with a wooden spoon or your hand, stir until all the flour is moistened. Knead the dough in the bowl until it comes together, then scrape it onto a lightly floured counter. Knead the dough for 5 minutes, enough to develop the gluten structure a little, adding as little of the reserved flour as possible to keep it from sticking. Use a bench scraper to scrape the dough and gather it together as you knead it. At this point, it will be very sticky. Cover it with the inverted bowl and allow it to rest for 20 minutes. (This resting time will make the dough less sticky and easier to work with.)

Knead the dough for another 5 minutes or until it is very smooth and elastic. It should still be tacky (sticky) enough to cling slightly to your fingers. If the dough is still very sticky, however, add some of the remaining reserved flour, or a little extra. (The dough will weigh about 19.5 ounces/559 grams.)

Both Methods

4 > Let the dough rise. Using an oiled spatula or dough scraper, scrape the dough into a 1 1/2-quart dough-rising container or bowl, lightly greased with cooking spray or oil. Push down the dough and lightly spray or oil the top. Cover the container with a lid or plastic wrap. With a piece of tape, mark the side of the container at approximately where double the height of the dough would be. Allow the dough to rise (ideally at 75° to 80°F) for 1 1/2 to 2 hours, until it has doubled.

Using an oiled spatula or dough scraper, scrape the dough onto a floured counter and press down on it gently to form a rectangle. It will be full of air and resilient. Try to maintain as many of the air bubbles as possible. Fold the dough from all four sides into a tight package, or give it 2 business letter turns, and set it back in the container. Again oil the surface, cover, and mark where double the height would now be. (It will fill the container fuller than before because it is puffier with air.) Allow the dough to rise for 1 to 2 hours or until doubled.

5 > Shape the dough and let it rise. Turn the dough onto a lightly floured counter and shape it into a loaf (see page 67 for illustrated directions). Place it in the prepared loaf pan; it will be about 1/2 inch from the top of the pan. Cover it with a large container or cover it loosely with oiled plastic wrap, and allow it to rise until the center is about 1 inch above the sides of the pan, 1 1/2 to 2 hours. If the dough is pressed with a fingertip the depression will very slowl fill in.

6 > Preheat the oven. Preheat the oven to 475°F 1 hour before baking. Have an oven shelf at the lowest level and place a baking stone or baking sheet on it, and a cast-iron skillet or sheet pan on the floor of the oven, before preheating.

7 > **Bake the bread.** Quickly but gently set the pan on the hot baking stone or hot baking sheet. Toss 1/2 cup of ice cubes into the pan beneath and immediately shut the door. Bake for 5 minutes. Turn the heat down to 375°F and bake for 15 minutes. Turn the heat down to 350°F and continue baking for 10 minutes or until the bread is medium golden brown and a skewer inserted in the middle comes out clean (an instant-read thermometer inserted into the center will read about 190°F). Halfway through baking, turn the pans around for even baking.

8 > **Glaze and cool the bread.** Remove the bread from the oven and set it on a wire rack. Brush it with the optional melted butter. Unmold and cool it top side up on a wire rack until barely warm, about 1 hour.

ULTIMATE FULL FLAVOR VARIATION

For the best flavor development, in Step 2, allow the sponge to ferment for 1 hour at room temperature and then refrigerate it for 8 to 24 hours. If using the hand mixing method, remove it from the refrigerator about 1 hour before mixing the dough.

POINTERS FOR SUCCESS

>   If not using the dry milk, you can replace the 1/2 cup of water with 1/2 cup milk, preferably nonfat.

UNDERSTANDING

Less butter is used here than in the Basic Soft White Sandwich Loaf because the banana enriches it with moisture and flavor.

Potato boiled in its skin has 79.8 percent water and banana has 75 percent, so the 1/2 cup of potato in the Potato Sandwich Loaf is replaced with 1/2 cup of banana and a little water. The banana causes the crust to brown a little faster so the heat is turned down toward the end of baking.

For calculation purposes if making this bread in larger quantity, it is useful to know that the banana peel represents about 25 percent of the weight of a banana.

This bread can initially bake at a higher temperature than the Soft White Sandwich Loaf because the banana gives it more structure, so it does not require as thick a crust.

THE DOUGH PERCENTAGE

Flour:	**100%** (includes the starch in the banana)
Water:	**62.3%** (includes the water in the butter, honey, and banana)
Yeast:	**1 %**
Salt:	**2.1%**
Butterfat:	**4.8%**

Sweet Potato Loaf

The flavor in this bread is so subtle you'd never know it contains a sweet potato. But the color is an orangey gold and the texture moist and soft without the slight chewiness that regular potato contributes. Yam and sweet potato are interchangeable. Less butter is needed than in the Basic Soft White Sandwich Loaf because the potato keeps the bread soft and moist.

TIME SCHEDULE

Dough Starter (Sponge): minimum 1 hour, maximum 24 hours
Minimum Rising Time: about 3 1/2 hours
Oven Temperature: 475°F
Baking Time: 25 to 30 minutes

Makes: an 8-by-4-by-4 1/2-inch-high loaf 19.5 ounces/555 grams

Dough Starter (Sponge)

INGREDIENTS	MEASURE	WEIGHT	
	volume	ounces	grams
1 medium sweet potato or yam, washed but not peeled		6 ounces	170 grams
Unbleached all-purpose flour (use only Gold Medal, King Arthur, or Pillsbury)	3/4 cup plus 1 tablespoon	4 ounces	117 grams
water, at room temperature (70° to 90°F)	1/2 cup plus 1 tablespoon	4.6 ounces	132 grams
honey	2 teaspoons	0.5 ounce	13 grams
instant yeast (see page 561 for brands)	1/4 teaspoon	--	0.8 gram

EQUIPMENT

an 8 1/2-by-4 1/2-inch loaf pan, lightly greased with cooking spray or oil;

a baking stone OR baking sheet

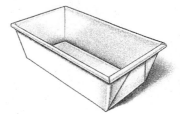

1 > Bake the potato and make the sponge. Preheat the oven to 375°F.

Bake the potato for 50 minutes or until tender. Cool slightly, then peel and put it through a ricer or strainer, or mash it. Measure or weigh out 1/2 cup (4.5 ounces).

In a mixer bowl or other large bowl, combine the flour, water, honey, and yeast. Whisk until very smooth, to incorporate air, about 2 minutes. The sponge will be the consistency of a thick batter. Scrape down the sides of the bowl and cover it with plastic wrap.

Flour Mixture

INGREDIENTS	MEASURE	WEIGHT	
	volume	ounces	grams
unbleached all-purpose flour (use only Gold Medal, King Arthur, or Pillsbury)	1 1/4 cups	6.3 ounces	180 grams
dry milk, preferably nonfat	2 tablespoons	0.7 ounce	20 grams
instant yeast	3/4 teaspoon	--	2.4 grams
unsalted butter, softened	4 teaspoons	0.6 ounce	18.5 grams
riced or mashed sweet potato or yam (from above)	1/2 cup	4.5 ounces	126 grams
salt	1 teaspoon	--	6.6 grams
Optional: melted butter	1/2 tablespoon	0.25 ounce	7 grams

2 > Combine the ingredients for the flour mixture and add to the sponge. In a medium bowl, whisk together the flour (reserve 2 tablespoons if mixing by hand), dry milk, and yeast. Sprinkle this on top of the sponge and cover tightly with plastic wrap. Allow it to ferment for 1 to 4 hours at room temperature. (During this time the sponge will bubble through the flour blanket in places: this is fine.)

3 > Mix the dough.

Mixer Method
Add the butter and mashed potato to the bowl. Mix with the dough hook on low speed (#2 if using a KitchenAid) for 1 minute or until the flour is moistened enough to form a rough dough. Scrape down any bits of dough. Cover the bowl with plastic wrap and allow the dough to rest for 20 minutes.

Sprinkle on the salt. Knead the dough on medium speed (#4 KitchenAid) for 7 to 10 minutes. It will be smooth, shiny, and tacky (slightly sticky) to the touch. With an oiled spatula, scrape down any dough clinging to the sides of the bowl. If the dough is not stiff, knead in a little flour. If it is not at all sticky, spray it with a little water and knead it in. (The dough will weigh about 21 ounces/600 grams.)

Hand Method

Add the butter, mashed potato, and salt to the bowl and, with a wooden spoon or your hand, stir until all the flour is moistened. Knead the dough in the bowl until it comes together, then scrape it onto a lightly floured counter. Knead the dough for 5 minutes, enough to develop the gluten structure a little, adding as little of the reserved flour as possible to keep it from sticking. Use a bench scraper to scrape the dough and gather it together as you knead it. At this point, it will be very sticky. Cover it with the inverted bowl and allow it to rest for 20 minutes. (This resting time will make the dough less sticky and easier to work with.)

Knead the dough for another 5 minutes or until it is very smooth and elastic. It should still be tacky (sticky) enough to cling slightly to your fingers. If the dough is still very sticky, however, add some of the remaining reserved flour, or a little extra. (The dough will weigh about 19.5 ounces/559 grams.)

Both Methods

4 > Let the dough rise. Using an oiled spatula or dough scraper, scrape the dough into a 2-quart dough-rising container or bowl, lightly greased with cooking spray or oil. Push down the dough and lightly spray or oil the top. Cover the container with a lid or plastic wrap. With a piece of tape, mark the side of the container at approximately where double the height of the dough would be. Allow the dough to rise (ideally at 75° to 80°F) until it has doubled, 1 1/2 to 2 hours.

Using an oiled spatula or dough scraper, scrape the dough onto a floured counter and gently press it down to form a rectangle. It will be full of air and resilient. Try to maintain as many of the air bubbles as possible. Pull out and fold the dough over from all four sides into a tight package, or give it 2 business letter turns, and set it back in the container. Again oil the surface, cover, and mark where double the height would now be. (It will fill the container fuller than before because it is puffier with air.) Allow the dough to rise for 1 1/2 to 2 hours or until doubled.

5 > Shape the dough and let it rise. Turn the dough onto a lightly floured counter and shape it into a loaf (see page 67 for illustrated directions). Place it in the prepared loaf pan; it will be about 1/2 inch from the top of the pan. Cover it with a large container, or cover it loosely with oiled plastic wrap, and allow it to rise until the center is about 1 inch above the sides of the pan, 1 1/2 to 2 hours. If the dough is pressed with a fingertip, the depression will very slowly fill in.

6 > Preheat the oven. Preheat the oven to 475°F 1 hour before baking. Have an oven shelf at the lowest level and place an oven stone or baking sheet on it, and a cast-iron skillet or sheet pan on the floor of the oven, before preheating.

7 > **Bake the bread.** Quickly but gently set the pan on the hot baking stone or hot baking sheet. Toss 1/2 cup of ice cubes into the pan beneath and immediately shut the door. Bake for 5 minutes. Lower the heat to 375°F and continue baking for 20 to 25 minutes or until the bread is medium golden brown and a skewer inserted into the middle comes out clean (an instant-read thermometer inserted into the center will read about 190°F). Halfway through baking, turn the pans around for even baking.

8 > **Glaze and cool the bread.** Remove the bread from the oven and set it on a wire rack. Brush the bread with the optional melted butter. Unmold and cool it top side up on a wire rack until barely warm, about 1 hour.

ULTIMATE FULL FLAVOR VARIATION

For the best flavor development, in Step 3, allow the sponge to ferment for 1 hour at room temperature and then refrigerate it for 8 to 24 hours. If using the hand mixing method, remove it from the refrigerator about 1 hour before mixing the dough.

POINTERS FOR SUCCESS

> If not using the dry milk, you can replace the water with 1/2 cup plus 1 tablespoon milk, preferably nonfat, scalded (brought to just under the boiling point) and cooled to lukewarm.

THE DOUGH PERCENTAGE

Flour:	100% (includes the starch contained in the sweet potato or yam)
Water:	64.1% (includes the water contained in the butter, honey, and sweet potato or yam)
Yeast:	0.94%
Salt:	1.9%
Butterfat:	4.4%

Cheddar Loaf

This bread is based on the Basic Soft White Sandwich Loaf recipe, so it has a light even crumb. The cheese gives the crust a dark golden brown color, and if you use orange Cheddar, the crumb will be an attractive orange gold. This bread makes the most fantastic ham sandwiches imaginable, spread with mayonnaise and sprinkled with a few fresh thyme leaves. It is also wonderful toasted and buttered, or for grilled cheese sandwiches as a double cheese sensation! The addition of cayenne pepper and mustard in the dough perks up the cheese flavor and leaves an enticing aftertaste to encourage the next bite.

TIME SCHEDULE

Dough Starter (Sponge): minimum 1 hour, maximum 24 hours
Minimum Rising Time: about 3 1/2 hours
Oven Temperature: 350°F
Baking Time: 45 to 50 minutes

Makes: an 8-by-4-by-4-inch-high loaf/22 ounces/628 grams

EQUIPMENT

an 8 1/2-by-4 1/2-inch loaf pan, lightly greased
with cooking spray or oil;

a baking stone OR baking sheet

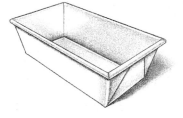

Dough Starter (Sponge)

INGREDIENTS	MEASURE	WEIGHT	
	volume	ounces	grams
unbleached all-purpose flour (use only Gold Medal, King Arthur, or Pillsbury)	1 cup plus 3 tablespoons	6 ounces	170 grams
water, at room temperature (70° to 90°F)	3/4 liquid cup plus 2 tablespoons (7 fluid ounces)	7.2 ounces	206 grams
malt powder or	1 tablespoon	0.3 ounce	9.3 grams
barley malt syrup or honey or	1 tablespoon	0.7 ounce	21 grams
sugar	1 tablespoon	0.5 ounce	12.5 grams
instant yeast (see page 561 for brands)	3/8 teaspoon	--	1.2 grams

1 > **Make the sponge.** In a mixer bowl or other large bowl, combine the flour, water, malt, honey, or sugar, and yeast. Whisk until very smooth, to incorporate air, about 2 minutes. The sponge will be the consistency of a thick batter. Scrape down the sides of the bowl and cover it with plastic wrap.

Flour Mixture and Dough

INGREDIENTS	MEASURE	WEIGHT	
	volume	ounces	grams
unbleached all-purpose flour (use only Gold Medal, King Arthur, or Pillsbury)	1 cup plus 2 tablespoons	5.7 ounces	160 grams
dry milk, preferably nonfat	2 tablespoons	0.7 ounce	20 grams
instant yeast	3/8 teaspoon	--	1.2 grams
sharp Cheddar cheese, grated	1 3/4 cups	4 ounces	113 grams
unsalted butter, softened	2 tablespoons	1 ounce	28 grams
Dijon mustard	2 teaspoons	scant 0.5 ounce	12 grams
cayenne pepper	1/8 teaspoon	--	--
salt	1 1/8 teaspoons	--	7.4 grams
Optional: melted butter	1/2 tablespoon	0.25 ounce	7 grams

2 > **Combine the ingredients for the flour mixture and add to the sponge.** In a medium bowl, whisk together the flour (reserve 2 tablespoons if mixing by hand), dry milk, and yeast. Sprinkle this on top of the sponge to cover it completely. Cover tightly with plastic wrap and allow it to ferment for 1 to 4 hours at room temperature. (During this time the sponge will bubble through the flour blanket in places: this is fine.)

3 > **Mix the dough.**

Mixer Method

Add the Cheddar, butter, mustard, and cayenne pepper to the bowl and mix with the dough hook on low speed (#2 if using a KitchenAid) until the flour is moistened enough to form a rough dough. Scrape down any bits of dough. Cover the bowl with plastic wrap and allow the dough to rest for 20 minutes.

Sprinkle on the salt and knead the dough on medium speed (#4 KitchenAid) for 7 to 10 minutes. It will be smooth and shiny and stick slightly to the bottom of the bowl but not feel sticky to the touch. If the dough is not stiff, knead in a little flour. If it is not at all sticky, spray on a little water and knead it in. (The dough will weigh about 24 ounces/684 grams.)

Hand Method

Add the Cheddar, butter, mustard, cayenne pepper, and salt to the bowl and, with a wooden spoon or your hand, stir until all the flour is moistened. Knead the dough in the bowl until it comes together, then scrape it onto a lightly floured counter. Knead the dough for 5 minutes, enough to develop the gluten structure a little, adding as little of the reserved flour as possible. Use a bench scraper to scrape the dough and gather it together as you knead it. At this point, it will be very sticky. Cover it with the inverted bowl and allow it to rest for 20 minutes. (This resting time will make the dough less sticky and easier to work with.)

Knead the dough for another 5 minutes or until it is very smooth and elastic. It should be soft but not stick to your fingers. If the dough is sticky, add some of the remaining reserved flour, or a little extra. (The dough will weigh about 24 ounces/ 684 grams.)

Both Methods

4 > **Let the dough rise.** Using an oiled spatula or dough scraper, scrape the dough into a 2-quart dough-rising container or bowl, lightly oiled with cooking spray or oil. Press down the dough and lightly spray or oil the top. Cover the container with a lid or plastic wrap. With a piece of tape, mark the side of the container at approximately where double the height of the dough would be. Allow the dough to rise (ideally at 75° to 80°F) until doubled, 1 1/2 to 2 hours.

Turn the dough out onto a lightly floured counter and press down on it gently to form a rectangle. It will be full of air and resilient. Try to maintain as many of the air bubbles as possible. Pull out and fold the dough over from all four sides into a tight package, or give it 2 business letter turns, and set it back in the container. Again oil the top, cover, and mark where double the height of the dough would now be. (It will fill the container fuller than before because it is puffier with air.) Allow it to rise a second time until doubled, 1 to 2 hours.

5 > Shape the dough and let it rise. Turn the dough out onto a lightly floured counter and shape it into a loaf (see page 67 for illustrated directions). Place it in the prepared loaf pan; it will be about 1/2 inch from the top of the pan. Cover with a large container, or cover it loosely with oiled plastic wrap, and allow it to rise until the center is about 1 inch above the sides of the pan, 1 1/2 to 2 hours. If the dough is pressed with a fingertip, the depression will very slowly fill in.

6 > Preheat the oven. Preheat the oven to 350°F 1 hour before baking. Have an oven shelf at the lowest level and place a baking stone or baking sheet on it, and a cast-iron skillet or sheet pan on the floor of the oven, before preheating.

7 > Bake the bread. Quickly but gently set the pan on the hot baking stone or hot baking sheet. Toss 1/2 cup of ice cubes into the pan beneath and immediately shut the door. Bake for 45 to 50 minutes or until the bread is medium golden brown and a skewer inserted in the middle comes out clean (an instant-read thermometer inserted into the center will read about 211°F). Halfway through baking, turn the pan around for even baking.

8 > Glaze and cool the bread. Remove the bread from the oven and set it on a wire rack. Brush the top of the bread with the optional melted butter. Unmold and cool it on a wire rack, top side up, until barely warm, about 1 hour.

ULTIMATE FULL FLAVOR VARIATION

For the best flavor development, in Step 2, allow the sponge to ferment for 1 hour at room temperature and then refrigerate it for 8 to 24 hours. If using the hand mixing method, remove it from the refrigerator about 1 hour before mixing the dough.

POINTERS FOR SUCCESS

>   If not using the dry milk, you can replace 1/2 cup of water with 1/2 cup milk, preferably nonfat.

UNDERSTANDING

Cheddar cheese contains 32.2 percent fat and 37 percent water, so the amount of water and butter in the Basic Soft White Sandwich Loaf recipe has been reduced to compensate.

THE DOUGH PERCENTAGE

Flour:	100%
Water:	76% (includes the water in the butter and cheese)
Yeast:	0.73%
Salt:	2.2%
Fat:	17.9% (includes the fat contained in the butter and cheese)

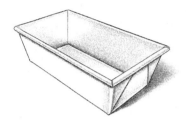

Ricotta Loaf

The bread is incredibly quick and easy to mix and thoroughly enjoyable. It is a pleasure just to touch the dough, which is as soft as a newborn's skin. It bakes into a pale yellow, soft crumb that can be sliced very thin. The flavor is ethereal and deeply complex.

This recipe came to me as a gift from Diego Mauricio Lopez of Colombia, South America.

TIME SCHEDULE

Starter: straight dough method
Rising Time: about 3 hours
Oven Temperature: 375°F
Baking Time: 40 to 50 minutes

Makes: an 8 1/2-by-5-by-4 1/2-inch-high loaf/34.2 ounces/970 grams

INGREDIENTS	MEASURE	WEIGHT	
	volume	ounces	grams
unbleached all-purpose flour (use only Gold Medal, King Arthur, or Pillsbury)	3 1/2 cups	17.5 ounces	500 grams
sugar	2 tablespoons	1 scant ounce	25 grams
instant yeast (see page 561 for brands)	1/2 tablespoon	--	4.8 grams
whole-milk ricotta, cold	1 cup plus 1 1/2 tablespoons	8.75 ounces	250 grams
unsalted butter, softened	7 tablespoons	3.5 ounces	100 grams
1 large egg, cold	3 tablespoons plus 1/2 teaspoon	2 ounces (in the shell)	57 grams
salt	1/2 tablespoon	--	10 grams
water, cold	1/2 liquid cup	about 4.2 ounces	118 grams
Optional: melted butter	1 tablespoon	0.5 ounce	14 grams

a 9-by-5-inch loaf pan, lightly greased with cooking spray or oil;

a baking stone OR baking sheet

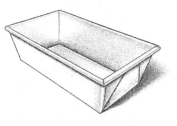

1 > Mix the dough. In a medium bowl, whisk together the flour, sugar, and yeast. Transfer to a food processor fitted with the dough blade. Add the ricotta, butter, egg, and salt and pulse about 15 times. With the motor running, add the cold water. Process for 60 to 80 seconds; be careful not to allow the dough to get hot. The dough should be soft but not sticky. If it is not soft, spray it with a little water and pulse it in. If it is sticky, transfer it to the counter and knead in a little flour at a time. After the first rise, it will become firmer and will be difficult to shape if it is not soft at this point. (The dough will weigh about 2 pounds, 5 ounces/1048 grams.)

2 > Let the dough rise. Place the dough in a 4-quart dough-rising container or bowl, lightly greased with cooking spray or oil. Push down the dough and lightly spray or oil the top. Cover the container with a lid or plastic wrap. With a piece of tape, mark the side of the container at approximately where double the height of the dough would be. Allow the dough to rise (ideally at 75° to 80°F) until doubled, 1 1/2 to 2 hours.

3 > Preheat the oven. Preheat the oven to 375°F 1 hour before baking. Have an oven shelf at the lowest level and place an oven stone or baking sheet on it, and a cast-iron skillet or sheet pan on the floor of the oven, before preheating.

4 > Shape the dough and let it rise. Turn the dough out onto a lightly floured counter and shape into a loaf (see page 67 for illustrated directions). Place it in the prepared loaf pan; it should be no higher than 1/2 inch from the top of the pan.

Cover the dough with a large container, or cover loosely with oiled plastic wrap, and allow it to rise until almost doubled, 45 minutes to 1 hour and 15 minutes. The center will be 1 inch higher than the sides of the pan, and when the dough is pressed gently with a fingertip, the depression will very slowly fill in.

5 > Slash and bake the bread. With a sharp knife or single-edged razor blade, make a long 1/2-inch-deep slash down the middle of the bread. Mist the dough with water and quickly but gently set the pan on the hot baking stone or hot baking sheet. Toss 1/2 cup of ice cubes into the pan beneath and immediately shut the door. Bake for 40 to 50 minutes or until the bread is golden and a skewer inserted in the middle comes out clean (an instant-read thermometer inserted into the center will read about 200°F). Halfway through baking, turn the pan around for even baking. After the first 30 minutes of baking, tent loosely with foil to prevent overbrowning.

6 > Cool the bread. Remove the bread from the oven and set it on a wire rack. Brush it with the optional melted butter, unmold it, and cool it top side up on the wire rack, until barely warm, at least 1 1/2 hours.

NOTE If you prefer to use a mixer, proceed as above but use room-temperature water. Mix with the dough hook on low speed (#2 if using a KitchenAid), and gradually add the water. When the flour is moistened, raise the speed to medium low (#3 KitchenAid) and knead for 10 minutes.

ULTIMATE FULL FLAVOR VERSION

If desired, in Step 4, after the dough has been shaped and placed in the loaf pan, it can be covered with oiled plastic wrap, placed in a 2-gallon freezer-weight plastic bag, and refrigerated for up to 2 days. It will develop more flavor, but it will take an extra 45 minutes to 1 hour to double in size before baking.

POINTERS FOR SUCCESS

> Have everything but the butter as cold as possible to prevent a buildup of heat in the processor. If the butter is not softened, the processor is likely to stall. Freezing the flour/sugar/yeast mixture for 15 minutes, or as long as you want, would help but is not absolutely necessary.

UNDERSTANDING

The instant yeast will not be killed by the cold water because the mixture heats up from the friction of the food processor blades within seconds.

THE DOUGH PERCENTAGE

Flour:	100%
Water:	70.2% (includes the water in the cheese and egg white)
Yeast:	0.96%
Salt:	2%
Fat:	17.5% (includes the fat in the cheese and egg yolk)

Cracked Wheat Loaf

For many years, Pepperidge Farm cracked wheat bread was my standard sandwich loaf, so I was disappointed when one day it was no longer on the shelf. I set out to create a replacement and eventually arrived at this one, which I find is more than its equal.

This bread is wheaty with an earthy sweetness, yet mildly sour, moist, soft, light, and golden with the subtle crackle of bulgur, steamed cracked wheat. The crust is velvety soft and especially delicious. This is perfect as sandwich bread, spread with butter, or toasted. And it makes a great open-faced quick lunch: toast it, top with a slice of muenster cheese, sprinkle with roughly crushed dried mild chile peppers and a little black pepper, and broil for a few seconds to melt the cheese.

If you love the flavor of whole wheat but prefer a softer, lighter loaf, this is the bread for you. Use the lecithin (available in health food stores and through the King Arthur catalogue) if you want to keep its soft moist texture for up to 3 days after baking.

TIME SCHEDULE

Dough Starter (Sponge): minimum 4 hours, maximum 24 hours
Minimum Rising Time: about 2 1/4 hours
Oven Temperature: 350°F
Baking Time: 45 to 55 minutes

Makes: an 8 1/2-by-5-by-5-inch-high loaf/30.5 ounces/875 grams

Dough Starter (Sponge)

INGREDIENTS	MEASURE	WEIGHT	
	volume	ounces	grams
bread flour	1/2 cup	2.75 ounces	78 grams
whole wheat flour	1/2 cup	2.5 ounces	72 grams
instant yeast (see page 561 for brands)	3/4 teaspoon	--	2.4 grams
sugar	1/2 tablespoon	--	6.2 grams
dry milk, preferably nonfat	1 tablespoon	--	8 grams
honey	1 tablespoon	0.7 ounce	21 grams
water, at room temperature (70° to 90°F)	1 liquid cup plus 2 tablespoons	9.3 ounces	266 grams

EQUIPMENT

a 9-by-5-inch loaf pan, lightly greased with cooking spray or oil;

a baking stone OR baking sheet

1 > **Make the sponge.** In a mixer bowl or other large bowl, combine the bread flour, whole wheat flour, yeast, sugar, dried milk, honey, and water. Whisk until very smooth, to incorporate air, about 2 minutes. The sponge will be the consistency of a thick batter. Scrape down the sides of the bowl and cover it with plastic wrap.

Flour Mixture

INGREDIENTS	MEASURE	WEIGHT	
	volume	ounces	grams
bread flour	2 cups	11 ounces	312 grams
sugar	1/2 tablespoon	--	6.2 grams
instant yeast	1/4 teaspoon	--	0.8 gram

2 > **Combine the ingredients for the flour mixture and add to the sponge.** In a medium bowl, whisk together the flour (reserve 1/4 cup if mixing by hand), sugar, and yeast. Sprinkle this on top of the sponge to cover it completely. Cover tightly with plastic wrap and allow it to ferment for 1 to 4 hours at room temperature. During this time, the sponge will bubble through the flour mixture in places: this is fine.

Bulgur and Finishing Ingredients

INGREDIENTS	MEASURE	WEIGHT	
	volume	ounces	grams
extra-coarse (#4) or coarse (#3) bulgur	1/2 cup	3 ounces	85 grams
boiling water	1/2 to 2/3 liquid cup	4 to 5.5 ounces	118–154 grams
granular lecithin or	1 tablespoon	--	6.4 grams
vegetable oil	1 tablespoon	--	13.5 grams
salt	1 3/4 teaspoons	--	11.5 grams
melted butter, preferably clarified	1 tablespoon	0.5 ounce	14 grams

3 > **Meanwhile, soak the bulgur.** Place the bulgur in a small bowl and pour the boiling water over it; use the smaller amount if a little crunch is desired. With the larger amount, the bulgur will be firm but not crunchy. Cover with plastic wrap and allow to sit until all the water is absorbed, about 1 hour, then refrigerate until ready to use.

4 > **Mix the dough.**

Mixer Method

Add the bulgur and optional lecithin or oil (if you want the bread to stay soft for up to 3 days) to the bowl. Mix with the dough hook on low speed (#2 if using a KitchenAid) for about 1 minute, until the flour is moistened enough to form a rough dough. Cover the bowl with plastic wrap and allow the dough to rest for 20 minutes.

Sprinkle on the salt and knead the dough on medium speed (#4 KitchenAid) for 10 minutes. (Drape plastic wrap over the top of the bowl to keep any of the bulgur from jumping out of the bowl before it gets a chance to be fully incorporated into the dough.) The dough should be very elastic and jump back when pressed with a fingertip, but still moist enough to cling slightly to your fingers. If it is still very sticky, knead in a little flour. If it is not at all sticky, spray it with a little water and knead it in. (The dough will weigh about 2 pounds, 1 3/4 ounces/964 grams.)

Hand Method

Add the bulgur, optional lecithin or oil, and salt to the bowl and, with a wooden spoon or your hand, stir until all the flour is moistened. Knead the dough in the bowl until it comes together, then scrape it onto a lightly floured counter. Knead the dough for 5 minutes, just to begin to develop the gluten structure, adding as little of the reserved flour as possible. Use a bench scraper to scrape the dough and gather it together as you knead it. At this point, it will be very sticky. Cover it with the inverted bowl and allow it to rest for 20 minutes. (This resting time will make the dough less sticky and easier to work with.)

Knead the dough until it is very smooth and elastic, another 10 minutes. It should still be tacky (sticky) enough to cling slightly to your fingers. If the dough is very sticky, add some of the remaining reserved flour, or a little extra. (The dough will weigh about 2 pounds, 1 3/4 ounces/964 grams.)

Both Methods

5 > **Let the dough rise.** Using an oiled spatula or dough scraper, scrape the dough into a 2-quart dough-rising container or bowl, lightly greased with cooking spray or oil. Lightly spray or oil the top and cover it with a lid or plastic wrap. With a piece of tape, mark the side of the container at approximately where double the height of the dough would be. Allow the dough to rise (ideally at 75° to 80°F) until doubled, 45 minutes to 1 1/2 hours.

Using an oiled spatula or dough scraper, scrape the dough out onto a floured counter and press down on it gently to form a rectangle. Give it a business letter turn, round the edges, and return it to the container. Oil the surface again, cover, and mark where double the height would now be. (It will fill the container fuller than before because it is puffier with air.) Allow the dough to rise until doubled, about 45 minutes to 1 hour. It will still be a little tacky (sticky).

6 > **Shape the dough and let it rise.** Turn the dough out onto a lightly floured counter. Shape into a loaf (see page 67 for see illustrated directions). Place it in the loaf pan; it will be about 1/2 inch from the top of the pan. Cover it with a large container, or cover loosely with oiled plastic wrap. Let the dough rise until almost doubled in bulk, 45 minutes to 1 1/2 hours. (The center will be about 1 1/4 inches higher than the sides of the pan.) When the dough is pressed gently with a fingertip, the depression will very slowly fill in.

7 > **Preheat the oven.** Preheat the oven to 350°F 1 hour before baking. Have an oven shelf at the lowest level and place an oven stone or baking sheet on it, and a cast-iron skillet or sheet pan on the floor of the oven, before preheating.

8 > **Slash, glaze, and bake the bread.** Brush the top of the dough with some of the melted butter. With a sharp knife or single-edged razor blade, make a 1/2-inch-deep lengthwise slash down the top of the dough.

Quickly but gently set the pan on the hot baking stone or hot baking sheet. Toss 1/2 cup of ice cubes into the pan beneath and immediately shut the door. Bake for 45 to 55 minutes or until the bread is pale golden brown and a skewer inserted into the middle comes out clean (an instant-read thermometer inserted into the center will read about 210°F).

9 > **Glaze and cool the bread.** Remove the bread from the oven and set it on a wire rack. Brush it with the remaining melted butter. Unmold it and cool it completely top side up on the wire rack.

ULTIMATE FULL FLAVOR VARIATION

For the best flavor development, in Step 2, allow the sponge to ferment for 1 hour at room temperature and then refrigerate it for 8 to 24 hours. If using the hand mixing method, remove it from the refrigerator about 1 hour before mixing the dough.

VARIATION

Buckwheat Loaf   Replace the whole wheat flour with buckwheat flour and the bulgur with coarse kasha. Use only 1/2 cup boiling water to soak the kasha.

POINTERS FOR SUCCESS

>   Brushing the dough with melted butter before baking produces a browner and more handsome crust.

UNDERSTANDING

Bulgur is steamed cracked wheat and needs only soaking to soften it. Cracked wheat must be cooked first or it will never soften adequately. A coarse grain is desirable because it provides more texture.

A high-protein bread flour gives the crumb a slightly chewier consistency which balances well with the slight crunch of the bulgur.

THE DOUGH PERCENTAGE

Flour:	100% (bread: 71.3%, whole wheat: 13.2%, cracked wheat: 15.5%)
Water:	70% to 77%
Yeast:	0.59%
Salt:	2.1%
Optional lecithin or oil:	2.4%

Flaxseed Loaf

Flax, a shiny dark brown oval seed, is an extraordinarily healthful grain, high in anti-oxidants. In bread, it contributes an appealing chewiness and, together with the honey and pumpernickel flour, extra flavor, making a pre-ferment (sponge) unnecessary.

This is an excellent sandwich bread and still more delicious lightly toasted, which brings out its flavor. Another virtue of this hearty bread is that it stays fresh for 3 days.

TIME SCHEDULE

Starter: straight dough method
Minimum Rising Time: about 1 3/4 hours
Oven Temperature: 375°F
Baking Time: 40 to 50 minutes

Makes: an 8 1/2-by-5-by-4 1/2-inch-high loaf/2 pounds 4.2 ounces/1027 grams

INGREDIENTS	MEASURE	WEIGHT	
	volume	ounces	grams
unbleached all-purpose flour (use only Gold Medal, King Arthur, or Pillsbury)	2 2/3 cups	13 ounces	374 grams
whole wheat flour	1 cup	5 ounces	144 grams
pumpernickel flour (coarse rye)	about 1/2 cup	2.5 ounces	71 grams
flaxseed	1/2 cup	2 ounces	58 grams
instant yeast (see page 561 for brands)	1 1/4 teaspoons	--	4 grams
honey	2 tablespoons	--	40 grams
water, warm (110° to 115°F)	1 3/4 liquid cups	14.6 ounces	414 grams
salt	2 teaspoons	--	13.2 grams
Optional: melted butter	1 tablespoon	0.5 ounce	14 grams

a 9-by-5-inch loaf pan, lightly greased with cooking spray or oil;

a baking stone OR baking sheet

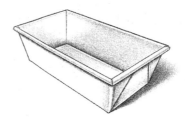

1 > Mix the dough.

Mixer Method

In the mixer bowl, whisk together the three flours, flaxseed, and yeast. Make a well in the center and add the honey. With the dough hook, on low speed (#2 if using a KitchenAid), gradually add the water. Continue mixing for about 1 minute or until all the dry ingredients are moistened enough to form a rough dough. Scrape down any bits of dough. Cover the bowl with plastic wrap and allow the dough to rest for 20 minutes.

Sprinkle on the salt and knead for 7 minutes on medium speed (#4 KitchenAid). The dough should be very elastic and jump back when pressed with a fingertip, but still moist enough to cling slightly to your fingers. If it is still very sticky, knead in a little flour. If it is not at all sticky, spray it with a little water and knead it in. (The dough will weigh about 2 pounds, 7 ounces/1103 grams.)

Hand Method

In a medium mixing bowl, with a wooden spoon or your hand, stir together the water, honey, flaxseed, pumpernickel flour, and yeast. Then stir in the salt, whole wheat flour, and all-purpose flour until the flour is moistened. Knead the dough in the bowl until it comes together, then scrape it onto a lightly floured counter. Knead the dough for 5 minutes, enough to develop the gluten structure a little, adding as little of the reserved flour as possible to keep it from sticking. Use a bench scraper to scrape the dough and gather it together as you knead it. At this point, it will be very sticky. Cover it with the inverted bowl and allow it to rest for 20 minutes. (This resting time will make the dough less sticky and easier to work with.)

Knead the dough for another 5 minutes or until it is very smooth and elastic. It should still be moist enough to cling slightly to your fingers. If the dough is very sticky, add some of the remaining reserved flour, or a little extra. (The dough will weigh about 2 pounds, 7 ounces/1103 grams.)

Both Methods

2 > **Let the dough rise.** Using an oiled spatula or dough scraper, scrape the dough into a 4-quart dough-rising container or bowl, lightly greased with cooking spray or oil. Push down the dough and lightly spray or oil the top. Cover the container with a lid or plastic wrap. With a piece of tape, mark the side of the container at approximately where double the height of the dough would be. Allow the dough to rise (ideally at 75° to 80°F) until doubled, about 1 hour.

3 > **Shape the dough and let it rise.** Turn the dough out onto a lightly floured counter and press down on it to flatten it slightly. Shape the dough it into a loaf (see page 67 for illustrated directions). Set it in the prepared loaf pan; it will be about 1/2 inch from the top of the pan. Cover it with a large container, or cover loosely with oiled plastic wrap, and allow it to rise until the center is about 1 inch higher than the sides of the pan, 45 to 60 minutes. When the dough is pressed gently with a fingertip, the depression will very slowly fill in.

4 > **Preheat the oven.** Preheat the oven to 375°F 1 hour before baking. Have an oven shelf at the lowest level and place an oven stone or baking sheet on it, and a cast-iron skillet or sheet pan on the floor of the oven, before preheating.

5 > **Slash and bake the dough.** With a sharp knife or single-edged razor blade, make a 1/2-inch-deep slash lengthwise down the top of the dough.

Quickly but gently set the pan on the hot baking stone or hot baking sheet. Toss 1/2 cup of ice cubes into the pan beneath and immediately shut the door. Bake for 40 to 50 minutes or until the bread is golden brown and a skewer inserted in the middle comes out clean (an instant-read thermometer inserted into the center will read about 190°F). Halfway through baking, turn the pan around for even baking.

6 > **Cool the bread.** Remove the bread from the oven and unmold it onto a wire rack. Turn top side up, brush it with melted butter, if desired, and allow it to cool until barely warm, about 2 hours.

POINTERS FOR SUCCESS

> Ground flaxseed can be substituted for the cracked flaxseed, but it will provide a less crunchy texture.

> If you want to make the dough ahead, refrigerate it overnight before shaping it. Be sure to press it down after the first 30 to 60 minutes in the refrigerator and then two or

three more times until it chills enough to cause the yeast to become dormant (this can take up to 4 hours), as this is a very lively dough!

UNDERSTANDING

Whole flaxseed isn't readily digested, so it is desirable to coarsely grind it in a wheat mill or blender to crack it. As flaxseed can become rancid very quickly, it is best to do this yourself rather than purchasing ground flaxseed.

This bread contains lower than the usual amount of yeast because the pumpernickel and whole wheat flours increase yeast activity.

Warm water is used in the dough because it helps to soften the whole-grain flours.

THE DOUGH PERCENTAGE

Flour:	100% (all-purpose: 57.8%, whole wheat: 22.2%, coarse rye: 11%, flaxseed: 9%)
Water:	64.8% (including the water in the honey)
Yeast:	0.62%
Salt:	2%

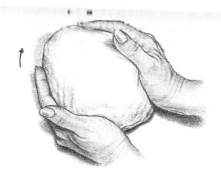

Hearth Breads

5.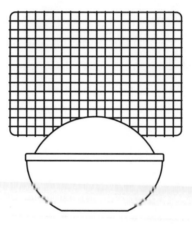

THE BREADS IN THIS CHAPTER ARE THE VARIETY THAT COME TO MIND WHEN one hears the term *artisan bread*. They have a chewy crumb, crunchy crust, and mostly rustic appearance. All of these breads are firm enough to be baked free-form on a baking stone or baking sheet, although most conform well to being baked in a more confined loaf shape if desired, such as the Basic Hearth Bread (page 305).

When bakers use the term *hearth*, they are referring to a wood-burning oven in which the bread is baked directly on its floor. A baking stone, pre-heated in a gas or electric oven, or a La Cloche clay bread baker simulates an artisan's hearth oven. I have given instructions for baking many of these breads in a clay baker and have also included special baking pan recommen-dations that will enable the home baker to produce artisan-quality baguettes.

The breads in this chapter are all yeast breads, but they are not at all dif-ficult to make. Most people's greatest fear of bread making is the all-too-real possibility of killing the yeast with water that is too hot or using water that is too cold to activate it. But now that instant yeast, which can be mixed in with the flour without the need to wake it up with water of the proper tempera-ture, is readily available, there is nothing left to fear. Just be sure to use the kind of flour specified in the recipe.

The yeast, flour, and water are all critical to the successful outcome of a yeast bread, but flour is the single most important ingredient—yet it is often taken for granted. The type of flour you use will determine both the flavor and the texture of your bread. It is fun to experiment with different flours, *but when you are making rustic breads for the first time, it is best to use the flour recommended in the recipe. It is also essential that the flour be fresh* (see page 553). Old flour may not "look" old, other than that it tends to lighten in color as it ages. And it may not smell bad. But it will have lost its ability to stretch (extensibility) and will not produce a good crumb. It may also have a rancid or other unpleasant flavor.

As far as weather is concerned, I work in an apartment with air conditioning, in a living room that is usually around 70°F and a kitchen that is almost always 80°F, and I've noticed little variation in the way my bread doughs behave. On a cold winter day, when the temperature in my kitchen may drop 5 degrees, I sometimes use hot water in my homemade plastic proof box, but that is the only adjustment I normally make. When I make bread in my country house in the summer, however, I usually reduce the yeast a little to compensate for the higher temperature. And in winter I have sometimes put bread dough near the fireplace to speed its rise.

Commercial bakers find a variation in 10 percent of the amount of water needed to be added to the dough (referred to as the hydration factor) because of variations in different crops of wheat used for flour, but that is not perceptible in small batches such as mine. Perhaps it is also because I make very wet doughs to begin with, and if the flour has a little more moisture, I may add a little more flour on the final shaping. I suspect that when people find there is a great variation in the amount of flour they use in different batches of the same recipe, it is because they are measuring with cups rather than weighing. When I weigh everything, I find that my doughs are the same each time by within a few grams. But the great thing about bread is that you can be creative, adding different ingredients or making a softer or stiffer dough by changing the amount of flour or water, and it will still be delicious. You can customize your bread by adding vital wheat gluten to make it more chewy, or by changing the proportion of types of flour, or by varying the design of the slash in the crust.

Many of these rustic breads involve making a dough starter, called a pre-ferment. This easy technique allows the initial amount of flour, water, and yeast to ferment and develop more flavor before adding it to the rest of the dough. Making a simple pre-ferment ahead enables you to make an exceptionally flavorful rustic bread in just a few hours when you are ready to bake. And it gives the bread not only more depth of flavor, but also moistness and improved texture.

There are two basic pre-ferments using commercial yeast in this chapter: the "sponge" and the "biga." Both are quicker, easier, and more reliable than the classic sourdough starter used in the following chapter.

A sponge is made simply by mixing all of the water in the recipe with equal parts flour (by volume) and half the yeast, then allowing it to ferment over a period of several hours to develop complexity and depth of flavor. If necessary, the fermenting time can be shortened to even just 1 hour and the bread will still be excellent. The longer refrigerated sponge is worth trying over a weekend or when you can be around for two days. The actual work involved is minimal and it's satisfying to know, as you go about other activities, that there is a bread starter rising and developing all sorts of wonderful flavors in the background.

A biga, which is simply a "mini dough" made with flour, yeast, and water that is mixed at least 6 hours before making the dough, is more practical for weekday baking, because it takes only minutes to put together and then can be refrigerated for up to 3 days until you are ready to bake. In these recipes, the biga is mixed by hand because it is too small a quantity for a stand mixer, but if you are making larger batches, it's fine to use a mixer with paddle attachment.

The essential difference between a bread made with a sponge and one made with a biga is the amount of water used. Generally, a sponge, which is like a thick pancake batter, is considered to be sweeter but more acidic, while a biga is more mellow and nutty, but this flavor difference is highly subjective. It is really more a matter of personal prefer which technique you choose.

There are also some breads in this chapter that are made without a sponge or a biga, but instead by what is known to professional bakers as the "straight dough method." This means that all the ingredients for the dough are mixed together at one time. Breads that derive their primary flavors from added ingredients, such as the Prosciutto Ring bread (page 370) or the Mantovana Olive Oil Bread (page 379), usually call for the straight dough method because they don't require the added flavor development offered by a dough starter.

One of the great challenges of making rustic loaves is producing the type that boasts big holes, such as the baguette, ciabatta, and pugliese. I have found that what produces this desirable crumb is:

> An acid dough (use of a dough starter and long cool rising)

> Underdeveloped gluten (from less mixing time)

> A high water percentage, to create a very wet dough

> A slow rise

> Gentle shaping

> An overnight rise of the shaped dough in the refrigerator

Some of the breads included in this chapter are made with the addition of whole or cracked grains, seeds, nuts, or dried fruits. A basic rustic bread dough can accommodate added grains, seeds, and nuts in a proportion of up to as much as 60 percent of the flour without becoming crumbly; my preference is between 10 and 33 percent. Seeds and grains will adds excellent flavor and texture as well as to fiber. When I sample a new bread that I find irresistible and would willingly forgo the rest of the meal in favor of it, invariably it contains seeds. Both seeds and nuts benefit from light toasting to bring out the flavor. Seeds, however, also require an overnight soaking to soften them so that they integrate better into the bread dough. I can't think of a single seed bread that is not enhanced by being spread with a little butter to temper the slight bitterness of the seeds. This natural bitterness is a great flavor accent—but the bitterness of rancidity is unpalatable. Because seeds, cracked grains, and nuts are extremely prone to rancidity, it is essential that they be fresh when purchased and then be stored in the refrigerator or freezer.

As a dessert lover, I find breads made with the dried fruit and nuts to be among the most appealing because they contains so many favorable elements: wheatiness from the flour, crunch from the nuts, and bright tart-sweetness from the dried fruit. And these breads, such as the Cranberry Walnut Bread (page 408) and the New Zealand Almond and Fig Bread (page 411), are show-stoppers—the perfect house gift when visiting friends.

Almost all homemade bread is best eaten the day it is baked, and that is why most of my recipes make just one loaf. For longer storage, I find that freezing and reheating is as close as one can get to fresh baked. If you have a large family, or are making bread for a party, by all means double the recipe if your mixer is large enough.

Keep in mind how fortunate you are. Most people will never know the simple but profound pleasure of eating a bread within hours after it comes out of the oven. It is the greatest reward of bread baking and a wonderful tradition and experience to share with your family.

UNDERSTANDING

The proportion of basic essential ingredients in hearth breads falls into the range of 46.5 to 89.2 percent water, 0.25 to 2 percent instant yeast, and 1.3 to 2.8 percent salt. These percentages are based on the Baker's Percentage, in which every ingredient is based on the flour, which is given the value of 100 percent. Some of these breads also contain between 2 and 22.9 percent oil.

Basic Hearth Bread

This rustic bread is the soul of simplicity, containing only flour, water, yeast, and salt, with the addition of honey for a little sweetness and a golden crust. It has a fairly chewy crumb and a wheaty flavor with the aroma and freshness of a summer day. It is one of the first breads I ever developed, and the secret to its wonderful flavor came from my editor at *Food & Wine* magazine, Susan Wyler, who told me that a small proportion of whole wheat flour makes a big contribution to the taste of white bread.

When I want a substantial sandwich loaf, I bake this bread in a loaf pan rather than free-form. And if you want to experiment with additions to bread, this is the one to use as your launching pad.

TIME SCHEDULE

Dough Starter (Sponge): minimum 1 hour, maximum 24 hours
Minimum Rising Time: about 3 hours
Oven Temperature: 475°F, then 425°F
Baking Time: 30 to 40 minutes

Makes: a 7 1/2-by-4-inch-high free-form loaf or
a 9-by-4 1/2-by-4 1/2-inch-high loaf
1 pound, 10 ounces/745 grams

EQUIPMENT:

a half sheet pan lined with a nonstick liner such as Silpain
or parchment, or sprinkled with flour or cornmeal, OR
a 10-by-5-inch loaf pan, lightly greased with cooking spray
or oil;

a baking stone OR baking sheet

Dough Starter (Sponge)

INGREDIENTS	MEASURE	WEIGHT	
	volume	ounces	grams
bread flour	1 cup	5.5 ounces	156 grams
whole wheat flour or kamut flour	1/4 cup	1.25 ounces	36 grams
instant yeast (see page 561 for brands)	3/8 teaspoon	--	1.25 grams
honey	1 1/4 teaspoons	--	9 grams
water, at room temperature (70° to 90°F)	about 1 1/3 liquid cups	11.2 ounces	322 grams

1 > **Make the sponge.** In a mixer bowl or other large bowl, place the bread flour, kamut or whole wheat flour, yeast, honey, and water. Whisk until very smooth, to incorporate air, about 2 minutes. The sponge should be the consistency of a thick batter. Scrape down the sides of the bowl. Set aside, covered with plastic wrap, while you make the flour mixture.

Flour Mixture

INGREDIENTS	MEASURE	WEIGHT	
	volume	ounces	grams
bread flour	1 3/4 cups plus 2 tablespoons	10.3 ounces	292 grams
instant yeast (see page 561 for brands)	1/2 teaspoon	--	1.6 grams
salt	1 1/2 teaspoons	0.4 ounce	10 grams

2 > **Combine the ingredients for the flour mixture and add to the sponge.** In a medium bowl, whisk together the bread flour (reserve 2 tablespoons if mixing by hand) and the instant yeast. Gently scoop it onto the sponge to cover it completely, cover tightly with plastic wrap, and allow to ferment for 1 to 4 hours at room temperature. (During this time, the sponge will bubble through the flour mixture in places; this is fine.)

3 > **Mix the dough.**

Mixer Method

With the dough hook, mix on low speed (#2 if using a KitchenAid) for about 1 minute, until the flour is moistened enough to form a rough dough. Scrape down any bits of dough. Cover the top with plastic wrap and allow the dough to rest for 20 minutes.

Sprinkle on the salt and knead the dough on medium speed (#4 KitchenAid) for about 7 minutes. The dough should be very elastic, smooth, and sticky enough to cling slightly to your fingers. If it is still very sticky, knead in a little flour. If it is not at all sticky, spray it with a little water and knead it in. (The dough will weigh about 28.5 ounces/810 grams.)

Hand Method

Add the salt and, with a wooden spoon or your hand, mix until the flour is moistened. Knead the dough in the bowl until it comes together, then scrape it out onto a lightly floured counter. Knead the dough for 5 minutes, enough to develop the gluten structure a little, adding as little of the reserved 2 tablespoons of flour as possible to keep it from sticking. Use a bench scraper to scrape the dough and gather it together as you knead it. At this point, it will be very sticky. Cover it with the inverted bowl and allow it to rest for 20 minutes. (This resting time will make the dough less sticky and easier to work with.)

Knead the dough for another 5 to 10 minutes, until it is very smooth and elastic. It should be barely tacky (sticky) to the touch. If the dough is still very sticky, add some of the remaining reserved flour. (The dough will weigh about 28.5 ounces/810 grams.)

Both Methods

4 > **Let the dough rise.** Using an oiled spatula or dough scraper, scrape the dough into an 2-quart dough-rising container or bowl, lightly greased with cooking spray or oil. Push down the dough and lightly spray or oil the top. Cover the container with a lid or plastic wrap. With a piece of tape, mark the side at where double the height of the dough would be. Allow the dough to rise (ideally at 75° to 80°F) until doubled, about 1 hour.

Using an oiled spatula or dough scraper, scrape the dough onto a floured counter and press down on it gently to form a rectangle. Give it 1 business letter turn, round the edges, and return it to the container. Oil the surface again, cover, and mark where double the height of the dough would now be. It will fill the container fuller than before because it is puffier with air. Allow to rise until doubled, 45 minutes to 1 hour.

5 > **Shape the dough and let it rise.** Turn the dough out onto a lightly floured counter and press it down to flatten it slightly. It will still be sticky, but use only as much flour during shaping as absolutely necessary. To make a free-form round loaf, round the dough into a ball about 6 inches by 2 1/2 inches high and set it on the prepared baking sheet or shape the dough into a rectangular loaf (see page 67 for illustrated directions), and place it in the prepared loaf pan (it will come to about 1/2 inch from the top of the pan).

Cover the shaped dough with a large container or oiled plastic wrap and allow it to rise until almost doubled, 45 minutes to 1 hour and 15 minutes. The free-form loaf will be about 8 inches by 3 inches high. In the loaf pan, the center should be 1 inch higher than the sides of the pan. When the dough is pressed gently with a fingertip, the depression will very slowly fill in.

6 > Preheat the oven. Preheat the oven to 475°F 1 hour before baking. Have an oven shelf at the lowest level and place a baking stone or baking sheet on it, and a cast-iron skillet or sheet pan on the floor of the oven, before preheating.

7 > Slash and bake the bread. If making a free-form loaf, with a sharp knife or single-edged razor blade, make several 1/2-inch-deep slashes in the top of the dough (see illustrations on page 81). (If baking the loaf in a bread pan, either make one long slash down the middle or leave it unslashed. Mist the dough with water and quickly but gently set the baking sheet or pan on the hot stone or hot baking sheet. Toss 1/2 cup of ice cubes into the pan beneath and immediately shut the oven door. Bake for 10 minutes. Lower the temperature to 425°F and continue baking for 20 to 30 minutes or until the bread is golden brown and a skewer inserted in the middle comes out clean (an instant-read thermometer inserted into the center will read about 200°F). Halfway through baking, turn the pan around for even baking. To give a free-form loaf an extra crisp crust, transfer it from the baking sheet to the stone and leave it in the oven for an extra 5 to 10 minutes, with the door propped ajar.

8 > Cool the bread. Remove the bread from the oven and transfer it to a wire rack. If using a pan, unmold the bread and turn top side up on the rack. Allow to cool completely.

VARIATIONS

Slightly Sour Artisan Loaf (my personal favorite). Replace the 3/8 teaspoon instant yeast in the sponge with 1/8 teaspoon Lalvain Pain de Campagne starter (see page 37). Increase the instant yeast in the flour mixture to 3/4 teaspoon. In Step 2, allow the sponge to sit at room temperature for at least 8 hours, or up to 12 hours, before mixing.

Velvety Buckwheat Bread **In the dough starter (sponge),** omit the whole wheat flour and use a total of 1 1/4 cups (6.7 ounces/192 grams) bread flour. Increase the yeast from 3/8 teaspoon to 1/2 teaspoon and replace the 1 1/2 cups of water with 3/4 cup (6.5 ounces/182 grams) sour cream. **In the flour mixture,** use only 1 1/4 cups (6.7 ounces/192 grams) bread flour and add 3/4 cup (3.5 ounces/100 grams) buckwheat flour. Bake at a lower temperature: 450°F for 5 minutes; then 400°F for 25 to 35 minutes or until the bread is golden brown and a skewer inserted into the middle comes out clean.

ULTIMATE FULL FLAVOR VARIATION

For the best flavor development, in Step 2, allow the sponge to ferment for 1 hour at room temperature, then refrigerate for 8 to 24 hours. If using the hand method, remove it from the refrigerator about 1 hour before mixing the dough. For even more flavor, refrigerate the finished dough overnight; take it out 1 hour before shaping it.

POINTERS FOR SUCCESS

>   It's fine to use a national brand *unbleached* all-purpose flour, such as Gold Medal, Hecker's, King Arthur, or Pillsbury, instead of bread flour, but these will produce a less chewy, slightly softer texture. The weight of the flour will be the same but you will need to add about 1/3 cup more if measuring by volume.

>   If working with a sticky dough alarms you, decrease the water from 1 1/2 cups to 1 1/4 cups and you will still have an excellent bread that will be firmer and a little smaller: 6 1/2 inches by 3 1/2 inches high free-form or, if baking it in a pan, use an 8 1/2-by-4 1/2-inch pan; the baked loaf will be 8 inches by 4 inches by 5 inches high. The weight of the dough will be about 24.5 ounces/700 grams.

UNDERSTANDING

The small amount of whole wheat flour (7.4 percent) adds a delicious flavor and lovely color to the bread without coarsening the texture. Kamut (see page 547), an ancient predecessor of wheat, is a suitable substitution for the whole wheat because it has less bitterness and will contribute a nutty sweetness. You can also use as much as 22.3 percent kamut (3/4 cup/3.75 ounces/108 grams) and only about 1/2 cup (3 ounces/84 grams) of bread flour in the sponge, but the bread will be slightly denser and much chewier because of the higher protein content (as high as 16 percent).

THE DOUGH PERCENTAGE

Flour:	100% (bread: 92.6%, whole wheat: 7.4%)
Water:	66.6%
Yeast:	0.57%
Salt:	2.1%

Heart of Wheat Bread

This has become my signature bread. I created it after essentially finishing the book—after putting together all the theory. It grew out of everything I understand about flour and bread baking and it is everything I want a bread to be, with a crisp chewy crust and a wheaty light but chewy crumb, cream colored and flecked with nutty sweet little bits of the germ. It was the one last idea I had to try after my husband had gently suggested that I slow down my bread production, as every crevice of our huge freezer was stuffed with bread, enough to last a good six months. The thought of making this bread inspires me to sing "America the Beautiful" while picturing the vast prairies of golden waves of wheat. But eating it inspires absolute and reverential silence!

If you love the fresh wholesome wheatiness of 100 percent whole wheat bread but dislike the bitter undertone and dense texture, here's how to have your wheat and eat it too: all you need to do is eliminate the bran. By using unbleached bread flour or all-purpose flour, which is whole wheat flour minus the germ and bran, and adding the same amount of germ that would be in whole wheat flour (about 2.5 percent), you get the exact equivalent of whole wheat flour minus the bitter bran. (Please note that a small amount of bran is not a bad thing—it can serve as an accent and has its place in some breads.)

You can start this bread as late as 11:00 A.M. on a weekend morning—it takes only 10 minutes to mix—and then leave it to ferment and develop wonderful flavors for 4 hours while you play tennis or go shopping. Then mix and knead it and let it rise once or twice: it takes only 45 minutes to an hour to double because of all the enzymatic activity from that lovely sweet wheaty germ. Shape it, let it rise for another hour, and bake it 30 minutes. Cool it for 1 hour, and it's ready for dinner. The whole process from beginning to end takes about 8 hours but the actual work involved is less than 1 hour. And it's equally wonderful if made ahead and stored uncut overnight in a brown paper bag, then reheated for 10 minutes in a 400°F oven for Sunday dinner. (In fact, the crust becomes perfectly crisp all around when treated this way.)

There's only one wine to consider as the perfect partner for this bread: a great burgundy, its equal in blending earthiness with the ethereal.

Dough Starter (Sponge): 4 hours
Minimum Rising Time: about 3 hours
Oven Temperature: 475°F, then 425°F
Baking Time: 30 to 40 minutes

Makes: an 8-inch-by 3 3/4-inch-high free-form loaf/
1 pound, 10 ounces/745 grams

EQUIPMENT:

a half sheet pan lined with a nonstick liner such as Silpain or parchment, or sprinkled with flour or cornmeal;

a baking stone OR baking sheet

Dough Starter (Sponge)

INGREDIENTS	MEASURE	WEIGHT	
	volume	ounces	grams
bread flour	1 cup	5.5 ounces	158 grams
fresh (not toasted) wheat germ (see page 548)	3 tablespoons	0.5 ounce	14 grams
instant yeast (see page 561 for brands)	3/8 teaspoon	--	1.25 grams
honey	1 1/4 teaspoons	--	9 grams
water, at room temperature (70° to 90°F)	about 1 1/3 liquid cups	11.2 ounces	322 grams

1 > **Make the sponge.** In a mixer bowl or other large bowl, place the bread flour, wheat germ, yeast, honey, and water. Whisk until very smooth, to incorporate air, about 2 minutes. The sponge should be the consistency of a thick batter. Scrape down the sides of the bowl. Set aside, covered with plastic wrap, while you make the flour mixture.

Flour Mixture

INGREDIENTS	MEASURE	WEIGHT	
	volume	ounces	grams
bread flour	2 cups	11 ounces	312 grams
instant yeast	1/2 teaspoon	--	1.6 grams
salt	1 1/2 teaspoons	0.4 ounce	10 grams

2 > Combine the ingredients for the flour mixture and add to the sponge. In a medium bowl, whisk together the bread flour (reserve 2 tablespoons if mixing by hand) and yeast. Gently scoop it onto the sponge to cover it completely, cover tightly with plastic wrap, and allow it to ferment for 4 hours at room temperature. (During this time, the sponge will bubble through the flour mixture in places; this is fine.)

3 > Mix the dough.

Mixer Method

With the dough hook, mix on low speed (#2 if using a KitchenAid) for about 1 minute, until the flour is moistened enough to form a rough dough. Scrape down any bits of dough. Cover the bowl with plastic wrap and allow the dough to rest for 20 minutes.

Sprinkle on the salt and knead the dough on medium speed (#4 KitchenAid) for about 7 minutes. The dough should be very elastic, smooth, and sticky enough to cling slightly to your fingers. If it is still very sticky, knead in a little flour. If it is not at all sticky, spray it with a little water and knead it in. (The dough will weigh about 28.5 ounces/810 grams.)

Hand Method

Add the salt and, with a wooden spoon or your hand, mix until the flour is moistened. Knead the dough in the bowl until it comes together, then scrape it onto a lightly floured counter. Knead the dough for 5 minutes, enough to develop the gluten structure a little, adding as little of the reserved 2 tablespoons flour as possible to keep it from sticking. Use a bench scraper to scrape the dough and gather it together as you knead it. At this point, it will be very sticky. Cover it with the inverted bowl and allow it to rest for 20 minutes. (This resting time will make the dough less sticky and easier to work with.)

Knead the dough for another 5 to 10 minutes or until it is very smooth and elastic. It should be sticky enough to cling slightly to your fingers. If the dough is very sticky, add some of the remaining reserved flour. (The dough will weigh about 28.5 ounces/810 grams.)

Both Methods

4 > Let the dough rise. Place the dough in an 2-quart dough-rising container or bowl, lightly greased with cooking spray or oil. Press down the dough and lightly spray or oil the top. Cover the container with a lid or plastic wrap. With a piece of tape, mark the side at where double the height of the dough would be. Allow the dough to rise (ideally at 75° to 80°F) until doubled, about 45 minutes.

Using an oiled spatula or dough scraper, scrape the dough onto a floured counter and press down on it gently to form a rectangle. Give it 1 business letter turn, round the edges, and return it to the bowl. Oil the surface again, cover, and mark where double the height of the dough would now be. It will fill the container fuller than before because it is puffier with air. Allow to rise until doubled, about 45 minutes to 1 hour.

5 > Shape the dough and let it rise. Turn the dough out onto a floured counter and press down on it gently to flatten it slightly. It will be sticky, but use only as much flour during shaping as absolutely necessary. Round the dough into a ball about 6 inches by 2 1/2 inches high (see illustrations, page 65) and set it on the prepared baking sheet. Cover it with a large container or oiled plastic wrap and allow it to rise until almost doubled, 45 minutes to 1 hour and 15 minutes. The dough will be about 8 inches by 3 inches high, and when it is pressed gently with a fingertip, the depression will very slowly fill in.

6 > Preheat the oven. Preheat the oven to 475°F 1 hour before baking. Have an oven shelf at the lowest level and place a baking stone or baking sheet on it, and a cast-iron skillet or sheet pan on the floor of the oven, before preheating.

7 > Slash and bake the bread. With a sharp knife or single-edged razor blade, make a 1/4-inch-deep cross in the top of the dough (see page 80). Mist the dough with water and quickly but gently set the baking sheet on the hot stone or hot baking sheet. Toss 1/2 cup of ice cubes into the pan beneath and immediately shut the door. Bake for 10 minutes. Lower the temperature to 425°F and continue baking for 20 to 30 minutes or until the bread is golden brown and a skewer inserted in the middle comes out clean (an instant-read thermometer inserted into the center will read about 200°F). Halfway through baking, with a heavy pancake turner, lift the bread from the pan and set it directly on the stone, turning it halfway around as you do so for even baking. For an extra crisp crust, leave the bread in the oven for an extra 5 or 10 minutes with the door propped ajar.

8 > Cool the bread. Remove the bread from the oven and transfer it to a wire rack to cool completely.

> It's fine to use a national-brand *unbleached* all-purpose flour such as Gold Medal, Hecker's, King Arthur, or Pillsbury instead of bread flour, but these will produce a less chewy, slightly softer texture. The weight of the flour will be the same, but you will need to add about 1/3 cup more flour if measuring by volume.

> Purchase the wheat germ at a health food store that does a brisk business so that it is fresh, and store it in the freezer.

UNDERSTANDING

This bread is based on the Basic Hearth Bread (page 305), in which the total amount of flour is 484 grams. The amount of germ contained in whole wheat flour is 2.5 percent, equal in that case to 12.1 grams, so all I needed to do was to add 12 grams wheat germ and subtract 12 grams from the total amount of flour (while eliminating the whole wheat flour). To make it easier for those who prefer measuring to weighing, I've rounded off the wheat germ to 3 tablespoons (14 grams/1 ounce), which comes to 2.9 percent germ.

This bread is 8 inches by 3 3/4 inches high instead of 7 1/2 inches by 4 inches high, as the Basic Hearth Bread is, because the wheat germ has a softening effect on the gluten.

I give this dough a 4-hour room-temperature fermentation to develop a mellow flavor rather than an overnight refrigerator rise, as I want the bread to taste of sweet wheaty tones without any underlying sourness.

THE DOUGH PERCENTAGE

Flour:	100%
Wheat germ	2.9%
Water:	66.6%
Yeast:	0.57%
Salt:	2.1%

Sacaduros

All of the wonderful bread at Restaurant Daniel in New York City is made in their pastry/bread kitchen by chef-boulanger Mark Fiorentino and baker Eli Cordeiro, who comes from Brazil. These unusual little rolls are my very favorite. They are called *sacaduros*, from the Portuguese *saca*, which means to take out, and *duro*, which means hard, referring to taking them out of the oven when they have a crisp hard crust. The buns were created by Eli based on a technique he learned in Brazil. Each is filled with a tiny cube of butter and fleur de sel, then the dough is pinched and folded six times to form a tidy little bundle. Each little bun is inverted into a bed of flour, and during baking, the dough unfolds a little, forming irregular petals and a beautiful contrast of golden dough against the powdery white sections where the flour has adhered. The crust is crunchy, the crumb soft and moist, and in the center is the tiny treat of a special filling.

These three-star-restaurant dinner rolls will delight the craftsperson.

TIME SCHEDULE

Rising Time: none
Oven Temperature: 475°F, then 400°F
Baking Time: 15 to 20 minutes

Makes: fourteen 2-by-2-inch-high buns

INGREDIENTS	MEASURE	WEIGHT	
	volume	ounces	grams
3/4 recipe Basic Hearth Bread dough (page 305)	--	about 1 pound	467 grams
flour for the shaped buns (page 312)	about 3 cups	about 1 pound	about 454 grams
butter and fleur de sel	14 1/2-inch cubes	about 1 ounce	24 grams

1 > Divide the dough. One at a time, pinch off 2-tablespoon (generous 1-ounce/33-gram) pieces of dough, keeping the remaining dough covered with a kitchen towel, and shape each one into a 1 1/2-inch ball (see pages 317–18). Flour your fingers if the dough is sticky, and cover the dough balls as you shape them.

2 > Prepare the flour bed. Fill a 13-by-9-inch baking pan about 1/2 inch deep with flour.

3 > Preheat the oven. Preheat the oven to 475°F 45 minutes before baking time. Have an oven shelf at the lowest level and place a baking stone or baking sheet on it, and a cast-iron skillet or sheet pan on the floor of the oven, before preheating.

4 > Fill and shape the buns. Working with one piece of dough at a time, on a lightly floured counter, gently flatten the dough into a 2-inch disk. Place a butter cube and a pinch of fleur de sel in the center. Gently but firmly pull 2 opposite edges of the dough, fold them over the center of the filling, and press down in the center just enough to seal the dough. The object is to seal the folded-over dough as you complete the shaping, but not to seal it so securely as to prevent it from opening up during baking. Pull the two other sides of the dough out and fold them over in the center, pressing as before to secure the dough. Repeat the process one more time, for a total of 6 pulls (three times); for the last two pulls, take only little pinches of dough. Turn the roll upside down and set it in the flour pan. Continue with the remaining dough. It should not take more than 30 minutes to shape the buns. If you are working more slowly, bake the ones you have finished after 30 minutes and pat the remaining dough balls down to keep them from overrising, then shape and bake them.

5 > Bake the buns. Lift each ball of dough out of the flour bed and, without dusting it off, set it flour side up on the prepared baking pan. Quickly but gently set the pan on the hot baking stone or hot baking sheet. Toss 1/2 cup of ice cubes into the pan beneath and immediately shut the door. Bake for 5 minutes. Lower the heat to 400°F and continue baking for 10 to 15 minutes or until the rolls are golden (an instant-read thermometer inserted in the center of a roll should read at least 190°F). Halfway through baking, turn the pan around for even baking.

6 > Cool the buns. Remove the buns from the oven and transfer to wire racks to cool completely.

STEP-BY-STEP ILLUSTRATIONS FOR MAKING A SACADURO:

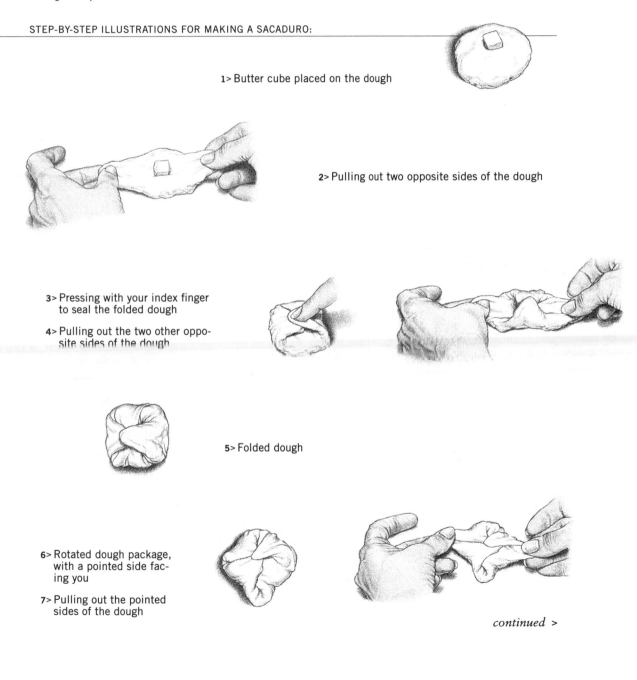

1> Butter cube placed on the dough

2> Pulling out two opposite sides of the dough

3> Pressing with your index finger to seal the folded dough

4> Pulling out the two other opposite sides of the dough

5> Folded dough

6> Rotated dough package, with a pointed side facing you

7> Pulling out the pointed sides of the dough

continued >

8> Dough with pointed sides folded over

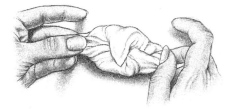

9> Pulling out the opposite pointed sides

10> The opposite pointed sides,
ends folded over

11> Dough package inverted and
placed in flour pan

12> A baked sacaduro

Potato Buttermilk Bread

I so loved the direct, wholesome simplicity of this bread on first taste that I immediately e-mailed its author, chef Rick Kangas, in Beaver Creek, Colorado, to tell him that it would become a part of my regular repertoire.

This bread uses the equivalent of twice the potato of the Potato Sandwich Loaf (page 266), so the earthy potato flavor really comes through. The sugar in the potato causes the crust to brown easily, contributing to the earthy quality. The slight sweetness also helps to mellow and balance the tangy, sort of cheese-like flavor from the dough starter and the buttermilk. The crumb has both a velvety moist quality from the potato and a chewy crustiness from the added vital wheat gluten, but rather than being dense it is light and airy. Because this bread loses most of its special flavor qualities on freezing, it is best eaten the day it is baked.

TIME SCHEDULE

Dough Starter (Biga): minimum 6 hours, maximum 3 days
Minimum Rising Time: about 2 1/2 hours
Oven Temperature: 475°F then 375°F
Baking Time: 30 to 40 minutes

Makes: a 7 1/2-by-4-inch-high round loaf/
1 pound, 8.6 ounces/642 grams

EQUIPMENT:

a half sheet pan lined with a nonstick liner such as Silpain or parchment, or sprinkled with flour or cornmeal;

a baking stone OR baking sheet

Dough Starter (Biga)

Makes: a scant 1/2 cup/4.7 ounces/134 grams

INGREDIENTS	MEASURE	WEIGHT	
	volume	ounces	grams
bread flour	**1/2 cup**	**2.6 ounces**	**75 grams**
instant yeast (see page 561 for brands)	**1/16 teaspoon**	**--**	**0.4 gram**
Optional: malt powder	1/2 teaspoon	--	1.6 grams
water, at room temperature (70° to 90°F)	**1/4 liquid cup**	**2 ounces**	**59 grams**

1 > Six hours or up to 3 days ahead, make the biga. In a small bowl, combine all the biga ingredients and stir with a wooden spoon for 3 to 5 minutes or until very smooth. The biga should still be tacky (sticky) enough to cling slightly to your fingers. Cover the bowl tightly with greased plastic wrap (or place it in a 2-cup food storage container with a lid) and set it aside until tripled and filled with bubbles. At room temperature, this will take about 6 hours. Stir it down and use it, or refrigerate it for up to 3 days before baking.

Dough

INGREDIENTS	MEASURE	WEIGHT	
	volume	ounces	grams
bread flour	**1 3/4 cups**	**10 ounces**	**284 grams**
potato flour	**1/3 cup plus 1 teaspoon**	**2.2 ounces**	**61 grams**
vital wheat gluten	**1/2 tablespoon**	**--**	**4.7 grams**
sugar	**1 teaspoon**	**--**	**4 grams**
instant yeast	**3/4 teaspoon**	**--**	**2.4 grams**
biga (from above)	*scant 1/2 cup*	*4.7 ounces*	*134 grams*
water, at room temperature (70° to 90°F)	**1/2 liquid cup**	**about 4.2 ounces**	**118 grams**
buttermilk	**1/2 liquid cup**	**4.2 ounces**	**121 grams**
salt	**1 1/2 teaspoons**	**--**	**10 grams**

2 > Mix the dough.

Machine Method
In the mixer bowl place the bread flour, potato flour, vital wheat gluten, sugar, yeast, and biga. With the dough hook, mix on low speed (#2 if using a KitchenAid) while

gradually adding the water and buttermilk, mixing until the flour is moistened enough to form a rough dough. Scrape down any bits of dough.

Cover the bowl with plastic wrap and allow the dough to rest for 20 minutes.

Sprinkle on the salt and knead the dough on low speed for 10 minutes (on a higher speed, the dough will climb out of the bowl). The dough will be fairly stiff and barely cling to your fingers. If it is not stiff enough, add a little flour. If it is too stiff, spray it with a little water and knead it in. (The dough will weigh about 25.7 ounces/731 grams.)

Hand Method

Remove the biga from the refrigerator about 1 hour before mixing the dough.

In a large bowl, whisk together 1 1/2 cups (8.2 ounces/234 grams) of the bread flour, the potato flour, vital wheat gluten, sugar, and yeast. Then whisk in the salt (this keeps the yeast from coming in direct contact with the salt, which would kill it). With a wooden spoon or your hand, stir in the biga. Gradually stir in the water and buttermilk until the flour is moistened.

Knead the dough in the bowl until it comes together, then scrape it onto a lightly floured counter. Knead the dough for 5 minutes, enough to develop the gluten structure a little, adding as little of the reserved 1/4 cup flour as possible to keep it from sticking. Use a bench scraper to scrape the dough and gather it together as you knead it. At this point, it will be very sticky. Cover it with the inverted bowl and allow it to rest 20 minutes. (This resting time will make the dough less sticky and easier to work with.)

Knead the dough for another 5 minutes or until it is very smooth and elastic, adding some of the remaining reserved flour, or a little extra, if it is sticky. The dough will be fairly stiff and should barely stick to your fingers. If it is not stiff enough, add a little flour. (It will weigh about 26.3 ounces/716 grams.)

Both Methods

3 > **Let the dough rise.** Place the dough in a 2-quart dough-rising container, or bowl lightly greased with cooking spray or oil. Push down the dough and lightly spray or oil the top. Cover the container with a lid or plastic wrap. With a piece of tape, mark the side of the container at approximately where double the height of the dough would be. Allow the dough to rise (ideally at 75°F to 80°F) until doubled, 1 1/2 to 2 hours.

4 > **Shape the dough and let it rise.** Turn the dough out onto a lightly floured counter and press down on it gently to flatten it slightly. Round the dough into a ball about 5 inches by 2 1/2 inches high and set it on the prepared baking sheet. Cover it with a large container or oiled plastic wrap. Allow the dough rise until almost doubled in

bulk, about 1 hour. It will be about 7 inches by 3 1/2 inches high and when it is pressed gently with a fingertip, the depression will very slowly fill in.

5 > **Preheat the oven.** Preheat the oven to 475°F 1 hour before baking. Have an oven shelf at the lowest level and place a baking stone or baking sheet on it, and a cast-iron skillet or sheet pan on the floor of the oven, before preheating.

6 > **Slash and bake the bread.** With a sharp knife or single-edged razor blade, make a 1/2-inch-deep slash across the top of the dough.

Mist the dough with water and quickly but gently set the sheet on the hot baking stone or hot baking sheet. Toss 1/2 cup of ice cubes into the pan beneath and immediately shut the door. Bake for 5 minutes. Lower the heat to 375°F and continue baking for 25 to 35 minutes or until the crust is deeply golden brown and a skewer inserted in the middle comes out clean (an instant-read thermometer inserted into the center will read about 212°F). Halfway through baking, with a heavy pancake turner, lift the bread from the pan and set it directly on the stone, turning it around as you do so for even baking.

7 > **Cool the bread.** Remove the bread from the oven and transfer to a wire rack to cool completely.

VARIATIONS

Potato Dill Bread   Add 2 tablespoons minced fresh dill (about 0.25 ounce/7 grams) to the dough when mixing it.

Tangy Cornbread   When corn flour or cornmeal is used instead of potato flour, it results in a bread with a pale yellow crumb and a subtle flavor that melds magnificently with a gilding of sweet butter. Replace the potato flour with an equal weight of corn-flour (1/2 cup minus 1 tablespoon) or cornmeal (1/2 cup minus 2 teaspoons).

ULTIMATE FULL FLAVOR VARIATION

For the best flavor development, in Step 1, allow the biga to ferment in a cool area (55° to 65°F) for 12 to 24 hours. After 12 hours, the starter will have tripled and be filled with bubbles; it will not deflate even after 24 hours at this cool temperature. (A wine cellar provides an ideal spot.)

POINTERS FOR SUCCESS

>   If time does not allow for a 1 1/2-to 2-hour rise, increase the instant yeast to 1 teaspoon.

THE DOUGH PERCENTAGE

Flour:	100% (bread: **84.5%**, potato: **14.4%**, vital wheat gluten: **1.1%**)
Water:	**67%**
Yeast:	**0.6%**
Salt:	**2.3%**

"Levy's" Real Jewish Rye Bread

Both of my parents were raised in the Bronx, but we lived in Manhattan when I was growing up. Whenever my father had an excuse to return to the Bronx, he'd never come back without a freshly baked loaf from his favorite bakery. I liked the rye bread, studded with constellations of caraway seeds, best. My grandmother, who lived with us, would serve it to me spread thickly with unsalted butter, the top paved with rounds of sliced red radishes, lightly sprinkled with kosher salt, crushed between her thumb and index finger. This is the way I prefer to eat rye bread even to this day. It has taken me years to get my rye bread to taste and feel just right. I like a wheaty flavor with not so much rye that it becomes bitter, and a chewy texture that is not so dense it becomes pasty. I love using La Cloche, the large unglazed earthenware platter with a dome-shaped top, especially for a double recipe, as, during baking, the bread rises to fill the dome, which gives it a lovely shape, moist texture, and very crunchy top. Of course, the bread is still delicious and beautiful made free-form.

For a 12-inch by 6-inch-high bread, double the recipe, but you will need to make the dough by hand or in a Bosch, Magic Mill, or commercial-sized mixer, as it is too much dough for the average stand mixer to handle.

TIME SCHEDULE

Dough Starter (Sponge): minimum 1 hour, maximum 24 hours
Minimum Rising Time: about 3 1/4 hours
Oven Temperature: 450°F, then 400°F
Baking Time: 45 to 55 minutes

Makes: a 7 3/4-by-4-inch-high round loaf/
1 3/4 pounds/794 grams

EQUIPMENT:

La Cloche Bread Baker OR a half sheet pan, either one sprinkled with cornmeal;

a baking stone OR baking sheet

Dough Starter (Sponge)

INGREDIENTS	MEASURE	WEIGHT	
	volume	ounces	grams
bread flour	3/4 cup	about 4 ounces	117 grams
rye flour	3/4 cup	3.3 ounces	95 grams
instant yeast (see page 561 for brands)	1/2 teaspoon	--	1.6 grams
sugar	1 1/2 tablespoons	0.6 ounce	18.7 grams

malt powder or
    barley malt syrup or honey, or
    sugar
	1/2 tablespoon	--	4.6 grams
			10.5 grams
			6.2 grams

water, at room temperature (70° to 90°F)	1 1/2 liquid cups	12.5 ounces	354 grams

1 > **Make the sponge.** In a mixer bowl or other large bowl, place the bread flour, rye flour, yeast, sugar, malt (or honey or sugar), and water. Whisk until very smooth, to incorporate air, about 2 minutes. The starter will be the consistency of a thick batter. Scrape down the sides of the bowl. Set it aside covered with plastic wrap while you make the flour mixture.

Flour Mixture

INGREDIENTS	MEASURE	WEIGHT	
	volume	ounces	grams
bread flour	2 1/4 cups	about 4.5 ounces	351 grams
instant yeast	1/2 plus 1/8 teaspoon	--	2 grams
caraway seeds	2 tablespoons	0.5 ounce	14 grams
salt	1/2 tablespoon	0.3 ounce	10.5 grams
vegetable oil	1/2 tablespoon	0.25 ounce	6.7 grams
cornmeal for sprinkling	about 2 teaspoons	about 0.5 ounce	about 16 grams
Optional, for serving: unsalted butter, softened fresh radishes, sliced fleur de sel or kosher salt	--	--	--

2 > Combine the ingredients for the flour mixture and add to the sponge. In a large bowl, whisk together the bread flour (reserve 1/4 cup if mixing by hand), rye flour, yeast, caraway seeds, and salt. Gently scoop it onto the sponge to cover it completely. Cover tightly with plastic wrap and allow it to ferment for 1 to 4 hours at room temperature. (During this time, the sponge will bubble through the flour mixture in places; this is fine.)

3 > Mix the dough.

Mixer Method
Add the oil and mix with the dough hook on low speed (#2 if using a KitchenAid) for about 1 minute, until the flour is moistened enough to form a rough dough. Raise the speed to medium (#4 KitchenAid) and mix for 10 minutes. The dough should be very smooth and elastic, and it should jump back when pressed with a fingertip. If the dough is at all sticky, turn it out onto a counter and knead in a little extra flour. (The dough will weigh about 2 pounds 1.7 ounces/965 grams.)

Hand Method
Add the oil and, with a wooden spoon or your hand, stir until the flour is moistened. Knead the dough in the bowl until it comes together, then scrape it onto a lightly floured counter. Knead the dough for 5 minutes, enough to develop the gluten structure a little, adding as little of the reserved flour as possible to keep it from sticking. Use a bench scraper to scrape the dough and gather it together as you knead it. At this point, it will be a little sticky. Cover it with the inverted bowl and

allow it to rest for 20 minutes. (This resting time will make the dough less sticky and easier to work with.)

Knead the dough for another 5 to 10 minutes or until it is very smooth and elastic. If the dough is sticky, add some of the remaining reserved flour, or a little extra. (The dough will weigh 2 pounds 1.7 ounces/965 grams.)

Both Methods

4 > Let the dough rise. Place the dough in a 2-quart dough-rising container or bowl, lightly greased with cooking spray or oil. Press down the dough and lightly spray or oil the top. Cover the container with a lid or plastic wrap. With a piece of tape, mark the side of the container at approximately where double the height of the dough would be. Allow the dough to rise (ideally at 75° to 80°F) until doubled, 1 1/2 to 2 hours.

Using an oiled spatula or dough scraper, scrape the dough out onto a floured counter and press down on it gently to form a rectangle. Give it 1 business letter turn. Oil the surface again, cover, and mark where double the height would now be. The dough will fill the container fuller than before because it is puffier with air. Allow rise a second time until doubled, about 45 minutes.

5 > Shape the dough and let it rise. Turn the dough out onto a lightly floured counter and press it down to flatten it slightly. Round the dough into a ball about 5 1/2 inches by 2 1/2 inches high (see page 65) and set it on the cornmeal sprinkled baking sheet, or La Cloche bottom. Cover it with a large container or oiled plastic wrap. Let the dough rise until almost doubled, about 1 hour to 1 hour and 15 minutes. It will be about 7 1/2 inches by 3 1/2 inches high, and when it is pressed gently with a fingertip the depression will very slowly fill in.

6 > Preheat the oven. Preheat the oven to 450°F 1 hour before baking. Have an oven shelf at the lowest level and place a baking stone or baking sheet on it before preheating. If not using La Cloche, place a cast-iron skillet or sheet pan on the floor of the oven to preheat. If using La Cloche, preheat the dome along with the oven.

7 > Slash and bake the bread. With a sharp knife or single-edged razor blade, make 1/4- to 1/2-inch-deep slashes in the top of the dough (I like to make 2 slashes about 6 inches apart in one direction and a second 2 slashes perpendicular to them). If using La Cloche, carefully place the hot top on the base and quickly but gently set it on the hot stone or hot baking sheet. Alternatively, mist the dough with water and quickly but gently set the baking sheet on the hot stone or hot baking sheet. Toss 1/2 cup of ice cubes into the pan beneath and immediately shut the door. Bake for 15 minutes. Then lower the temperature to 400°F and continue baking for 30 to 40 minutes or until the bread is golden brown and a skewer inserted into the middle comes out clean (an instant-read thermometer inserted into the center will read about 190°F). If not using La Cloche, halfway through baking, with a heavy pancake turner, lift the bread from the pan and set it directly on the stone, turning it around as you do so for even baking. If using La Cloche, remove the dome for the last 5 to 10 minutes of baking.

8 > **Cool the bread.** Remove the bread from the oven, and transfer to a wire rack to cool completely.

ULTIMATE FULL FLAVOR VARIATION

For the best flavor development, in Step 2, allow the sponge to ferment for 1 hour at room temperature, then refrigerate it for 8 to 24 hours. If using the hand mixing method, remove it from the refrigerator about 1 hour before mixing the dough.

POINTERS FOR SUCCESS

>   For a double recipe, you will need to bake the bread for 50 to 65 minutes after lowering the temperature to 400°F.

UNDERSTANDING

I prefer bread flour to unbleached all-purpose flour for this bread because it results in a chewier texture.

I do not use the autolyse technique (allowing the dough to rest and hydrate—absorb the water) before adding the salt, because I am not concerned with keeping the dough as moist as possible. I want a relatively stiff dough, which results in a dense texture.

I use cornmeal for the bottom of the bread simply out of deference to tradition.

THE DOUGH PERCENTAGE

Flour:	100% (bread: 83.1%, rye: 16.9%)
Water:	62.9%
Sugar:	3.3%
Yeast:	0.64%
Caraway seeds:	2.5%
Salt:	1.9%
Oil:	1.2%

Authentic Pumpernickel Bread

This bread recipe has been evolving for years. It was a challenging recipe to develop. I did it for my father, who longed for the pumpernickel of yesteryear, no longer to be found, but I was working at a disadvantage because I had never really liked pumpernickel bread. I found it too dense and bitter, and I'd always assumed it was the pumpernickel flour responsible for these qualities. To my surprise, I learned that pumpernickel flour is merely coarsely ground rye and that the bitterness in many recipes comes from the molasses. I played with the quantities of molasses, coffee, cocoa, and caramel powder to get the desirable dark color and flavor without too much bitterness, and I added both vital wheat gluten, to get the characteristic chew, and a higher proportion of bread flour, to make it less dense. I also discovered that the old baker's tradition of adding *"altus brat,"* or a small quantity of stale pumpernickel bread soaked in water and squeezed dry, does indeed contribute significant depth of flavor, though you can still make an excellent version without it. And, as usual, when you create a recipe you end up making it to your own taste and you, loving it. So does Dad, probably because it's mine.

TIME SCHEDULE

Dough Starter (Sponge): minimum 3 hours, maximum 24 hours
Minimum Rising Time: about 3 hours
Oven Temperature: 400°F, then 375°F
Baking Time: 35 to 40 minutes

Makes: a 7 1/2-4-inch-high round loaf/
1 pound, 10.5 ounces/755 grams

a half sheet pan OR La Cloche Bread Baker, either one lined with a
nonstick liner such as Silpain or parchment, or sprinkled with flour
or cornmeal;

a baking stone OR baking sheet

Dough Starter (Sponge)

INGREDIENTS	MEASURE	WEIGHT	
	volume	ounces	grams
bread flour	1/2 cup	2.75 ounces	78 grams
pumpernickel flour	1/2 cup	2.5 ounces	71 grams
instant yeast (see page 561 for brands)	3/4 teaspoon	--	2.4 grams
caraway seeds	1/2 tablespoon	--	3.5 grams
water, at room temperature (70° to 90°F)	1 liquid cup plus 2 tablespoons (9 fluid ounces)	9.25 ounces	265.5 grams
cider vinegar	1 tablespoon	0.5 ounce	15 grams

malt powder or
  barley malt syrup or honey, or
  sugar
	1 tablespoon	0.3 ounce
		0.7 ounce
		0.5 ounce
			9.3 grams
			21 grams
			12.5 grams

molasses	1 tablespoon	0.7 ounce	22 grams

1 > **Make the sponge.** In a mixer bowl or other large bowl, whisk together the bread
flour, pumpernickel flour, yeast, and caraway seeds. Whisk in the water, vinegar,
malt, honey, or sugar, and molasses until very smooth, to incorporate air, about
2 minutes. The sponge will be the consistency of a thick batter. Set it aside, covered
with plastic wrap, while you make the flour mixture.

Flour Mixture

INGREDIENTS	MEASURE	WEIGHT	
	volume	ounces	grams
bread flour	1 1/2 cups	8.2 ounces	234 grams
pumpernickel flour	1/2 cup	2.5 ounces	71 grams
instant yeast	3/8 teaspoon	--	1.2 grams
vital wheat gluten	2 tablespoons	0.6 ounce	18 grams
caramel powder (see page 568)	2 tablespoons	0.6 ounce	18 grams
cocoa	2 tablespoons	scant 0.5 ounce	12 grams
sugar	1 tablespoon	scant 0.5 ounce	12.5 grams
instant espresso powder	1 teaspoon	--	1.5 grams
vegetable oil	1/2 tablespoon	0.25 ounce	6.7 grams
salt	1 3/4 teaspoons plus 1/8 teaspoon	--	12.3 grams

2 > Combine the ingredients for the flour mixture and add to the sponge. In a medium bowl, whisk together the bread flour (reserve 1/4 cup if mixing by hand), pumpernickel flour, yeast, vital wheat gluten, caramel powder, cocoa, sugar, and instant espresso. Sprinkle this mixture over the top of the sponge. Cover tightly with plastic wrap and allow it to ferment for 1 hour to 4 hours at room temperature. (During this time the sponge will bubble up through the flour mixture in places; this is fine.)

3 > Mix the dough.

Mixer Method
Add the oil and mix with the dough hook on low speed (#2 if using a KitchenAid) for 5 minutes. The dough will pull away from the bowl but cling to your fingers. Cover the bowl with plastic wrap and allow the dough to rest for 20 minutes.

Sprinkle on the salt and knead the dough on medium speed to (#4 KitchenAid) for 2 more minutes. Empty the dough onto a lightly floured counter and knead it, adding a little extra flour only if necessary to keep it from sticking. The dough should be a little tacky (slightly sticky) but not cling to your fingers. Adding too much flour, however, will make it drier and heavier (this is especially true of pumpernickel bread). (The dough will weigh about 1 pound, 13 ounces/820 grams.)

Hand Method
Add the oil and salt, and, with a wooden spoon or your hand, stir until all of the flour is moistened. Knead the dough in the bowl until it comes together, then scrape it onto a lightly floured counter. Knead the dough for 5 minutes, enough to develop

the gluten structure a little, adding as little of the reserved 1/4 cup of flour as possible to keep it from sticking. Use a bench scraper to scrape the dough and gather it together as you knead it. At this point, it will be very sticky. Cover it with the inverted bowl and allow it to rest for 20 minutes. (This resting time will make the dough less sticky and easier to work with.)

Knead the dough for another 5 minutes or until it is very smooth and elastic. The dough should be a little tacky (slightly sticky) but not cling to your fingers. If the dough is sticky, add some of the remaining reserved flour, or a little extra. Adding too much flour, however, will make it drier and heavier (this is especially true of pumpernickel bread). (The dough will weigh about 1 pound, 13 ounces/820 grams.)

Both Methods

4 > **Let the dough rise.** Place the dough in a 2-quart dough-rising container or bowl, lightly greased with cooking spray or oil. Push down the dough and lightly spray or oil the top. Cover the container with a lid or plastic wrap. With a piece of tape, mark the side of the container at approximately where double the height of the dough would be. Allow the dough to rise (ideally at 75° to 80°F) until doubled, 1 to 2 hours.

Scrape the dough out onto a floured counter and press down on it gently to form a rectangle. Give it 1 business letter turn, round the edges, and set it back in the container. Oil the surface again, cover, and mark where double the height would now be. (It will fill the container fuller than before because it is puffier with air.) Allow the dough to rise until doubled, 1 to 1 1/2 hours.

5 > **Shape the dough and let it rise.** Turn the dough out onto a lightly floured counter and press it down to flatten it slightly. Shape it into an 5-inch by 3-inch-high ball (see page 65). Set the dough on the prepared baking sheet or La Cloche bottom. Cover it with a large container or oiled plastic wrap. Let the dough rise until almost doubled, about 1 hour. (It will be 7 inches by 4 inches high), and when it is pressed gently with a fingertip, the depression will very slowly fill in.

Optional Shiny Glaze

Makes: a generous 1/4 cup (enough for 2 loaves)

INGREDIENTS	MEASURE	WEIGHT	
	volume	ounces	grams
water	1/4 cup plus 2 tablespoons, divided	--	--
cornstarch	1/2 tablespoon	--	--
Optional: sesame seeds, preferably raw	1/2 tablespoon	--	--

6 > **Prepare the optional glaze (for a high gloss).** In a small saucepan, bring the 1/4 cup of water to a boil. Meanwhile, whisk together the remaining 2 tablespoons water and the cornstarch. When the water is boiling, whisk in the cornstarch mixture. Return it to a boil, whisking constantly, and boil, whisking, until it thickens and turns translucent. Remove from the heat. (The glaze can be made ahead and set aside, covered; reheat before using.

7 > **Preheat the oven.** Preheat the oven to 400°F 1 hour before baking. Have an oven shelf at the lowest level and place a baking stone or baking sheet on it before pre-heating. If not using La Cloche, place a cast-iron skillet or sheet pan on the floor of the oven to preheat. If using La Cloche, preheat the dome along with the oven.

8 > **Glaze, slash, and bake the bread.** If using the glaze, brush it over the entire sur-face of the bread. With a sharp knife or single-edged razor blade, make several 1/4- to 1/2-inch-deep slashes in the top of the dough. (I like to make 2 slashes about 2 1/2 inches apart in one direction and a second slash perpendicular to them). Sprinkle with the sesame seeds, if desired.

Quickly but gently set the baking sheet on the hot stone or hot baking sheet. Toss 1/2 cup of ice cubes into the pan beneath and immediately shut the door. Bake for 15 minutes. Lower the temperature to 375°F and continue baking for 20 to 30 minutes or until a skewer inserted in the middle comes out clean (an instant-read thermometer inserted into the center will read about 204°F). Halfway through bak-ing, turn the pan around for even baking.

Alternatively, if using La Cloche, carefully place the *hot* top on the base and quickly but gently set it on the hot stone or hot baking sheet. Bake for 10 minutes. Lower the temperature to 400°F and continue baking for 30 to 35 minutes or until a skewer inserted in the center comes out clean (an instant-read thermometer inserted in the center will read about 204°F).

9 > **Glaze and cool the bread.** Remove the bread from the oven and transfer it to a wire rack. Rewarm the glaze and brush the bread with a second coat, if desired. Allow the bread to cool completely.

VARIATIONS

Denser Pumpernickel   Replace 1 cup (5.5 ounces/156 grams) of the bread flour with 1 cup (5 ounces/144 grams) whole wheat flour.

Raisin Pumpernickel   Place 1 cup (5 ounces/144 grams) of raisins in a small bowl and add 1/3 cup hot water. Cover with plastic wrap and allow to sit until softened, stirring once, for 30 minutes. (Don't soak longer, or the raisins will lose their texture.) Drain the raisins, reserving the liquid. Use 1/4 cup of the raisin water to replace 1/4 cup of the water in the recipe.

After the dough is mixed, allow it to rest, covered, for 10 minutes to relax the gluten. Then press or roll it into a rectangle about 10 inches by 15 inches. Sprinkle it with the raisins and, starting from a short end, roll it up. Knead it for a few minutes to incorporate the raisins evenly.

Altus Brat The addition of "old bread" provides an extra flavor dimension and slightly moister crumb. The shaped dough and bread will be slightly larger (5 1/2 inch by 3 inches high for the dough, 8 inches by 4 1/2 inches high for the baked bread); it will weigh about 32.5 ounces/924 grams. If you use "old bread" you need to add more extra flour to balance the added liquid.)

For about 1/2 cup (4.2 ounces/120 grams) "old bread," use about 1 slice crustless (2.25 ounces/63 grams) pumpernickel bread (stale, even several days old, is fine). Tear it into pieces and soak it overnight at room temperature in about 1/4 cup of water. When ready to mix the dough, squeeze out any excess moisture, and add the bread when adding the oil. You will probably need to add about 2 1/2 tablespoons (1 ounce/28 grams) flour.

ULTIMATE FULL FLAVOR VARIATION

For the best flavor development, in Step 2, allow the sponge to ferment for 1 hour at room temperature, then refrigerate it for 8 to 24 hours. If using the hand mixing method, remove it from the refrigerator about 1 hour before mixing the dough.

THE DOUGH PERCENTAGE

Flour:	Flour: **100%** (bread: **66.1%**, coarse rye: **30.1%**)
vital wheat gluten:	**3.8%**
Caraway seeds:	**0.7%**
Water:	**60.5%** (includes the vinegar)
Yeast:	**0.76%**
Salt:	**2.6%**
Oil:	**1.4%**

Baguette

The baguette is the definitive fingerprint of the bread baker. And as I worked on this book, it served for me as the basis of all bread baking (the way the pound cake did in *The Cake Bible*). No bread could be more simple or, conversely, more difficult to perfect. All the dough contains is flour, water, yeast, and salt. And so it's all about those few ingredients, plus temperature, and timing, and gentle but firm shaping, and baking.

I wasn't planning to include baguettes in this book for two reasons: I didn't think they could be made successfully in a home oven, and I can buy wonderful ones within five minutes of my home. But people who did not live in areas where they could find good baguettes pleaded with me to come up with a good recipe.

My goal was a light crumb with large holes and a splinteringly crisp but tender crust. It took me over twenty-five tries to get right, but the result was the lightest, crispest, and best baguette I've ever had. I took a loaf to Michael Batterberry when I was visiting *Food Arts* magazine, and when we broke off a piece, it showered crumbs all over the papers on his desk. I didn't know whether to be horrified or triumphant, but when I saw the look of delighted comprehension in his eyes, I was reassured as to my choice! We both knew that this was the real thing. And now the baguette seems like one of the easiest of all doughs.

The secret to the big holes and fine crust: the right kind of flour (and not over three months old), a very wet dough, a slow rise, maintaining the bubbles during shaping, and overnight "retarding" in the refrigerator after shaping.

I tried many recipes. My final recipe was inspired by the recipe from Acme Bakery in Maggie Glezer's wonderful book, *Artisan Bread*. Most baguette recipes use the straight-dough technique, avoiding dough starters. But that recipe uses two different starters, a scrap dough, or pâte fermentée (the French equivalent of the Italian biga), and a poolish (a thin sponge) for great depth of flavor. Maggie came up with a very clever and useful technique of diluting the yeast in order to measure the very small quantity needed.

Plan to start this dough the night before. If you start at 8:00 P.M., you will be able to go to sleep by 11:00 and the poolish will be ready to use by 7:30 to 8:00 the next morning. (For a different schedule, use 4 teaspoons of the yeast mixture for the poolish—there will be enough—and it will be ready in just 5 to 5 1/2 hours.) Timing is for a room temperature of 75°F.

(**A note on the color photograph of the baguettes:** The week we took the photographs for this book was the coldest week of the New York winter (January 2003). It was so cold in the studio that none of the breads was rising fast enough to catch the fading winter light. For this reason, we had to call The French Culinary Institute for an emergency delivery of freshly baked baguettes. Your baguettes will be as beautiful, but they will not have the exact appearance or length of one baked in a commercial deck oven.)

TIME SCHEDULE

Dough Starter (scrap dough and poolish): minimum 11 1/2 hours, maximum 16 hours
Minimum Rising Time: 4 hours
Oven Temperature: 450°F
Baking Time: 30 minutes (plus 5 minutes with oven off)

Makes: two 14-inch-long baguettes, 2 1/4 inches wide by 2 inches high, about 7 ounces/200 grams each

EQUIPMENT:

a heavy-duty stand mixer with dough hook attachment;

two-section baguette pan, nonstick or greased lightly with cooking oil or spray OR a Steam Baking Master (see page 589) OR a baking stone or baking sheet

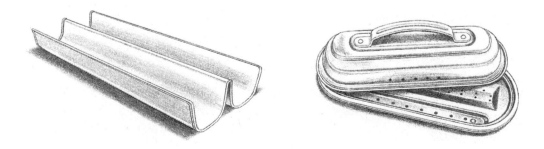

Scrap Dough (Pâte Fermentée)

Makes: about 3.5 ounces/100 grams

INGREDIENTS	MEASURE	WEIGHT	
	volume	ounces	grams
water, at warm room temperature (75° to 90°F)	1/4 liquid cup	2 ounces	59 grams
instant yeast (see page 561 for brands)	1/8 teaspoon	--	0.4 gram
unbleached all-purpose flour, preferably King Arthur European-style artisan flour, or Gold Medal or Pillsbury	1/4 cup plus 2 1/2 tablespoons	2 ounces	57.5 grams
salt	3/16 teaspoon	--	1.2 grams

1 > A day ahead, make the scrap dough (pâte fermentée). Place the water in a small bowl and stir in the yeast. Stir again before using.

In a small bowl, stir together the flour and salt. Add 2 tablespoons plus 2 teaspoons of the yeast water. Reserve the rest for the poolish (starter).

Stir this very soft and sticky dough until it is smooth and comes away from the sides of the bowl, about 5 minutes. Cover tightly with plastic wrap and let it ferment at room temperature for about 3 hours, then refrigerate it until the next morning.

Dough Starter (Poolish)

Makes: about 5.3 ounces/150 grams

INGREDIENTS	MEASURE	WEIGHT	
	volume	ounces	grams
unbleached all-purpose flour, preferably King Arthur European-style artisan flour, or Gold Medal or Pillsbury	1/2 cup plus 1/2 tablespoon	2.6 ounces	75 grams
instant yeast mixture (from above)	1/2 tablespoon	0.26 ounce	7.5 grams
water, at room temperature (70° to 90°F)	1/4 liquid cup plus 1 1/2 tablespoons	2.4 ounces	67.5 grams

2 > Meanwhile, make the poolish. Place the flour in a 2-cup measure and add 1/2 tablespoon of the reserved yeast water to the flour (discard the little that remains). Add the room-temperature water and stir until incorporated. The poolish will be a very gloppy batter. Cover with plastic wrap and let ferment for 11 1/2 to 16 hours, depending on the room temperature, or until there are a lot of bubbles on the top, some of which are beginning to pop, and the poolish is just beginning to sink. It will have slightly more than tripled. (You could also let it rise in a Ball jar or other small

(2-cup capacity) container, marking with tape how high it should rise; it will start off at 1/2 cup and rise to 1 2/3 cups.)

Dough

INGREDIENTS	MEASURE	WEIGHT	
	volume	ounces	grams
unbleached all-purpose flour, preferably King Arthur European-style artisan flour, or Gold Medal or Pillsbury	1 cup plus 3 tablespoons	6 ounces	170 grams
instant yeast	1/8 teaspoon	--	0.4 gram
water, room temperature (70° to 90°F)	3 fluid ounces (6 tablespoons)	about 3 ounces	90 grams
poolish (from above)	--	*about 5.3 ounces*	*150 grams*
scrap dough (from above)	--	*about 3.5 ounces*	*about 100 grams*
salt	1 teaspoon	--	6.6 grams

3 > **Make the dough.** In the mixer bowl, whisk together the flour and yeast. Stir the water into the poolish to loosen it, and add this to the flour mixture. With a wooden spoon, mix just until well combined, 2 to 3 minutes. The dough will be very rough and sticky but it will pull away from the bowl. Cover with plastic wrap and allow it to rest for 20 minutes.

With oiled fingers, tear the scrap dough into a few pieces, and add it and the salt to the dough. Knead on medium speed (#4 if using a KitchenAid) for about 7 minutes. The dough should be tacky (sticky) enough to cling slightly to your fingers. If it is still very sticky, knead in a little flour. If it is not at all sticky, spray with a little water and knead it in. (The dough will weigh about 17.6 ounces/500 grams.)

4 > **Let the dough rise.** Using an oiled spatula or dough scraper, scrape the dough into a 2-quart dough-rising container or bowl, lightly greased with cooking spray or oil. Push down the dough and lightly spray or oil the top. Cover the container with a lid or plastic wrap. With a piece of tape, mark the side of the container at approximately where double the height of the dough would be. Allow the dough to rise (ideally at 75° to 80°F) until it has doubled, 2 to 3 hours. During the first hour, give the dough a gentle business letter turn every 20 minutes, for a total of three times, to redistribute the yeast and gently strengthen the gluten. Then leave the dough undisturbed for the remaining fermentation so that it becomes light and airy.

Please see illustrations on pages 70–71 for shaping a baguette.

5 > Preshape the dough and let it rest. Turn the dough out onto a lightly floured counter and cut it in half. (Don't worry if each one is not exactly the same size; patching would make the dough stretchy and hard to shape without losing air bubbles.) Gently pat each piece into a rectangle, they shape it into a stubby log by rolling the top edge down to the middle, then pushing it back slightly with your thumbs. Repeat this rolling motion two more times, ending with the seam at the bottom edge of the dough (see page 70 for more detail). Use a bench scraper to move each loaf to a lightly floured counter, seam side down. Cover with oiled plastic wrap and allow to sit for about 30 minutes or until relaxed and extensible (when you pull the dough gently, it stretches without tearing).

6 > Shape the dough and let it rise. Working with one piece of dough at a time, gently pat and stretch it into an 8-by-5-inch rectangle. Fold the bottom over, a little past the center and fold the top down to the center. With the side of your hand, seal the dough in the center, creating a trough. Then bring the top down to the bottom and seal using the heel of your hand or your thumbs, pressing only on the seam to maintain as much air as possible in the rest of the dough. Try to keep the length at about 8 inches. Allow the loaves to rest covered (or place in a couche) for 30 to 45 minutes, until very light and soft enough to stretch.

Gently stretch each piece of dough to 14 inches and set each one into a baguette pan depression or place in the Steam Master. Cover with oiled plastic wrap (if not using Saran original brand, then set in a large clean garbage bag) and refrigerate for 5 to 14 hours.

About 1 1/2 hours before you are ready to bake the baguettes, remove them from the refrigerator and let them sit until almost doubled, 1 to 1 1/2 hours. When the dough is pressed gently with a fingertip, the depression will very slowly fill in. In a baguette pan, the top of the dough will not quite reach the plastic wrap if is stretched taut over the sides of the mold. When the dough has risen, remove the plastic wrap and allow the surface to dry for 5 minutes, for easier slashing.

7 > Preheat the oven. Preheat the oven to 450°F 1 hour before baking. Have an oven shelf at the lowest level and place a baking stone or baking sheet on it before preheating. If not using a Steam Master, put a cast-iron skillet or sheet pan on the floor of the oven to preheat.

8 > Slash and bake the bread. With a sharp knife or single-edged razor blade, make about three long 1/4- to 1/2-inch-deep diagonal slashes down the length of each loaf. Mist with water and quickly but gently set the pan on the baking stone or baking sheet. If using the Steam Master, add water to the pan; if not, toss 1/2 cup of ice cubes into the pan beneath. Immediately shut the door, and bake for 30 minutes. Halfway through baking, turn the pan around for even baking. If the crust is not deeply golden after 30 minutes, remove the baguettes from the pan and set them on the stone or the baking sheet. Turn the oven up to 475°F and bake for 5 minutes or until golden. Turn off the oven, prop the door slightly ajar with a wooden spoon, and allow the bread to sit for another 5 minutes to allow the steam to escape and a crisp side crust to form.

9 > **Cool the bread.** Remove the breads from the oven and transfer them to wire racks to cool for 10 minutes.

POINTERS FOR SUCCESS

> If using Gold Medal or Pillsbury flour, you can replace 1 to 3 percent of the flour with whole wheat flour (1 teaspoon to 1 tablespoon/3 to 9 grams) to approximate the lovely flavor the King Arthur European-style flour gives.

> If the shaped baguette dough sits refrigerated for 5 hours or longer, it will develop larger holes and a crisper, more blistery crust. If desired, however, you can omit the refrigeration and bake the baguettes after about an hour at room temperature after shaping, when they have almost doubled.

UNDERSTANDING

The Steam Baking Master and the curved baguette pans produce bread with the prettiest rounded shape. The Steam Master also produces the crispest and most attractive crust.

The flour in the scrap dough and the poolish is 78 percent of the total flour used in the rest of the dough.

One of the secrets to large holes in the baguette crumb is to shape it into a loaf about half the desired finished size and let it proof 30 minutes, then very gently pull it to full length. This opens and stretches the holes. Be very gentle when shaping, though, so as to keep in as much air as possible!

SUGGESTED TIME SCHEDULE FOR DINNER BAGUETTES

7:30 to 8:00 a.m.: mix the dough

8:00 to 8:20: autolyse

8:20 to 8:35: machine mix

8:35 to 11:30: let rise, with 3 turns in the first hour

11:30 to 12:00: divide, preshape, and let rest

12:00 to 12:15: final shaping

12:15 to 12:45: rest, and pull to lengthen the dough

12:45 to 5:45: refrigerate (5 hours, or refrigerate longer, up to 1 3/4 hours before dinner)

5:45 to 6:45: let sit at room temperature

6:45 to 7:15: bake

VARIATION

Baguettes au Chocolat   When he was teaching at the Baking Center in Minneapolis, master baker Didier Rosado made a wonderful breakfast treat for his students: ficelles (thin baguettes) with butter and grated flakes of chocolate. Regular baguettes will work as well.

Cut each warm baguette into 2 pieces, and split each one lengthwise in half. Spread each piece with 2 teaspoons (9.2 grams) unsalted butter and grate about 4 grams (about a tablespoon) of milk chocolate on top, using a melon baller or a peeler. The thin flurries of chocolate will melt immediately on contact.

THE DOUGH PERCENTAGE

Flour:	100%
Water:	67.5%
Instant yeast:	0.25%
Salt:	2.2%

Spicy Herbed Bread Sticks

Zoe's, my favorite New York City neighborhood restaurant, makes the most delicious bread sticks (*grissini* in Italian). Skinny as twigs, crisp, spicy and herby, they are displayed towering above the tall glasses that hold them at the bar. This is their special recipe.

TIME SCHEDULE

Starter: straight dough method
Resting Time: 6 to 12 hours
Oven Temperature: 375°F
Baking Time: 12 to 16 minutes per batch

Makes: about 68 bread sticks/13 ounces/376 grams

INGREDIENTS	MEASURE	WEIGHT	
	volume	ounces	grams
bread flour	2 1/4 cups	12.25 ounces	351 grams
instant yeast (see page 561 for brands)	1/2 teaspoon	--	1.6 grams
salt	1 1/8 teaspoons	--	7.4 grams
black pepper	1 teaspoon	--	--
white pepper	1/2 teaspoon	--	--
garlic powder	1/2 teaspoon	--	--
grated Parmigiano-Reggiano	1/2 cup loosely packed	0.75 ounce	20 grams
herbs, such as chives, rosemary, thyme, sage, and/or marjoram, minced	2 tablespoons	0.25 ounce	7 grams
Tabasco	1/2 teaspoon	--	--
water, at room temperature (70° to 90°F)	1 liquid cup	8.4 ounces	236 grams
cornmeal for dusting	--	--	--
fine sea salt	--	--	--

EQUIPMENT:

3 half sheet pans lined with Silpat or parchment and sprinkled with cornmeal (if you have only 2 pans, work with one batch of dough at a time)

1 > **Mix the dough 6 to 12 hours ahead.**

Mixer Method

In the mixer bowl, combine the flour, yeast, salt, black pepper, white pepper, garlic powder, grated cheese, minced herbs, and Tabasco. With the dough hook, on low speed (#2 if using a KitchenAid), gradually add the water, then continue mixing just until the dough pulls away from the bowl; do not overmix. Transfer the dough to a floured counter and knead it lightly, adding extra flour if the dough is at all sticky. (The dough will weigh about 21.75 ounces/625 grams.)

Hand Method

In a large bowl, combine the flour, yeast, salt, black pepper, white pepper, garlic powder, grated cheese, minced herbs, and Tabasco. Mixing with a wooden spoon or your hand, gradually add the water, then continue mixing just until the dough cleans the sides of the bowl; do not overmix. Transfer the dough to a floured counter and knead it lightly, adding extra flour if the dough is at all sticky. (The dough will weigh about 21.75 ounces/625 grams.)

Both Methods

2 > **Let the dough rise.** Place the dough in a 1-quart or larger dough-rising container or bowl, lightly greased with cooking spray or oil. Push down the dough and lightly spray or oil the top. With a piece of tape, mark the side of the container at approximately where double the height of the dough would be. Cover the container with a lid or plastic wrap and refrigerate for 6 to 12 hours. After the first hour or two, gently deflate the dough; check again after a few hours and deflate it again if the dough is rising to more than double, or place a weight on top of the container.

3 > **Preheat the oven.** Preheat the oven to 375°F 1 hour before baking. Have one oven rack at the lowest level and a second oven rack one level above it before preheating.

4 > **Shape the dough.** Cut the dough into 4 pieces and shape each one into a ball, then flatten each one on a counter sprinkled with cornmeal. Work with two pieces of

dough at a time, keeping the others covered and refrigerated. Pass one piece of dough through a pasta machine on the widest setting: the dough will be about 1/8 inch thick. Dredge the sheets of dough in more cornmeal as necessary as you work to prevent the dough from sticking. Allow the first piece to dry slightly while you run the second piece through the machine.

Run the first piece of dough through the fettuccine (1/4-inch-wide) cutter. Gently separate the strands, lay them on the cornmeal-dusted counter, and toss to coat them with the cornmeal. Lay the strands on a prepared baking sheet, trimming them to fit if necessary (but try not to stretch them or make them too thin), leaving a little space between the strands as they expand slightly during baking, to ensure crispness. Spray or brush all over with olive oil and dust each with a pinch or two of fine sea salt and more cornmeal.

5 > **Bake the bread sticks.** Bake for 12 to 16 minutes or until golden. The bread sticks are done when they start to curve away from the parchment but are still a little flexible; avoid overbrowning, which could make them bitter.

6 > **Cool and recrisp the bread sticks.** Transfer the bread sticks to racks to cool, and allow the pans to cool completely before the next batch. (There is no need to change the parchment or remove the cornmeal for the second batch.) Then roll, cut, and bake the remaining dough.

When all the bread sticks are baked and the oven has cooled, place them, still on racks, in the oven with the pilot light, or set on the lowest possible heat, for about an hour or until totally crisp.

7 > **Cool the bread sticks again.** Remove the bread sticks from the oven and cool them completely on the wire racks.

STORE   Store the bread sticks in an airtight container for no more than 4 days.

POINTERS FOR SUCCESS

>   It's fine to use a food processor to chop the herbs if you add some of the flour mixture along with them.

>   If the dough overrises, it will tear the strands of gluten and be too weak and inelastic to roll out. If this should happen, you can knead in more bread flour and water until the dough becomes stretchy again, but it is much easier simply to deflate the dough during the first few hours of refrigerated rest.

> Don't use Silpain to line the pans, as cornmeal, which gives a nice crunch to the outside of the bread sticks, gets stuck in the little holes and is hard to wash out.

THE DOUGH PERCENTAGE

Flour:	100%
Water:	67.2%
Yeast:	0.45%
Salt:	2.1%

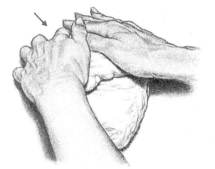 

Brinna's Pugliese

My friend Brinna Sands of King Arthur Flour calls this her "daily bread," but she also mentioned that she is continuously learning and changing things and that the wonderful thing about bread is that it is adaptable. In her words:

"The struggle I'm having is that this bread flies in the face of all the whole grains, levains, and starters I've been committed to over the years. It is, after all, a primarily white yeast-leavened loaf that is the antithesis of all things I used to hold important. But everyone loves it. I love it. It's terrific right out of the oven, half an hour out of the oven, the next day, the day after that, and finally as toast, bread pudding, strata, croutons, crumbs. . . . What makes it so compelling? Why do I make it over and over again? I'm not sure I have the answer. I'm not sure I want to know the answer!"

A biga is simply a dough starter made with just flour, yeast, and water, that is mixed at least 12 hours before mixing the dough to give it more depth of flavor, moistness, and chewiness. Brinna always has a biga sitting in her refrigerator, waiting for the next loaf.

This is a very wet dough, so it is best mixed in a stand mixer or bread machine. Brinna prefers the bread machine, saying there is less oxygenation, and also that it provides a perfect environment to proof the mixed dough. I give both methods in the recipe.

This bread is exceptionally light and full of holes! The addition of a small amount of pumpernickel flour (coarse rye) adds delightfully to its wonderful flavor.

TIME SCHEDULE

Dough Starter (Biga): minimum 6 hours, maximum 3 days
Rising Time: about 2 hours and 15 minutes
Oven Temperature: 450°F, then 400°F
Baking Time: 30 to 35 minutes

Makes: a 7-by-4-inch-high round loaf/1 pound, 2 ounces/510 grams

EQUIPMENT:

a bread machine OR a heavy-duty stand mixer with dough
hook attachment;

a large half sheet pan lined with a nonstick liner such as
Silpain or parchment;

a baking stone OR baking sheet;

an 8-inch banneton OR colander

Dough Starter (Biga)

Makes: about 3/4 cup/7 ounces/200 grams

INGREDIENTS	MEASURE	WEIGHT	
	volume	ounces	grams
instant yeast (see page 561 for brands)	1/8 teaspoon	--	0.4 gram
water, at room temperature (70° to 90°F)	3 fluid ounces (6 ~~teaspoons~~) *tablespoon*	3 ounces	88.5 grams
unbleached all-purpose flour (use only Gold Medal, King Arthur, or Pillsbury)	1/2 cup	2.5 ounces	71 grams
pumpernickel flour (coarse rye)	1/3 cup	1.5 ounces	42.5 grams
salt	1/4 teaspoon	--	1.7 grams

1 > **Six hours or up to 3 days ahead, make the biga.** In a small bowl, combine all the
ingredients for the biga in the order listed, and stir the mixture with a wooden spoon
for about 3 minutes or until it is very smooth and pulls away from the sides of the
bowl. It should still be tacky (sticky) enough to cling slightly to your fingers. Cover
the bowl tightly with oiled plastic wrap (or place it in a 1-quart food storage container with a lid) and set it aside until doubled and filled with bubbles. At room temperature, this will take about 6 hours. Then stir it down and use it, or refrigerate up
to 3 days before baking. (If using a bread machine, it can be mixed in the bread
machine, covered with plastic wrap, and left the bread machine until ready to mix,
no more than 6 hours. Be sure to scrape in bits of dough sticking to the sides.)

Dough

INGREDIENTS	MEASURE	WEIGHT	
	volume	ounces	grams
water, at room temperature (70° to 90°F)	3/4 liquid cup	6.25 ounces	177 grams
unbleached all-purpose flour (use only Gold Medal, King Arthur, or Pillsbury)	1 1/2 cups plus 1 1/2 tablespoons	8 ounces	227 grams
instant yeast	3/4 teaspoon	--	2.4 grams
biga (from above)	*about 3/4 cup*	*7 ounces*	*200 grams*
salt	3/4 teaspoon	--	5 grams

2 > **Mix the dough.**

Bread Machine Method

Add the water, flour, and yeast to the biga. Program the machine to mix for 3 minutes and knead for 10 minutes, and allow it to go through the 3 minutes of mixing, then press the pause button. (You want it to pause for 20 minutes, so try to catch it just before 10 minutes and the moment the machine starts up again, press "pause" a second time for another 10-minute pause.)

Add the salt and allow the machine to continue into the knead cycle for 10 minutes. The dough will be very sticky. Let the dough rise in the machine until doubled, about 1 hour and 15 minutes to 1 1/2 hours.

Mixer Method

Place the biga in the mixer bowl and mix with the dough hook on low speed (#2 if using a KitchenAid) for about 1 minute, until the flour is moistened enough to form a rough dough. Scrape down any bits of dough. Cover the top of the bowl with plastic wrap and allow the dough to rest for 20 minutes.

Sprinkle on the salt and knead the dough on medium speed (#4 KitchenAid) for about 7 minutes. The dough will be very sticky.

Using an oiled spatula or dough scraper, scrape the dough into an 2-quart dough-rising container or bowl, lightly greased with cooking spray or oil. Push down the dough and lightly spray or oil the top. Cover the container with a lid or plastic wrap. With a piece of tape, mark the side of the container at approximately where double the height of the dough would be. Allow the dough to rise (ideally at 75° to 80°F) until doubled, about 1 hour and 15 minutes to 1 1/2 hours.

Both Methods

3 > **Shape the dough and let it rise.** Turn the dough out onto a lightly floured counter and press down on it gently to flatten it slightly. Round the dough into a ball (see

page 65), dusting it with as little flour as possible to keep it from sticking and keeping as much air as possible in the dough. (It will weigh about 21 ounces/600 grams.)

Set the ball of dough upside down in an 8-inch banneton *bottom side up* or a colander lined with a floured cloth. Cover the banneton or colander with a large container or oiled plastic wrap and let the dough rise (ideally at 75° to 80°F) until almost doubled, about 1 hour. In an 8-inch banneton, the center of the dough will rise to 1 inch above the sides. When the dough is pressed gently with a fingertip the depression will very slowly fill in.

4 > Preheat the oven. Preheat the oven to 450°F 1 hour before baking. Have an oven shelf at the lowest level and place a baking stone or baking sheet on it, and a cast-iron skillet or sheet pan on the floor of the oven, before preheating.

5 > Slash and bake the bread. Remove the plastic wrap and gently invert the dough onto the prepared baking sheet. (If you used a colander and floured towel and the risen bread is more than 1 inch below the top, you will need to support the bread when inverting it so that it doesn't fall and deflate. Cut a cardboard circle that is small enough to fit into the colander and touch the surface of the bread. Place a piece of parchment on top of the bread, place the cardboard on top, and invert the bread onto the cardboard. Then slide the bread, still on the parchment, onto the baking sheet.) With a sharp knife or single-edged razor blade, make several 1/4- to 1/2-inch-deep slashes in the top of the dough (see pages 80–81).

Quickly but gently set the baking sheet on the hot baking stone or hot baking sheet. Toss 1/2 cup of ice cubes into the pan beneath and immediately shut the oven door. Bake for 15 minutes. Turn down the heat to 400°F and continue baking for 15 minutes or until the bread is deeply golden brown and a skewer inserted in the middle comes out clean (an instant-read thermometer inserted into the center will read about 204°F). Halfway through baking, with a heavy pancake turner, lift the bread from the pan and set it directly on the stone, turning it around as you do so for even baking.

6 > Cool the bread. Remove the bread from the oven, and transfer it to a wire rack to cool completely.

ULTIMATE FULL FLAVOR VARIATION

For the best flavor development, in Step 1, allow the biga to ferment in a cool area (55° to 65°F) for 12 to 24 hours. (A wine cellar provides an ideal spot.) After 12 hours, it will have doubled and be filled with bubbles; it will not deflate even after 24 hours at this cool temperature.

The addition of pumpernickel flour to the biga gives it a little more acidity, resulting in a slightly more mildly sour flavor and more open crumb. The small amount of salt is added to slow down the action of the yeast slightly, as pumpernickel flour ferments faster than wheat flour.

This biga only doubles rather than triples on fermentation because the rye flour makes it less extensible (stretchy).

THE DOUGH PERCENTAGE

Flour:	100% (all-purpose: 87.5%, pumpernickel: 12.5%)
Water:	78%
Yeast:	0.82%
Salt:	1.9%

Tuscan Low-Salt Bread

When I had the good fortune to be a presenter at the Melbourne Food and Wine Festival, I got to know many of Australia's best bakers. Phillippa Grogan of Phillippa's Bakery in Armadale, a suburb of Melbourne, gave me a tasting of her amazing breads and fabulous pastries, as well as a midnight visit to the bread ovens, where her husband was baking the bread. It was there that I changed my opinion of Tuscan bread. Because of an ancient government tax levied on products containing salt, this bread is traditionally made without the salt. Although it's ideally suited to the zesty, salty Tuscan sauces and sausages, I usually find unsalted bread too flat in flavor. But when Phillippa told me that it was their most popular bread, I tasted and reconsidered. Her husband uses 1 percent salt, which makes a considerable difference. The low amount of salt means that the yeast can rise uninhibited, making it possible to use less yeast and derive more flavor from the flour. Eliminate the salt entirely if you wish to be traditional, but note that the rising times will be a little shorter.

TIME SCHEDULE

Dough Starter (Biga): minimum 6 hours, maximum 3 days
Rising Time: about 3 hours
Oven Temperature: 425°F
Baking Time: 15 to 25 minutes

Makes: an 8-by-6-by-1/2-inch-high loaf/1 pound/454 grams

EQUIPMENT:

a heavy-duty stand mixer with dough hook attachment;

a half sheet pan lined with a nonstick liner such as Silpain or parchment, well dusted with flour;

a baking stone OR baking sheet

Dough Starter (Biga)

Makes: scant 1/2 cup/4.7 ounces/134 grams

INGREDIENTS	MEASURE	WEIGHT	
	volume	ounces	grams
unbleached all-purpose flour (use only Gold Medal, King Arthur, or Pillsbury)	1/2 cup plus 1/2 tablespoon	2.6 ounces	75 grams
instant yeast (see page 561 for brands)	1/16 teaspoon	--	0.2 gram
Optional: malt powder	1/2 teaspoon	--	1.6 grams
water, at room temperature (70° to 90°F)	1/4 liquid cup	2 ounces	59 grams

1 > **Six hours or up to 3 days ahead, make the biga.** In a small bowl, combine all the ingredients for the biga and stir the mixture with a wooden spoon for 3 to 5 minutes or until it is very smooth and comes away from the sides of the bowl. The dough should still be tacky (sticky) enough to cling slightly to your fingers. Cover the bowl tightly with oiled plastic wrap (or place it in a 2-cup food-storage container with a lid) and set aside until tripled and filled with bubbles. At room temperature, this will take about 6 hours. Stir the biga down and use it, or refrigerate it for up to 3 days before baking.

Dough

INGREDIENTS	MEASURE	WEIGHT	
	volume	ounces	grams
unbleached all-purpose flour (use only Gold Medal, King Arthur, or Pillsbury)	1 3/4 cups	8.5 ounces	244 grams
instant yeast	1/2 teaspoon	--	1.6 grams
biga (from above)	*scant 1/2 cup*	*4.7 ounces*	*134 grams*
water	2/3 liquid cup	5.5 ounces	155 grams
salt	1/2 teaspoon	--	3.3 grams

2 > **Mix the dough.** In the mixer bowl place the flour, yeast, and biga. Mixing with the dough hook on low speed (#2 if using a KitchenAid), gradually add the water, then mix until the flour is moistened enough to form a rough dough. Scrape down any bits of dough. Cover the bowl with plastic wrap and allow the dough to rest for 15 to 20 minutes.

Sprinkle on the salt and knead the dough on medium-low speed (#3 KitchenAid) for 7 minutes. The dough should be very elastic, smooth, and sticky

Authentic Pumpernickel Bread > page 329 (background)
Authentic Pumpernickel Bread, sliced,
with smoked salmon, cream cheese, and dill

Dimpled ciabatta dough
ready to bake > page 357

Ciabatta with soppressata > page 355

Stages of biga (dough starter) for Pugliese > page 361: (*top*): just mixed; (*bottom*): tripled and fully risen

Pugliese > page 360

Tyrolean Ten-Grain
Torpedo > page 394

Prosciutto Ring with Chianti
> page 370

New Zealand Almond and Fig Bread

> page 411

enough to cling slightly to your fingers. If it is still very sticky, knead in a little flour. If it is not at all sticky, spray it with a little water and knead it in. (The dough will weigh about 18 ounces/510 grams.)

3 > Let the dough rise. Using an oiled spatula or dough scraper, scrape the dough into a 2-quart dough-rising container or bowl, lightly greased with cooking spray or oil. Push down the dough and lightly spray or oil the top. Cover the container with a lid or plastic wrap. With a piece of tape, mark the side of the container at approximately where triple the height of the dough would be. Allow the dough to rise (ideally at 75° to 80°F) until tripled, about 3 hours.

4 > Preheat the oven. Preheat the oven to 475°F 1 hour before baking. Have an oven shelf at the lowest level and place an oven stone or baking sheet on it, and a cast-iron skillet or sheet pan on the floor of the oven, before preheating.

5 > Shape the bread and let it rise. With an oiled dough scraper or spatula, gently turn the dough out onto the prepared pan, without deflating it. It should be about 8 inches by 6 inches by about 1 1/4 inches high. Dust the surface of the dough well with flour and allow it to rise until 1 1/2 inches high, about 30 minutes.

6 > Bake the bread. Quickly but gently set the baking sheet on the hot baking stone or hot baking sheet. Toss 1/2 cup of ice cubes into the pan beneath and immediately shut the door. Bake for 15 to 25 minutes or until the bread is golden and a skewer inserted in the middle comes out clean (an instant-read thermometer inserted into the center will read about 200°F).

7 > Cool the bread. Remove the bread from the oven, and transfer it to a wire rack to cool completely.

ULTIMATE FULL FLAVOR VARIATION

For the best flavor development, in Step 1, allow the biga to ferment in a cool area (55° to 65°F) for 12 to 24 hours. (A wine cellar is usually this temperature range so it provides an ideal spot.) After 12 hours, it will have tripled and be filled with bubbles; it will not deflate even after 24 hours at this cool temperature.

POINTERS FOR SUCCESS

> For larger holes, it is important not to overmix the dough and develop too much gluten.

THE DOUGH PERCENTAGE

Flour:	100%
Water:	67%
Yeast:	0.56%
Salt:	1%

Ciabatta
(*Ciabatta de Donna*, or Lady's Slipper)

This is the bread that, after the focaccia (page 205), has highest water content and is therefore the very lightest in texture. The contrast of the crisp firm crust and soft open crumb is a delightful shock to the senses. It took enormous effort to conquer this bread, and I learned volumes about the texture of bread in the process.

Ciabatta (The name means "slipper" in Italian) is a relatively flat, shapeless bread with a fine crisp crust, wrinkled by a special shaping technique (taught to me by master baker David Norman when he was an instructor at the French Culinary Institute), and boasting large holes in the interior. The holes proved the biggest challenge, to the point that it came to seem Zen-like to be working so hard to achieve empty space. The quest led me once again to Brinna Sands, of King Arthur Flour, who taught me one of the most important lessons about this particular dough: in order to create an open crumb, you must have a very moist dough. Before this, I had always kneaded bread by hand. But she explained that in order to achieve this very sticky dough, it is best to use a mixer or bread machine, or one will be tempted to add too much flour. Another interesting thing I discovered in my ten-day obsession with ciabatta was that developing too strong a framework (gluten) would make a tighter crumb, so that it is better to use a flour that is very extensible (ideally unbleached all-purpose), with lower protein-forming gluten than bread flour, and not to knead it too long. This flour also results in a more tender and less chewy crumb, similar to that of the ciabatta found in Italy, where the flour is lower in protein. All my many *ciabatta* looked the same on the outside but it wasn't until the ninth one that I found was what I was looking for after cutting it open—big beautiful holes.

Once mastered, this bread will enable you to sail through other wet dough breads that bake into light loaves with large holes, such as Pugliese (page 360) and focaccia.

Dough Starter (Biga): minimum 6 hours, maximum 3 days
Minimum Rising Time: about 2 3/4 hours
Oven Temperature: 475°F, then 450°F
Baking Time: 30 minutes

Makes: an 11-by-5-by-2 to 2 1/2-inch-high loaf/
about 10.5 ounces/300 grams

EQUIPMENT:

a heavy-duty stand mixer with paddle attachment;

a half sheet pan lined with a nonstick liner such as
Silpain or parchment, or sprinkled with flour or
cornmeal;

a baking stone OR baking sheet

Dough Starter (Biga)

Makes: scant 1/2 cup/4.7 ounces/134 grams

INGREDIENTS	MEASURE	WEIGHT	
	volume	ounces	grams
unbleached all-purpose flour (use only Gold Medal, King Arthur, or Pillsbury)	1/2 cup plus 1/2 tablespoon	2.6 ounces	75 grams
instant yeast (see page 561 for brands)	1/16 teaspoon	--	0.2 gram
Optional: malt powder	1/2 teaspoon	--	1.6 grams
water, at room temperature (70° to 90°F)	1/4 liquid cup	2 ounces	59 grams

1 > Six hours or up to 3 days ahead, make the dough starter (biga). In a small bowl, combine all the ingredients for the biga and stir the mixture with a wooden spoon for 3 to 5 minutes or until it is very smooth and comes away from the sides of the bowl. It will be slightly sticky to the touch. Cover the bowl tightly with oiled plastic wrap (or place the biga in a 2-cup food storage container with a lid) and set it aside until tripled and filled with bubbles. At room temperature, this will take about 6 hours. Stir it down and use it or refrigerate it for up to 3 days before baking. (Remove it to room temperature for 1 hour before mixing the dough.)

Dough

INGREDIENTS	MEASURE	WEIGHT	
	volume	ounces	grams
unbleached all-purpose flour (use only Gold Medal, King Arthur, or Pillsbury)	scant 1 cup (plus flour for shaping)	4.75 ounces	136 grams
instant yeast	1/4 teaspoon	--	0.8 gram
salt	1/2 teaspoon	--	3.3 grams
water	1/2 liquid cup	about 4 ounces	118 grams
biga (from above)	*scant 1/2 cup*	*4.7 ounces*	*134 grams*

2 > **Mix the dough.** In the mixer bowl, whisk together the flour and yeast. Then whisk in the salt (this keeps the yeast from coming in direct contact with the salt, which would kill it). Add the water and biga. Using the paddle attachment, mix on low speed (#2 if using a KitchenAid) for a few seconds, just until all the flour is moistened. Raise the speed to medium-high (#6 KitchenAid) and beat for 3 minutes. At first the dough will be very moist and soft, almost soupy. Gradually it will start to develop strands of gluten. Lower the speed to medium (#4 KitchenAid) and continue beating for 2 minutes. If the dough hasn't pulled away from the bowl after the first 3 minutes, scrape down the sides of the bowl and beat on medium-high (#6 KitchenAid) for another 2 minutes. If it still doesn't pull away from the bowl, beat in a little flour 1 teaspoon at a time on low speed (#2 KitchenAid). The dough should cling to your fingers if touched.

3 > **Let the dough rise.** Using an oiled spatula or dough scraper, scrape the dough into a 1-quart food storage container, lightly greased with cooking spray or oil (I detach the paddle from the machine and use it to lift out the dough, as it usually clings to the paddle in a long elastic strand). (The dough will weigh about 13.6 ounces/386 grams.) Push down the dough and lightly spray or oil the top. Cover the container with a lid or plastic wrap. With a piece of tape, mark the side of the container at approximately where triple the height of the dough would be. Allow the dough to rise (ideally at 75° to 80°F) until tripled, 1 1/4 to 2 hours.

4 > **Shape the dough and let it rise.** Sift a generous amount of flour onto a counter in a rectangle at least 10 inches by 8 inches. With an oiled spatula, gently scrape the dough onto the flour, and sift more flour on top. Handle the dough gently at all times to maintain as much air in it as possible. Using the palms of your hands against the sides of the dough, push it together slightly. Using your fingertips, make large deep dimples in the dough about 1 inch apart, elongating it. Push the sides together a second time. (This process wrinkles the bottom of the dough, which will become the top when inverted, and creates the classic lines in the crust.)

Carefully lift up the dough and invert it onto the prepared baking sheet. It will be 10 to 11 inches in length. Push in the sides so that the dough is about 4 1/2 inches wide. It will be between 1/2 inch and 1 inch high. Sift flour over the top and cover the dough with a large container, or cover loosely with plastic wrap. Allow it to rise a warm spot until 1 to 1 1/2 inches high, 1 1/2 to 2 hours.

5 > **Preheat the oven.** Preheat the oven to 475°F 1 hour before baking. Have an oven shelf at the lowest level and place a baking stone or baking sheet on it, and a cast-iron skillet or sheet pan on the floor of the oven, before preheating.

6 > **Bake the bread.** Remove the container or plastic wrap and quickly but gently set the baking sheet on the hot baking stone or hot baking sheet. Toss 1/2 cup of ice cubes into the pan beneath and immediately shut the door. Bake for 5 minutes. Lower the temperature to 450°F and continue baking for 20 minutes or until the bread is deep golden brown (an instant-read thermometer inserted in the center will read about 214°F). Halfway through baking, turn the pan around for even baking. Turn off the oven, prop the door open with a wooden spoon wrapped in foil, and allow the bread to sit for 5 minutes.

7 > **Cool the bread.** Remove the bread from the oven and transfer it to a wire rack to cool completely. Brush off the flour from the surface.

VARIATION

Oval Cloud Rolls   Ciabatta dough also makes wonderfully light dinner rolls. Sift the flour (after weighing or measuring it) so that it is as light as possible. Use 1 tablespoon less water in the dough, so that the rolls will maintain their shape. Beat the dough with the paddle attachment for 15 to 18 minutes on medium-high speed (#6 KitchenAid) to develop more gluten. Allow the dough to rise for 2 to 2 1/2 hours.

To shape the rolls, cut the dough into 4 equal pieces (about 2.75 ounces each). Shape them gently into ovals about 3 1/2 inches by 2 1/2 inches by 1 1/4 inches high. (Try to maintain as much air as possible in the dough, and do not dimple it.) Allow the rolls to rise until 1 1/2 inches high.

Bake the rolls for 20 minutes or until deep golden brown. They will rise to 2 1/2 inches high and 3 inches wide but will still be 3 1/2 inches long.

ULTIMATE FULL FLAVOR VARIATION

For the best flavor development, in Step 1, allow the biga to ferment in a cool area (55° to 65°F) for 12 to 24 hours. (A wine cellar provides an ideal spot.) After 12 hours, it will have tripled and be filled with bubbles; it will not deflate even after 24 hours at this cool a temperature.

> The type of flour determines the consistency of the crumb. For the softest, most gauze-like crumb, use Pillsbury or Gold Medal *unbleached* all-purpose flour. For a soft but slightly firmer crumb, use King Arthur all-purpose flour. If you prefer a much chewier ciabatta, replace the all-purpose flour with an equal weight of bread flour (the volume will be 1/2 cup for the biga and 3/4 cup plus 2 tablespoons for the dough).

> If you prefer a puffy 3-inch-high bread, omit the dimpling technique, which deflates some of the bubbles, and have the final length be 9 inches. The loaf will spread during rising but shrink in and rise up during baking. (It will no longer resemble a slipper.)

> For *stirato*, shape the dough by pulling it into a long, baguette-shaped loaf.

> Sifting extra flour over the shaped ciabatta gives it an attractive appearance. The flour already coating the dough tends to be absorbed into the dough. I like to set a piece of parchment or wax paper along either side of the dough when applying the flour and remove the paper before baking, as flour left on the pan liner would burn.

> After a total of 15 minutes of baking, you can lift the ciabatta off the parchment and bake it directly on the baking stone or baking sheet to ensure the crispest possible bottom.

> The final 5 minutes in the oven with the heat off and the door open ensures a crisp top crust.

UNDERSTANDING

The biga makes the dough more moist and tender and will extend the shelf life to a second day. It is brought to room temperature before adding it to the dough to minimize gluten development.

THE DOUGH PERCENTAGE

Flour:	100%
Water:	83.9%
Yeast	0.53%
Salt:	2%

Pugliese

Pugliese, ciabatta, and pizza/focaccia are our most popular Italian breads. The dough for pugliese is actually almost identical to that of ciabatta and has close to the same exceptionally high water content, which produces the characteristic large holes in the crumb. The holes are smaller in the pugliese, however, because the dough is strengthened by stretching and folding the dough at intervals during rising. This technique, demonstrated by Peter Reinhart in his book *The Bread Baker's Apprentice*, is an excellent way of maintaining as much air as possible in the dough while developing the protein structure (gluten) of the dough. It also makes the bread more chewy than the ciabatta.

Pugliese was named after Puglia, or the Apulia region of Italy, where it originated, but I have encountered versions of this bread throughout Sicily as well. The Sicilian versions were all made with part durum flour. This flour is the hardest of all wheat varieties and though low in gluten-forming protein, it gives the bread an especially delicious nutty/sweet flavor, pale golden crumb, and exceptionally fine, chewy crust.

Much as I usually favor bread and butter, I have to admit that the ideal accompaniment to this particular bread is a light drizzle of Italian extra virgin olive oil

TIME SCHEDULE

Dough Starter (Biga): minimum 6 hours, maximum 3 days
Minimum Rising Time: about 3 hours
Oven Temperature: 500°F, then 450°F
Baking Time: 20 to 25 minutes

Makes: a 6 1/2-by-3-inch-high round loaf/
13 ounces/370 grams

EQUIPMENT:

a heavy-duty stand mixer with dough hook attachment;

a half sheet pan lined with a nonstick liner such as Silpain or parchment, or sprinkled with flour or cornmeal;

a baking stone OR baking sheet

an 8-inch banneton OR a colander lined with a towel

Dough Starter (Biga)

Makes: scant 1/2 cup/4.7 ounces/134 grams

INGREDIENTS	MEASURE	WEIGHT	
	volume	ounces	grams
unbleached all-purpose flour (use only Gold Medal, King Arthur, or Pillsbury)	1/2 cup plus 1/2 tablespoon	2.6 ounces	75 grams
instant yeast (see page 561 for brands)	1/16 teaspoon	--	0.2 gram
Optional: malt powder	1/2 teaspoon	--	1.6 grams
water, at room temperature (70° to 90°F)	1/4 liquid cup	2 ounces	59 grams

1 > **Six hours or up to 3 days ahead, make the starter (biga).** In a small bowl, combine all the ingredients for the biga and stir the mixture with a wooden spoon for 3 to 5 minutes or until it is very smooth and pulls away from the sides of the bowl. The biga should still be tacky (sticky) enough to cling slightly to your fingers. Cover the bowl tightly with oiled plastic wrap (or place it in a 2-cup food storage container with a lid) and set aside until tripled and filled with bubbles. At room temperature, this will take about 6 hours. Stir it down and use it, or refrigerate it for up to 3 days before baking.

Dough

INGREDIENTS	MEASURE	WEIGHT	
	volume	ounces	grams
unbleached all-purpose flour (use only Gold Medal, King Arthur, or Pillsbury)	1/2 cup	2.5 ounces	71 grams
durum flour	1/2 cup (plus flour for shaping)	2.5 ounces	71 grams
instant yeast (see page 561 for brands)	1/2 teaspoon	--	1.6 grams
salt	3/4 teaspoon	--	5 grams
water, at room temperature (70° to 90°F)	1/2 liquid cup	about 4 ounces	118 grams
biga from above	*scant 1/2 cup*	*4.7 ounces*	*134 grams*

2 > **Mix the dough.** In the mixer bowl, whisk together the all-purpose flour, durum flour, and yeast. Then whisk in the salt (this keeps the yeast from coming into direct contact with the yeast, which would kill it). Add the water and the biga. Using the paddle attachment, mix on low speed for about 1 minute, until the flour is moistened enough to form a rough dough. Change to the dough hook, raise the speed to medium (#4 KitchenAid), and beat for 5 minutes to form a smooth, sticky dough. If the dough does not pull away from the bowl after 5 minutes, beat in more flour 1 teaspoon at a time. The dough should still stick to the bottom of the bowl and cling to your fingers. If it is not sticky, spray it with a little water and knead it in.

3 > **Let the dough rise.** Sprinkle durum flour generously onto a counter in a 6-inch square. Using a wet or oiled spatula or dough scraper, scrape the dough onto the flour, and dust the top of it with more flour. (The flour will be absorbed into the wet dough.) Allow it to rest for 2 minutes.

With floured hands, pull out two opposite sides of the dough to stretch it to double its length, and give it a business letter turn. Dust it again with flour, cover it with plastic wrap, and allow it to rest for 30 minutes.

Repeat the stretching, folding, and flouring a second time, and again allow the dough to rest for 30 minutes.

Repeat the stretching, folding, and flouring a third time, then round the edges of the dough. Using an oiled spatula or dough scraper, transfer the dough to a 2-quart dough-rising container or bowl, lightly greased with cooking spray or oil. Cover the container with a lid or plastic wrap. Using a piece of tape, mark the side of the container at approximately where triple the height of the dough could be. Allow the dough to rise (ideally at 75° to 80°F) until tripled, about 2 hours.

4 > Preheat the oven. Preheat the oven to 500°F. 1 hour before baking. Have an oven shelf at the lowest level and place an oven stone or baking sheet on it, and a cast-iron skillet or sheet pan on the floor of the oven, before preheating.

5 > Shape the dough and let it rise. Dust a counter well with durum flour. With floured hands or a floured dough scraper, gently transfer the dough to the counter. Handling the dough very gently, to maintain as much air as possible, round it into a ball (see page 65).

Gently set the dough seam side up in a floured banneton or a colander lined with a floured towel. Pinch together the seam if necessary. Sprinkle the top lightly with flour, and cover with a large container, or cover loosely with oiled plastic wrap. Allow the dough to rise until it has increased by about 1 1/2 times, to 1 1/2 hours. (In the banneton, it will just begin to push up the plastic.)

6 > Bake the bread. Remove the container or plastic wrap, invert the lined baking sheet on top of the banneton or colander, and invert the dough onto the sheet. (If you used a colander and floured towel and the risen bread is more than 1 inch below the top, you will need to support the bread when inverting it so that it doesn't fall and deflate. Cut a cardboard circle small enough to fit into the colander and touch the surface of the bread. Place a piece of parchment on top of the bread, place the cardboard on top, and invert the bread onto the cardboard. Slide the bread, still in the parchment, onto the baking sheet.) Or, if using a cornmeal-sprinkled baking sheet, invert the dough directly onto it. Quickly but gently set the sheet on the baking stone or baking sheet. Toss 1/2 cup of ice cubes into the pan beneath and immediately shut the door. Bake for 5 minutes. Lower the temperature to 450°F and continue baking for 15 to 25 minutes or until the bread is deep golden brown (an instant-read thermometer inserted into the center will read about 205°F). Halfway through baking, with a heavy pancake turner, lift the bread from the pan and set it directly on the stone, turning it around for even baking.

7 > Cool the bread. Remove the bread from the oven and transfer it to a wire rack to cool completely.

ULTIMATE FULL FLAVOR VARIATION

For the best flavor development, in Step 1, allow the biga to ferment in a cool area (55° to 65°F) for 12 to 24 hours. (A wine cellar provides an ideal spot.) After 12 hours, it will have tripled and be filled with bubbles; it will not deflate even after 24 hours at this cool temperature.

UNDERSTANDING

Durum flour is finely milled from the endosperm of durum wheat. It is sometimes marketed as "extra-fancy" pasta flour or "farina grade." Semolina, also from durum wheat, is a much coarser grind and will not work for this bread.

THE DOUGH PERCENTAGE

Flour:	100% (bread: 74%, durum: 26%)
Water:	80.4%
Yeast:	0.79%
Salt:	2.2%

Golden Semolina Torpedo

Semolina is an exceptionally high-protein flour, finely milled from the endosperm of durum wheat. It is considered to be the ideal flour for pasta because the high protein gives it more bite. When it comes to bread making, most bakers use it in combination with a relatively high protein unbleached flour to supply a more extensible (stretchy) gluten to improve texture. However, 100 percent semolina is so deeply golden and delicious I'm willing to accept a few cracks in the crust to have the full impact of this amazing flavor. Semolina has a heavenly sweetness of wheat, with a golden color and an incredibly fine, delicate, but firm crumb. The crust is not crisp but satisfyingly chewy.

In order to avoid the risk of toughening this bread it is best to knead the dough by hand. This is a particular pleasure because it happens to be an exceptionally satiny bread dough. Less mixing also serves to maximize its exceptional flavor.

The bread is so special it's a shame to put anything on it that would mask its flavor, but a thin gilding of butter or a little ricotta works well to enhance the natural sweetness of the durum wheat.

TIME SCHEDULE

Dough Starter (Sponge): minimum 1 hour, maximum 24 hours
Minimum Rising Time: about 2 hours
Oven Temperature: 425°F (450°F if using La Cloche), then 400°F.
Baking Time: 30 to 40 minutes

Makes: an 11-by-4-by-2 1/2-inch-high loaf/13.2 ounces/375 grams

La Cloche Italian Bread Baker, lined with a nonstick liner, such as Silpain or sprinkled with cornmeal, OR a nonstick Italian bread pan (see page 590);

a baking stone OR baking sheet

Dough Starter (Sponge)

INGREDIENTS	MEASURE	WEIGHT	
	volume	ounces	grams
durum flour	2/3 cup	3.5 ounces	100 grams
instant yeast (see page 561 for brands)	1/8 teaspoon	--	0.4 gram
water, at room temperature (70° to 90°F)	3/4 liquid cup	6.25 ounces	177 grams

1 > **Make the sponge.** In a medium bowl, whisk together the durum flour and instant yeast. Whisk in the water, then whisk until very smooth, to incorporate air, about 2 minutes. The sponge will be the consistency of a thick batter. Scrape down the sides of the bowl. Set aside, covered with plastic wrap, while you make the flour mixture.

Flour Mixture

INGREDIENTS	MEASURE	WEIGHT	
	volume	ounces	grams
durum flour	1 cup	5.5 ounces	155 grams
instant yeast	3/8 teaspoon	--	1.4 grams
salt	3/4 plus 1/8 teaspoon	--	5.8 grams
bread flour for kneading	1 to 2 tablespoons	0.3 to 0.6 ounce	9 to 18 grams

2 > **Combine the ingredients for the flour mixture and add to the starter.** In a medium bowl, whisk together 1/4 cup (1.3 ounces/38 grams) of the durum flour and the yeast. Then whisk in the salt (this keeps the yeast from coming into direct contact with the salt, which would kill it). Gently scoop it onto the sponge to cover it completely. Cover tightly with plastic wrap and allow it to ferment for 1 to 4 hours at room temperature. (During this time, the sponge will bubble through the flour mixture in places; this is fine.)

3 > Mix the dough. Using a wooden spoon or your hand, gradually mix the sponge into the flour mixture until all of the flour is moistened. Knead the dough in the bowl until it comes together, then scrape it onto a counter floured with some of the reserved flour. Knead the dough for 5 minutes, enough to develop the gluten structure a little, adding more of the reserved 1/4 cup of flour as needed to keep the dough from sticking. Use a bench scraper to scrape the dough and gather it together as you knead it. The dough should still be tacky (sticky) enough to cling slightly to your fingers. Cover it with the inverted bowl and allow it to rest for 20 minutes. (This resting time will make the dough less sticky and easier to work with.)

Knead the dough for another 5 minutes or until it is very smooth and elastic, adding more of the reserved flour as necessary. It's fine if the dough is a tiny bit tacky (sticks to your hand a little), but you should be able to form it into a firm ball that holds its shape. (The dough will weigh about 15 ounces/427 grams.)

4 > Let the dough rise. Place the dough in a 1-quart dough-rising container or a bowl lightly greased with cooking spray or oil. Push down the dough and lightly spray or oil the top. Cover the container with a lid or plastic wrap. With a piece of tape, mark the side of the container at approximately where double the height of the dough, would be. Allow the dough to rise (ideally at 75° to 80°F) until doubled, 1 1/2 to 2 hours.

5 > Shape the dough and let it rise. Turn the dough out onto a lightly floured counter and gently press down on it to shape it into a 7-by-6-inch rectangle. Then shape it into an 9-inch-long torpedo-shaped loaf (batard; see page 69). Set it into the prepared La Cloche or place it on the prepared baking pan. Cover it with a large container, or cover loosely with oiled plastic wrap: Let the dough rise until almost doubled, about 1 hour to 1 hour and 15 minutes. It will be about 10 1/2 to 11 inches long by 4 inches wide by 2 1/4 inches high. (In La Cloche, the very center will be about the height of its sides.) When the dough is pressed gently with a fingertip, the depression will very slowly fill in.

6 > Preheat the oven. Preheat the oven to 450°F, or 425°F if using La Cloche, 1 hour before baking. Have an oven shelf at the lowest level and place an oven stone or baking sheet on it before preheating. If not using La Cloche, place a cast-iron skillet or sheet pan on the floor of the oven to preheat. If using La Cloche, preheat the top along with the oven.

7 > Slash and bake the bread. With a sharp knife or single-edged razor blade, make three 1/4- to 1/2-inch-deep long diagonal slashes in the top of the dough (see page 81).

If using La Cloche, carefully place the hot La Cloche top on the base and quickly but gently set it on the hot stone or hot baking sheet. Bake for 15 minutes. Remove the La Cloche top, lower the temperature to 400°F, and bake for 15 to 25 minutes longer or until the bread is golden brown and a skewer inserted in the middle comes out clean (an instant-read thermometer inserted in the center will read about 200°F).

Alternatively, mist the dough with water and quickly but gently set the baking pan on the hot stone or hot baking sheet. Toss 1/2 cup of ice cubes into the pan beneath and immediately shut the door. Bake for 20 minutes. Lower the temperature to 400°F and continue baking for 10 to 20 minutes or until the bread is golden brown and a skewer inserted in the middle comes out clean (an instant-read thermometer inserted into the center will read about 208°F). Halfway through baking, with a heavy pancake turner, lift the bread from the pan and set it directly on the stone, turning it around as you do so for even baking.

8 > Cool the bread. Remove the bread from the oven, and transfer it to a wire rack to cool completely.

ULTIMATE FULL FLAVOR VARIATION

For the best flavor development, in Step 2, allow the sponge to ferment for 1 hour at room temperature, then refrigerate it for 8 to 24 hours. Remove it from the refrigerator about 1 hour before mixing the dough.

If desired, for even fuller flavor, the dough can be refrigerated overnight after shaping. Cover it with plastic wrap greased with cooking spray or oil and allow it to sit at room temperature for 20 to 30 minutes or until it begins to puff slightly. Then refrigerate it overnight. Let stand at room temperature for 30 minutes, or until it is 2 1/4 inches high, before baking.

POINTERS FOR SUCCESS

> This is a delicate bread and should not be allowed to overrise, or it will collapse when slashed. In fact, slightly underproofing it is desirable, as the slashes will open up more widely to reveal the beautiful yellow crumb. (Underproofing is when the depression made by a finger pressed into the dough gradually fill in, as opposed to a full proof, when the depression remains.)

> Because durum is low in gluten-forming protein, the dough needs to be stiff enough to hold its shape well during rising and baking but then has a tendency to dry and crack on the top crust. If you want to prevent this, you can substitute an equal volume or weight of bread flour for 2 tablespoons (0.7/19 grams) of the durum flour.

UNDERSTANDING

Although this bread is made with silky soft durum flour not the coarse granular semolina flour (see page 546), it is still traditionally referred to as semolina bread. I love the taste of 100 percent durum flour, but if you replace some of it with *unbleached* all-purpose flour, you will have a better-shaped loaf that loses less moisture (weight) when baking and holds its shape better.

THE DOUGH PERCENTAGE

Flour:	100%
Water:	69.4% to 74.5%
Yeast:	0.62%
Salt:	2.2%

Prosciutto Ring

I cannot tell you how many times I have stopped at my neighborhood Italian bakery, Zito's, and bought one of their rings of "lard bread." Tearing off "just one more piece" as I walk home, I usually go through at least a quarter of it. I never in my wildest dreams expected to be able to get this recipe, let alone reproduce it in my home oven. But one day I dared to ask and as luck would have it, Anthony Zito, one of the owner's sons, was there. We discovered that my father was making bagel peels on the Bowery at the same time his father opened his bakery on Bleecker Street in 1924 and that our families were both old-time New Yorkers. In fact, when my aunt Ruth was first married, she lived over Zito's! To my delight, not only did Anthony describe the recipe in detail, it turned out to be sublimely simple. So much flavor comes from the prosciutto and black pepper that the bread requires no starter preferment, and since it's intended to be a coarse, rustic bread, it only gets one rise. This makes it exceptionally quick to prepare. I also tried, with great success, to mix it in the food processor, which makes it even quicker and easier still, but it works equally well with every method, so I have listed them all, as each is slightly different. (Zito's mixes the dough in a commercial mixer, but they cut in the prosciutto with a bench scraper.)

Because the texture of this bread should be chewy this is a fairly stiff dough. It will be slightly more chewy if you use bread flour instead of unbleached all-purpose. If desired, pork cracklings can be added and baked ham or even turkey ham substituted for the prosciutto.

My addition, the bacon fat brushed on top, gives the bread a slightly smoky flavor. Either bacon fat or butter produces a velvety, crisp crust.

Starter: straight dough method
Rising Time: about 1 hour
Oven Temperature: 450°F, then 400°F
Baking Time: 30 to 35 minutes

Makes: an 8 1/2-by-2-inch-high ring/
1 pound, 5 ounces/596 grams

INGREDIENTS	MEASURE	WEIGHT	
	volume	ounces	grams
bread flour or	**2 cups plus 3 tablespoons**	12 ounces	340 grams
unbleached all-purpose flour (use only Gold Medal, King Arthur, or Pillsbury)	2 1/4 cups plus 2 tablespoons		
malt powder or	**1 tablespoon**	**0.3 ounce**	**9.3 grams**
barley malt syrup or honey or	1 tablespoon	0.7 ounce	21 grams
sugar	1 tablespoon	0.5 ounce	12.5 grams
instant yeast (see page 561 for brands)	**3/4 teaspoon**	--	**2.4 grams**
coarsely cracked black pepper	**scant 1/2 teaspoon**	--	**0.8 gram**
salt	**3/4 teaspoon**	--	**5 grams**
water, room temperature (70° to 90°F) (or cold, if using a food processor)	**1 liquid cup**	**8.3 ounces**	**236 grams**
prosciutto, trimmed of excess fat, sliced not too thin and cut into 1/4- to 1/2-inch pieces	**3/4 cup**	**3 ounces**	**85 grams**
bacon fat or	**4 teaspoons**	**0.6 ounce**	**18.6 grams**
butter, melted			

EQUIPMENT:

a nonstick liner such as Silpain or parchment;

a baking stone OR baking sheet

1 > Mix the dough.

Food Processor Method
In the bowl of a food processor fitted with the metal blade, combine the flour malt (or honey or sugar), yeast and pepper, and process for a few seconds to mix. Then

add the salt (this keeps the yeast from coming in direct contact with the salt, which would kill it) and process again for a few seconds. With the motor running, gradually pour in the cold water. Process for 45 seconds after the dough comes together. It should be slightly tacky (sticky).

Scrape the dough onto a lightly floured counter and lightly flour the dough. Press it into a rectangle and sprinkle it with the prosciutto. Roll up the dough and knead it to incorporate the prosciutto evenly. (The dough will weigh about 1 1/2 pounds/675 grams.)

Dust the dough lightly with flour and cover it with plastic wrap. Allow it to relax for 20 minutes.

Mixer Method

In the mixer bowl, whisk together the flour, malt (or honey or sugar), yeast, and black pepper. Then whisk in the salt (this prevents the yeast from coming into direct contact with the salt, which would kill it). With the dough hook, on low speed (#2 if using a KitchenAid), add the water and mix for about 1 minute, until the flour is moistened. Knead the dough on medium speed (#4 KitchenAid) for 7 minutes.

Add the prosciutto and mix on low speed (#2 KitchenAid) for 1 minute or until evenly incorporated. The dough should be very elastic and jump back when pressed with a fingertip. It should still be a little tacky (sticky) but not cling to your fingers. If the dough is very sticky, knead in a little flour. If it is not sticky at all, spray it with a little water and knead it in. (The dough will weigh about 1 1/2 pounds/675 grams.)

Dust the dough lightly with flour and cover it with plastic wrap. Allow it to relax for 20 minutes.

Hand Method

In a large bowl, whisk together the flour, malt (or honey or sugar), pepper, and yeast. Then whisk in the salt (this keeps the yeast from coming into direct contact with the salt, which would kill it). Add the water and stir, with a wooden spoon or your hand, until the flour is moistened.

Empty the dough onto a counter and knead it for 10 minutes or until it is very elastic and jumps back when pressed with a fingertip. Knead in the prosciutto. The dough should be a little tacky (sticky) but not cling to your fingers. If it is very sticky, knead in a little flour. (The dough will weigh about 1 1/2 pounds/675 grams.)

Dust the dough lightly with flour and cover it with plastic wrap. Allow it to relax for 20 minutes.

Bread Machine Method

In the bread machine container, place the water, salt, malt (or honey or sugar), flour, black pepper, and yeast, in that order. Put it through the dough cycle (mix 3 minutes, knead 5 minutes). Let the dough rest for 20 minutes.

Add the prosciutto and do a second dough cycle (mix 3 minutes, knead 5 minutes.) The dough should be a little tacky (sticky) but not cling to your fingers. If necessary, remove it from the machine and knead in a little more flour. (The dough will weigh about 1 1/2 pounds/675 grams.)

All Methods

2 > **Shape the dough and let it rise.** Turn the dough out onto a lightly floured counter, if it's not already on the counter. Roll it into an 18-inch-long rope. Shape it into a ring, overlapping ends by 2 inches, and press lightly to seal them; the ring will be about 7 inches in diameter and 1 1/4 inches high, with a 3-inch hole in the center.

Set the bread on the Silpain or parchment and cover it with a large container or oiled plastic wrap. Allow the dough to rise (ideally at 75° to 80°F) until almost doubled, about 1 hour. It will be almost 9 inches across by 1 1/2 inches high, and when it is pressed gently with a fingertip, the depression will very slowly fill in.

3 > **Preheat the oven.** Preheat the oven to 450°F 1 hour before baking. Have an oven shelf at the lowest level and place a baking stone or baking sheet on it, and a cast-iron skillet or sheet pan on the floor of the oven, before preheating.

4 > **Glaze and bake the bread.** Shortly before baking, brush the dough all over with the melted bacon fat or butter. (Do not slash the dough.) Using the Silpain liner, lift the ring onto the hot baking stone or hot baking sheet; or use a peel if it is on parchment. Toss 1/2 cup of ice cubes into the pan beneath and immediately close the door. Bake for 20 minutes. Turn down the heat to 400°F and continue baking for 10 to 15 minutes or until the bread is deep golden brown (an instant-read thermometer inserted into the center will read about 211°F). Halfway through baking, with a heavy pancake turner, lift the bread from the Silpain or parchment and set it directly on the stone, turning it around as you do so for even baking. When the bread is baked, turn off the oven, prop the door slightly ajar, and leave the bread in the oven for 5 minutes.

5 > **Glaze and cool the bread.** Remove the bread from the oven, and transfer it to a wire rack. Brush with another coat of melted bacon or butter, and cool completely. The texture of this bread is most appealing when torn rather than cut.

STORE This bread stays fresh for 2 days at room temperature.

UNDERSTANDING

For the food processor method, using cold (or refrigerated) water at about 46°F will result in a dough of about 84°F after processing. This is a stiff dough, so it really heats up during mixing. It cools to 79°F after kneading in the prosciutto. It is also possible to freeze the water for 5 to 10 minutes before adding it so that the initial temperature of the mixed dough is below 80°F. The cold water does not harm the yeast, because it heats up so quickly. Freezing the flour for at least 15 minutes will also help to keep the dough cooler during mixing.

THE DOUGH PERCENTAGE

Flour:	100%
Water:	69.4%
Yeast:	0.7%
Salt:	1.5%

Beer Bread

Dark beer gives bread an incredibly soft texture, subtle mellow flavor, beautiful mahogany crust, and dark golden crumb. The beer does not result in an identifiably beery flavor; in fact, if one didn't know, one might not guess what mysterious ingredient provides such an appealing depth of flavor. This bread is so flavorful it doesn't require a lengthy dough starter, though refrigerating the proofed dough or shaped bread overnight will make it even more delicious.

TIME SCHEDULE

Starter: straight dough method
Minimum Rising Time: about 2 1/2 hours
Oven Temperature: 450°F, then 400°F (if using La Cloche, 475°F, then 425°F)
Baking Time: 45 to 55 minutes (in La Cloche 25 to 30 minutes)

Makes: a 7-by-3 1/2/ to 4-inch-high round loaf/
1 pound, 5.5 ounces/612 grams

INGREDIENTS	MEASURE	WEIGHT	
	volume	ounces	grams
instant yeast (see pages 561 for brands)	**1 1/4 teaspoons**	--	**4 grams**
malt powder or	**1 tablespoon**	**0.3 ounce**	**9.3 grams**
barley malt syrup or	1 tablespoon	0.7 ounce	21 grams
sugar	1 tablespoon	0.5 ounce	12.5 grams
bread flour	**2 1/2 cups less 1 tablespoon**	**about 13.5 ounces**	**380 grams**
whole wheat flour	**3 tablespoons plus 1 teaspoon**	**about 1 ounce**	**30 grams**
dark beer, such as Bass or Beck's, at room temperature (or cold if using a food processor)	**1 liquid cup plus 2 tablespoons (9 fluid ounces)**	**9 ounces**	**255 grams**
salt	**1 1/4 teaspoons**	--	**8.3 grams**

a half sheet pan lined with a nonstick liner, such as Silpain or parchment, OR La Cloche Bread Baker;

a baking stone OR baking sheet

1 > Mix the dough.

Mixer Method

In the mixer bowl, whisk together the yeast, malt or sugar, all but 2 tablespoons of the bread flour, and the whole wheat flour. With the dough hook, mix on low speed (#2 if using KitchenAid) to blend. Add the beer and mix on low speed for about 1 minute, until the flour is moistened enough to form a rough dough. Scrape down any bits of dough. Cover the bowl with plastic wrap and allow the dough to rest for 20 minutes.

Sprinkle on the salt, and knead the dough on medium speed (#4 KitchenAid) for 7 minutes. If the dough doesn't pull away from the bowl, add the remaining 2 tablespoons of flour toward the end. The dough should be very elastic and smooth (this putty-colored dough is one of the softest doughs I've ever felt). If it is not at all sticky, knead in a little flour. If it is stiff, spray it with a little water and knead it in. (The dough will weigh about 1 1/2 pounds/686 grams.)

Hand Method

In a large mixing bowl, whisk together the yeast, malt or sugar, all but 1/4 cup of the bread flour, and the whole wheat flour. Then whisk in the salt (this keeps the yeast from coming in direct contact with the salt, which would kill it).

With a wooden spoon or your hand, gradually stir in the beer until the flour is moistened. Knead the dough in the bowl until it comes together, then scrape it onto a lightly floured counter. Knead the dough for 5 minutes, enough to develop the gluten structure a little, adding as little of the reserved 1/4 cup of flour as possible to keep it from sticking. Use a bench scraper to scrape the dough and gather it together as you knead it. At this point, it will be very sticky. Cover it with the inverted bowl and allow it to rest for 20 minutes. (This resting time will make the dough less sticky and easier to work with.)

Knead the dough for another 5 minutes or until it is very elastic, soft, and smooth. If the dough is sticky, add some of the remaining reserved flour, or a little extra. (The dough will weigh about 1 1/2 pounds/686 grams.)

Food Processor Method

In the bowl of a food processor fitted with the metal blade, combine the yeast, malt or sugar, all but 2 tablespoons of the bread flour, and the whole wheat flour. Process for 30 seconds to mix. Add the beer and salt and process for 45 seconds. If the dough does not pull away from the sides of the bowl, add the remaining 2 tablespoons flour and pulse it in. (The dough will weigh about 1 1/2 pounds/686 grams.)

All Methods

2 > **Let the dough rise.** Place the dough in a 2-quart dough-rising container or bowl, lightly greased with cooking spray or oil. Push down the dough and lightly spray or oil the top. Cover the container with a lid or plastic wrap. With a piece of tape, mark the side of the container at approximately where double the height of the dough would be. Allow the dough to rise (ideally at 75° to 80°F) until doubled, 1 1/2 to 2 hours.

3 > **Shape the dough and let it rise.** Turn the dough out onto a lightly floured counter and press down on it gently to flatten it slightly. Round the dough into a ball about 5 inches by 2 1/2 inches high (see page 65) and set it on the prepared baking sheet. Cover it with a large container, or cover loosely with oiled plastic wrap. Let the dough rise until almost doubled, 1 to 1 1/2 hours. It should be almost 7 inches in diameter and 3 inches high, and when it is pressed gently with a fingertip, the depression will very slowly fill in.

4 > **Preheat the oven.** Preheat the oven to 450°F, or 475°F if using La Cloche, 1 hour before baking. Have an oven shelf at the lowest level and place a baking stone or baking sheet on it before preheating. If not using La Cloche, place a cast-iron or skillet sheet pan on the floor of the oven to preheat. If using La Cloche, preheat the top along with the oven.

5 > **Slash and bake the bread.** With a sharp knife or single-edged razor blade, make 1/4- to 1/2-inch-deep slashes in the top of the dough (I like to make the "lantern" slash for this bread; see page 81).

Mist the dough with water and quickly but gently set the baking sheet on the hot stone or hot baking sheet. Toss 1/2 cup of ice cubes into the pan beneath and immediately shut the door. Bake for 15 minutes. Lower the temperature to 400°F and continue baking for 30 to 40 minutes or until the bread is golden brown and a skewer inserted in the middle comes out clean (an instant-read thermometer inserted into the center will read about 200°F). Halfway through baking, turn the pan around for even baking.

Alternatively, if using La Cloche, carefully place the hot Cloche top onto the base and quickly but gently set it on the hot stone or hot baking sheet. Bake for 10 minutes. Remove the Cloche top, lower the temperature to 425°F and continue baking for 15 to 20 minutes or until the bread is golden brown and a skewer inserted in the middle comes out clean (an instant-read thermometer inserted into the center will read about 202°F).

6 > Cool the bread. Remove the bread from the oven and transfer it to a wire rack to cool completely.

STORE   This bread keeps well for 2 days at room temperature, wrapped airtight.

POINTERS FOR SUCCESS

>   Beer is tricky to measure accurately because of the foam. Weigh it, or allow it to sit until flat before measuring. (The 2 tablespoons of flour reserved in both the machine and hand method allow for variance if measuring the beer rather than weighing it.)

>   I don't use honey for this bread because the beer darkens the crust, and honey would make it too brown or even burn.

>   I have tried both hard apple cider and unpasteurized apple cider in place of the beer, and although the crumb was acceptable, the flavor was undesirable (in the first case, unpleasant, and in the second, uninteresting).

THE DOUGH PERCENTAGE

Flour:	100% (bread: **92.7%**, whole wheat: **7.3%**)
Water:	57.2%
Yeast:	1%
Salt:	2%

Mantovana Olive Oil Bread

This bread is a local specialty of Mantua, Italy, where it is served with cured meats and antipasti, but it is fantastically flavorful on its own. It has a great moist, soft texture with an even, slightly open crumb. The flavor of the sesame seeds predominates.

Susan Huxter teaches this bread at her school near Capetown, South Africa.

TIME SCHEDULE

Starter: straight dough method
Minimum Rising Time: about 2 1/2 hours
Oven Temperature: 450°F, then 400°F
Baking Time: 45 to 50 minutes

Makes: a 7 1/2-by-4-inch-high round loaf/
1 pound, 8.7 ounces/700 grams

INGREDIENTS	MEASURE	WEIGHT	
	volume	ounces	grams
unhulled sesame seeds	3 tablespoons	1 ounce	28 grams
sunflower seeds	3 tablespoons	1 ounce	28 grams
poppy seeds	3 tablespoons	1 ounce	28 grams
cracked flaxseed	2 1/2 tablespoons	1 ounce	27 grams
bread flour	1 2/3 cups	8.7 ounces	250 grams
whole wheat bread	scant 2/3 cup	3 ounces	88 grams
instant yeast (see page 561 for brands)	3/4 teaspoon	--	2.4 grams
water, at room temperature (70° to 90°F)	1 liquid cup plus 2 tablespoons (9 fluid ounces)	9.4 ounces	266 grams
extra virgin olive oil	1/4 liquid cup	about 2 ounces	54 grams
salt	1 1/8 teaspoons	--	7.4 grams

EQUIPMENT:

a half sheet pan lined with a nonstick liner such as Silpain or parchment, or sprinkled with flour or cornmeal;

a baking stone OR baking sheet

1 > Toast the seeds. Preheat the oven to 325°F.

Spread the sesame and sunflower seeds on a small cookie sheet. Toast them for about 7 minutes, stirring once or twice, just until they begin to color. Combine them with the flaxseed and set them aside until cool.

2 > Mix the dough.

Mixer Method

In the mixer bowl, whisk together the bread flour, whole wheat flour, yeast, and seeds. With the dough hook, on low speed (if using a #2 KitchenAid), gradually add the water and then the olive oil, and mix until the flour is moistened enough to form a rough dough. Scrape down any bits of dough. Cover the bowl with plastic and allow the dough to rest for 20 minutes.

Sprinkle on the salt and knead the dough on medium speed (#4 KitchenAid) for 10 minutes. It will pull away from the bowl but will still be sticky enough to cling to your fingers. If it is still very sticky, knead in a little flour. If it is not sticky, spray it with a little water and knead it in. (It will weigh about 27.25 ounces/772 grams.)

Hand Method

In a large bowl, whisk together all but 1/4 cup of the bread flour, the whole wheat flour, yeast, and seeds. Then whisk in the salt (this keeps the yeast from coming in direct contact with the salt, which would kill it).

Stirring with a wooden spoon or your hand, gradually add the water and then the olive oil, mixing until the flour is moistened. Knead the dough in the bowl until it comes together, then scrape it onto a lightly floured counter. Knead the dough for 5 minutes, enough to develop the gluten structure a little, adding as little of the reserved flour as possible to keep it from sticking. Use a bench scraper to scrape the dough and gather it together as you knead it. At this point, it will be very sticky. Cover it with the inverted bowl and allow it to rest for 20 minutes. (This resting time will make the dough less sticky and easier to work with.)

Knead the dough for another 5 minutes or until it is very smooth and elastic. It should still be sticky enough to cling to your fingers. If the dough is really wet, add some of the remaining reserved flour, or a little extra. (It will weigh about 27.25 ounces/772 grams.)

Both Methods

3 > Let the dough rise. Using an oiled spatula or dough scraper, scrape the dough into a 4-quart dough-rising container or bowl, lightly greased with cooking spray or oil. Push down the dough and lightly spray or oil the top. Cover the container with a lid or plastic wrap. With a piece of tape, mark the side of the container at approximately where double the height of the dough would be. Allow the dough to rise (ideally at 75° to 80°F) until doubled, 1 1/2 to 2 hours.

Using an oiled spatula or dough scraper, scrape the dough out onto a floured counter and press down on it gently to form a rectangle. It will be full of air and resilient; try to maintain as many of the air bubbles as possible. Fold the dough from all four sides into a tight package (see page 60) or give it 2 business letter turns and round the edges. Set it back in the container. Oil the surface again, cover, and mark where double the height would now be. It will fill the container fuller than before because it is puffier with air. Allow it to rise until doubled, about 1 hour.

4 > Shape the dough and let it rise. Turn the dough out onto a lightly floured counter and round it into a 5-inch ball. Set it on the prepared baking sheet. Cover it with a large container, or cover loosely with oiled plastic wrap. Let the dough rise until almost doubled, about 1 hour. It will be about 7 inches by 3 1/2 inches high, and when it is pressed gently with a fingertip, the depression will very slowly fill in.

5 > Preheat the oven. Preheat the oven to 450°F 1 hour before baking. Have an oven shelf at the lowest level and place a baking stone or baking sheet on it, and a cast-iron skillet or sheet pan on the floor of the oven, before preheating.

6 > Slash and bake the bread. With a sharp knife or single-edged razor blade, make 1/4- to 1/2-inch-deep slashes in the top of the dough (I like to make 2 slashes in one direction and a second slash perpendicular to them).

Mist the dough with water and quickly but gently set the pan on the hot baking stone or hot baking sheet. Toss 1/2 cup of ice cubes into the pan beneath and immediately shut the door. Bake for 5 minutes. Lower the heat to 400°F and continue baking for 40 to 45 minutes or until golden (an instant-read thermometer inserted into the center will read about 200°F). Halfway through baking, with a heavy pancake turner, lift the bread from the pan and set it directly on the stone, turning it around as you do so for even baking.

7 > **Cool the bread.** Remove the bread from the oven, and transfer it to a wire rack to cool completely.

POINTERS FOR SUCCESS

> Whole flaxseed is not absorbed by the body, so it is desirable to crack it by grinding it coarse in a wheat mill or blender. As flax becomes rancid very quickly, it is best to do this yourself rather than purchasing ground flax, which also contributes less texture than the coarse-ground seeds.

> At the end of Step 3, you can refrigerate the dough for 4 hours, or up to overnight, for maximum flavor development. Let it stand at room temperature for 1 hour before shaping.

THE DOUGH PERCENTAGE

Flour:	100% (bread: **68.5%**, whole wheat: **24.1%**, flax: **7.4%**)
Seeds:	**23%**
Water:	**72.9%**
Yeast:	**0.71%**
Salt:	**2%**
Oil:	**14.5%**

Olive Bread

I discovered this bread when baking colleague and friend Flo Braker introduced me to Kurtis Baguley at Scavulo's, in the Sir Francis Drake Hotel in San Francisco. I loved his olive bread so much I flew back to New York with a prototype and some of his starter in my carry-on bag. Luckily I had double-bagged the starter, because it was so lively it broke through the first freezer-weight bag! After many tries, conversations with Kurtis, and different types of flour, I finally reproduced his bread to my satisfaction.

Out of sheer sentiment and determination, I kept that sourdough starter going for close to nine years, until I discovered that a biga is much less work and makes just as good an olive bread. No mere description can do total justice to this bread. I could mention its crisp crust and moist light crumb, and that it is juicy with flavorful olives, but it's not enough. It is the synergy of textures and flavors that makes this bread so wonderful.

It takes under two minutes to mix this dough in a food processor and it produces just as good a texture as any other method. If you double the recipe, use the plastic dough blade instead of the metal blade.

TIME SCHEDULE

Dough Starter (Biga): minimum 6 hours, maximum 3 days
Minimum Rising Time: 2 hours
Oven Temperature: 475°F, then 425°F, then 375°F (if using La Cloche 450°F, then 400°F)
Baking Time: 25 minutes

Makes: a 6 1/2-by-3 1/2-inch-high round loaf/
15 ounces/431 grams

a half sheet pan lined with a nonstick liner such as
Silpain or sprinkled with flour or cornmeal, OR
La Cloche Bread Baker;

an 8-inch banneton OR a colander lined with a towel;

a baking stone OR baking sheet

Dough Starter (Biga)

Makes: scant 1/2 cup/4.7 ounces/134 grams

INGREDIENTS	MEASURE	WEIGHT	
	volume	ounces	grams
unbleached all-purpose flour (use only Gold Medal, King Arthur, or Pillsbury)	1/2 cup plus 1/2 tablespoon	2.6 ounces	75 grams
instant yeast (see page 561 for brands)	1/16 teaspoon	--	0.2 gram
Optional: malt powder	1/2 teaspoon	--	1.6 grams
water, at room temperature (70° to 90°F)	1/4 liquid cup	2 ounces	59 grams

1 > Six hours or up to 3 days ahead, make the biga. In a small bowl, combine all the
ingredients for the biga and stir the mixture with a wooden spoon for 3 to 5 minutes
or until it is very smooth and comes away from the sides of the bowl. It will be tacky
(slightly sticky) to the touch. Cover the bowl tightly with oiled plastic wrap (or place
the biga in a 2-cup food storage container with a lid) and set it aside until tripled and
filled with bubbles. At room temperature, this will take about 6 hours. Stir it down
and use it, or refrigerate it for up to 3 days before baking. If using the food processing, the biga must be refrigerated for at least 1 hour before using.

Dough

INGREDIENTS	MEASURE	WEIGHT	
	volume	ounces	grams
unbleached all-purpose flour (use only Gold Medal, King Arthur, or Pillsbury)	1 1/3 cups	6.5 ounces	186 grams
instant yeast (see page 561 for brands)	1/2 teaspoon	--	1.6 grams
biga (from above)	*scant 1/2 cup*	*4.7 ounces*	*134 grams*

INGREDIENTS	MEASURE	WEIGHT	
	volume	ounces	grams
water, at room temperature (or cold if using a processor)	7 tablespoons plus 1 teaspoon	3.7 ounces	106 grams
salt	1/2 teaspoon	--	3.3 grams
Kalamata olives (or a mix of Kalamata and oil-cured, herbed Moroccan)	6 tablespoons (1/3 cup pitted)	2.1 ounces	60 grams 46 grams up to 55 grams pitted
unbleached all-purpose flour	1 tablespoon	0.3 ounce	9 grams

2 > Mix the dough.

Mixer Method

In the mixer bowl, place the flour, yeast, and biga. With the dough hook, on low speed (#2 if using a KitchenAid), gradually add the water, mixing until the flour is moistened enough to form a rough dough. Scrape down any bits of dough. Cover the bowl with plastic wrap and allow the dough to rest for 20 minutes.

Sprinkle on the salt and knead the dough on medium speed (#4 KitchenAid) for 7 minutes. The dough should be very elastic but still moist enough to cling slightly to your fingers. If it is still very sticky, knead in a little flour. If it is not at all sticky, spray it with a little water and knead it in. Allow the dough to relax, covered, for 10 minutes.

Food Processor Method

Place the cold biga in the bowl of a food processor fitted with the metal blade (plastic if doubling the recipe) and add the flour and yeast. With the motor running, add the salt and then the cold water. Once the dough pulls away from the bowl, continue processing for 45 seconds. The dough should be very elastic but still moist enough to cling slightly to your fingers. If it is still very sticky, pulse in a little flour. If it is not at all sticky, spray it with a little water and pulse it in. Allow the dough to relax, covered, for 10 minutes.

Hand Method

If the biga has been refrigerated, remove it from the refrigerator about 1 hour before mixing the dough.

In a large bowl, whisk together but 2 tablespoons of the 1 1/3 cups (6.5 ounces/186 grams) of flour and the instant yeast. Then whisk in the salt (this keeps the yeast from coming in direct contact with the salt, which would kill it). With a wooden spoon or your hand, stir in the biga and the water until the flour is moistened. Knead the dough in the bowl until it comes together, then scrape it onto a lightly floured counter. Knead the dough for 5 minutes, enough to develop the gluten structure a little, adding as little of the reserved flour as possible to keep it from sticking. Use a bench scraper to scrape the dough and gather it together as you knead it. At this point, it will be very sticky. Cover it with the inverted bowl and allow it to rest for 20 minutes. (This resting time will make the dough less sticky and easier to work with.)

Knead the dough for another 5 minutes or until it is very smooth and elastic. It should still be moist enough to cling slightly to your fingers. If it is very sticky, add some of the remaining reserved flour, or a little extra. Allow the dough to relax covered, for 10 minutes.

All Methods

3 > **Add the olives.** Coarsely chop the olives. Place them in a small bowl and toss them with the 1 tablespoon flour.

Turn the dough out onto a lightly floured counter (if it's not already on the counter). Press down on it gently to form a rectangle, and scatter the olives all over it. Roll it up and knead it to distribute the olives evenly (some will come to the surface). As the olives start releasing their moisture, you may need to add flour to keep the dough from sticking to the counter; add it by the tablespoon only if necessary. The dough should still be sticky enough barely to cling to your fingers. (The dough will weigh about 17 ounces/480 grams.)

4 > **Let the dough rise.** Place the dough in a 1-quart dough-rising container or bowl, lightly greased with cooking spray or oil. Press down the dough and lightly spray or oil the top. Cover the container with a lid or plastic wrap. With a piece of tape, mark the side of the container at approximately where double the height of the dough would be. Allow the dough to rise (ideally at 75° to 80°F) until doubled, 1 to 1 1/2 hours.

5 > **Shape the dough and let it rise.** Turn the dough out onto a lightly floured counter and shape it into a ball (see page 65). Place it seam side up in a floured banneton or a colander lined with a floured cloth. Pinch together the seam if necessary. Spray the dough with oil or lightly sprinkle the top with flour. Cover it with a large container or cover loosely with oiled plastic wrap, and allow it to rise until almost doubled, 1 to 2 hours. (The center will be above the sides of the banneton, if using one.) When the dough is pressed gently with a fingertip, the depression will very slowly fills in.

6 > **Preheat the oven.** Preheat the oven to 475°F, or 450°F if using La Cloche, 1 hour before baking. Have an oven shelf at the lowest level and place an oven stone or baking sheet on it before preheating. If not using La Cloche, place a cast-iron skillet or

sheet pan on the floor of the oven to preheat. If using La Cloche, preheat the dome along with the oven.

Remove the container or plastic wrap. If you are using a Silpain-lined baking sheet, invert it on top of the banneton or colander and gently invert the dough onto the sheet. (If you used a colander and the risen bread is more than 1 inch below the top, you will need to support the bread when inverting it so that it doesn't fall and deflate. Cut a cardboard circle small enough to fit into the colander and touch the surface of the bread. Place a piece of parchment on top of the bread, place the cardboard on top, and invert the bread onto the cardboard. Then slide the bread, still on the parchment, onto the baking sheet.) Or, if using La Cloche or a cornmeal-sprinkled baking sheet, gently invert the dough onto it.

7 > **Slash and bake the bread.** With a sharp knife or single-edged razor blade, make 1/4- to 1/2-inch-deep slashes in the top of the dough (see page 80). I like to make a cross going all the way across the dough in each direction almost to the edge. (This dough is very airy, so use a light hand to make a mark first and then go over it with the tip of the knife or the razor. You can also use scissors to cut through the dough.)

If using La Cloche, carefully place the hot Cloche dome onto the base and quickly but gently set it on the hot stone or hot baking sheet. Bake for 10 minutes. Lower the temperature to 400°F and bake for 5 minutes. Remove the dome and bake for 15 minutes or until the bread is pale golden brown and a skewer inserted in the middle comes out clean (an instant-read thermometer inserted into the center will read about 207°F).

Alternatively, quickly but gently set the baking sheet on the hot stone or hot baking sheet. Toss 1/2 cup of ice cubes into the pan beneath and immediately shut the door. Bake for 5 minutes. Lower the oven to 425°F and bake for another 10 minutes. Lower the oven to 375°F and bake for 10 minutes more or until the bread is pale golden brown and a skewer inserted in the middle comes out clean (an instant-read thermometer inserted into the center will read about 207°F). Halfway through baking, turn the pan around for even baking.

8 > **Cool the bread.** Remove the bread from the oven and transfer it to a wire rack to cool completely.

STORE   This bread is still excellent on the second day at room temperature, if stored wrapped airtight.

VARIATION

Puttanesca Bread   This idea came to me when my spell-check changed the word *prosciutto* to *prostitute* (*puttanesca* in Italian)! Capers and olives, so delicious in a pasta sauce, are also terrific in bread, and it makes an extraordinary sardine sandwich. The best capers are those packed in salt. Soak about 2 tablespoons of salt-packed capers in water for about 15 minutes, drain, and add to the dough along with the olives.

ULTIMATE FULL FLAVOR VARIATION

For the best flavor development, in Step 1, allow the biga to ferment in a cool area (55° to 65°F) for 12 to 24 hours. (A wine cellar provides an ideal spot.) After 12 hours, it will have tripled and be filled with bubbles; it will not deflate even after 24 hours at this cool a temperature.

POINTERS FOR SUCCESS

> If using food processor, freezing the flour for the dough for 15 minutes (or as long as you want) would only help, but it is not absolutely necessary, as the cold biga and the cold water help to keep the finished dough under 85°F. With frozen flour, it will be around the ideal 78°F.

> Don't use parchment for lining the pan—it would stick to this dough.

> If oil-cured olives are not available, it's easy to make your own. Simply mix the olives with enough olive oil to coat them, and toss them with herbs of your choice, such as chopped rosemary and thyme, and a smashed garlic clove. Refrigerated, they will keep for several weeks.

> Baked in La Cloche, this bread has a crisper crust but the color is slightly more golden and handsome without it.

THE DOUGH PERCENTAGE

Flour:	100%
Water:	63.2%
Yeast:	0.69%
Salt:	1.3%

Mushroom Bread

This bread is baked in the shape of a mushroom. My Aunt Margaret is a mycologist (mushroom expert) as well as an artist, so it was inevitable that she would bake bread in the shape of a mushroom. This idea stayed vivid in my mind for twenty years before it occurred to me one day how delicious it would be to add mushrooms. I tried using pulverized dried porcinis, but the flavor was too intense. Duxelles, the butter-enriched sautéed minced mushroom mixture, however, gave the bread the woodsy mushroom taste I was hoping for. (The duxelles can be made up to three months ahead and frozen.)

Use either a bread steamer (see page 591) or large coffee can to give the bread a mushroom shape.

This bread makes a great display set on a bread board at the dinner table. And the "stem" cuts into beautiful rounds for serving.

TIME SCHEDULE

Duxelles: about 1 hour
Dough Starter (Sponge): minimum 1 hour, maximum 24 hours
Minimum Rising Time: 2 1/4 hours
Oven Temperature: 400°F
Baking Time: 45 to 55 minutes

Makes: a 4-by-8 1/2-inch-high loaf (with a 5-inch "cap")/
1 pound, 12.5 ounces/808 grams

EQUIPMENT:

an ovenproof glass bread steamer (4 inches in diameter and 6 1/4 inches high) OR a 5-inch-high coffee can, lightly greased with cooking spray or oil;

a baking stone OR baking sheet

Duxelles

Makes: about 1 1/4 cups/7.5 ounces/212 grams

INGREDIENTS	MEASURE	WEIGHT	
	volume	ounces	grams
white mushrooms (buy 2 ounces extra to allow for trimming)	4 cups, lightly packed (after mincing)	12 ounces	340 grams
unsalted butter	4 tablespoons	2 ounces	57 grams
1 medium garlic clove, lightly smashed	--	--	--
salt	3/4 teaspoon, or to taste	--	--
black pepper	1/8 teaspoon	--	--

Clean the mushrooms by brushing off any dirt with a damp paper towel and cutting off the tough stem ends. If using a food processor, cut any large mushrooms into quarters and then process until finely minced. Or mince the mushrooms very fine by hand.

In a large skillet, melt the butter over medium heat. Add the mushrooms, garlic, and salt and cook, covered, over low heat for 5 minutes. The mushrooms will have released a lot of water. Uncover and continue cooking for about 30 minutes, stirring occasionally, until the mushrooms have turned dark brown and all the water has evaporated. Add more salt if desired. Stir in the pepper. Remove the garlic and discard it. Let cool.

Dough Starter (Sponge)

INGREDIENTS	MEASURE	WEIGHT	
	volume	ounces	grams
bread flour	1 cup	5.5 ounces	156 grams
instant yeast (see page 561 for brands)	3/8 teaspoon	--	1.2 grams

malt powder or
  barley malt
  sugar
	1 teaspoon	--	3.1 grams
			7 grams
			8.3 grams

water, at room temperature (70° to 90°F)	1 liquid cup	8.3 ounces	236 grams

1 > **Make the sponge.** In a mixer bowl or other large bowl, place the bread flour, yeast, malt or sugar, and water. Whisk until very smooth, to incorporate air, about 2 minutes. The sponge will be the consistency of a thick batter. Scrape down the sides of the bowl. Set aside, covered with plastic wrap, while you make the flour mixture.

Flour Mixture

INGREDIENTS	MEASURE	WEIGHT	
	volume	ounces	grams
bread flour	2 cups plus 1 tablespoon	11.2 ounces	322 grams
whole wheat flour	2 tablespoons plus 2 teaspoons	about 0.75 ounce	24 grams
instant yeast (see page 561 for brands)	3/8 teaspoon	--	1.2 grams
salt	1 teaspoon	0.2 ounce	6.6 grams
Duxelles (page 390), at room temperature	1 cup firmly packed	6 ounces	170 grams

2 > Combine the ingredients for the flour mixture and add to the sponge. In a medium bowl, whisk together the bread flour (reserve 1/4 cup if mixing by hand), whole wheat flour, and yeast. Gently scoop it onto the sponge to cover it completely. Cover tightly with plastic wrap and allow it to ferment for 1 to 4 hours at room temperature. (During this time, the sponge will bubble up through the flour mixture in places; this is fine.)

3 > Mix the dough.

Mixer Method

With the dough hook, mix on low speed (#2 KitchenAid) until the flour is moistened enough to form a rough dough. Scrape down any bits of dough. Cover the bowl with plastic wrap and allow the dough to rest for 20 minutes.

Add the salt and duxelles and mix on low speed until incorporated. Raise the speed to medium (#4 KitchenAid) and knead for 7 minutes. The dough should be very elastic and jump back when pressed down on it with a fingertip, but still moist enough to cling slightly to your fingers. If it is still very sticky, knead in a little flour. If it is not at all sticky, spray it with a little water and knead it in. (The dough will weigh about 2 pounds/913 grams.)

Hand Method

Add the salt and duxelles and, with a wooden spoon or your hand, mix until the flour is moistened. Knead the dough in the bowl until it comes together, then scrape it onto a lightly floured counter. Knead the dough for 5 minutes, enough to develop the gluten structure a little, adding as little of the reserved flour as possible to keep it from sticking. Use a bench scraper to scrape the dough and gather it together as you knead it. At this point, it will be very sticky. Cover it with the inverted bowl and allow it to rest for 20 minutes. (This resting time will make the dough less sticky and easier to work with.)

Knead the dough for another 5 minutes or until it is very smooth and elastic. It should still be moist enough to cling slightly to your fingers. If it is very sticky, add some of the remaining reserved flour, or a little extra. (The dough will weigh about 2 pounds/913 grams.)

Both Methods

4 > Let the dough rise. Using an oiled spatula or dough scraper, scrape the dough into a 2-quart dough-rising container or bowl lightly greased with cooking spray or oil. Push down the dough and lightly spray or oil the top. Cover the container with a lid or plastic wrap. With a piece of tape, mark the side of the container at approximately where double the height of the dough would be. Allow the dough to rise (ideally at 75° to 80°F) until doubled, 1 to 1 1/2 hours.

Using an oiled spatula or dough scraper, scrape the dough onto a floured counter and press down on it gently to form a rectangle. Give it 1 or 2 business letter turns, round the edges, and set it back in the container. Oil the surface again, cover, and mark where double the height would now be. (It will fill the container fuller than before because it is puffier with air.) Allow the dough to rise until doubled, about 30 to 45 minutes.

5 > Shape the dough and let it rise. Turn the dough out onto a counter dusted lightly with flour. Roll it into a cylinder and push it down into the prepared bread steamer or coffee can. (If using the coffee can, fill it only two-thirds full and reserve the remaining 3/4 cup dough for rolls: See Little Round Rolls, page 252). Use your fingers to make sure that it is pushed all the way down to the bottom of the steamer or can. Cover with a large container or oiled plastic wrap. Let the dough rise until doubled, about 1 hour. The center should be 1 1/2 inches above the top of the container and the dough should "mushroom" over the sides. When it is pressed gently with a fingertip the depression will not fill in.

6 > Preheat the oven. Preheat the oven to 400°F 1 hour before baking. Have an oven shelf at the lowest level and place a baking stone or baking sheet on it, and a cast-iron skillet or sheet pan on the floor of the oven, before preheating.

7 > Bake and glaze the bread. Quickly but gently set the container on the hot baking stone or hot baking sheet. Toss 1/2 cup of ice cubes into the pan beneath and immediately shut the door. Bake for 55 to 65 minutes or until golden (an instant-read thermometer inserted into the center will read about 210°F). Halfway through baking, turn the pan around for even baking.

8 > Cool the bread. Remove the bread from the oven, unmold it onto a wire rack, and turn right side up. For a shiny surface, brush "mushroom cap" with 1 teaspoon of melted butter. Allow to cool completely.

ULTIMATE FULL FLAVOR VARIATION

For the best flavor development, in Step 2, allow the sponge to ferment for 1 hour at room temperature, then refrigerate it for 8 to 24 hours. If using the hand mixing method, remove it from the refrigerator about 1 hour before mixing the dough.

UNDERSTANDING

Although this bread has a relatively low percentage of liquid, it has a moist texture from the duxelles. If well wrapped, it will stay fresh for up to 3 days at room temperature.

THE DOUGH PERCENTAGE

Flour:	Flour: **100%** (bread: **95.2%**, whole wheat: **4.8%**)
Water:	**47%**
Yeast:	**0.48%**
Salt:	**1.3%**
Butterfat:	**7.2%**

Tyrolean Ten-Grain Torpedo

Many years ago, Peter Kump (founder of The Institute of Culinary Education in New York City) and I arranged a special trip for food professionals to his son, Christopher, and Margaret Fox's Café Beaujolais in Mendocino, California. It was there that I discovered this extraordinary bread, unlike any I had ever tasted: wheaty, chewy but light in texture, with an appealing flavor and crunch from the many grains within.

Turning to Peter during lunch, I asked him if he supposed I could get the recipe. "I'm sure they will give it to you," replied Peter, smiling optimistically (anyone who knew Peter will remember his characteristic expression). "They got it from an Austrian baker near our castle in Austria." Peter was right, but it took over ten years, as it was one of their top sellers and top secret! In the interim, I tried extrapolating the recipe from the description of ingredients on their mail-order list for the bread. It turns out that all I needed to do was buy their ten-grain cereal mix and add extra sunflower seeds! So I now have two versions, their Austrian Sunflower Bread and mine.

The secret to the chewy but light texture is the addition of vital wheat gluten, available in many supermarkets and in health food stores.

This bread is thoroughly satisfying on its own, but it is also excellent with sandwich meats such as ham or turkey.

TIME SCHEDULE

Dough Starter (Sponge): minimum 8 hours, maximum 24 hours
Minimum Rising Time: about 2 1/2 hours
Oven Temperature: 450°F
Baking Time: 25 to 30 minutes

Makes: a 12-by-5-by-3 1/4-inch-high-loaf/
1 pound, 5.7 ounces/622 grams

EQUIPMENT:

a heavy-duty stand mixer with dough hook attachment;

a half sheet pan lined with a nonstick liner such as Silpain or parchment, or sprinkled with flour or cornmeal;

a baking stone OR baking sheet

Dough Starter (Sponge)

INGREDIENTS	MEASURE	WEIGHT	
	volume	ounces	grams
bread flour	2/3 cup	3.5 ounces	100 grams
instant yeast (see page 561 for brands)	1/4 teaspoon	--	0.8 gram

malt powder or
  barley malt syrup or honey or
  sugar
	1/2 tablespoon	--	4.6 grams
			10.5 grams
			6.2 grams

water, at room temperature (70° to 90°F)	3/4 liquid cup	6.2 ounces	177 grams

1 > **Nine hours ahead or the night before, make the sponge.** In the mixer bowl, place the flour, yeast, malt (or honey or sugar), and water. Whisk until very smooth, to incorporate air, about 2 minutes. The sponge will be the consistency of a thick batter. Scrape down the sides. Set it aside, covered with plastic wrap, while you make the flour mixture.

Flour Mixture

INGREDIENTS	MEASURE	WEIGHT	
	volume	ounces	grams
bread flour	1 1/4 cups plus 1/2 tablespoon	7 ounces	200 grams
instant yeast	3/4 teaspoon	--	2.4 grams
Optional: vital wheat gluten	4 teaspoons	--	12 grams

2 > **Combine the ingredients for the flour mixture and add to the sponge.** In a medium bowl, whisk together the flour, yeast, and vital wheat gluten, if you are using it. Spoon this mixture lightly on top of the sponge to cover it completely. Cover

it tightly with plastic wrap. Allow to ferment for 1 hour at room temperature and then for 8 to 24 hours in the refrigerator. (During this time, the sponge will bubble through the flour mixture; this is fine.)

Grains

INGREDIENTS	MEASURE	WEIGHT	
	volume	ounces	grams
ten-grain cereal mix (see Pointers for Success)	1/2 cup plus 2 tablespoons	about 3.5 ounces	100 grams
hot water	1/2 liquid cup minus 1 tablespoon	3.5 ounces	100 grams
salt	1 1/4 teaspoons	--	8.3 grams
Optional: white rye or medium rye flour for dusting	--	--	--

3 > Meanwhile, 8 hours ahead or the night before, soak the grains. Place the grain mixture in a medium bowl, add the hot water, and stir until thoroughly combined. Cool to room temperature, then cover and refrigerate for 8 or up to 24 hours.

4 > Mix the dough. With the dough hook, mix on low speed (#2 if using a KitchenAid) for about 1 minute, until the flour is moistened. Raise the speed to medium (#4 KitchenAid) and knead for 7 minutes. The dough will be very sticky. Allow it to rest for 20 minutes.

Add the salt and seed mixture (including any liquid that remains in the bowl) and knead for another 3 to 5 minutes or until evenly incorporated. The dough should be just barely tacky (slightly sticky). If it is still very sticky, knead in a little flour. If it is not at all sticky, spray it with a little water and knead in it. (The dough will weigh about 24 ounces/680 grams.)

5 > Let the dough rise. Place the dough in a 2-quart dough-rising container or bowl, lightly greased with cooking spray or oil. Push down the dough and lightly spray or oil the top. Cover the container with a lid or plastic wrap. With a piece of tape, mark the side of the container at approximately where double the height of the dough would be. Allow the dough to rise (ideally at 75° to 80°F) until doubled, 1 1/2 to 2 hours.

Using an oiled spatula or dough scraper, scrape the dough out onto a floured counter and press down on it gently to form a rectangle. Give it 1 or 2 business letter turns to redistribute the grains. Round the edges and set it back in the container. Oil the surface again, cover, and mark where double the height of the dough would now be. (It will fill the container fuller than before because it is puffier with air.) Allow it to rise until doubled, about 45 minutes to 1 hour.

6 > Shape the dough and let it rise. Turn the dough out onto a lightly floured counter and press or roll it into a rectangle. Shape it into an 11-inch-long by 2-inch-high torpedo-shaped loaf (batard; see page 69). Set it on the prepared baking sheet and cover it with a large container, or cover loosely with oiled plastic wrap. Let the dough rise until doubled, about 40 to 50 minutes. It will be about 12 inches long by 5 inches wide by 2 1/2 inches high, and when it is pressed gently with a fingertip, the depression will very slowly fill in.

7 > Preheat the oven. Preheat the oven to 450°F 1 hour before baking. Have an oven shelf at the lowest level and place a baking stone or baking sheet on it, and a cast-iron skillet or sheet pan on the floor of the oven before preheating.

8 > Slash and bake the bread. For a decorative effect and ease in slashing, dust the top of the dough lightly with the rye flour. With a sharp knife or single-edged razor blade, make three 1/4- to 1/2-inch-deep diagonal slashes in the top of the dough (see page 81).

Slide the dough, on its liner, onto the hot baking stone or hot baking sheet. Toss 1/2 cup of ice cubes into the pan beneath and immediately shut the door. Bake for 25 to 30 minutes or until the bread is golden brown and a skewer inserted in the middle comes out clean (an instant-read thermometer inserted into the center will read about 208°F). Halfway through baking, using a sturdy pancake turner, turn the bread around for even baking.

9 > Cool the bread. Remove the bread from the oven and transfer it to a wire rack to cool completely.

VARIATION

Café Beaujolais Austrian Sunflower Bread   Use only 1/4 cup (1.4 ounces/40 grams) cereal mix plus 6 tablespoons (2 ounces/55 grams) sunflower seeds, toasted together.

NOTES   *To make your own ten-grain/seed cereal mix,* mix equal volumes of

coarse buckwheat, toasted
pumpkin seeds, toasted
sunflower seeds, toasted
soy nugget granules, toasted
polenta
barley flakes
flaxseed
millet

steel-cut oats
cracked wheat

To toast seeds and buckwheat: Preheat the oven to 325°F. Spread the pumpkin seeds, sunflower seeds, and buckwheat on a baking sheet and toast, stirring once or twice, for 7 minutes or until the sunflower seeds just begin to darken.

POINTERS FOR SUCCESS

>   You can order the Café Beaujolais mix (www.cafebeaujolais.com, or 707/937-5614), make one yourself (see Notes), or use a ten-grain cereal mix from the health food store.

>   This is a very sticky dough and needs to be well kneaded before you add the seeds and grains, so it is best made in an electric mixer.

>   The less flour worked into the dough, the lighter and more open the crumb.

>   Soy contains lipoxidase, which oxidizes (combines with oxygen) the unsaturated fats in flour, creating unpleasant flavors and bleaching the flour. The enzyme is inactivated by toasting the soy; otherwise, it is best to avoid using it in bread.

UNDERSTANDING

When the dough is first mixed, it is very soft and sticky, making it easier to incorporate the grain mix. More flour is added with the grain mix to bring it to the correct consistency. Vital wheat gluten really shines here, as it strengthens the protein network of the dough enough to support the large amount of grains that otherwise tend to cut through gluten strands, resulting in an unpleasantly dense bread.

The raised bread starts off 5 inches wide but actually pulls in to 4 1/2 inches during baking because of the strength of the gluten.

THE DOUGH PERCENTAGE

Flour:	100% (includes the cereal and vital wheat gluten)
Instant yeast:	1.1%
Water:	67.2%
Salt:	2.7%
Seeds and grains:	33.3%

Swedish Limpa Bread

This is beautiful golden brown loaf, slightly darker at the edges of the slashes in the crust, with a fine crumb. The ale and molasses impart a slight bitter sweetness, together with a haunting undertone of spice from the fennel, anise, and orange zest.

This bread tastes best the first two days after baking, but it stays moist for as long as four.

Special thanks to my friend Mark Moody's Swedish mother, who inspired this recipe.

TIME SCHEDULE

Starter: straight dough method
Minimum Rising Time: about 2 hours
Oven Temperature: 375°F, then 350°F (or 350°F the whole time for the large loaf)
Baking Time: 20 to 25 minutes for the small loaves, 45 to 55 minutes for the large loaf

Makes: two 9 3/4-by-4-by-3-inch-high loaves,
about 1 pound/468 grams each
or one 13-by-5-by-3 1/2-inch-high loaf,
about 2 pounds/937 grams

EQUIPMENT:

a half sheet pan lined with a nonstick liner
such as Silpain or parchment, or sprinkled with
flour or cornmeal;

a baking stone OR baking sheet

Molasses Mixture

INGREDIENTS	MEASURE	WEIGHT	
	volume	ounces	grams
light molasses	6 tablespoons (3 fluid ounces)	about 4 ounces	120 grams
bitter ale, at room temperature	10 fluid ounces (1 1/4 liquid cups)	10 ounces	284 grams
unsalted butter	3 tablespoons	1.5 ounces	42 grams
salt	2 1/4 teaspoons	--	15 grams

1 > **Make the molasses mixture.** In a small saucepan, stir together the molasses, ale, butter, and salt. Heat over low heat, stirring constantly, until the butter is melted. Remove from the heat and allow to cool to room temperature. Pour it into a 2-cup liquid measure.

Flour Mixture

INGREDIENTS	MEASURE	WEIGHT	
	volume	ounces	grams
unbleached all-purpose flour (use only Gold Medal, King Arthur, or Pillsbury)	2 cups	10 ounces	284 grams
rye flour	2 cups	9 ounces	255 grams
orange zest, finely grated (from about 1 orange)	2 teaspoons	--	4 grams

malt powder or
  barley malt syrup or honey or
  sugar
	2 tablespoons
	2 tablespoons
	2 tablespoons
		0.6 ounce
		1.5 ounces
		scant 1 ounce
			18.6 grams
			42 grams
			25 grams

aniseed	1 teaspoon	--	2 grams
fennel seeds	1 teaspoon	--	2.4 grams
instant yeast, preferably SAF gold (for sweet doughs) (see page 561 for other brands)	1 tablespoon plus 1/2 teaspoon	--	11.2 grams

2 > **Combine the flour mixture.** In the mixer bowl or other large bowl, combine the all-purpose flour (reserve 1/4 cup if mixing by hand), rye flour, orange zest, malt (or honey or sugar), aniseed, fennel seeds, and yeast. Whisk to blend.

3 > **Mix the dough.**

Mixer Method

With the dough hook, mix on low speed (#2 if using a KitchenAid) while slowly adding the cooled liquid mixture, for about 1 minute, until the flour is moistened enough to form a rough dough. Scrape down any bits of dough. Cover the bowl with plastic wrap and allow the dough to rest for 20 minutes.

Knead the dough on medium speed (#4 KitchenAid) for 7 minutes. The dough should be very elastic, silky-smooth, and very soft but not sticky. If it is still sticky, knead in a little flour. If it is not sticky at all, spray it with a little water and knead it in. (The dough will weigh about 36 ounces/1017 grams.)

Hand Method

Using a wooden spoon or your hand, gradually stir in the cooled liquid mixture until all the flour is moistened. Knead the dough in the bowl until it comes together, then scrape it onto a lightly floured counter. Knead the dough for 5 minutes, enough to develop the gluten structure a little, adding as little of the reserved flour as possible to keep it from sticking. Use a bench scraper to scrape the dough and gather it together as you knead it. At this point, it will be very sticky. Cover it with the inverted bowl and allow it to rest for 20 minutes. (This resting time will make the dough less sticky and easier to work with.)

Knead the dough for another 5 minutes or until it is silky-smooth and elastic. It should be very soft but not sticky. If necessary, add some of the remaining reserved flour, or a little extra. (The dough will weigh about 36 ounces/1017 grams.)

Both Methods

4 > Let the dough rise. Place the dough in an oiled 2-quart dough-rising container or bowl, lightly greased with cooking spray or oil. Press down the dough and lightly spray or oil the dough. Cover the container with a lid or plastic wrap. With a piece of tape, mark the side of the container at approximately where double the height of the dough would be. Allow the dough to rise (ideally at 75° to 80°F) until doubled, 1 to 2 hours.

5 > Shape the dough and let it rise. Turn the dough out onto a lightly floured counter. Cut it in half if you are making 2 loaves. Give the dough a business letter turn and allow it to rest, covered, for 30 minutes or until relaxed and extensible (when you pull it gently, it stretches without tearing).

Shape the dough into 2 football-shaped loaves about 8 inches long by 3 inches wide by 2 inches high or 1 football-shaped loaf 11 1/2 inches by 3 1/2 inches by 2 1/2 inches high (see page 69). Set the shaped dough on the lined baking sheet (If making 2 loaves, set them 2 inches apart) and cover with a large container or oiled plastic wrap. Let the dough rise until almost doubled, about 1 hour to 1 hour and 15 minutes. The small loaves will be 9 1/2 inches by 3 3/4 inches by 2 1/2 inches high, a large loaf 12 inches by 4 inches by 2 3/4 inches high. When the dough is pressed gently with a fingertip, the depression will very slowly fill in.

6 > Preheat the oven. Preheat the oven to 375°F, or 350°F if making 1 large loaf, 30 minutes before baking. Have an oven shelf at the lowest level and place an oven stone or baking sheet on it, and a cast-iron skillet or sheet pan on the floor of the oven, before preheating.

7 > Slash and bake the bread. With a sharp knife or single-edged razor blade, make 4 diagonal 1/4- to 1/2-inch-deep slashes in the top of each smaller loaf, or 5 in the large loaf. The dough will rise and open up along the cuts significantly, so make the slashes long enough to prevent the dough from bursting unevenly.

Mist the dough with water and quickly but gently set the baking sheet on the hot baking stone or hot baking sheet. Toss 1/2 cup of ice cubes into the pan beneath and immediately shut the door. Bake for 5 minutes. Lower the temperature to 350°F and continue baking for 15 to 20 minutes for smaller loaves, 45 to 55 minutes for the large loaf or until the bread is golden brown and a skewer inserted in the middle comes out clean (an instant-read thermometer inserted into the center will read about 190°F). Halfway through baking, turn the pan around for even baking.

8 > Cool the bread. Remove the bread from the oven and transfer it to a wire rack to cool completely.

STORE The bread keeps well for 4 days at room temperature if well wrapped.

POINTERS FOR SUCCESS

> If desired, for deeper flavor, the dough can be refrigerated after its first rise for up to 14 hours. Let it stand at to room temperature for 1 hour before shaping.

UNDERSTANDING

Because the dough contains a high amount of molasses in addition to malt, honey, or sugar, it is preferable to use a yeast designed specifically for sweet doughs. If you use regular instant yeast or active dry yeast, the first rising may take as long as 3 hours.

This bread needs to bake at a lower temperature than most breads because it tends to brown easily, and if overbrowned, it becomes bitter.

THE DOUGH PERCENTAGE

Flour:	Flour: **100%** (all-purpose: **52.7%**, rye: **47.3%**)
Seeds:	**0.9%**
Water:	**59.2%** (includes the water in the molasses and butter)
Yeast:	**2%**
Salt:	**2.8%**
Butterfat:	**6.3%**

Raisin Pecan Bread

This delicious bread is practically a meal in itself and when I serve it at home, my husband, Elliott, and I usually make it the centerpiece of our dinner. Of all my breads, this is his favorite.

The secret of the fine texture and tangy sweet/sour flavor is the ground pecans and the raisin water added to the dough. The resulting bread is dense, chewy though fine-textured, and studded with the sweet, moist raisins and the soft crunch of additional broken pecans. (Walnuts can be substituted if you prefer their slightly bitter flavor and extra crunch.) This bread is so perfectly pleasing it could be eaten for dessert, spread with a thin layer of softened sweet butter or cream cheese, or just "plain" (which, is this instance, is probably a contradiction in terms). It also makes the most terrific sandwich of curried chicken salad prepared with little bits of tart apple. In three-star Paris restaurants, this bread is traditionally served with the cheese course. It pairs especially well with Pierre Robert.

TIME SCHEDULE

Dough Starter (Sponge): minimum 1 1/2 hours, maximum 24 hours
Minimum Rising Time: about 3 1/2 hours
Oven Temperature: 400°F, then 375°F
Baking Time: 45 to 55 minutes

Makes: a 12-by-5-by-3-inch-high free-form loaf
(13 1/2 inches by 4 1/2 inches by 3 inches high in La Cloche)/
2 pounds/930 grams

EQUIPMENT:

La Cloche Italian Bread Baker OR a baking sheet, either one lined with a nonstick liner such as Silpain or parchment, or sprinkled with flour or cornmeal;

a baking stone OR baking sheet

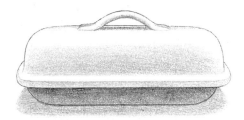

Raisins

INGREDIENTS	MEASURE	WEIGHT	
	volume	ounces	grams
raisins	1 cup	5 ounces	144 grams
hot water	1/3 liquid cup	2.75 ounces	78 grams

1 > Soak the raisins. Place the raisins in a small bowl and add the water. Cover with plastic wrap and allow to sit, stirring once, until softened and plump, about 30 minutes. Drain the raisins, reserving the liquid in a 1-cup liquid measure. (You should have about 1/4 cup.) Add enough warm water to equal 1 cup. If planning to mix the dough the next day, cover the raisins and water with plastic wrap and refrigerate them overnight, then bring to room temperature before using.

Dough Starter (Sponge)

INGREDIENTS	MEASURE	WEIGHT	
	volume	ounces	grams
bread flour	1 cup	5.5 ounces	156 grams
instant yeast (see page 561 for brands)	1/2 teaspoon	--	1.6 grams
water, at room temperature (70° to 90°F)	1 liquid cup (including raisin soaking water)	8.25 ounces	236 grams

malt powder or
  barley malt syrup or honey or
  sugar
	1 tablespoon	0.3 ounce
		0.7 ounce
		0.5 ounce
			9.3 grams
			21 grams
			12.5 grams

2 > Make the sponge. In a large bowl or the mixer bowl, place the bread flour, yeast, water, and malt (or honey or sugar). Whisk until very smooth, to incorporate air, about 2 minutes. The sponge will be the consistency of a thick batter. Scrape down the sides of the bowl. Set aside, covered with plastic wrap, while you make the flour mixture.

Flour Mixture

INGREDIENTS	MEASURE	WEIGHT	
	volume	ounces	grams
bread flour	1 1/4 cups	7 ounces	196 grams
whole wheat flour, preferably stone-ground	about 1/3 cup	1.75 ounces	50 grams
instant yeast	3/4 teaspoon	--	2.4 grams
pecans, finely ground	1/2 cup	1.5 ounces	42.7 grams
salt	1 1/4 teaspoons	--	8.3 grams
granular lecithin or	1 tablespoon	0.25 ounce	6.4 grams
vegetable oil	1 tablespoon	about 0.5 ounce	13.5 grams
pecan halves, coarsely broken	1 1/2 cups	5.25 ounces	150 grams

3 > Combine the ingredients for the flour mixture and add to the sponge. In a medium bowl, combine 1 cup (5.5 ounces/156 grams) of the bread flour, the whole wheat flour, yeast, and ground pecans. Spoon this mixture lightly on top of the sponge. Cover it tightly with plastic wrap and allow to ferment for 1 to 4 hours at room temperature. (During this time, the sponge will bubble through the flour mixture in places; this is fine.)

4 > Mix the dough.

Hand Method

Add the salt and, with a wooden spoon or your hand, stir the flour mixture into the sponge. Stir in the lecithin or oil, the broken pecans, and the raisins, and mix to distribute them throughout the dough. Knead the dough in the bowl until it comes together, then scrape it onto a lightly floured counter. Knead the dough for 5 minutes, enough to develop the gluten structure a little, adding as little of the remaining 1/4 cup (1.5 ounces/40 grams) flour as possible to keep it from sticking. Use a bench scraper to scrape the dough and gather it together as you knead it. At this point, it will be very sticky. Cover it with the inverted bowl and allow it to rest for 20 minutes. (This resting time will make the dough less sticky and easier to work with.)

Knead the dough for another 5 minutes or until it is very smooth and elastic. It should be soft but not cling to your fingers. If the dough is sticky, add some of the remaining reserved flour, or a little extra. (The dough will weigh about 2 1/4 pounds/1010 to 1020 grams.)

Mixer Method

Add the lecithin or oil to the dough and mix with the dough hook on low (#2 if using a KitchenAid) for about 1 minute, until the flour is moistened enough to form a soft, rough dough. Scrape down any bits of dough. Cover the bowl with plastic wrap and allow the dough to rest for 20 minutes.

Sprinkle on the salt and knead the dough on medium speed (#4 KitchenAid) for 7 minutes. The dough should be smooth and elastic. If after the first 3 minutes the dough still appears sticky and does not begin to pull away from the bowl, add a little of the remaining 1/4 cup (5.5 ounces/156 grams) of bread flour, a tablespoon at a time.

Sprinkle the counter lightly with a little more flour, turn the dough out on top of it, and cover it with plastic wrap. Allow to sit for 10 minutes to relax the gluten.

Roll the dough into a rectangle about 10 inches by 15 inches. Sprinkle the raisins and pecans evenly over the dough and, starting from the short end, roll up the dough as you would a jelly roll. (Do not use the mixer to mix in the raisins and nuts, as they will break down and produce a dark, compact crumb.)

Form the dough into a ball and knead it lightly. After the raisins are added, the dough will become a little tacky (sticky) and will need a little more of the extra flour.

Both Methods

5 > **Let the dough rise.** Place the dough in a 2-quart dough-rising container or bowl, lightly greased with cooking spray or oil. Push down the dough and lightly spray or oil the top. Cover the container with a lid or plastic wrap. With a piece of tape, mark the side of the container at approximately where double the height of the dough would be. Allow the dough to rise (ideally at 75° to 80°F) until doubled, 1 1/2 to 2 hours.

Using an oiled spatula or dough scraper, scrape the dough out onto a floured counter and press down on it gently to form a rectangle. Give it a business letter turn, round the edges, and set it back in the container. (It will fill the container fuller than before because it is puffier with air). Oil the surface again, cover, and mark where double the height of the dough would now be. Allow the dough to rise until doubled, about 1 1/2 hours.

6 > **Shape the dough and let it rise.** Turn the dough out onto a lightly floured counter and press down or roll it into a rectangle. Shape it into a 10- to 11-inch-long torpedo-shaped loaf (batard; see page 69). Set the dough on the La Cloche bottom or the prepared baking sheet. Cover it with a large container, or cover loosely with oiled plastic wrap. Let the dough rise until doubled, about 1 hour. The free-form loaf will be about 12 inches long by 4 inches wide by 3 inches high. When the dough is pressed gently with a fingertip the depression will very slowly fill in.

7 > **Preheat the oven.** Preheat the oven to 400°F 1 hour before baking. Have an oven shelf at the lowest level and, if not using La Cloche, place a baking stone or baking sheet on it, and a cast-iron skillet or sheet pan on the floor of the oven before preheating. If using La Cloche, preheat the top along with the oven.

8 > Slash and bake the bread. Remove the container or plastic and allow the dough to sit for 5 minutes to dry slightly.

With a sharp knife or single-edged razor blade, make 1/4- to 1/2-inch-deep parallel slashes in the top of the dough (I like to make about 5 short crosswise slashes).

If using La Cloche, carefully place the hot Cloche top onto the base and quickly but gently set it in the oven. Bake for 10 minutes. Lower the temperature to 375°F and continue baking for 30 to 35 minutes, until the bread is golden and a skewer inserted in the middle comes out clean (an instant-read thermometer inserted into the center will read about 190°F).

Alternatively, mist the dough with water and quickly but gently set the baking sheet on the hot stone or hot baking sheet. Toss 1/2 cup of ice cubes into the pan beneath and immediately shut the door. Bake for 5 minutes. Lower the heat to 375°F and continue baking for 40 to 50 minutes or until the bread is golden, and a skewer inserted in the middle comes out clean (an instant-read thermometer inserted into the center will read about 190°F). Halfway through baking, turn the pan around for even baking.

9 > Cool the bread. Remove the bread from the oven and transfer it to a wire rack to cool completely, at least 2 hours.

ULTIMATE FULL FLAVOR VARIATION

For the best flavor development, in Step 3, allow the sponge to ferment for 1 hour at room temperature, then refrigerate it for 8 to 24 hours. If using the hand mixing method, remove it from the refrigerator about 1 hour before mixing the dough.

CRANBERRY WALNUT VARIATION

In this variation I have replaced mellow pecans with the sharp crunch of walnuts, and the sweetness of raisins with the tang of dried cranberries. The cranberries give the crumb a lovely rosy hue. If using malt syrup instead of malt powder, however, it will produce a browner crumb.

To make this bread, simply replace the raisins with an equal voume or weight of dried cranberries, and replace the ground and broken pecans with a total of 2 cups/7 ounces/200 grams walnuts. Lightly toast the walnuts on a baking sheet in a pre-heated oven at 325°F for about 7 minutes to bring out their flavor and keep them from turning blue in the bread. Transfer them to a clean towel and, while still hot, rub them to remove as much of the bitter skin as possible. Coarsely break up 1 1/2 cups and set them aside. Process the remaining 1/2 cup walnuts with the whole wheat flour, for about a minute, until finely ground. Proceed as for the raisin pecan bread.

\>   To grind pecans fine, place the 1/2 cup pecans and 1 cup of the bread flour in a food processor and process for about 30 seconds.

\>   For extra flavor, you can toast the nuts very lightly (5 minutes at 325°F), but keep in mind that those that come to the surface of the bread will darken in the oven.

\>   Don't soak the raisins for longer than 30 minutes, or they will lose their texture. If using the new "moist baking raisins," there is no need to soak them.

\>   Don't set La Cloche on a preheated baking stone, as this bread tends to brown faster than most and could overbrown.

\>   The lecithin (see page 567) will extend the bread's freshness for a second day.

\>   *Unbleached* all-purpose flour could be used for this bread, but I prefer bread flour, which produces a crumb that is more firm to the chew and is more compatible with the texture of the raisins and nuts.

UNDERSTANDING

Soaking the raisins not only softens them but also produces a naturally sweetened liquid that permeates the dough and turns the crust a magnificent golden brown. During the final kneading, a little of the softened raisins will be integrated into the dough, making it moister.

I Iand mixing is my first choice for this dough so that the raisins can be added to the dough early on in the mixing process. This way, they can be integrated more into the dough without losing their shape entirely, as would happen with the mixer method if they were added at this point.

This bread takes longer to rise than usual because of the extra weight of the whole wheat flour, raisins, and nuts.

A softer dough results in a lighter texture, ideal for this bread. Don't work in too much flour.

NOTE   The recipe can be doubled to make an 18-by-7-by-4-inch-high loaf. Bake at 375°F for 50 to 60 minutes or until the bread tests done.

THE DOUGH PERCENTAGE

Flour:	Flour: **100%** (bread: **87.6%**, whole wheat: **12.4%**)
Water:	**58.7%**
Yeast:	**1%**
Salt:	**2%**
Oil:	**3.4%**

New Zealand Almond and Fig Bread

My husband, Elliott, and I celebrated our twenty-fifth anniversary with a long-awaited trip to New Zealand. We loved the country and adored the people, but it would have been worth the trip just for this amazing bread by Dean Brettschnelder, a professional baker. The recipe has since appeared in a book he wrote with our mutual friend Lauraine Jacobs, former president of the International Association of Culinary Professionals. This stunning bread is encrusted with sliced almonds and gilded with an apricot glaze. The crumb is dense and studded with chopped almonds and dried figs, with one whole fig implanted right in the center, which, when cut, resembles a heart.

The bread is delicious without further adornment, but it is also perfect with a blue cheese. My favorites are mild Cambozola blue and Saga blue.

TIME SCHEDULE

Dough Starter (Sponge): minimum 1 hour, maximum 24 hours
Minimum Rising Time: about 3 1/2 hours
Oven Temperature: 425F, then 375°F (if using La Cloche, 450°F, then 400°F)
Baking Time: 40 to 45 minutes

Makes: a 6-by-3-inch-high round loaf/
1 pound, 7.75 ounces/679 grams

EQUIPMENT:

La Cloche Bread Baker OR a half sheet pan, either one lined with a nonstick liner such as Silpain or parchment, or sprinkled with flour or cornmeal;

a baking stone OR baking sheet

Dough Starter (Sponge)

INGREDIENTS	MEASURE	WEIGHT	
	volume	ounces	grams
bread flour	3/4 cup	about 4 ounces	117 grams
instant yeast (see page 561 for brands)	1/2 teaspoon	--	1.6 grams
sugar	3/4 teaspoon	--	3.1 grams
water, at room temperature (70° to 90°F)	3/4 liquid cups	6.2 ounces	177 grams

1 > **Make the sponge.** In a mixer bowl or other large bowl, place the flour, yeast, sugar, and water. Whisk until very smooth, to incorporate air, about 2 minutes. The sponge will be the consistency of a thick batter. Scrape down the sides of the bowl. Set it aside, covered with plastic wrap, while you make the flour mixture.

Flour Mixture

INGREDIENTS	MEASURE	WEIGHT	
	volume	ounces	grams
bread flour	3/4 cup plus 2 table-spoons for kneading	4 ounces plus 0.6 ounces	117 grams plus 19 grams
whole wheat flour	1/2 cup	2.5 ounces	72 grams
instant yeast	1/2 teaspoon	--	1.6 grams
oil	2 teaspoons	--	9 grams
salt	1 1/4 teaspoons	0.25 ounce	8.3 grams
unblanched slivered (not sliced) or whole almonds, coarsely chopped	1 cup	2.6 ounces	75 grams
dried Mission figs, stems removed, cut into 1/4- to 1/2-inch pieces, plus 1 whole fig for décor	1/2 cup	2.6 ounces	75 grams

2 > **Combine the ingredients for the flour mixture and add to the sponge.** In a medium bowl, whisk together the bread flour (reserve 1/4 cup if mixing by hand), whole wheat flour, and yeast. Sprinkle this on top of the sponge and cover it tightly with plastic wrap. Allow it to ferment for 1 to 4 hours at room temperature. (During this time the sponge will bubble through the flour mixture in places; this is fine.)

3 > **Mix the dough.**

Mixer Method
Add the oil and mix with the dough hook on low speed (#2 if using a KitchenAid) until the flour is moistened enough to form a rough dough. Scrape down any bits

of dough. Cover the bowl with plastic wrap and allow the dough to rest for 20 minutes.

Sprinkle on the salt and knead the dough on medium speed (#4 KitchenAid) for 7 minutes. It will be smooth and shiny and cling slightly to your fingers. If it is still very sticky, knead in a little flour. If it is not at all sticky, spray it with a little water and knead in it. (It will weigh about 17 ounces/490 grams.) Allow the dough to rest for 10 minutes.

Turn the dough out onto a lightly floured counter and roll it into a rectangle about 9 inches by 14 inches. Sprinkle with the chopped almonds and cut-up figs. Roll up the dough and knead it for a few minutes to incorporate the almonds and figs evenly. Shape it into a ball.

Hand Method

Add the oil and salt and, with a wooden spoon or your hand, mix until the flour is moistened. Knead the dough in the bowl until it comes together, then scrape it onto a lightly floured counter. Knead the dough for 5 minutes, enough to develop the gluten structure a little, adding as little of the reserved 1/4 cup of flour as possible to keep it from sticking. Use a bench scraper to scrape the dough and gather it together as you knead it. At this point, it will be very sticky. Cover it with the inverted bowl and allow it to rest for 20 minutes. (This resting time will make the dough less sticky and easier to work with.)

Knead the dough for another 5 minutes or until it is very smooth and elastic. It should still be moist enough to cling slightly to your fingers. If it is very sticky, add some of the remaining reserved flour, or a little extra. (The dough will weigh about 17 ounces/490 grams.) Allow the dough to rest for 10 minutes.

Roll the dough into a rectangle about 9 inches by 14 inches, and sprinkle with the almonds and cut-up figs. Roll up the dough and knead it for a few minutes to incorporate the almonds and figs evenly. Shape it into a ball.

Both Methods

4 > **Let the dough rise.** Set the dough in a 4-quart dough-rising container or bowl, lightly greased with cooking spray or oil. Press down the dough and lightly spray or oil the top. Cover the container with a lid or plastic wrap. With a piece of tape, mark the side of the container at approximately where double the height of the dough would be. Allow the dough to rise (ideally at 75° to 80°F) until doubled, about 1 1/2 hours.

Using an oiled spatula or dough scraper, scrape the dough out into a floured counter, and press down on it gently to form a rectangle. Fold the dough into a tight package or give it 2 business letter turns, and set it back in the container. Oil the surface again, cover, and mark where double the height of the dough would now be. It will fill the container fuller than before because it is puffier with air. Allow the dough to rise until doubled, about 1 hour.

Almonds and Apricot Glaze

INGREDIENTS	MEASURE	WEIGHT	
	volume	ounces	grams
sliced almonds	1 cup	2.6 ounces	75 grams

Apricot Glaze

INGREDIENTS	MEASURE	WEIGHT	
	volume	ounces	grams
apricot jelly	3 tablespoons	1.75 ounces	50 grams
water	2 tablespoons	1 ounce	30 grams

5 > Shape the dough, encrust it with almonds, and let it rise. Turn the dough out onto a lightly floured counter and press down on it gently to flatten it slightly. Round the dough into a 4 1/2-inch ball (see page 65) and lightly spray or brush the surface with water. Scatter the almonds on a counter. Roll the ball of dough in the almonds to cover it completely, pressing the nuts into the dough. Firmly push the whole fig, pointed end down, into the center so that it is submerged as deeply as possible into the dough. The loaf will measure 5 inches by 2 1/2 inches high.

Place it on the baking sheet or the La Cloche base. Cover it with a large container, or cover loosely with oiled plastic wrap. Let the dough rise until doubled, about 1 hour to 1 hour and 15 minutes. It will be about 5 1/2 inches by 3 inches high, and when it is pressed gently with a fingertip, the depression will very slowly fill in. Press any remaining almonds into the empty spaces created by the dough's expansion.

6 > Preheat the oven. Preheat the oven to 425°F, or 450°F if using La Cloche, 1 hour before baking. Have an oven shelf at the lowest level and place an oven stone or baking sheet on before preheating. If using La Cloche, preheat the dome along with the oven.

7 > Bake the bread. If using La Cloche, carefully place the hot dome onto the base and quickly but gently set it on the hot stone or hot baking sheet. Bake for 10 minutes. Lower the temperature to 400°F and continue baking for 30 to 35 minutes or until the bread is golden brown and a skewer inserted in the middle comes out clean (an instant-read thermometer inserted into the center will read about 190°F).

Alternatively, quickly but gently set the baking sheet on the hot stone or hot baking sheet. Bake for 5 minutes. Lower the temperature to 375°F and continue baking for 35 to 40 minutes or until the bread is golden brown and a skewer inserted into the middle comes out clean (an instant-read thermometer inserted into the center will read about 190°F.) If the nuts begin to brown, tent the loaf loosely with aluminum foil. Halfway through baking, turn the pan around for even baking.

8 > **Glaze the bread.** Meanwhile, in a small saucepan, mix the apricot jelly and water together. Bring to a boil and simmer for 1 to 2 minutes, stirring constantly. With a spoon, press the preserves through a strainer to make a smooth glaze.

When the bread is done, remove it from the oven and brush it with the hot apricot glaze. Return it to the oven for 1 minute to set the glaze.

9 > **Cool the bread.** Remove the bread from the oven and transfer it to a wire rack to cool completely.

ULTIMATE FULL FLAVOR VARIATION

For the best flavor development, in Step 2, allow the sponge to ferment for 1 hour at room temperature, then refrigerate it for 8 to 24 hours. If using the hand mixing method, remove it from the refrigerator about 1 hour before mixing the dough.)

POINTERS FOR SUCCESS

> *Unbleached* all-purpose flour could be used for this bread, but I prefer bread flour, which produces a crumb with a chewier texture, more compatible with the texture of the figs and nuts.

> *Slivered almonds* are thicker than sliced almonds and when chopped offer a coarser texture to the crumb. They are easier to chop than whole almonds, which also work well. If unblanched, meaning the nuts still have their brown skin, they add a little more flavor. Sliced almonds make the most beautiful decoration for the outside of the loaf.

THE DOUGH PERCENTAGE

Flour:	100% (bread: **77.9%**, whole wheat: **22.1%**)
Water:	54.5%
Yeast:	0.98%
Salt:	2.6%
Oil:	2.8

Walnut Fougasse

I developed the recipe for this traditional French ladder or lattice-shaped bread many years ago. With the availability of instant yeast, I changed the method of making the sponge, which is now very easy to prepare. The resulting bread, crisp, deeply walnutty, dense, and chewy, is identical to that produced with the original laborious and traditional method of proofing a biscuit-dough–consistency sponge by floating it in a bowl of warm water until it rises.

This bread is moist and full-flavored eaten by itself, and it is a fabulous complement to Roquefort cheese and Sauternes or port.

TIME SCHEDULE

Starter: Straight Dough Method
Rising Time: 1 1/2 hours
Oven Temperature: 425°F
Baking Time: 20 to 25 minutes

Makes: a 15-by-10-by-1 1/4-inch-high loaf
1 pound, 9 to 9.6 ounces/740 to 760 grams

INGREDIENTS	MEASURE	WEIGHT	
	volume	ounces	grams
unbleached all-purpose flour (use only Gold Medal, King Arthur, or Pillsbury)	3 cups plus a scant 1/4 cup	1 pound	454 grams
instant yeast (see page 561 for brands)	1 3/4 teaspoons	--	5.6 grams
salt	1/2 tablespoon	0.3 ounce	10 grams
skim milk scalded and cooled to room temperature or warm	1 1/4 liquid cups	10.3 ounces	295 grams
walnut oil	1/2 liquid cup, divided	3.75 ounces	107 grams
walnuts, coarsely broken	3/4 cup	2.6 ounces	75 grams

EQUIPMENT:

a half sheet pan OR a baking sheet at least 15 inches long;

a baking stone OR baking sheet.

1 > Mix the dough.

Mixer Method

In the mixer bowl, whisk together the flour, and yeast. Then whisk in the salt, (this keeps the yeast from coming in direct contact with the salt, which would kill it). With the dough hook on low speed (#2 if using a KitchenAid), add the milk and 2 tablespoons of the oil, then mix for about 1 minute, until the flour is moistened enough to form a rough dough. On medium speed (#4 KitchenAid), knead the dough for 7 minutes. The dough should be very elastic and just barely tacky (sticky). Allow the dough to rest, covered, for 15 minutes.

    Empty the dough onto a counter and knead in the walnuts. If the dough is sticky, knead in a little flour. (The dough will weigh almost 2 pounds/858 grams.)

Hand Method

In a medium bowl, whisk all but 1/4 cup of the flour together with the yeast. Then whisk in the salt (this prevents the yeast from coming in direct contact with the salt, which would kill it). With a wooden spoon or your hand, mix in the walnuts, the milk, and 2 tablespoons of the oil until the flour is moistened. Knead the dough in the bowl until it comes together, then scrape it onto a lightly floured counter. Knead the dough for 5 minutes, enough to develop the gluten structure a little, adding as little of the reserved flour as possible to keep it from sticking. Use a bench scraper to scrape the dough and gather it together as you knead it. At this point, it will be very sticky. Cover it with the inverted bowl and allow it to rest for 20 minutes. (This rest will make the dough less sticky and easier to work with.)

    Knead the dough for another 5 minutes or until it is very smooth and elastic and no longer sticky. If necessary, add some of the remaining reserved flour, or a little extra. (The dough will weigh almost 2 pounds/858 grams.)

Both Methods

2 > Let the dough rise. Coat a 2-quart dough-rising container or bowl with 2 tablespoons of the remaining walnut oil. Roll the dough in the container to coat all sides.

Push down the dough and cover the container with a lid or plastic wrap. With a piece of tape, mark the side of the container at approximately where double the height of the dough would be. Allow the dough to rise (ideally at 75° to 80°F) until doubled, 45 minutes to 1 hour.

Turn the dough out onto a counter and gently press down on it to flatten it. Knead in another tablespoon of the oil. Return it to the oiled container, cover, and mark where double the height of the dough would now be. (It will fill the container fuller than before because it is puffier with air.) Allow the dough to rise a second time until doubled, 30 to 45 minutes.

Again turn the dough out onto the counter and gently press down on it to flatten it. Knead in another tablespoon of the oil. Return it to the oiled container, cover, and mark the side again. Allow it to rise a third time until doubled, about 30 minutes.

3 > Preheat the oven. Preheat the oven to 425°F 1 hour before baking. Have an oven shelf at the lowest level and place an oven stone or baking sheet on it before preheating.

4 > Shape the dough and let it rise. Turn the dough out onto a lightly floured counter and gently pat or roll it into a rectangle. Give it a business letter turn, cover it with plastic wrap, and allow it to rest for 30 minutes or until relaxed and extensible (when you pull it gently, it will stretch without tearing).

With a pastry brush or plastic wrap, coat the baking sheet with 1 tablespoon of the remaining oil. Set the dough on it and, with your fingers or a rolling pin, press out the dough to an oval about 9 inches by 15 inches by 1/2 inch thick. Brush it with the remaining tablespoon of walnut oil. With a sharp knife, score 7 diagonal slashes about 3 inches long and 2 inches apart, 3 on either side and 1 at the bottom, radiating around the bread. Use scissors to cut through to the bottom of the pan. With your fingers, push the slashes open wide. Allow the dough to rise for about 15 minutes or until it is 3/4 inch high. If the openings have closed a little, stretch them open again.

5 > Bake the bread. Set the baking sheet on the hot stone or hot baking sheet. Bake the fougasse for 20 to 25 minutes or until crisp and golden brown (an instant-read thermometer inserted into the center will read about 212°F). Halfway through baking, turn the pan around for even baking.

6 > Cool the bread. Remove the pan from the oven. Use a large pancake turner to loosen the bread and lift it from the pan to a wire rack to cool completely.

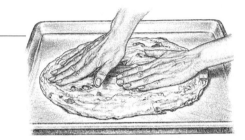

1> Pressing out the dough

2> Slashing the dough

3> Cutting open the slashes with scissors

4> Stretching open the cuts

POINTERS FOR SUCCESS

> Be sure the walnut oil is fresh; it turns rancid easily. Always store the oil in the refrigerator, where it will keep for months.

> In place of the skim milk, you can substitute 1 cup plus 2 tablespoons (9.3 ounces/266 grams) of warm water and 1/3 cup (50 grams) *gappe*, the browned milk

solids from clarified butter, or 1/4 cup (about 1.5 ounces/40 grams) dry milk, preferably nonfat. If you don't have a full 1/3 cup of *gappe*, add just a tablespoon, in addition to the skimmed milk, for extra impact.

> If you prefer less oil, use a total of 1/3 cup (2.5 ounces/72 grams). The bread will be a little less compact and moist. When using *gappe*, if there is still butterfat clinging to it, I use 1 tablespoon less oil (i.e., 7 tablespoons).

> The flavor and texture of this bread actually improves after standing for 6 to 18 hours.

UNDERSTANDING

A high proportion of yeast is used to compensate for the yeast-retarding effect of the oil.

The walnuts are not toasted because if they were, those on the surface would overbrown and become bitter.

An all-purpose flour on the lower protein side is best for this bread, because it is dense. A higher-protein flour would make it undesirably chewy.

The optional *gappe*, the browned milk solids (protein) resulting from clarified butter, contributes a special richness of flavor. It also compensates for the tendency of the high amount of oil to slow down the rising of the dough. Skim milk will serve the same purpose, but it will not contribute much flavor.

This bread is baked soon after shaping, resulting in its unique texture. Despite the large amount of oil, the bread is not at all greasy.

This bread loses a lot more weight on baking than most because of the large surface area for evaporation.

THE DOUGH PERCENTAGE

Flour:	100%
Water:	58.6%
Yeast:	1.2%
Salt:	2.2%
Oil:	15.9% to 22.9%

Walnut Onion Bread

The dough for this bread, originating in southern Burgundy, France, is practically identical to that for Walnut Fougasse (page 416). The only difference is that this dough uses only half the walnut oil and includes chopped onion. But the texture is entirely different, because of the smaller amount of oil and because this loaf is allowed to have the usual full rise, rather than baking it 15 minutes after shaping. As a result, instead of a dense chewy bread, it's a moist, light, almost cake-like loaf.

TIME SCHEDULE

Starter: straight dough method
Rising Time: about 1 1/2 hours
Oven Temperature: 400°F (if using La Cloche, 425°F, then 400°F)
Baking Time: 30 to 35 minutes

Makes a 12 1/2-by-5-by-3 1/4-inn high loaf/
1 3/4 pounds/807 grams

INGREDIENTS	MEASURE	WEIGHT	
	volume	ounces	grams
unbleached all-purpose flour (use only Gold Medal, King Arthur, or Pillsbury)	2 3/4 cups plus 1 tablespoon	14 ounces	400 grams
instant yeast (see page 561 for brands)	1/2 tablespoon	--	4.8 grams
salt	1/2 tablespoon	--	10 grams
skimmed milk (scalded and cooled to room temperature or warm) or water (room temperature or warm) plus dried milk, preferably non-fat	1 liquid cup or 1 cup 1/4 cup	8.5 ounces 8.3 ounces 1.5 ounces	242 grams 236 grams 40 grams
walnut oil or olive oil	1/4 cup	about 1.75 ounces	54 grams
walnuts, coarsely broken	3/4 cup	2.6 ounces	75 grams
onion, finely chopped	1/2 cup	2.5 ounces	70 grams
Optional: cornmeal	about 2 teaspoons	--	--

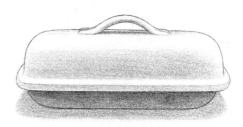

La Cloche Italian Bread Baker OR a baking sheet, either one lined with a nonstick liner such as Silpain or parchment, or sprinkled with flour or cornmeal;

a baking stone OR baking sheet

1 > Mix the dough.

Mixer Method

In the mixer bowl, whisk together the flour and yeast. Then whisk in the salt (this keeps the yeast from coming in direct contact with the salt, which would kill it.) Make a well in the center and add the milk and oil. (If using dry milk, add it to the flour, and pour the water into the well.) With the dough hook, mix on low speed (#2 if using a KitchenAid) for about 1 minute, until the flour is moistened. On medium speed (#4 KitchenAid), knead for 7 minutes. The dough should be very elastic and bounce back when pressed with a fingertip, but still moist enough to cling slightly to your fingers. If it is still very sticky, knead in a little flour. If it is not at all sticky, spray it with a little water and knead it. (The dough will weigh about 1 pound, 9 1/4 ounces/721 grams.)

Hand Method

In a medium bowl, whisk together 2 1/3 cups (11.7 ounces/330 grams) of the flour and the yeast. Then whisk in the salt (this keeps the yeast from coming in direct contact with the salt, which could kill it.) Add the milk and oil. (If using dry milk, add it to the flour, and pour the water into the well.) Using a wooden spoon or your hand, gradually mix the liquid into the flour. Knead the dough in the bowl until it comes together, then scrape it onto a lightly floured counter. Knead the dough for 5 minutes, just to begin to develop the gluten structure, adding as little of the remaining flour as possible. Use a bench scraper to scrape the dough and gather it together as you knead it. At this point, it will be very sticky. Cover it with the inverted bowl and allow it to rest for 20 minutes. (This resting time will make the dough less sticky and easier to work with.)

Knead the dough for another 5 minutes or until it is very smooth and elastic but moist enough to cling slightly to your fingers. If necessary, add some of the remaining reserved flour, or a little extra. (The dough will weigh about 1 pound, 9 1/4 ounces/721 grams.)

Both Methods

2 > Let the dough rise. Using an oiled spatula or dough scraper, scrape the dough into a 2-quart dough-rising container or bowl, lightly greased with cooking spray or oil. Push down the dough and lightly spray or oil the top. Cover the container with a lid or plastic wrap. With a piece of tape, mark the side of the container at approximately where double the height of the dough would be. Allow the dough to rise (ideally at 75° to 80°F) until doubled, 1 1/2 to 2 hours.

Using an oiled spatula or dough scraper, scrape the dough onto a floured counter, and press down on it gently to form a large rectangle. Sprinkle on the walnuts and onions. Roll up the dough and knead it to incorporate these ingredients, adding a little more flour to keep it from sticking. The dough should still feel tacky (a little sticky). (It will weigh about 885 grams/31 ounces.)

3 > Preshape the dough and let it rest. Move the dough onto a freshly floured clean area of the counter and gently pat it into a rectangle. Shape it into a log by rolling the top edge down to the middle, then pushing it back slightly with your thumbs. Repeat this rolling motion 2 more times, ending with the seam at the bottom edge of the dough. Use a bench scraper to move it to another freshly floured clean area of the counter, seam side down. Cover it with oiled plastic wrap and allow it to sit for about 30 minutes or until relaxed and extensible (when you pull it gently, it stretches without tearing).

4 > Shape the dough and let it rise. Press or roll the dough into a rectangle and shape it into a 10-inch-long torpedo-shaped loaf (batard; see page 69). Set it onto the La Cloche bottom or the prepared baking sheet and cover it with a large container, or cover loosely with oiled plastic. Let the dough rise until almost doubled, 30 minutes to an hour. It will be about 11 inches by 4 1/2 inches by 2 1/2 inches high, and when it is pressed gently with a fingertip, the depression will very slowly fill in.

5 > Preheat the oven. Preheat the oven to 400°F, or 425°F if using La Cloche, 1 hour before baking time. Have an oven shelf at the lowest level and place a baking stone or baking sheet on it before preheating. If not using La Cloche, place a cast-iron skillet or sheet pan on the floor of the oven to preheat. If using La Cloche, preheat the top along with the oven.

6 > Slash and bake the bread. With a sharp knife or single-edged razor blade, make three 1/4- to 1/2-inch deep diagonal slashes in the top of the dough (see page 81).

If using La Cloche, carefully place the hot Cloche top onto the base and quickly but gently set it on the hot stone or hot baking sheet. Bake for 10 minutes. Lower the temperature to 400°F and bake for 10 minutes. Remove the cover and continue baking for 10 to 15 minutes, or until the bread is golden brown and a skewer inserted into the middle comes out clean (an instant-read thermometer inserted into the center will read about 212°F).

Alternatively, mist the dough with water and quickly but gently set the baking sheet on the hot stone or hot baking sheet. Toss 1/2 cup of ice cubes into the pan beneath and immediately shut the door. Bake for 30 to 35 minutes or until golden brown and a skewer inserted in the middle comes out clean (an instant read thermometer inserted into the center will read about 212°F). Halfway through baking, turn the pan around for even baking.

7 > **Cool the bread.** Remove the bread from the oven, and transfer it to a wire rack to cool completely.

> Be sure that the walnut oil has the sweet pleasant aroma of walnuts and is not rancid.

> If you prefer, the onions can be omitted; in that case, no flour will be required when kneading in the walnuts.

UNDERSTANDING

The oil and high moisture content give this bread an almost cake-like tenderness. You could use 2 1/2 cups of bread flour in place of the all-purpose, but the bread will be less tender and more chewy.

A high proportion of yeast is used to compensate for the yeast-retarding effect of the oil.

The walnuts are not toasted because if they were, those on the surface would overbrown and become bitter.

THE DOUGH PERCENTAGE

Flour:	100%
Water:	69% (includes the water in the onions)
Yeast:	1.2%
Salt:	2.5%
Oil:	13%

6.

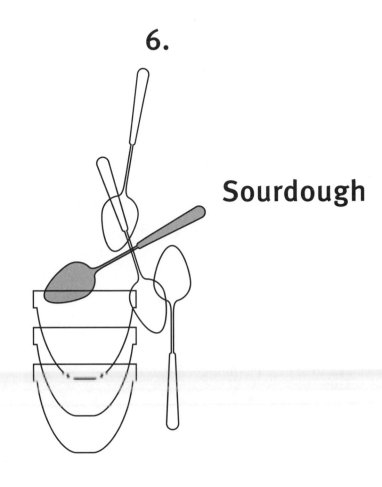

Sourdough

SOURDOUGH BREAD IS THE SOUL OF ARTISAN HEARTH BREAD, THE WELLSPRING or ancestor of all yeast bread.

Sourdough bread is bread that is made from a starter (pre-ferment), a mixture of flour, water, and yeast that flavors the bread and makes it rise. A sourdough starter often is cultured from wild yeast and the bacteria present on the flour. The starter produces a bread that is high in natural acidity, giving the bread a distinctive tang and a crumb that is moist but does not mold readily.

I wasn't intending to include sourdough made with noncommercial yeast starter in this book. It seemed too difficult and unpredictable. I also feared making my readers become prisoners to a feeding (yeast-refreshing) schedule of flour and water needed to keep the fermenting starter alive. My editor was surprised and disappointed at my decision, but it was my father who protested with indignation, saying that the book would not be complete without it. I argued that I wanted the predictability of commercial yeast to fit in with my own often erratic schedule and the busy lifestyles of my readers as well. I even had myself convinced that I enjoyed the subtlety of the bread produced by using the commercial sourdough starters such as Lalvain dry sourdough starter every bit as much as any artisan sourdough I had ever tasted. I went so far as to insist that I felt more than satisfied with the complexity and flavors offered by pre-ferments that are far quicker than sourdough, such as biga, poolish, and the simple sponge, because sourdough bread usually tasted too sour. But now that I have succeeded in coaxing wild yeast and favorable bacteria out of what seems like thin air into my bread, and produced a stable and mature starter for the first time, I recommend that every bread baker experience the thrill of watching a mixture of flour and water ferment into an starter that can cause a loaf of bread to rise. It is the final frontier, the Zen of bread making.

Making your own successful starter is really very simple. All you need is some organic rye flour (from the health food store), bread flour, unchlorinated water (let your tap water sit for 6 hours uncovered if it smells like chlorine, or use bottled water to be on the safe side), patience, and time. It takes about a week to achieve a starter that has an adequate population of yeast together with a good balance of flavorful friendly bacteria (from the environment), and another two weeks until it is fully mature and able to be the sole leavening of your bread.

One of the great benefits of a sourdough bread, including one made with a commercial sourdough starter, is that because of the acidity of the starter, even on the fifth day after baking, the bread is moist and its flavor still potent. This is not the case with most other yeast breads. But the major benefit is that the flavor of a sourdough bread is not merely sour: it is multidimensional and complex. The word that came to me when I tasted the first bread produced from my newly created sourdough starter was *beguiling*. I was hooked. Sourdough bread from my own starter is now a permanent part of my bread repertoire. And it is not at all difficult to maintain the starter. Perhaps the only difficult part is throwing out the ever-present excess starter, because as the starter is fed (refreshed) with flour and water to keep it alive and active, it continues to grow and expand to a far greater quantity than is practical, especially for home baking. Every time I send excess active starter down the drain, I feel a pang of regret.

Homemade sourdough bread has a distinctly sour flavor, but it doesn't have to be overpoweringly sour. The degree of acidity in your bread depends on how often you refresh the starter and what percentage of the starter you use in the bread dough (usually between 15 and 40 percent). I've come to appreciate a more sour flavor on occasion, particularly with a strong flavorful cheese, such as Gorgonzola, because the bread's assertive flavor enables it to hold its own and not be overpowered.

Maintaining a sourdough culture takes only a few minutes once a week. Starting the culture, however, takes about a week. The growing starter needs to be fed at specific and often difficult to predict intervals. If you do not have the sort of schedule that allows you to be present during as much of this first week as would be necessary, purchase a starter (see Sources, page 572) or adopt one from a friend (there's always more than enough to share). If you do decide to make your own, you will increase your chances of creating a successful starter by cultivating it during a cool time of year, as cool temperatures attract the most desirable type of bacteria. Once the starter is established, usually by the fifth day, it no longer needs to be kept at cooler temperatures. (The fifth day of my starter's life, when I heard it explode out of the Ball jar because the plastic wrap was too tight, was a moment I will always treasure—because it was then that I knew for sure it was alive.)

The great fallacy of sourdough, however, is that many people feel they are bringing an organism to life, that is more "natural" than commercial yeast. *All yeast is natural*: it is never a synthesized product. The difference between "wild" yeast and "domesticated" (commercial) yeast is that the commercial yeast is harvested from a specific strain, derived from the brewing industry, and is therefore more hardy and consistent. Many strains of wild yeast reside on the particles of flour, particularly organic rye flour, in great abundance. In fact, a single gram (about 1/28 of an ounce) of flour contains about 13,000 wild yeast cells and about 320 lactic bacteria cells.

For me, the most fascinating aspect of sourdough culture is the symbiotic relationship between the wild yeast and the lactic bacteria, called *lactobacilli*. These bacteria are responsible for converting maltose, a complex sugar formed by the enzyme action on the starch in the flour, into a variety of acids, primarily lactic acid and acetic acid. Because all acids taste sour, these acids are largely responsible for the special flavor of sourdough bread. The wild yeast can coexist in perfect harmony with the lactobacilli because unlike commercial yeast, wild yeast can survive in this acid environment. Also unlike commercial yeast, wild yeast cannot metabolize maltose, so it consumes other sugars present in the flour and ignores the maltose vital to the life of the lactobacilli. It is this balance and interplay of yeast and bacteria that is responsible for the unique flavor and texture of a sourdough bread.

If you like the pronounced tangy taste and complexity of a wild yeast sourdough bread and enjoy the unpredictability in rising time, you will delight in the drama of creating and maintaining a sourdough culture. And, after all, what wild creature is totally predictable?!

The lactobacilli, beyond being fundamental to the production of a sourdough culture, are also responsible for maintaining the health of a mature sourdough culture, by producing an antibiotic that protects it from contamination by other harmful bacteria. These harmful bacteria, which can form at the earlier stages of a developing (immature) starter, produce streaks of color. If this happens, the starter should be thrown out.

When making a bread using only a wild yeast starter, the minimum amount of starter required to raise the dough is 15 percent of the entire weight of the dough. If you like a very sour flavor, you can use up to 40 percent. (Over 40 percent, and the acidity will compromise the strength of the gluten, resulting in a dense, flat loaf.) If you prefer a less sour flavor, another way to achieve this while maintaining much of the flavor complexity is to increase the amount of flour and water used to refresh and strengthen the starter prior to baking. Normally I increase (expand) the starter by eight times its original weight before using it each time.

A wild yeast starter will always raise the dough more slowly than a commercial starter, because there is a far smaller concentration of yeast in the sourdough culture. (There are about two hundred billion yeast cells in just a tablespoon of commercial dry yeast, compared to nearly a billion in a whole cup of sourdough culture.) This slow rise is part of what creates interesting and complex flavors. My basic sourdough bread making schedule is about 36 hours from start to finish, but 95 percent of this is waiting time and requires no active participation. For example, if I want to have sourdough for dinner on Wednesday night, I take my starter out of the refrigerator first thing Tuesday morning. I feed it flour and water and remove part of it to store for the next batch. I allow the starter for the bread to sit until doubled, usually about

8 hours. I feed it a second time and allow it to sit in a cool spot overnight until at least doubled. (At 75°F, it will take about 6 hours, but it can sit for 12 hours before beginning to deflate. If I don't plan to mix the dough within 12 hours, I refrigerate it—for up to 24 hours is fine—and remove it 1 hour before mixing the dough. If I want to go to bed and it hasn't yet doubled, I set it in a cool area, 55° to 60°F, until the next morning.) On Wednesday morning I mix the dough. The first rising takes about 6 hours (this is for the basic sourdough bread—others, such as the pumpernickel, may take longer). I then shape the bread and set it to rise a second time, about 3 hours. Baking takes 30 minutes and cooling about 1 hour. (If I want to save the baked bread until the following day, I put it in a brown paper bag after it is cooled and fold over the opening. When I am ready to eat it, I crisp the crust by setting it on the oven rack in a preheated 350°F oven for about 10 minutes, slice it, and eat it warm.)

If you find this process difficult to fit into your schedule, you can change it by either slowing it down by chilling the dough, known as *retarding*, or speeding it up by adding a small amount of commercial yeast. Retarding the dough also develops a more complex and sour flavor and slightly increases volume.

Retarding or chilling the dough

A shaped loaf can be refrigerated before baking, following either of two different time schedules:

1> Allow the shaped loaf to rise at warm room temperature (75° to 80°F) for 1 hour. Then refrigerate it for up to 24 hours. Remove it to room temperature 3 hours before baking and let stand until it has almost doubled.

2> Allow the loaf to rise at warm room temperature (75° to 80°F) for 3 to 4 hours or until it has almost doubled (when pressed gently with a fingertip, the depression will very slowly fill in). Then refrigerate it for up to 24 hours. Remove 30 minutes before baking.

Adding Commercial Instant Yeast

It is possible to speed up the rising process of a sourdough by about 25 percent without sacrificing flavor or acidity by adding no more than 0.06 percent of the total weight of the flour (this includes the flour in the starter) in commercial instant yeast. This comes to 1/16 teaspoon/0.2 gram for the average 17.5-ounce/500-gram loaf. (For professional bakers who may use cake yeast instead of the dry instant yeast, the equivalent amount of yeast to add is 0.2 percent of the total weight of the flour. It is equal to one-seventh the amount of yeast normally used in the recipe.)

For a recipe using a total of about 2 cups (10.6 ounces/300 grams) bread flour, add 1/16 teaspoon (0.2 gram) instant yeast.

You must add the yeast after the first 3 minutes of kneading the dough. If you add it too soon, the acidity in the sourdough starter might kill the commercial yeast. On the other hand, if you add too much commercial yeast, it will raise the pH level of the dough (make it more alkaline and less acid), resulting in a less sour bread.

POINTERS FOR SUCCESS FOR MAKING A SOURDOUGH STARTER

>   Use organic rye or organic whole wheat flour. (Organic white flour will also work, but the process will be much slower.)

>   Use unchlorinated water (bottled water is fine).

>   Have everything that will touch the starter spotlessly clean (including your hands) so as not to contaminate it. (Once the starter is active, it will be much more resistant to contamination.)

>   During culturing, the starter will give off many aromas, including cheese, citrus/tangerine, apple, and, when fully mature, fresh paint. If streaks of color appear, however, the starter is contaminated. Throw it out and start again.

NOTE   If you can't be home during the first week and still want to make your own starter, a less exacting method that may also work is to feed the starter every 12 hours for about 5 days, pouring off and throwing out some of it when the jar gets too full. If it doubles in 12 hours, it is active and ready to use.)

MAKING A SOURDOUGH STARTER (LEVAIN) FROM SCRATCH

EQUIPMENT

a 4-cup glass canning jar OR 4-cup glass measuring cup;

large heavy plastic spoon OR clean wooden spoon;

plastic wrap

INGREDIENTS

organic rye flour or organic whole wheat flour; bread flour; and bottled water

Days 1 through 5

DAY 1

In an immaculately clean bowl, combine **a scant cup/4.2 ounces/120 grams organic rye flour** and **1/2 cup/4.2 ounces/120 grams bottled water**. With a clean hand or spoon, stir until the flour is moistened and a stiff dough is formed. If there are still loose flour particles after 2 minutes, add more water by the droplet. Scrape the starter into the 4-cup container. You will have about 1 cup/8.5 ounces/240 grams. Cover it tightly with plastic wrap (it's fine to use the ring that screws onto the canning jar to keep the plastic wrap in place) and place it in a cool area (65°F) for 48 hours. (If you don't have a cool area, let it sit for only 24 hours [until Day 2] and feed it the same way as described for Day 3.)

DAY 2

There will be no visible change in the color or texture of the starter.

DAY 3

The consistency of the starter will now resemble a thick pancake batter and there may be a few bubbles in the surface. With a clean spoon, remove and throw out about half of the starter (about 1/2 cup/4.25 ounces/120 grams).

Stir in: **a scant 1/2 cup/about 2 ounces/60 grams bread flour** and **1/4 liquid cup/about 2 ounces/60 grams bottled water.**

You will again have 8.5 ounces/240 grams of starter, but it will have expanded in volume from just under 8 fluid ounces to about 10 fluid ounces. Cover again tightly with plastic wrap and leave at room temperature (70° to 75°F) for 24 hours. (After 12 hours, the starter may have increased by one and a half, to 14 fluid ounces, and have lots of bubbles. Don't be concerned if it then deflates and falls.)

DAY 4

The starter may give off a faint citrus aroma. With a clean spoon, again scoop and throw out about half of the starter (about 1/2 cup/4.25 ounces/120 grams).

Stir in: **a scant 1/2 cup/about 2 ounces/60 grams bread flour** and **1/4 liquid cup/about 2 ounces/60 grams bottled water.**

You will again have 8.5 ounces/240 grams of starter, about 10 fluid ounces in volume. Cover it with plastic wrap, but not tightly, as gases should now be forming that need to escape. Leave it at room temperature (70° to 75°F) for 24 hours.

DAY 5

If the starter is active, it will have increased in volume to at least 3 cups, or even 4 cups. It will dome and then start to recede. (If it is not yet at this point, continue throwing out half the starter and feeding it with the **scant 1/2 cup/about 2 ounces/60 grams bread flour** and **1/4 liquid cup/about 2 ounces/60 grams bottled water** every 24 hours until it reaches this state of activity.)

With a clean spoon, again remove and throw out about half of the starter (about 1/2 cup/4.25 ounces/120 grams).

Stir in: **a scant 1/2 cup/about 2 ounces/60 grams bread flour** and **1/4 liquid cup/about 2 ounces/60 grams bottled water.**

You will now have about 1 cup/8.5 ounces/240 grams of active starter. (You may feel the impulse to give it a name. Give in to it: I named mine Billo.) Cover it with plastic wrap and let it sit at warm room temperature (75 to 80°F) for about 4 hours or until it has almost doubled. You can now "expand" it (feed with flour and water) for baking bread or refrigerate it overnight and start expanding it the next day. If you don't plan to use it for several days, feed it again to double it, let it sit for 1 hour, and then refrigerate it.

This starter will mature over the next few weeks, gaining in strength and flavor. For the first 2 weeks, store at least 1 cup (8.5 ounces/240 grams) of it and feed it at least three times a week. After 2 weeks of regular feeding (equal weights flour and water or, by volume, 1 1/2 times flour to water, to at least double it; when the jar gets half-full, pour off half), at least three times a week, the culture is mature and bread made from it will be more mellow and complex. You can now switch to once-a-week feeding if you only make bread once a week.

Once your starter is mature, all you need to store is enough for 1 or 2 loaves plus enough to start the next batch (about a full 3/4 cup/7 ounces/200 grams). If you plan to bake in larger quantities, simply increase the amount you store by throwing out less of it before each feeding.

Stiff starter versus liquid starter

Once the starter is active (after Day 5), you have the choice at any point thereafter of storing it as a liquid sourdough starter or a stiff sourdough starter.

To convert this liquid starter to a stiff starter, add 3/4 cup/(4.25 ounces/120 grams) flour to 1 cup/8.5 ounces/240 grams of the liquid starter. With a wooden spoon, stir the starter until all the flour is incorporated. Empty it into a bowl and knead it for about 2 minutes. If it is sticky, knead in more flour until it is very firm. If, after 2 minutes, it is too dry and crumbly, add water by the droplet. It is best to make it very stiff, because the acidity in the starter will cause it to soften as it stands and it will stick to your fingers when you are ready to use it to make the bread. Set this stiff starter in an oiled container with a lid. Grease the top of the dough with cooking spray or oil and cover it tightly. Store at room temperature or refrigerate it.

I prefer a stiff starter, but this is strictly a matter of personal preference. According to some theories, the yeast in the sourdough starter develops faster in a liquid starter than in a stiff starter, but from my observation, it's neck and neck: a stiff starter rises faster and deflates more slowly. I believe this is because the gluten (protein) structure of the stiff starter supports the rise caused by the carbon dioxide formed as a result of the yeast consuming the sugar in the flour.

Many bakers, including me, feel that a stiff starter produces a less sour flavor than one with a liquid consistency, but others (including my husband—empirically) disagree, arguing that a stiff culture tends to develop more acetic acid, whereas a liquid starter will have a higher production of the milder lactic acid. Some compromise by maintaining a liquid starter, converting it into a stiff starter as necessary the day before mixing dough.

Clearly the perception of sour is highly subjective. But to my mind, the most significant degree of sourness comes more from the specifics of storage, rebuilding, temperature during proofing, and the amount used than from the state of the original starter, stiff or liquid. The degree of sourness of liquid starter compared to stiff starter may also depend on the age of the starter.

A comparison of stiff starter to liquid starter

A stiff starter is one-third water and two-thirds flour by weight (50 percent hydration). This means that 100 grams of stiff starter contain 33.35 grams water and 66.65 grams flour (or 3 times flour to water by volume).

A liquid starter is half water and half flour by weight, or by volume, 1 1/2 times the water in flour (100 percent hydration). This means that 100 grams of liquid starter contain 50 grams water and 50 grams flour.

Since it is the flour component of the starter that feeds the yeast and bacteria, the goal is always to maintain the same amount of flour in the starter. Since a liquid starter has less flour per volume or weight than a stiff starter, more of the liquid starter will be needed to replace it, but the extra water will need to be removed from the rest of the recipe. So to interchange liquid for stiff, or vice versa, you need to increase or decrease the amount of starter to arrive at the same amount of flour and increase or decrease the amount of water called for in the rest of the dough. This means that a recipe using starter equal to 30 percent of the total weight of the flour and water (including what is contained in the starter) will require 5.25 ounces/150 grams of stiff starter or 7 ounces/200 grams of liquid starter.

Here's how to convert a liquid starter to a stiff starter: By weight, if a recipe calls for, for example, 5.25 ounces/150 grams stiff starter, and you have a liquid starter, you will need to increase the amount of starter called for by one and a third times (meaning 7 ounces/200 grams liquid starter) and then remove the amount of extra water you have added (one-quarter of the weight of the liquid starter, which is 1.75 ounces/50 grams) from the rest of the dough. Or to convert it by volume, simply stir flour into the liquid starter a teaspoon at a time. When it becomes stiff enough to touch without sticking to your fingers, knead it with your hand, adding flour until it is no longer sticky.

Here's how to convert a stiff starter to a liquid starter: If a recipe calls for, for example, 7 ounces/200 grams liquid starter, and you have a stiff starter, you will need to decrease the amount of starter by three-quarters (which equals 1.75 ounces/150 grams stiff starter) and add water equal to one-third the weight of the stiff starter (1.7 ounces/50 grams) to the rest of the dough.

Pros and Cons of a Liquid Sourdough Starter

> When changing amount of liquid starter used, it is easy to calculate how much flour and water to add or remove from the rest of the dough since it is equal parts flour and water by weight.

> It is easy to refresh (feed) the liquid starter by stirring the flour and water directly into the starter, rather than having to transfer it to another container and knead it in.

> A liquid starter ferments (cultures) more quickly, but it "burps" and loses gas and is more prone to collapse.

> A liquid starter produces bread with slightly larger holes.

Pros and Cons of a Stiff Sourdough Starter

> It ferments more quickly, but it holds the gases better and is slower to collapse.

> It is less messy, making it easier to measure and work with. Also, it doesn't stick to the bowl or mixing spoon, guaranteeing that all of it is added to the mixture.

> It produces bread with a more golden crumb.

Maintaining (Refreshing) a Sourdough Starter

To feed the yeast in a starter in order to keep it alive, you need to give the starter enough flour and water to at least double its weight or volume. Although cleanliness is always a virtue, once the starter is established, there is far less risk of contamination by other bacteria.

NOTE 1 cup of stiff or (if stirred down) liquid sourdough starter equals 8.5 ounces/240 grams, or about 1 ounce/15 grams per 1 tablespoon. (This is 1 cup in a dry measuring cup; in a glass measure, it may read as more.)

SCHEDULE FOR REFRESHING (FEEDING) A STIFF SOURDOUGH STARTER TO KEEP IT ALIVE

Allow the (refrigerated) starter to sit at room temperature (70° to 80°F) for 1 hour before feeding it. You will be increasing it by 2 1/2 times, from 50 grams to 125 grams.

Remove a **scant 1/4 cup/1.75 ounces/50 grams** of the starter and place it in a small bowl. Discard the rest. Add **1/3 cup/1.75 ounces/50 grams flour** and **1 tablespoon plus 2 teaspoons/1 scant ounce/25 grams water.**

Mix with a wooden spoon and then your hand, or with the paddle attachment of an electric mixer on low speed (#2 if using a KitchenAid) until a smooth dough forms. It should be the consistency of biscuit dough—firm and not sticky to the touch. Adjust it if necessary with a little flour or a few droplets of water. (The starter should be very stiff because the acidity in the starter causes it to soften on standing.)

Transfer the starter to a lightly oiled container with a lid. Lightly oil the surface of the starter.

If planning to feed and store for 1 day before using, let the starter increase in volume by about 1 1/2 times, 2 hours or so, then refrigerate.

If planning to feed and store for 3 days before using, let it increase in volume by about 1 1/4 times, 1 hour or so, then refrigerate.

If planning to store for 1 week before using, let it increase in volume just slightly, about 30 minutes, then refrigerate.

SCHEDULE FOR REFRESHING (FEEDING) A LIQUID SOURDOUGH STARTER TO KEEP IT ALIVE

Because of the sticky nature of a liquid starter, the easiest way to refresh it is by pouring off about half of it and then feeding it equal weights of flour and water to at least double its weight. If you are measuring volume, you will need 1 1/2 times more flour than water (For example, for 1 liquid cup of water, you will need 1 1/2 cups of flour.)

Mix with a firm plastic or wooden spoon until smooth. After several weeks, when the top part of the container gets crusty with dried starter, pour the starter into a clean jar.

TIMETABLE

If planning to feed and store the starter for 1 day before using, let it increase by about 1 1/2 times, 5 hours or so, then refrigerate.

If planning to feed and store the starter for 3 days before using, let it increase by about 1 1/4 times, 3 hours or so, then refrigerate.

If planning to store the starter for 1 week before using, let it increase just slightly, about 1 hour, then refrigerate.

If planning to store the liquid starter for more than a week before using, you should convert it into a stiff starter. *To the 1 cup/8.5 ounces/240 grams of liquid starter, add*

3/4 cup/4.25 ounces/120 grams flour. You can then convert it back into a liquid starter by adding 1/2 cup/4.25 ounces/120 grams water.

OLD STARTERS

A starter is active, and ready to be used, when it will it at least double in size within 8 hours after it is fed. Different starters will reach this point in different amounts of time, but if the starter can't double itself, it surely won't raise your bread. However, if a starter has not been fed, it may still be possible to restore it.

To Revive a Neglected Stiff Sourdough Starter

A stiff starter will probably keep for a month, refrigerated. If longer than that, to restore it to its original potency, you will need to refresh (feed) it in the usual way, throwing out excess and doubling it every 24 hours until it can double in volume in 6 to 8 hours. Until that point, don't feed it more than every 24 hours, because the yeast needs a chance to multiply before the next feeding.

To Revive a Neglected Liquid Sourdough Starter

The standard technique for restoring an old liquid starter is first to pour off the liquid formed on the top (which contains the alcohol "waste" produced by the yeast) and then to throw out all but 20 percent of what remains. Put the remainder in a 1-quart canning jar and feed it equal weights flour and water to double it (by volume, flour is 1 1/2 times water, so for every cup of starter, feed it 3/4 cup flour and 1/2 cup water) every 24 hours. When it comes close to the top of the jar, pour off half and continue feeding it until it will double in volume in 6 to 8 hours.

Expanding a Sourdough Starter for Baking

The stored (refrigerated) starter needs to be fed flour and water to expand (increase) it to at least triple its original size before using it, to keep it from being too acidic. I increase my starter by 8 times in two stages, throwing out some after the first feeding so that I don't end up with a lot more than I need for the amount of the final bread dough (see the recipe on page 444).

Expanding a Stiff Starter

The day before baking, first thing in the morning, give the starter its first feeding so that it can have its second feeding by early afternoon and be ready to use to mix the dough by end of the day, or to rest overnight and be used to mix the dough the next morning. Ideally, you want to use the starter at its peak, when it is active but not deflated. (A stiff starter will stay at its peak for many hours. If the starter is overly mature, most of the sugar in the flour will have been consumed by the yeast, which will result in a paler crust (as there is less sugar to caramelize during baking) and less flavor in the baked bread. If it is not mature enough, there will not be enough yeast, so it will take longer to raise the bread.

Expanding a Liquid Starter

If using a liquid starter, it is practical to do the first feeding 8 hours before the end of the day, then give it the second feeding. It can then ferment and rise overnight at room temperature (70° to 80°F) for about 10 to 12 hours.

HOW TO USE A SOURDOUGH STARTER IN PLACE OF COMMERCIAL YEAST IN OTHER RECIPES

If you enjoy the flavor that a sourdough starter adds to bread, you may want to convert some of your favorite recipes so you can use it instead of commercial yeast.

When adding sourdough starter to a recipe, you are, of course, adding the flour and water, as well as the wild yeast and bacteria, contained in the sourdough, so you need to reduce the amount of flour and water in the rest of the recipe as appropriate and eliminate the commercial yeast (or reduce it to no more than 0.2 percent of the total weight of the flour). When worked out by weight, this is a very easy calculation. (If you have a liquid starter, convert it to a stiff starter.)

In order for the sourdough starter to be about 30 percent of the total flour and water component of the finished dough, you need to:

1 > Total the weights of the flour and water in the recipe.

2 > Multiply the flour and water total by 30 percent to get the amount of starter needed.

3 > Since the starter is one-third water and two-thirds flour (by weight), divide the total amount of starter by 3 to get the amount of water it contains and by 1 1/2 to get the flour. Subtract those amounts from the total water and total flour in the dough.

Flour: 100 grams
Water: 68 grams
Salt: 3.7 grams
Yeast: 0.5 grams

Total flour and water equals 168 grams. The amount of starter at 30 percent of the total flour and water (168 grams) would be 50.4 grams. Round it off to **50 grams. This is the amount of starter to use.**

The 50 grams of starter contains 16.6 grams water and 33.3 grams flour (it's one-third water and two-thirds flour, i.e., 1 part water to 2 parts flour) so those are the amounts you need to remove from the rest of the recipe.

Subtract the 33.3 grams flour from the 100 grams of flour used in the recipe, for a total of **66.7 additional grams flour to be added to the starter.**

Subtract the 16.6 grams from the 68 grams of water used in the recipe, for a total of **51.4 additional grams of water to be added to the starter.**

Eliminate the yeast, and **the salt remains the same.**

(Obviously there is no need to use a sponge starter, as the sourdough starter provides all the flavor needed.) You can also replace the biga (and yeast) in a recipe with equal volume or weight of stiff sourdough starter.

When to Add the Sourdough Starter

If mixing the dough by machine, it is best to mix the rest of the dough, (except the salt) and knead it for 3 minutes, enough to develop the gluten structure a little. Allow it to rest (autolyse) for 20 minutes, then knead in the sourdough starter. Add the salt after the sourdough starter is mixed into the dough, as direct contact with salt is harmful to the yeast. In addition, the salt should be added at the end because it draws water from the dough and causes the dough to become stiffer.

It is best to add the sourdough to the partially kneaded dough for two reasons. One is that the starter has already been kneaded during feeding, so it requires less additional kneading. The other is that the acidity of the starter softens the gluten-forming proteins of the dough, so it's better to give them a chance to develop first.

If mixing the dough by hand, it is easiest to add the starter in the beginning to the liquid in the recipe to break it up. This ensures that it will incorporate it evenly into the dough.

**THE 8 BASIC STEPS IN MAKING SOURDOUGH BREAD FROM
A SOURDOUGH SEED STARTER (CULTURE)**

The basic process of making sourdough bread involves feeding the yeast in a sourdough seed starter a mixture of flour and water to make it active enough to raise the bread. The feeding is referred to as refreshing when you are planning to store the sourdough seed starter for future use. It is referred to as expanding when you are preparing the seed starter to make the sourdough bread.

1   Feed (refresh) some of the sourdough seed starter for future bread.
2   Feed (expand) some of the sourdough seed starter for the bread you are making.
3   Feed (expand) the sourdough seed starter for this bread a second time.
4   Mix the dough.
5   Let the dough rise.
6   Shape the dough and let it rise.
7   Bake the bread.
8   Cool the bread.

POINTERS FOR SUCCESS IN MAKING SOURDOUGH

>   When mixing the dough with the machine method, add a stiff sourdough starter before adding the salt. Once the salt is added, the dough becomes firmer, so the starter would take longer to mix evenly into the rest of the dough.

>   Sourdough is a very sticky dough until the last few minutes of kneading. To prevent sticking, it helps to use your fingertips, not the palms of your hands. Use a bench scraper to scrape the dough and gather it together as you knead it.

>   If measuring instead of weighing a stiff sourdough starter, the dough will measure more in a solid measuring cup than it will in a liquid measuring cup.

> Round bannetons are baskets or containers with air holes used for shaping sourdough loaves while rising, to give the soft, slack dough extra support. They can be beautiful willow baskets from France, unlined or lined with coarse woven cloth, or they can even be plastic baskets or colanders lined with clean kitchen towels. The unlined willow baskets will leave an attractive design on the crust of the bread. It is important to have a container that allows the dough to breathe. Otherwise, the moisture of the dough may cause it to stick to the cloth, and the dough will collapse and deflate when unmolded. The recipes in this chapter all use an 8-inch round banneton. Larger bannetons or colanders can be used for these amounts of dough, but when unmolding the dough before baking, you will need to support the dough with a cardboard round or plate held against its surface so that it doesn't fall several inches, which would make it deflate.

> Bread flour is used for making sourdough bread because it has higher gluten-forming protein content than all-purpose flour and will give more structure to the loaf. The acidity of the sourdough starter makes the dough very slack, and the extra structure provided by the bread flour helps to counteract this and support the rise.

> Keep the shaped dough covered with oiled plastic wrap to prevent the outside from drying, which would impede rising.

> Allow the shaped dough to proof just long enough so that it almost keeps a dent when pressed. Overproofing may cause the dough to collapse and result in a pale crust and limited shelf life. Slight underproofing is preferable. If significantly underproofed, however, the crust will burst open unevenly during baking and the loaf will have less volume.

> Don't use a food processor to mix the dough for a sourdough bread, as the buildup of heat will probably destroy the wild yeast sourdough culture. (Even 100°F is hot enough to kill it.)

Using a Bread Machine for Sourdough
A bread machine can work very well to mix and knead one loaf of sourdough bread, but use only a model that has a programmable dough feature that does not heat the bread during mixing.

To use a bread machine, if it's been refrigerated, let the starter stand at room temperature for 1 hour before mixing the dough.

Place the water and the flour called for in the bread machine bowl. Program the machine to a manual cycle. After the 3-minute mix, immediately hit the pause button, so that the dough can rest 20 minutes for the autolyse. (Since "pause" is usually only 10 minutes, set a timer for 9 minutes so you can press the button a second time, before the machine starts kneading the dough.) Add the salt when the kneading cycle begins, at the end of the 20-minute pause. Scrape the corners of the bowl when flour or dough collects in them during kneading. Allow the machine to knead the dough for about 1 minute. Then add the stiff sourdough starter, torn into 4 pieces. Continue kneading for 7 minutes

UNDERSTANDING

The proportion of basic essential ingredients in sourdough breads falls into the range of 60.5 to 68 percent water, 15 to 40 percent dough starter, and 1.7 to 2.5 percent salt. These percentages (except for the starter, which is based on the entire amount of flour and water in the recipe, including the dough starter) are based on the Baker's Percentage, in which every ingredient is based on flour, which is given the value of 100 percent.

Basic Sourdough Bread

This bread is as homespun as bread can get, using a stiff sourdough starter cultivated from wild yeast. It has a characteristic sourdough profile: tangy, complex flavor; thin, crisp crust; and springy moist crumb with uneven holes of moderate size.

I love this small loaf because of the size of the whole slices when cut. Also, for those who may have just one banneton (dough-rising basket), I wanted to provide a recipe for just one loaf. A loaf of this size is ideal for two people for three days, with a few slices to share with anyone who comes by to visit. If your family is larger, you will want to double the recipe.

Sharing the sourdough starter for bread is a time-honored tradition around the world. I got my first starter from Kurtis Baguley, a baker in San Francisco. And when my friend Angelica Pulvirenti asked me for a bread recipe to use on her boyfriend's boat, one that was easy and had good keeping qualities (so it wouldn't mold from the humidity), I gave her this recipe and some of my starter to make it. She was especially delighted because sharing a bread starter was a long-standing custom in a small village near Ragusa, Sicily, where she grew up. She said that her mother, at the end of baking day, always passed some of her unbaked bread dough to her friends. She loved the sense of community this imparted and is thrilled that she and I are continuing it.

TIME SCHEDULE

Stiff Sourdough Starter: minimum 13 hours, maximum 34 hours
Minimum Rising Time: about 9 hours
Oven Temperature: 475°F, then 450°F
Baking Time: 25 to 30 minutes

Makes: a 6-by-3 1/2-inch-high round loaf/
about 15 ounces/430 grams

EQUIPMENT:

a heavy-duty mixer with dough hook attachment;

an 8-inch banneton OR small colander lined with a towel;

a half sheet pan lined with a nonstick liner such as Silpain or parchment;

a baking stone OR baking sheet

Stiff Sourdough Starter

INGREDIENTS	MEASURE	WEIGHT	
	volume	ounces	grams
sourdough starter	1/3 cup	2 3/4 ounces	75 grams
(for storing)	(scant 1/4 cup)	(1.75 ounces)	(50 grams)
(for this bread)	(1 tablespoon plus 2 teaspoons)	(1 scant ounce)	(25 grams)
FLOUR AND WATER FOR FEEDING THE STARTER			
bread flour	1 1/3 cups, divided	7 ounces	200 grams
water, at room temperature (70 to 90°F)	1/2 cup minus 1 tablespoon, divided	3.5 ounces	100 grams

The day before baking, first thing in the morning, feed (expand) the sourdough starter. (It will be ready to use or to rest refrigerated overnight after about 14 hours.) Allow the starter to sit at room temperature (70° to 80°F) for 1 hour before feeding it.

The Storage Starter

First, feed (refresh) and store some of the sourdough seed starter for future batches of bread (you will be increasing it by 2 1/2 times, from 50 grams to 125 grams):

Begin by tearing off **a scant 1/4 cup (1.75 ounces/50 grams) of the starter**. It will be soft and stretchy. Place it in a small bowl.

Add **1/3 cup (1.75 ounces/50 grams) of the flour** and **1 tablespoon plus 2 teaspoons (1 scant ounce/25 grams) of the water**. With a wooden spoon and then your hand, mix and knead together until all the flour is absorbed. The starter should be the consistency of a stiff biscuit dough. If after about 2 minutes of kneading there are still loose particles of flour, add water by the droplet. (Don't worry, too much water won't hurt it—but during fermentation and resting, the dough becomes softer, and it is easier to work with the starter when it is firm and not sticky, so you don't lose any on your fingers or the bowl.)

Place this starter in a lightly oiled 1-cup storage container with a lid. Lightly oil the surface of the starter. Allow the starter to start to ferment at warm room temperature (75° to 80°F) before storing it in the refrigerator. If you are planning to bake more bread soon, you want the starter to ferment longer at room temperature so it will be more active sooner. If you are not planning to bake more bread for several days, you want to slow down the fermentation by refrigerating it sooner so that the yeast doesn't consume all the added flour.

If baking bread the next day or the day after feeding the starter, refrigerate the starter after 2 hours at room temperature.

If baking bread 3 days after feeding the starter, refrigerate the starter after 1 hour at room temperature.

If baking bread 1 week after feeding the starter, refrigerate the starter after 30 minutes at room temperature.

The Starter for the Bread

1 > **Give the starter the first feeding and allow it to ferment and rise (you will be increasing the starter by 4 times, from 25 grams to 100 grams).** Tear off a **scant 2 tablespoons (1 scant ounce/25 grams) of the sourdough starter** (discard any remaining starter) and place it in a small bowl.

Add **1/3 cup (1.75 ounces/50 grams) of the flour** and **1 tablespoon plus 2 teaspoons (1 scant ounce/25 grams) of the water.** With a wooden spoon and then your hand, mix and knead together until all the flour is absorbed. If after about 2 minutes of kneading there are still loose particles of flour, add water by the droplet. The starter should be a rough dough that is very stiff but holds together, with no loose flour particles. It will measure a rounded 1/3 cup and weigh 3.5 ounces/100 grams.

Transfer the starter to an oiled 1-cup glass measure. Oil the top and press it down into the cup. It should measure about 1/3 cup in the glass measure. Cover the measuring cup tightly with greased plastic wrap and let rise (ideally at 75° to 80°F) until it has doubled, to 2/3 cup, 6 to 8 hours.

2 > **Give the starter the second feeding and allow the yeast to ferment and rise (you will be increasing it by 4 times, from 50 grams to 200 grams).** Tear off **a scant 1/4 cup (1.75**

ounces/50 grams) of the starter and discard the remainder. Tear the starter into a few pieces and place in a medium bowl. Add the remaining **2/3 cup (3.5 ounces/100 grams) flour** and **3 1/2 tablespoons (1.75 ounces/50 grams) water**. With a wooden spoon and then your hand, mix and knead together until all the flour is absorbed. If after about 2 minutes of kneading there are still loose particles of flour, add water by the droplet. The starter should be a rough dough that is very stiff but holds together, with no loose flour particles. You will have a full 3/4 cup (7 ounces/200 grams).

Transfer the starter to an oiled 2-cup glass measure. Oil the top and press it down into the cup. It should measure about 3/4 cup in the glass measure. Cover the measuring cup tightly with greased plastic wrap and let rise (ideally at 75° to 80°F) until it has doubled, to 1 1/2 cups, about 6 hours. Refrigerate the starter if you are not ready to mix the dough—up to 20 hours.

Dough

INGREDIENTS	MEASURE	WEIGHT	
	volume	ounces	grams
bread flour	1 1/4 cups	7 ounces	200 grams
water, at room temperature (70 to 90°F)	2/3 liquid cup	5.5 ounces	154 grams
stiff sourdough starter (from above)	*2/3 cup*	*5.25 ounces*	*150 grams*
salt	1 scant teaspoon	scant 0.25 ounce	6 grams

3 > **Mix the dough.**

Mixer Method

If you have refrigerated the starter, remove it to room temperature 1 hour before mixing the dough.

In the mixer bowl, place the flour. With the dough hook, on low speed (#2 if using a KitchenAid), gradually add the water until the flour is moistened enough to form a rough dough. Continue kneading on low speed for 3 minutes, enough to develop the gluten structure a little. Scrape down any bits of dough. Cover the bowl with plastic wrap and allow the dough to rest for 20 minutes.

With oiled fingers, tear off 2/3 cup (5.25 ounces/150 grams) of the starter; discard the rest. Tear it into 4 pieces, roughly the same size. On low speed, knead it into the dough, about 2 minutes. Add the salt and continue kneading for 1 minute. Raise the speed to medium (#4 KitchenAid) and knead for 3 minutes. The dough will be barely tacky (sticky), smooth, and very elastic. If it is still very sticky, knead in a little flour. If it is not at all sticky, spray it with a little water and knead it. (The dough will measure about 2 cups and weigh about 17.7 ounces/502 grams.)

Hand Method

If it has been refrigerated, remove the starter to room temperature 1 hour before mixing the dough.

With oiled fingers, tear off 2/3 cup (5.25 ounces/150 grams) of the starter; discard the rest. Tear it into 4 pieces, roughly the same size, and place it in a mixing bowl.

With a wooden spoon, stir in the water, stirring for a few seconds to soften the starter, then add all but 2 tablespoons of the flour and the salt. Continuing with the wooden spoon or using your hand, mix until the flour is moistened. Knead the dough in the bowl until it comes together, then scrape it onto a lightly floured counter. Knead the dough for 5 minutes, enough to develop the gluten structure a little, adding as little of the reserved 2 tablespoons flour as possible to keep it from sticking. (To prevent sticking, it helps to use your fingertips, not the palms of your hands.) Use a bench scraper to scrape up the dough and gather it together as you knead it. At this point, it will be very sticky. Cover it with the inverted bowl and allow it to rest for 20 minutes. (This rest will make the dough less sticky and easier to work with.)

Knead the dough for another 5 to 10 minutes or until it is very smooth and elastic. It should be barely tacky (sticky) to the touch. If the dough is still very sticky, add some or all of the remaining reserved flour or a little extra. (The dough will measure about 2 cups and weigh about 17.7 ounces/502 grams.)

Both Methods

4 > **Let the dough rise.** Using an oiled spatula or dough scraper, scrape the dough into a 4-cup glass measuring cup or 1-quart food storage container, lightly greased with cooking spray or oil. Press down the dough so you can get an accurate measure, and lightly spray or oil the top. It will come to 2 cups. Cover the measuring cup with plastic wrap; or cover the container with a lid and, with a piece of tape, mark the side of the container at approximately where double the height of the dough would be. Allow the dough to rise (ideally at 75° to 80°F) for 1 hour. It will only have risen a little.

Scrape the dough onto a lightly floured counter. Gently push it down to deflate it, and stretch it into a rectangle (the exact size is not important). Give it 2 business letter turns. It will be soft and stretchy but a little firmer after each turn. Return the dough to the greased container and lightly spray or oil the top. Cover the container with a lid or plastic wrap and allow it to rise for another hour.

Stretch the dough again, give it 2 business letter turns, and return it to the container. Grease the top, cover, and allow it to rise until doubled, to 4 cups (1 quart), 4 to 5 hours.

5 > **Shape the dough and let it rise.** Without deflating it, turn the dough out onto a floured counter and round it into a ball (see page 65). Set it in a floured banneton or

a colander lined with a floured towel, seam side up. Pinch together the seam if it starts to pull apart. In the banneton, the dough will be about 2 inches from the top.

Spray the dough with oil or sprinkle lightly with flour and cover it with a large container or plastic wrap. Let the dough rise ideally at (75° to 80°F.) until almost doubled, 3 to 4 hours. When it is pressed gently with a fingertip, the depression will very slowly fill in. In the banneton, the center of the dough will be 3/4 to 1 inch from the top.

6 > Preheat the oven. Preheat the oven to 475°F 1 hour before baking. Have an oven shelf at the lowest level and place an oven stone or baking sheet on it, and a cast-iron skillet or sheet pan on the floor of the oven, before preheating.

7 > Slash and bake the dough. Very gently invert the dough onto the prepared baking sheet. (If you are using a colander and the risen bread is more than 1 inch below the top, you will need to support the bread when inverting it so that it doesn't fall and deflate. Cut a cardboard circle small enough to fit into the colander and touch the surface of the bread. Place a piece of parchment on top of the bread, place the cardboard on top, and invert it onto the cardboard. Then slide the bread, still on the parchment, onto the baking sheet.) For a more evenly rounded bread, it's fine to leave the dough unslashed. If you like the rustic appearance of a slashed top crust, with sharp scissors, sharp knife, or a single-edged razor blade, slash a 1/4-inch-deep cross in the dough. Because the skin of the dough is very dry, it will be difficult to slash; use a gentle hand so as not to deflate the dough.

Quickly but gently set the baking sheet on the hot baking stone or hot baking sheet. Toss 1/2 cup of ice cubes into the pan beneath and immediately shut the door. Bake for 5 minutes. Lower the oven to 450°F and continue baking for 10 minutes. With a heavy pancake turner, lift the bread from the pan and set it directly on the stone, turning it around as you do so for even baking. Continue baking for 10 to 15 minutes or until the crust is deeply burnished and a skewer inserted into the middle comes out clean (an instant-read thermometer inserted into the center will read about 212°F). For a very crisp crust, prop the open door slightly ajar for the last 5 minutes of baking.

8 > Cool the bread. Remove the bread from the oven, and transfer it to a wire rack to cool completely.

VARIATIONS

Quicker Sourdough Bread (with added commercial yeast)   If your schedule requires speeding up the process (by about 25 percent), or if you feel more secure with the added reliability of commercial yeast, you can add up to 0.06 percent of the total weight of the flour in this recipe (including the flour contained in the starter). The total weight is 300 grams; 0.06 percent of 300 grams is about 0.2 gram or about 1/16 teaspoon instant yeast. This should be added after the autolyse (the 20-minute rest before the final mixing). At this low a percentage, it will not affect the acidity or flavor of the sourdough, but if it were added at the beginning, the commercial yeast would likely be killed by the acidity of the sourdough starter.

Basic Sourdough Bread with Extra Flavor and Keeping Quality   If desired, you can replace 2 tablespoons (0.7 ounce/20 grams) of the bread flour with an equal measure or weight of whole wheat, kamut, or rye flour. (This is 6.5 percent of the total amount of flour in the recipe.)

French Country Boule   Reduce the bread flour in the dough to 3/4 cup plus 2 tablespoons (4.5 ounces/130 grams) and add 1/3 cup (1.5 ounces/40 grams) medium rye flour and 3 tablespoons (1 ounce/30 grams) whole wheat flour.

ALTERING THE PERCENTAGE OF STARTER

In a very cold room, when yeast will take a long time to ferment, or a very warm one, when yeast will take a shorter time to ferment, you may want to adjust the amount of sourdough starter used in the dough.

To reduce the amount of stiff sourdough starter from 30 percent to 20 percent:

Reduce the starter to a rounded 1/3 cup (3.5 ounces/100 grams). To the rest of the dough, add 1 full tablespoon (about 1 ounce/16.6 grams) water and 3 1/2 tablespoons (1 full ounce/33.3 grams) flour.

To increase the amount of stiff sourdough starter from 30 percent to 40 percent:

Increase the starter to a full 3/4 cup (7 ounces/200 grams). From the rest of the dough, subtract 1 full tablespoon (about 1 ounce/16.6 grams) water and 3 1/2 tablespoons (1 full ounce/33.3 grams) flour.

POINTERS FOR SUCCESS

>   If you need more starter—to make 2 loaves at once, for example—in Step 2, rather than discarding half, use the full 100 grams and increase it to 400 grams.

THE DOUGH PERCENTAGE

Flour:	100%
Water:	68%
Dough Starter:	30%
Salt:	2%

Sourdough Rye

It is amazing how the flavor of a sourdough starter intensifies and enhances the unique flavor of rye bread. Another benefit of the sourdough culture is that it keeps this bread fresh and moist for up to 5 days at room temperature. As long as I have an active sourdough starter handy, this is my first choice of rye bread to bake.

TIME SCHEDULE

Stiff Sourdough Starter: minimum 13 hours, maximum 34 hours
Minimum Rising Time: about 8 1/2 hours
Oven Temperature: 450°F, then 400°F
Baking Time: 45 minutes

Makes: an 8-by-4-inch-high round loaf/
about 1 pound, 75 ounces/846 grams

EQUIPMENT:

a heavy-duty mixer with dough hook attachment;

a half sheet pan sprinkled with cornmeal or lined with a nonstick liner such as Silpain or parchment;

a baking stone OR baking sheet

Stiff Sourdough Starter

INGREDIENTS	MEASURE	WEIGHT	
	volume	ounces	grams
sourdough starter (for storing) (for this bread)	**1/3 cup** (scant 1/4 cup) (1 tablespoon plus 2 teaspoons)	**2.75 ounces** (1.75 ounces) (1 scant ounce)	**75 grams** (50 grams) (25 grams)
FLOUR AND WATER FOR FEEDING THE SEED STARTER			
bread flour	**about 2 cups**	**10.6 ounces**	**300 grams**
water, at room temperature (70 to 90°F)	**about 2/3 liquid cup**	**5.3 ounces**	**150 grams**

The day before baking, first thing in the morning, feed (expand) the sourdough starter. (It will be ready to use or to rest refrigerated overnight after about 14 hours.) Allow the starter to sit at room temperature (70° to 80°F) for 1 hour before feeding it.

The Storage Starter

First, feed (refresh) and store some of the starter for future batches of bread (you will be increasing it by 2 1/2 times, from 50 grams to 125 grams):

Begin by tearing off **a scant 1/4 cup (1.75 ounces/50 grams) of the seed starter.** It will be soft and stretchy. Place it in a small bowl.

Add **1/3 cup (1.75 ounces/50 grams) of the flour** and **1 tablespoon plus 2 teaspoons (1 scant ounce/25 grams) of the water.** With a wooden spoon and then your hand, mix and knead together until all the flour is absorbed. The starter should be the consistency of a stiff biscuit dough. If after about 2 minutes of kneading there are still loose particles of flour, add water by the droplet. (Don't worry, too much water won't hurt it—but during fermentation and resting, the dough becomes softer, and it is easier to work with the starter when it is firm and not sticky, so you don't lose any on your fingers or the bowl.)

Place this starter in a lightly oiled 1-cup storage container with a lid. Lightly oil the surface of the starter. Allow the starter to start to ferment at warm room temperature (75° to 80°F) before storing it in the refrigerator. If you are planning to bake more bread soon, you want the starter to ferment longer at room temperature so it will be more active sooner. If you are not planning to bake more bread for several days, you want to slow down the fermentation by refrigerating it sooner so that the yeast doesn't consume all the added flour.

If baking bread the next day or the day after feeding the starter, refrigerate the starter after 2 hours at room temperature.

If baking bread 3 days after feeding the starter, refrigerate the starter after 1 hour at room temperature.

If baking bread 1 week after feeding the starter, refrigerate the starter after 30 minutes at room temperature.

The Starter for the Bread

1 > **Give the starter the first feeding and allow it to ferment and rise (you will be increasing the starter by 4 times, from 25 grams to 10 grams).** Tear off **a scant 2 tablespoons (1 scant ounce/25 grams) of the sourdough seed starter** (discard any remaining starter) and place it in a small bowl.

Add **1/3 cup (1.75 ounces/50 grams) of the flour** and **1 tablespoon plus 2 teaspoons (1 scant ounce/25 grams) of the water.** With a wooden spoon and then your hand, mix and knead together until all the flour is absorbed. If after about 2 minutes of kneading there are still loose particles of flour, add water by the droplet. The starter should be a rough dough that is very stiff but holds together, with no loose flour particles. It will measure a rounded 1/3 cup and weigh 3.5 ounces/100 grams.

Transfer the starter to an oiled 1-cup glass measure. Oil the top and press it down into the cup. It should measure about 1/3 cup in the glass measure. Cover the measuring cup tightly with greased plastic wrap and let rise (ideally at 75° to 80°F) until it has doubled, to 2/3 cup, 6 to 8 hours.

2 > **Give the starter the second feeding and allow the yeast to ferment and rise** (you will be increasing it by 4 times, from 100 grams to 400 grams). Tear off **a scant 1/2 cup (3.5 ounces/100 grams) of the starter** and discard the remainder. Tear the starter into a few pieces and place in a medium bowl.

Add the remaining **1 1/4 cups plus 1/2 tablespoon (7 ounces/200 grams) flour** and scant **1/2 cup (3.5 ounces/100 grams) water.** With a wooden spoon and then your hand, mix and knead together until all the flour is absorbed. If after about 2 minutes of kneading there are still loose particles of flour, add water by the droplet. The starter should be a rough dough that is very stiff but holds together with no loose flour particles. You will have a full 1 1/2 cups (14 ounces/400 grams).

Transfer the starter to an oiled 4-cup glass measure. Oil the top and press it down into the cup. It should measure about 1 1/2 cups in the glass measure. Cover the measuring cup tightly with greased plastic wrap and let rise (ideally at 75° to 80°F) until it doubled, to 3 cups, about 6 hours. Refrigerate the starter if you are not ready to mix the dough—up to 18 hours.

Dough

INGREDIENTS	MEASURE	WEIGHT	
	volume	ounces	grams
bread flour	about 1 1/2 cups	about 8 ounces	230 grams
medium rye flour	3/4 cup	3.3 ounces	95 grams
water, at room temperature (70° to 90°F)	1 liquid cup	about 8 ounces	232 grams
stiff sourdough starter (from above)	*1 1/2 cups*	*12.7 ounces*	*360 grams*
caraway seeds	2 tablespoons	0.5 ounce	14 grams
salt	1/2 tablespoons	0.3 ounce	10.5 grams

3 > **Mix the dough.**

Mixer Method

If you have refrigerated the starter, remove it to room temperature 1 hour before mixing the dough.

In the mixer bowl, place the flours. With the dough hook, on low speed (#2 if using a KitchenAid), gradually add the water until the flour is moistened enough to form a rough dough. Continue kneading on low speed for 3 minutes, enough to develop the gluten structure a little. Scrape down any bits of dough. Cover the bowl with plastic wrap and allow the dough to rest for 20 minutes.

With oiled fingers, tear off 1 1/2 cups (12.7 ounces/360 grams) of the starter; discard the rest. Tear it into 4 pieces, roughly the same size. On low speed (#2 KitchenAid), knead it into the dough, about 2 minutes. Add the caraway seeds and salt and knead for 1 minute. Raise the speed to medium (#4 KitchenAid) and knead for 3 minutes. The dough will be barely tacky (sticky), smooth, and very elastic. If it is still very sticky, knead in a little flour. If it is not at all sticky, spray it with a little water and knead it. (The dough will measure a little under 4 cups and weigh about 33 ounces/940 grams.)

Hand Method

If it has been refrigerated, remove the starter to room temperature 1 hour before mixing the dough.

With oiled fingers, tear off 2/3 cup (5.25 ounces/150 grams) of the starter; discard the rest. Tear it into 4 pieces, roughly the same size, and place it in a mixing bowl.

With a wooden spoon, stir in the water, stirring for a few seconds to soften the starter, then add all but 2 tablespoons of the flour, the caraway seeds, and salt. Continuing with the wooden spoon or using your hand, mix until the flour is moistened. Knead the dough in the bowl until it comes together, then scrape it onto a lightly floured counter. Knead the dough for 5 minutes, enough to develop the gluten structure a little, adding as little of the reserved 2 tablespoons flour as possible to keep it from sticking. (To prevent sticking, it helps to use your fingertips, not the palms of your hands.) Use a bench scraper to scrape up the dough and gather it together as you knead it. At this point, it will be very sticky. Cover it with the inverted bowl and allow it to rest for 20 minutes. (This rest will make the dough less sticky and easier to work with.)

Knead the dough for another 5 to 10 minutes or until it is very smooth and elastic. It should be barely tacky (sticky) to the touch. If the dough is still very sticky, add some or all of the remaining reserved flour, or a little extra. (The dough will measure a little under 4 cups and weigh about 33 ounces/940 grams.)

Both Methods

4 > Let the dough rise. Using an oiled spatula or dough scraper, scrape the dough into a 2-quart dough-rising container or bowl, lightly greased with cooking spray or oil. Press down the dough so you can get an accurate measure, and lightly spray or oil the top. It will come to a little under 1 quart. Cover with a lid or plastic wrap and, with a piece of tape, mark the side of the container at approximately where double the height of the dough would be. Allow the dough to rise (ideally at 75° to 80°F) for 1 hour. It will only have risen a little.

Scrape the dough out onto a lightly floured counter. Gently push it down to deflate it and stretch it into a rectangle. Give it 2 business letter turns. It will be soft and stretchy but a little firmer after each turn. Return the dough to the greased container and lightly spray or oil the top. Cover the container with a lid or plastic wrap and allow it to rise for another hour.

Stretch the dough again, give it 2 business letter turns, and return it to the container. Grease the top, cover, and allow it rise until doubled, to almost 2 quarts, 3 1/2 to 5 hours.

5 > Shape the dough and let it rise. Turn the dough onto a lightly floured counter and press it down to flatten it slightly without deflating it. Round the dough into a ball about 6 inches by 3 inches high and set it on the prepared baking sheet (see page 451). Cover it with a large container or oiled plastic wrap. Let the shaped dough rise (ideally at 75° to 80°F) until almost doubled, 3 to 4 hours. It will be about 7 1/2 inches by 3 inches high, when it is pressed gently with a fingertip, the depression will very slowly fill in.

6 > Preheat the oven. Preheat the oven to 450°F 1 hour before baking. Have an oven shelf at the lowest level and place an oven stone or baking sheet on it, and a cast-iron skillet or sheet pan on the floor of the oven, before preheating.

7 > **Slash and bake the dough.** With a sharp knife or single-edged razor blade, slash a 1/4- to 1/2-inch-deep cross in the dough. Quickly but gently set the baking sheet on the hot baking stone or hot baking sheet. Toss 1/2 cup of ice cubes into the pan beneath and immediately shut the door. Bake for 5 minutes. Lower the oven to 400°F and continue baking for 15 minutes. With a heavy pancake turner, lift the bread from the pan and set it directly on the stone, turning it around as you do so for even baking. Continue baking for 35 minutes or until the crust is tawny brown and a skewer inserted in the middle comes out clean (an instant-read thermometer inserted into the center will read about 190°F). For a very crisp crust, prop the oven door slightly ajar for the last 5 minutes of baking.

8 > **Cool the bread.** Remove the bread from the oven and transfer it to a wire rack to cool completely.

VARIATIONS

USING A LIQUID SOURDOUGH STARTER

If you have a liquid sourdough starter, it's easy to make it into a stiff sourdough starter for this recipe; see page 434 for instructions. Then allow it to sit until doubled, 6 to 8 hours, and use it in place of the stiff sourdough starter, starting at Step 2, the first feeding.

Quicker Sourdough Rye (using added commercial yeast) If your schedule requires speeding up the process (by about 25 percent), or if you feel more secure with the added reliability of commercial yeast, it you can add up to 0.06 percent of the total weight of the flour in this recipe (including the flour contained in the starter). The total weight is 565 grams; 0.06 percent of 565 grams is about 0.3 grams or about a full 1/16 teaspoon instant yeast. This should be added after the autolyse (the 20-minute rest before the final mixing). At this low a percentage, it will not affect the acidity or flavor of the sourdough, but if it were added at the beginning, the commercial yeast would likely be killed by the acidity of the sourdough.

ALTERING THE PERCENTAGE OF STARTER

The amount of sourdough starter in this recipe is 39.25 percent of the total flour and water (including what is contained in the starter). In warmer months, you may want to decrease the starter to 30 percent so that the dough rises more slowly, for maximum flavor. (I would not decrease it to less than 30 percent, as the sour flavor is so desirable in this bread.)

To reduce the amount of stiff sourdough starter to 30 percent:
Reduce the starter to a full cup (9.7 ounces/275 grams). To the rest of the dough, add 2 tablespoons (1 ounce/28 grams) water and 1/4 cup plus 2 tablespoons (2 ounces/56.6 grams) flour.

UNDERSTANDING

This is the same basic recipe as the "Levy's" Real Jewish Rye Bread on page 324, but I left out the sugar, malt, oil, and commercial yeast because the sourdough starter provides the complexity of flavor and moistness these ingredients added.

THE DOUGH PERCENTAGE

Flour:	100% (bread: **83.1%**, rye: **16.9%**)
Water:	**62.9%**
Dough Starter:	**39.25%**
Salt:	**1.9%**

Sourdough Pumpernickel

Most recipes for pumpernickel bread (including the Authentic Pumpernickel Bread on page 329) use a little vinegar to replicate the underlying sour taste of the Old World pumpernickel bread made with sourdough starter, like this one. This is basically the identical recipe to the one using packaged yeast but in its place I use sourdough starter. I do omit the oil, because the sourdough starter produces enough moist elasticity in the dough. You can also omit the coffee and cocoa and still have a fabulous pumpernickel, because the sourdough gives the bread so much flavor dimension.

This heavy dough takes longer than most other sourdoughs to rise, so if your schedule does not allow for this extra time, see the added commercial yeast variation below.

This bread has fantastic keeping qualities. I discovered this when I sent my father and aunt Ruth three trial slices in a padded envelope (to test the water before committing to the expense of FedExing a whole loaf). It somehow took an entire week to get from New York City to Pompano Beach, Florida, but, according to my father, it was still perfectly moist and fresh.

TIME SCHEDULE

Stiff Sourdough Starter: minimum 13 hours, maximum 34 hours
Minimum Rising Time: about 12 hours
Oven Temperature: 400°F, then 375°F
Baking Time: 35 to 40 minutes

Makes: a 7 1/2-by-4-inch-high round loaf/
about 1 pound, 13.75 ounces/846 grams

EQUIPMENT:

a heavy-duty mixer with dough hook attachment;

a half sheet pan lined with a nonstick liner such as Silpain or parchment;

a baking stone OR baking sheet

Stiff Sourdough Starter

INGREDIENTS	MEASURE	WEIGHT	
	volume	ounces	grams
sourdough starter	1/3 cup	2 3/4 ounces	75 grams
(for storing)	(scant 1/4 cup)	(1 3/4 ounces)	(50 grams)
(for this bread)	(1 tablespoon plus 2 teaspoons)	(scant 1 ounce)	(25 grams)
FLOUR AND WATER FOR FEEDING THE STARTER			
bread flour	about 2 cups	10.6 ounces	300 grams
water, at room temperature (70 to 90°F)	about 2/3 liquid cup	5.3 ounces	150 grams

The day before baking, first thing in the morning, feed (expand) the sourdough starter. (It will be ready to use or to rest refrigerated overnight after about 14 hours.) Allow the starter to sit at room temperature (70° to 80°F) for 1 hour before feeding it.

The Storage Starter

First, feed (refresh) and store some of the starter for future batches of bread dough (you will be increasing it by 2 1/2 times from 50 grams to 125 grams):

Begin by tearing off **a scant 1/4 cup (1.75 ounces/50 grams) of the starter.** It will be soft and stretchy. Place it in a small bowl.

Add **1/3 cup (1.75 ounces/50 grams) of the flour** and **1 tablespoon plus 2 teaspoons (1 scant ounce/25 grams) of the water.** With a wooden spoon and then your hand, mix and knead together until all the flour is absorbed. The dough should be the consistency of a stiff biscuit dough. If after about 2 minutes of kneading there are still loose particles of flour, add water by the droplet. (Don't worry, too much water won't hurt it but during fermentation and resting, the dough becomes softer and it is easier to work with the starter when it is firm and not sticky, so you don't lose any on your fingers or the bowl.)

Place this starter in a lightly oiled 1-cup storage container with a lid. Lightly oil the surface of the starter. Allow the starter to start to ferment at warm room temperature (75° to 80°F) before storing it in the refrigerator. If you are planning to bake more bread soon, you want the starter to ferment longer at room temperature so it will be more active sooner. If you are not planning to bake more bread for several days, you want to slow down the fermentation by refrigerating it sooner so that the yeast doesn't consume all the added flour.

If baking bread the next day or the day after feeding the starter, refrigerate the starter after 2 hours at room temperature.

If baking bread 3 days after feeding the starter, refrigerate the starter after 1 hour at room temperature.

If baking bread 1 week after feeding the starter, refrigerate the starter after 30 minutes at room temperature.

The Starter for the Bread

1 > Give the starter the first feeding and allow it to ferment and rise (you will be increasing the starter by 4 times, from 25 grams to 100 grams). Tear off **a scant 2 tablespoons (1 scant ounce/25 grams) of the sourdough seed starter** (discard any remaining starter) and place it in a small bowl.

Add **1/3 cup (1.75 ounces/50 grams) of the flour** and **1 tablespoons plus 2 teaspoons (1 scant ounce/25 grams) of the water**. With a wooden spoon and then your hand, mix and knead together until all the flour is absorbed. If after about 2 minutes of kneading there are still loose particles of flour, add water by the droplet. The starter should be a rough dough that is very stiff but holds together, with no loose flour particles. It will measure a rounded 1/3 cup and weigh 3.5 ounces/100 grams.

Transfer the starter to an oiled 1-cup glass measure. Oil the top and press it down into the cup. It should measure about 1/3 cup in the glass measure. Cover the measuring cup tightly with greased plastic wrap and let rise (ideally at 75° to 80°F) or until it has doubled, to 2/3 cup, 6 to 8 hours.

2 > Give the starter the second feeding and allow the yeast to ferment and rise (you will be increasing it by 4 times, from 100 grams to 400 grams). Tear off **a scant 1/2 cup (3.5 ounces/100 grams) of the starter** and discard the remainder. Tear the starter into a few pieces and place in a medium bowl.

Add the remaining **1 1/4 cups plus 1/2 tablespoon (7 ounces/200 grams) flour** and **scant 1/2 cup (3.5 ounces/100 grams) water**. With a wooden spoon and then your hand, mix and knead together until all the flour is absorbed. If after about 2 minutes of kneading there are still loose particles of flour, add water by the droplet. The starter should be a rough dough that is very stiff but holds together with no loose flour particles. You will have a full 1 1/2 cup (14 ounces/400 grams).

Transfer the starter to an oiled 4-cup glass measure. Oil the top and press it down into the cup. It should measure about 1 1/2 cups in the glass measure. Cover the measuring cup tightly with greased plastic wrap and let rise (ideally at 75° to 80°F). Or until it has doubled, to 3 cups about 6 hours. Refrigerate the starter if you are not ready to mix the dough—up to 18 hours.

The Dough

INGREDIENTS	MEASURE	WEIGHT	
	volume	ounces	grams
stiff sourdough starter (from above)	*1 cup plus 2 tablespoons*	*9.5 ounces*	*270 grams*
bread flour	3/4 cup plus 2 tablespoons	4.7 ounces	134 grams
pumpernickel flour	1 cup	5 ounces	142 grams

malt powder or
  barley malt syrup or honey or
  sugar
	1 tablespoon	0.3 ounce
		0.7 ounce
		0.5 ounce
			9.3 grams
			21 grams
			12.5 grams

vital wheat gluten	2 tablespoons	0.6 ounce	18 grams
caramel powder	2 tablespoons	0.6 ounce	18 grams
cocoa	2 tablespoons	scant 0.5 ounce	12 grams
sugar	1 tablespoon	scant 0.5 ounce	12.5 grams
instant espresso powder	1 teaspoon	--	1.5 grams
caraway seeds	1/2 tablespoon	--	3.5 grams
molasses	1 tablespoon	0.7 ounce	22 grams
water, at room temperature (70° to 80°F)	3/4 liquid cup	about 6 ounces	173 grams
salt	1 3/4 teaspoons plus 1/8 teaspoon	--	12.3 grams

3 > Mix the dough.

Mixer Method

If you have refrigerated the starter, remove it to room temperature 1 hour before mixing the dough.

In the mixer bowl, whisk together the bread flour, pumpernickel flour, malt (or honey or sugar), vital wheat gluten, caramel powder, cocoa, sugar, instant espresso powder, and caraway seeds. Add the molasses. With the dough hook, on low speed (#2 if using a KitchenAid), gradually add the water until the flour is moistened enough to form a rough dough. Continue kneading on low speed for 3 minutes, enough to develop the gluten structure a little. Scrape down any bits of dough. Cover the bowl with plastic wrap and allow the dough to rest for 20 minutes.

With oiled fingers, tear off 1 1/2 cups (12.7 ounces/360 grams) of the sourdough starter; discard the rest. Tear it into 4 pieces, roughly the same size. On low speed (#2 KitchenAid), knead it into the dough, about 2 minutes. Add the salt and continue kneading for 1 minute. Raise the speed to medium (#4 KitchenAid) and knead for 3 minutes. It will be barely tacky (sticky), smooth, and very elastic. If it is still very sticky, knead in a little flour. If it is not at all sticky, spray it with a little water and knead it. The dough should be very smooth and firm. (The dough will measure about 3 cups and weigh about 29.5 ounces/835 grams.)

Hand Method

If it has been refrigerated, remove the starter to room temperature 1 hour before mixing the dough.

In a medium bowl, whisk together all but 2 tablespoons of the bread flour, the pumpernickel flour, malt (or honey or sugar), vital wheat gluten, caramel powder, cocoa, sugar, instant espresso powder, caraway seeds, and salt. Set aside.

With oiled fingers, tear off 2/3 cup (5.25 ounces/150 grams) of the sourdough starter; discard the rest. Tear it into 4 pieces, roughly the same size, and place in a large mixing bowl.

With a wooden spoon, stir in the water, stirring for a few seconds to soften the starter. Add the molasses, then gradually stir in the flour mixture, mixing until the flour is moistened. Knead the dough in the bowl until it comes together, then scrape it onto a lightly floured counter. Knead the dough for 5 minutes, enough to develop the gluten structure a little, adding as little of the reserved 2 tablespoons flour as possible to keep it from sticking. (To prevent sticking, it helps to use your fingertips, not the palms of your hands.) Use a bench scraper to scrape up the dough and gather it together as you knead it. At this point, it will be very sticky. Cover it with the inverted bowl and allow it to rest for 20 minutes. (This rest will make the dough less sticky and easier to work with.)

Knead the dough for another 5 to 10 minutes or until it is very smooth and elastic. It should be barely tacky (sticky) to the touch. If the dough is still very sticky, add some or all of the remaining reserved flour. The dough should be very smooth and firm. (The dough will measure about 3 cups and weigh about 29.5 ounces/835 grams.)

Both Methods

4 > **Let the dough rise.** Using an oiled spatula or dough scraper, scrape the dough into a 2-quart dough-rising container or bowl, lightly greased with cooking spray or oil. Press down the dough so you can get an accurate measure, and lightly spray or oil the top. It will come to 3 cups. Cover with a lid or plastic wrap and, with a piece of tape, mark the side of the container at approximately double the height the dough

would be. Allow the dough to rise (ideally at 75° to 80°F) for 1 hour. It will only have risen a little.

Scrape the dough out onto a lightly floured counter. Push it down to deflate it, and roll it into a rectangle (the exact size doesn't matter). (This is stiff, not very stretchy, dough, so rolling it with a pin is better than stretching or pressing it with your hand.) Give it 1 business letter turn; it will be a little firmer after the turn. Return the dough to the greased container and grease the top lightly with cooking spray or oil. Cover the container with a lid or plastic wrap and allow it to rise for another hour.

Rolling the dough again, give it 1 business letter turn, and return it to the container. Grease the top, cover it, and allow rise until doubled, to 6 cups, 6 to 8 hours.

5 > Shape the dough and let it rise. Turn the dough out onto a lightly floured counter and press it down to flatten it slightly. Round the dough into a ball about 6 inches by 3 inches high (see page 65) and set it on the prepared baking sheet. Cover it with a large container or oiled plastic wrap. Let the dough rise (ideally at 75° to 80°F) until almost doubled, 4 to 5 hours. It will be about 7 inches by 3 inches high, and when it is pressed gently with a fingertip the depression will very slowly fill in.

Optional Shiny Glaze

Makes: full 1/4 cup (enough for 2 loaves)

INGREDIENTS	MEASURE	WEIGHT	
	volume	ounces	grams
water	1/4 cup plus 2 tablespoons, separated	--	
cornstarch	1/2 tablespoon	--	--
Optional: sesame seeds, preferably raw	1/2 tablespoon	--	--

6 > Prepare the optional glaze. In a small saucepan, bring the 1/4 cup water to a boil. Meanwhile, whisk together the remaining 2 tablespoons water and the cornstarch. When the water is boiling, whisk in the cornstarch mixture. Return it to a boil, whisking constantly until it thickens and turns translucent. Remove from the heat. (The glaze can be made ahead, cooled, and covered; reheat before using).

7 > Preheat the oven. Preheat the oven to 450°F 1 hour before baking. Have an oven shelf at the lowest level and place an oven stone or baking sheet on it, and a cast-iron skillet or sheet pan on the floor of the oven, before preheating.

8 > Slash and bake the dough. Brush the glaze on the bread, coating the entire surface. Cover the remaining glaze and set aside. With a sharp knife or single-edged razor blade, slash a 1/4- to 1/2-inch-deep cross in the dough.

Quickly but gently set the baking sheet on the hot baking stone or hot baking sheet. Toss 1/2 cup of ice cubes into the pan beneath and immediately shut the door. Bake for 5 minutes. Lower the oven to 400°F and continue baking for 15 minutes. With a heavy pancake turner, lift the bread from the pan and set it directly on the stone, turning it around as you do so for even baking. Continue baking for 35 minutes or until the crust is dark brown and a skewer inserted in the middle comes out clean (an instant-read thermometer inserted into the center will read about 190°F). For a very crisp crust, prop the oven door slightly ajar for the last 5 minutes of baking.

9 > Cool the bread. Remove the bread from the oven and transfer it to a wire rack. Brush it with a second coat of the glaze and allow it to cool completely.

VARIATIONS

USING A LIQUID SOURDOUGH STARTER

If you have a liquid sourdough starter, it's easy to make it into a stiff sourdough starter for this recipe; see page 434 for instructions. Then allow it to sit until doubled, 6 to 8 hours, and use it in place of the stiff sourdough starter, starting at Step #2.

Quicker Sourdough Pumpernickel (using added commercial yeast)   If your schedule requires speeding up the process (by about 25 percent), or if you feel more secure with the added reliability of commercial yeast, you can add up to 0.06 percent of the total weight of the flour in this recipe (including the flour contained in the starter). The total weight is 474 grams; 0.06 percent of 474 grams is almost 0.3 gram or about a full 1/16 teaspoon instant yeast. This should be added after the autolyse (the 20-minute rest before the final dough mixing). At this low a percentage, it will not affect the acidity or flavor of the sourdough, but if it were added at the beginning, the commercial yeast would likely be killed by the acidity of the sourdough starter.

Raisin Pumpernickel   In a small bowl, place 1 cup (5 ounces/144 grams) of raisins and add 1/3 cup hot water. Cover with plastic wrap and allow to sit until softened, stirring once, for 30 minutes. (Don't soak longer, or the raisins will lose their texture.) Drain the raisins, reserving the liquid in a 1-cup liquid measure. (You should have about 1/4 cup.) Use this water to replace 1/4 cup of the water in the recipe.

After the dough is mixed, allow it to rest, covered, for 10 minutes to relax the gluten. Then roll it into a rectangle about 10 inches by 15 inches. Sprinkle it with the raisins, and, starting from a short end, roll it up. Knead it for a few minutes to incorporate the raisins evenly. The dough will measure 3 1/2 cups instead of 3 cups.

POINTERS FOR SUCCESS

> The amount of stiff sourdough starter in this recipe is 37.5 percent. I don't decrease it in warmer months, because I don't want to diminish the sour flavor in this bread. Also, the density of the dough causes it to rise more slowly than most other sourdough breads.

THE DOUGH PERCENTAGE

Flour:	100% (bread: **66.1%**, coarse rye: **30.1%**, vital wheat gluten: **3.8%**)
Water:	60.5%
Dough Starter:	37.5%
Salt:	2.6%

Sourdough Wheat Bread with Seeds

I fell head over heels in love with this rustic bread at my first dinner at The French Laundry restaurant in Yountville, California, in Napa Valley. I discovered that it was made by a bakery in nearby Petaluma called Della Fattoria. It is down-to-earth, dense, wheaty, crunchy with seeds, and wonderfully wholesome, with a distinctly sour depth of flavor, and it wholly holds its own against the imaginatively refined cuisine of Thomas Keller. I was sure I'd never succeed in getting the recipe and would have been perfectly content to buy the bread, but since distance made this impractical, I begged for the recipe. Since bread bakers are the most generous human beings on earth, particularly Della Fattoria baker Kathleen Weber, she FedExed me not only several loaves of the bread and the detailed recipe, but also the flours and some of the actual starter she had created for it. Knowing how afraid I was at the time of making bread with only a wild yeast starter and no added yeast, she wrote these loving words of encouragement: "Don't worry, just fuss over it a little bit and tell it what a wonderful piece of magic it is, and that in fact you expect it to turn straw into gold. After all, this is alchemy. And please don't worry. Remember, there is plenty of starter where that came from." Kathleen feels that a bread made with no commercial yeast will taste more rich and nutty rather than sour.

The La Cloche Bread Baker (see page 577) simulates the bakery's enviable brick ovens built by Kathleen's husband, Ed, and creates its most beautiful golden color. This was the first bread I made using no commercial yeast, and watching it rise to perfection was like flying to the moon and being at one with the universe.

Stiff Sourdough Starter: about 36 hours
Minimum Rising Time: 5 hours
Oven Temperature: 450°F, then 400°F (if using La Cloche, 475°F, then 450°F)
Baking Time: 25 to 35 minutes

Makes: two 9-by-5 3/4-by-3-inch-high loaves,
1 3/4 pounds/795 grams each

EQUIPMENT:

2 La Cloche Bread Bakers OR 1 La Cloche Bread Baker and a baking sheet, OR 1 half sheet pan, all lined with nonstick liners such as Silpain or parchment, and/or sprinkled with flour or cornmeal;

a baking stone OR baking sheet

Whole Wheat Stiff Sourdough Starter

INGREDIENTS	MEASURE	WEIGHT	
	volume	ounces	grams
stiff sourdough starter	1/2 cup minus 1 tablespoon	3.75 ounces	106 grams
FLOUR AND WATER FOR FEEDING THE STARTER			
bread flour	1 full cup	6 ounces	168 grams
whole wheat flour	4 1/2 tablespoons	1 1/2 ounces	42 grams
water, at room temperature (70° to 90°.)	about 1/2 liquid cup	3 3/4 ounces	102 grams

Two nights before baking day, remove the starter from the refrigerator and let it sit overnight in a cool place (60° to 70°F).

The day before baking, first thing in the morning, expand (feed) the dough starter.
1 > Give the starter the first feeding (you will be increasing it by 2 times, from 106 grams to 212 grams. Place the starter it in a small bowl.

Add: **about 5 tablespoons plus 2 teaspoons (2 ounces/56 grams) of the bread flour, 1 1/2 tablespoons (1/2 ounce/14 grams) of the whole wheat flour, and 2 1/2 tablespoons (1.25 ounce/36 grams) of the water.** With a wooden spoon and then your hand, mix and knead together until all the flour is absorbed. The dough should be the consistency of a stiff biscuit dough. If after about 2 minutes of kneading there are still loose particles of flour, add water by the droplet. (Don't worry, too much water won't hurt it—but during fermentation and resting the dough becomes softer—it's easier to work with the starter when it is firm and not sticky so you don't lose any on your fingers or the work bowl.)

(Note: to store the starter for future baking at this point, rather than making the bread now: place the starter into a oiled 1-cup storage container and oil the top of the dough. Cover tightly with a lid. Allow the starter to ferment at warm room temperature [75° to 80°F] for 30 minutes if planning to store for 1 week, 1 hour if planning to store for 3 days, or 2 hours if planning to bake within 2 days. Then refrigerate until ready to proceed.)

2 > Give the starter the second feeding and allow it to ferment and rise (you will be increasing the starter by 2 times, from 212 grams to 424 grams). Tear off 3/4 cup plus 2 tablespoons (7.5 ounces/212 grams) of the starter; discard the rest. Place the starter in a medium bowl.

Add the remaining scant **3/4 cup (4 ounces/112 grams) bread flour, 3 tablespoons (1 ounce/28 grams) whole wheat flour,** and **1/3 liquid cup (2 1/2 ounce/72 grams) water.** With a wooden spoon and then your hand, mix and knead it together until all the flour is absorbed. If after about 2 minutes of kneading there are still loose particles of flour, add water by the droplet. The starter should be a rough dough that is very stiff but holds together with no loose flour particles. It will measure about 1 3/4 cups and weigh 15 ounces/424 grams.

Save some of the starter for future baking:

Tear off 1/2 cup minus 1 tablespoon (3 3/4 ounces/106 grams) of the stiff sourdough starter. Place this starter in a lightly oiled 1-cup storage container with a lid. Lightly oil the surface of the starter. Allow the starter to start to ferment at warm room temperature (75° to 80°F) before storing it in the refrigerator. If you are planning to bake more bread soon, you want the starter to ferment longer at room temperature so it will be more active sooner. If you are not planning to bake more bread for several days, you want to slow down the fermentation by refrigerating it sooner so that the yeast doesn't consume all the added flour.

If baking bread the next day or the day after feeding the starter, refrigerate the starter after 2 hours at room temperature.

If baking bread 3 days after feeding the starter, refrigerate the starter after 1 hour at room temperature.

If baking bread 1 week after feeding the starter, refrigerate the starter after 30 minutes at room temperature.

Store the rest of the starter overnight:

Set 3/4 cup plus 1 tablespoon (7 ounces/200 grams) of the remaining starter in another oiled container (discard any remaining starter). Allow it to sit overnight in a cool place, 60° to 70°F. It will have puffed slightly.

Seeds and Grain

INGREDIENTS	MEASURE	WEIGHT	
	volume	ounces	grams
pumpkin seeds	3 tablespoons	--	25.4 grams
natural sesame seeds	3 tablespoons	--	28.4 grams
sunflower seeds	3 tablespoons	--	25.4 grams
polenta	3 tablespoons	--	33 grams
flaxseed	3 tablespoons	--	33 grams

3 > **Toast the seeds.** Preheat the oven to 325°F.

Spread the pumpkin seeds, sesame seeds, and sunflower seeds on a cookie sheet and toast for 7 minutes or until the sunflower seeds just begin to darken. Place them in a small bowl and allow them to cool. Add the polenta and flaxseed.

Dough

INGREDIENTS	MEASURE	WEIGHT	
	volume	ounces	grams
whole wheat flour (freshly ground or under 3 months old)	about 2 1/2 cups	12.6 ounces	357 grams
bread flour	2 cups plus 3 tablespoons	12 ounces	342 grams
wheat germ	1 tablespoon plus 1/2 teaspoon	0.3 ounce	10 grams
wheat bran	1 tablespoon plus 2 teaspoons	--	5 grams
water, at room temperature (70° to 90°F)	2 1/2 liquid cups	20 ounces	567 grams
honey	4 teaspoons	1 ounce	28 grams
stiff sourdough starter (from above)	*3/4 cup plus 1 tablespoon*	*7 ounces*	*200 grams*
salt	1 tablespoon	0.7 ounce	21 grams

4 > **Mix the dough.** In the mixer bowl, place the whole wheat flour, bread flour, wheat germ, wheat bran, water, and honey. With the dough hook, mix on low speed (#2 if using a KitchenAid) for 5 minutes to form a rough dough. Cover the bowl with plastic wrap and allow the dough to rest for 20 minutes.

Tear the starter it into 6 pieces, roughly the same size, and add to the dough. On low speed (#2 KitchedAid), knead it into the dough for 2 minutes. Add the salt and knead for 1 minute. Raise the speed to medium (#4 KitchenAid) and knead for 2 minutes. Add the seed mixture and knead on low speed (#2 KitchenAid) for 2 to 3 minutes or until incorporated. The dough will be very sticky but should pull away from the bowl. If it doesn't, knead in a little flour 1 tablespoon at a time. (The dough will weigh about 3 2/3 pounds/1680 grams.)

5 > Let the dough rise. Place the dough in a 4-quart dough-rising container or bowl, lightly greased with cooking spray or oil. Push down the dough and lightly spray or oil the top. Cover the container with a lid or plastic wrap. Allow the dough to rise (ideally at 75° to 80°F) until it has puffed slightly, to just over 2 quarts, 1 1/2 to 2 hours.

Turn the dough out onto a lightly floured counter and press it down to flatten it slightly. With a rolling pin, roll it into a long rectangle (the exact size doesn't matter). Give it a business letter turn. Turn it 45 degrees so that the closed side is facing to your left, and repeat the rolling and folding process 4 times, for a total of 5 turns. With each turn, the dough will become more elastic. Set it back in the container. Oil the top of the dough, cover it, and allow it to rise a second time until it puffs a little more than the first rise, to 3 quarts, 1 1/2 to 2 hours.

6 > Preshape the dough and let it rest. Turn the dough onto a lightly floured counter and cut it in half. Gently pat each piece into a rectangle and shape it into a stubby log by rolling the top edge down to the middle, then pushing it back slightly with your thumbs. Repeat this rolling motion two more times, ending with the seam at the bottom edge of the dough (see page 67). Use a bench scraper to move the logs of dough to a clean, lightly floured part of the counter, seam side down. Cover with oiled plastic wrap and allow to sit for about 30 minutes or until relaxed and extensible (when you pull the dough gently, it stretches without tearing).

7 > Shape the dough and let it rise. Press or roll each log into a rectangle and then shape into a 7 3/4-inch-long torpedo-shaped loaf (batard; see page 69). Set them on the prepared Cloche bottom(s) and/or on the baking sheet, leaving ample space between the 2 loaves for rising. *If you have only one La Cloche, set the second shaped loaf on a lined baking sheet and "retard" it by letting it rise in a cooler area (65° to 70°F). Place it in a warmer area when the first loaf goes into the oven. After removing the first loaf, replace the Cloche dome in the oven to preheat until the second loaf is ready to bake.* Cover with a large container or oiled plastic wrap and let rise (ideally at 75° to 80°F) until the dough puffs a bit more than the first 2 rises, about 2 to 2 1/2 hours. Each loaf will be about 8 1/2 inches by 5 1/2 inches wide. The dough will feel buoyant to the touch, and when pressed gently with your fingertip, it will spring back.

8 > Preheat the oven. Preheat the oven to 450°F, or 475°F if using La Cloche, 1 hour before baking. Have an oven shelf at the lowest level and place a baking stone or baking sheet on it before preheating. If not using La Cloche, place a cast-iron skillet or sheet pan on the floor of the oven to preheat. If using La Cloche, preheat the dome along with the oven.

9 > Slash and bake the bread. With a sharp knife or single-edged razor blade, make two or three 1/4- to 1/2-inch-deep diagonal slashes in the top of each loaf (see page 81).

If using La Cloche, carefully place the hot Cloche dome onto the base and quickly but gently set it on the hot stone or hot baking sheet. Bake for 10 minutes. Remove the dome, lower the temperature to 450°F, and continue baking for 15 to 20 minutes or until the bread is golden brown and a skewer inserted into the middle comes out clean (an instant-read thermometer inserted into the center will read about 190°F).

Alternatively, quickly but gently set the baking sheet on the hot stone or hot baking sheet. Toss 1/2 cup of ice cubes into the pan beneath and immediately shut the door. Bake for 15 minutes. With a heavy pancake turner, lift the breads from the pan and set directly on the stone, turning them around as you do so for even baking. Lower the temperature to 450°F and continue baking for 15 to 20 minutes or until the crust is tawny brown and a skewer inserted into the middle comes out clean (an instant-read thermometer inserted into the center will read about 190°F).

10 > Cool the bread. Remove the bread(s) from the oven and transfer to wire racks to cool completely.

VARIATION

Quicker Sourdough Seeded Wheat (using added commercial yeast) If your schedule requires speeding up the process (by about 25 percent), or if you feel more secure with the added reliability of commercial yeast, you can add up to 0.06 percent of the total weight of the flour in this recipe (including the added bran and germ and the flour contained in the starter). The total weight is 847 grams; 0.06 percent of 847 grams is 0.5 gram or 1/8 plus a scant 1/16 teaspoon/0.5 gram instant yeast. This should be added just before the seed mixture. At this low a percentage, it will not affect the acidity or flavor of the sourdough, but if it were added at the beginning, the commercial yeast would likely be killed by the acidity of the sourdough.

> It is imperative to use fresh whole wheat flour, as the bread will not rise if the flour is too old, unless commercial yeast is added.

UNDERSTANDING

The recipe Kathleen sent me called for a proportion of "reduced-bran flour," but as that flour is usually very difficult to obtain, I have created the equivalent flour by using bread flour and adding the appropriate amount of wheat bran and germ. Be sure to store the bran and germ in the refrigerator or freezer as they, particularly the germ, are highly prone to rancidity.

Once the seed mixture is added, the dough should not be kneaded much, as the seeds will cut through the gluten. The rolling and turning is a more gentle process.

This bread uses a very low amount of stiff sourdough starter, only 17.2 percent, which results in its appealingly dense texture and mildly sour flavor. Because it is part whole wheat flour, it is somewhat more active than an all-white flour starter, so less can be used. If you would prefer a lighter texture and more sour flavor, it's fine to increase the starter by as much as double. You will need to add 3/4 teaspoon/5 grams more salt to balance the extra flour and water.

This starter is the same as the basic stiff sourdough starter but it has part whole wheat flour. It too has the same consistency of a stiff biscuit dough, soft but not sticky. It also has double the weight of flour to water (or, by volume, 3 parts flour to 1 part water), 2 1/2 ounces/70 grams flour to 1 1/4 ounces/35 grams water.

If you have a stiff sourdough starter made with all-white wheat (bread flour), it's fine to use it here. By the time you have fed it twice, it will have plenty of whole wheat flour.

If you have an active liquid starter, you can turn it into a stiff sourdough starter simply by stirring in about half its weight of bread flour until it is firm enough to knead for a few minutes on a counter to the consistency of stiff biscuit dough. (It is difficult to give an exact volume amount of flour to add because the liquid starter is hard to measure accurately.)

THE DOUGH PERCENTAGE

Flour:	100% (bread: 47.9%, whole wheat: 50%, added bran and germ: 2.1%)
Seeds:	17.2%
Water:	67.7%
Dough Starter:	17.2%
Salt:	2.5%

Low-Risk Sourdough Bread

What a happy day it was when I discovered Lalvain in the King Arthur catalogue. This ideal starter from France, which contains a blend of yeast and bacteria, comes in powdered form and needs only to be mixed with water twelve hours before mixing a dough. When I baked my first bread using the version called Pain de Campagne, I was amazed to discover that it is a truly viable substitution for anyone who does not want to go to the effort of starting his or her own sourdough culture.

For a delicious, mild yet complex flavor, use the starter the day after mixing it and allow the shaped and risen bread to sit refrigerated overnight. For a true San Francisco–style tangy bread with large holes, use the Lalvain French Sourdough starter and let it sit for 1 week after mixing.

In order to produce a bread with the characteristic large open holes, this needs to be an exceptionally sticky dough and is therefore best made in a mixer.

TIME SCHEDULE

Liquid Sourdough Starter: minimum 12 hours, maximum 1 week
Minimum Rising Time: about 3 1/2 hours
Oven Temperature: 475°F, then 450°F
Baking Time: 25 to 30 minutes

Makes: a 7-by-3-inch-high round loaf/
about 14.75 ounces/421 grams

EQUIPMENT:

a heavy-duty mixer with dough hook attachment;

a banneton OR a small colander lined with a towel;

a half sheet pan lined with a nonstick liner such as Silpain or parchment;

a baking stone OR baking sheet

Liquid Sourdough Starter

Makes: 1 scant cup/8.5 ounces/240 grams

INGREDIENTS	MEASURE	WEIGHT	
	volume	ounces	grams
water, at room temperature (70° to 90°F)	1/2 liquid cup (4 fluid ounces)	4.25 ounces	120 grams
Lalvain Pain de Campagne starter (see page 37)	1/8 teaspoon	--	0.4 gram
bread flour	2/3 cup	3.5 ounces	100 grams
whole wheat flour or kamut flour	2 tablespoons	0.7 ounce	20 grams

1 > **Make the starter.** In a small bowl, combine all the ingredients and whisk until very smooth, to incorporate air, about 2 minutes. The starter will be the consistency of a thick batter. Scrape down the sides of the bowl.

Cover the bowl tightly with greased plastic wrap (or place the starter in a 2-cup food-storage container with a lid) and place it in a warm spot (70° to 80°F). Allow it to sit for at least 12 hours or up to 20 hours. It will be full of bubbles and will have risen by about one-third. It is ready to use, or it can be refrigerated for up to 7 days. If using the mixer method, chill for 1 hour.

Dough

INGREDIENTS	MEASURE	WEIGHT	
	volume	ounces	grams
liquid sourdough starter (from above)	*1 scant cup*	*scant 8.5 ounces*	*240 grams*
bread flour	1 1/4 cups	6.5 ounces	186 grams
instant yeast (see page 561 for brands)	1/4 teaspoon	--	0.8 gram

INGREDIENTS	MEASURE	WEIGHT	
	volume	ounces	grams
water, at room temperature (70° to 90°F)	6 tablespoons (3 fluid ounces)	about 3 ounces	88 grams
salt	3/4 teaspoon	--	5.2 grams

2 > Mix the dough.

Mixer Method

With an oiled spatula or dough scraper, scrape the cold liquid sourdough starter into the mixer bowl. Add the flour and yeast. With the dough hook on low speed (#2 if using a KitchenAid), gradually add the water and mix until the flour is moistened enough to form a rough dough. Continue kneading for 3 minutes, enough to develop the gluten structure a little. Scrape down any bits of dough. Cover the bowl with plastic wrap and allow the dough to rest for 20 minutes.

Sprinkle on the salt and knead on medium speed (#4 KitchenAid) for 3 minutes. The dough will still be sticky enough to cling to your fingers and very elastic. If it is very sticky, knead in a little flour. If it is not at all sticky, spray it with a little water and knead it. (The dough will measure about 2 cups and weigh about 17.7 ounces/ 502 grams.)

Hand Method

If it has been refrigerated, remove the starter to room temperature 1 hour before mixing the dough.

With an oiled spatula or dough scraper, scrape the starter into a large mixing bowl. With a wooden spoon, stir in the water, then stir in all but 2 tablespoons of the flour and the salt. Continuing with the wooden spoon or using your hand, mix until the flour is moistened. Knead the dough in the bowl until it comes together, then scrape it onto a lightly floured counter. Knead the dough for 5 minutes, enough to develop the gluten structure a little, adding as little of the reserved 2 tablespoons flour as possible to keep it from sticking. (To prevent sticking, it helps to use your fingertips, not the palms of your hands.) Use bench scraper to scrape the dough and gather it together as you knead it. At this point, it will be very sticky. Cover it with the inverted bowl and allow it to rest for 20 minutes. (This rest will make the dough less sticky and easier to work with.)

Knead the dough for another 5 to 10 minutes or until it is very smooth and elastic. It should be barely tacky (sticky) to the touch. If the dough is still very sticky, add some or all of the remaining reserved flour or a little extra. (The dough should measure about 2 cups and weigh about 17.7 ounces/502 grams.)

Both Methods

3 > **Let the dough rise.** Using an oiled spatula or dough scraper, scrape the dough into a 4-cup glass measuring cup or 1-quart food-storage container, lightly greased with cooking spray or oil. Press down the dough and lightly spray or oil the top. Cover the measuring cup with plastic wrap; or cover the container with a lid and, with a piece of tape, mark the side of the container at approximately where double the height of the dough would be. Allow the dough to rise (ideally at 75° to 80°F) for 1 hour. (It will not yet have doubled.)

Scrape the dough onto a lightly floured counter. Gently push it down to deflate it, and stretch it into a rectangle (the exact size isn't important). Give it 2 business letter turns. It will be very soft and stretchy, but it will become a little firmer after each turn. Return the dough to the greased container and grease the top lightly with cooking spray or oil. Cover the container with a lid or plastic wrap and allow it to sit for another hour.

Stretch the dough again, give it 2 business letter turns, and return it to the container. Continue to let it rise until doubled.

4 > **Shape the dough and let it rise.** Without deflating it, turn the dough out onto a floured counter and round it into a ball (see page 65). Set it in a floured banneton or colander lined with a floured towel, seam side up. Pinch the seam together if it starts to open. In the banneton, the dough will be about 2 inches from the top.

Spray the dough with oil or sprinkle lightly with flour and cover it with a large container or plastic wrap. Let the dough rise until almost doubled, 1 1/2 to 2 hours. When it is pressed gently with a fingertip, the depression will very slowly fill in. (Alternatively, you can refrigerate the risen shaped dough for up to 20 hours before baking it. This will develop more sour flavor should you desire it—and possibly fit better into your schedule. Remove it from the refrigerator 30 minutes before baking.)

5 > **Preheat the oven.** Preheat the oven to 475°F 1 hour before baking. Have an oven shelf at the lowest level and place an oven stone or baking sheet on it, and a cast-iron skillet or sheet pan on the floor of the oven, before preheating.

6 > **Slash and bake the dough.** Very gently invert the dough onto the prepared baking sheet. (If you are using a colander, and the risen bread is more than 1 inch below the top, you will need to support the bread when inverting it so that it doesn't fall and deflate. Cut a cardboard circle small enough to fit into the colander and touch the surface of the bread. Place a piece of parchment on top of the bread, place the cardboard on top, and invert onto the cardboard. Then slide the bread, still on the parchment, onto the baking sheet.) For a more evenly rounded bread, it's fine to leave the dough unslashed. If you like the rustic appearance of a slashed top crust, with

sharp scissors, a sharp knife, or a single-edged razor blade, slash a 1/4-inch-deep cross in the dough. Because the skin of the dough is very dry, it will be difficult to slash; use a gentle touch so as not to deflate the dough. (I find that small sharp scissors work best.)

Quickly but gently set the baking sheet on the hot baking stone or hot baking sheet. Toss 1/2 cup of ice cubes into the pan beneath and immediately shut the door. Bake for 5 minutes. Lower the oven to 450°F and continue baking for 20 to 25 minutes or until deep brown and a skewer inserted into the middle comes out clean (an instant-read thermometer inserted into the center will read about 212°F). Halfway through baking, with a heavy pancake turner, lift the bread from the pan and set it directly on the stone, turning it halfway around as you do so for even baking. For a very crisp crust, prop the oven door slightly ajar for the last 5 minutes of baking.

7 > **Cool the bread.** Remove the bread from the oven and transfer it to a wire rack to cool completely.

UNDERSTANDING

If you use the starter cold from the refrigerator, and add the remaining flour and water at room temperature, the dough will be about 75°F after mixing, which is the ideal temperature.

THE DOUGH PERCENTAGE

Flour:	100% (bread: 93.5, whole wheat: 6.5%)
Water:	68%
Yeast:	0.39%
Salt:	1.7%

French Country Sourdough Boule

This fantastic *boule* is the one taught at the French Culinary Institute in New York City. It boasts a deep brown, chewy crust and a nicely distributed open and springy crumb. To my taste, it is just sour enough without being overwhelmingly so, enabling it also to be nicely complex in flavor. This is a very wet and sticky dough, so it is best made in a mixer. In fact, the dough is so soft it almost puddles, and each time I make it I think it will never rise—but then it reliably balloons to 3 1/2 inches in height. I have worked out this recipe using the excellent packaged French sourdough starter called Lalvain Pain de Campagne starter to make it possible for people who don't have their own sourdough starter to make this wonderful bread.

TIME SCHEDULE

Liquid Sourdough Starter: minimum 12 hours, maximum 6 days
Minimum Rising Time: 3 hours
Oven Temperature: 475°F, then 450°F
Baking: 25 to 30 minutes

Makes: a 6 3/4-by-3 1/2-inch-high round loaf
14.5 ounces/410 grams

EQUIPMENT:

a heavy-duty stand mixer with dough hook attachment;

a banneton OR a small colander lined with a towel;

a half sheet pan lined with a nonstick liner such as Silpain or parchment;

a baking stone OR baking sheet

Liquid Sourdough Starter

Makes: 1/3 cup/3.5 ounces/100 grams

INGREDIENTS	MEASURE	WEIGHT	
	volume	ounces	grams
bread flour	1/3 cup	1.75 ounces	50 grams
Lalvain Pain de Campagne starter (see page 37)	1/16 teaspoon	--	0.2 gram
water, at room temperature (70° to 90°F)	3 1/2 tablespoons	1.75 ounces	50 grams

1 > **Make the starter.** In a small bowl, combine all the ingredients and stir the mixture with a wooden spoon for 3 to 5 minutes or until very smooth. It will be very liquid.

Cover the bowl tightly with greased plastic wrap (or place the starter in a 1-cup food-storage container with a lid) and place it in a warm spot (70° to 90°F). Allow it to sit for at least 12 hours, or up to 20 hours. It will be full of bubbles and will have risen by about one-third. It is ready to use to make the dough, or it can be refrigerated for up to 3 days.

Dough

INGREDIENTS	MEASURE	WEIGHT	
	volume	ounces	grams
liquid sourdough starter (from above)	*full 1/4 cup*	*3.5 ounces*	*100 grams*
water	2/3 liquid cup	5.3 ounces	150 grams
bread flour	1 cup	5 ounces	156 grams
medium rye flour	1/3 cup	1.5 ounces	40 grams
whole wheat flour	3 tablespoons	1 ounce	29 grams
instant yeast (see page 561 for brands)	1/4 teaspoon	--	0.8 gram
salt	3/4 plus 1/8 teaspoon	--	5.8 grams

2 > **Mix the dough.** Place the starter in the mixer bowl and stir in the water.

In a medium bowl, whisk together the bread flour, rye, whole wheat, and yeast. Sprinkle this mixture on top of the liquid in the mixer bowl. With the dough hook, mix on low speed (#2 if using a KitchenAid) until the flour is moistened enough to form a rough dough. Scrape down any bits of dough. Cover the top of the bowl with plastic wrap and allow the dough to rest for 20 minutes.

Sprinkle on the salt and knead the dough on medium speed (#4 KitchenAid) for 10 minutes. It will be exceptionally sticky and very elastic. If it does not cling to your fingers, spray it with a little water and knead it in. (It should weigh about 16.25 ounces/461 grams—but only if you wet your fingers and get every last smidgen.)

3 > Let the dough rise. Using an oiled spatula or dough scraper, scrape the dough into a 2-quart dough-rising container or bowl, lightly greased with cooking spray or oil. Push down the dough and lightly spray or oil the top. Cover the container with a lid or plastic wrap. With a piece of tape, mark the side of the container at approximately where double the height of the dough would be. Allow the dough to rise (ideally at 75° to 80°F) until doubled, 1 1/2 to 2 hours.

Using an oiled spatula or dough scraper, scrape the dough onto a floured counter and press down on it gently to form a rectangle. Give the dough 2 business letter turns and set it back in the container. Oil the surface again, cover, and mark where double the height of the dough would now be. (It will fill the container fuller than before because it is puffier with air.) Allow to rise until doubled, about 1 hour.

4 > Shape the dough and let it rise. Turn the dough out onto a lightly floured counter and press it gently to flatten it slightly. Round the dough into a ball (see page 65), dusting with as little flour as possible to keep it from sticking. It will still be very sticky. Set it in a banneton or a small colander lined with a floured cloth and cover it with a large container or oiled plastic wrap. Let it rise until almost doubled, about 1 hour. When the dough is pressed gently with a fingertip the depression will very slowly fill in. (In the banneton, the center of the loaf should come to the top of the banneton sides or a little above.)

5 > Preheat the oven. Preheat the oven to 475°F 1 hour before baking. Have an oven shelf at the lowest level and place a baking stone or baking sheet on it, and a cast-iron skillet or sheet pan on the floor of the oven, before preheating.

6 > Slash and bake the bread. Very gently invert the dough onto the prepared baking sheet. (If you are using a colander and the risen bread is more than 1 inch below the top, you will need to support the bread when inverting it so that it doesn't fall and deflate. Cut a cardboard circle small enough to fit into the colander and touch the surface of the bread. Place a piece of parchment on top of the bread, place the cardboard on top, and invert onto the cardboard. Then slide the bread, still on the parchment, onto the baking sheet.) With small sharp scissors, a sharp knife, or a single-edged razor blade, make 1/4-inch-deep slashes in the top of the dough (see pages 80–81). Because the skin of the dough is very dry, it will be difficult to slash; use a gentle touch so as not to deflate the dough.

Quickly but gently set the baking sheet on the hot baking stone or hot baking sheet. Toss 1/2 cup of ice cubes into the pan beneath and immediately shut the door.

Chocolate Sticky Buns > page 502

Traditional Challah > page 516

Traditional Challah, sliced

Stud Muffin > page 528

Sliced Stud Muffin with prosciutto

Monkey Bread > page 506

Chocolate Almond Swirl Kugelhopf
> page 522

Wheaten Croissants with orange
marmalade > page 533

Bake for 5 minutes. Lower the oven to 450°F and continue baking for 20 to 25 minutes or until the bread is deep brown and a skewer inserted in the middle comes out clean (an instant-read thermometer inserted into the center will read about 212°F). Halfway through baking, with a heavy pancake turner, lift the bread from the pan and set it directly on the stone, turning it around as you do so for even baking.

7 > **Cool the bread.** Remove the bread from the oven and transfer it to a wire rack to cool completely.

ULTIMATE FULL FLAVOR VERSION

If desired, at the end of Step 3, the dough can be placed in an oiled freezer-weight plastic bag and refrigerated overnight. It will develop more flavor, but be sure to let it sit at room temperature for 1 1/2 hours before shaping.

UNDERSTANDING

When I refrigerated the finished dough for 2 days, the baked bread rose to only 2 1/2 inches, making it denser and more chewy. It tasted very tangy and delicious. (It took 3 1/2 hours to rise after shaping.)

This dough has less than half the commercial yeast normally used because of the Lalvain sourdough starter and the rye flour, which speed the rising.

If you have an active sourdough starter, you can certainly use it to replace the Lalvain and instant yeast in this recipe, and eliminate the added yeast entirely. (See the variation on page 450 of the Basic Sourdough Recipe.) It will take much longer to rise, 6 to 7 hours for the first rise and about 3 hours for the shaped rise.

You can vary the proportion of whole wheat to all-purpose flour depending on how wheaty a taste you crave, but keep in mind that the whole wheat also adds bitterness.

THE DOUGH PERCENTAGE

Flour:	100% (bread: 75%, rye: 14.5, whole wheat: 10.5%)
Water:	72.7%
Yeast:	0.36%
Salt:	2.1%

The Brioche Family of Breads

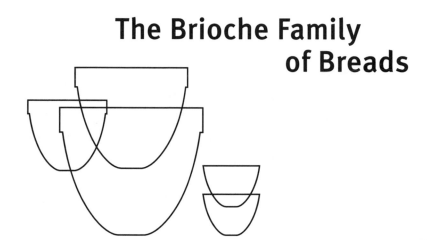

THE BRIOCHE DOUGH IS SO SOFT AND SILKY, I LOOK FORWARD TO MAKING IT just to enjoy the feel of it under my hands. The finished dough is so full of life it requires constant deflating during its maturing rest in the refrigerator. When I worked with the legendary chocolate makers the Bernachons in Lyon, France, translating their book *A Passion for Chocolate*, I learned a new word for handling brioche dough. Papa Bernachon advised me to remember to *rompre* the dough at frequent intervals while it was chilling. When I asked him the meaning of *rompre* he looked puzzled. He sought the help of several bakers in his kitchen to translate the term but they could not, so I watched for its meaning as they lifted the dough and tossed it over on itself a few times to suppress its vigorous rise. It was an indelible lesson in witnessing the vigor of brioche dough.

Brioche is, of course, wonderful eaten on its own, but it is also the basis for a host of bread creations from kugelhopf and challah (both a less rich brioche) to panettone (a super-rich brioche). The entire family of egg-and-butter-rich doughs is among people's favorites and these breads are an inevitable feature of celebration and holiday tables, especially at Thanksgiving and Christmas. And what could be more welcome than sticky buns (also made from brioche dough) for Sunday brunch?

Although I wrote about brioche in *The Cake Bible* and *The Pie and Pastry Bible*, I am offering it once again because no book on bread would be complete without it. Also, I have more to say! I've improved the basic recipe and technique and, more important, I have significantly improved my recipe for sticky buns, a personal favorite. I now caramelize the sugar topping before setting the unbaked buns on top of it, to make the caramel deeper, more intense, and more gooey. And I've also perfected the texture of the buns, achieving a crisp outside crust and soft but not doughy crumb, by baking them in a special mold with individual cups (you can also use "Texas" muffin pans). I love the sticky bun so much, I've come up with two new versions that rival the original: a luscious chocolate sticky bun and a maple walnut sticky bun.

Of all the egg breads in this chapter, the Stud Muffin (page 528) has the least egg, only 10 percent, compared to brioche, which has 66 percent. Less egg would normally result in a less airy texture, but this is not the case here because the Stud Muffin has large holes resulting from the cubes of cheese that melt into the crumb, leaving behind air spaces, resulting in the kind of structure normally provided by egg.

The two recipes in this chapter that don't contain eggs are the Wheaten Croissants (page 533) and the Monkey Bread (page 506). Aside from this absence of egg, croissant and brioche have the same ingredients. flour, yeast, salt, sugar, milk, and butter. There are only two significant differences: croissant dough contains almost double the amount of butter and has only milk as the liquid component, whereas the liquid for brioche dough comes mostly from eggs, with only a little milk. The eggs in the brioche dough give it an airy cake-like crumb, while the large amount of butter in the croissant dough, and the way in which it is rolled and layered into the dough, gives it its flaky crumb.

Monkey Bread is not actually a legitimate member of the brioche family because the dough used to make it is the Soft White Bread dough from Chapter 4. It is similar in texture to the soft and airy brioche, but it is less rich since it has no egg and less butter. However, it is in this chapter because its filling of brown sugar, raisins, pecans, and butter make it akin to sticky buns. While I chose this dough for Monkey Bread because the richness of the filling balances well with a less rich dough, you could, of course, if you prefer, use brioche dough in its place.

POINTERS FOR SUCCESS SPECIFIC TO BRIOCHE FAMILY BREADS

> Do not allow the dough to rise more than the number of times recommended in the recipes, or the rise will weaken the structure and cause the bread to be heavy.

> Be sure to chill the dough thoroughly before deflating it, or the butter will leak out. If this should happen inadvertently, chill the dough for 1 hour and knead the butter back into the dough.

> When shaping the dough, be sure to brush off any excess flour, or it will form a hard thin line inside the soft dough.

> Steam is not used when an egg glaze is used, as it would dull the glaze.

> Slashing the top of the loaf prevents it from opening unattractively at the sides.

> Wait until the breads are completely cool before cutting to prevent collapse.

> Cut these breads with an electric knife or a serrated knife to avoid compressing and crushing the airy crumb.

UNDERSTANDING

The proportion of basic essential ingredients in egg breads fall into the range of 39 to 77.2 percent water, 0.83 to 2.2 percent instant yeast, 0.52 to 2.5 percent salt, and 12.1 to 53.7 percent butterfat or oil. These percentages are based on the Baker's Percentage, in which every ingredient is based on flour which is given the value of 100 percent. However, here the water and fat percentages include what is contained in any added ingredient, such as eggs and butter.

Because eggs and butter contribute so much flavor, I use a shorter sponge time than for some of the other breads, but if it is more convenient to make the sponge the night ahead, it's fine to let it sit for 1 hour at room temperature and then refrigerate it for up to 24 hours before mixing (cold from the refrigerator). There will be no perceptible difference in flavor or texture.

Basic Brioche

This is my basic brioche recipe, soft, light, and intensely buttery. For those who desire even more butter, it can be increased to 6 ounces, which will also make the crumb finer, denser, and more cake-like. This is actually a very easy dough to make, especially in a bread machine, which handles this small amount of dough perfectly.

TIME SCHEDULE

Dough Starter (Sponge): minimum 1 1/2 hours, maximum 24 hours
Minimum Rising Time: 10 hours
Oven Temperature: 425°F (350°F for the loaf)
Baking Time: 10 to 15 minutes for small brioche, 35 to 40 minutes for the loaf

Makes: 16 small brioche (or one 8 1/2-by-4 1/2-by-4 1/2-inch-high loaf)/
17.5 ounces/500 grams

Dough Starter (Sponge)

INGREDIENTS	MEASURE	WEIGHT	
	volume	ounces	grams
water, at room temperature (70° to 90°F)	2 tablespoons	1 ounce	29.5 grams
sugar	1 tablespoon	scant 0.5 ounce	12.5 grams
instant yeast (see page 561 for brands)	1/4 teaspoon	--	0.8 gram
unbleached all-purpose flour (use only Gold Medal, King Arthur, or Pillsbury)	1/2 cup	2.5 ounces	71 grams
1 large egg	--	2 ounces (weighed in the shell)	58 grams

EQUIPMENT:

a heavy-duty mixer with dough hook attachment;

sixteen 2 3/4-inch brioche molds (OR an 8 1/2-by-4 1/2-inch loaf pan if making one loaf), lightly greased with cooking spray or oil or well buttered;

a baking stone OR baking sheet

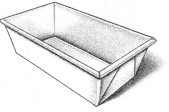

1 > **One day or up to 2 days ahead, make the dough.** In the mixer bowl, place the water, sugar, instant yeast, flour, and egg. Whisk by hand until very smooth, to incorporate air, about 3 minutes. The sponge will be the consistency of a very thick batter. (At first the dough may collect inside the whisk, but just shake it out and keep whisking. If it's too thick to whisk, it means you've added too much flour and will need to add a little of the eggs to be added Step 3.) Scrape down the sides of the bowl and set it aside, covered with plastic wrap.

Flour Mixture

INGREDIENTS	MEASURE	WEIGHT	
	volume	ounces	grams
unbleached all-purpose flour (use only Gold Medal, King Arthur, or Pillsbury)	1 cup plus 1 1/2 tablespoons	5.5 ounces	156 grams
sugar	2 tablespoons	about 0.75 ounce	25 grams
instant yeast	1 1/4 teaspoons	--	4 grams
salt	1/2 teaspoon	--	3.3 grams
2 large eggs, cold	--	4 ounces (weighed in the shells)	113 grams
unsalted butter, very soft	8 tablespoons	4 ounces	113 grams

2 > **Combine the ingredients for the flour mixture and add to the sponge.** In a small bowl, whisk the flour with the sugar and yeast. Then whisk in the salt (this keeps the yeast from coming in contact with the salt, which would kill it). Sprinkle this mixture on top of the sponge. Cover it tightly with plastic wrap and let it stand for 1 1/2 to 2 hours. (During this time, the sponge will bubble through the flour mixture in places; this is fine.)

3 > Mix the dough. Add the 2 cold eggs and mix with the dough hook on low (#2 if using a KitchenAid) for about 1 minute or until the flour is moistened. Raise the speed to medium (#4 KitchenAid) and beat for 2 minutes. Scrape the sides of the bowl with an oiled spatula and continue beating for about 5 minutes longer or until the dough is smooth and shiny but very soft and sticky. It will mass around the dough hook but not pull away from the bowl completely.

Add the butter by the tablespoon, waiting until each addition is almost completely absorbed before adding the next tablespoon, beating until all the butter is incorporated. The dough will be very soft and elastic and will stick to your fingers unmercifully, but don't be tempted to add more flour at this point; it will firm considerably after chilling. (The dough will weigh about 19 ounces/536 grams.)

4 > Let the dough rise. Using an oiled spatula or dough scraper, scrape the dough into a 1-quart dough rising container or bowl, greased lightly with cooking spray or oil. Lightly spray or oil the top of the dough and cover the container with a lid or plastic wrap. With a piece of tape, mark the side of the container at approximately where double the height of the dough would be. Allow the dough to rise until doubled, 1 1/2 to 2 hours.

5 > Chill the dough. Refrigerate the dough for 1 hour to firm it; this will prevent the butter from separating.

Gently deflate the dough by stirring it with a rubber scraper or spatula, and return it to the refrigerator for another hour so that it will be less sticky and easier to handle.

6 > Deflate the dough and allow it to rest, chilled. Turn the dough out onto a well-floured surface and press or roll it into a rectangle, flouring the surface and dough as needed to keep it from sticking. The exact size of the rectangle is not important. Give the dough a business letter turn, brushing off any excess flour, and again press down or roll it out into a rectangle. Rotate it 90 degrees so that the closed side is facing to your left. Give it a second business letter turn and round the corners. Dust it lightly on all sides with flour. Wrap it loosely but securely in plastic wrap and then place it in a large zip-seal bag. Refrigerate for at least 6 hours or up to 2 days to allow the dough to ripen (develop flavor) and firm.

7 > Shape the dough and let it rise. Remove the dough from the refrigerator and gently press it down to deflate it. Cut the dough into 16 pieces (a scant 1 1/4 ounces/33 grams each). Without a scale, the easiest way to divide the dough evenly is to lightly flour your hands and roll it into a long cylinder. Cut it in half, then continue cutting each piece in half until there are 16 pieces.

Pinch off a little less than one-quarter of each piece, for the topknot. Roll each larger piece of dough into a ball and press it into a prepared brioche mold. With lightly floured hands, shape each of the dough pieces reserved for the topknots into an elongated pear form. Using your index finger, make a hole in the center of each brioche, going almost to the bottom of the mold, and insert the elongated part of a topknot deeply into the hole. Cover the molds loosely with oiled plastic wrap and let rise (ideally at 75° to 80°F) until the edges of the dough reach the tops of the molds, about 1 hour. (See page 493 for step-by-step illustrations.)

8 > Preheat the oven. Preheat the oven to 425°F 1 hour before baking. Have an oven shelf at the lower level and place a baking stone or baking sheet on it before preheating.

Egg Glaze (if making a large loaf, glaze is optional)

INGREDIENTS	MEASURE	WEIGHT	
	volume	ounces	grams
1 large egg yolk	1 tablespoon	--	--
cream or milk	1 teaspoon	--	--

9 > Glaze and bake the brioche. Lightly beat together the egg yolk and cream for the glaze. Brush the top of the brioche with the egg glaze, being careful not to drip any on the side of the pans, or it will impede rising. Allow it to dry for 5 minutes and then brush a second time with the glaze. Use greased scissors or a small sharp knife to make a 1/4-inch-deep cut all around the base of the topknot so it will rise to an attractive shape.

Set the molds on a baking sheet and place them on the hot stone or hot baking sheet. Bake for 10 to 15 minutes, or until a skewer inserted under a topknot comes out clean (an instant-read thermometer inserted into the center will read about 190°F).

10 > Cool the brioche. Remove the brioche from the oven and unmold them onto a wire rack. Turn top side up and allow them to cool until barely warm.

NOTE   The small brioche can be reheated in a 350°F oven for 5 minutes.

ULTIMATE FULL FLAVOR VARIATION

For the best flavor development in Step 2, allow the sponge to ferment for 1 hour at room temperature, then refrigerate it for up to 24 hours.

VARIATIONS

Black Pepper Brioche   When I tasted this brioche, filled with lobster salad, at Larry Forgione's An American Place years ago, I imagined that it would be a great counterpoint to the smokiness of bacon. It does indeed make an amazingly delicious BLT! Simply add 1 1/2 teaspoons (4 grams) coarse or butcher's grind black pepper along with the salt.

Sweet Potato Brioche   This delightful version was inspired by Julia Carter, who used to be Susan Spicer's pastry chef at Bayona Restaurant in New Orleans. Sweet potato, or yam, adds a beautiful golden color and moister texture to the brioche, without adding the eggy flavor that more egg would produce. The flavor of the sweet potato, however, is so subtle as to be unnoticeable.

Add 1/2 cup (about 4.5 ounces/126 grams) of sieved baked sweet potato or yam to the dough when adding the cold eggs. The overall sugar can be decreased by 1 tablespoon to compensate for the sweetness of the potato.

Brioche Loaf   The basic recipe, or the above variations, can be baked as one large loaf. Follow the recipe as written through Step 6, then proceed as directed below.

7 > **Shape the dough and let it rise.** Deflate the dough as directed, then press or roll the dough into a rectangle about 7 1/2 inches long and 5 inches wide. Roll it down from the top in 3 turns, being sure to brush off any excess flour, pressing with your thumbs to seal the dough (see illustrations on page 493). Place it seam side down in the prepared pan, pressing it down firmly. Cover it lightly with oiled plastic wrap and allow it to rise until the top of the dough reaches the top of the pan, 1 1/2 to 2 hours.

8 > **Preheat the oven.** Preheat the oven to 350°F 30 minutes before baking. Have an oven shelf at the lowest level and place a baking stone or baking sheet on it before preheating.

9 > **Glaze (if desired), slash, and bake the brioche loaf.** For a shiny top crust, brush with the optional egg glaze. With a sharp knife or single-edged razor blade, make a 1/4- to 1/2-inch-deep lengthwise slash in the dough, starting about 1 inch from one end of the pan and going to within 1 inch of the other end.

Set the pan on the hot stone or hot baking sheet. Bake for 35 to 40 minutes or until golden brown and a skewer inserted into the center comes out clean (an instant-read thermometer inserted into the center will read about 190°F).

10 > **Cool the brioche loaf.** Remove the brioche from the oven and unmold it onto a wire rack. Turn top side up and allow it to cool until barely warm, at least 2 hours.

Giant Brioche

Makes: a 9-inch-by-5-inch-high round loaf/2 1/4
pounds/1047 grams

EQUIPMENT:

**a 2-quart brioche mold, well buttered or greased
with cooking spray or oil**

Make a double recipe of Basic Brioche dough
(2 pounds 6 ounces/1 kilogram, 80 grams), fol-
lowing the recipe as written through Step 6. Shape and let rise as in Step 7 (page
489). Glaze and bake as in Steps 8 and 9, but after 5 minutes at 425°F turn down the
oven to 375°F and continue baking for 45 to 55 minutes or until a skewer inserted
under the topknot comes out clean. (An instant-read thermometer inserted into the
center will read about 190°F.) After about 20 minutes at 375°F, or when the top crust
is brown, tent it loosely with foil, shiny side out. Cool for several hours until barely
warm.

Dairy Dinner Challah

People often complain that challah seems dry. This one isn't, because it's a true brioche,
made with butter. According to kashruth (kosher) laws, bread made with butter or
dairy products cannot be eaten when meat is served at the same meal. So break with
tradition, and serve fish instead of chicken one Friday night. This challah will still be
moist the next morning, ready to be lightly toasted and topped with smoked salmon.

Makes: a 9-by-5-inch-high round loaf/
2 1/4 pounds/1047 grams

EQUIPMENT:

**a 9-by-3-inch cake pan, well buttered (a 2-inch-high pan will also
work, but the top decoration may spread apart a little)**

Make a double recipe of Basic Brioche dough (2 pounds 6 ounces/1 kilogram, 80 grams),
following the recipe as written through Step 6, then proceeding as directed below.

7 > **Shape the dough and let it rise.** Remove the dough from the refrigerator. Flatten
it gently so as not to activate the gluten, making it stretchy. For a loaf with a braided
top, divide the dough into 3 equal parts. Roll each on a lightly floured counter into a

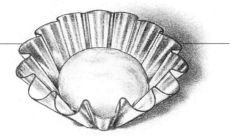

1> The dough ball in the mold

2> Shaping the topknot

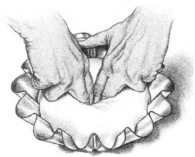

3> Making a hole in the center of the dough ball

4> Inserting the topknot deep into the hole

5> Snipping a 1/4-inch cut all around the base of the topknot

6> Inserting an instant-read thermometer into the center of the baked brioche

rope about 26 inches long. (If the dough is very elastic, allow it to rest, covered with plastic wrap, for 5 to 10 minutes.) For the most symmetrical loaf, braid the dough starting from the center and working toward each end, pinching it at the ends (see page 73). Coil the braid into the pan, starting at the center, and tucking the end underneath. Or, for an elegant snail shape, make one long thick rope and coil it around in the same manner.

8 > **Glaze the dough and let it rise.** Brush the dough with the egg glaze, going deep into the crevices. Cover and refrigerate the remaining glaze. Cover the dough with a plastic box (page 588) or oiled plastic wrap and allow it to rise in a warm place until the dough has reached the top of the pan, about 1 1/2 to 2 hours.

9 > **Preheat the oven.** Preheat the oven to 425°F 1 hour before baking. Have an oven shelf at the lowest level and place a baking stone or baking sheet on it before preheating.

Egg Glaze

INGREDIENTS	MEASURE	WEIGHT	
	volume	ounces	grams
lightly beaten egg	1 to 2 tablespoons	--	--
poppy seeds	1 tablespoon	0.33	9 grams

10 > **Glaze and bake the challah.** Brush the challah again with the egg glaze, going well into the crevices; be careful not to drip any down the side of the pan, or it will impede rising. Sprinkle the challah with the poppy seeds.

Place the pan onto the hot baking stone or hot baking sheet and bake for 5 minutes. Lower the heat to 375°F and continue baking for 50 to 55 minutes or until the bread is golden and a skewer inserted into the middle comes out clean (an instant-read thermometer inserted into the center will read about 190°F). After about 20 minutes at 375°F, or when the top crust is brown, tent it loosely with foil.

11 > **Cool the challah.** Remove the pan from the oven and unmold the challah onto a wire rack. Turn it top side up to cool completely.

Convenience Brioche

To make the dough in a bread machine with a programmable setting and pause button, after mixing the sponge (Step 1), scrape it into the bread machine container and sprinkle the flour blanket on top, as in Step 2. Add the cold eggs (Step 3) and mix the dough for 3 minutes, then let it proceed through the knead cycle for about 8 minutes, or until the dough is smooth, shiny, and elastic. You will need to pause the machine a few times to scrape out any flour or dough that collects in the corners of the container. Add the softened butter at once and continue the kneading cycle until it is incorporated, about 3 minutes, pausing and scraping down the sides if necessary.

For the first rise (Step 4), turn off the machine and let the dough rise (with the lid closed) until approximately doubled, 1 1/2 to 2 hours. Remove the container from the machine, cover it with plastic wrap, and refrigerate it for 1 hour (Step 5). Return the container to the bread machine (you can leave the plastic wrap in place) and deflate the dough by pressing the mix button and mixing for about 30 seconds. Return the container to the refrigerator for 1 hour. Then proceed from Step 6, deflating and chilling the dough.

POINTERS FOR SUCCESS

> In a superb article on brioche in *Pleasures of Cooking,* the cookbook author Paula Wolfert recommends melting and browning about one-fifth of the butter (2 tablespoons) for an extra rich, delicious flavor.

> On some mixers there may not be an adjustment to raise the bowl, and the dough hook may not work as well for this small amount of dough; if this is the case, use the paddle beater.

> If after unmolding a brioche loaf the sides are still pale in color, place the loaf directly on the oven rack and continue baking for about 5 minutes to brown the sides and make them firm to prevent collapse.

> If a deeper shine is desired, the brioche can be double-glazed by brushing with the glaze immediately after shaping and then a second time just before baking. This also serves to prevent the dough from drying out during rising.

UNDERSTANDING

This dough is exceptionally wet. Just enough extra flour is added to be able to handle it for shaping, resulting in a very light, soft bread. I do not use the food processor for this dough because it is so sticky that it is very difficult to remove from the bowl and blade; it also lifts up the blade when incorporating the butter.

THE DOUGH PERCENTAGE

Flour:	100%
Water:	55.4% (includes the water in the butter and egg white)
Yeast:	2.1%
Salt:	1.5%
Fat:	47.7% (includes the fat in the egg yolk)

Sticky Caramel Buns

A sticky bun has everything: a buttery soft moist crumb, plump sweet raisins, nutty pecans, and, most wonderful of all, sticky/chewy caramel. My favorite caramel for these buns uses light brown sugar, preferably muscovado for the best flavor. Adding heavy cream helps to keep the caramel smooth so that during baking some of it is absorbed into the dough and the rest coats the tops.

Sticky buns are at their very best within minutes after baking. I discovered this simply out of impatience! But they stay fresh, if stored airtight at room temperature, for up to two days, and a few minutes in a 350°F oven will restore them almost to their original glory.

Consider the professional method below of making sticky buns using a Flexipan Texas-size cupcake mold. The pan is an investment, but it will probably last a lifetime and once you try it, you'll never go back to any other method. Each bun will have a perfect round shape and every last bit of caramel topping floats out without coaxing. And baking the buns in individual cups gives them a wonderfully crisp outside crust.

TIME SCHEDULE

Advance Preparation: make the dough 1 to 2 days ahead
Minimum Rising Time: 1 to 2 hours
Oven Temperature: 375°F
Baking Time: 25 to 30 minutes

Makes: 12 buns

EQUIPMENT:

a 9-by-13-inch baking pan, lightly greased;

a baking stone OR baking sheet.

Sticky Bun Filling

INGREDIENTS	MEASURE	WEIGHT	
	volume	ounces	grams
raisins	1/2 cup	2.5 ounces	72 grams
dark rum	2 tablespoons	1 ounce	28 grams
boiling water	1/4 liquid cup	2 ounces	60 grams
pecans, toasted and coarsely chopped	1/4 cup	1 ounce	28 grams
light brown sugar	1/4 cup (firmly packed)	2 ounces	56 grams
granulated sugar	1 tablespoon	0.5 ounce	13 grams
cinnamon	2 teaspoons	--	9.6 grams

1 > **Make the sticky bun filling.** Place the raisins in a small heatproof bowl. Add the rum and boiling water, cover, and let stand for at least 1 hour to plump the raisins. When ready to fill the dough, drain the raisins, reserving the soaking liquid for the glaze.

In another bowl, combine the chopped nuts, sugars, and cinnamon.

Sticky Bun Topping and Dough

INGREDIENTS	MEASURE	WEIGHT	
	volume	ounces	grams
unsalted butter, softened	1/4 cup	2 ounces	56 grams
light brown sugar	1/2 cup (firmly packed)	4 ounces	112 grams
Lyle's golden syrup or light corn syrup	1 tablespoon	0.75 ounce	21 grams
heavy cream, heated until warm or hot	3 tablespoons	1.5 ounces	42 grams
1 recipe Basic Brioche dough (page 487)	--	*about 19 ounces*	540 grams
lightly beaten egg	1 tablespoon	about 0.5 ounce	16 grams
pecan halves	1/2 cup	2 ounces	56 grams

2 > **Make the sticky bun topping.** In a small heavy saucepan, off the heat, stir together the butter, brown sugar, and syrup until the sugar is moistened. Bring to a boil over low heat, stirring constantly. Simmer, without stirring, for 5 minutes (only 3 minutes if using a cast-iron pan, as it will continue cooking). There will be many bubbles and the caramel will be dark brown; do not allow it to get too brown. If you are using a thermometer, it should be 244°F. Pour in the heavy cream and swirl the pan to mix it in. Continue simmering for 3 minutes, swirling the pan occasionally, or if you are using a thermometer, until it returns to 244°F. Pour the syrup evenly into the prepared pan. Cool completely.

3 > Fill the dough. Roll out the dough on a well-floured surface into a 14-by-12-inch rectangle. Move it around from time to time to make sure it is not sticking, and add more flour if necessary. Brush it with the lightly beaten egg, right up to the edges, and sprinkle it with the sugar mixture and drained raisins. Roll it up from a long end, brushing off excess flour as you go (it helps to use a long ruler slipped slightly under the dough to lift and roll it). Push in the ends so that they are the same thickness as the middle and the roll is 12 inches long. For ease in slicing, you can slide the dough onto a baking sheet and refrigerate it for 30 minutes, or freeze it for 5 to 10 minutes covered with plastic wrap.

4 > Cut the dough and let the buns rise. Using a piece of dental floss or heavy kitchen string, or a sharp knife, cut the roll into 4 pieces, then cut each piece into thirds (each piece will be about 1 inch thick). Place 3 pecan halves onto one cut end of each bun and place pecan side down in the prepared pan. Push down the tops so that the sides of the buns touch. Cover with oiled plastic wrap. Let the buns rise in a warm place (ideally 75° to 85°F) until they double, 1 to 2 hours. They should be airy and puffy and about 3/4 inch from the top of the pan. (Note: If you want to bake the sticky buns the following day, as soon as they are shaped, refrigerate them for up to 14 hours. They will take about 2 1/2 hours to rise before baking. You can speed the rising to about 1 1/2 hours by placing them in a proof box with hot water; see page 588.)

Sticky Bun Glaze

INGREDIENTS	MEASURE	WEIGHT	
	volume	ounces	grams
reserved raisin soaking liquid	--	--	--
unsalted butter	1 tablespoon	0.5 ounce	14 grams

5 > Make the sticky bun glaze. In a small saucepan, boil the reserved raisin liquid over medium heat, stirring constantly to prevent scorching, until reduced to 1 1/2 to 2 tablespoons, or reduce in a 2-cup heatproof measuring cup in a microwave oven on high power. Add the butter and stir until melted. (It should be no more than warm when brushed onto the buns.)

6 > Preheat the oven. Preheat the oven to 375°F 1 hour before baking. Have an oven shelf at the lower level and place a baking stone or baking sheet on it before preheating.

7 > Glaze and bake the buns. Brush the buns with the glaze. Place the pan on the hot stone or hot baking sheet and bake for 10 minutes. To keep the buns from becoming

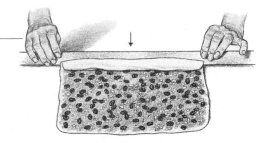

1> Rolling up the dough from a long side, using a ruler

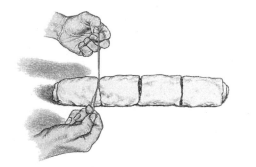

2> Cutting the dough with dental floss

3> Buns placed in a rectangular pan

4> Buns placed in a copper tarte Tatin pan

too brown, cover them loosely with foil, and continue baking for 15 to 20 minutes or until a skewer inserted in the center comes out clean (an instant-read thermometer inserted into the center will read about 180°F).

8 > Cool the buns slightly. Remove the pan from the oven and allow the buns to cool in the pan for 3 minutes, then unmold them onto a serving plate or foil-lined counter. If any of the topping sticks to the pan, lift it off with a metal spatula and apply it to the buns. They can be eaten at once or cooled and reheated later. Reheat loosely wrapped in foil, in a 350°F oven for 15 minutes, or wrapped in a damp paper towel in a microwave oven on high power for 30 seconds.

THE PROFESSIONAL WAY

Use a Flexipan number 1601 mold—the mold has 15 cups, so either make 1 1/2 times the recipe and make each bun a little larger, or simply make the basic recipe and pour a tablespoon of water into each empty cup. If your oven is not large enough to hold a full-size sheet pan, the Flexipan can be cut apart. You could also use Texas muffin pans, but they are more conical and I prefer the shape of the Flexipan molds.

Set the Flexipan on the sheet pan. When the topping is done, pour it into a 1-cup measure. If you have used a nonstick pan and captured all of the caramel, you will have 3/4 cup, or 1 tablespoon per sticky bun; (if you increased the caramel recipe by 1 1/2 times you will have a generous cup). Pour the caramel into 15 of the cups if you made 1 1/2 times the recipe, or into 12 of the cups if using the basic recipe. If you work quickly, the caramel will stay fluid, but if it starts to thicken too much, simply put it in the microwave oven for a few seconds to liquefy it again. Allow the caramel to cool completely in the pan.

Set the (nut-encrusted) buns on top of the caramel (alternatively, you can place the nuts directly on the caramel) and then cover the top with plastic wrap. Allow the buns to rise until double. They will not reach the top of the mold but will be light and airy.

Bake as above and unmold immediately when done. To unmold, place a second sheet pan on top of the mold and invert the pans. Lift off the Flexipan (or muffin pan).

Maple Bungee Buns

When I attended college in Burlington at the University of Vermont I was introduced to the favorite local flavor combination of maple and walnut. It stayed in my taste memory to create this sticky bun variation.

Pure maple syrup forms hard crystals during baking, so I like to use a good brand of syrup with maple flavoring for these buns. Not only does it result in a perfect sticky texture, it also offers a rounder, more mapley flavor. The syrup is made from corn syrup, which contains fructose, preventing crystallization. Using maple sugar in the filling makes for the most complete maple flavor.

To make this variation, omit the glaze and replace the pecans with walnuts.

For the topping, replace the light brown and granulated sugars with 1/2 cup/6 ounces/170 grams maple-flavored syrup, such as Log Cabin. In a small, heavy saucepan over medium heat, bring the butter and syrup to a boil, stirring constantly, and simmer on low heat for about 8 minutes, swirling the pan or stirring occasionally with a heat-proof spatula. There will be many bubbles. If you are using a thermometer it should register 230°F. Stir in the heavy cream and broken nuts and continue simmering for 3 to 5 minutes, swirling the pan occasionally, until, if you are using a thermometer, it reaches 244°F. Pour the syrup evenly into the prepared pan.

For the filling, if desired, you can replace the light brown sugar with maple sugar. Proceed as for sticky buns.

POINTERS FOR SUCCESS

> If using a very strong specialty cinnamon, use only 1 1/2 teaspoons.

> You can also bake the buns in a round pan. My favorite is a 9 1/2-inch (bottom measurement) by 2-inch-high copper tart Tatin pan (see page 591). (Place 8 buns evenly around the perimeter of the pan and 4 in the middle.) You can also use a 10-by-2-inch cake pan. For half the dough, use a 7-by-2-inch cake pan or an 8-inch tarte Tatin or cake pan with a ball of crumpled foil in the center.

> Be sure to brush off all the flour from each bun before placing them in the pan, or they will shrink away from each other while baking.

> Lyle's golden syrup has a slightly tart flavor and I find it to be more delicious than corn syrup.

UNDERSTANDING

Although this dough is given a long chilling time when making brioche, for sticky buns it's fine to use it after 2 hours or once it is well chilled, as there is so much flavor in the filling the subtle difference in the flavor of the dough from longer chilling would be unnoticed.

Chocolate Sticky Buns

Walnuts and chocolate meld with caramel and brioche for a delectable variation on the traditional sticky bun. I developed this for the chocoholic and fell in love with them! Don't serve these for breakfast, it's too early in the day to have everyone swooning to the floor.

TIME SCHEDULE

Advance Preparation: make the dough 1 to 2 days ahead
Minimum Rising Time: 1 to 2 hours
Oven Temperature: 375°F
Baking Time: 20 to 30 minutes

Makes: 12 buns

EQUIPMENT:

a 9-by-13-inch baking pan, lightly greased;

a baking stone OR baking sheet

Sticky Bun Chocolate Ganache Filling

INGREDIENTS	MEASURE	WEIGHT	
	volume	ounces	grams
fine-quality semisweet chocolate, broken into pieces	--	2 ounces	56 grams
heavy cream, heated until warm or hot	2 tablespoons	1 ounce	28 grams
Lyle's golden syrup or corn syrup	1 tablespoons	0.7 ounce	21 grams
1 large egg white	2 tablespoons	1 ounce	30 grams

1 > **Make the sticky bun filling.** In a small microwave proof bowl, place the chocolate and microwave it, stirring every 15 seconds, until almost completely melted. Then stir until melted. (Or melt in a double boiler over very hot, but not simmering, water.) Stir in the heavy cream and syrup until completely uniform in color. Gently stir in the egg white until incorporated.

Set aside to firm up for at least 2 hours, or refrigerate just until set. It should be firm but spreadable.

Sticky Bun Topping and Dough

INGREDIENTS	MEASURE	WEIGHT	
	volume	ounces	grams
unsalted butter, softened	1/4 cup	2 ounces	56 grams
light brown sugar	1/2 cup (firmly packed)	4 ounces	112 grams
Lyle's golden syrup or light corn syrup	1 tablespoon	0.75 ounce	21 grams
heavy cream, heated until warm or hot	3 tablespoons	1.5 ounces	42 grams
coarsely broken walnut pieces (not toasted)	3/4 cup	3 ounces	85 grams
1 recipe Basic Brioche dough (page 487)	--	*about 19 ounces*	*540 grams*
chocolate chips (semisweet or milk chocolate)	1 scant cup	6 ounces	170 grams

2 > **Make the sticky bun topping.** In a small heavy saucepan, off the heat, stir together the butter, brown sugar, and syrup until the sugar is moistened. Bring to a boil over low heat, stirring constantly. Simmer for 5 minutes (only 3 minutes if using a cast-iron pan as it will continue cooking), without stirring. There will be many bubbles and the caramel will be dark brown; do not allow it to get too brown. If you are using a thermometer, it should register 244°F. Pour in the heavy cream and swirl the pan to mix it in. Continue simmering for 3 minutes, swirling the pan occasionally, or if you are using a thermometer, until it returns to 244°F. Pour the syrup evenly into the prepared pan. Sprinkle the broken walnut pieces on top of the caramel. Cool completely.

3 > **Fill the dough.** Roll out the dough on a well-floured surface into a 14-by-12-inch rectangle. Move it around from time to time to make sure it is not sticking, and add more flour if necessary. Spread it evenly with the chocolate ganache filling, going right up to the edges on all sides. Sprinkle it evenly with the chocolate chips. Roll it up from a long end, brushing off excess flour as you go (a long plastic ruler is very

helpful for lifting the dough evenly and supporting it while rolling). Push in the ends so that they are the same thickness as the middle and the roll is 12 inches long. For ease in slicing, you can slide the dough onto a baking sheet and refrigerate it for 30 minutes, or freeze it for 5 to 10 minutes, covered with plastic wrap.

4 > Cut the dough and let the buns rise. Using a piece of dental floss or heavy kitchen string, or a sharp knife, cut the roll into 4 pieces, then cut each piece into thirds (each piece will be about 1 inch thick). Place them in the prepared pan and push the tops down so that the sides touch. Cover with oiled plastic wrap and let the buns rise (ideally at 75° to 85°F) until they double, 1 to 2 hours. (In a tart Tatin pan [see Pointers for Success], the highest point of the dough will be about 3/4 inch from the top of the pan.) The dough will be airy and puffy. (Note: If you want to bake the sticky buns the following day, as soon as they are shaped, refrigerate them for up to 14 hours. They will take about 2 1/2 hours to rise before baking. You can speed the rising by placing them in a proof box with hot water; see page 588.)

5 > Preheat the oven. Preheat the oven to 375°F 45 minutes before baking. Have an oven shelf at the lower level and place a baking stone or baking sheet on it before preheating.

6 > Bake the buns. Place the pan on the hot stone or hot baking sheet and bake for 10 minutes. To keep the buns from becoming too brown, cover them loosely with foil, and continue baking for 15 to 20 minutes or until a skewer inserted in the center comes out clean (an instant-read thermometer inserted into the center will read about 180°F).

7 > Cool the buns. Remove the buns from the oven and allow them to cool in the pan for 3 minutes, then unmold them onto a serving plate or foil-lined counter. If any of the topping sticks to the pan, lift it off with a metal spatula and apply it to the buns. They can be eaten while still warm or allowed to sit for a few hours to set the chocolate. They can also reheated, loosely wrapped in foil, in a 350°F oven for 15 minutes, or, wrapped in a damp paper towel, in a microwave oven on high power for 30 seconds.

THE PROFESSIONAL WAY

Use a Flexipan number 1601 mold—the mold has 15 cups, so either make 1 1/2 times the recipe and make each bun a little larger, or simply make the basic recipe and pour a tablespoon of water into each empty cup. If your oven is not large enough to hold a full-size sheet pan, the Flexipan can be cut apart. You could also use Texas muffin pans, but they are more conical and I prefer the shape of the Flexipan molds.

Set the Flexipan on the sheet pan. When the topping is done, pour it into a 1-cup measure. If you have used a nonstick pan and captured all of the caramel, you will have 3/4 cup, or 1 tablespoon per sticky bun; if you increased the caramel recipe by 1 1/2 times, you will have a generous cup. Pour the caramel into 12 of the containers. If you work quickly, the caramel will stay fluid, but if it starts to thicken too much, simply put it in the microwave oven for a few seconds to liquefy it again. Sprinkle 1 tablespoon of the walnuts into each cup. Allow the caramel to cool completely.

Set the buns on top of the caramel and then cover the top with plastic wrap. Allow the buns to rise until double. They will not reach the top of the mold but will be light and airy.

Bake as above and unmold immediately when done. To unmold, place a second sheet pan on top of the mold and invert the pans. Lift off the Flexipan (or muffin pan).

POINTERS FOR SUCCESS

> You can also bake the buns in a round pan. My favorite round pan is a 9 1/2-inch (bottom measurement) by 2-inch-high copper tarte Tatin pan (see page 591). Place 8 buns around the perimeter of the pan and 4 in the middle. You can also use a 10-by-2-inch-high round cake pan. For half the dough, use a 7-by-2-inch cake pan or an 8-inch tarte Tatin or cake pan with a ball of crumpled foil in the center.

> Be sure to brush off all the flour from each bun before placing them in the pan, or they will shrink away from each other while baking.

> Lyle's golden syrup has a slightly tart flavor and I find it to be more delicious than corn syrup.

Monkey Bread

This bread consists of clusters of sticky buns layered in an angel food pan and baked. Each person gets to tear off a bun with cinnamon sugar, rum raisins, and toasted pecans clinging to it. The bread's name is believed to have come from the haphazard way in which the balls of dough are piled into the pan. And, in fact, the more irregular the size of the buns, the more fun to eat.

TIME SCHEDULE

Dough Starter (Sponge): minimum 1 hour, maximum 24 hours
Rising Time: about 2 1/2 hours
Oven Temperature: 350°F
Baking Time: 60 to 70 minutes

Makes: about ninety 1 1/2-inch buns

EQUIPMENT:

a heavy-duty stand mixer with dough hook attachment;

a 10-inch (12-cup) two-piece angel food pan, lightly sprayed with nonstick vegetable coating;

a baking stone OR baking sheet

Dough Starter (Sponge)

INGREDIENTS	MEASURE	WEIGHT	
	volume	ounces	grams
unbleached all-purpose flour (use only Gold Medal, King Arthur, or Pillsbury)	2 cups plus 6 1/2 tablespoons	12 ounces	341 grams
water, at room temperature (70° to 90°F)	scant 1 3/4 cups	14.3 ounces	405 grams
honey	2 tablespoons plus 1 teaspoon	1.5 ounces	45 grams
instant yeast (see page 561 for brands)	3/4 teaspoon	--	2.4 grams

1 > **Make the sponge.** In the mixer bowl, preferably with the whisk attachment (#4 if using a KitchenAid), beat together the flour, water, honey, and yeast until very smooth, to incorporate air, about 3 minutes. The sponge will be the consistency of a thick batter. Scrape down the sides of the bowl and set it aside, covered with plastic wrap.

Flour Mixture

INGREDIENTS	MEASURE	WEIGHT	
	volume	ounces	grams
unbleached all-purpose flour (use only Gold Medal, King Arthur, or Pillsbury)	2 cups plus 3 tablespoons	11 ounces	311 grams
dry milk, preferably nonfat	1/4 cup plus 2 tablespoons	about 2 ounces	60 grams
instant yeast	3/4 teaspoon	--	2.4 grams
unsalted butter, softened	9 tablespoons	4.5 ounces	128 grams
salt	2 1/2 teaspoon	--	16.6 grams

2 > **Combine the ingredients for the flour mixture and add to the sponge.** In a medium bowl, whisk together the flour, dry milk, and yeast. Sprinkle this on top of the sponge and cover it tightly with plastic wrap. Allow it to ferment for 1 to 4 hours at room temperature. (During this time, the sponge will bubble through the flour mixture in places; this is fine.)

3 > **Mix the dough.** Add the butter and mix with the dough hook on low speed (#2 KitchenAid) until the flour is moistened. Then mix on medium speed (#4 Kitchen Aid) for 3 minutes. Allow the dough to rest for 20 minutes.

Sprinkle on the salt and knead the dough on medium speed (#4 KitchenAid) for 10 minutes. It should be smooth, shiny, and slightly sticky to the touch. (It will weigh about 45.2 ounces/1282 grams.)

4 > **Let the dough rise.** Place the dough in a 4-quart dough-rising container or bowl, lightly greased with cooking spray or oil. Push down the dough and lightly spray or oil the top. Cover the container with a lid or plastic wrap. With a piece of tape, mark the side of the container at approximately where double the height of the dough would be. Allow the dough to rise (ideally at 75° to 80°F) until doubled about 1 1/2 hours.

Scrape the dough out onto a lightly floured counter and press or roll it gently into a rectangle. (The exact size is not important.) It will be full of air and resilient; try to maintain as much of the air bubbles as possible by not pressing too hard. Fold the dough into a tight package or give it 2 business letter turns and set it back in the container. Oil the surface again, cover, and mark where double the height of the dough would now be. Allow it to double, about 1 hour.

Filling

INGREDIENTS	MEASURE	WEIGHT	
	volume	ounces	grams
raisins	1 cup	5 ounces	144 grams
dark rum	1/4 liquid cup	--	--
boiling water	1/2 liquid cup	--	--
pecans, toasted and coarsely broken	1 1/2 cups	6 ounces	168 grams
unsalted butter	16 tablespoons	8 ounces	227 grams
light brown sugar	1 cup (firmly packed)	7.6 ounces	217 grams
cinnamon	4 teaspoons	0.3 ounce	8.6 grams

5 > **Make the filling.** Place the raisins in a small heatproof bowl. Add the rum and boiling water, cover, and let stand for at least 1 hour. When ready to roll the dough, drain the raisins, reserving the liquid for the glaze.

In a medium microwaveable bowl (or saucepan), melt the butter with the brown sugar and cinnamon, stirring once or twice (or constantly if over direct heat). Set aside to cool until just warm.

6 > **Shape the dough and let it rise.** Turn the dough out onto a lightly floured counter and divide it in half. Return one half to the greased bowl, cover, and set it aside. Pinch off small pieces of the remaining dough, flouring your fingers lightly if necessary, and roll them on the lightly floured counter into 1-inch balls (0.5 ounce/14 grams each). It is fine and even desirable for them to vary slightly in size. Cover the shaped balls with oiled plastic wrap while rolling the rest of the dough.

Dip the balls one at a time in the butter/sugar mixture and set them in the prepared pan, placing them slightly apart, as they will expand during rising. After forming the first layer, scatter in some of the pecans and raisins. (Use all of the raisins before finishing with the final layer, as they tend to overbrown when on top.) Stir the butter/sugar mixture often to keep it from separating. When all the balls from the first batch of dough are arranged, cover the pan with plastic wrap and refrigerate it while you roll the second batch of dough into balls.

Continue making layers with the balls as before, reheating the butter/sugar mixture if necessary to keep it liquid. The layers of balls will be uneven, as the balls will vary in size, but when completed they will fill the pan three-quarters full. Drizzle any remaining butter/sugar mixture on top. Cover the pan with a large container, or loosely with oiled plastic wrap, and allow the rolls to rise until they reach the top of the pan, 50 to 60 minutes.

7 > Preheat the oven. Preheat the oven to 350°F 45 minutes before baking. Have an oven shelf at the lowest level and place a baking stone or baking sheet on it.

8 > Bake the bread. Set the pan on the hot baking stone. Bake for 60 to 70 minutes or until the bread is golden and a skewer inserted in the middle comes out clean (an instant-read thermometer inserted into the center will read about 190°F). After the first 50 minutes, place a sheet of foil on top to prevent overbrowning.

9 > Glaze and unmold the bread. While the rolls are baking, boil the raisin liquid down to about 2 tablespoons, or until syrupy (use a 2-cup microwaveproof measure or a small saucepan).

Remove the bread from the oven and set the pan on a rack. Brush the raisin syrup evenly over the top. Allow the bread to cool on the rack for 10 minutes. Unmold by setting the pan on top of a canister that is smaller than the side portion of the pan and pushing the sides down firmly and evenly. Then invert it onto a rack and reinvert it onto a serving plate. Serve immediately, or while still warm (it will stay warm for about an hour). Encourage people to use their fingers to break off the warm buns. (The bread resembles an attractive Roman ruin as it is consumed.)

ULTIMATE FULL FLAVOR VARIATION

For the best flavor development, in Step 2, allow the sponge to ferment for 1 hour at room temperature, then refrigerate it for 8 to 24 hours.

POINTERS FOR SUCCESS

> You can omit the dry milk and instead use nonfat or whole milk, scalded and cooled to lukewarm, to replace the water in the sponge.

> Toast the pecans on a baking sheet in a preheated 325°F oven for 7 minutes to bring out their flavor.

UNDERSTANDING

A little extra salt is used in this dough to balance the sweetness.

THE DOUGH PERCENTAGE

Flour:	100%
Water:	66.3% (includes the water in the butter and honey)
Yeast:	0.83%
Salt:	2.5%
Butterfat:	15.9%

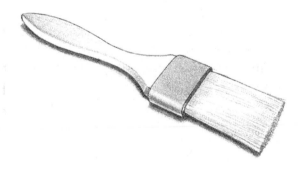

Panettone with Chestnuts

I adapted this recipe from my basic brioche dough, adding an extra egg yolk, replacing the egg white with water, using the maximum butter, and replacing the sugar with syrup to hold the moistness. The mystery ingredient here is fiori di Sicilia ("flowers of Sicily"), an extract unlike any other, containing notes of jasmine, citrus, and vanilla (see Sources, page 572). If you are not a fan of chestnuts, omit them and double the raisins—or use an equivalent amount of chopped candied fruit, if that is your preference. This bread is not to be missed. And it is the silkiest, most sensual dough you will ever put your hands to.

This sweet bread keeps well frozen or at room temperature for as long as four days. When it starts to dry out, place cut slices in a 350°F oven for about 2 minutes and it will soften immediately. It is also great lightly toasted. It may be gilding the lily, but it is sublime with butter.

This recipe is best made in a heavy-duty electric mixer, and it can be doubled. Although you can use a coffee can or a 6-cup soufflé dish with a collar, the beautiful paper pans from Italy work best and make a lovely presentation (see Sources, page 598).

TIME SCHEDULE

Dough Starter (Sponge): minimum 1 1/2 hours, maximum 24 hours
Rising Time: about 7 1/2 hours
Oven Temperature: 350°F
Baking Time: 55 to 65 minutes
Standing Time: at least 8 hours

Makes: a 5 1/2-by-6 1/2-inch-high loaf (5 1/2 inches by 6 inches if baked in a paper liner)/1 pound-11.5 ounces/778 grams

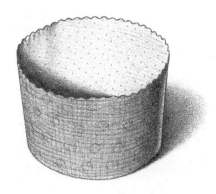

EQUIPMENT:

a heavy-duty mixer with paddle attachment;

a 6-by-4-inch paper panettone pan, OR a 6-inch-high coffee can, greased and lined with parchment, OR a greased soufflé dish with a collar

Filling

INGREDIENTS	MEASURE	WEIGHT	
	volume	ounces	grams
6 large or 16 small chestnuts in syrup	2/3 cup	4.2 ounces	120 grams
raisins, preferably "moist raisins for baking"	1/4 cup	1.25 ounces	36 grams
unbleached all-purpose flour(use only Gold Medal, King Arthur, or Pillsbury)	2 tablespoons	0.6 ounce	18 grams

1 > **Make the filling.** Drain the chestnuts, reserving the syrup, and crumble them coarsely. In a small bowl, combine them with the raisins and flour and toss to mix. Cover and set aside.

Dough Starter (Sponge)

INGREDIENTS	MEASURE	WEIGHT	
	volume	ounces	grams
water, at room temperature (70° to 90°F)	1/2 liquid cup	4 ounces	118 grams
reserved syrup from the chestnuts (or Lyle's golden syrup or corn syrup)	1 tablespoon	0.7 ounce	20 grams
instant yeast (see page 561 for brands)	3/4 teaspoon	--	2.4 grams
unbleached all-purpose flour (use only Gold Medal, King Arthur, or Pillsbury)	3/4 cup	3.5 ounces	100 grams
2 large egg yolks	--	1.25 ounces	36 grams

2 > **Early in the morning or the night before, make the sponge.** In the mixer bowl, place the water, syrup, yeast, flour, and egg yolks and whisk until very smooth, to incorporate air, about 2 minutes. The sponge will be consistency of a very thick batter. Scrape down the sides of the bowl and set aside, covered with plastic wrap.

Flour Mixture and Dough

INGREDIENTS	MEASURE	WEIGHT	
	volume	ounces	grams
unbleached all-purpose flour (use only Gold Medal, King Arthur, or Pillsbury)	1 cup plus 1 1/2 tablespoons	5.5 ounces	156 grams
instant yeast	3/4 teaspoon	--	2.4 grams
Optional: granular lecithin	1 tablespoon	--	6 grams
dry milk	1 1/2 tablespoons	--	14 grams
salt	1/2 teaspoon	--	3.3 grams
reserved syrup from the chestnuts (or Lyle's golden or corn syrup)	2 tablespoons	about 1.5 ounces	40 grams
3 large egg yolks (cold)	3 fluid ounces	2 ounces	54 grams
fiori di Sicilia or: pure vanilla extract	1/2 teaspoon 1 teaspoon	--	--
pure orange oil or: grated orange zest	1 teaspoon 1 tablespoon	--	-- 6 grams
unsalted butter, very soft	10 tablespoons	5 ounces	142 grams

3 > **Combine the ingredients for the flour mixture and add to the sponge.** In a small bowl, whisk together the flour and yeast, then add the lecithin, dry milk, and salt. Sprinkle this mixture on top of the sponge to cover it completely. Cover tightly with plastic wrap and let it stand for 1 1/2 to 2 hours. (During this time, the sponge will bubble through the flour mixture in places; this is fine.)

4 > **Mix the dough.** Add the syrup, egg yolks, and extracts (or oil) with the paddle attachment, and beat on low speed (#2 if using a KitchenAid) for about 1 minute or until the flour is moistened. Raise the speed to medium (#4 KitchenAid) and beat for about 5 minutes or until the dough is smooth and shiny but still very soft and sticky. It will not pull away from the bowl completely.

Add the butter by the tablespoon, waiting until each addition is almost completely absorbed before adding the next tablespoon, beating until all the butter is incorporated. The dough will be very soft and elastic and will almost completely pull away from the bowl. Scrape the sides of the bowl, cover with plastic wrap, and allow it to rest for 10 minutes.

Scrape the dough onto a very lightly floured counter and pat it into a rectangle. The exact size is unimportant. Sprinkle on the chestnut/raisin mixture, draw up the sides of the dough to enclose it, and knead briefly until incorporated. Don't be concerned if the mixture is not evenly distributed, as the "turns" after rising will accomplish this. (The dough will weigh about 28.7 ounces/816 grams.)

5 > **Let the dough rise.** Transfer the dough to a 2-quart dough-rising container or bowl, lightly greased with cooking spray or oil. Lightly spray or oil the top of the dough and cover it with a lid or plastic wrap. With a piece of tape, mark the side of the container at approximately where double the height of the dough would be. Cover it with a large plastic box or cover the bowl tightly with plastic wrap and allow the dough to rise (ideally at 75° to 80°F) until doubled in bulk, 1 1/2 to 2 hours.

6 > **Chill the dough.** Refrigerate the dough for 1 hour to firm it; this will prevent the butter from separating.

Gently deflate the dough by stirring it with a rubber scraper, and return it to the refrigerator for another hour so that it will be less sticky and easier to handle.

7 > **Deflate the dough and allow it to rest, chilled.** Turn the dough out onto a lightly floured surface and press or roll it into a rectangle (the exact size is not important), lightly flouring the top of the dough if needed. Give the dough 1 business letter turn, brushing off any excess flour, and again press or roll it out into a rectangle. Rotate it 45 degrees so that the closed side is facing to your left. Give it a second business letter turn and round the corners. Wrap it loosely but securely in oiled plastic wrap and then place it in a large zip-seal bag, or wrap it in foil, and refrigerate it for at least 6 hours, or up to 2 days, to allow the dough to ripen (develop flavor) and firm.

8 > **Shape the dough and let it rise.** Turn the dough out onto a lightly floured surface. Round it into a ball, trying to keep as much air as possible in the dough. Set it into the paper panettone pan, coffee can, or soufflé dish. It will be about 2 1/2 inches high.

Set it in a plastic box with a cup of hot water (see page 588), or cover it loosely with greased plastic wrap. Let rise in a warm spot (ideally 75° to 80°F) until almost doubled, 2 to 3 hours. It should come to the top of the paper or be about 4 inches high in the coffee can or soufflé dish. (The dough is slow to rise, as it was shaped cold from the refrigerator and takes at least an hour to come to room temperature.)

9 > **Preheat the oven.** Preheat the oven to 325°F 45 minutes before baking. Have an oven shelf at the lower level and place a baking stone or baking sheet on it before preheating.

10 > **Bake the panettone.** Uncover the dough and let the surface dry for 5 minutes to crust. Then use greased sharp scissors to snip a 1-inch-deep cross into the top of the dough.

Place the pan on the hot stone or hot baking sheet and bake for 60 to 65 minutes or until a skewer inserted into the middle comes out clean (an instant-read thermometer inserted into the center will read about 195°F). Tent the bread with foil after the first 30 minutes of baking to prevent overbrowning.

11 > Cool the panettone. Remove the bread from the oven and transfer to a rack to cool, still in its pan, for 30 minutes. Or, if using the paper pan, allow it to cool completely in the pan.

If using a coffee can or soufflé dish, unmold the bread and finish cooling it, top side up, on a soft pillow on the counter (covered with a piece of plastic wrap to keep it clean); the pillow gently supports the fragile crust until it firms up on cooling.

When it is cool, wrap the bread in airtight plastic wrap or foil and then in a freezer-weight storage bag. Allow it to mellow for at least 8 hours for the best flavor.

ULTIMATE FULL FLAVOR VARIATION

For the best flavor development, in Step 3, allow the sponge to ferment for 1 hour at room temperature, then refrigerate it for 8 to 24 hours.

POINTERS FOR SUCCESS

> If desired, melt and brown about one-fifth of the butter (2 tablespoons if using 10 tablespoons) for an extra rich, delicious flavor.

THE DOUGH PERCENTAGE

Flour:	100%
Water:	57.7% (includes the water in the butter and chestnut syrup)
Yeast:	1.8%
Salt:	1.3%
Fat:	53.7% (includes the fat in the egg yolk)

Traditional Challah

In all the years I was growing up, I cannot remember a Friday night without a loaf of challah sitting on the table and the long serrated bread knife by its side. Grandma didn't bake the challah on our Sabbath table, she bought it from a kosher bakery in the neighborhood. I remember it with fondness because of its appealingly plump four-braided symmetry, but the cottony texture was not appealing to me. I would eat one small slice drizzled with a little honey and never wanted more. Usually I ate it out of reverence for the ceremony (I remember the Hebrew prayer for bread to this day). So when I set out to formulate my own challah recipe, it was only that braided appearance I was trying to duplicate. Challah is actually a brioche, with more egg and less liquid and fat. In order to add moistness and extend the shelf life, I replaced the sugar with honey, thinking that since it was so compatible as a topping it might be appropriate as a sweetener for the dough itself. I discovered that not only did it improve the flavor, it also gave it a more golden crumb and a firmer texture. Here then is my idea of a pareve (dairy-free) challah at its best.

TIME SCHEDULE

Dough Starter (Sponge): minimum 1 hour, maximum 24 hours
Minimum Rising Time: 10 hours
Oven Temperature: 350°F
Baking Time: 45 to 55 minutes

Makes: a 14-by-6-by-4 1/2-inch-high loaf
(a 3-braid challah will be 17 inches long)
3 pounds, 2 ounces/1415 grams

EQUIPMENT:

an 18-by-12-inch baking sheet, lightly greased with cooking spray or oil or lined with Silpat or parchment;

a baking stone OR baking sheet

Dough Starter (Sponge)

INGREDIENTS	MEASURE	WEIGHT	
	volume	ounces	grams
unbleached all-purpose flour (use only Gold Medal, King Arthur, or Pillsbury)	1 cup	5 ounces	142 grams
instant yeast (see page 561 for brands)	1 teaspoon	--	3.2 grams
water, at room temperature (70° to 90°F)	2/3 liquid cup	5.5 ounces	156 grams
honey	2 tablespoons	about 1.5 ounces	40 grams
3 large eggs, at room temperature	scant 2/3 liquid cup	5.25 ounces	150 grams (weighed without shells)

1 > Early in the morning or the night ahead, make the sponge. In a mixer bowl or other large bowl, place the flour, water, honey, and eggs. Whisk until very smooth to incorporate air, about 2 minutes. The sponge will be the consistency of a very thick batter. Scrape down the sides of the bowl and set aside, covered with plastic wrap.

Flour Mixture and Dough

INGREDIENTS	MEASURE	WEIGHT	
	volume	ounces	grams
unbleached all-purpose flour (use only Gold Medal, King Arthur, or Pillsbury)	4 2/3 cups (plus 2 to 3 tablespoons for kneading)	23.3 ounces (plus 0.7 ounce)	662 grams (plus about 20 grams)
instant yeast (see page 561 for brands)	1 1/4 teaspoons	--	4 grams
salt	1 tablespoon	0.7 ounce	19.8 grams
2 large eggs (cold)	6 tablespoons (3 fluid ounces)	3.5 ounces	100 grams (weighed without shells)
corn oil	1/3 liquid cup	2.5 ounces	72 grams
honey	6 tablespoons (3 fluid ounces)	4.25 ounces	120 grams
cider vinegar	1 tablespoon	--	--

2 > Combine the ingredients for the flour mixture and add to the sponge. Whisk the flour and the yeast. Then whisk in the salt (this keeps the yeast from coming in direct contact with the salt, which would kill it). Sprinkle this mixture on top of the sponge. Cover it tightly with plastic wrap and let it stand for 1 to 4 hours at room temperature. (During this time, the sponge will bubble through the flour mixture in places; this is fine.)

3 > Mix the dough.

Mixer Method

Add the eggs, oil, honey, and vinegar. With the dough hook, beat on medium speed (#4 if using a KitchenAid) for about 5 minutes or until the dough is smooth and shiny. Lightly sprinkle some of the flour for kneading onto a counter and scrape the dough onto it. Knead the dough, adding a little flour if necessary so that it is just barely tacky (sticky). (The dough will weigh about 3 pounds 5 ounces/1504 grams.)

Hand Method

Add the eggs, oil, honey, and vinegar. With a wooden spoon or your hand, stir the mixture until the flour is moistened. Knead the dough in the bowl until it comes together, then scrape it onto a floured counter. Knead the dough for 5 minutes, just to begin to develop the gluten structure, adding as little of the extra flour as possible. Use a bench scraper to scrape the dough and gather it together as you knead it. At this point, it will be very sticky. Cover it with the inverted bowl and allow it to rest for 20 minutes. (This rest will make the dough less sticky and easier to handle.)

Knead the dough for 5 minutes or until it is very elastic and bounces back when pressed with a fingertip. Add a little more flour if necessary so that it is just barely tacky (sticky). (The dough will weigh about 3 pounds, 5 ounces/1504 grams.)

Both Methods

4 > Let the dough rise. On a lightly floured countertop, round the dough into a ball. Place the dough in a 4-quart dough-rising container or bowl, lightly greased with cooking spray or oil. Push down the dough and lightly spray or oil the top. Cover the container with a lid or plastic wrap. With a piece of tape, mark the side of the container at approximately where double the height of the dough would be. Allow the dough to rise (ideally at 75° to 80°F) until it has doubled, 1 to 2 hours.

Gently deflate the dough by pushing it down and give it a business letter turn. Return the dough to the container. Oil the surface again, cover, and mark where double the height would now be. (It will fill the container fuller than before because it is puffier with air.) Allow to rise a second time until doubled, about 45 minutes to an hour.

Flatten the dough by pressing down on it gently, so as not to activate the gluten, making it stretchy.

5 > **Shape the dough** (see pages 72–74).

Three-Braided Challah
Divide the dough into 3 equal pieces. Cover with plastic wrap and allow to rest for 10 minutes.

One at a time, roll each piece of dough under your palms into as long a rope as possible, at least 13 inches. (Keep the rest of the dough covered while you work with each piece.) Lift the rope of dough up at one end with one hand and use the other hand to pull and stretch it gently downward to form a 15- to 16-inch-long rope, flouring your hands lightly if the dough is sticky. Taper the ends so that they are narrower than the rest of the rope, as this part of the dough tends to bunch up and be too fat.

For the most symmetrical braid, start at the middle and braid out to each end, pulling and stretching the dough slightly as you go. Moisten the ends with a little water, pinch the strands together at each end of the braid, and tuck each end under a little, then push the ends in slightly so that the loaf is about 15 inches long and wider in the middle. Place the loaf on the prepared baking sheet.

Four-Braided Challah
Divide the dough into 4 equal pieces. Cover with plastic wrap and allow to rest for 10 minutes.

One at time, roll each piece of dough under your palms into as long a rope as possible, at least 12 inches. (Keep the rest of the dough covered while you work with each piece.) Lift the rope of dough up at one end with one hand and use the other hand to pull and stretch it gently downward to form a 14- to 15-inch-long rope, flouring your hands lightly if the dough is sticky. Taper each end of the dough rope to about 5 inches down so that it is narrower than the rest of the rope, as this part of the dough tends to bunch up and be too fat.

Lay the ropes side by side on the counter, pinch them together at the tops, and braid them, pulling and stretching the dough slightly as you go. Keep pinching the ends together, as they tend to pull apart as you braid; pull the dough more as you come to the end of the braid so that it comes to more of a point. Pinch the ropes together at the end of the braid. Moisten the pinched ends with a little water to help them hold together during rising, and tuck them under a little at each end, then push the ends in a little so that the loaf is about 12 inches long by 3 inches high. Place the loaf on the prepared baking sheet.

Egg Glaze

INGREDIENTS	MEASURE	WEIGHT	
	volume	ounces	grams
lightly beaten egg	**2 tablespoons**	--	**33 grams**
water	**1 teaspoon**	--	--
Optional: poppy seeds	4 teaspoons	0.50 gram	12 grams

6 > Glaze the bread and let it rise. In a small bowl, lightly whisk together the egg and water. Brush the loaf lightly with the glaze, and cover it loosely with greased plastic wrap. Cover the egg glaze and refrigerate it. Allow the loaf to rise (ideally at 75° to 85°F) until doubled, about 1 hour. It will be 1 inch longer, 1/2 inch wider, and 3/4 inch higher.

7 > Preheat the oven. Preheat the oven to 350°F 45 minutes before baking. Have an oven shelf at the lowest level and place a baking stone or baking sheet on it before preheating.

8 > Glaze and bake the challah. Remove the plastic wrap and brush the challah all over with the egg glaze, going well into the crevices of the braid. Sprinkle the top with the poppy seeds, if desired, tilting the pan slightly so you have access to the sides.

Quickly but gently set the baking sheet on the hot baking stone or hot baking sheet. Bake for 20 minutes. Tent loosely with a large sheet of heavy-duty aluminum foil and continue baking for 25 to 35 minutes or until the bread is deep golden brown and a skewer inserted into the middle comes out clean (an instant-read thermometer inserted into the center will read about 190°F).

9 > Cool the challah. Remove the pan from the oven and, using a peel or two large pancake turners, transfer the challah to a wire rack to cool completely.

NOTE The challah can be baked as two 9-inch loaves instead of one large one. Since there is less dough for each loaf, it will be easier to use the 3-strand braid (roll them to 10 to 11 inches long). Baking time will be 30 to 35 minutes, and the baked breads will measure 13 inches by 5 inches by 3 inches.

The challah can also be baked as 3 single-strand braids, using a special knotting technique (see page 75).

NOTE If you prefer to use sugar rather than honey, use 2/3 cup (4.7 ounces/132 grams) and increase the water to 3/4 cup (6.2 ounces/177 grams). A 4-braid loaf made with sugar will be 14 inches by 7 inches by 5 inches high.

ULTIMATE FULL FLAVOR VARIATION

For the best flavor development, in Step 2, allow the sponge to ferment for 1 hour at room temperature, then refrigerate it for 8 to 24 hours. If using the hand mixing method, remove it from the refrigerator 1 hour before mixing the dough.

POINTERS FOR SUCCESS

> If desired, for maximum flavor development, the dough can be wrapped loosely with plastic wrap, placed in a 2-gallon plastic bag, and refrigerated overnight. Allow it to sit at room temperature for 30 minutes before shaping.

> The 3-braid loaf is most symmetrical if started from the center.

> To prevent overbrowning, don't use a dark pan for this bread.

UNDERSTANDING

You can see from the percentage of water why challah is usually such a dry bread. The addition of honey and oil and the lecithin from the egg yolk help considerably to add moisture. The texture of this bread is best the day it is made, but, if desired, you can add 1 to 2 tablespoons of granular lecithin to extend the keeping qualities, or freeze any leftover bread. It reheats perfectly and the flavor even seems to improve!

The vinegar both strengthens and relaxes the gluten in the dough, making it easier to stretch into long strands. It also adds a subtle depth of flavor.

This dough needs to be firm enough to hold the braid well. It is best to allow the shaped bread to rise until doubled so that there is less oven spring and, therefore, fewer pale unglazed parts.

THE DOUGH PERCENTAGE

Flour:	100%
Water:	39% (includes the water in the egg whites and honey)
Yeast:	0.9%
Salt:	2.4%
Oil:	12.1% (includes the fat in the egg yolks)

Chocolate Almond Swirl Kugelhopf

In Europe, kugelhopf is traditionally a dry bread, baked in a fluted tube pan, meant to be dunked in coffee. Since we are not a nation of "dunkers," I came up with this much moister version with a delicious swirl of chocolate "schmear" filling. The "schmear" recipe was given to me by baker Norbert Grave when I admired it at the Mandalay Bay resort in Las Vegas. He said he had formulated it at a Jewish bakery where he'd worked in Great Neck, Long Island, to make use of the ever-present leftover cake crumbs by moistening them with chocolate and almond paste. But the "schmear" works perfectly with fresh cake crumbs too. And, I discovered that with the addition of an egg, the filling would expand along with the rising dough and not form gaps. I used the same technique to create the Chocolate Sticky Buns (page 502). If you like poppy seeds, see the poppy seed filling variation that follows.

Instead of using the traditional kugelhopf pan, I like to use Nordicware's Rose Bundt® pan. This soft bread dough molds beautifully into the petaled crevices, resulting in a stunning giant rose with a surprise spiral of delicious filling.

TIME SCHEDULE

Dough Starter (Sponge): minimum 20 minutes, maximum 24 hours
Minimum Rising Time: 40 minutes
Oven Temperature: 350°F
Baking Time: 55 to 65 minutes

Makes: an 8-by-5-inch-high loaf/2 pounds, 10.75 ounces/1 kilogram, 214 grams
(3 pounds, 4.5 ounces/1 kilogram, 500 grams with poppy seed filling)

EQUIPMENT:

a heavy-duty mixer with paddle attachment;

a 9 to 10-cup kugelhopf or tube pan, OR a Rose Bundt® pan, well buttered or greased with cooking spray or oil;

a baking stone OR baking sheet

Chocolate Schmear Filling

Makes: 1 1/3 cups 12.6 ounces 360 grams

INGREDIENTS	MEASURE	WEIGHT	
	volume	ounces	grams
cake crumbs, fresh or stale	1 cup (loosely packed)	4 ounces	113 grams
almond paste	3 tablespoons	1.5 ounces	42 grams
unsalted butter, softened	4 tablespoons	2 ounces	56 grams
1 large egg	3 tablespoons	2 ounces	56 grams (weighed in the shell)
Lyle's golden syrup or corn syrup	1 tablespoon	0.7 ounce	20 grams
fine-quality dark chocolate, melted		3 ounces	85 grams

1 > Make the "schmear." In a food processor fitted with the steel blade, process the cake crumbs, almond paste, butter, egg, and syrup for a few seconds or until smooth. Add the melted chocolate and process for another few seconds until uniformly blended. Cover and allow to sit for at least 1 hour (or refrigerate for up to several hours) to firm.

Dough Starter (Sponge)

INGREDIENTS	MEASURE	WEIGHT	
	volume	ounces	grams
unbleached all-purpose flour (use only Gold Medal, King Arthur, or Pillsbury)	1/2 cup	2.7 ounces	78 grams
instant yeast (see page 561 for brands)	1 1/4 teaspoons	--	4 grams
milk, scalded and cooled to warm or room temperature	1/2 liquid cup	4.2 ounces	121 grams

2 > Make the sponge. In the mixer bowl, place the flour, yeast, and milk. With the whisk beater, beat on medium speed (#4 if using a KitchenAid), for about 3 minutes or until very well mixed. Scrape down the sides of the bowl and set aside, covered with plastic wrap.

Flour Mixture

INGREDIENTS	MEASURE	WEIGHT	
	volume	ounces	grams
unbleached all-purpose flour (use only Gold Medal, King Arthur, or Pillsbury)	2 3/4 cups	13.7 ounces	392 grams
sugar	3 tablespoons	1.25 ounces	40 grams
instant yeast	1 teaspoon	--	3.2 grams
salt	1 teaspoon	--	6.6 grams

3 > Combine the ingredients for the flour mixture and add to the sponge. In a medium bowl, whisk together the flour, sugar, and yeast. Then whisk in the salt (this keeps the yeast from coming in direct contact with the salt, which would kill it). Sprinkle this on top of the sponge and cover it tightly with plastic wrap. Allow it to stand for 1 to 4 hours at room temperature. (During this time, the sponge will bubble through the flour mixture in places; this is fine.)

Dough

INGREDIENTS	MEASURE	WEIGHT	
	volume	ounces	grams
2 large eggs (cold)	6 tablespoons (3 full fluid ounces)	4 ounces	113 grams (weighed in the shell)
milk, scalded and chilled	1/4 liquid cup	2 ounces	60 grams
unsalted butter, very soft	5 tablespoons	2.5 ounces	70 grams
melted butter, preferably clarified	2 tablespoons	about 0.7 ounce	24 grams

4 > Mix the dough. Add the eggs, milk, and softened butter and beat with the dough hook on low speed (#2 KitchenAid) for about 1 minute or until the flour is moistened. Raise the speed to medium (#4 KitchenAid) and knead for about 7 minutes or until the dough is smooth, shiny, and very elastic. It should be a little tacky (sticky) but not enough to stick to your fingers. If necessary, knead in a little extra flour. (The dough will weigh about 30 ounces/850 grams.)

5 > Let the dough rest. Using an oiled spatula or dough scraper, scrape the dough onto a lightly floured counter. Lightly flour the top and cover it with plastic wrap.

Let it rest for 30 minutes or until extensible (when you pull it up gently, it stretches without tearing).

6 > **Fill the dough and let it rise.** Remove the plastic wrap. With a rolling pin, roll the dough into a rectangle 16 to 17 inches by 12 to 14 inches, flouring the counter as necessary to keep it from sticking. Using an offset metal spatula, spread the chocolate filling evenly over the dough, leaving a 1/2-inch margin at the top and bottom and 1/4 inch on the sides. Roll up the dough, from a long edge, using a long plastic ruler to help support the dough as you roll it (slip the edge of the ruler slightly under the dough and use it to lift up and roll the dough). With each roll, dust any flour from the bottom of the dough and press gently all along the top of the dough to keep it from separating. Work carefully, without rushing! Then pinch the edge of the dough firmly to make a tight seam; if it doesn't hold well, brush the seam lightly with water. Turn the dough seam side down and pinch the ends of the dough firmly together. Lift the dough and coil it into the prepared pan, overlapping the ends by about 2 inches: start with the seam side up, as this will be the bottom of the bread when unmolded. The dough will fill the pan two-thirds to three-quarters full. Cover the pan with a large plastic box or oiled plastic wrap and let rise (ideally at 70° to 80°F) until the dough puffs and the center is at least level with the top of the pan, 40 minutes to 1 1/2 hours.

7 > **Preheat the oven.** Preheat the oven to 350°F 45 minutes before baking. Have an oven shelf at the lowest level and place a baking stone or baking sheet on it, and a cast-iron skillet sheet pan on the floor of the oven, before preheating.

8 > **Bake the kugelhopf.** Quickly but gently set the kugelhopf pan on the hot stone or baking sheet. Toss 1/2 cup of ice cubes into the pan beneath and immediately shut the door. Bake for 55 to 65 minutes or until golden brown (an instant-read thermometer inserted into the center will read about 180°F). The seam will open slightly, revealing some of the chocolate filling, which is fine. After 30 minutes, turn the pan around, and cover loosely with foil if it is already golden brown.

9 > **Glaze and cool the kugelhopf.** Remove the kugelhopf from the oven and brush the top with enough of the melted butter to cover the entire surface. Unmold the kugelhopf onto a rack and brush it all over with the remaining melted butter. Cool until warm or room temperature. Slice and serve with softened unsalted butter, if desired.

VARIATION

Poppy Seed Filling

Ground poppy seeds make a wonderful filling. They can be ground in a special poppy seed mill or a spice mill or blender, but for the best texture, they should not be so finely ground that they become a paste. Solo brand poppy seed filling, available in many supermarkets, makes an excellent substitute for homemade. You will need to buy 2 cans. Measure out 3/4 cup plus 1 tablespoon (18 ounces/517 grams), and stir in the lightly beaten egg.

Makes: 2 cups (almost 20 ounces/567 grams), without the raisins

INGREDIENTS	MEASURE	WEIGHT	
	volume	ounces	grams
milk	1/2 cup	4.2 ounces	121 grams
poppy seeds, ground	about 1 2/3 cups whole, 2 2/3 cups ground	8 ounces	227 grams
sugar	2/3 cup	4.6 ounces	132 grams
lemon zest, finely grated	1/2 teaspoon	--	--
lemon juice, freshly squeezed	2 1/2 tablespoons	--	39 grams
1 large egg, lightly beaten	3 tablespoons	1.75 ounces	50 grams
Optional: golden raisins, plumped in 1/4 cup of warm water and drained	1/2 cup	2.5 ounces	72 grams

In a small saucepan, heat the milk until hot. Stir in the poppy seeds until they absorb the milk (a few seconds). Remove from the heat and stir in the sugar, lemon zest, and lemon juice until incorporated. Cool the filling to room temperature.

Stir in the egg until evenly incorporated, then stir in the optional raisins. The filling can be made several days ahead, covered, and refrigerated. If desired, the soaking water from the raisins can be used in the dough to replace an equal volume of water. Fill the kugelhopf, as directed in the recipe.

ULTIMATE FULL FLAVOR VARIATION

For the best flavor development, in Step 3, allow the sponge to ferment for 1 hour at room temperature, then refrigerate it for 8 to 24 hours.

POINTERS FOR SUCCESS

> The cake crumbs for the "schmear" filling can be from any butter cake, either homemade or a good-quality frozen one, such as Sara Lee plain or chocolate swirl pound cake.

> If necessary the whole milk can be replaced with dry milk and water. In the sponge, use 2 tablespoons (0.7 ounce/20 grams) dry milk plus 1/2 cup (4 ounces/118

grams) water. In the dough, use 1 tablespoon (0.3 ounce/10 grams) dry milk plus 1/4 cup water. (The dough will weigh 31 ounces/887 grams.)

>   If the outside is pale when you unmold the kugelhopf, place it on a baking sheet, raise the heat to 400°F, and bake for 5 minutes or just until golden.

>   The flavor and texture of the bread improves on standing for 8 hours, but be sure to store it airtight, covering the cut portions with plastic wrap.

UNDERSTANDING

This bread is like a firmer, less rich brioche because the dough contains less liquid (48.2 percent compared to 55.4 percent), one-third the egg, and about one-third less fat. The result is a denser and less moist bread but one that can support a delicious filling.

THE DOUGH PERCENTAGE

Flour:	100%
Water:	48.2%
Yeast:	1.6%
Salt:	1.4%
Fat:	15.7% (includes the fat in the milk and egg yolk)

Stud Muffin

This three-cheese bread looks like a soufflé—that never falls. It was inspired by a recipe from Perugia, Italy, by cookbook author Jane Freiman, called torta di Pasqua, or Easter cake. When sliced, it reveals a crumb that is almost lacy, with many medium-sized pockets that become coated with melted Gruyère. My favorite part of this bread is the crispy bits of Gruyère that work their way to the outside of the dough and melt and brown on the crust, so I stud the top surface all over with extra little cubes of it before baking, hence its name.

Prosciutto is a traditional accompaniment, laid on thin slices of the bread to serve as an appetizer, but I've also discovered a combination that serves brilliantly as a cheese course: inch-thick strips of the bread spread with Époisses (a runny pungent French cheese), and a glass of Burgundy. Eat this, and swoon with pleasure!

This dough is very quick to mix in a food processor. It requires a long slow rise, but the actual work involved is minimal. You will need either a soufflé dish or large coffee can to bake it.

TIME SCHEDULE

Dough Starter (Sponge): minimum 1 hour, maximum 24 hours
Minimum Rising Time: 11 hours
Oven Temperature: 350°F
Baking Time: 45 to 50 minutes

Makes: a 7-by-5 1/2-inch-high round loaf/
2 pounds, 2.7 ounces/992 grams

EQUIPMENT:

a 2-quart soufflé dish (7 inches by 3 1/2 inches high)
OR a 6-inch-high coffee can, well greased;

a baking stone OR baking sheet

Dough Starter (Sponge)

INGREDIENTS	MEASURE	WEIGHT	
	volume	ounces	grams
unbleached all-purpose flour (use only Gold Medal, King Arthur, or Pillsbury)	1 cup plus 1 1/2 tablespoons	5.5 ounces	156 grams
instant yeast (see page 561 for brands)	3/4 teaspoon	--	2.4 grams
water, at room temperature (70° to 90°F)	3/4 liquid cup	6.2 ounces	177 grams

1 > **Make the sponge.** In a mixer bowl or medium bowl, place the flour, yeast, and water. Whisk until very smooth, to incorporate air, about 2 minutes. The sponge will be the consistency of a thick batter. Scrape down the sides of the bowl. Cover it tightly with plastic wrap and allow it to stand for 1 to 4 hours at room temperature.

Dough

INGREDIENTS	MEASURE	WEIGHT	
	volume	ounces	grams
Parmigiano-Reggiano, cut into 1-inch or smaller chunks	--	2 ounces	56 grams
imported Romano cheese, cut into 1-inch or smaller chunks	--	2 ounces	56 grams
unbleached all-purpose flour (use only Gold Medal, King Arthur, or Pillsbury)	2 cups plus a scant 1/2 cup	12 ounces	343 grams
instant yeast (see page 561 for brands)	1 1/4 teaspoons	--	4 grams
salt	1 teaspoon	--	6.6 grams
black pepper	1 1/2 teaspoons	--	3.8 grams
unsalted butter, softened	4 tablespoons	2 ounces	56 grams
water (cold if using a food processor, room temperature if using a mixer)	1/2 liquid cup	4 ounces	118 grams
1 large egg (cold if using the processor, room temperature if using the mixer)	--	2 ounces (weighed in the shell)	56 grams
imported Gruyère cheese, cut into 1/4-inch dice	1/2 cup plus 2 tablespoons, divided	2.5 ounces	70 grams

Glaze

INGREDIENTS	MEASURE	WEIGHT	
	volume	ounces	grams
lightly beaten egg	1 teaspoon	--	--

2 > **Mix the dough.**

Food Processor Method

In a food processor fitted with the metal blade, process the Parmesan and Romano cheeses until finely grated (powdery). Transfer to a bowl, and switch to the dough blade.

In a medium bowl, whisk together all but a scant 1/4 cup of the flour, the yeast, salt, and black pepper. Empty it into the food processor, and scrape the sponge on top. Add the butter.

In a measuring cup with a spout, whisk together the cold water and egg. With the machine running, slowly pour the mixture into the feed tube. Stop the machine, add the grated Parmesan and Romano, and process for about 15 seconds, until the dough forms a soft, shaggy ball. If the dough does not form a ball, add some or all of the remaining flour by the tablespoon, processing in 4-second bursts. The dough should feel slightly sticky.

Empty the dough onto a lightly floured counter and flatten it into a rectangle. Press 1/2 cup of the Gruyère cubes onto the dough, roll it up, and knead it to incorporate evenly. The dough will weigh about 2 pounds 5 ounces/1050 to 1060 grams.

Mixer Method

Grate the Parmesan and Romano cheeses with a hand grater. In a measuring cup with a spout, whisk together the water and egg.

In a medium bowl, whisk together all but a scant 1/4 cup of the flour, the yeast, salt, and black pepper. Sprinkle this mixture over the sponge.

Add the softened butter and mix with the dough hook on low speed (#2 if using a KitchenAid) while gradually adding the water/egg mixture until the flour is moistened, about 1 minute. Add the Parmesan and Romano cheeses, raise the speed to medium (#4 KitchenAid), and knead the dough for 5 minutes or until elastic and bouncy. The dough should be slightly sticky. If it does not pull away from the bowl, beat in some or all of the remaining flour by the tablespoon. The dough should feel slightly sticky.

Empty the dough onto a lightly floured counter and flatten it into a rectangle. Press 1/2 cup of the Gruyère into the dough, roll it up, and knead it to incorporate evenly. (The dough will weigh about 2 pounds 5 ounces/1050 to 1060 grams.)

Both Methods

3 > **Let the dough rise.** Place the dough in a 2-quart dough-rising container or bowl, lightly greased with cooking spray or oil. Push down the dough and lightly spray or oil the top. Cover the container with a lid or plastic wrap. With a piece of tape, mark the side of the container at approximately where double the height of the dough would be.

Refrigerate the dough. Allow it to chill for at least 8 hours or up to 2 days to firm and ripen (develop flavor). Pat it down two or three times after the first hour or two, until it stops rising. Once the dough is cold, it will stop rising.

4 > Shape the dough and let it rise. Turn the dough out onto a counter and knead it lightly. Round it into a ball (see page 65). Push it down into the prepared mold; it will fill the soufflé dish or the coffee can half-full. Cover it lightly with a piece of wax paper and let it rise in a warm area (80° to 85°F) until it almost triples, about 3 to 4 hours. (To reduce the rising time to 2 hours, place it in a proofer without water; see page 588.) The center should be at least 1/2 inch, preferably 1 inch, above the top of the dish or can.

5 > Preheat the oven. Preheat the oven to 350°F 45 minutes before baking. Have an oven shelf at the lowest level and place a baking stone or baking sheet lined with foil on it before preheating.

6 > Glaze, stud, and bake the bread. Brush the surface of the dough with the lightly beaten egg, being careful not to brush it over the top of the dish or can, which would impede rising. Gently insert the remaining 2 tablespoons Gruyère cubes into the dough using a chopstick; first gently twist it into the dough to make a shallow hole, then use the chopstick to push in a cheese cube; it should be visible.

Place the dish or can on the hot stone or hot baking sheet. Bake for 45 to 50 minutes or until the bread is golden and a skewer inserted in the middle comes out clean (an instant-read thermometer inserted into the center will read about 190°F).

7 > Cool and unmold the bread. Remove the pan from the oven and set it on a wire rack for 10 minutes.

With the tip of a sharp knife, loosen the sides of the bread where the cheese may have crusted on and unmold the bread onto its side onto a soft pillow (covered with a piece of plastic wrap to keep it clean) on the counter to finish cooling. This will prevent the soft fragile sides from collapsing; turn it a few times to speed cooling, but always leave it on its side. It will take about 1 hour to cool completely.

ULTIMATE FULL FLAVOR VARIATION

For the best flavor development, in Step 1, allow the sponge to ferment for 1 hour at room temperature, then refrigerate it for 8 to 24 hours. If using the mixer method, remove it from the refrigerator 30 minutes before mixing the dough.

POINTERS FOR SUCCESS

> The bread stays moist and soft for 2 days but is great lightly toasted or heated for 3 to 4 minutes in a 400°F oven to remelt the cheese.

THE DOUGH PERCENTAGE

Flour:	**100%**
Water:	**77.2%** (includes the water in the cheese and egg white)
Yeast:	**1.3%**
Salt:	**1.3%**
Fat:	**19.2%** (includes the fat in the cheese and egg yolk)

Wheaten Croissants

A well-made croissant has a crisp crust and a somewhat flaky crumb that is soft but never doughy. Croissant is actually the missing link between puff pastry and brioche. Take puff pastry dough, add a little extra liquid, add some yeast, and you have croissant dough. Take brioche dough, add as much as almost double the butter, replace the eggs with milk, and you have the makings of croissant dough. Some people think of a croissant as a pastry, others as a bread. Most don't think much about it at all, they just eat it with great pleasure.

Since this recipe first appeared in *The Pie and Pastry Bible*, I have received countless e-mails from home bakers eager to make the dough but unable to find the "reduced-bran whole wheat" called for. I used that flour because it offers a sweet, slightly nutty flavor and beautiful golden color without the bitterness or heaviness of texture of 100 percent whole wheat flour. Reduced-bran flour, available commercially in large quantities, is simply whole wheat flour with most (98 percent) of its sweet, flavorful germ still in it but only 20 percent of its bran—just enough to add flavor intensity without bitterness. Once I investigated flour milling in depth, I realized that it's a simple matter to add this amount of germ and bran back to white flour to make your own reduced-bran flour! This recipe makes it possible. In fact, since I am adding the coarse bran and germ separately, I incorporate them into the butter package. The butter coats their sharp edges and help to keep them from cutting through the gluten network of the dough. Of course, if you prefer a traditional croissant, just omit the germ and bran.

Now that high-fat European-style butter is nationally available to home bakers, it makes it a lot easier to produce quality croissants. Because the butter is more pliable even when cold, it's easier to roll the dough. I also find I prefer the lighter texture of a croissant dough made with less of this rich butter.

Classic croissants are given a total of four turns (business letter folds). But if the butter starts breaking through the dough, it's fine to stop after three turns; you will still have plenty of flaky layers. The fact that the butter breaks through the dough layers is what makes the croissant so much more tender than puff pastry, where the butter layers remain perfectly intact.

TIME SCHEDULE

Dough: minimum 2 hours, maximum 12 hours
Minimum Rising Time: 4 hours
Oven Temperature: 450°F, then 400°F
Baking Time: 20 to 25 minutes

Makes: twelve to fourteen 5-by-2 1/2-by-1 1/2-inch-high croissants

INGREDIENTS	MEASURE	WEIGHT	
	volume	ounces	grams
unbleached all-purpose flour (use only Gold Medal, King Arthur, or Pillsbury)	2 cups	10 ounces	284 grams
wheat germ	1 tablespoon	--	4 grams
wheat bran	2 teaspoons	--	2 grams
instant yeast (see page 561 for brands)	1 1/2 teaspoons	--	4.8 grams
sugar	2 tablespoons	scant 1 ounce	25 grams
salt	1 teaspoon	--	6.6 grams
milk, scalded and cooled to room temperature (70° to 90°F)	3/4 cup	6.3 ounces	181 grams
unsalted butter, preferably a higher-fat European-style butter, such as Vermont Cultured, Plugra, or Land O' Lakes "ultra"	12 tablespoons	6 ounces	170 grams

EQUIPMENT:

a heavy-duty mixer with dough hook attachment;

2 large baking sheets OR half sheet pans, lined with Silpat or parchment;

optional: two 18-by-2-inch-high sheet pans, for proof boxes

1 > Mix the flour, germ, and bran for the butter square. In a small bowl, whisk together 1 tablespoon of the flour, the wheat germ, and wheat bran. Cover and set aside.

2 > Make the dough. In the mixer bowl, whisk together the remaining flour, the yeast, and the sugar. Then whisk in the salt (this keeps the yeast from coming in direct contact with the salt, which would kill it). With the dough hook, add the milk and mix, starting on low speed (#2 if using a KitchenAid), until the dry ingredients are moistened. Raise the speed to medium (#4 KitchenAid) and knead for 4 minutes. The dough will be silky-smooth and have pulled away from the sides of the bowl, but it will still cling to your fingers slightly. (The dough needs to be soft and not too elastic to make it easier to roll and so the butter package will not break through.)

Place the dough in a 1-quart or larger food-storage container or bowl, lightly greased with cooking spray or oil. Press down the dough and lightly spray or oil the top. Cover the container with a lid or plastic wrap. Allow the dough to rise (ideally at 75° to 80°F) for 30 minutes.

Using an oiled spatula, gently fold the dough by lifting it from the sides and pressing it into the middle to deflate it slightly. Cover and refrigerate it for a minimum of 2 hours, or up to overnight.

3 > Make the butter square. Place the bran mixture on a sheet of plastic wrap and put the butter on top of it. Wrap the plastic wrap loosely around it. Pound the butter lightly with a rolling pin to flatten and soften it, then knead it together with the bran mixture, using the plastic wrap and your knuckles to avoid touching the butter directly. Work quickly, and as soon as the bran mixture is incorporated, shape it into a 4 1/2-inch square (no thicker than 3/4 inch). At this point, the butter should still be cool but workable—60°F. Use it at once, or keep it cool. The butter must not be colder than 60°F when rolled into the pastry, or it will break through the dough and not distribute evenly. A cool cellar, or a wine cellar, is an ideal place to maintain this temperature. Alternatively, refrigerate it, but then allow it to soften slightly before using it. The butter should be cool but malleable.

4 > Roll the dough and make the butter package. Roll out the dough on a well-floured surface to an 8-inch square. Place the butter square diagonally in the center of the dough square and, with the back of the knife, lightly mark the dough along the edges of the butter. Remove the butter and roll each marked corner of the dough into a flap. (The dough will be slightly elastic.) Moisten these flaps lightly with water and replace the butter on the dough. Wrap it securely by stretching the flaps just so they overlap slightly. Wrap it in plastic wrap and refrigerate for no longer than 30 minutes.

5 > Turn the dough. Place the dough seam side up on a well-floured surface. Keeping it lightly floured, gently roll the dough package into a long rectangle 7 inches by 16 inches. Brush off all the flour from the surface of dough and give it a business letter turn. Wrap the dough in plastic wrap and refrigerate it for 40 minutes before the next turn. (Mark the number of turns on a slip of paper, as the fingertip impressions in the dough used for puff pastry would disappear in this yeast dough as rises.)

For each turn, clean the work surface and reflour it. Position the dough so that the closed side is facing to your left, and press down on the edges of the dough with the rolling pin to help keep them straight. (The upper part tends to roll out more than the bottom part.) Roll and fold the dough a second time exactly the same way, but this time turn it over occasionally to keep the seams and edges even. Be sure to roll into all four corners of the dough, and use a pastry scraper to even the edges. Do a total of 4 turns, resting the dough for 40 minutes between each. Don't worry if the butter breaks through. Just cover the exposed butter layer with flour and keep going. This dough contains so much more butter than a pie dough that a little extra flour won't make much difference to the texture.

After the last turn, refrigerate the dough for at least 2 hours before rolling it.

6 > Shape the croissants. Remove the dough from the refrigerator and allow it to sit for 15 minutes.

Roll the dough on a floured counter to a rectangle about 14 inches by 24 inches. Brush off all the flour. Fold the dough over lengthwise so that it is about 6 inches by 22 inches. Using a pizza wheel or sharp knife, trim one short side on an angle (reserve the scraps), cutting through the two layers, then make another diagonal cut to make a triangular piece of dough with a 5-inch base. Continue making diagonal cuts to form triangles down the entire length of the dough. Make a 1/2-inch notch in the center of the base of each triangle. Open up the two layers of each triangle and cut in half to form 2 triangles.

Shape the croissants one at a time, keeping the rest of the triangles covered with plastic wrap.

Use the scraps to make 12 to 14 balls (depending on the number of triangles) the size of green grapes (about 4 grams each). Scissors work best to cut the dough for the balls. Keep these covered with plastic wrap too.

To shape the croissants, gently stretch each triangle to about 9 inches long: first pull the base sideways—gently but firmly—then, holding the base in your left hand, use your thumb and two fingers of your right hand to work down the length of the dough, elongating it. Place the triangle on the counter with the narrow point toward you. Shape one of the little balls of dough into a 1 1/4-inch-long football, and place it at the base of the triangle. Roll the base over the football to encase it by about 1/2 inch. Continue rolling with the fingers of your left hand, keeping the triangle stretched with your right hand. Place the croissant on the lined half sheet pan, with the point underneath. Curve in the sides so that they turn in on the side of the croissant opposite the point. Keep the croissants covered with plastic wrap while you shape the others. Set 6 to 7 croissants evenly spaced on each pan, so there will be room for them to expand to the baked size of 5 inches by 2 1/2 inches.

Egg Glaze

INGREDIENTS	MEASURE	WEIGHT	
	volume	ounces	grams
1 large egg	3 tablespoons	2 ounces	56 grams
water	1 tablespoon	--	--

7 > **Glaze the croissants and let them rise.** Lightly beat together the egg and water for the glaze. Brush the croissants with the glaze. Cover and refrigerate the remaining glaze. If you have two large plastic containers or 2-inch-deep 18-inch sheet pans, invert them over the croissants. Alternatively, cover them lightly with very well-oiled plastic. Let rise (ideally at 75° to 85°F) until the croissants double in size and are very light in texture, about 2 hours. (At 70°F, they can take as long as 3 to 4 hours to rise.)

8 > **Preheat the oven.** Preheat the oven to 450°F 1 hour before baking. Have an oven shelf at the lower level.

9 > **Glaze and bake the croissants.** Gently brush the croissants again with the egg glaze, being careful to use a light touch so as not to deflate them. Place the croissants in the oven and turn the oven down to 400°F. Bake for 10 minutes. Reverse the position of the two sheets, turning them around as you do so, and continue baking for 10 to 15 minutes or until the croissants are golden brown (an instant-read thermometer inserted into the center will read about 210°F). The texture will be slightly doughy inside, but on cooling they will continue to cook through perfectly.

10 > **Cool the croissants.** Remove the croissants from the oven and transfer them to racks to cool for 20 to 30 minutes. They are best eaten warm (when the outside is crisp and light, the center soft and tender) or within 3 hours after baking:

VARIATION

Chocolate-Filled Croissants (Pains au Chocolat) Rectangles of Wheaten Croissant dough wrapped around small rectangles of bittersweet chocolate make a delectable variation on the traditional white-flour *pains au chocolat.* They are most delicious when eaten still warm from the oven when the chocolate is still slightly melted. Of course, they can be reheated to achieve this same effect.

Use your favorite bittersweet chocolate. I prefer a milder chocolate, not one that is too bittersweet, as it would contrast too sharply with the dough.

Makes: 12 *pains au chocolat*

INGREDIENTS	MEASURE	WEIGHT	
	volume	ounces	grams
1 recipe Wheaten Croissant dough (above)	--	27 ounces	765 grams
dark chocolate, such as Cluizel (60%), Valrhona Gastronomie (61%), or Scharffen Berger (62%)	--	6 ounces	170 grams

EQUIPMENT:

2 large baking sheets or half sheet pans lined with Silpat or parchment;

optional: two 8-by-2-inch-high sheet pans for proof boxes

1 > Shape the *pains au chocolat*. Remove the dough from the refrigerator and allow it to sit for 15 minutes. Meanwhile, with a sharp knife, cut the chocolate into coarse chunks.

Roll the dough on a floured counter to a rectangle 6 inches by 24 inches. Using a pizza wheel or sharp knife, cut the dough lengthwise in half. Cut each rectangle crosswise into 4-inch pieces. You will now have twelve 4-by-3-inch rectangles of dough.

Brush off all the flour from the dough. Shaping the *pains* one at a time, keeping the rest of the dough covered with plastic wrap, set a row of the little chunks of chocolate on each piece of dough close to a longer edge of the dough and, starting from that long side, roll up the dough so that it encloses the chocolate. Moisten the end of the dough with a bit of water, and place the *pain* seam side down on the lined baking sheet. Space the *pains* at least 2 inches apart.

Egg Glaze

INGREDIENTS	MEASURE	WEIGHT	
	volume	ounces	grams
1 large egg	3 tablespoons	2 ounces	56 grams
water	1 tablespoon	--	--

2 > Glaze the *pains au chocolats* and let them rise. Lightly beat together the egg and water for the glaze. Brush the *pains au chocolat* with the egg glaze. Cover and refrigerate the remaining glaze. If you have large plastic containers or 2-inch-deep by 18-inch sheet pans, invert them over the *pains*. Alternatively, cover them lightly with very well oiled plastic. Let rise (ideally at 75° to 85°F) until the *pains au chocolat* double in size and are very light in texture, about 2 hours. (At 70°F, they can take as long as 3 to 4 hours to rise.)

3 > Preheat the oven. Preheat the oven to 450°F 1 hour before baking. Have an oven shelf at the lower level.

4 > Glaze and bake the *pains au chocolat*. Gently brush the *pains au chocolat* with the egg glaze, being careful to use a light touch so as not to deflate them. Place the *pains au chocolat* in the oven and turn the oven down to 400°F. Bake for 10 minutes. Reverse the position of the two sheets, turning them around and as you do so, continue baking for 10 to 15 minutes or until the *pains* are golden brown (an instant-read thermometer inserted into the center will read about 210°F). The texture will be slightly doughy inside but on cooling will continue to cook through perfectly.

5 > Cool the *pains au chocolat*. Remove the *pain au chocolats* from the oven and transfer them to racks to cool for 20 to 30 minutes. They are best eaten warm (when the outside is crisp and light, the center soft and tender) or within 3 hours after baking.

POINTERS FOR SUCCESS

> Higher-fat European-style butters, such as Vermont Cultured butter, Plugra, or Land O'Lakes "ultra" butter, contain less water than our regular butter so they stay pliant in the dough even when cold. Vermont Cultured butter contains 86 percent fat, the highest butterfat of all American brands. Because it is "cultured," it has a lower pH level (higher acidity), which makes it especially soft and pliant, ideal for rolling into the dough without breaking through the layers.

> Flour with too high a protein content (over 12.5 percent) makes it harder to roll the dough and results in a chewy texture. It is also important not to knead the dough to the point where it becomes very elastic, as with each rolling and folding it becomes more stretchy and harder to roll.

> If you have a Cuisinart mini processor, you can reduce the size of the bran and germ by processing them with the 1 tablespoon of the flour before adding it to the butter.

> If you prefer to use dry milk instead of liquid milk, substitute 3 tablespoons (1 ounce/30 grams) dry milk plus 3/4 liquid cup (6.25 ounce/177 grams) water.

> You can use up to 9 ounces/255 grams butter. It's easier to roll the dough if you use the smaller amount listed in the recipe. I prefer the lighter texture it gives the croissants, and the flavor is still very buttery.

> A tutove (ridged) rolling pin can be used, for added ease in rolling, for the first four turns, after which the dough layer becomes too thin, and the butter could break through.

> Make each turn after 40 minutes of chilling, but no longer. If the dough is too cold, when you roll it, the outside of the dough softens while the center remains firm, which makes it hard to roll and destroys some of the layering. Once you have completed all the turns, however, the butter is evenly dispersed in thin sheets so the dough stays evenly pliant.

> Brush off all loose flour when rolling, and keep the unused dough covered to avoid crusting, which would cause separation of the rolled layers during baking. The inside of the croissant should consist of numerous little open cells with no visible striations.

> If the room is cool (68°F or under), it is desirable to leave the rolled dough covered on the counter for up to 30 minutes to relax before the final shaping.

> After cutting the dough triangles or rectangles, you can set them on a baking sheet, cover them tightly with plastic wrap, and refrigerate for several hours, or up to overnight. Remove them from the refrigerator and allow them to soften for about 10 minutes before shaping them. Alternatively, you can shape them, set them on the baking sheets, cover them tightly with plastic wrap, and refrigerate them. Allow them to rise until doubled before baking.

> Although a tightly rolled croissant with the classic 7 distinct sections is attractive, I find that the texture is lighter and better if they are not rolled too tightly.

> After proofing and egg glazing the croissant (so your fingers won't stick to the dough), to get a more pronounced curve, very gently recurve the ends inward.

> Unbaked croissant dough can be refrigerated for 2 days. Baked croissants or *pains au chocolat* can be held at room temperature for a day or frozen for several months. Reheat them in a preheated 300°F oven for 5 minutes (8 minutes if frozen).

> If you have cushioned cookie sheets or enough to stack one on top of the other to make a double-layered baking sheet, it helps keep the bottoms of the croissants or *pains* from getting too brown.

THE DOUGH PERCENTAGE

Flour:	100%
Water:	64% (includes the water in milk and butter)
Yeast:	1.65%
Salt:	2.3%
Butterfat:	73.4 to 75.3% (depending on the type of butter)

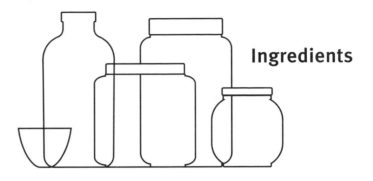

Ingredients

What is bread at its most elemental level?

Referred to ubiquitously as "the staff of life," bread satisfies on such a primal level I've often felt that I would be happy on a diet of bread and wine alone (although cheese would always be welcome, as would a little sweet butter to enhance the flavor of the bread). My American Heritage dictionary actually defines bread as "... *regarded as necessary for sustaining life.*" I'm convinced that this refers to more than just nutrition.

There are many types of bread, including flatbreads, such as pita, which often don't contain yeast, and quick breads, such as banana bread, which usually use baking powder or baking soda instead of yeast and are more like cakes in texture. But to me, when I think of bread, first and foremost it is a free-form or shaped loaf of yeast-raised dough with a crust and a chewy crumb.

There are many delightful things that can be added to basic bread dough to make it special, but the true miracle of bread is that it takes only four essential, and inexpensive ingredients (plus temperature control and timing) to produce a soul-satisfying good loaf. The ever-present magic is that one of these ingredients (the yeast) is visibly very much alive, and if using whole wheat flour, the enzymes in the germ contained are active as well. **The four essential ingredients are: unbleached wheat flour, water, yeast, and salt.**

Essential Ingredient #1: Flour

Although the U.S. government code of federal regulations considers the word *flour* when used alone to refer to wheat flour, the dictionary definition of flour is "*a fine, powdery foodstuff obtained by grinding and sifting the meal of a grain, especially wheat, used chiefly in baking.*" The word is thought to have evolved from the word "flower," so-called because it is produced from the best part of the grain. The term *flour*, however, also often applies to food substances that are not grains, such as the fine powders made from grinding nuts, dried legumes, potatoes, or corn. (In my opinion, most alternative grains and legumes are used as flour in bread primarily for nutritional or health reasons, such as allergies to wheat flour, and in most cases are far less desirable in terms of texture, volume, color, or flavor.) Wheat flour is the only flour that contains a sufficient amount of the proteins glutenin and gliadin. When they are combined with water to make a dough, they form gluten, an elastic network that enables the gases produced by the yeast to expand without breaking through the dough, resulting in a high rise and chewy crumb. The protein glutanin is thought to be responsible for elasticity in the dough—the capability to spring back when stretched. The protein gliadin is responsible for extensibility in the dough—the ability of the dough to stretch. When the two are combined, they are capable of absorbing three times their weight in water. This explains why a flour containing a high degree of protein will require more water to make a workable dough.

THE THREE MOST CRITICAL CRITERIA FOR FLOUR ARE

> Variety

> Protein content

> Freshness

Variety

Wheat flour is the foundation of most breads and, therefore, the most important ingredient. A grain (also referred to as a kernel or berry) of wheat flour is amber in color (think "America the Beautiful," and "amber waves of grain"). The wheat grain has an oval shape and consists of the three main parts:

1   The **bran**, the hard, fibrous outer coating that surrounds the wheat grain. It contains phenolic acid, which makes it bitter.

2   The **endosperm**, the inner part of the wheat grain. It contains the starch from which our basic white flour is made.

3   The **germ**, located at the bottom of the oval wheat grain. It is high in oil, with a sweet/nutty flavor.

A grain of wheat is a complete universe unto itself. It is 83 to 85 percent endosperm, 2.5 percent germ, and 12.5 to 14.5 percent bran. When harvested, a grain of wheat may appear dry and lifeless, but unless it is very old it is alive and can remain alive, in a dormant state, for several years! As in any seed, the *germ* is the "potential life," or embryo, of the grain, capable of *germinating* and producing more wheat, even after it is picked. When combined with water, it is awakened from dormancy and will begin to sprout. The endosperm, the starch/protein component, is the germ's food and the bran is the protective layer that contains it.

When baking bread with flour ground from the whole wheat grain, it is necessary for the germ to still be alive when ground to make bread with good texture and flavor. The germ is viable for only a few weeks after grinding, which is why whole wheat flour over six weeks old is no longer good for baking bread.

Wheat varieties

There are many varieties of wheat, and millers often blend them to achieve their desired results. However, the two basic types of wheat grown are **soft wheat** and **hard wheat**.

The term *hard* refers to the structure of the wheat kernel; that of hard wheat is harder than that of soft wheat. Most hard wheat flours have a high protein content. All soft wheat flours have a low protein content. Most nationally available brands of all-purpose flour are made with hard wheat flour. All-purpose flour from the South is usually made with soft wheat flour.

Hard wheat flours are usually used for yeast raised breads, whereas soft flours are usually used for chemically leavened (baking powder or baking soda) quick breads, biscuits, cakes, and so forth.

Hard wheat is mostly grown in the northern Great Plains, Minnesota, the Dakotas, and Canada. Hard wheat is planted in the spring and harvested in late summer, so it is called **spring wheat**.

Soft wheat flour is grown in regions such as the Carolinas, where the winters are mild and dry. The wheat is planted in the fall and harvested in late spring, and it is called **winter wheat** because its major growing period is during the winter. It can be either a hard wheat or soft wheat variety.

Spring wheat flour results in bread with a redder crust than bread made with **winter wheat flour**, which yields a more golden crust. **Spring wheat** also provides a slightly bitter afternote.

When you purchase whole wheat or flour, you may see the term *red wheat* or *white wheat*. These refer to the color of the bran, or outer coating, of the wheat kernel. **Red wheat** has been around for centuries, but **white (whole) wheat** was developed only about twenty years ago as the result of efforts to produce a wheat without the bitter phenolic acid contained in the bran but with its other nutritional attributes.

Current theories are that white flour is more digestible than whole wheat and that whole wheat flour's major benefit is the laxative benefits of fiber. If you prefer the flavor or health benefits of whole wheat flour, I recommend using the traditional red whole wheat. If you find it bitter, use a lower proportion to get the wheaty flavor with just a slight accent of bitterness. I find the white whole wheat lacking in flavor. There is no difference in flavor, however, between red wheat and white wheat bread or all purpose flours, as the bran and germ are removed during milling.

White wheat flour is appealing to millers because when they separate the bran and germ from the endosperm of the grain to grind it to produce white flour, they can use the portion of the endosperm that is closest to the bran without it showing up as dark specks the way it would with red wheat flour. This is called a higher extraction rate. Flour that is ground with portions of the endosperm closer to the bran usually has a higher mineral (ash) content. Another advantage to white wheat flour is that there is less phenolic acid in the bran, so it is less apt to turn rancid. Apart from that, the hardness (gluten-forming protein) of red and white wheat flours will be similar if both are from winter wheat. Some mills offer flours with a blend of red and white.

Of all the wheat flour varieties, **hard red spring wheat** usually has the highest percentage of gluten-forming protein. **Hard red winter wheat**, however, is the flour preferred by most artisan bakers, because of its higher extensibility. Before the artisan bread movement, American bakers valued elasticity (the ability to stretch and shrink back to its original size), which can hold up to machine methods of mixing dough, while French bakers, such as the world-renowned Lionel Poilane, who spearheaded the artisan bread movement, valued extensibility (the ability of the dough to stretch in a relaxed way without shrinking back to its original shape).

Durum wheat

Durum is a variety of wheat with the highest protein content of all wheat flour, but durum flour does not form gluten that is as elastic or stretchy (extensible) as other hard wheat flours. It is, therefore, usually used in combination with all-purpose or bread flour. Because of its high protein content, if it is overworked, it will produce an excessively chewy bread. Both durum flour and **semolina** are ground from the endosperm of durum wheat, but durum flour is finely ground and semolina is coarsely ground. Durum flour gives a lovely golden color and absolutely delicious flavor to bread. The golden breads of Sicily all contain a high percentage of durum flour. Durum flour is sometimes labeled "extra-fancy pasta flour" or "patent durum flour," or "farina grade." It is as silky-fine as all-purpose or bread flour.

Kamut
This grain is the Egyptian ancestor of today's wheat. Kamut flour lacks the bitterness associated with whole wheat while at the same time contributing a delicious sweet nuttiness to bread. I now use kamut in place of whole wheat for many of my recipes.

Wheat flours
There are two basic types of flour produced from all the varieties of wheat, **whole wheat flour,** which is made by grinding the entire grain, and **white wheat flour** (usually referred to as white flour), which is produced from only the endosperm.

White flour comes in several types suited to different uses, from cakes to breads. The different types are determined not only by the protein content of the flour but also by the portion of the grain's endosperm that is used.

The milling process (for all wheat flour), known as the gradual reduction method, involves grinding, sifting, and separating the flour multiple times. The separating allows the miller to segregate different parts of the flour from the endosperm. The interior of the endosperm contains no bran and has the least amount of protein. Although there is no special government classification, in the industry this is referred to as *short patent flour.* Short patent flour made from soft wheat is the type of flour used to produce cake flour. *Long patent flour* is produced from the part of the endosperm closer to the bran and is therefore higher in protein. It is used for all-purpose flour. Long patent flour made from hard wheat is used for bread flour. *Clear flour* (sometimes referred to as common flour) is considered to be a lower grade than these because it contains some of the bran. Toward the end of the milling process, some of the bran is reduced to particles and is no longer separated out, and the result is "clear flour." The bran raises the mineral (ash) content but not the gluten-forming protein content, so clear flour is usually made from a hard wheat to maximize its strength. It is this flour, in combination with rye flour, that sets the old-style Jewish rye bread, with its compact coarseness of crumb, apart from other breads.

Most flours are closer to what is referred to as **long patent** or **straight grade,** derived from a 75 percent "extraction." (Short patent flour, by contrast is only 45 percent extraction.) The extraction percentage refers to the amount of the entire grain retained in the flour.

Ash content

The ash content (also referred to as the mineral content on the package) of flour is related to fiber and flavor. Since the minerals are concentrated in the outer layers of the wheat berry, a flour processed from parts of the wheat berry closest to the bran has a higher ash content. Flour with a higher ash content is darker in color, because of the bran particles. These provide both an increase in flavor and in fermentation capability. French flour generally has a higher ash content than American flour, although some millers, such as some of those who mill flour for King Arthur, produce a "European-style" flour of this type.

Reduced-bran whole wheat flour

Some millers also produce for commercial sources what they call **reduced-bran flour, which contains about 98 percent of the raw germ and only 20 percent of the bran.** Although it's not available to consumers, you can make your own in two different ways, either by sifting out part of the bran from the whole wheat flour or by adding wheat bran and wheat germ to unbleached all-purpose or bread flour. Of course, if you sift out part of the bran from whole wheat flour, you will also lose some of the flavorful and nutritious germ. Alternatively, if you make your own blend, you will usually need to find germ that is very fresh, as the high oil content makes it extremely prone to rancidity. **Stabilized wheat germ,** however, available from King Arthur, has been treated to give it a shelf life of up to a year (in a cool, dry place) without altering its taste as would the toasted germ available in supermarkets. You can add up to 10 percent germ to white flour to make reduced-bran whole wheat flour. (If the germ has not been toasted or "stabilized," there is a lot of the enzyme activity that would cause decomposition of the flour and a decrease in volume of the loaf if the germ is in excess of 10 percent.)

To make 3.5 ounces/100 grams (about 3/4 cup) reduced-bran flour, use 93 percent unbleached all-purpose, 5 percent germ, and 2 percent bran. For example:

93 grams bleached all-purpose flour (about 2/3 cup)
5 grams germ (2 teaspoons)
2 grams bran (2 teaspoons)

BASIC VARIETIES OF WHITE WHEAT FLOUR USED IN BREADS AND QUICK BREADS

NOTE The term *organic flour* refers to agricultural growing methods and is more a philosophical/environmental issue than a quality issue. Because there is the potential of bugs in organic flour (as storage bins are not sprayed with insecticides), it should be stored as for whole wheat—either no more than 3 months at cool room temperature or up to a year in the freezer.

High-gluten flour: Generally made from the highest gluten-forming protein wheat, which is hard red spring. Since there are no government standards for this type of flour, it may vary in protein content.

Bread flour: Made from hard red winter wheat or a blend of hard wheats.

All-purpose flour: A mix of hard and soft wheats.

Instant or quick-mixing flour: Wondra flour, produced by General Mills, is a bleached all-purpose flour that has been processed in a special way that makes it possible to dissolve it instantly in liquid. It makes terrific popovers that have a spongy, almost cake-like texture.

Unbleached and bleached all-purpose and cake flour: The natural pigments present in wheat flour give it its creamy color and wheaty aroma. This is destroyed by bleaching. Most all-purpose flour is not bleached by chlorine bleach, which weakens the proteins, but some are. Also, a softer variety of wheat is used in some brands of bleached flour. Consequently, it is best to use only unbleached flour for making bread.

Milling techniques

There are several different ways of milling flour. The roller milling machinery of large-scale high-production flour mills heats the grains, resulting in a certain measure of deterioration. This damage affects the water-absorption capacity of the flour, as well as speeding up fermentation and reducing the stretching capacity (extensibility) of the dough. Artisan bread bakers prefer flour produced by specialty mills that use the traditional stone-grinding method, which does not damage the grain in this way. Flour that is labeled "stone-ground" has been ground between heavy, slowly rotating mill stones.

Another method of milling is the hammermill, which is a grinder with a screen. The wheat goes into the center, where the shaft turns (driven by a motor) "hammers" at the end of the motor shaft. Metal projections sling out from centrifugal force and beat the wheat through the screen. This method produces a higher degree of uniformity than stone grinding, with less damaging heat generated than in roller milling. Stone grinding, however, is preferable for bread flour, because hammermilling leaves particles of the endosperm that are not reduced down enough to absorb water (hydrate) properly, with the result that the flour produced behaves like a lower protein flour than it actually is.

Since I never have enough room in my freezer to store flour, and whole wheat flour has only a three month shelf life if not frozen, for the small proportion of whole wheat flour I use in my breads, I usually prefer to grind it myself in a home flour mill.

But, when I do buy whole wheat flour, my favorite is Kenyon's stone-ground (see Sources, page 572). It is a hard wheat flour with flecks of bran that are unusually large and flat, giving breads a lot of texture and a beautiful speckled appearance. The milling process used is what produces the texture (in their cornmeal as well); it is unusual in that their millstones are made of very hard westerly granite from Rhode Island and are flat rather than grooved. The grains are "shaved" down between the stones, resulting in the flatter particles as opposed to the more granulated grind that results from the chopping action of the grooved stones.

To speed up production, some mills first coarsely grind the wheat between millstones and then pass it through roller mills. Unfortunately, there is no government restriction against labeling this flour as stone-ground, since that was part of the process.

Protein Content and Brands

There is a great variance from brand to brand in terms of varieties, consistency of quality, and methods of milling, and since the type of flour used is so critical to the taste and texture of the bread, I have listed the flours that have given me the best results. All are national brands and can be found in most supermarkets or mail-ordered. Regional brands may be much lower in protein and may produce loaves that do not rise well due to lack of good structure. However, there are many wonderful flours, some from smaller mills, such as Heartland (see Sources, page 572), around the country and abroad, and once you've mastered a recipe, it's fun and interesting to experiment with other brands of flours.

Flour's protein content can vary from harvest to harvest. King Arthur Flour has a justly earned reputation for consistency, valued particularly by commercial bakers where variation would be readily apparent in the large batches of dough they produce. It is impossible to determine the exact protein content from what is listed on the bag, because it is given as an approximate percentage for only a very small portion size and it is allowed to vary within the 1 ounce/30 grams, so when multiplied to 3.5 ounces/100 grams the variance is magnified.

APPROXIMATE RANGE OF PROTEIN IN NATIONALLY AVAILABLE FLOURS

Note that millers can achieve different protein contents by buying and blending different wheats which are classified by protein content. When manufacturers order flour in bulk, they get the specifications but still usually need to adjust their formulas.
Gold Medal unbleached all-purpose flour: 10 to 12%, usually 10.5%
Gold Medal bread flour: 12.1 to 12.6%, usually 12.3%

Pillsbury unbleached all-purpose flour: 10.5 to 11.5%
Pillsbury bread flour: 11 1/2 to 12 1/2%
King Arthur high-gluten (Sir Lancelot) flour: 14%
King Arthur bread flour (all hard red spring wheat): 12.7%
King Arthur all-purpose flour (all hard red winter wheat): 11.7%
King Arthur whole wheat flour: 14%
King Arthur white whole wheat flour: 13%
King Arthur Italian-style flour: 7.4%
King Arthur European-style Artisan flour (contains organic whole wheat and ascorbic acid): 11.7%
King Arthur French-style Flour (contains high-ash hard white wheat): 11.5%
King Arthur organic flour: 11.7%

King Arthur all-purpose flour has a higher percentage of protein than most other all-purpose flours, but the others listed above will perform about the same, with perhaps a slightly less chewy crumb. Most recipes that call for bread flour will work well with an equal weight of unbleached all-purpose flour and simply be a little less chewy. Because lower-protein unbleached all-purpose flour is usually more stretchable (extensible), you may even get more volume than with the higher-protein bread flour.

To replace bread flour with all-purpose flour, by volume:
1 cup bread flour = 1 cup plus 1 1/2 tablespoons all-purpose flour.

Vital wheat gluten
Vital wheat gluten is removed from the flour by a washing process. It is then added to flours to increase their strength (adding 1 percent of the weight of the flour in vital wheat gluten increases the protein content by 0.6 percent). It will result in a more chewy crumb and provide more support for added ingredients that cut through the gluten, such as seeds and grains. When I use it, I add from 1/2 teaspoon to 2 teaspoons per cup of flour (1 to 4 percent of the weight of the flour). If adding vital wheat gluten to your own recipes, you will also need a little more water, as this higher-protein wheat gluten is capable of absorbing more liquid (equal in weight to the amount of the vital wheat gluten). If you add too much vital wheat gluten, the crumb will be very chewy. Hodgson Mill recommends a maximum of 3 tablespoons per 4 cups of flour (which would be a shade more than 2 teaspoons per cup at the high end) but they report that some people use as much as 2 tablespoons per cup. And if you are experimenting with alternative grains that do not contain gluten-forming protein, you will want to start with as much as 1 tablespoon per cup of flour (6 percent).

Vital wheat gluten will keep refrigerated for up to 16 months. To test its vitality, place 1 teaspoon of it in a small bowl and gradually stir in 1 scant teaspoon cold water until the wheat gluten is completely moistened. It should form a putty-like mass that can be stretched to 1 or 2 inches before breaking apart.

Malting and enzymes

All of the flours listed above (except King Arthur organic flour) contain malted barley flour, which is added to make enzyme activity consistent during fermentation and the rising process. The germ has the highest enzyme content. Dark-colored flours have higher enzymatic activity than lighter-colored flours, because they contain more particles from the outer layer of the grain (the bran also contains some enzymes). The amylase and protease enzymes in flour are important factors in the development of a dough. Amylase has the potential to act upon some of the starch to convert it into a simple sugar that feeds the yeast and flavors the bread. The starch, which is a complex carbohydrate, is contained in the endosperm. Protease has the important function of converting a portion of the proteins into a soluble form, adding to the elasticity of the gluten by mellowing and softening it.

Diastatic versus nondiastatic barley malt

Diastatic barley malt contains the alpha-amylase enzymes that convert the starch in flour to sugar, to feed the yeast during fermentation of the dough. Nondiastatic barley malt does not contain this active enzyme, so it can be added in larger quantities as a flavor enhancer. If too much diastatic barley malt is added to a dough, there will be too much breakdown of the starch and the result will be a sticky dough and gummy bread with an overly brown crust, from the residual sugar (bakers sometimes use a small amount of diastatic malt to improve crust color). Since the flour I use is already malted, I use nondiastatic barley malt for its flavor. The listing on the flour bag will indicate if it contains malted barley flour. Organic flour is not usually malted and so will benefit from a small amount of diastatic malt to supplement the enzymes present in the flour.

If you want to experiment with diastatic malt, if using malted flour start with only 0.5 percent the weight of the flour (about 1/8 teaspoon per cup). If the flour isn't malted, start with 0.75 to 1 percent the weight of the flour (about 1/4 teaspoon per cup). It is best to divide the malt between the dough starter (pre-ferment) and the rest of the dough, but keep in mind that it takes 45 minutes to an hour for diastatic malt to become functional in a mixed dough, and then the enzymes in the diastatic malt require at least 8 hours to work effectively.

Ascorbic acid

Gold Medal and Pillsbury bread flour and King Arthur European-style flour contain a very tiny amount of ascorbic acid, an oxidizing agent added to strengthen the gluten. This is important when a dough does not have a long fermentation to strengthen it or when it is being retarded (held at a cool temperature) for an extended period of time, such as the baguette dough. During baking, the ascorbic acid completely dissipates, leaving no aftertaste.

Other wheat flours or derivatives

Cracked wheat is produced by cracking the entire wheat grain into small pieces.

Bulgur is produced by removing the bran from the grains, cracking them, partially steaming them, and then drying them.

Graham flour originally was simply coarsely milled whole wheat flour, but today it can also contain extra bran or even a certain percentage of rye flour.

Freshness

I have to confess that for years I never believed flour could get stale, as long as I couldn't smell any off flavors, but I was dead wrong. I learned the now-unforgettable lesson when developing the recipe for the baguette. No matter what I tried, I couldn't get those lovely open holes in the crumb. I called everyone I could think of, and somewhere along the line someone suggested that maybe it was the flour. What I was using was three years old. I bought a new batch and the favorable results forever changed the way I think about the shelf life of any dry ingredient. I learned that unless you freeze flour, it is essential to date it the moment you bring it into the house and then ruthlessly throw it out after 3 months if it's whole wheat or rye, after one year if it's white flour. No ifs, ands, or buts. As flour ages, it loses its strength. If it isn't stored airtight, it will absorb air in a humid environment or dry out in a dry environment. Only cake flour, which is chlorine bleached, seems to have a virtually indefinite shelf life, if stored airtight. Flour isn't expensive enough to risk wasting your time with an expired one.

Excess oxidation is the enemy of good bread. In the mixing phase, a certain amount of incorporated air is desirable, but in ground flour, undesirable oxidation starts to takes place from the moment the grain is cracked and exposed to air. This is why the whole unground grain can keep for as long as five years, if cleaned and kept dry and cool, but whole wheat flour keeps for only about 3 months. A common practice in milling is to moisten the grains to make separation of the bran easier. One of the benefits of this practice is that the bran flakes into attractive little pieces instead of powdering and merely darkening the bread. If the moistening and drying is done quickly, there is no down side, but if not, the moisture is likely to activate enzymes that will cause the flour to deteriorate more quickly.

If you are in doubt as to whether your whole grains are still viable after prolonged storage, soak some of the grains in water. If most of them don't start to germinate (sprout) after 2 or 3 days, the grain is no longer alive and should be discarded.

How fresh is too fresh? Before aging, wheat flour is referred to as "green." There is a big debate over freshly ground whole wheat and aging vis-a-vis the absorption capability of water when mixing the dough. According to Joe Lindley of Lindley Mills in Graham, North Carolina, "Whole wheat is better within the first three or four days after it is ground flavor and nutrition wise, but it won't be noticeable in home baking to 95 percent of people. After five days, there is a less stable product because of enzyme activity. Three weeks later, it is already more consistent. Using new-crop wheat that hadn't aged a month or one and a half months could be a problem with large-scale baking so bromation was used to enabled bakers to use flour right from the mill. This artificially aged it, improving the grain and texture of the bread. Nowadays this is accomplished by another chemical process, referred to as ADA. Flour will age naturally if allowed to stand for eight to twelve weeks. By the time the consumer receives it, the aging will be sufficient."

When making a dough with a very short process time as opposed to one with a long dough starter (pre-ferment), aging of the flour is important because new flour can be weak and produce loaves with little volume. However, most of my doughs are made with a pre-ferment, which helps the flour to mature, and in any event the percentage of whole wheat (that might be freshly ground) is very low.

Storage: It is best to store flour and other grains in airtight containers or freeze them in freezer-weight plastic bags. If the flour comes in a bag, leave it in the bag and place it in a freezer-weight plastic bag. Flour will lose or gain moisture if not stored airtight. If stored airtight in the freezer, most grains will keep for up to 2 years.

Other grains

Ezekiel Flour: This is a blend of different flours, the name inspired by the Bible, Ezekiel 4:9, where God tells the prophet: "Take wheat and barley, beans and lentils, millet and spelt; put them in a single vessel and make bread out of them."

White Rice Flour: This silky-soft flour is ideal for dusting work surfaces when shaping the dough. Because it does not absorb liquid quickly, it is ideal to keep it from sticking. It is also great for dusting bannetons to keep the dough from sticking, and it tends to clump less on the dough than wheat flour. It can substitute for 5 percent of wheat flour used in the bread without affecting the quality. It is very prone to rancidity and best used soon after grinding or stored in the refrigerator or freezer.

Red, Purple, and Green Rice Flours: These exquisite rice flours give a beautiful color to the bread as well as subtle flavor. The red rice is Bhutanese, the purple Forbidden Rice, and the green is roasted Kaipen, a fresh water algae, finely milled with rice. (See Lotus Foods in Sources, page 572.)

Rye Flour: Rye is a strong-flavored grain. Rye flour is low in gluten-forming protein, so, unlike bread made with wheat flour, its structure is based more on starch than on protein. Rye flour is almost always used in combination with wheat flour to give the bread a better, more airy structure and to contribute flavor to the wheat flour. The carbo-hydrate portion of rye flour contains a gummy substance called pentosan that results in breads with a sticky crumb if more than 20 percent rye flour is used in the dough. In addition, the germ and bran of rye are exceptionally high in amylase enzymes, which add to gumminess by breaking down the starch. This same quality, however, makes rye a desirable flour to use as part of a dough starter (pre-ferment). A long, cool pre-fermenta-tion deve lops acidity in the dough that serves to counteract the potential stickiness.

White rye flour is milled from the center of the endosperm and has little, if any, of the characteristic rye flavor. Medium rye flour is generally milled from the entire endosperm, but may sometimes be a flour that is finely milled from the entire rye berry. **Dark rye flour** is milled from the outer part of the endosperm, which contains some of the bran. **Pumpernickel** or **rye meal**, milled from the entire rye grain, is the darkest of the rye flours. **Pumpernickel** is usually ground coarse; **rye meal** can be fine, medium, or coarse. Rye chops are the equivalent of cracked wheat, in that they are the whole rye berry that has been coarsely cracked. Any rye flour containing the whole grain is prone to rancidity, though not quite as readily as wheat flour since rye is lower in phenolic acid. It is therefore best to store it in the freezer if you won't be using it within 3 months.

Spelt (*farro* in Italian): An ancient grain, spelt, which has a slightly nutty flavor, is related to wheat but is sometimes tolerated by those who have wheat-related allergies. Using it as the only flour in a bread will make the crumb very dense. It has a high pro-tein content, but because it is a fragile sort of protein, it can be substituted for whole wheat flour without compromising texture in recipes where only a small percentage is used in proportion to a high-protein white wheat flour. However, although it has its fans, I find that in bread it produces a slightly odd, unpleasant flavor.

Triticale (*pronounced "tritaKAYlee"*): Developed in Scotland, this grain is a hybrid of wheat and rye. The goal was to produce a flour that had rye's superior nutri-tive value and wheat's better baking qualities. Triticale has a high protein content, but the protein is weak.

Other flours

Flours from varying sources can be added to bread doughs for increased nutritional value, but I find that they often have a bitter or strange aftertaste and most are extremely prone to rancidity. Health food stores are a good source of grains and flours, but as there is no way to assess freshness, it is safer to grind your own flour from the grains or mail-order them and store in the freezer.

Barley Flour: This can be substituted for 5 percent of the wheat flour in bread.

Buckwheat Flour: Buckwheat is actually a seed, not a grain, that is in the rhubarb family. It has a strong, earthy, slightly bitter flavor. The flour is best used in combination with bread flour, both to cut its flavor intensity and to supply gluten-forming protein to give the bread good structure. Coarse or medium-grind buckwheat, available in supermarkets and health food stores, makes an excellent substitute for the bulgur in the Cracked Wheat Loaf (page 289).

Corn: I adore the flavor corn flour gives to bread and cornmeal gives to muffins. The variety of corn used to produce cornmeal is the highly starchy but more flavorful field corn. It may be yellow, white, or even blue. Blue corn has an almost identical flavor to yellow but offers its intriguing blue/gray color. It is usually ground finer than yellow and as a result absorbs slightly more liquid. White corn has a milder flavor than yellow or blue.

A kernel of corn is made up of the same basic components as a grain of wheat: the hull, the endosperm, and the germ. Cornmeal, like wheat flour, also comes as whole-grain or degerminated and hulled. Whole-grain meal has a much fuller and more delicious flavor, without the bitterness associated with whole wheat flour. Because of the oil in the germ, cornmeal and corn flour are very prone to rancidity and so should be ordered from a mill and stored in the freezer. The best varieties are stone-ground, hammermilled, or steel cut, grinding methods that avoid deteriorating heat.

Corn is dried and ground to varying degrees, from coarse to medium to fine cornmeal to the powdery fine flour. **Corn flour** is not the same as cornstarch, which is only the starch component of the kernel. Corn flour can be difficult to find. If you have a flour mill, you can grind it yourself from dried corn kernels. Kenyon's Grist Mill (see Sources, page 572) sells the dried corn kernels. Or you can grind coarse cornmeal to flour consistency. Alternatively, Gary Leavitt of Kitchen Resource, who represents the Bosch mixers and flour mill, recommends grinding (unpopped) popping corn, saying it is a little sweeter in flavor. Because of its high oil content, however, it requires a flour mill with an air-cooling system, such as the Bosch.

Legume Flour: Dried legumes such as peas, beans, peanuts, chickpeas, and soybeans can be ground into flour. Generally, legume flour can be substituted for 5 to 15 percent of the wheat flour in a dough without loss of quality. Neutrally flavored white beans, pea beans, or navy beans do not alter the flavor of the bread, and produce a very soft bread because they contain no gluten-forming proteins and can be ground exceptionally fine.

Unheated soy flour contains lipoxygenase, an enzyme that oxidizes unsaturated fats in flour, creating off flavors and bleaching the flour. This type should be purchased from a reputable source and should be either refrigerated, for up to 2 weeks, or frozen, for up to 1 year. The recommended amount to use is up to 0.5 percent the weight of the wheat flour in the dough. (Because the lipoxygenase has been deactivated in the heated variety, it can be used in a slightly larger amount, up to 2 to 3 percent.) Soy is added to bread to increase protein (for nutritional purposes), to extend the shelf life, and to make the bread softer.

Millet Flour: Ground to a flour, millet can be substituted for 25 percent of the wheat flour in bread. Unground, the small seeds make a flavorful and appealing addition to breads.

Oat Flour: Because it contains 17 percent protein, oat flour can be substituted for as much as 30 percent of the wheat flour in bread.

Potato Flour: Potato flour is ground from dried whole potatoes. It can replace up to 15 percent of the wheat flour in bread.

The advantage of using potato flour is that you can add more of it without having to add excess water, and then use a larger amount of buttermilk as part of the liquid as in the Potato Buttermilk Bread (page 319). Also it is less chewy. The advantage of using (plain) mashed potatoes is that you can use the potato boiling water for extra flavor. Thus, both potato flour and mashed potato produce a very flavorful bread. I find the flour an easier solution.

TO SUBSTITUTE MASHED (OR RICED) POTATOES FOR POTATO FLOUR

By weight: Use 4.9 times the weight of the flour in mashed potatoes and subtract 79.8 percent of its weight from the water used in the recipe.

By volume: Use 3.3 times the volume of the potato flour in mashed potatoes and subtract 85 percent of its volume in water from the recipe.

Example:
To substitute mashed (or riced) potatoes for 1 cup (6 ounces/172 grams) potato flour, use 3 1/3 cups (29.5 ounces/844 grams) of mashed potatoes and subtract 2 3/4 cups plus 1 1/2 tablespoons (23.5 ounces/673.3 grams) water from the recipe.

TO SUBSTITUTE POTATO FLOUR FOR MASHED (OR RICED) POTATOES

By weight: Use 20.2 percent of the weight of the mashed potatoes in potato flour and add 79.8 percent of their weight in water.

By volume: Use 30 percent the volume of the mashed potatoes in potato flour and add 86 percent of their volume in water.

Example:

To substitute potato flour for 1 cup mashed (or riced) potatoes, use 5 tablespoons (about 1.7 ounces/51.5 grams) potato flour plus 3/4 cup plus 2 tablespoons (about 7 ounces/203.5 grams) water

Essential Ingredient #2: Water and Other Liquids

When bread doesn't turn out as anticipated, people are usually very quick to blame the water. While it's true that a very heavily chlorinated water will affect the dough, it is rare to encounter such water, since most types of chlorine dissipate when exposed to air. If in doubt, simply leave the water uncovered for a few hours, and the chlorine will probably vanish. (This is particularly important when working with a starter made from wild yeast.) The minerals in very hard water or the lack of minerals in very soft water, however, may noticeably affect the taste and texture of bread. Very hard water will toughen the dough and slow down fermentation, and very soft water will soften the dough and make it sticky. If your water quality is suspect, use bottled water. You don't want one too high in minerals, neither do you want distilled water, which has none at all. Alternatively, you can adjust the salt level, which will affect the gluten structure: increase it slightly if using soft water or decrease it slightly if using water. Obviously, in areas where there is sulfur in the water, that will give an unpleasant taste to the bread. Otherwise, begin with tap water and go from there.

I call for warm water in some recipes and room temperature water (70° to 90°F) in others. I don't want to risk anyone's adding too hot water (above 120°F which would kill the yeast) or cold water which would not activate it fully. For room-temperature water, simply let it sit for at least 30 minutes.

Potato water from boiling potatoes makes an excellent addition to bread dough. Not only does it impart a delicious subtle flavor, it also keeps the bread moist. **Beet water** turns the crumb the most gorgeous shade of rose and the crust a rosy golden brown. Other vegetable cooking water can also be used, but then it is more for health virtues than flavor, as the taste is usually very subtle.

Milk contributes flavor, strengthening of the gluten (which results in higher volume), and browning of the crust, from the lactose it contains. The lactose sugar is not consumed by the yeast, so it is available for caramelization during baking, giving the crust a good color. The protease enzyme in milk, however, slows down yeast production and can cause breakdown of the protein in the flour, resulting in a sticky and weakened dough. But this enzyme is deactivated by heat, which makes it advisable to scald the milk (bring it to just under the boiling point—small bubbles appear around the edges) and then allow it to cool until only warm before adding it to the dough. Actually, I find it much easier to use the Baker's Special Dry Milk from King Arthur. Unlike "instant" dried milk, it is heated to a high enough temperature during production to deactivate the protease. It will not reconstitute in liquid so must be added to the flour. To substitute it for regular milk in recipes, use 1/4 cup (about 1 1/2 ounces/40 grams) plus 1 cup of water per cup of milk. Up to 8.2 percent of the weight of the flour is the recommended amount; I use 6 percent in my soft white sandwich loaves.

Buttermilk makes a wonderful addition to bread dough because of its mellow delicious flavor and dough-strengthening acidity. I prefer liquid buttermilk, which has much more flavor than the powdered variety. **Sour cream** has a similar mellow flavor and dough-strengthening acidity, and it also has almost eleven times the butterfat. The extra butterfat tenderizes the dough very slightly and adds moisture and shelf life to the baked bread.

Beer produces a luxuriously supple dough and lovely flavor. Encouraged by my success with beer and ale, I went on to try hard cider, which was a flavor disaster, and then apple cider, which was merely insipid. That has discouraged me from trying other fruit juices, at least for the time being. Champagne, which I expected to be wonderful, gave one loaf huge attractive holes from the natural acidity of the grapes, but the vague champagne flavor in the bread was surprisingly just short of awful. (I persevered through three tries and variations before giving up.)

Eggs are sometimes used to enrich bread and replace some of the liquid. Although they are certainly liquid in the raw state, when the dough is baked, the egg yolk and white, of course, solidify; in addition, the albumin in the egg white has a drying effect. That is why breads like challah, which are high in egg, can be so dry just a few hours after baking, and why they benefit from the addition of water-retaining (hygroscopic) honey or sugar. But what eggs in bread lack in moisture they make up for in flavor and color, particularly the bright orange yolks of true free-range eggs. Furthermore, the lecithin in the egg yolk has a softening effect on the crumb and produces a finer crumb, while the egg white makes it lighter in texture.

Cheeses, particularly soft cheeses such as cottage or ricotta, have a high moisture content (see the chart on pages 569–70) and add delicious flavor to bread dough.

Essential Ingredient #3: Yeast

Breads that are made with baking powder or baking soda, which are chemical leavening agents, are called **quick breads** because they are baked immediately after mixing. **Yeast breads**, rather than relying on chemical reaction to produce carbon dioxide to leaven the bread (make it rise), rely on the metabolic action of yeast known as *fermentation*. Yeast is a microscopic single-cell organism present in the air. When added to flour and water, it feeds on the sugar in the flour's carbohydrates. In the process, the yeast multiplies and grows, producing alcohol, which flavors the dough, and carbon dioxide, which is held by the gluten network of the dough and creates the structure of the bread. If fermentation takes place for a prolonged period of time at a cool temperature, acetic acid is also produced, which adds flavor and strengthens the dough.

Before commercial yeast was available, bread baking relied on airborne wild yeasts to ferment flour and water. The "starters" made from wild yeast are often maintained for years, but there are widely diverging opinions on "natural yeast" versus commercial yeast (see the Sourdough chapter, page 425, for more detail). Some believe that the strain of natural yeast developed in a specific environment, such as the strain used to create the famous San Francisco sourdough bread, loses its individual attributes when transferred to another location with different water, bacteria, and airborne yeast strains. Others think that a strong yeast strain can fight off invasion from other strains and maintain its character, particularly if a small percentage of commercial yeast is added to boost the natural one. And some believe that these cultures can be kept going for years while others think that a starter or yeast culture should be discarded after a few months because aging causes it to lose its strength and flavor attributes. Wild starters, which by nature lack the consistency of commercial starters, are also more fragile or susceptible to higher fermentation temperatures (I experienced this firsthand when mixing a dough made with one in a food processor).

In her book *The Italian Bread Baker*, Carol Field writes that the yeast in the air resulting from a lot of bread baking adds to the bread. After several years of baking bread just about every day I can testify to this. Bread now seems to rise faster and improve in flavor in my kitchen.

I use commercial yeast in all my bread baking except when I make sourdough bread from my own sourdough culture. Commercial yeast is derived from varying strains of the yeast called *Saccharomyces cervisiae*, used in the brewing industry. When it comes to commercial sourdough culture, the flavor that pleases me most comes from the powdered starters called Lalvain du Jour starters. These are produced in France, and there are two types available: Pain de campagne LA–2 (my favorite, containing the lactobacillus *pedio-*

coccus pentosaceu) and French Sourdough LA–4 (containing the lactobacillus *brevis* and lactobacillus *plantarum*, similar to the San Francisco–type bacteria). Both of these starters also contain *Saccharomyces cervisiae*, brewer's yeast. These starters require only 12 hours to develop, as opposed to the lengthy process of keeping a wild yeast starter alive and fed. For me this is not a viable alternative, because I find the flavor to be so excellent. They also require the addition of commercial yeast, such as instant yeast.

For breads where I don't want any sour flavor, I use 100 percent instant yeast. In most cookbooks, this type is referred to as "instant" yeast, but sometimes you will see it called "rapid-rise." I see this as a misnomer, because used in correct proportion, it does not speed the fermentation of the dough (which would be undesirable for full flavor development). Because of the manufacturing process, there are fewer dead yeast cells in instant yeasts than in active dry yeast. This special process also enables the yeast to "wake up" more quickly and makes it possible to use less yeast.

Instant yeast is available nationally in supermarkets under the following brand names:

Fleischmann's Bread Machine Yeast or Rapid Rise
Red Star's QuickRise
Red Star's Instant Active Dry
SAF Instant
SAF Gourmet Perfect Rise

If unopened, instant yeast will keep at room temperature for up to two years. Once it's opened, it is best to store it in the freezer. If you buy it in bulk, it is best to transfer a small amount to another container for regular use and freeze both the larger and smaller amount to ensure maximum shelf life, which is at least 1 year.

This type of yeast, which can be added directly to the flour without dissolving and soaking (hydrating) it in water, is an enormous boon to the home baker, because it all but eliminates the possibility of killing the yeast by using water that is too hot. Note, however, that the yeast will die if subjected to ice-cold water. It is fine to whisk the yeast into the flour before adding the water, but the yeast can also be soaked (hydrated) in warm water (at least three times its volume) for ten minutes if allowed to come to room temperature first if the yeast has been frozen.

Compared to fresh compressed yeast, instant yeast increases the relaxing (slackening) of the gluten during mixing. This adds to the gluten's extensibility, but ascorbic acid is usually added to ensure its strength.

Active dry yeast, with its higher amount of dead yeast cells, is favored by pizza dough makers because the dead yeast cells contain *glutathione*, which relaxes the gluten bonds, adding further to extensibility—making it easier to stretch out the dough. Dead yeast cells add a desirable flavor as well.

YEAST CONVERSIONS

To convert recipes calling for instant yeast to active dry yeast: Use 1.25 times the weight; or, for 1 teaspoon instant yeast, use about 1 1/4 teaspoons active dry yeast.

To convert recipes calling for active dry yeast to instant yeast: Use 0.67 times the weight; or, for 1 teaspoon active dry yeast, use 3/4 teaspoon instant yeast.

To convert recipes calling for fresh compressed yeast to instant yeast: Use 0.32 times the weight; or, for 1 packed tablespoon (21 grams) fresh yeast, use 2 teaspoons instant yeast.

Though it is necessary to soak (hydrate) active dry yeast, it actually is not necessary to "proof" it. Proofing is done as reassurance that the yeast is still active. It is necessary to add a small amount of sugar to the water in order to have the yeast foam to demonstrate that it is alive and active. It is equally unnecessary but acceptable to soak (hydrate) instant yeast. You will need at least 4 times the weight, or 3 times the volume, of the yeast in water.

To proof 1 teaspoon dry yeast: Dissolve about 1/4 teaspoon sugar in 1 to 3 tablespoons of the water in the recipe, warmed only to hot bath temperature (110°F). Sprinkle the yeast on top and stir to dissolve it. Set it in a warm spot for 10 to 20 minutes. As the yeast activates, it will rise to the surface and will have a crown of bubbles.

Osmotolerant yeast is a special form of dry yeast designed for doughs with high amounts of sugar, because sugar competes with the more traditional types of yeast for available water. The two brands available through catalogues are Fermipan Brown and SAF Gold. Alternatively, instant yeast can be substituted but you need to use more.

Essential Ingredient #4: Salt

Jeffrey Steingarten said it best in his book *The Man Who Ate Everything*: "Nearly all recipes call for about 2 percent salt compared to the weight of the flour—much more, and you kill the yeast and bacteria; much less, and the yeast grow without restraint and exhaust themselves too soon. Salt also strengthens the gluten, keeping it elastic in the corrosive acid environment of *pain au levain* and helping the bread rise. Can it be mere chance that the chemically ideal level of salt is precisely the amount that makes bread taste best?"

All I would add (the French have a great expression used to describe opinionated people that translates as always having to add one's grain of salt!) is that because salt contributes to the moisture retention of bread, it also keeps it fresh longer. Incidentally, too much salt would toughen the crust, but the right amount aids in making it crisp and crusty. Oh yes, a few final grains: the presence of salt improves the color of the crust by slowing down the rate of the yeast's consumption of the sugar. And salt also helps to preserve the color and flavor of the flour. Finally, during warm weather, 0.2 to 0.3 percent salt is added to the starter to slow down yeast activity and thereby prevent overacidity.

I use sea salt because it is uniodized, as the iodized variety can give an unpleasant taste to the bread. Fine sea salt is easier to measure (if not weighing), and it integrates more readily into the dough than coarse sea salt. It's very difficult to measure salt accurately for two reasons: measuring spoons vary from brand to brand, and salt is extremely hygroscopic: that is, it will readily grab water from the air, increasing its weight. Using the same scale and the same salt, I have found a teaspoon to vary between 5.2 grams and 6.6 grams. When you find the level of salt that you prefer, if not weighing the salt, for consistency, it is best always to use the same measuring spoon. But whether measuring by weight or volume, in very humid conditions it may be desirable to add a little extra salt, or, conversely, in very dry conditions, a little less.

Other Ingredients Commonly Used in Bread

Various flavorful ingredients such as sugar, honey, butter, and olive oil (as well as eggs, described above) are employed to create more tender and richer breads with finer crumb, usually considered to be "special occasion" breads. Some of these breads can stand in quite nicely for cakes, as on the baking spectrum they come fairly close though they are neither quite as tender nor as rich.

Sweeteners
Sugar: It irks me no end to hear the statement "sugar is sugar." Sugar is not sugar any more than flour is flour. The varieties are manifold, explained in a fifteen-thousand word article I wrote for *Food Arts* magazine. It is permanently posted on my website, www.thecakebible.com, for anyone interested in learning about the subject in depth.

What is essential to know about sugar and other sweeteners in bread baking is that in high proportions, not only do they limit the yeast activity, they also limit the amount of gluten that can be developed in the flour. This is because, like yeast, they compete with the flour for the water necessary for gluten formation. Because of this water-retention ability, called hygroscopicity, sugar also serves to hold in moisture, making the crumb softer and keeping the bread fresher longer. And, although too much sugar (in excess of 13 percent of the weight of the flour) will decrease the strength of the dough and be detrimental to the development of the yeast, a moderate amount (6 percent of the flour) increases the strength of the dough and provides extra food for the yeast, thereby increasing fermentation. (A good example of the opposite effect is the Basic Brioche, on page 495. The 16.5 percent sugar used requires 2.1 percent yeast, four times as much as the amount of yeast, but in this bread, the reduction in gluten strength is desirable because it makes for a very tender crumb.)

A bread that is made without the addition of any sugar but is allowed a long fermentation will have a sweet, wheaty quality. Breads that contain a high proportion of whole wheat flour or rye flour, however, benefit from some sugar to balance the slight bitterness of the grain.

I never use refined sugar for bread baking because the dead-white color is not necessary as it is in some sweet baked goods and all it would add flavorwise is sweetness. I prefer the partially refined sugars, such as the golden fine granulated sugar from Florida Crystals or Billington's "Golden Baker's Sugar (See Sources, page 572), and the coarser turbinado sugar, such as Sugar in the Raw, which offer much more interesting flavor. When I use light brown sugar, I choose muscovado from the volcanic soil of the island of Mauritius, off the coast of India (see Sources).

Always store brown sugar in an airtight container. If it gets hard, make a small shallow cup from a piece of aluminum foil and set it on top of the sugar. Tear a paper towel in half, wet it, and squeeze out most of the water. Set it on top of the foil, not touching the sugar. Cover the container tightly, and within several hours the sugar will have drawn the moisture from the towel and become soft and loose again.

Other Sweeteners

Honey is an ideal sweetener for bread for several reasons. It ferments more slowly than other syrups, which is beneficial to flavor development. It caramelizes more readily than sugar, resulting in a more golden brown crust. And it is extremely moisture-retentive (hygroscopic) because of its high fructose component, which aids greatly in keeping the bread moist, and antibacterial, which helps to keep it fresh and free from mold. Some honey, however, is so strongly antibacterial it will kill the yeast. It is therefore safer to use mild, mellow clover honey, but it is fun to experiment with other varieties, as they can add interesting flavor notes. Personal favorites are thyme honey from Greece, blue borage honey from New Zealand, and wildflower honey from New York State.

I agonized for years each time I tried to replace sugar with honey in a recipe, or honey with sugar. It is confusing because fructose is a sweeter sugar than sucrose, so you actually need less honey than sugar by volume, but because honey also contains 17.2 percent water, which is heavy, that smaller volume of honey will weigh more than the sugar you are replacing. That is, by weight you need to use more honey than sugar to get equal sweetness but by volume you need less. It also means that you have to adjust the water content of the recipe.

One day I sat down for a couple of hours and laboriously, but I hope definitively, worked out the equivalencies of sugar and honey by both volume and weight.

When replacing sugar with honey, for 1 cup of sugar you will need 80 percent the volume, or about 3/4 cup of honey, but you will also need to remove 3 tablespoons of water from the recipe. By weight, you will need to multiply the sugar by 128 percent to get the weight of the honey and then multiply the weight of the honey by 17.2 percent to determine how much liquid to remove from the recipe.

When replacing honey with sugar, for 1 cup of honey you will need 125 percent the volume or about 1 1/4 cups of sugar plus 1/4 cup of water. By weight, you will need to multiply the honey by 78 percent to get the weight of the sugar and also multiply the weight of the honey by 17.2 percent to determine how much water to add to the recipe.

Because honey is essentially a supersaturated solution (water that holds an extra amount of sugar), it tends to crystallize over time. It is best stored at room temperature or in the freezer. Crystallized honey can be reliquified easily by placing the container in warm water until the crystals dissolve or by microwaving it in the jar with the lid off, stirring every 30 seconds. (One cup will take 2 to 3 minutes on high power.)

Maple syrup lends its distinctive maple flavor to bread, but the intensity depends on the type of syrup used. Grade A pure maple syrup is so mild it barely has a maple flavor. Grade B pure maple syrup, which King Arthur sells as "Cooking Maple," offers a much more intense flavor, as does a good-quality syrup with maple flavoring.

Molasses has a unique flavor that is essential to pumpernickel bread. However, I much prefer the lighter variety to the darker, which I find overpoweringly bitter.

Barley malt syrup is barely sweet, but it is used both for its flavor and its moisture-retaining quality. It is valued by bakers because, unlike sucrose or other sugars, it does not interfere with gluten development.

Fat

The two main fats I add to breads are butter and oil. A small amount of fat, such as the 1.2 percent added to the rye bread, actually increases the volume of a loaf by lubricating the gluten strands and enabling them to expand more, but a larger amount of fat will reduce the volume of the loaf by making it heavier and more compact. Breads made with the addition of fat also have a softer crumb and crust and longer shelf life. Excess fat, however, coats the flour particles, preventing them from absorbing the water necessary for gluten formation and in effect "overtenderizes" the dough. Excess fat also prevents the yeast from getting to the flour, thereby lengthening or in extreme cases even preventing fermentation.

When a larger proportion of fat is added, such as butter in a brioche, where the total fat content is 47.7 percent of the flour, the dough is mixed first in order to develop the gluten before coating it with the fat.

Unsalted butter is preferable to salted both to make it possible to control the amount of salt added to the dough and for its fresher flavor. I recommend a top-quality butter such as Horizon Organic, Hotel Bar, or Land O'Lakes. I prefer to weigh butter, as when unwrapped, a 4-ounce stick of butter often weighs only 3.86 ounces. For spreading, I adore the barely salted (0.3 percent salt), extraordinarily flavorful Vermont Butter & Cheese Company butter (see Sources, page 572), the type of butter known as *demi-sel* in France. The U.S. government standard for butter is that it must contain a minimum of 80 percent butterfat. The European standard for unsalted butter is 83 percent minimum. Vermont Butter & Cheese Company butter contains 86 percent fat, the highest butterfat of all American brands. Because it is "cultured," it has a higher acidity (lower pH), which makes it softer—a desirable quality when it is used chilled.

With very few exceptions, I prefer spreading bread with butter rather than dipping it in oil after the bread is baked, as butter heightens and accentuates the flavor of the bread. Olive oil imparts a very intense flavor of its own that, though divine, can mask the more subtle flavor of some breads.

Among my favorite **olive oils** are the Tuscan oils of Montecastelli, in particular the Simone Santini (see Sources, page 572), and of Laudemia. Also worth seeking out are the very fruity Sicilian olive oils. All these oils are best stored in a cool area. **Walnut** oil is a fabulous addition to Walnut Fougasse (page 416) and Walnut Onion Bread (page 421). Walnut oil is very prone to rancidity and must be stored in the refrigerator. When I am looking for a more neutral background sort of oil to add to a dough, I use **safflower** or **corn oil**. I also store these oils in the refrigerator to prevent rancidity.

Lecithin, naturally present in egg yolks, is available in granular or liquid form. It is derived from soy and is used to soften the crumb and extend the shelf life of bread. I prefer the granular variety for ease in weighing or measuring, but liquid lecithin is incorporated more easily into the bread with hand kneading. Both are extremely prone to rancidity and should be stored in the refrigerator, where they will keep for up to 1 year. The recommended amount is 1 tablespoon of lecithin (either granular or liquid) for 3 cups of flour (remove 1 tablespoon of oil from the recipe if using it).

Cooking spray, which is mostly oil and lecithin, is ideal for keeping the dough from sticking to a dough-rising container or crusting and drying out.

Baker's Joy is a soy oil/lecithin–based spray that also contains flour, making it ideal for keeping quick breads and scones from sticking to the baking pan. It can also be used to grease the dough-rising container.

Special Additions

Dried fruits such as raisins, cranberries, figs, and pears blend beautifully with the soft chewy crumb of a firm bread. I like to soften them slightly in hot water and then use the water in the sponge (dough starter), which seems to please the yeast because it speeds fermentation. The "baking raisins" from Sun-Maid are extra moist and are a pleasure to use as they don't require waiting time for softening. They also don't discolor dough as much as soaked raisins do. Some bakers don't soak dried fruit because the fruit will soften to a certain extent during baking, stealing a little moisture from the dough, but this is a matter of personal preference.

Seeds and small **whole grains**, such as millet, pumpkin, sesame, sunflower, and poppy, add both a delightful texture and flavor to bread. They are best stored in the refrigerator or freezer as they are rich in oil and prone to rancidity. Poppy seeds become bitter when old. **Poppy seed filling** for rolls or the kugelhopf (page 525) can be made or purchased. Solo makes a canned filling that is fully as good as homemade.

Flaxseed, a shiny dark brown oval grain, is extraordinarily healthful. Its oil is high in antioxidants, but the nutrients are not readily absorbed by the body unless it is cracked or ground. This can be accomplished easily in a wheat mill or blender. As flaxseed becomes rancid very quickly, it is best to do this yourself rather than purchasing cracked or ground flaxseed.

Nuts that are soft, such as pecans, or a little crisper, such as walnuts, blend beautifully with the crumb of the bread and can even be ground fine and used as part of the flour (see Raisin Pecan Bread, page 404, and Cranberry Walnut Bread, page 408). Almonds are delicious both in bread and as a coating (see New Zealand Almond and Fig Bread, page 411). Some people also enjoy hazelnuts in bread, but I find them too firm and overpowering.

Chocolate combined with a yeast dough that is not high in sugar, such as Chocolate-Filled Croissants (*Pains au Chocolate*, page 537), can be combative if it is too bitter but wonderful when the chocolate is well balanced and mellow. The percentage of cocoa solids in the chocolate does not necessarily indicate the degree of bitterness. Quality of flavor comes more from the variety of beans used and the methods of production. Some chocolates with a high percentage of cocoa solids, such as Valrhona Grand Cru Guanaja, at 70.5 percent, are more mellow to my taste than some chocolates with a lower percentage of cocoa solids, such as their Manjari, at 64 percent. Another Valrhona chocolate that is more widely available to the consumer, and an excellent choice, is the 61 percent Le Noir Gastronomie. (Williams-Sonoma carries it; it is labeled as Extra Bitter when sold in bulk to the trade.)

Other favorite chocolates to use in bread are the 60 percent Cluizel Dark Chocolate and the 62 percent Scharffenberger Semisweet Chocolate.

Olives, particularly the Greek kalamata and the small oil-cured Moroccan, are fantastic chopped and added to bread.

Blueberries make the best muffins, especially if you use the hard-to-find tiny, flavorful, wild Maine variety. I was thrilled this year to find a source for frozen ones, which keep well for months in the freezer. They should be added frozen to the muffin batter. To my taste the dried blueberries have very little blueberry flavor.

Coloring, such as BlackJack Caramel Color or Burnt Sugar, which are in liquid form, or powdered caramel color, is the secret to near-black pumpernickel bread. These natural colorings are made from caramelizing corn syrup or sugar until black. At this point they have lost all of their sweetening powder and merely serve as coloring. It pays to be conservative, as a little goes a long way and too much will add bitterness. The suggested amounts, indicated on the product, are 2 teaspoons per 6 cups of flour for the liquid coloring and 2 teaspoons per 1 cup for the powdered coloring.

Extracts, such as pure vanilla extract, pure orange oil, and fiori di Sicilia provide the extra magic perfumed touch for many quick breads and holiday breads, such as Panettone with Chestnuts (page 511). Fiori di Sicilia, which translates as "flowers of Sicily," contains vanilla and citric oil and also a mysterious haunting floral note—that a recent trip to Sicily revealed possibly to be broom, the little yellow flower that grows on the volcanic lava of Mt. Etna.

When using **candied ginger**, crystallized ginger from Fouquet's in Paris, which is Thai ginger, and Australian ginger are my first choices. I also love the convenience of the excellent-quality mini ginger chips from King Arthur, made from Chinese ginger. They are not as moist, nor quite as vibrant, but they are still an excellent product and so much easier than having to chop the moister larger pieces of the other gingers.

Spices, such as nutmeg and pepper, are always more vibrant when ground fresh. My favorite cinnamon is the Korintje cassia from Indonesia. It is the variety that is most often sold as cinnamon in supermarkets. I also like the more powerful Vietnamese cinnamon, but when using specialty cinnamons, which are more aromatic, be sure to use no more than three-quarters the amount specified in the recipe.

To keep spices fresh, store them in a cool, dark area (not near the stove.)

Water, Fat, and Fiber Contents of Basic Ingredients Used in Bread

Liquids
beer: 92.1% water
buttermilk: 90.5% water, 1.75% fat
milk: 87.4% water, 3.6% fat
sour cream: 71.5% water, 19% fat
heavy cream: 56.6% water, 36% fat

Sweeteners and Syrups
barley malt powder: 5.2% water
sugar: 0.5% water
barley malt syrup: 15% water
honey: 17.2% water (but behaves like 12.9% in bread dough)
molasses: 24% water
glucose: 15 to 19.7% water
corn syrup: 24% water

Fats
butter: 15.5% water, 81% fat
oil: 100% fat

Eggs
egg white: 87.6% water
yolk: 51% water, 30.6% fat

Vegetables and Fruit
carrots: 88.2% water, 10.7% carbohydrate/fiber
potato: 79.8% water, 20.2% starch/fiber
pumpkin (canned): 90.2% water, 7.6% carbohydrate/fiber
sweet potato: 63.7% (baked in skin) 33.4% carbohydrate/fiber, 10% sugar
banana: 75.7% water, 22.7% carbohydrate/fiber
cranberries: 87.9% water

Cheese
cottage cheese: 79% water, 0.3 fat%
Cheddar: 37% water, 32% fat
Parmigiano-Reggiano: 30% water, 26% fat
Swiss: 39% water, 28% fat

Weights

NOTE the weight of flour will vary slightly from year to year in relation to the variations in supply of wheat available to the miller.

INGREDIENT	OUNCES	GRAMS
Fats	**1 Cup**	
butter	8	227
clarified butter	6.9	195
olive, safflower, or walnut oil	7.6	215
Sugars	**1 Cup**	
granulated sugar	7	200
light brown sugar	7.7	217
Flours and Other Dry Ingredients	**1 Cup**	
cake flour: sifted	3.5	100
lightly spooned	4	114
all-purpose flour (dip-and-sweep)	5	142
bread flour and durum flour		
(dip-and-sweep)	5.5	156
whole wheat flour (dip-and-sweep)	5	144
whole wheat flour, finely milled:		
lightly spooned	5	145
dip-and-sweep	5.3	150
Wondra rapid-dissolve flour		
(lightly spooned)	4.4	124
rye flour	4.6	130
buckwheat flour:		
lightly spooned	4.2	119
dip-and-sweep	4.7	133

INGREDIENT	OUNCES	GRAMS
potato flour	6	172
corn flour	4.7	134
cornmeal	4.5	128
mashed (riced) potato	9	255
mashed (riced) sweet potato	8.8	252
mashed banana	8	227
Nuts	**1 Cup**	
almonds:		
whole	6.7	191
slivered	4.2	120
sliced or coarsely chopped	2.6	75
finely ground	3.7	107
powder-fine	3	89
walnuts and pecans:		
halves	3.5	100
coarsely chopped	4	114
finely ground	3	85
Liquids	**1 Cup**	
water	8.3	236.35
heavy cream	8.2	232
milk, buttermilk, sour cream, and		
half-and-half	8.5	242
Syrups	**1 Tablespoon**	
barley malt	0.7	20
molasses	0.7	20
Lyle's refiner's syrup	0.7	20
corn syrup	0.7	20
Eggs		
1 large in shell	2	56.7
1 large without shell (3T + 1/2t)	1.7	50
1 large egg white (2 T)	1	30
1 large egg yolk (3 1/2t)	0.6	18.6
Miscellaneous		
raisins	5	144
"baking raisins"	6	170

INGREDIENT	VOLUME	GRAMS
instant yeast	1 teaspoon	3.2
salt	1 teaspoon	5.7
malt powder	1 teaspoon	3.1
vital wheat gluten	1 teaspoon	3
baking powder	1 teaspoon	4.9
baking soda	1 teaspoon	5
cream of tartar	1 teaspoon	3.1

INGREDIENT	VOLUME	GRAMS
dry milk	1 tablespoon	10
wheat germ	1 tablespoon	4.5
wheat germ, toasted	1 tablespoon	8.4
lecithin powder	1 tablespoon	6.4
cinnamon	1 tablespoon	6.5
caraway seeds	1 tablespoon	7
poppy seeds	1 tablespoon	9
extracts	1 teaspoon	4
citrus zest, grated	1 teaspoon	2

NOTE Salt is extremely water-retentive (hygroscopic), and also depending on the measuring spoon, may vary between 5 to 7 grams per teaspoon.

NOTE When whole wheat flour is freshly ground it will be aerated and weigh only about 118 grams per cup, measured by dipping the cup in and sweeping off the excess flour.

INGREDIENT SOURCES

The King Arthur catalogue carries many of the specialty ingredients listed in this chapter. They also offer specialty flours such as high-gluten and durum flour in consumer-size bags!

Flours and Grains
Anson Mills: www.ansonmills.com, 803-467-4122
Bob's Red Mill (natural raw wheat germ from red spring wheat, corn flour): www.bobs redmill.com, 800-349-2173
General Mills: www.gmiflour.com, 800-426-2760 technical, 800-288-1624 sales
Kalustyan: www.kalustyans.com, 212-685-3451
Kamut Association: www.kamut.com, 800-644-6450
Kenyon's Grist Mill: www.kenyonsgristmill.com, 401-783-4054
King Arthur Flour Baker's Catalogue: www.kingarthurflour.com, 800-827-6836
Heartland Mill: www.heartlandmill.com, 800-232-8533
Integral Yoga: 212-243-2642
Lotus Foods: www.lotusfoods.com, 510-525-3137
Milling and Baking News: www.world-grain.com
Montana Flour and Grains (kamut): www.montanaflour.com, 406-622-5436
Sourdough International (to purchase sourdough cultures): www.sourdo.com
Sultan's Delight: www.sultansdelight.com, 800-852-5046

White Lily Foods Company: www.whitelily.com, 800-264-5459
For the gluten intolerant: www.livingwithout.com

Miscellaneous

Artisanal Cheese Center: www.artisanalcheese.com

The Mozzarella Company: www.mozzco.com, 800-798-2954

Baker's Joy: Alberto-Culver Company, www.alberto.com, 800-333-0005

Butter: Vermont Butter & Cheese Company, www.vtbutterandcheeseco.com, 800-884-6287

Cheese: Murray's Cheese, www.murrayscheese.com, 800-692-4339

Crystallized ginger: Fouquet, www.fouquet.fr

Sugars: India Tree, www.indiatree.com, 800-369-4848

La Cuisine: www.lacuisineus.com, 800-521-1176

Solo poppy seed filling: www.solofoods.com, 708-482-8250

Tuscan olive oil: www.montecastelli.com

Vanilla: www.vanilla.com

Williams-Sonoma: www.williamssonoma.com, 800-541-2233

Maine blueberries: Wyman's, www.wymans.com, 800-341-1758

Albert Uster Imports, Inc. (mostly large-quantity purchase): www.auiswiss.com, 800-231-8154

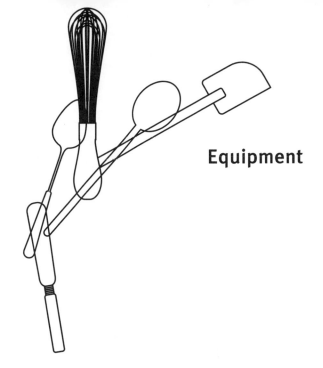

Equipment

Bread baking requires less equipment than most other types of baking. Even on this list of essential pieces of equipment, there are several things you could do without and still be able to make terrific bread. But to give you the ability to make all breads with ease and optimal results, these are my recommendations.

THE BAKER'S DOZEN ESSENTIAL PIECES OF EQUIPMENT FOR BREAD BAKING

1 > A baking stone

2 > An instant-read thermometer

3 > A scale for large quantities or solid measuring cups

4 > A scale for small quantities or measuring spoons

5 > A heavy-duty stand mixer

6 > A bench scraper

7 > Pans: loaf (8 1/2 by 4 1/2 and 9 by 5 inches) and half sheet

8 > Pan liners: Silpain, Silpat, or parchment

9 > A wire rack

10 > Two long rulers

11 > A dough-rising container (ideally two, a 2-quart and a 4-quart)

12 > A timer

13 > Heavy-duty pot holders

Ovens

An oven, of course, is a given. People are always asking me about my preference in ovens, and it's getting harder to answer by the year because so many changes are taking place. In fact, no two ovens are alike, any more than two breads are alike, and the oven of my dreams is yet to be manufactured. (Manufacturers take note: Ask bakers what they WANT in an oven.) Also, it's not safe to assume that the oven recommended by a friend is the same one now being manufactured, even if it has the same model number. I consider the single most common denominator in baking failure to be the oven.

Generally speaking, the temperature in electric ovens fluctuates less than in gas ovens. Electric ovens, however, often release hot air through a vent, which is a disadvantage for bread during the first ten minutes of baking because moisture is carried out along with the air, unless the vent can be covered. It becomes an advantage at the end of baking, though, when you want to get rid of the moisture to achieve a crisp crust. If your oven has a convection option, use it just to preheat faster. Once the oven is preheated, turn it to conventional heat so that the convection currents don't blow out the moist air. At the end of baking, turn the oven back to convection to rid the oven of moisture.

Two designs put you at a disadvantage when baking bread: The first is ovens that activate the broiler unit both when the oven is preheating and when it switches modes from bake to convection. The second is ovens with exposed bottom heating coils.

Toaster ovens can be terrific for reheating bread. Small models work well for individual slices. Larger models, such as the Cuisinart convection toaster oven, are big enough to reheat an **entire loaf** yet small enough to preheat in just a few minutes. (The Cuisinart is even large enough to bake bread in a standard loaf pan.)

Baking Stone

Since every oven I have ever used (with the exception of the one in Proctor and Gamble's test laboratory kitchen) has been in one way or another uneven, I put a baking stone at the head of my list of essential equipment. A baking stone accomplishes five important things in baking bread:

Baking stone

1 > The stone absorbs the oven's heat and helps to maintain constancy of heat during baking. The stone helps to compensate for normal oven heat fluctuation and also helps the bread to bake more evenly.

2 > When you open the oven door to turn the bread around for even baking, the temperature drops 25 to 50 degrees. Because the stone retains heat so well, the oven will recover its heat faster.

3 > The baking stone radiates heat, making baking more even.

4 > When a bread dough is placed directly on the stone or its pan is set directly on the stone, it will start to rise more quickly (improved oven spring), producing a bread with a greater rise.

5 > When the dough is placed directly on the stone, the stone absorbs moisture from the bottom crust, helping to make it crisp.

La Cloche Bread Bakers

The La Cloche clay bread baking containers give you the option of having a perfectly even small oven within your standard oven. These unglazed stone containers with domed covers simulate a beehive brick oven. The large, round, bell-shaped La Cloche can bake a bread as large as 10 inches by 5 1/2 inches high. The long, narrow **La Cloche Italian Bread Baker** bakes breads 13 1/2 inches by 4 1/2 inches by 3 inches high.

La Cloche Bread Baker

The La Cloche is not the ideal baking container for all breads. For one, a loaf pan won't fit into either of the Cloches. Also, the best results involve preheating the dome, and handling a large hot dome can be tricky. But these will give you the most attractively even golden brown crust and largest size without having to steam the oven. Actually, I ignore the instructions to soak the cloche top. After an hour of soaking, it absorbs only 10 grams of water, which is less than 1/2 ounce. Instead, preheat the dome along with the oven. I like to do the final rising of the dough in the base, so in order to provide the greatest initial burst of heat for rising (called oven spring), I preheat an oven stone instead of preheating the La Cloche base.

It's fine to sprinkle the base with cornmeal or flour to

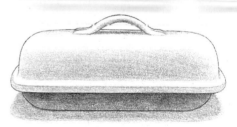

La Cloche Italian Bread Baker

Octagonal Silpat liner in the La Cloche Bread Baker

keep the dough from sticking to it, but I prefer to line it with a Silpat. The octagonal liner exactly fits the bottom of the round Cloche. And I a use nonstick liner for the rectangular Cloche, cut or folded to fit. Because La Cloche absorbs the moisture from the bread, it will cause parchment to stick to the bottom of the bread, so should be avoided; and the bread should not be misted before baking.

Breads baked in La Cloche usually weigh a little more because they retain more moisture (*King Arthur and Sassafras,* see Sources, page 598).

POINTERS FOR SUCCESS USING LA CLOCHE BREAD BAKERS

> Raise the baking temperature given by 25 degrees.

> If you have preheated the dome, the baking time will be about 5 minutes less than usual.

> Remove the dome for the last 5 to 10 minutes of baking to allow moisture to evaporate and to crisp the crust and give it more color. (I remove the bread from the base and set it directly on the baking stone, and I prop the oven door partially ajar.)

Stone or Quarry Tiles

The most even ovens are those with the shortest dimension from top to bottom. If your oven is high, however, you can turn that into an advantage because it means you can set a baking stone or a layer of quarry tiles on both the bottom and top racks. Measure the interior of your oven before you purchase baking stones or quarry tiles. To ensure proper air circulation, be sure to allow 2 inches of clearance space between the stone or tiles and the oven walls on all sides.

The ideal minimum-size stone is 16 1/2-by-14 1/2-by-1/2 inch thick (*King Arthur,* see Sources, page 598), because it will accommodate a half sheet pan. The interior of your oven needs to be at least 20 by 18 inches to accommodate this stone and still have good air circulation.

I also have a Gaggenau oven that has a pizza stone insert that rests on its own heating element. This is the only kind of stone that is effective in an oven like this, which has a fan that is almost continuously blowing and releasing out hot air. Stones that merely sit on the oven shelf, and rely only on ambient heat will not maintain their temperature well in this type of oven.

NOTE   I also bake pies and tarts on my baking stone. If I suspect that a pie might have sticky juices that will bubble out of the pan, I cover the stone with foil to keep it from staining the stone and smoking up the oven, otherwise, I set the pan directly on the stone. When baking cakes, I move the oven stone to the floor of the oven, to promote even heat, but I place the cake pan(s) on the oven rack, for the circulation of air needed for baking cakes. If baked directly on the stone they tend to have undesirably thick bottom crusts.

Thermometers

Instant-Read Thermometers

A quality probe thermometer is ideal for taking the temperature of raw dough, baked breads, and myriad other items. The one I find most reliable is the English battery-operated *Thermapen 5F* thermometer, with a range of −50°F to 550°F (*King Arthur,* see Sources, page 598).

Thermapen instant-read thermometer

Oven Thermometers

I use a laboratory cable thermometer from Omega (model #HH22). It is very expensive but far more accurate than any oven thermometers designed for the home baker I have tested. And since it has two probes, it can be used for two ovens at the same time. It is important that you buy an oven thermometer you can read without opening the oven, so as not to cause the temperature to drop. There is also an optional probe attachment for the Omega thermometer that can be used as an instant-read thermometer for the bread, roasts, sugar syrups, or other uses.

For battery-operated thermometers, change the battery at least twice a year. Don't wait for it to stop working. As the battery runs out, accuracy decreases.

Scales

I have been searching a long time for affordable home scales that are reliably accurate. I'm delighted that the swiss Soehnle scales not only are far less expensive than laboratory scales, they are both accurate and beautifully designed.

My number one scale is the **Soehnle Futura,** which weighs in both ounces and grams. It weighs up to 4 pounds 6 ounces/2 kilograms in 1-gram (1/28 of an ounce) increments up to 1000 grams, and 2 gram increment after that. Each one is calibrated, and the Futura model can actually be rinsed under running water. The only minor problem I have with the

Soehnle Futura scale

Soehnle scales is that, like most battery-operated scales, that they are designed to turn off after a few minutes when not in use in order to save battery power. This can be a problem if you are in the middle of weighing several ingredients into the same bowl and aren't working quickly enough. The way around this is to touch the bowl or the top of the scale lightly, which lets it know you haven't finished and will keep it turned on.

Soehnle Ultra scale

For minute ingredient amounts, such as yeast or salt, the small **Soehnle Ultra** is a treasure. It weighs in 0.1-gram increments up to 200 grams.

The Futura is readily available in gourmet stores and catalogues, but the Ultra can be purchased only through the website (*Soehnle*, see Sources, page 598).

Measuring Cups and Spoons

Solid Measuring Cups

Measuring cups used to measure dry ingredients such as flour, or solid ingredients such as butter or cheese, have smooth rims, without pour spouts. This enables you to run the blade of a metal spatula or knife across the top in order to measure a level cup evenly and accurately.

Foley stainless steel measuring cups

Foley stainless steel cups are the most attractive and among the most accurate (except for the 2-cup size, which measures slightly under). Tupperware's heavy-duty plastic cups are also excellent and include the very useful 2/3-cup and 3/4-cup sizes.

Liquid Measuring Cups

Liquid measuring cups have a spout. I prefer heatproof glass to plastic as these can also be used to heat liquids in the microwave oven.

The most accurate and well-marked heatproof measuring cups I have found are made by **Oven Basics**, available in some supermarkets. When shopping for liquid measuring cups, look for ones with level markings. A cup of water, read below the meniscus (the curved upper surface), should

Glass liquid measuring cup

weigh close to 8 ounces. In addition to measuring liquid, these cups are ideal for pouring hot syrups and caramel. The glass handles remain cool to the touch and the spouts help you control the way the liquid pours. I use my 1-cup measures the most, but the 2-cup and 4-cup are useful as well.

Measuring Spoons

Foley stainless measuring spoons (not the oval ones) and **Tupperware** heavy-duty plastic spoons are the most accurate. I especially like the Tupperware spoons because they include the odd but frequently called for 1/8-teaspoon, 1/2-tablespoon, and 4-teaspoons sizes. Tupperware spoons are scaled slightly larger than the Foley, but both are within an acceptable range. I have found other brands of measuring spoons, to be somewhat smaller than these two types and below the acceptable range of accuracy.

Foley stainless steel measuring spoons

The set of spoons called a pinch, dash, and smidgen are ideal for measuring the formerly immeasurable. (A pinch equals 1/8 teaspoon, a dash equals 1/16 teaspoon, and a smidgen equals 1/32 teaspoon.) They don't have a brand name, but are carried by Crate and Barrel.

Pinch, dash, and smidgen measuring spoons

Mixers

Heavy-Duty Stand Mixers

KitchenAid and Kenwood stand mixers come equipped with a paddle beater, a dough hook, and a whisk beater. Unless the dough is a very liquid one (such as the Focaccia dough), I prefer to use the dough hook rather than the paddle attachment. When mixing very small amounts of dough in a large mixer, the paddle attachment often works better because it reaches closer to the bottom of the bowl. The whisk attachment can be used for beating air into a sponge dough starter.

KitchenAid: Devoted as I have been to my trusty K5 (5-quart) model over the years, the Professional 6-quart is now my first choice. Its

KitchenAid® mixer with water jacket attachment

motor has 60 percent more power and the bowl has 20 percent more capacity. The wider bowl provides more access, and the pouring shield is the most effective I've used. It also has far more stability on the counter. And it handles small amounts of dough or batter almost as easily as large amounts.

Kenwood Mixer: The Kenwood 5 1/2-quart mixer is an excellent stand mixer. A larger 6.9-quart model with a more powerful motor is now also available.

Spiral-Type Mixers

These are heavy-duty stand mixers that are designed to simulate the powerful spiral-type mixers used in commercial bakeries. These mixers can handle as much as 12 pounds of dough but can also knead as little as 1 pound. They are ideal for mixing and kneading bread, and they also come with attachments such as whisk beaters designed for mixing cake and other batters.

Bosch Universal: This mixer has a plastic bowl with a lid and comes equipped with a specially designed stainless steel dough hook. It also has an optional stainless steel dough hook with smaller blades for mixing doughs under 3 pounds.

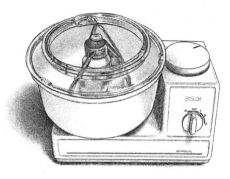

Bosch Universal mixer

Electrolux Magic Mill: This mixer has a heavy stainless steel bowl that rotates when the machine is turned on. It comes equipped with a specially designed dough hook for up to 4 pounds of dough. This dough hook moves back and forth from the side to the center of the bowl as the bowl circles around, giving it a sort of dual action. The mixer also comes with a large roller and dough scraper for larger amounts of dough. The roller has grooves designed to simulate the action of fingers. It as well moves back and forth as the bowl circles. The scraper is used in conjunction with the roller to scrape the sides of the bowl.

Scrapers

Bench scraper

Metal bench scrapers are excellent for cleaning counters without scratching the surface of your coun-

Electrolux Magic Mill "Assistant" mixer

tertop. They're also great for gathering, moving, and cutting bread or pastry doughs.

Plastic dough scrapers (*cornes* in French) are ideal for scraping dough out of bowls because of their flexibility (*King Arthur, J. B. Prince, La Cuisine*, see Sources, page 598).

Metal bench scraper

Basic Pans

Most of the pans mentioned in this section are available through King Arthur or the manufacturers' websites. For others, see Sources, page 598.

Plastic dough scraper

Bread Pans

Loaf pans are a very personal choice. I value a heavy-weight pan that is nonstick, as most loaf pans are today. The Alfred clay pans are my first choice because they bake so evenly and give an attractive golden brown color and ever so slightly rough texture to the sides of the loaf. As clay is breakable, my second choice would be the All-Clad loaf pans, which also bake evenly. Other excellent pans include the T-Fal loaf pan, whose sides are the most straight, great for sandwich loaves; Chicago Metallic, a nice heavy weight, made of aluminum and steel; and the Doughmakers, lighter in weight, but it makes a fine loaf. Pans such as All-Clad and those that are dark require a baking temperature 25°F lower than that specified in the recipe. Flexible loaf pans made from 100% FDA approved food-grade platinum silicone offer an excellent alternative to metal. They are totally non-stick, and are lightweight yet bake evenly.

Alfred clay pan

All-Clad loaf pan

Because the slope of a loaf pan varies so much, the internal capacity of these pans varies significantly. The less sharp the angle, the greater the capacity. (A loaf pan with a sharp angle is wider and longer measured at the top of the pan than it is when measured at the bottom of the pan.) It is best to measure the

T-Fal—a straight-sided loaf pan

capacity of your loaf pan by pouring water into it from an accurate glass measure. Here are the approximate volumes of many of the basic pans on the market today:

Dough Makers' loaf pan

3 7/8-by-2 1/2-by-1 5/8-inches high (mini pans for individual loaves): 1/2 cup

5 3/4 by 3 1/8 inches: 2 cups

8 by 4 inches: 4 cups

8 1/2 by 4 1/2 inches: 6 cups

9 by 5 inches: 7 cups

Specific brands

Dough Makers: 8 1/2-by-4 1/2-inch pan is 5 cups.

Lékué: 9 by 4 inch pan is 6 cups.

Chicago Metallic: 9-by-5-inch pan is 7 cups; 11-by-6 1/2-by 3 1/4-inch pan is 10 cups.

T-Fal: 9-by-5-inch pan is 8 1/2 cups.

All-Clad: 8 1/2-by-4 1/2-inch pan is 5 3/4 cups; 10-by-5 inch pan is 8 cups.

Alfred: 8 1/2-by-4 1/2-inch pan is 6 cups; 10 1/2-by-4 1/2-inch pan is 9 1/2 cups.

A rule of thumb for determining the size of pan to use: Check the volume of the dough after the first rise, when it has doubled. (If you are using a dough-rising container with volume marks on it, simply go by that. If using a bowl, pour water up to the mark where it has risen and measure it.) The loaf pan should hold about three-quarters the volume of the risen loaf. Light and airy doughs can be a little more than three-quarters and dense loaves can be a little less, as they will rise less.

Aluminum Sheet Pans and Heavy-Gauge Aluminum Rimless Cookie Sheets

For breads baked at over 375°F, it is best to use a half sheet pan with rolled edges, which prevent warping. Sheet pans have 1-inch-high sides, but these do not interfere with the browning of the sides of the bread since the bread is not close to the sides of the pan. For breads baked at 375°F and under, it's fine to use heavy-gauge rimless cookie sheets.

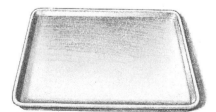

Half sheet pan

The standard half sheet pan commonly referred to in recipes as 17 by 12 inches is actually 17 3/4 by 13 inches measured across the top, from the outside edges, and 16 1/2 by 11 3/4 inches measured across the bottom.

For most bread baking, I prefer the kind of sheet pan that has perforations on its underside because that helps crisp the bottom crust.

Half sheet pan with 2-inch-high sides

If you don't have a baking stone, it is better to preheat a heavy baking sheet rather than just setting the pan of bread on the oven rack. If you have a second half-size baking sheet, invert it on the rack before preheating, then set the bread on the second sheet pan directly on top of that.

A half sheet pan with 2-inch-high sides works well if you are pouring boiling water into a pan to steam the oven. When using ice cubes to create steam in the oven, I prefer a cast-iron skillet.

Pan Liners

The development of **silicone nonstick liners** has changed the way professionals bake, making it unnecessary to use grease, flour, or cornmeal on the baking sheets. And now these are available to home bakers as well. Professional-quality liners, with care, will last a lifetime. They can withstand indirect heat up to 550°F (don't put them on the stovetop or under the broiler).

Silicone nonstick liners are made in France and they come in two types: **Silpat** and **Silpain**. The names are a clue as to what they are best suited for. The "sil" in Silpat represents silicone and the "pat" is short for *pâtisserie*. The "pain" in Silpain is French for bread. The Silpat is a semi-transparent beige and has a solid texture with a woven fiberglass center layer. The Silpain is black with little air holes. If it is set in a perforated sheet pan, it allows air circulation to crisp the bottom crust. The dark color of the Silpain also aids in the browning of the bottom crust. (In fact, with some breads, it is advisable to remove them from the Silpain toward the end of baking and place them on the oven rack to prevent overbrowning.)

Both of these liners come in 11 1/2-by-16 1/2-inch sheets, which fit perfectly into half-size sheet pans and can be set on top of cookie sheets. Both liners also come in a variety of other shapes. I use the 10-inch octagonal Silpat to line the bottom of the round La Cloche bread baker. It fits neatly into the bottom and slightly up the sides of the base. I use the Silpain pizza sheet for individual 7-inch pizzas. You can make six pizzas at a time in the separate 7-inch depressions, or you can cut the molds into individual pieces, to bake one pizza at a time. The rough surface of the Silpain makes it easy to spread the dough, and the little holes ensure a crisp bottom crust when set on a baking stone. The shallow depressions encourage a beautifully rolled edge to the dough. The Silpat is available in specialty stores or through catalogues such as Williams Sonoma and King Arthur. The Silpain is only available directly from DeMarle, the manufacturer, and J. B. Prince (see Sources, page 598).

Parchment can be used in place of silicone liners and sheet pans because it will slide off the baking peel onto the oven stone (silicone sticks to the peel). It doesn't work in La Cloche for soft breads such as Olive Bread (page 383) unless greased, as it would stick to the bread. If baking bread on parchment, it is best to remove it from the parchment after it has set (15 to 20 minutes) so the bottom of the bread doesn't steam. The only advantage parchment has over a Silpain or Silpat is that it is disposable and cheaper (in the short run at least).

Round wire cooling rack

Roul'pat is a nonstick work surface ideal for kneading, rolling, and shaping dough. Avoid putting it in the oven. If heated, it will slide on the counter!

Cooling Racks

I specify wire racks for cooling bread because wood, though beautiful, can warp from heat in combination with moisture. I have an assortment of round and rectangular wire racks but the exact size or shape is of no significance: the purpose of using racks to cool bread is to allow air to circulate around the bread. This speeds cooling and keeps the crust crisp.

Rectangular wire cooling rack

Rulers

Rulers are useful for measuring dough, both when rolling it to a specific size and for determining the degree of proofing by the height of the dough in the bread pan.

Dough-Rising Containers

After dough is mixed and kneaded, it must be allowed to rise until doubled. It can be set in a bowl, but I prefer to use acrylic containers with tight-fitting lids. (I sometimes put a heavy weight on top of the lid so that if I forget to push down the dough in time it will not overrise.) The containers have markings on their sides making it easy to tell when the dough has doubled.

Clear acrylic dough-rising containers

Acrylic containers are available from restaurant suppliers and websites (see Sources, page 598). They are very durable and not expensive. The brand I like best is Cambro. The sizes I use the most often are the 1-quart, 2-quart, and 4-quart; the 6-quart is perfect for storing a 5-pound bag of flour.

Heavy-duty Pot Holders

Most bread bakes at a very high temperature, so heavy-duty pot holders are very important, especially if using and preheating La Cloche clay domes. I find the Ritz cotton terrycloth pot holders that are two-ply with a pocket are the safest, because for very high heat I can hold them from the outside, instead of slipping my hands into the center, and have double protection. Asbestos mitts also offer excellent protection, but if your hands are small, as are mine, they are too unwieldy. I like to use Duncan's Kitchen Grips oven mitts. They are made of a rubber compound and are easy to keep clean.

Timers

West Bend's Triple Timer/Clock (item #40053) is a fantastic and inexpensive timer. Each of the three channels times up to 24 hours, and if by chance you don't hear it or don't turn it off, it will start counting the time that has elapsed since you should have (this is referred to as a count-up timer). I keep a little notepad by the timer so I can remember what I am timing on which channel. If you prefer a single-channel timer, choose item #40044 instead. (See Sources, page 598.)

West Bend's triple timer/clock

Nice to Have

Spatulas and Stirring Devices (most are available from King Arthur)
Metal Spatulas: A small metal spatula with wooden handle and a narrow 4-inch blade is one of the most-used tools in my kitchen. It is ideal for leveling measuring

spoons with dry ingredients and for helping to unmold quick breads. Small and large angled or offset spatulas are also handy for spreading batters, evenly in pans.

Small and Large Rubber Spatulas: Nothing takes the place of these for scraping bowls with liquid ingredients. Because they can retain odors, I have a separate set designated for baking. They come in many colors, so it's easy to determine which is which. I tend to use darker colors for savory cooking and paler ones for baking. I prefer the flat ones, and I use a spoon instead of curved spatulas.

High-Heat Rubber Spatulas: These spatulas are indispensable for stirring hot mixtures up to 500°F. The handles stay cool to the touch, and they can even be used for making caramel. Ones with white or translucent blades make it easy to judge the exact color of the caramel.

Wire Whisks: Medium-sized wire whisks, 8 to 10 inches in circumference, are the type most often used for bread baking. The best kind for whisking a dough starter (sponge) is a sturdy one with just five to seven loops, not the fine wire piano balloon whisks used for whisking egg whites (*La Cuisine*, see Sources, page 598).

Steam Makers

A small **spray bottle**, available in any hardware store, is handy for misting the surface of a loaf.

Proof Boxes

An acrylic container that is large enough to cover most loaves of dough as they are rising makes it unnecessary to cover the dough with greased plastic wrap to keep it from drying out. King Arthur carries a 12-inch-square-by-7-inch-high box and a 19-by-14-by-5 1/4-inch-high box. Both are made of thick acrylic. You can also purchase plastic or acrylic boxes of a similar size, at office supply stores. You can even use a cardboard box. Cut off the top so you will be able to see the bread's progress as it rises, and slip the box into a large plastic bag to contain the moisture.

Spray bottle

Bannetons or Dough-Rising Baskets and Couches

Bannetons are round or oblong baskets or containers used for shaping bread doughs while they are rising to give them extra support. They may be beautiful willow baskets from France, unlined or lined with coarse woven cloth, or they may even be plastic baskets or colanders lined with clean kitchen towels. The unlined willow baskets leave an attractive design on the crust of the bread. It is important to have a porous container so that the dough can breathe; otherwise, the moisture of the dough may cause it to stick to the cloth and the dough will collapse and deflate when unmolded. The bannetons used for the recipes in this book are the 8-inch-round and the 15-inch-long banneton. Larger bannetons (or colanders) could also be used, but when unmolding the dough before baking, you will need to support it with a cardboard round or plate held against its surface so that it doesn't fall several inches, which would make it deflate.

The word *couche* means bed in French, and that is the name given to the cloth that is folded to make a bed for long bread doughs, such as baguettes, to rest during rising. It is made of the same special coarse fiber cloth used to line bannetons and needs to be dusted with flour in the same way. A slim narrow board or baker's peel is used to roll the dough from the cloth and then onto the baking stone (*Chef's Boutique, French Baking Machines, King Arthur*, see Sources, page 598).

Cloth-lined banneton

Willow banneton

Spiral willow banneton

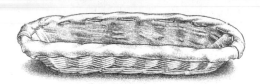

Cloth-lined oblong banneton

Colander lined with a kitchen towel—an improvised banneton

Specialty Bread Pans

The Steam Baking Master is a nonstick aluminized steel pan with a perforated steaming tray that makes it unnecessary to worry about steaming the oven, because you simply pour a little hot water into the pan underneath. It produces the best 14-inch baguettes made in a home oven, with a per-

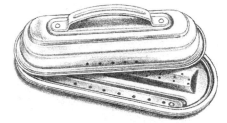

Steam Baking Master

fectly crisp crust. It also serves as a proofing box for the baguette dough to rise in, and it's a handy pan for reheating the bread (*King Arthur*, see Sources, page 598).

The triple baguette pan from Chicago Metallics, made of a combination of steel and aluminum, is also nonstick. It is a good alternative to the Steam Baking Master if you don't mind steaming the oven by hand, with ice cubes or boiling water, because the pan is perforated, which aids in creating a crisp crust. It will make three baguettes but also works fine for just one. **Double baguette pans**, even without perforations, are preferable to baking a baguette dough directly on a stone in a home oven because the slightly curved sides support the dough and result in the best shape. Chicago Metallics also makes a double perforated **Italian bread pan** (*King Arthur*, see Sources, page 598).

The Pullman pan, used for Pain de Mie (page 256), is a straight-sided long pan with a lid. These come in different lengths. The one you need for the recipe is 16 inches by 4 inches by 4 inches, with a 6-cup capacity. Be sure to insert the lid with the curved end farthest from you down, so that when sliding the lid open it does not scrape across the bread! (*J. B. Prince*, see Sources, page 598).

The Rose Bundt® Pan by Nordicware is a 10-cup capacity nonstick tube pan in the shape of a full-blown rose. I use it for the kugelhopf on page 522.

The Bundt® mini loaf pan has four 2-cup-capacity loaf depressions designed to resemble braided loaves.

The flat **carbon steel round pans** with slightly

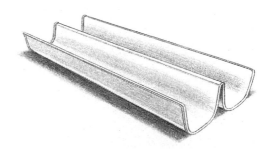

Double baguette pan

Pullman loaf pan

Rose Bundt® pan

Carbon steel baking pan

raised edges from France are perfect for baking pizzas or free-form round loaves. I like the 9 1/2-inch size for pizza for two or 7-inch loaves and the 12 1/2-inch size for larger pizzas (*La Cuisine*, see Sources, page 598).

Ovenproof Glass Bread Pans

The Bread Steamer, a 4-by-6 1/4-inch-high glass pan by Catamount Glass, is sold as a bread steamer for New England steamed bread but I use to make Mushroom Bread (page 389). It's well worth the investment because not only is this an exceptionally delicious bread, it makes a stunning centerpiece, especially on the holiday table (*King Arthur*, see Sources, page 598).

The classic 7-by-3 1/2-inch-high 2-quart **soufflé dish** is what I use for the Stud Muffin (page 528). You can also use a straight-sided ovenproof 2-quart casserole or a French ceramic soufflé dish (*La Cuisine*, see Sources, page 598).

Sticky Bun Pans

The Flexipan Texas muffin–sized mold (#1601) with 15 depressions, each 3 5/16 inches by 2 3/4 inches by 2 inches high, is the ideal pan for sticky buns (*DeMarle* or *J. B. Prince*, see Sources, page 598).

My favorite **rectangular baking pans** (9 inches by 13 inches) are by All-Clad and by Doughmakers.

The classic 9 1/2-inch (bottom measurement) **tart Tatin pan,** copper lined with tin, is ideal for the most even caramelization of sticky buns. The only problem with this pan is that when the sticky buns are unmolded, it is difficult to lift off the pan. Sur La Table designed and produced the perfect Tatin pan, adding handles to make lifting off the pan a breeze. It is lined with a thin layer of stainless steel that does not interfere with the conduction of heat and holds up better to the high temperature necessary for producing caramel. The 8-inch Tatin pan is about half the size of the larger one.

6-cup Texas muffin–sized mold

a 9 by 13-inch rectangular baking pan

Copper tart Tatin pan

Popover Pans

It wasn't until this pan was invented that I could turn out a perfect high-rising, crisp popover. The secret is the six tall dark metal nonstick cups connected by heavy wires that keep them spaced far enough apart so that the popovers don't steam and collapse. A **mini popover pan**, with twelve half-size popover cups, is also available (*King Arthur*, see Sources, page 598).

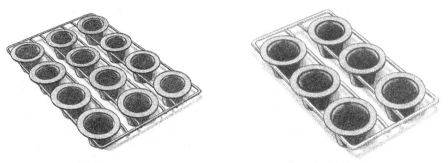

Mini popover pan   Standard-size popover pan

Dutch Baby Pan

This 11-inch steel pan with curved sides makes the most spectacular Dutch babies (*Fante's, King Arthur*, see Sources, page 598).

Corn-Finger Molds

These cast-iron molds are made for baking Corn Fingers (page 115) into perfect little corn-on-the-cob shapes. The molds are so attractive they also make excellent kitchen décor hung on the wall. (The handles have openings in them, no doubt for just this purpose.) If you are a collector, look for them in antiques stores, but the ones being produced today seem identical (*Lehman's*, see Sources, page 598).

Black steel Dutch baby pan

Cutting Devices

Pizza-Cutting Wheel: The heavy-duty type with a large 4-inch wheel offers steady, even pressure for cutting through the crust. It is great for cutting bread dough as well (*La Cuisine*, see Sources, page 598).

Cast-iron corn-finger mold

Dough Slashers: These are a matter of personal preference. Some bakers like the **lame**, which is like a curved razor blade on a handle; it is available in an inexpensive disposable version (*King Arthur*, see Sources, page 598). I prefer to use a very sharp thin-bladed **chef's knife** or a **single-edged razor blade**. For very soft doughs, I mark the surface with a knife tip and then use sharp shears to cut through the dough.

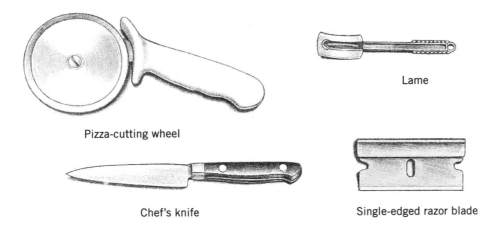

Pizza-cutting wheel

Lame

Chef's knife

Single-edged razor blade

Joyce Chen Shears: These small sharp shears with orange or white handles are indispensable for cutting and slashing dough and for numerous other kitchen tasks. (Available at gourmet stores and *King Arthur*, see Sources, page 598)

Bread Knives: Serrated knives work best for cutting through both hard and soft bread crusts. For soft breads, I find that either an electric knife or the Furi 10-inch-long blade (*King Arthur*, see Sources, page 598), with gently rounded instead of pointed serrations, works well. For hard crusts, I use the Leifheit 8-inch serrated blade, with sharp serrations. It is an exceptionally well-weighted and balanced knife (*Leifheit*, see Sources, page 598).

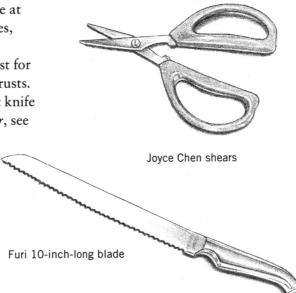

Joyce Chen shears

Furi 10-inch-long blade

The Baker's Peel

This is a large flat paddle used to slide loaves in and out of the oven. It is no doubt heresy to say that I prefer a metal peel with wooden handle (*King Arthur*, see Sources, page 598) to an all-wood peel, because my father had the monopoly on bagel peel production in the greater New York area in the 1940s. But knowing him, his peels were surely made of cured heavy wood that would not warp, unlike the present-day ones.

Baker's peel

Rolling Pins

When rolling bread dough to deflate it or to enlarge it before sprinkling on ingredients and rolling up the dough, as for sticky buns, a standard medium-weight French rolling pin, untapered and without handles, 1 3/4 inches in diameter and almost 20 inches long, works well. My favorite is the solid white plastic pin from France. The plastic makes it easy to wash without risk of warping (*La Cuisine*, see Sources, page 598).

For small amounts of dough, such as for the Paratha (page 232), it's great to have a 9-by-3/4-inch-diameter pin or an artist's "brayer," used for linoleum block prints.

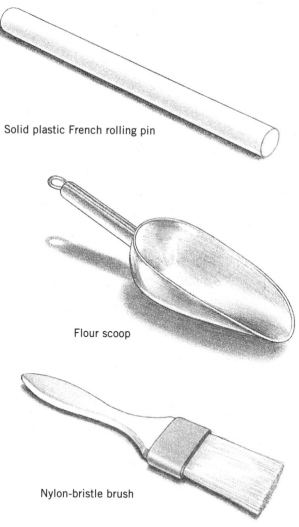

Solid plastic French rolling pin

Flour scoop

Nylon-bristle brush

Flour Scoops

The beautifully designed stainless steel scoops carried by King Arthur (see Sources, page 598) are a pleasure to use because the tapered rounded ends make it easy to add or remove small amounts of flour. They can also be used to measure flour if you run a metal spatula or knife across the straight-edged top. They come in 1/4-cup, 1/2-cup, and 1-cup sizes.

Brushes

Small natural or nylon bristle pastry

brushes or feathers work well both for brushing off excess flour from doughs and for glazing them. (*Available at gourmet stores or catalogues such as King Arthur, La Cuisine*, see Sources, page 598).

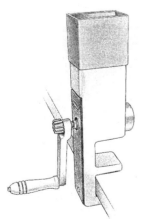

Feathers for brushing

Flour Mills

If you bake with whole grains or grains other than white wheat flour, you will sooner or later want to own a home flour mill, most of all to ensure the freshness of the flour. The choice of which mill really depends on how you will use the mill.

For small quantities, the hand-cranked **Back to Basics Grain Mill** is an absolute gem. It clamps to the counter (if the counter isn't too thick) and easily adjusts from coarse to fine.

If you do a moderate amount of grinding, don't require a truly coarse grind, and already own a KitchenAid mixer, the answer is the **KitchenAid grain mill** attachment.

If you do a large amount of grinding, you will treasure the heavy-duty **Diamant Grain Mill** imported from Denmark. With its huge 16-inch wheel, it grinds quickly and finely, from chickpeas to rice. For me, it, more than any other piece of machinery, is the symbol of bread baking, as it all begins here with the grinding of the flour. This mill is beautiful enough to stand in as functional sculpture. Not everyone, however, will appreciate the teal color. (It's carried by Lehman's, their "Non-Electric Catalog" is a treasure trove of beautiful and functional retro items. See Sources, page 598.)

For true high-speed milling (referred to as micromilling), but without excessive heating of the flour, for those who want to turn out a great deal of flour in the shortest

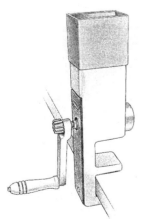

Back to Basics Grain Mill

Diamant Grain Mill

Nutrimill Grain Mill

amount of time, the **Nutrimill** by Bosch will seem like a miracle. This modern-day home electric mill simulates stone milling, in which one stone is stationary and the other rotates. It has two stainless steel heads, each with ten intertwining teeth, and if used on low speed, they grind at a lower temperature than stone grinding. The mill is self-cleaning because of the air-cooling, and it can grind (depending on the coarseness of the grind) 100 pounds an hour. It will grind anything from chickpeas to rice, and it is the only mill I know of that can handle popping corn.

Grinders

Small inexpensive hand **spice grinders** are ideal for small quantities of spices or seeds. One of my favorites is made by Oxo. If you have a spare electric coffee grinder, that can also be used.

A poppy seed grinder is an adorable old-fashioned hand grinder that looks like a miniature meat grinder. It is a luxury specialty item, but boy does it do the job! That is because it is designed expressly to grind poppy seeds uniformly into a fine fluff without risk of causing the oils to exude. If you are a lover of poppy seeds, this functional little item is a must (*King Arthur*, see Sources, page 598).

Electric Griddles

The Farberware are the most even griddles I've ever encountered. The heating coil, which is imbedded and sealed into the metal, runs the full length of the griddle. Crumpets, English muffins, pancakes, or anything else you cook on these griddles will brown evenly. I prefer the rectangular model for the size and shape but the round model is probably the only one that has the nonstick finish, which is of an excellent quality, and this requires less butter to prevent sticking.

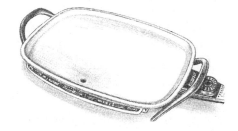

Farberware electric griddle

FoodSaver by Tilia

A food vacuum is a necessary luxury for me because of my erratic baking schedule and passion for freshness. I use the containers to keep baked breads at their freshest, as well as for flour, yeast, chemical leavening, seeds, spices, nuts, and many other things. The customer service help line is one of the best of any I've ever encountered, both knowledgeable and friendly.

Ceramic Woven Bread Basket/Warmer

This is fun item and makes a great gift, especially if presented with a fresh loaf of bread or stacks of rolls set inside. I find it so attractive I've placed mine permanently on the dining room table. It doubles as a fruit bowl, but its real use is as a bread warmer because it can be placed in the oven while the bread is baking and then set on a trivet on the table, keeping the bread or rolls warm throughout dinner. It comes in both oval and round shapes (*King Arthur, Williams Sonoma*, see Sources, page 598).

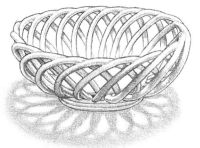

Ceramic woven bread basket/warmer

Flour Wand

I use a flour wand whenever I want to sprinkle the counter with flour to keep the dough from sticking. It is essentially a coiled spring with a handle; when expanded, it picks up flour, and when waved over the dough, it dispenses the finest dusting of flour over the counter or the dough (*King Arthur*, see Sources, page 598).

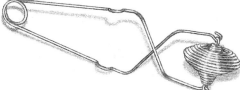

Flour wand

Bread Boards

Having a father who was a skilled cabinetmaker, I developed a great love of wood. Charles Shackelton and his master craftsmen work a great deal in cherry, making exquisite dining room tables and other furniture. He also makes beautiful bread boards. And his wife, Miranda, makes equally beautiful pottery in her studio next door. They are very special people; if in the area, do visit their shop (see Sources, page 598). Also check antiques stores for bread boards with elaborate carving.

Antique wooden cutting board

Countertops

Marble, granite, wood, Formica—they all work for bread. My preference is marble or granite for kneading dough because it seems to stick slightly less, requiring less flour. But when shaping bread I prefer wood, as its slightly rougher surface grabs the dough a little, helping to firm it into shape.

Plastic Wrap and Storage Bags

When covering rising dough or wrapping baked bread for the freezer, the "original" Saran brand plastic wrap and Glad Press n' Seal are the only ones I know of that are manufactured to be airtight. Freezer-weight zip-seal storage bags, with all air expelled before sealing, are the best choice for storing the wrapped bread. Once the bread is frozen firm, you can rebag it using a vacuum sealer, which will prevent freezer burn and vastly increase storage life.

Decorative Baking Paper

Using Italian or panettone paper to bake the Panettone with Chestnuts (page 511) is not only a nice way to package it as a holiday gift but also serves to keep the bread fresh, because it remains adhered to the sides. Finding the right size of panettone paper, however, is not easy. King Arthur and La Cuisine carry the size I like, which measures about 6 inches by 4 inches high.

EQUIPMENT SOURCES

This is a list of suggested sources; however, addresses and phone numbers can change over the years and some places stop carrying certain items. If you can't find what you are looking for from this list, the Internet is a great way to locate hard-to-find items and, of course, e-Bay is ideal for locating things that are no longer available retail.

Gourmet Stores
Broadway Panhandler: 477 Broome Street, New York, NY 10013; 212-966-3434
The Complete Kitchen: 118 Greenwich Avenue, Greenwich, CT 06830; 203-869-8384
Fante: 1006 South Ninth Street, Philadelphia, PA 19147; 800-878-5557
King Arthur Flour Baker's Catalogue: www.kingarthurflour.com, 800-827-6836
La Cuisine: 323 Cameron Street, Alexandria, VA 22314; 800-521-1176
Lehman's: www.lehmans.com, 888-438-5346
J. B. Prince: 36 East 31st Street, 11th floor, New York, NY 10016; 212-683-3553 (food service quantities only)
Sur La Table: www.surlatable.com, 800-240-0853
Williams-Sonoma: www.williams-sonoma.com, 800-541-2233

Mixers
Electrolux of Sweden: www.magicmillusa.com, 800-243-9078
KitchenAid: www.kitchenaid.com, 800-541-6390
Kitchen Resource: www.boschmixers.com, 800-MYBOSCH (692-6724)

Pan Liners, Flexipan, and Silicone Pans
Demarle Inc.: www.demarleusa.com, 609-395-0219
Lékué: www.gourmetcatalog.com, 214-855-0005

Bannetons
French Baking Machines: 609-860-0577
Technobake System, Inc.: www.chefsboutique.com, 609-466-4588

Miscellaneous

Back to Basics: www.backtobasicsproducts.com, 801-572-1982 (grain mills)

Dough containers: http://sdc2.sdccorp.com/smartstore

Duncan Industries: www.kitchengrips.com

Charles Shackleton and Miranda Thomas: www.shackletonthomas.com, 800-245-9901 (bread boards)

Nordicware: www.nordicware.com (bread pans)

Omega: www.omega.com, 800-826-6342 (oven thermometers)

Sassafras®: 800-537-4941

Soehnle scales: www.scalesexpress.com or www.leifheitusa.com, 866-695-3434 for nearest retailer

Leifheit bread knife: www.leifheitusa.com, or 866-695-3434, for nearest retailer

The Chef's Catalog: www.chefscatalog.com, 800-884-CHEF

The Doughmakers: www.doughmakers.com, 888-386-8517 (bread pans)

Tupperware: www.tupperware.com

West Bend: www.housewares@westbend.com 262-334-6949

Glossary of Bread Baking Terms

When you overhear bread bakers talking it often sounds like a foreign language, because their conversation is peppered with so many terms unique to the industry. Some actually are foreign words (mostly French) but most are merely familiar terms used in a different way. All professions have "jargon"—a terminological shorthand designed for communicating quickly and precisely with a minimum of words. I have used many of these bread bakers' terms throughout the book, such as "tacky" and "extensible" and put the more familiar translation in parenthesis ("slightly sticky" and "stretchy"). Here is a glossary of commonly used bread-baking terms to make you feel completely at home when you enter the world of bread baking.

NOTE Ingredient and equipment terms are detailed fully in the chapters starting on pages 543 and 575.

active dry yeast: Commercial dried yeast that contains a higher amount of dead yeast cells than instant yeast. This yeast requires soaking in warm water to activate it.

altus brat: Old bread added to bread dough, usually pumpernickel, to give more complexity of flavor.

autolyse: The rest, usually 20 minutes, given to the dough after the initial mixing, to give it a chance to absorb the water more evenly before developing the dough fully.

barm: A fully mature dough starter created from wild yeast.

benching: Allowing the dough to rest before shaping.

biga: A stiff pre-ferment or dough starter close to the consistency of dough, created from commercial yeast.

bannetons: Round or oblong baskets or containers used for shaped bread dough during the final rise, to give extra support and a rustic floured crust.

batard: A torpedo or football-shaped loaf.

bloom: *See* grigne.

boule: A round ball-shaped loaf.

chef: A dough starter created from wild yeast at the stage before it becomes fully mature or active.

couche: A word for bed in French, this is the name given to the cloth that is folded to make a bed for long bread doughs, such as baguettes, to rest during rising.

crumb: The interior structure of a baked loaf.

degas: To deflate or press down or punch down the dough to release air.

desem: The Flemish word for a fully mature dough starter created from wild yeast.

dimpling: Pressing indentations into the dough with your fingers.

dividing the dough: Cutting the dough into smaller pieces for shaping.

dormancy: A state of slowed down yeast activity in the dough produced by chilling.

dough elasticity: Springiness—the ability of the dough to spring back when pulled or stretched.

dough extensibility: The ability of the dough to stretch without pulling back.

enriched dough: Dough containing fat, dairy, eggs, or sugar.

expanding the dough starter: Feeding it with flour and water to increase its quantity.

fermentation: The yeast-produced breakdown of sugar in the flour into carbon dioxide and alcohol. This term is generally used to refer to the first rise of the dough.

flour blanket: When flour is sprinkled on top of a sponge or batter consistency pre-ferment to cover it completely.

friction factor: The amount of heat produced by a mixer or processor when bread dough is mixed.

glazing: Brushing the shaped, risen dough with egg wash, melted fat, or a cornstarch mixture to produce a shine to the baked bread.

gluten: The protein network produced when flour that contains gluten-forming proteins is mixed with water.

grigne: The French word for "grin," referring to the opening of the baked dough where it has been slashed. This is called "bloom" in English.

hydration: The percentage of water contained in a dough.

hygroscopicisty or hygroscopic: Refers to ingredients that retain moisture, such as honey.

inoculating the dough: Adding sourdough culture to dough.

instant yeast: Dry yeast that is produced to contain more live yeast cells than active dry yeast. Instant yeast does not require "proofing," or soaking in warm water to activate it, and can be added directly to the flour in a mixture. Instant yeast is nationally available in supermarkets under the following brand names:

Fleischmann's Bread Machine Yeast or Rapid Rise
Red Star's QuickRise
Red Star's Instant Active Dry
SAF Instant
SAF Gourmet Perfect Rise

kneading: The second stage of more vigorous mixing of the dough after it has come together to form a mass.

lame: A curved razor blade used to slash bread dough.

laminated dough: A dough that contains a high percentage of fat that is layered into it.

lean dough: A dough that contains little or no fat, eggs, or sugar.

levain: The French word for leavening, it refers to a fully mature dough starter created from wild yeast. It can be batter consistency or a stiff dough consistency.

madre bianca, or mother: A fully mature dough starter created from wild yeast.

misting: Spraying the dough with water before baking.

pâte fermentée: Old dough, i.e., dough that has already undergone its first fermentation or rising.

peel: A large, flat paddle used to slide loaves in and out of the oven. (A bagel peel is a narrower paddle designed to move bagels around in the oven for even baking and to remove them when baked.)

peeling: The process of transferring bread from the peel to the oven.

poolish: A batter-consistency pre-ferment or dough starter created from commercial yeast, usually consisting of equal weight flour and water. It is made the same day or the day before the bread is baked and is always fermented at room temperature to produce milder lactic flavors.

pre-ferments (or dough starters): Start the fermenting process before the final mixing of the dough, extending the length of fermentation and allowing more flavor to develop.

preshaping: Rounding the dough and allowing it to relax afterward so that the dough is not too elastic to shape well.

primary bulk fermentation: The first rising of the dough before it is divided and/or shaped.

proofer or proof box: A contained environment to raise the dough, both temperature and humidity controlled.

proofing: Refers to both the development of yeast when activated with warm water (*see* active dry yeast) and the final rising of shaped dough, also referred to as secondary fermentation.

refreshing the sourdough starter: "Feeding" it with flour and water.

retarding dough: Chilling the dough to slow down fermentation and allow complex flavors to develop.

rich dough: Dough containing 20 percent or more fat.

ripening dough: Chilling the dough and allowing it to rest to develop more complex flavors.

rounding the dough: Tucking under the edges of the dough to form a smooth skin or outer surface.

scaling: Weighing the dough.

seed culture: A dough starter created from wild yeast at the stage before it becomes fully mature or active.

slashing (scoring or slitting): Making cuts or slashes in the dough to release the steam during baking.

soaker: A mixture consisting of whole or coarsely milled grains and/or seeds and water, which softens them and activates the enzymes in the grains that convert starch in the grains to sugar.

sourdough culture or sourdough starter: A fully mature dough starter created from wild yeast. It can be a batter consistency, referred to as a liquid starter, or a stiff consistency, referred to as a stiff starter.

sourdough bread: Naturally leavened (risen) bread (made with wild yeast as opposed to commercial yeast).

sponge: A batter consistency pre-ferment or dough starter created from commercial yeast (some bakers use the term sponge to mean any form of pre-ferment).

spritzing: Spraying the dough with water before baking.

straight dough or direct dough method: Mixing the dough without a pre-ferment.

strong flour: Flour that contains a high amount of gluten-forming proteins.

tacky: Refers to dough that is slightly sticky. It does not stick to your fingers but feels like it might.

taring (pronounced "tairing"): Removing the weight of a container or ingredient on a scale by pressing a button, which enables you to determine the weight of the next ingredient added to it.

turning the dough: This process is a gentle way to stretch and develop the gluten of a dough by pulling and stretching or rolling it and then folding it into a tight package.

window pane test: Also referred to as membrane test, used for moist dough to determine if adequate gluten development has taken place. A small piece of dough when stretched will form a translucent membrane without tearing.

Bibliography

Books

Raymond Calvel, *The Taste of Bread*, translated by Ron Wirtz. Gaithersburg, Md.: Aspen Publishers, 2001.

Helen Charley, *Food Science*. New York: John Wiley & Sons, 1982.

Shirley O. Corriher, *CookWise*. New York: William Morrow and Company, 1997.

Suzanne Dunaway, *No Need to Knead: Handmade Italian Breads in 90 Minutes*. New York: Hyperion, 1999.

Carol Field, *The Italian Baker*. New York: Harper & Row, 1985.

Maggie Glezer, *Artisan Baking Across America*. New York: Artisan, 2000.

Pauline C. Paul and Helen H. Palmer, *Food Theory and Applications*. New York: John Wiley & Sons, 1972.

Peter Reinhart, *The Bread Baker's Apprentice*. Berkeley, Calif.: Ten Speed Press, 2001.

Amy Scherber and Toy Kim Dupree, *Amy's Bread*. New York: William Morrow and Company, 1996.

Alan Scott and Daniel Wing, *The Bread Builders*. White River Junction, Vt.: Chelsea Green Publishing Co., 1999.

Gail Sher, *From a Baker's Kitchen*. Berkeley and Los Angeles, Calif.: Aris Books, 1984.

Nancy Silverton, *Breads from the La Brea Bakery*. New York: Villard Books, 1996.

Jeffrey Steingarten, *The Man Who Ate Everything*. New York: Alfred A. Knopf, 1998.

William J. Sultan, *Practical Baking*. Westport, Conn.: AVI Publishing Co., 1980.

Reay Tannahill, *Food in History*. New York: Crown Trade Paperbacks, 1989.

Bernice K. Watt and Annabel L. Merrill, *Composition of Foods: Agriculture Handbook No 8*. Washington, D.C.: United States Department of Agriculture, 1963.

Magazines and Reprints

Maggie Glezer, "Baking a Flatbread with an Inlay of Herbs," *Fine Cooking*, November 1998.

Tim Huff, "Creating Artisan Breads," *General Mills Bakers Flour*, November 1999.

Kay Rentschler and Julia Collin, "Understanding and Using Yeasts," *Cook's Magazine*, January and February 2001.

Didier Rosada, "Exploring the Life of a Sourdough," *Modern Baking's Bread and Rolls Handbook*, supplement to *Modern Baking*, November 1999.

Didier Rosada, "Pre-Ferments (Part One)," *Bread Lines, The Bread Baker's Guild of America*, Volume 8, Issue 1, February 2000.

Didier Rosada, "Pre-Ferments (Part Two)," *Bread Lines, The Bread Baker's Guild of America*, Volume 8, Issue 2, May 2000.

Baker's Special Websites

Reggie and Jeff Dworkin, *Bread Bakers' Digest*: www.bread-bakers.com

The Bread Bakers Guild of America: www.bbga.org

Index

When a recipe has more than one reference, the first page number, in **boldface**, refers to the recipe itself; page numbers which follow refer to other discussion of the recipes.
Page numbers in *italics* refer to illustrations.

A

Wolfert, Paula, 54, 495
Wonder Bread, 244
Wondra flour, 180, 549
    weight of, 570
Wood countertops, 597
Wooden spoons, 47
Wyler, Susan, 305
Wyman's, 573

Y

Yams
    sweet potato biscuits, 136–38
    sweet potato loaf, 276–79
Yeast, 29, 560–62
    active dry, 561–62
        proofing, 562
        substituting for instant yeast, 562
        substituting instant yeast for, 562
    adding to dough, timing of, 55
    amount of
        with added ingredients, 44
        freezing dough and, 65
        for high-altitude baking, 89
    amount used, 31
    in biga, 35–36
    chilling of, 30
    commercial (brewer's), 560, 561
        adding to sourdough bread dough, 430–31,
            449–50, 456, 464, 471
        in pre-ferments, 31, 302
        replacing with sourdough starter, 439–40
        in sourdough starters, 37, 38
    conversion between types of, 562
    in The Dough Percentage, 40–41
    fermentation and, 29–30, 560
    fresh compressed (cake)

in sourdough starters, 36
    substituting instant yeast for, 562
    hydrating, 562
    instant (rapid-rise), 561
        adding to dough, 54
        brand names of, 561
        gluten and, 561
        for hearth breads, 300
        in poolish, 34–35
        shelf life of, 561
        in sourdough starters, 37, 38
        substituting active dry yeast for, 562
        substituting for active dry or fresh compressed
            yeast, 562
        temperature and, 561
        weight of, 571
    killing of, by salt, 45
    osmotolerant, 562
    proofing, 562
    wild, 426–27, 560
        commercial yeast versus, 428
        in sourdough starters, 36, 37
Yeast breads
    ingredient proportions in, 94
    little, ingredient proportions in, 95–96
    see also specific breads and types of breads

Z

Zest
    citrus, grated, weight of, 572
    grating, 123
Zesters, 123
Zito, Anthony, 370
Zito's bakery, 370
Zoe's restaurant, 342
Zucchini bread, 105